The Ethics of Lawyers

The International Library of Essays in Law and Legal Theory
Series Editor: Tom D. Campbell

Schools

Natural Law, Vols I & II *John Finnis*
Justice *Thomas Morawetz*
Law and Economics, Vols I & II *Jules Coleman and Jeffrey Lange*
Critical Legal Studies *James Boyle*
Marxian Legal Theory *Csaba Varga*
Legal Reasoning, Vols I & II *Aulis Aarnio and D. Neil MacCormick*
Legal Positivism *Mario Jori*
American Legal Theory *Robert Samuel Summers*
Postmodernism and Law *Dennis Patterson*
Law and History *David Sugarman*
Law and Language *Fred Schauer*
Sociological Theories of Law *Kahei Rokumoto*
Rights *Carlos Nino*
Law and Psychology *Martin Lyon Levine*
Feminist Legal Theory, Vols I & II *Frances Olsen*
Law and Society *Roger Cotterrell*
Contemporary Criminological Theory *Francis T. Cullen and Velmer S. Burton Jr.*

Areas

Criminal Law *Thomas Morawetz*
Tort Law *Ernest J. Weinrib*
Contract Law, Vols I & II *Larry Alexander*
Anti-Discrimination Law *Christopher McCrudden*
Consumer Law *Iain Ramsay*
International Law *Martti Koskenniemi*
Property Law, Vols I & II *Elizabeth Mensch and Alan Freeman*
Constitutional Law *Mark V. Tushnet*
Procedure *D.J. Galligan*
Evidence and Proof *William Twining and Alex Stein*
Company Law *Sally Wheeler*
Privacy, Vols I & II *Raymond Wacks*
Lawyers' Ethics *David J. Luban*
Administrative Law *D.J. Galligan*
Child Law *Harry D. Krause*
Family Law, Vols I & II *Harry D. Krause*
Welfare Law *Peter Robson*
Medicine and the Law *Bernard M. Dickens*
Commercial Law *Ross Cranston*
Environmental Law *Michael C. Blumm*
Conflict of Laws *Richard Fentiman*
Law and Religion *Wojciech Sadurski*
Human Rights Law *Philip Alston*
European Community Law, Vols I & II *Francis Snyder*
Tax Law, Vols I & II *Patricia D. White*
Media Law *Eric Barendt*
Labour Law *David L. Gregory*
Alternative Dispute Resolution *Michael D.A. Freeman*

Legal Cultures

Comparative Legal Cultures *Csaba Varga*
Law and Anthropology *Peter Sack*
Hindu Law and Legal Theory *Ved Nanda*
Islamic Law and Legal Theory *Ian Edge*
Chinese Law and Legal Theory *Michael Palmer*
Russian Legal Theory *W. Butler*
Common Law *Michael Arnheim*
Japanese Law and Legal Theory *Koichiro Fujikura*
Law and Development *Anthony Carty*
Jewish Law and Legal Theory *Martin P. Golding*
Legal Education *Martin Lyon Levine*
Civil Law *Ralf Rogowski*
African Law and Legal Theory *Gordon Woodman and Akintunde Obilade*

Future Volume
Cumulative index

The Ethics of Lawyers

Edited by

David Luban

Morton and Sophia Macht Professor of Law;
Research Scholar, Institute for Philosophy and Public Policy,
University of Maryland

NEW YORK UNIVERSITY PRESS
REFERENCE COLLECTION

Manufactured in Great Britain

First published in the U.S.A. in 1994 by
NEW YORK UNIVERSITY PRESS
Washington Square
New York NY 10003

Library of Congress Cataloging-in-Publication Data
The ethics of lawyers / edited by David Luban.
p. cm. – (The international library of essays in law and legal theory. Areas : 25)
'New York University Press reference collection.'
Includes bibliographical references.
ISBN 0–8147–5066–4
1. Legal ethics – United States. I. Luban, David, 1949–
II. Series.
KF306.A5E87 1994
174' .3'0973–dc20 94–30377
CIP

Contents

Acknowledgements vii
Series Preface ix
Introduction xi

PART I ROLE DIFFERENTIATED MORALITY

1 Richard Wasserstrom (1975), 'Lawyers as Professionals: Some Moral Issues', *Human Rights*, **5**, pp. 1–24. 3
2 Gerald J. Postema (1980), 'Moral Responsibility in Professional Ethics', *New York University Law Review*, **55**, pp. 63–89. 27

PART II NEUTRAL PARTISANSHIP: JUSTIFICATIONS AND CRITIQUES

3 Stephen L. Pepper (1986), 'The Lawyer's Amoral Ethical Role: A Defense, A Problem, and Some Possibilities', *American Bar Foundation Research Journal*, **1986**, pp. 613–35 57
4 Monroe H. Freedman (1978), 'Personal Responsibility in a Professional System', *Catholic University Law Review*, **27**, pp. 191–205. 81
5 Charles Fried (1976), 'The Lawyer as Friend: The Moral Foundations of the Lawyer-Client Relation', *Yale Law Journal*, **85**, pp. 1060–89. 97
6 Edward A. Dauer and Arthur Allen Leff (1977), 'Correspondence: The Lawyer as Friend', *Yale Law Journal*, **86**, pp. 573–84. 127
7 David Luban (1983), 'The Adversary System Excuse', in David Luban (ed.), *The Good Lawyer: Lawyers' Roles and Lawyers' Ethics*, Totowa, New Jersey: Rowman & Allanheld, pp. 83–122. 139
8 William H. Simon (1978), 'The Ideology of Advocacy: Procedural Justice and Professional Ethics', *Wisconsin Law Review*, pp. 30–144. 179

PART III MORAL PSYCHOLOGY

9 Thomas L. Shaffer (1987), 'The Legal Ethics of Radical Individualism', *Texas Law Review*, **65**, pp. 963–91. 297

10 Anthony T. Kronman (1987), 'Living in the Law', *University of Chicago Law Review*, **54**, pp. 835–76. 327

11 Carrie Menkel-Meadow (1985), 'Portia in a Different Voice: Speculations on a Women's Lawyering Process', *Berkeley Women's Law Journal*, **1**, pp. 39–63. 369

PART IV ETHICAL IDEALS AND INSTITUTIONAL REALITIES

12 Deborah L. Rhode (1985), 'Ethical Perspectives on Legal Practice', *Stanford Law Review*, **37**, pp. 589–652. 397

13 Mark J. Osiel (1990), 'Lawyers as Monopolists, Aristocrats, and Entrepreneurs', *Harvard Law Review*, **103**, pp. 2009–66. 461

Name Index 519

Acknowledgements

The editor and publishers wish to thank the following for permission to use copyright material.

Catholic University Law Review for the essay: Monroe H. Freedman (1978), 'Personal Responsibility in a Professional System', *Catholic University Law Review*, **27**, pp. 191–205. Professor Freedman has updated his article in his book, *Understanding Lawyers' Ethics* (Matthew Bender 1990).

Harvard Law Review for the essay: Mark J. Osiel (1990), 'Lawyers as Monopolists, Aristocrats, and Entrepreneurs', *Harvard Law Review*, **103**, pp. 2009–66. Copyright © 1990 by The Harvard Law Review Association.

New York University Law Review for the essay: Gerald J. Postema (1980), 'Moral Responsibility in Professional Ethics', *New York University Law Review*, **55**, pp. 63–89.

Stephen L. Pepper (1986), 'The Lawyer's Amoral Ethical Role: A Defense, A Problem, and Some Possibilities', *American Bar Foundation Research Journal*, 1986, pp. 613–35. Copyright © Stephen L. Pepper.

Rowman & Allanheld for the essay: David Luban (1983), 'The Adversary System Excuse', in David Luban (ed.), *The Good Lawyer: Lawyers' Roles and Lawyers' Ethics*, pp. 83–122.

Stanford Law Review and Fred B. Rothman & Company for the essay: Deborah L. Rhode (1985), 'Ethical Perspectives on Legal Practice', *Stanford Law Review*, **37**, pp. 589–652. Copyright © 1985 by the Board of Trustees of the Leland Stanford Junior University.

Texas Law Review for the essay: Thomas L. Shaffer (1987), 'The Legal Ethics of Radical Individualism', *Texas Law Review*, **65**, pp. 963–91. Copyright © 1987 by the Texas Law Review Association.

The University of California Press for the essay: Carrie Menkel-Meadow (1985), 'Portia in a Different Voice: Speculations on a Women's Lawyering Process', *Berkeley Women's Law Journal*, **1**, pp. 39–63. Copyright © 1985 by Berkeley Women's Law Journal.

The University of Chicago Law Review for the essay: Anthony T. Kronman (1987), 'Living in the Law', *University of Chicago Law Review*, **54**, pp. 835–76.

Wisconsin Law Review for the essay: William H. Simon (1978), 'The Ideology of Advocacy: Procedural Justice and Professional Ethics', *Wisconsin Law Review*, pp. 30–144. Copyright © 1978, by the Board of Regents of the University of Wisconsin System. Reprinted by permission of Wisconsin Law Review.

The Yale Law Journal Company and Fred B. Rothman and Company for the essay: Charles Fried (1976), 'The Lawyer as Friend: The Moral Foundations of the Lawyer-Client Relation', *Yale Law Journal*, **85**, pp. 1060–89; Edward A. Dauer and Arthur Allen Leff (1977), 'Correspondence: The Lawyer as Friend', *Yale Law Journal*, **86**, pp. 573–84.

Every effort has been made to trace all the copyright holders, but if any have been inadvertently overlooked the publishers will be pleased to make the necessary arrangement at the first opportunity.

Series Preface

The International Library of Law and Legal Theory is designed to provide important research materials in an accessible form. Each volume contains essays of central theoretical importance in its subject area. The series as a whole makes available an extensive range of valuable material which will be of considerable interest to those involved in the research, teaching and study of law.

The series has been divided into three sections. The Schools section is intended to represent the main distinctive approaches and topics of special concern to groups of scholars. The Areas section takes in the main branches of law with an emphasis on essays which present analytical and theoretical insights of broad application. The section on Legal Cultures makes available the distinctive legal theories of different legal traditions and takes up topics of general comparative and developmental concern.

I have been delighted and impressed by the way in which the editors of the individual volumes have set about the difficult task of selecting, ordering and presenting essays from the immense quantity of academic legal writing published in journals throughout the world. Editors were asked to pick out those essays from law, philosophy and social science journals which they consider to be fundamental for the understanding of law, as seen from the perspective of a particular approach or sphere of legal interest. This is not an easy task and many difficult decisions have had to be made in order to ensure that a representative sample of the best journal essays available takes account of the scope of each topic or school.

I should like to express my thanks to all the volume editors for their willing participation and scholarly judgement. The interest and enthusiasm which the project has generated is well illustrated by the fact that an original projection of 12 volumes drawn up in 1989 has now become a list of some 60 volumes. I must also acknowledge the vision, persistence and constant cheerfulness of John Irwin and the marvellous work done by Mrs Margaret O'Reilly and Sonia Hubbard.

TOM D. CAMPBELL
Series Editor
The Faculty of Law
The Australian National University

Introduction

Moral suspicions about the practice of law are hardly new. Consider Socrates's argument in the *Gorgias* that lawyers' 'rhetoric is to justice what cookery is to medicine' (465c)[1] – both substitute the merely beguiling for the wholesome – or his claim in the *Theaetetus* (172e–173b) that the lawyer is

> . . . a slave disputing about a fellow slave before a master sitting in judgment. . . . Hence he acquires a tense and bitter shrewdness; he knows how to flatter his master and earn his good graces, but his mind is narrow and crooked. An apprenticeship in slavery has dwarfed and twisted his growth and robbed him of his free spirit, driving him into devious ways . . . ; so, turning from the first to lies and requital of wrong with wrong, warped and stunted, he passes from youth to manhood with no soundness in him and turns out, in the end, a man of formidable intellect – as he imagines.[2]

Consider this medieval anthem to Saint Ive, patron saint of lawyers (quoted by Fried in his essay reproduced as Chapter 5 in the present collection):

Sanctus Yvo erat Brito	Saint Ive was a Breton
Advocatus sed non latro	A lawyer but not a thief
Res miranda populo![3]	A miraculous thing to the people!

Consider also Louis XII's quip that 'Lawyers use the law as shoemakers use leather; rubbing it, pressing it, and stretching it with their teeth, all to the end of making it fit their purposes'.[4] Or Kant: 'The jurist, who has taken as his symbol the scales of right and the sword of justice, usually uses the latter not merely to keep any extraneous influences away from the former, but will throw the sword into one of the scales if it refuses to sink. . . .'[5] Or Macaulay, who, in his biographical essay on Bacon, described a lawyer as one who would, 'with a wig on his head, and a band round his neck, do for a guinea what, without those appendages, he would think it wicked and infamous to do for an empire'.[6]

Finally, consider the lawyer jokes that have become a staple of popular culture:

> *Question*: Why did the scientist substitute lawyers for laboratory rats in experiments?
> *Answers*: Because it's too easy to get emotionally attached to rats. Because lawyers reproduce faster. Because there are some things rats just won't do.
> *Question*: How do you tell when a lawyer is lying?
> *Answer*: His lips move.

Several themes recur throughout the age-old litany of lawyer-bashing: lawyers are greedy and charge too much; lawyers have little respect for law or justice; lawyers stir up quarrels; lawyers are untruthful. Finally, there is the complaint of

Macaulay but also of the punch line above: 'There are some things rats just won't do'. In other words, lawyers suspend their sense of morality in pursuing their clients' interests, in zealously supporting causes both righteous and wicked, seemingly without regard for the difference. It is this last contention that forms the jumping-off point for many of the essays collected here.

The aim of this volume is to make easily available some of the most influential philosophical essays on legal ethics. Like other volumes in the *International Library of Essays in Law and Legal Theory*, we restrict ourselves to self-standing essays, omitting excerpts from books and treatises. We aim, as well, to include essays that will be of interest throughout the English-speaking world, and are thus not exclusively tied to the law of a single jurisdiction. In this volume, the latter consideration has led us to omit some of the most interesting writing on lawyers' ethics, for the subject has flourished as an object of scholarly interest primarily in the United States, and most of the literature addresses problems specific to the somewhat atypical American legal profession. (It is atypical for a variety of reasons, including the lack of distinction between barristers and solicitors, the detailed formal ethical codes regulating American lawyers, the underpinnings of the American concept of legal representation in the Bill of Rights to the Constitution, and the unparalleled size and power of American law firms and, more generally, of the American legal profession).[7] Although most of the essays in the present collection are written by Americans, and discuss primarily American examples, their arguments do not turn on features particular to American law, and their interest is not parochial.

Considerations of space have compelled us to omit numerous essays on legal ethics that are equally as worthy of inclusion as those reproduced here.[8] In this Introduction I shall attempt to do two things: first, to introduce the essays in the collection and, second, to survey some of the contemporary literature that we have omitted.

The problem of role differentiated morality

'Can a good lawyer be a good person?' Thus, provocatively, begins Charles Fried's essay in this volume (Chapter 5). It is a strange and, one might think, needlessly pugnacious question. Notwithstanding the tradition of lawyer-bashing, there seems little reason to doubt that the profession of law attracts a mix of human types – the good, the bad, the ugly – much the same as in any other profession. If any among us can lay claim to human goodness, why should it not be a lawyer?

Yet there are some things rats just won't do. A magazine portrait of a successful criminal lawyer whose clientele includes numerous organized crime figures describes his defence of a gangster whose motto was 'No corpus delecti, no investigation', and whose 'practice was to dismember the bodies of his murder victims and dispose of the parts in plastic garbage bags'.[9] The lawyer explains that he draws many of his finest oratorical inspirations from Martin Luther King. In this case, he borrowed from one of King's most moving books to craft a closing argument that associated the prosecution witnesses with 'cesspools of perjury' and portrayed his client as someone who just wanted to be allowed to live. 'I had the jurors crying,' the lawyer recalls. 'I had tears in my own eyes. I loved it. Didn't work, though.'[10] The cynical appropriation of King's phrases to impugn the prosecution witnesses on behalf of a vicious murderer seems hard to reconcile with what we ordinarily associate with human goodness.

In one of the best-known articles in the literature of legal ethics, Monroe Freedman argues that criminal defence lawyers should present perjurious client testimony as though it is true, brutally cross-examine truthful prosecution witnesses to make them appear to be liars, and counsel clients about the law knowing that they will rearrange their recollections to conform to available defences.[11] Such actions, many people are inclined to think, are inconsistent with moral rectitude, however we choose to flesh out that concept. Freedman, of course, understood this perfectly, and the aim of his provocative article was to lay out candidly what he believes to be logical implications of the adversary system – implications that the Bar has long endorsed in practice but obfuscated in theory.

An important point about these examples is that, in the eyes of most lawyers, they do not represent professional pathologies, illegalities or malpractice.[12] On the contrary, they represent what is arguably professional obligation – the ideal of a good lawyer. Hence the force of Fried's question.

Wasserstrom's essay in this volume (Chapter 1) sketches a philosophical approach to this question that has influenced a great deal of subsequent discussion. According to Wasserstrom, the inconsistency between professional obligation and our everyday views of moral propriety can be justified only under the assumption that lawyers operate under a 'role differentiated morality'. By this he means the idea that social and occupational roles have unique rights and obligations attached to them – the idea that F. H. Bradley described a century ago as the morality of 'my station and its duties'. It seems plausible, of course, that morality should be role differentiated: otherwise, how could morality accommodate the complexity of social existence? At the same time, however, it seems like special pleading to insist that what is wicked and infamous to do for an empire becomes obligatory once the barrister has placed the wig on his head and the band round his neck. As Wasserstrom puts it in another essay, there is 'a comprehensiveness, a universalistic dimension of morality, that is at odds with the more particularistic focus and direction of the kind of reasoning that occurs within and through the perspective of roles'.[13]

Alan Goldman has usefully distinguished between weak and strong role differentiation.[14] Every social role imposes duties unique to that role. Mostly, however, these duties supplement, but do not contradict, general moral obligations. This yields a kind of role differentiation, but only a weak and uncontroversial kind. Teachers, for example, have special responsibilities to improve their pupils' minds, but this role obligation raises no moral problems. The problematic aspect of lawyers' ethics, however, consists in duties (such as demolishing the truthful witness) that *contradict* rather than *supplement* everyday morality. Such are strongly differentiated role obligations, and it is these latter that are philosophically problematic.

The distinction between weak and strong role differentiation may be used advantageously to reformulate Wasserstrom's problem. The division of roles within society indeed requires special role obligations, but most of these are weakly role differentiated and do not offend more universal moral values. Legal ethics, however, at least insofar as it imposes strongly role differentiated duties, requires a justification that goes beyond the general appeal to division of labour.

Wasserstrom singles out two aspects of legal practice that raise substantial moral problems. The first is the aspect we have just been discussing: the lawyer's energetic furthering of causes that may be unworthy, or the use of lawful, but offensive, tactics in advancing client interests. The second is the lawyer's generally paternalistic attitude toward clients. In the present volume we include mostly essays that address only the first of these issues; the second has, in any case, attracted a much smaller philosophical literature.[15]

Wasserstrom examines several arguments on behalf of lawyers' unique role differentiated morality; though he finds some merit to these arguments, he concludes that they have probably been pushed further than they warrant. For example, he agrees that there are good reasons for assigning zealous advocates to criminal defendants, because of the unequal line-up between state and defendant, the particularly serious nature of criminal punishment and – in the United States – the constitutional rights of the accused. However, he doubts that these reasons extend to non-criminal matters (a point with which Luban also agrees in Chapter 7). And, in any case, Wasserstrom insists that there is a substantial moral price-tag attached to the morality of lawyers.

Neutral partisanship

At least three of the authors represented in this volume agree on the main troubling features in the lawyer's role morality. Simon characterizes the ethic of zealous advocacy by two principles which he terms the principles of *neutrality* and *partisanship*. The former states that a lawyer is not responsible for the morality of the client's cause; the latter states that the lawyer must 'work aggressively to advance his client's ends'. Luban likewise characterizes zealous advocacy by these two principles, taking his formulations from Murray Schwartz. who styled them the principles of *non-accountability* and *professionalism*.[16] Postema and Luban call the conjunction of these two principles the *standard conception of the lawyer's role*. However, subsequent authors have objected that there is nothing 'standard' about this view at all, particularly in non-advocacy lawyering roles, and it may well be that legal practice contains counter-traditions and alternative conceptions.[17] Carrie Menkel-Meadow, for example, suggests that the rapidly increasing feminization of the legal profession might lead to a less adversarial approach to legal practice, and Robert Gordon, David Luban, and William Simon have argued that there is a long-standing tradition of professionalism in the Bar that is quite distinct from these two principles.[18] In view of these and similar observations, it may be best to abandon the term 'standard conception' and describe the Simon–Schwartz characterization of legal professionalism simply as *neutral partisanship*.

As Simon observes in his essay (Chapter 8), what is unique to legal ethics is the two principles taken together, not either of the principles taken separately. Politicians and soldiers are supposed to be zealous partisans, but they are not supposed to be neutral toward the ends they advance. (Mercenary soldiers and opportunist politicians are an exception, but it is far-fetched to treat these as serious candidates for professional ethics.) Likewise, physicians and bureaucrats are supposed 'to serve the general public without regard to the ends of those who seek their help', but they are not supposed to be one-sided partisans. The neutral partisanship role, which requires single-minded zeal while simultaneously disavowing moral responsibility, combines principles that are arguably inconsistent. Moreover, as Wasserstrom and Postema point out, neutral-partisan legal practice in effect leases out the lawyer's 'moral faculties' of speech, judgement and deliberation, which makes the ideal even more problematic. What bothers us about the mob lawyer is not simply his representation of a ruthless murderer, but his delight in appropriating a treasured part of Americans' collective moral heritage – the words of Martin Luther King – for a purely instrumental purpose. The fact that the lawyer's oratory brought tears to his own eyes makes the whole performance seem even more cynical. Of course, fabricated emotion belongs to another profession besides law – acting – but actors do not mean their audience to mistake the play for reality, and act on that mistake, as the lawyer so obviously does.

Defences of neutral partisanship

How can neutral partisanship be justified? Defenders have generally relied upon three kinds of arguments to justify their conception of the lawyer's role: arguments focused on the *legal system* and the lawyer's part in making it work; arguments focused on the *client* and the client's autonomy; and arguments focused on the *lawyer*, and the lawyer's distinctive moral interests.

The adversary system

As Luban points out, most lawyers in common-law jurisdictions confronted by the charge that they are mere 'hired guns' will explain that their role as neutral partisan is a requirement of the adversary system, which assigns each party the responsibility of making its own case in the most effective way possible.

To illustrate the way in which the argument from the adversary system works, let us turn to one of the best-known books in the legal ethics literature, Freedman's *Lawyers' Ethics in an Adversary System* (1975). Freedman develops his arguments from two central ideas: the importance of the adversary system as a defence of civil liberties (a point to which we shall return) and the centrality of the lawyer's duty of confidentiality to adversary advocacy. According to Freedman, the obligation of zealous advocacy imposed by the adversary system requires lawyers to find out all the facts of the client's case. The client cannot be expected to know which facts are relevant and which are not, and so the client must be reassured that it is safe to reveal anything to his lawyer. Hence the importance of confidentiality, without which the lawyer cannot offer this reassurance.

Having grounded confidentiality in the requirements of the adversary system, Freedman's best-known controversial conclusions seem to follow logically. Thus, he argues that if a lawyer is required to blow the whistle on client perjury, a trilemma of inconsistent obligations results: the lawyer is supposed to keep client confidences, find out all the facts of the case, and reveal to the court that the client has committed perjury. If the lawyer is to honour confidentiality as well as the whistle-blowing requirement, he or she will be compelled to avoid finding out facts inconsistent with what the client plans to testify, thereby violating the requirement of full investigation. If the lawyer honours the duty of full investigation and the whistle-blowing requirement, he or she will be forced to reveal client confidences by informing the judge that the client's perjurious testimony is inconsistent with what the lawyer has learned in private. Since the adversary system imposes obligations of full investigation and confidentiality, it is the whistle-blowing requirement that must go.[19]

Similarly, Freedman points out that if a lawyer refuses to discredit truthful opposing witnesses in cross-examination, then the lawyer is using confidential client information (that the witness is telling the truth) against the client. Although both of Freedman's arguments can be questioned, they carry a great deal of plausibility, and help one understand how the adversary system may generate a strongly differentiated role morality.

A natural response to such arguments is to question the value of the adversary system. In *Lawyers' Ethics in an Adversary System*, Freedman focuses his justification of the adversary system on the criminal defence function. He argues that the advocate serves a crucial political role, for he or she may be the sole protector of the defendant's rights against the awesome power of the state – a power graphically illustrated in case names such as *State v. Jones, People v. Smith, Regina v. Robinson*. Freedman frequently invokes the Bill of Rights to the American Constitution in his argument, but he is plainly taking a more general civil-libertarian position: the right to counsel, the right to due process of law and the right against self-incrimination represent values central to all liberal legal systems, and are not just American idiosyncracies. These values represent two aspects of liberalism: a mistrust of the power of the state based on the historical fact that this power is so often abused, and a celebration of individual human dignity.

Luban agrees with Freedman, but argues that the values Freedman invokes are particular to the criminal defence function and that, in non-criminal as well as non-litigation contexts, the adversary system is much more problematic. Canvassing a number of arguments for the adversary system – that it is the best way of ascertaining the truth, that it is the best defence of legal rights, that it embodies a rational system of moral division of labour, that it creates a morally valuable relationship between lawyer and client, that it enjoys the consent of the governed, and that it is an ineradicable part of national traditions in those jurisdictions that have adopted it – Luban concludes that they all fail. Instead, he defends the adversary system by the pragmatic argument that it is no worse than its alternatives, and that one should stay with one's own system unless alternatives are demonstrably better. He argues that this justification of the adversary system is insufficient to excuse much of the morally problematic behaviour associated with lawyers' role differentiated morality. Only in the criminal defence context, where the justification of the adversary system is principled and not merely pragmatic, can the lawyer's unique role morality be justified. Related criticisms of the adversary system excuse may be found in the essays of Postema, Rhode, and Wasserstrom.

Subsequent discussion of these criticisms has moved in five contrasting directions. In his 1988 book, *Lawyers and Justice: An Ethical Study*, Luban observes that the liberal principles that strongly justify the adversary system in criminal defence rest on the David-and-Goliath contest (to use Rhode's image) between individuals and the state. But, he continues, similar contests can occur when Goliath is a large and powerful institution other than the state – a multinational corporation, for example. Thus, the argument for neutral partisanship in criminal defence can be extended to other David-and-Goliath contests that raise the same liberal concern for individual rights against powerful institutions posing standard threats to them. Conversely, criminal cases can pit Goliath against Goliath; indeed, occasionally it is an understaffed, underfunded governmental agency opposing a powerful private enterprise that is the true David. In such cases, the liberal fear-of-the-state argument fails. Thus, Luban modifies his position from 'The Adversary System Excuse', distinguishing between a 'criminal defense paradigm' and 'a civil suit paradigm', which does not always correspond to the legalistic criminal–civil distinction. Indeed, although Luban accepts Freedman's argument that respect for individual dignity requires lawyers to keep client confidences, he argues that such considerations cannot underwrite a duty of confidentiality for organizational clients, and advocates abolishing the corporate attorney–client privilege.

In his second book, *Understanding Lawyers' Ethics* (1990), Freedman undertakes a careful defence of the adversary system. He argues (a) that the values of dignity and autonomy served by the criminal defence lawyer have counterparts in civil litigation, where cases often establish new rules of public law; (b) that alternatives to the adversary system are weaker than their proponents suggest – in particular, because they frequently require excessive deference to state bureaucracies; and (c) that cross-cultural empirical studies have shown that the adversary system best corresponds with people's sense of fairness.[20]

By contrast, William Simon has argued that neutral partisanship should be abandoned even in criminal defence.[21] Simon criticizes writers (such as Freedman and Luban) fixated on 'the bogey of the state', arguing that:

> ... the image of the lonely individual facing Leviathan is misleading. Let us grant the lonely part even though some defendants have lots of friends. But, what about the state? Libertarian rhetoric tends to suggest that the individual defendant takes on the entire state. But, of course, the state has other concerns besides this defendant. From the state's point of view, the defendant may be part of an enormous class of criminal defendants and suspects with which it can hardly begin to cope.
>
> It is more plausible to portray the typical defendant as facing a small number of harassed, overworked bureaucrats.[22]

Simon proceeds to criticize other premises and arguments for neutral partisanship in criminal defence. To arguments for zealous criminal defence based on concerns about individual dignity, Simon complains that proponents have neglected to take into account the victims of crimes: 'A viable ideal of dignity has to make room for respect for the rights of others and, at least in our system, for acceptance of punishment when the individual violates such rights.'[23]

At a more philosophical level, Rob Atkinson has criticized the metaethical and political assumptions that undergird both Luban's and Simon's critiques of neutral partisanship.[24] Luban accepts Wasserstrom's and Goldman's formulation of the basic problem of legal ethics as a conflict between the lawyer's role differentiated morality and common morality; moreover, both he and Simon argue that the advocate's role morality undermines 'the legal ideals of transcendence and universality'.[25] Thus, neutral partisanship is both morally and legally problematic. Atkinson observes that both these criticisms rest on a conflict between the lawyer's role differentiated behaviour and more universal public norms; in effect, both presuppose the existence of such public norms – norms of morality and norms of political authority. Yet neither Luban nor Simon offers a satisfactory response to sceptics who doubt the existence or, less drastically, the verifiability, of such norms. Atkinson goes on to argue in great detail that Luban's efforts to draw concrete conclusions from his general argument fail because he is continually forced to help himself to norms that 'we' would accept, when in fact these norms are far from obvious: Luban's arguments therefore beg the question.

Although Atkinson believes that Luban and Simon have successfully undermined neutral partisanship, he complains that they have not provided a satisfactory metaethics. This alternative he describes as a 'fideist' or existentialist conception of ethics, in which lawyers acknowledge that the source of value lies ultimately in one's own will. Atkinson draws the further implication that the fideist can avoid the dangers of arrogance and arbitrariness only by discussing ethical issues in communities of those with similar commitments. This communitarian side of fideism is something that Atkinson finds absent in Luban's and Simon's theories. In this respect Atkinson's view is very similar to that of Shaffer, whose essay (Chapter 9) likewise accuses Luban of an unacceptable ethical individualism.[26]

Another important criticism of the metaethical underpinnings of Luban's argument – one which applies with equal force to the parallel arguments of Wasserstrom and Postema – is provided by David Wasserman, who demonstrates that, contrary to Luban's own expectation, Luban's injunction to balance the demands of professional role against common morality will almost always lead lawyers to abandon their role obligations, even in the criminal defence context.[27] In the face of Wasserman's criticism, Luban subsequently revised his theory to give more presumptive weight to the demands of the role differentiated morality than 'The Adversary System Excuse' would suggest.[28]

A final line of argument against critics of adversary ethics has been offered by Stephen Ellmann, who objects that Luban's 'pragmatic justification' of the adversary system is a strong justification – strong enough to underwrite role differentiated morality.[29] The fact that a pragmatic justification consists merely of the comparative judgement that a system is no worse than its alternatives is no objection, for the comparative judgement 'may be a very important criterion indeed'.[30] To this Luban replies:

> Important, yes – for determining whether the system ought to be replaced. Important for determining the strength of role obligations? No, for the moral worth of acts performed in an institutional setting surely turns on the characteristics of that institution, not on the characteristics of alternative institutions in other societies.[31]

Client autonomy

Ellmann's principal worry is that abandoning the stance of moral neutrality toward the client's ends injures client autonomy. In his contribution to this collection (Chapter 3), Pepper likewise argues that client autonomy, not the adversary system, is the central issue in the defence of neutral partisanship – what Pepper calls the lawyer's 'amoral ethical role'. Since involvement with the legal system is among the most salient features in contemporary life, first-class citizenship requires an ability that only lawyers possess to navigate the legal system. If lawyers interpose themselves as censors of autonomously chosen client ends, refusing to assist ends with which they disagree, clients will be denied the full measure of autonomy that the law permits them. Pepper's argument makes no assumption about whether the client and lawyer are involved in adversarial or non-adversarial business: the central point is that when a lawyer's conscience frustrates a lawful client objective, the lawyer has become an impediment to client autonomy over and above the impediments the law itself mandates.[32] If the law is democratic, lawyers who abandon neutral partisanship therefore represent an anti-democratic element. Echoing Wasserstrom, Pepper complains that client autonomy will be frustrated by an oligarchy of lawyers.

To this argument four responses have appeared in the literature. First, one might generalize Simon's previously cited objection to aggressive criminal defence, that client autonomy is not the only moral value, and argue that when enhancing a client's autonomy injures others, it remains to be shown that the gain in autonomy excuses the wrong.[33] More fundamentally, Shaffer in his contribution to this volume (Chapter 9) criticizes the entire emphasis on autonomy, which he denigrates as 'the legal ethics of radical individualism'. In Shaffer's view, the individualist picture that gives pride of place to autonomy in our value-scheme is 'sad, corrupting, and untruthful'.

Second, the 'oligarchy' argument may rest on an imperfect analogy; as Alan Goldman has remarked,

> [t]he major fallacy in this argument . . . is the implicit assumption that lawyers act as a corporate body to determine collectively how clients may act. In fact they do not form such a body. They do not vote on how cases should be pursued, but rather act as individuals whose moral opinions may differ among themselves. . . . If an individual lawyer refuses to do for a client that which he feels the client has no right to do, the client can always seek another lawyer.[34]

Of course, Pepper might with justice reply that seeking another lawyer does not mean finding another lawyer and, more importantly, that in a liberal society client autonomy should rest on a firmer foundation than the bland prediction that lawyers' moral opinions will differ among themselves. Indeed, it would seem hypocritical for a lawyer who refuses to help a client on moral grounds to hope that some other lawyer will take the client's case; yet, without this hope, Pepper's concerns about lawyers collectively frustrating client autonomy seem quite real.

Third, Rhode points out that concerns for individual autonomy are unrealistic in the majority of cases. In line with Freedman, Luban, and Wasserstrom, she acknowledges the importance of individual autonomy in criminal defence and some public interest law, but argues that in the more typical cases when the client is an organization, the appeal to individual autonomy is a *non sequitur*. Moreover, Rhode finds it difficult to square the Bar's professions of concern about individual autonomy with a distribution of legal services by market mechanisms. A well known American criminal defence attorney once quipped that his credo is 'reasonable doubt for a reasonable price'. However, 'autonomy if you can afford it' scarcely seems a recipe for guaranteeing first-class citizenship to all. Of course, Pepper need not tie his moral argument to a defence of the market for legal services and, in any event, he might object that it scarcely excuses a lawyer's interference with a client's autonomy to note that others in society likewise lack autonomy.

In his contribution to the present volume (Chapter 4), Freedman, like Pepper, grounds the lawyer's role in the demands of client autonomy. However, Freedman places equal weight on the lawyer's autonomy, and this leads him to a position that amounts to a fourth line of criticism of Pepper. For Freedman, honouring the lawyer's autonomy means that the lawyer must have discretion to reject cases that offend his or her conscience. (Freedman would presumably criticize, on moral grounds, the cab-rank rule governing barristers in most of the common-law world except the United States.) From this discretion it follows that a lawyer *can* be morally criticized for electing to represent a client, and thus Freedman rejects the principle of neutrality insofar as it applies to the initial choice of client.[35]

The moral interests of the lawyer

Freedman's essay bridges concerns about client autonomy with the third line of defence of neutral partisanship, which focuses on the moral interests of the lawyer. In 'The Lawyer as Friend' (Chapter 5), Charles Fried analogizes the lawyer-client relationship to friendship, and then goes on to press two points. First, each of us has a right to lavish disproportionate attention on our own friends, even if that attention would do more good if it were distributed more broadly. We are not obligated to treat everyone in the world equally, as though our personal relationship with them is morally irrelevant. It is an essential component of the good life to be able to pay special attention to one's family, loved ones and friends, and to deny us that right would be to infringe on basic aspects of our moral personality.

Fried's second point is that lavishing care on our friends is praiseworthy because friendship is itself a source of moral value. Reasoning by analogy, Fried concludes that, since clients are 'special-purpose friends', an advocate cannot be criticized for favouring their interests. Indeed, since it is supererogatory to help anyone to whom we have no pre-existent obligation, it follows that the lawyer's decision to help one client rather than another should be praised and not criticized.

Fried's argument has attracted numerous comments and criticisms, of which Dauer and Leff's and Simon's are included in the present volume (Chapters 6 and 8). Edward Dauer and Arthur Leff object that the friendship analogy is weak, since lawyers and friends share only a single similarity, that of adopting another's interests as one's own. 'In effect,' they argue, 'a lawyer is like a friend even to this limited extent because, for Professor Fried, a friend is like a lawyer.' In the same vein, George Fletcher has accused Fried of neglecting 'the elements of time and interwoven identity that bind friends together and thus make friendship plausible. His illusion that one chooses friends in the way one chooses a lawyer, or a lawyer in the way one develops a friendship, sidesteps reality for the sake of argument.'[36] William Simon goes further. Focusing on the fact that, typically, a lawyer becomes the client's 'friend' only for payment, Simon maintains that Fried has formulated the classical definition not of friendship but of prostitution.

By contrast, Susan Wolf agrees with much of Fried's argument, although she objects that, by using it to defend neutral partisanship, Fried has drawn the wrong conclusion.

> If one adopts some interests as one's own, it would seen one becomes to that extent personally accountable for them. Thus, if the interests are immoral, one can be personally blamed for having them. If, on the other hand, the lawyer is not to be blamed for the immorality of the client's goals, this would have to be because these goals are *not* identified with the lawyer's goals.[37]

Moreover, Derek Parfit has tellingly criticized Fried's optimistic view that, since helping people is supererogatory, lawyers cannot be criticized for their choice of whom to help. By way of a counter-example, Parfit observes that, although it is supererogatory to run into a burning building to carry out a rescue, we would rightly criticize someone who heroically ran into the building to rescue Fried's umbrella rather than Fried himself.[38]

Despite these objections, many lawyers will recognize a substantial grain of truth in Fried's insistence on the personal and intimate character of legal services, which implies a large measure of trust on the part of the client. However compelling one finds the criticisms of Fried's formal arguments, they leave untouched the sense, shared by many lawyers, that the analogy of lawyer-as-friend accurately describes their own professional lives.

Moral psychology

This last point brings to the fore an issue that political arguments about the adversary system and individual rights often neglect – namely, the underpinnings of legal ethics in moral psychology. The essays in this volume by Postema, Kronman, Shaffer, and Menkel-Meadow address this issue.

Postema's essay (Chapter 2) is closest in its immediate connection with the preceding discussion of neutral partisanship and role differentiated morality. In Chapter 2 and a sequel,[39] Postema criticizes neutral partisanship for requiring of lawyers a psychologically unwholesome detachment of their professional selves from their moral personalities. In an often-cited early essay on legal ethics, Charles Curtis appealed to the Stoic tradition exemplified by Montaigne to defend the advocate's detachment; Curtis suggested that this salutary stoical detachment could be achieved either by treating litigation as a mere game or by reducing one's concerns to pride in craft.[40] Montaigne wrote:

> The mayor and Montaigne have always been two, with a very clear separation. For all of being a lawyer or a financier, we must not ignore the knavery there is in such callings. An honest man is not accountable for the vice or stupidity of his trade.[41]

In this way, 'I have been able to take part in public office without departing one nail's breadth from myself'.[42] These two quotations exemplify the strategy of moral detachment that Postema believes to underlie neutral partisanship. In the later essay, Postema observes that Montaigne has actually described two distinct versions of detachment: a strategy of *schizophrenia*, of splitting one's moral self into distinct professional and non-professional halves, and a strategy of *restricted identification*, of investing one's selfhood only in the non-professional half.[43] Postema argues that neither strategy is capable of sustaining one's integrity as a moral being and, for this reason, he rejects neutral partisanship. In its place, Postema proposes that lawyers regard themselves as occupying a *recourse role*. This term, which Postema takes from Mortimer and Sanford Kadish's *Discretion to Disobey*, denotes a role which incorporates among its distinctive moral requirements an understanding that the role-occupant has discretion to depart from them when circumstances warrant.

Kronman, in Chapter 10, aims to answer the question that began Fried's essay – can a good lawyer be a good person? – but pursues it in a direction entirely different from Fried's emphasis on rights and autonomy. Kronman asks why a person would wish to be a lawyer and argues that two common answers – money-making and status on the one hand, or the desire to pursue public interest objectives on the other – cannot be the whole story, since both are instrumental reasons for practising law and neither describes anything intrinsically rewarding about law practice. Kronman finds the intrinsic rewards of law practice to lie in the exercise of practical judgement and the consequent development of the lawyer's character.

Philosophers as diverse as Aristotle, Kant and Wittgenstein have all observed that the faculty of judgement, or practical wisdom (in Aristotle's terms), cannot be understood as a computational capacity that can be encapsulated in a set of rules or formulae. Since one needs good judgement to know when a particular case falls under one rule rather than another, if judgement were entirely rule-governed that would imply an infinite regress of rules. Judgement is a basic cognitive and moral capacity, irreducible to reason or understanding. Kronman analyses judgement as a capacity that combines sympathy and detachment: one is a good judge of human affairs when one can sympathetically place oneself in the shoes of another, while nevertheless retaining an outsider's objectivity toward the other's situation. It is the pre-eminent quality that distinguishes good lawyers from mere legal technicians: as Lincoln Caplan has recently written about 'superlawyer' Joseph Flom, Flom's partners 'are impressed above all by . . . his large quota of the vague but bankable resource that lawyers call good judgement'.[44] And, according to Kronman, it is in the cultivation and exercise of judgement that the rewards intrinsic to law practice lie.

However, sympathetic detachment, Kronman argues, inevitably means that a lawyer must occupy a role much broader than that of hired gun. The lawyer is a counsellor and an adviser, and his or her sympathetic appreciation of other people – clients and non-clients alike – which is a necessary prerequisite to being a good adviser, will inevitably lead the lawyer to serve as a brake on destructive client schemes. Thus, Kronman's identification of the value of lawyering with the exercise of detached sympathy leads him to a vision of legal practice much broader than neutral partisanship.[45] A successful lawyer necessarily possesses good judgement which inevitably leads him to a public-spirited standpoint. (One wonders, however, whether Kronman has not conjured the successful Mafia lawyer out of existence!)

Shaffer, in Chapter 9, adopts and extends Kronman's focus on character in surprising ways. In this essay, as well as in numerous other writings, he argues that character cannot be understood in isolation from the community that forms it and imparts significance to it. In Chapter 9, Shaffer systematically criticises views of legal ethics that neglect community and focus on the protection of individual autonomy and individual rights. In a subsequent book, he writes,

> Rights language in legal ethics may also be wrong, but, before that issue is even considered, it is shallow. When I attempt to contribute to such conversations I *feel* shallow; when I listen to them I feel that I belong somewhere else.[46]

In an equally memorable aphorism, he writes: 'An ethic that is not found in a community is not an ethic; it is only somebody's idea.'[47] The essay in this volume connects several related themes: that individuals exist first (morally and ontologically) in communities; that moral ideas take form within communities not as philosophical theories but as stories; that these stories are the raw material for detailed judgements about what to do; that ethics is a matter of the virtue and character that guide judgement rather than of rules and precepts; and last, but in many ways the most important, that any view of legal ethics which denies these facts is likely to lead lawyers into wrong action that disserves clients.

Consistent with the themes he raises, Shaffer does not offer an abstract or quasi-deductive argument for these conclusions. Rather, he develops them out of a story in which a family's lawyer, confronted with a divisive family issue, can follow two paths: the path of 'radical individualism', which interprets the family rift as a clash between individual clients that poses an intolerable conflict of interest for the lawyer; or the path that recognizes families *as* families, that finds communitarian categories such as 'family' completely natural as a moral vocabulary and that recognizes families as moral entities with which a lawyer can work. In confirmation of Shaffer's suspicion that mainstream legal ethics can fall into grotesque distortions by its innate suspicion of non-individualistic thinking, let me relate an incident that has happened virtually every time I have taught Shaffer's essay to law students. When I ask what guidance the American ethics codes give them in Shaffer's John-and-Mary problem, they flip nervously through the rules until, finally, someone answers that the controlling standard is the American Bar Association's rule entitled 'Organization as Client'. This rule principally concerns how corporate lawyers should respond when officers of the client corporation are engaged in unlawful behaviour that can harm the corporation. Having latched on to this analogy, the students then set to work determining who are the 'duly authorized constituents' and 'highest authority in the organization' consisting of John and Mary's family. A lawyer, one is tempted to conclude, is someone whose trained incapacity leads him to answer the question, 'What is a family?' with the response, 'It's like a corporation, only smaller'!

Yet this is not to say that Shaffer's argument is wholly persuasive, nor that his solution to the John-and-Mary problem is the wisest. One might doubt that the 'estate planning issue . . . is whether this family is equal to the truth of what it is': indeed, one might wonder whether 'the truth of what the family is' is an unambiguous Platonic form waiting to be discovered. One might wonder whether the interventionist course that Shaffer commends would be the right answer if Mary had legitimate reasons for doubting whether her marriage could survive the confrontation of the issue. Suppose, for example, that Mary reveals to the lawyer that, as an unmarried teenager before she met John, she bore a child who was subsequently adopted by acquaintances of her parents. It is this child to whom she wishes to make a bequest, but it seems likely to her that if John learned this profound secret now, it would undermine their marriage. Should the lawyer insist that the family confront the issue to determine whether it is equal to the truth of what it is? Elsewhere Shaffer has written that 'the goal and purpose of a virtuous life in a profession is to help others become good persons'.[48] This view, the diametrical opposite of neutral partisanship, may seem too overbearing and represent too great a declaration of independence of the lawyer's responsibilities from the client's preferred ends.[49]

Many of the communitarian, narratively-based, and anti-rights themes in Shaffer's essay are also recognizable components of what is often called 'difference feminism' – the view, made famous by Carol Gilligan's *In a Different Voice*, that women adopt a more relation-oriented and less entitlement-based style of moral thinking than men. In *The Merchant of Venice* it is Portia who argues in court for mercy over legalism, and Menkel-Meadow's title 'Portia in a Different Voice' (Chapter 11) sounds the principal themes of her pioneering essay in feminist legal ethics: that feminist moral theory can, and should, transform legal ethics and that the feminization of the legal profession (an international demographic phenomenon) may well influence the Bar's traditional approaches to a variety of ethical problems in practice.[50] In addition to those features previously mentioned, Menkel-Meadow proposes that Portia in a different voice will be less enthralled with the warrior-adversary culture and more interested in various forms of alternative dispute resolution.

Numerous empirical studies have cast doubt on the validity of Gilligan's analysis;

but of course this is beside the point when Gilligan's concerns are raised as a normative argument about how people – men as well as women – ought to behave, rather than as a description of how they in fact behave. Deborah Rhode has argued that difference feminism is best understood as a set of normative prescriptions that does itself a disservice when it masquerades as a descriptive anthropology (or gynology): 'we can affirm concerns that resonate with women's experiences, but on the basis of feminist commitments, not biological categories.'[51] Rhode adds:

> When last I delivered comments along these lines, a fellow panelist responded with ill-disguised impatience and possibly unintended irony, 'so what do women want?' My instinct, then as now, was to fight the question. A more useful inquiry, I suggested, is what feminists want.[52]

An example will illustrate the point. Gilligan suggests that, confronted with a clash of valid entitlement-claims, men are liable to weigh them against each other, while women are more likely to examine the underlying situation that led the parties to enter the claims, with a view to resolving the problem without being forced into a zero-sum game. Whether Gilligan is right or wrong about how men and women address the problem, it makes perfect sense for feminists – men as well as women – to argue that the latter approach is clearly superior. Of course, like Shaffer's interventionist approach to the John-and-Mary problem, such efforts at reformulating client ends to finesse confrontational entitlement claims may often run contrary to client wishes and expectations; feminist legal ethics, like the approaches of Kronman and Shaffer, requires lawyers to maintain independence from client ends.

The independence of lawyers

Indeed, one way of formulating many of the issues we have been discussing is to ask whether, in what ways, and to what extent lawyers should be independent of their clients. 'Of their clients' is crucial to this question, for the independence of the Bar *from the state* is a different and much less controversial matter. To lawyers, independence from the state represents a jealously guarded freedom – a central achievement of nineteenth-century liberalism, and one that has often been threatened by anti-liberal regimes eager to convert lawyers into informants and deputy prosecutors.

In a sense, it is unfortunate that independence from the state/independence from clients seems to offer such a tidy dichotomy, one that appears in official rhetoric whenever the lawyer's role as advocate is contrasted with his or her role as 'officer of the court'. For this either-or schema makes the ideal of independence from clients seem tantamount to abandoning liberalism and converting the lawyer into a tool of the state. Plainly, however, this is not what critics of neutral partisanships have in mind: serving the client's ends, whatever they may be, and serving the state's ends, whatever *they* may be, are surely not the sole alternatives. Rather, advocates of independence from the client want lawyers to bring to their representation other values besides unswerving client loyalty: moral values, legal values, political values, religious values. Those who pursue Wasserstrom's concerns about role differentiated morality want lawyers to exercise independent moral judgement. Writers such as Shaffer focus on religious values when they argue that '[f]aithfulness means that a lawyer imagines that she is first of all a believer and is then a lawyer'.[53] Simon, in an essay not included here, has argued that lawyers should exercise discretion on behalf of values inherent in the law (which can include natural law, and hence by no means make the lawyer a servant of the state).[54] And Robert Gordon, in an essay entitled simply 'The Independence of Lawyers', has argued that lawyers should remain independent of their clients on behalf of political values distinct from subservience to the state.[55]

Gordon's essay is the most fully developed and articulate defence of a civic republican vision of legal practice. In its contemporary revival, civic republicanism is usually understood as the opponent of interest-group politics and of the assimilation of political life to market morality. Civic republicans claim that the notion of the common good is a meaningful one; they also argue that it is essential to a viable political order that citizens concern themselves with the common good, for the common good will not be achieved through the guidance of the Invisible Hand. Thus, political life requires at least some people to develop a kind of civic virtue that transcends the pursuit of self-interest, or even of the one-sidedly private interest of a client. Gordon's extensive historical investigations of American corporate lawyers in the nineteenth and early twentieth centuries have persuaded him that the civic republican tradition has always been an important stand in the American Bar's self-understanding, and in 'The Independence of Lawyers' he endeavours to revive this tradition as a lawyerly ideal in the context of contemporary corporate practice.[56] Consequently, the examples on which he focuses are drawn mostly from the realm of law furthest removed from courtroom advocacy: so-called 'compliance counselling' – that is, counselling business clients about how, and to what extent, to comply with intrusive regulations. Gordon offers telling criticisms of the various arguments lawyers rely on to justify adopting a neutral-partisan stance toward the counselling role. He aims to vindicate a vision of legal ethics along the lines of de Tocqueville, Brandeis, Durkheim, and Parsons – a role in which the lawyer serves as a mediator between selfish client interests and the public interests embodied in the law.[57]

This image of the lawyer contrasts sharply with another that has been defended by various sociologists of the profession, most notably Richard Abel and his colleagues.[58] The latter view considers lawyers as self-interested economic agents whose claims to professionalism (whether professionalism is understood along the lines of neutral partisanship or civic republicanism) are not so much a contrast to commercialism as a refined form of it. Where overtly commercial occupations try to control their market from the demand side, by offering particularly attractive goods or prices, professionals aim to control their market from the supply side, by erecting barriers to entry by competitors. Hence unauthorized practice statutes and licensure requirements.

In Chapter 13, Mark Osiel offers important criticisms of both Abel's lawyer-as-entrepreneur metaphor and the lawyer-as-aristocrat metaphor offered in different forms by Gordon, Rhode, Simon, and Luban. Examining sources and data from numerous countries, Osiel argues that neither model explains the behaviour patterns of lawyers. Instead, Osiel proposes an alternative metaphor, that of the lawyer-as-heliotrope. By this he means that lawyers gravitate in the direction of whatever the dominant source of power and authority is in a community. In countries such as France and Germany, where the dominant source of power and authority has long been the state bureaucracy, lawyers tend toward greater independence from their clients and greater alignment toward these bureaucracies. In the United States, by contrast, the dominant source of power and authority has been the private sector – the world of business, finance, and commerce – and, consequently, lawyers have aligned themselves with the interests of business clients.

Osiel argues that Gordon's 'independence of lawyers' thesis is sociologically naive if it means (as Gordon and other critics of neutral partisanship intend) that lawyers should exercise long-term social control over their clients. Gordon maintains that lawyers have much more power than they are willing to admit to themselves, and much of his argument is devoted to overcoming what we might call the 'objection from helplessness', the lame excuse that lawyers are powerless to interfere with their clients. Osiel agrees with Gordon that lawyers have achieved great wealth and power, but observes that the lawyer's power is wholly derivative: it is the clients who are the source of the lawyer's power, prestige and wealth, and, to the extent that lawyers endeavour to exercise social control over their clients, they risk undermining the very power to which Gordon appeals. Gordon's civic-republican project, on Osiel's analysis, resembles the fabled machine that turns itself off.

Rhode's essay (Chapter 12) which, like Osiel's, focuses attention on the social and economic bases of professional ideologies, explores in detail a number of hypocritical and self-serving arguments that the American Bar frequently advances when it fears that its perquisites and privileges are being threatened; one of her principal themes is that 'current ideology miscasts professional expedients as moral necessities'. She is, however, less pessimistic than Osiel about the possibilities of professional reform. In part, she believes that criticizing the ideological hypocrisies and inconsistencies that, in her view, underlie typical Bar rhetoric can have some limited efficacy; in part, she believes that education and socialization focusing on alternative norms can help. Yet, in Rhode's view, practical proposals are also necessary, and 'the only generalization applicable to all such proposals is that their design and evaluation ought not to rest solely under bar control' because historical experience demonstrates that the Bar is too likely to place its own interests first.[59] Both in Chapter 12 and elsewhere, Rhode advocates lay participation in the regulation of lawyers.

Jurisprudential themes

Much of the writing discussed so far has examined legal ethics from the point of view of moral philosophy. Yet the subject also has another philosophical dimension, as a branch of jurisprudence. If the lawyer is indeed an 'officer of the court' and an interpreter of the law, how we understand legal practice will clearly depend on how we understand the nature of law itself. To a certain extent, the converse is also true:

since lawyers are often the boundary-point, or point of contact, between the brooding omnipresence of the law and the citizens and transactions of everyday life, the practice of law may implicitly define the terms of the rule of law. Two of the essays in this volume explicitly address jurisprudential themes: these are Simon's classic essay 'The Ideology of Advocacy' (Chapter 8) and Pepper's essay 'The Lawyer's Amoral Ethical Role' (Chapter 3).

Simon aims to criticize the postulates of neutral partisanship by demonstrating that their jurisprudential underpinnings cannot support them. There is little point in trying to summarize Simon's complex argument – the longest in this book – in this Introduction. Suffice it to say that Simon examines three distinct schools of jurisprudential thought, arguing that the efforts of each to justify neutral partisanship lead to contradictions. The first, legal positivism, is, of course, familiar. The second two will be less familiar to readers unfamiliar with American jurisprudence. 'Purposivism' is Simon's term for the neo-Aristotelian view that law must be understood as a purposive endeavour, not simply as the fiat of an arbitrary sovereign will, as positivists insist. Purposivism is implicit in functionalist sociology, such as that of Durkheim and Parsons, but it is most closely associated with the thought of Lon Fuller (who at one point co-authored a quasi-official defence of the adversary system and the form of lawyers' ethics it entails).[60] The final group of theories which Simon examines he terms 'ritualism': it is the view that law achieves its aim of securing social order by symbolic affirmations of its own legitimacy. Ritualism is not a jurisprudential theory of the same centrality as positivism or even purposivism, but it may well offer an accurate account of the origins of adjudicatory institutions, and the ritualist analysis appears in the writings of some of the best-known legal realists of the 1930s and 1940s (such as Thurman Arnold and Karl Llewellyn). For the most part, of course, realists aimed to debunk atavistic or irrational 'ritual' remnants in the law on pragmatic grounds. Arnold's and Llewellyn's refinement to this general programme was the observation that such atavistic or irrational remnants might be pragmatically justifiable as symbolic affirmations of legitimacy; it is this refinement of realism that Simon takes as his target.

The heart of the matter for Simon is that neutral partisanship does a demonstrably inadequate job of securing basic legal values, whether those values are understood on positivist, purposivist or ritualist lines. At the end of the essay, Simon proposes an alternative to neutral partisanship that he sketches in a rather perfunctory way, calling it 'nonprofessional advocacy'. In the aftermath of his highly influential essay, Simon was frequently criticized for offering an argument that was purely negative, excoriating neutral partisanship while offering only a sketchy and hazy alternative.[61] Several years later, Simon responded by writing 'Ethical Discretion in Lawyering'[62] in which he developed his alternative in considerable detail.

Simon's alternative fits roughly into the purposivist school of thought: essentially, he argues that, when lawyers understand that institutional mechanisms are likely to fail in a given case, they should exercise ethical discretion to remedy the situation. For example, if a tax lawyer knows that the client's documents will never be audited because the tax authority is understaffed, she should refuse to adopt legally controversial positions in these documents, even though she would be willing to advocate them in an adversary hearing. For, in this case, there will never be an adversary adjudication of them. If, on the other hand, the lawyer knows that the government will have an opportunity to challenge her controversial positions, she may assert them even if she personally finds them specious. Thus, in each case, Simon wants the lawyer to ask herself questions such as these: 'How are the institutions I am dealing with supposed to work? Are they actually working that way? What are the policies that the laws relevant to my case are meant to fulfil?' By answering these questions, the lawyer will be able to decide on the ethical stance best calculated to advance the values of the legal system.

Simon sharply distinguishes his view from that of moral philosophers such as Wasserstrom, Postema or Luban, arguing that lawyers should exercise discretion to perfect values inherent in the law rather than to assuage their own consciences. However, Simon's notion of 'values inherent in the law' is a broad one, including natural law principles that appear nowhere in positive law,[63] so it may be that the contrast he draws is not as sharp as it initially appears.

His system is also open to three interconnected criticisms: first, the criticism of Shaffer and Atkinson that Simon's lawyer solves her ethical problems by solitary ratiocination rather than by drawing on the traditions and collective wisdom of a moral community; second, the worry that Simon requires lawyers to engage in a kind of sophisticated analysis of the policies and purposes underlying laws that is far more appropriate to a professor than to a harried practitioner; and, third, that he seems to assume that the question 'what are the policies and purposes underlying this law or this institution?' typically has a determinable answer.

This last point opens Simon to criticism from the direction of legal realism. For the realists, the law consists of predictions of what courts and officials will do, regardless of legislative policies and purposes. This raises Pepper's concern that 'if one combines the dominant "legal realism" understanding of law with the traditional amoral role of the lawyer, *there is no moral input or constraint in the present model of the lawyer-client relationship*'. For the neutral-partisan lawyer does not pass moral judgement on client projects, but only judgement on whether they are legal; thus, if the law is ambiguous and indeterminate, no judgement is left. This realist objection can also be taken from another direction. Pepper worries that lawyers' advice about what is legal will not constrain clients; but lawyers, too, are supposed to be constrained by the law. The central idea of zealous advocacy is that the lawyer is supposed to do everything possible for the client, provided it is legal. On a realist understanding of law, however, this constraint comes close to dissolving. So, at any rate, argues David Wilkins in 'Legal Realism for Lawyers'.[64] The consequence may well be that neither lawyer nor client faces any constraints at all.

One possible response is to reject the realists' predictive theory of law and insist that the bounds of the law are neither as porous nor as dependent on judges' subjective wills as realists typically claim. Another is to argue that, while realism is by and large correct, there is sufficient practical consensus over policies and purposes that engaging in the kind of policy analysis Simon recommends is the best way to predict what courts and officials will do.

Among the most interesting post-realist jurisprudential theories of legal ethics is that of Susan Koniak[65] who adopts the jurisprudential vision elaborated by the late Robert Cover.[66] For Cover, law is more than a system of rules, determinate or not – fundamentally, it is a system of meaning. However, legal rules take on meaning only when they are embedded within the narratives of a community. Since modern societies consist of multiple communities, the state's official set of narratives is only one alternative and is not necessarily the most authoritative one. Certainly, the state has coercive force at its disposal but, contrary to the positivists' view, might does not make right: violence is the antithesis of meaning. In practice, other subcommunities, including the Bar, offer their competing narrative visions of the law, and, if courts do not exercise a firm and wise 'jurispathic' function of killing off some of the rival visions, there simply is no univocal law. In the midst of a Babel of alternative efforts to impart legal meaning, coercion and violence (by the state) too often settle matters.

Cover's jurisprudence contains elements of realism, communitarianism and purposivism; in his insistence that the state's version of the law is no more authoritative than others, it has a decidedly anti-authoritarian and anti-positivist strain as well. Koniak uses Cover's ideas to explore running battles in America between the Bar and the state over the limits of confidentiality. She accuses courts of abdicating their job of imparting legal meaning to the norms governing lawyers – an abdication that leaves the norms underdetermined and the parties in constant ferment. Koniak defends the right of the Bar to stand up to the state on behalf of its own moral vision of appropriate legal process: however, she disagrees with the Bar both on the substance of its normative vision (confidentiality *über alles*) and its unwillingness to protest abuses of the legal process when they affect the welfare of anyone except lawyers.

The relevance of Koniak's very original approach to Simon's 'ethical discretion' thesis is fourfold. First, her picture of competing interpretive communities reinforces the concern that a lawyer's inquiry into the principles and policies underlying law will not yield a univocal answer. Second, her insistence that the state's interpretations of law are no more authoritative than the Bar's (or other groups') implies that we cannot solve the interpretive problem by automatically accepting the state's version of policy. Third, however, her observation that legal meaning appears only within communities (recall Shaffer's aphorism that '[a]n ethic that is not found in a community is not an ethic; it is only somebody's idea') implies that multiple interpretations of law represent more than mere anarchy. This rules out a radically relativist argument against Simon, based on the proposition that any policy whatever might underlie the law. Finally, Koniak's argument that the legal authority of alternative interpretations should be determined by moral argument suggests that Simon's theory may require the kind of moral inquiry Simon hopes to avoid by substituting legal values for moral ones in a lawyer's deliberations.

Inevitably, a survey such as this, which aims to set the essays in the present volume within the context of a larger intellectual history, suffers from significant omissions. Obviously, the editor's own interpretation of the history of contemporary legal ethics scholarship has coloured the discussion contained in this Introduction, as well as in the selection of articles that follow. I state this both as a caution to the reader and as an apology to the many important writers whose work I have not discussed or included here. However, I do not wish to close without at least citing two essays whose focus on the history of American legal ethics made them inappropriate for the present volume, but whose arguments commend them to any serious student of legal ethics. These are Geoffrey C. Hazard (1991), 'The Future of Legal Ethics', *Yale Law Journal* **100**, p. 1239 and L. Ray Patterson (1980), 'Legal Ethics and the Lawyer's Duty of Loyalty', *Emory Law Journal* **29**, p. 909.

Notes

1. Plato (1961), *Gorgias*, in Edith Hamilton & Huntington Cairns (eds), *The Collected Dialogues of Plato*, p. 247.
2. Plato, *Theaetetus*, in *The Collected Dialogues of Plato*, at p. 879.
3. Quoted in David Mellinkoff (1973), *The Conscience of a Lawyer*, p. 13.
4. Quoted in Tuli Kupferberg (1978), 'An Insulting Look at Lawyers Through the Ages', *Juris Doctor*, **8**, Oct.-Nov., at p. 62.
5. Immanuel Kant (1991) 'Perpetual Peace' in Hans Reiss (ed.), *Kant: Political Writings*, 2nd edn, trans. H. B. Nisbet, p. 115.
6. Thomas Babington Macaulay (1900), 'Macaulay's Essay on Bacon', in G. Trevelyan (ed.), *The Works of Lord Macaulay*, **6**, p. 163.
7. It is for this reason that we have chosen to omit the increasingly sophisticated literature (much of it developed by economic analysts of law) concerning the regulation of lawyers, despite the fact that many of the essays in the collection advance proposals to which this literature is quite germane. Although it is germane, the literature is largely American in focus, and the differences among national regulatory regimes are sufficiently deep that many of the arguments would seem parochial.
8. In addition, we have chosen mostly articles that are unavailable through the widely used electronic data bases.
9. Frederic Dannen (1994), 'Annals of the Law: Defending the Mafia', *The New Yorker*, 21 February, p. 69.
10. Ibid.
11. Monroe H. Freedman (1969), 'Professional Responsibility of the Criminal Defense Lawyer: The Three Hardest Questions', *Michigan Law Review*, **64**, p. 1469. In his subsequent book *Lawyers' Ethics in an Adversary System* (1975), Freedman changed his view regarding the third of these issues.
12. The possible exception is Freedman's defence of presenting perjurious client testimony, about which American courts divided until the 1980s, when a series of changes in Bar ethics rules and court opinions unequivocally rejected the practice. Professor Freedman, however, continues to argue that the Bar and the courts have got this issue wrong – that sound professional ethics, as well as a proper reading of the Bill of Rights in the American Constitution, require lawyers to present perjurious client testimony. Otherwise, Freedman argues, the lawyer will be compelled to use client confidences against the client.
13. Richard Wasserstrom (1983), 'Roles and Morality', in David Luban (ed.), *The Good Lawyer: Lawyers' Roles and Lawyers' Ethics*, p. 28.
14. Alan Goldman, (1980), *The Moral Foundations of Professional Ethics*.
15. Goldman discusses the paternalism of physicians toward their patients, but not of lawyers toward their clients. See, however, Stephen Ellmann (1987), 'Lawyers and Clients', *UCLA Law Review*, **34**, p. 717; David Luban (1981), 'Paternalism and the Legal Profession', *Wisconsin Law Review*, p. 454; Marcy Strauss (1987), 'Toward a Revised Model

of Attorney-Client Relationships: The Argument for Autonomy', *North Carolina Law Review*, **65**, p. 315; Dennis Thompson (1980), 'Paternalism in Medicine, Law, and Public Policy', in Daniel Callahan and Sissela Bok (eds), *Ethics Teaching in Higher Education*, p. 246.

16. Murray L. Schwartz (1978), 'The Professionalism and Accountability of Lawyers', *California Law Review*, **66**, p. 673. In *Lawyers and Justice*, Luban combines Simon's and Schwartz's terminology, referring to the principles of non-accountability and partisanship.
17. See especially Ted Schneyer (1984), 'Moral Philosophy's Standard Misconception of Legal Ethics', *Wisconsin Law Review*, p. 1529, but also Stephen Ellmann (1990), 'Lawyering for Justice in a Flawed Democracy', *Columbia Law Review*, **90**, p. 116, and M. B. E. Smith (1990), 'Should Lawyers Listen to Philosophers About Legal Ethics?', *Law and Philosophy*, **9**, p. 67. Luban has replied to Schneyer's criticisms in *Lawyers and Justice*, supra note 16, pp. 397–403, to Ellmann's (1990) in 'Partisanship, Betrayal and Autonomy in the Lawyer-Client Relationship: A Reply to Stephen Ellmann', *Columbia Law Review*, **90**, pp. 1006–12, and to Smith's (1990–91) in 'Smith Against the Ethicists', *Law and Philosophy*, **9**, p. 417.
18. David Luban, 'Partisanship, Betrayal and Autonomy', supra note 17, pp. 1012–17; (1988), 'The *Noblesse Oblige* Tradition in the Practice of Law', *Vanderbilt Law Review*, **41**, p. 717; Robert W. Gordon, *Lawyers as the American Aristocracy* (unpublished Holmes lectures), 'The Independence of Lawyers', *Boston University Law Review*, **68**, p. 1; (1988); William H. Simon (1985), 'Babbitt v. Brandeis: The Decline of the Professional Ideal', *Stanford Law Review*, **37**, p. 565; Robert W. Gordon and William H. Simon (1992), 'The Redemption of Professionalism', in Robert L. Nelson, David M. Trubek & Rayman L. Solomon (eds), *Lawyers' Ideals/Lawyers' Practices*, p. 230.
19. See Freedman (1990), *Understanding Lawyers' Ethics*, pp. 109–41.
20. Ibid. at pp. 13–42. See also Stephan Landsman (1984), *The Adversary System: A Description and Defense.*
21. William H. Simon (1993), 'The Ethics of Criminal Defense', *Michigan Law Review*, **91**, p. 1707. See also the reply by David Luban (1993), 'Are Criminal Defenders Different?' *Michigan Law Review*, **91**, p. 1729 and Simon's (1993) rejoinder 'Further Reflections on Libertarian Criminal Defense', *Michigan Law Review*, **91**, p. 1767.
22. Simon, 'The Ethics of Criminal Defense', p. 1707.
23. Ibid. at p. 1713.
24. Rob Atkinson (1992), 'Beyond the New Role Morality for Lawyers', *Maryland Law Review*, **51**, p. 853.
25. William H. Simon (1980), 'Homo Psychologicus: Notes on a New Legal Formalism', *Stanford Law Review*, **32**, p. 541.
26. See Shaffer's essay, Chapter 9 in this volume, at note 4.
27. David Wasserman (1990), 'Should a Good Lawyer Do the Right Thing? David Luban on the Morality of Adversary Representation', *Maryland Law Review*, **49**, pp. 394–404.
28. David Luban (1990), 'Freedom and Constraint in Legal Ethics: Some Mid-Course Corrections to *Lawyers and Justice*', *Maryland Law Review*, **49**, pp. 432–35, 443–52.
29. Stephen Ellmann (1990), 'Lawyering for Justice in a Flawed Democracy', *Columbia Law Review*, **90**, pp. 143–44.
30. Ibid. at 144 n. 53.
31. Luban, supra note 17 at p. 1020.
32. A similar argument appears in a splendid essay by Alan Donagan that has not received the attention it is due: 'Justifying Legal Practice in the Adversary System', in *The Good Lawyer*, supra note 13 at pp. 128–33. Donagan, however, employs the argument to justify the adversary system, but rejects neutral partisanship.
33. For versions of this argument see David Luban (1986), 'The Lysistratian Prerogative: A Response to Stephen Pepper', *American Bar Foundation Research Journal*, p. 639, and Luban, supra note 17 at pp. 1035–43.
34. Goldman, *The Moral Foundations*, supra note 14 at pp. 129–30.

35. In this Freedman repudiates his earlier position to the contrary in *Lawyers' Ethics in an Adversary System*.
36. George P. Fletcher (1993), *Loyalty: An Essay on the Morality of Relationships*, p. 180.
37. Susan Wolf (1983), 'Ethics, Legal Ethics, and the Ethics of Law', in *The Good Lawyer*, supra note 13 at p. 59 n. 4.
38. Charles Fried and Derek Parfit (1979), 'Correspondence', *Philosophy and Public Affairs*, **8**, p. 396.
39. Gerald J. Postema (1983), 'Self-Image, Integrity, and Professional Responsibility', in *The Good Lawyer*, supra note 13 at p. 286.
40. Charles P. Curtis (1951), 'The Ethics of Advocacy', *Stanford Law Review*, **4**, pp. 19–23.
41. Michel de Montaigne (1958), 'Of Husbanding Your Will', in Donald Frame (ed.), *Complete Essays of Montaigne*, p. 774.
42. Ibid. at p. 770.
43. Postema, 'Self-Image, Integrity, and Professional Responsibility', supra note 39 at pp. 292–93.
44. Lincoln Caplan (1993), *Skadden: Power, Money, and the Rise of a Legal Empire*, p. 3.
45. Kronman offers an extended development of these ideas in *The Lost Lawyer: Failing Ideals of the Legal Profession* (1993).
46. Thomas L. Shaffer and Mary M. Shaffer (1991), *American Lawyers and Their Communities: Ethics in the Legal Profession*, p. 13.
47. Ibid. at p. 130 n. 4.
48. Ibid. at p. 94.
49. For further discussion of these issues, see Russell G. Pearce (1994), 'Family Values and Legal Ethics: Competing Approaches to Conflicts in Representing Spouses', *Fordham Law Review*, **62**, p. 1253.
50. See also Rand Jack and Dana Crowley Jack (1989), *Moral Vision and Professional Decisions: The Changing Values of Women and Men Lawyers*; Deborah L. Rhode (1988), 'Perspectives on Professional Women', *Stanford Law Review*, **40**, p. 1163; Rhode (1993), 'Missing Questions: Feminist Perspectives on Legal Education', *Stanford Law Review*, **45**, p. 1547; Leslie Bender (1990), 'From Gender Difference to Feminist Solidarity: Using Carol Gilligan and an Ethic of Care in Law', *Vermont Law Review*, **15**, p. 1.
51. Rhode, 'Missing Questions', supra note 50 at p. 1554.
52. Ibid. at p. 1563.
53. Supra note 46 at p. 198.
54. William H. Simon (1988), 'Ethical Discretion in Lawyering', *Harvard Law Review*, **101**, p. 1083.
55. Robert W. Gordon (1988), 'The Independence of Lawyers', *Boston University Law Review*, **58**, p. 1.
56. For another historical account of civic-republican themes in nineteenth-century American legal ethics, see Russell G. Pearce (1992), 'Rediscovering the Republican Origins of the Legal Ethics Codes', *Georgetown Journal of Legal Ethics*, **6**, p. 241. See also Robert W. Gordon (1990), 'Corporate Law Practice as a Public Calling', *Maryland Law Review*, **49**, p. 255.
57. See Durkheim's *The Division of Labor in Society* (trans. George Simpson 1933) and *Professional Ethics and Civil Morals* (1957), as well as Parsons' 'The Professions and Social Structure' and 'A Sociologist Looks at the Legal Profession', both in *Essays in Sociological Theory* (rev. edn 1954).
58. Richard L. Abel (1989), *American Lawyers*; (1988) *The Legal Profession in England and Wales*; Richard L. Abel and Philip S. C. Lewis (1989), *Lawyers in Society*, 4 vols.
59. There is, however, some evidence that this plausible proposition is not invariably true. See particularly Terence C. Halliday (1989), 'Legal Professions and the State: Neocorporatist Variations on the Pluralist Theme of Liberal Democracies', in Richard L. Abel and Philip S. C. Lewis (eds), *Lawyers in Society: Comparative Theories*, **3**; Terence C. Halliday (1987), *Beyond Monopoly: Lawyers, State Crises, and Professional Empowerment*.

60. Lon Fuller and John D. Randall (1958), 'Professional Responsibility: Report of the Joint Conference of the ABA and AALS', *American Bar Association Journal,* **44**, p. 1160.
61. It is worth noting that this became something of a stock criticism of writing in *Critical Legal Studies*, and Simon's essay was the first *CLS* discussion of legal ethics.
62. Supra note 54.
63. Ibid. at p. 1115.
64. David B. Wilkins (1990), 'Legal Realism for Lawyers', *Harvard Law Review,* **104**, p. 469.
65. Susan P. Koniak (1992), 'The Law Between the Bar and the State', *North Carolina Law Review,* **70**, p. 1389; Koniak (1993), 'When Courts Refuse to Frame the Law and Others Frame It to Their Will', *Southern California Law Review,* **66**, p. 1075.
66. See Martha Minow, Michael Ryan and Austin Sarat (eds) (1993), *Narrative, Violence, and the Law: The Essays of Robert Cover.*

Part I

Role Differentiated Morality

[1]

Articles

LAWYERS AS PROFESSIONALS: SOME MORAL ISSUES

RICHARD WASSERSTROM*

In this paper I examine two moral criticisms of lawyers which, if well-founded, are fundamental. Neither is new but each appears to apply with particular force today. Both tend to be made by those not in the mainstream of the legal profession and to be rejected by those who are in it. Both in some sense concern the lawyer-client relationship.

The first criticism centers around the lawyer's stance toward the world at large. The accusation is that the lawyer-client relationship renders the lawyer at best systematically amoral and at worst more than occasionally immoral in his or her dealings with the rest of mankind.

The second criticism focuses upon the relationship between the lawyer and the client. Here the charge is that it is the lawyer-client relationship which is morally objectionable because it is a relationship in which the lawyer dominates and in which the lawyer typically, and perhaps inevitably, treats the client in both an impersonal and a paternalistic fashion.

To a considerable degree these two criticisms of lawyers derive, I believe, from the fact that the lawyer is a professional. And to the extent to which this is the case, the more generic problems I will be exploring are those of professionalism generally. But in some respects, the lawyer's situation is different from that of other professionals. The lawyer is vulnerable to some moral criticism that does not as readily or as easily attach to any other professional. And this, too, is an issue that I shall be examining.[1]

---

* B.A. 1957, Amherst College; M.A. 1958, Ph.D. 1960, University of Michigan; LL.B. 1960, Stanford. Professor of Law and Professor of Philosophy, University of California School of Law, Los Angeles. This article is a revised version of a lecture given at Amherst College in 1974 as a part of the Copeland Colloquium series on morality and the professions.

[1] Because of the significance for my analysis of the closely related concepts of a profession and a professional, it will be helpful to indicate at the outset what I take to be the central features of a profession.

But first there is an ambiguity that must be noted so that it can be dismissed. There is one sense of "professional" and hence of "profession" with which I am not concerned. That is the sense in which there are in our culture, professional

Although I am undecided about the ultimate merits of either criticism, I am convinced that each is deserving of careful articulation and assessment, and that each contains insights that deserve more acknowledgment than they often receive. My ambition is, therefore, more to exhibit the relevant considerations and to stimulate additional reflection, than it is to provide any very definite conclusions.

I.

As I have indicated, the first issue I propose to examine concerns the ways the professional-client relationship affects the professional's stance toward the world at large. The primary question that is presented is whether there is adequate justification for the kind of moral universe that comes to be inhabited by the lawyer as he or she goes through professional life. For at best the lawyer's world is a simplified moral world; often it is an amoral one; and more than occasionally, perhaps, an overtly immoral one.

To many persons, Watergate was simply a recent and dramatic

athletes, professional actors, and professional beauticians. In this sense, a person who possesses sufficient skill to engage in an activity for money and who elects to do so is a professional rather than, say, an amateur or a volunteer. This is, as I have said, not the sense of "profession" in which I am interested.

I am interested, instead, in the characteristics of professions such as law, or medicine. There are, I think, at least six that are worth noting.

(1) The professions require a substantial period of formal education—at least as much if not more than that required by any other occupation.

(2) The professions require the comprehension of a substantial amount of theoretical knowledge and the utilization of a substantial amount of intellectual ability. Neither manual nor creative ability is typically demanded. This is one thing that distinguishes the professions both from highly skilled crafts—like glassblowing—and from the arts.

(3) The professions are both an economic monopoly and largely self-regulating. Not only is the practice of the profession restricted to those who are certified as possessing the requisite competencies, but the questions of what competencies are required and who possesses them are questions that are left to the members of the profession to decide for themselves.

(4) The professions are clearly among the occupations that possess the greatest social prestige in the society. They also typically provide a degree of material affluence substantially greater than that enjoyed by most working persons.

(5) The professions are almost always involved with matters which from time to time are among the greatest personal concerns that humans have: physical health, psychic well-being, liberty, and the like. As a result, persons who seek the services of a professional are often in a state of appreciable concern, if not vulnerability, when they do so.

(6) The professions almost always involve at their core a significant interpersonal relationship between the professional, on the one hand, and the person who is thought to require the professional's services: the patient or the client.

illustration of this fact. When John Dean testified before the Select Senate Committee inquiring into the Watergate affair in the Spring of 1973, he was asked about one of the documents that he had provided to the Committee. The document was a piece of paper which contained a list of a number of the persons who had been involved in the cover-up. Next to a number of the names an asterisk appeared. What, Dean was asked, was the meaning of the asterisk? Did it signify membership in some further conspiracy? Did it mark off those who were decision makers from those who were not? There did not seem to be any obvious pattern: Ehrlichman was starred, but Haldeman was not; Mitchell was starred, but Magruder was not. Oh, Dean answered, the asterisk really didn't mean anything. One day when he had been looking at the list of participants, he had been struck by the fact that so many of them were lawyers. So, he marked the name of each lawyer with an asterisk to see just how many there were. He had wondered, he told the Committee, when he saw that so many were attorneys, whether that had had anything to do with it; whether there was some reason why lawyers might have been more inclined than other persons to have been so willing to do the things that were done in respect to Watergate and the cover-up. But he had not pursued the matter; he had merely mused about it one afternoon.

It is, I think, at least a plausible hypothesis that the predominance of lawyers was not accidental—that the fact that they were lawyers made it easier rather than harder for them both to look at things the way they did and to do the things that were done. The theory that I want to examine in support of this hypothesis connects this activity with a feature of the lawyer's professionalism.

As I have already noted, one central feature of the professions in general and of law in particular is that there is a special, complicated relationship between the professional, and the client or patient. For each of the parties in this relationship, but especially for the professional, the behavior that is involved is to a very significant degree, what I call, role-differentiated behavior. And this is significant because it is the nature of role-differentiated behavior that it often makes it both appropriate and desirable for the person in a particular role to put to one side considerations of various sorts—and especially various moral considerations—that would otherwise be relevant if not decisive. Some illustrations will help to make clear what I mean both by role-differentiated behavior and by the way role-differentiated behavior often alters, if not eliminates, the significance of those moral considerations that would obtain, were it not for the presence of the role.

Being a parent is, in probably every human culture, to be involved in role-differentiated behavior. In our own culture, and once again in most, if not all, human cultures, as a parent one is entitled, if not obligated, to prefer the interests of one's own children over those of children generally. That is to say, it is regarded as appropriate for a parent to allocate excessive goods to his or her own children, even though other children may have substantially more pressing and genuine needs for these same items. If one were trying to decide what the right way was to distribute assets among a group of children all of whom were strangers to oneself, the relevant moral considerations would be very different from those that would be thought to obtain once one's own children were in the picture. In the role of a parent, the claims of other children vis-à-vis one's own are, if not rendered morally irrelevant, certainly rendered less morally significant. In short, the role-differentiated character of the situation alters the relevant moral point of view enormously.

A similar situation is presented by the case of the scientist. For a number of years there has been debate and controversy within the scientific community over the question of whether scientists should participate in the development and elaboration of atomic theory, especially as those theoretical advances could then be translated into development of atomic weapons that would become a part of the arsenal of existing nation states. The dominant view, although it was not the unanimous one, in the scientific community was that the role of the scientist was to expand the limits of human knowledge. Atomic power was a force which had previously not been utilizable by human beings. The job of the scientist was, among other things, to develop ways and means by which that could now be done. And it was simply no part of one's role as a scientist to forego inquiry, or divert one's scientific explorations because of the fact that the fruits of the investigation could be or would be put to improper, immoral, or even catastrophic uses. The moral issues concerning whether and when to develop and use nuclear weapons were to be decided by others; by citizens and statesmen; they were not the concern of the scientist *qua* scientist.

In both of these cases it is, of course, conceivable that plausible and even thoroughly convincing arguments exist for the desirability of the role-differentiated behavior and its attendant neglect of what would otherwise be morally relevant considerations. Nonetheless, it is, I believe, also the case that the burden of proof, so to speak, is always upon the proponent of the desirability of this kind of role-differentiated behavior. For in the absence of special reasons why parents ought to prefer the interests of their children over those of children in general, the moral point of view surely requires that the claims and needs of all children receive equal consideration. But we take the rightness of parental preference so for granted, that we often neglect, I think, the fact that it is anything but self-evidently morally appropriate. My own view, for example, is that careful reflection shows that the *degree* of parental preference systematically encouraged in our own culture is far too extensive to be morally justified.

All of this is significant just because to be a professional is to be enmeshed in role-differentiated behavior of precisely this sort. One's role as a doctor, psychiatrist, or lawyer, alters one's moral universe in a fashion analogous to that described above. Of special significance here is the fact that the professional *qua* professional has a client or patient whose interests must be represented, attended to, or looked after by the professional. And that means that the role of the professional (like that of the parent) is to prefer in a variety of ways the interests of the client or patient over those of individuals generally.

Consider, more specifically, the role-differentiated behavior of the lawyer. Conventional wisdom has it that where the attorney-client relationship exists, the point of view of the attorney is properly different—and appreciably so—from that which would be appropriate in the absence of the attorney-client relationship. For where the attorney-client relationship exists, it is often appropriate and many times even obligatory for the attorney to do things that, all other things being equal, an ordinary person need not, and should not do. What is characteristic of this role of a lawyer is the lawyer's required indifference to a wide variety of ends and consequences that in other contexts would be of undeniable moral significance. Once a lawyer represents a client, the lawyer has a duty to make his or her expertise fully available in the realization of the end sought by the client, irrespective, for the most part, of the moral worth to which the end will be put or the character of the client who seeks to utilize it. Provided that the end sought is not illegal, the lawyer is, in essence, an amoral technician whose peculiar skills and knowledge in respect to the law are available to those with whom the relationship of client is established. The question, as I have indicated, is whether this particular and pervasive feature of professionalism is itself justifiable. At a minimum, I do not think any of the typical, simple answers will suffice.

One such answer focuses upon and generalizes from the criminal defense lawyer. For what is probably the most familiar aspect of this role-differentiated character of the lawyer's activity is that of the defense of a client charged with a crime. The received view within the profession (and to a lesser degree within the society at large) is that having once agreed to represent the client, the lawyer is under an obligation to do his or her best to defend that person at trial, irrespective, for instance, even of the lawyer's belief in the client's innocence. There are limits, of course, to what constitutes a defense: a lawyer cannot bribe or intimidate witnesses to increase the likelihood of securing an acquittal. And there are legitimate questions, in close cases, about how those limits are to be delineated. But, however these matters get resolved, it is at least clear that it is thought both appropriate and obligatory for the attorney to put on as vigorous and persuasive a defense of a client believed to be guilty as would have been mounted by the lawyer thoroughly convinced of the client's innocence. I suspect that many persons find this an attractive and admirable feature of the life of a legal professional. I know that often I do. The justifications are varied and, as I shall argue below, probably convincing.

But part of the difficulty is that the irrelevance of the guilt or innocence of an accused client by no means exhausts the altered perspective of the lawyer's conscience, even in criminal cases. For in the course of defending an accused, an attorney may have, as a part of his or her duty of representation, the obligation to invoke procedures and practices which are themselves morally objectionable and of which the lawyer in other contexts might thoroughly disapprove. And these situations, I think, are somewhat less comfortable to confront. For example, in California, the case law permits a defendant in a rape case to secure in some circumstances an order from the court requiring the complaining witness, that is the rape victim, to submit to a psychiatric examination before trial.[8] For no other crime is such a pretrial remedy available. In no other case can the victim of a crime be required to undergo psychiatric examination at the request of the defendant on the ground that the results of the examination may help the defendant prove that the offense did not take place. I think such a rule is wrong and is reflective of the sexist bias of the law in respect to rape. I certainly do not think it right that rape victims should be singled out by the law for this kind of special pretrial treatment, and I am skeptical about the morality of any involuntary psychiatric examination of witnesses. Nonetheless, it appears to be part of the role-differentiated obligation of a lawyer for a defendant charged with rape to seek to take advantage of this particular rule of law—irrespective of the independent moral view he or she may have of the rightness or wrongness of such a rule.

Nor, it is important to point out, is this peculiar, strikingly amoral behavior limited to the lawyer involved with the workings of the criminal law. Most clients come to lawyers to get the lawyers to help them do things that they could not easily do without the assistance provided by the lawyer's special competence. They wish, for instance, to dispose of their property in a certain way at death. They wish to contract for the purchase or sale of a house or a business. They wish to set up a corporation which will manufacture and market a new product. They wish to minimize their income taxes. And so on. In each case, they need the assistance of the professional, the lawyer, for he or she alone has the special skill which will make it possible for the client to achieve the desired result.

And in each case, the role-differentiated character of the lawyer's way of being tends to render irrelevant what would otherwise be morally relevant considerations. Suppose that a client desires to make a will disinheriting her children because they opposed the war in Vietnam. Should the lawyer refuse to draft the will because the lawyer thinks this a bad reason to disinherit one's children? Suppose a client can avoid the payment of taxes through a loophole only available to a few wealthy taxpayers. Should the lawyer

[8] Ballard v. Superior Court, 64 Cal. 2d 159, 410 P.2d 838, 49 Cal. Rptr. 302 (1966).

refuse to tell the client of a loophole because the lawyer thinks it an unfair advantage for the rich? Suppose a client wants to start a corporation that will manufacture, distribute and promote a harmful but not illegal substance, *e.g.*, cigarettes. Should the lawyer refuse to prepare the articles of incorporation for the corporation? In each case, the accepted view within the profession is that these matters are just of no concern to the lawyer *qua* lawyer. The lawyer need not of course agree to represent the client (and that is equally true for the unpopular client accused of a heinous crime), but there is nothing wrong with representing a client whose aims and purposes are quite immoral. And having agreed to do so, the lawyer is required to provide the best possible assistance, without regard to his or her disapproval of the objective that is sought.

The lesson, on this view, is clear. The job of the lawyer, so the argument typically concludes, is not to approve or disapprove of the character of his or her client, the cause for which the client seeks the lawyer's assistance, or the avenues provided by the law to achieve that which the client wants to accomplish. The lawyer's task is, instead, to provide that competence which the client lacks and the lawyer, as professional, possesses. In this way, the lawyer as professional comes to inhabit a simplified universe which is strikingly amoral—which regards as morally irrelevant any number of factors which nonprofessional citizens might take to be important, if not decisive, in their everyday lives. And the difficulty I have with all of this is that the arguments for such a way of life seem to be not quite so convincing to me as they do to many lawyers. I am, that is, at best uncertain that it is a good thing for lawyers to be so professional—for them to embrace so completely this role-differentiated way of approaching matters.

More specifically, if it is correct that this is the perspective of lawyers in particular and professionals in general, is it right that this should be their perspective? Is it right that the lawyer should be able so easily to put to one side otherwise difficult problems with the answer: but these are not and cannot be my concern as a lawyer? What do we gain and what do we lose from having a social universe in which there are professionals such as lawyers, who, as such, inhabit a universe of the sort I have been trying to describe?

One difficulty in even thinking about all of this is that lawyers may not be very objective or detached in their attempts to work the problem through. For one feature of this simplified, intellectual world is that it is often a very comfortable one to inhabit.

To be sure, on occasion, a lawyer may find it uncomfortable to represent an extremely unpopular client. On occasion, too, a lawyer may feel ill at ease invoking a rule of law or practice which he or she thinks to be an unfair or undesirable one. Nonetheless, for most lawyers, most of the time, pursuing the interests of one's clients is an attractive and satisfying way to live in part just because the moral world of the lawyer is a simpler, less complicated, and less ambiguous world than the moral world of ordinary life. There is, I think, something quite seductive about being able to turn aside so many ostensibly difficult moral dilemmas and decisions with the reply: but that is not my concern; my job as a lawyer is not to judge the rights and wrong of the client or the cause; it is to defend as best I can my client's interests. For the ethical problems that can arise within this constricted point of view are, to say the least, typically neither momentous nor terribly vexing. Role-differentiated behavior is enticing and reassuring precisely because it does constrain and delimit an otherwise often intractable and confusing moral world.

But there is, of course, also an argument which seeks to demonstrate that it is good and not merely comfortable for lawyers to behave this way.

It is good, so the argument goes, that the lawyer's behavior and concomitant point of view are role-differentiated because the lawyer *qua* lawyer participates in a complex institution which functions well only if the individuals adhere to their institutional roles.

For example, when there is a conflict between individuals, or between the state and an individual, there is a well-established institutional mechanism by which to get that dispute resolved. That mechanism is the trial in which each side is represented by a lawyer whose job it is both to present his or her client's case in the most attractive, forceful light and to seek to expose the weaknesses and defects in the case of the opponent.

When an individual is charged with having committed a crime, the trial is the mechanism by which we determine in our society whether or not the person is in fact guilty. Just imagine what would happen if lawyers were to refuse, for instance, to represent persons whom they thought to be guilty. In a case where the guilt of a person seemed clear, it might turn out that some individuals would be deprived completely of the opportunity to have the system determine whether or not they are in fact guilty. The private judgment of individual lawyers would in effect be substituted for the public, institutional judgment of the judge and jury. The amorality of lawyers helps to guarantee that every criminal defendant will have his or her day in court.

In addition, of course, appearances can be deceiving. Persons who appear before trial to be clearly guilty do sometimes turn out to be innocent. Even persons who confess their guilt to their attorney occasionally turn out to have lied or to have been mistaken. The adversary system, so this argument continues, is simply a better method than any other that has been established by which to determine the legally relevant facts in any given case. It is certainly a better method than the exercise of private judgment by any particular individual. And the adversary system only works if each party to the controversy has a lawyer, a person whose institutional role it is to argue, plead and present the merits of his or her case and the demerits of the opponent's. Thus if the adversary system is to work, it is necessary that there be lawyers who will play their appropriate, professional, institutional role of representative of the client's cause.

Nor is the amorality of the institutional role of the lawyer restricted to the defense of those accused of crimes. As was indicated earlier, when the lawyer functions in his most usual role, he or she functions as a counselor, as a professional whose task it is to help people realize those objectives and ends that the law permits them to obtain and which cannot be obtained without the attorney's special competence in the law. The attorney may think it wrong to disinherit one's children because of their views about the Vietnam war, but here the attorney's complaint is really with the laws of inheritance and not with his or her client. The attorney may think the tax provision an unfair, unjustifiable loophole, but once more the complaint is really with the Internal Revenue Code and not with the client who seeks to take advantage of it. And these matters, too, lie beyond the ambit of the lawyer's moral point of view as institutional counselor and facilitator. If lawyers were to substitute their own private views of what ought to be legally permissible and impermissible for those of the legislature, this would constitute a surreptitious and undesirable shift from a democracy to an oligarchy of lawyers. For given the fact that lawyers are needed to effectuate the wishes of clients, the lawyer ought to make his or her skills available to those who seek them without regard for the particular objectives of the client.

Now, all of this certainly makes some sense. These arguments are neither specious nor without force. Nonetheless, it seems to me that one dilemma which emerges is that if this line of argument is sound, it also appears to follow that the behavior of the lawyers involved in Watergate was simply another less happy illustration of lawyers playing their accustomed institutional role. If we are to approve on institutional grounds of the lawyer's zealous defense of the apparently guilty client and the lawyer's effective assistance of the immoral cheat, does it not follow that we must also approve of the Watergate lawyer's zealous defense of the interests of Richard Nixon?

As I have indicated, I do not think there is any easy answer to this question. For I am not, let me hasten to make clear, talking about the easy cases—about the behavior of the lawyers that was manifestly illegal. For someone quite properly might reply that it was no more appropriate for the lawyer who worked in the White House to obstruct justice or otherwise violate the criminal law than it would be for a criminal defense lawyer to shoot the prosecution witness to prevent adverse testimony or bribe a defense witness in order to procure favorable testimony. What I am interested in is all of the Watergate behavior engaged in by the Watergate lawyers that was not illegal, but that was, nonetheless, behavior of which we quite properly disapprove. I mean lying to the public; dissembling; stonewalling; tape-recording conversations; playing dirty tricks. Were not these just effective lawyer-like activities pursued by lawyers who viewed Richard Nixon as they would a client and who sought, therefore, the advancement and protection of his interests—personal and political?

It might immediately be responded that the analogy is not apt. For the lawyers who were involved in Watergate were hardly participants in an adversary proceeding. They were certainly not participants in that institutional setting, litigation, in which the amorality of the lawyer makes the most sense. It might even be objected that the amorality of the lawyer *qua counselor* is clearly distinguishable from the behavior of the Watergate lawyers. Nixon as President was not a client; they, as officials in the executive branch, were functioning as governmental officials and not as lawyers at all.

While not wholly convinced by a response such as the above, I am prepared to accept it because the issue at hand seems to me to be a deeper one. Even if the involvment of so many lawyers in Watergate was adventitious (or, if not adventitious, explicable in terms of some more benign explanation) there still seems to me to be costs, if not problems, with the amorality of the lawyer that derives from his or her role-differentiated professionalism.

As I indicated earlier, I do believe that the amoral behavior of the *criminal* defense lawyer is justifiable. But I think that jurisdiction depends at least as much upon the special needs of an accused as upon any more general defense of a lawyer's role-differentiated behavior. As a matter of fact I think it likely that many persons such as myself have been misled by the special features of the criminal case. Because a deprivation of liberty is so serious, because the prosecutiorial resources of the state are so vast, and because, perhaps, of a serious skepticism about the rightness of punishment even where wrongdoing has occurred, it is easy to accept the view that it makes sense to charge the defense counsel with the job of making the best possible case for the accused—without regard, so to speak, for the merits. This coupled with the fact that it is an adversarial proceeding succeeds, I think, in justifying the amorality of the criminal defense counsel. But this does not, however, justify a comparable perspective on the part of lawyers generally. Once we leave the peculiar situation of the criminal defense lawyer, I think it quite likely that the role-differentiated amorality of the lawyer is almost certainly excessive and at times inappropriate. That is to say, this special case to one side, I am inclined to think that we might all be better served if lawyers were to see themselves less as subject to role-differentiated behavior and more as subject to the demands of the moral point of view. In this sense it may be that we need a good deal less rather than more professionalism in our society generally and among lawyers in particular.

Moreover, even if I am wrong about all this, four things do seem to me to be true and important.

First, all of the arguments that support the role-differentiated amorality of the lawyer on institutional grounds can succeed only if the enormous degree of trust and confidence in the institutions themselves is itself jusified. If the institutions work well and fairly, there may be good sense to deferring important moral concerns and criticisms to another time and place, to the level of institutional criticism and assessment. But the less certain we are entitled to be of either the rightness or the self-corrective nature of the larger institutions of which the professional is a part, the less apparent it is that we should encourage the professional to avoid direct engagement with the moral issues as they arise. And we are, today, I believe, certainly entitled to be quite skeptical both of the fairness and of the capacity for self-correction of our larger institutional mechanisms, including the legal system. To the degree to which the institutional rules and practices are unjust, unwise or undesirable, to that same degree is the case for the role-differentiated behavior of the lawyer weakened if not destroyed.

Second, it is clear that there are definite character traits that the professional such as the lawyer must take on if the system is to work. What is less clear is that they are admirable ones. Even if the role-differentiated amorality of the professional lawyer is justified by the virtues of the adversary system, this also means that the lawyer *qua* lawyer will be encouraged to be competitive rather than cooperative; aggressive rather than accommodating; ruthless rather than compassionate; and pragmatic rather than principled. This is, I think, part of the logic of the role-differentiated behavior of lawyers in particular, and to a lesser degree of professionals in general. It is surely neither accidental nor unimportant that these are the same character traits that are emphasized and valued by the capitalist ethic—and on precisely analogous grounds. Because the ideals of professionalism and capitalism are the dominant ones within our culture, it is harder than most of us suspect even to take seriously the suggestion that radically different styles of living, kinds of occupational outlooks, and types of social institutions might be possible, let alone preferable.

Third, there is a special feature of the role-differentiated behavior of the lawyer that distinguishes it from the comparable behavior of other professionals. What I have in mind can be brought out through the following question: Why is it that it seems far less plausible to talk critically about the amorality of the doctor, for instance, who treats all patients irrespective of their moral character than it does to talk critically about the comparable amorality of the lawyer? Why is it that it seems so obviously sensible, simple and right for the doctor's behavior to be narrowly and rigidly role-differentiated, *i.e.*, just to try to cure those who are ill? And why is it that at the very least it seems so complicated, uncertain, and troublesome to decide whether it is right for the lawyer's behavior to be similarly role-differentiated?

The answer, I think, is twofold. To begin with (and this I think is the less interesting point) it is, so to speak, intrinsically good to try to cure disease, but in no comparable way is it intrinsically good to try to win every lawsuit or help every client realize his or her objective. In addition (and this I take to be the truly interesting point), the lawyer's behavior is different in kind from the doctor's. The lawyer—and especially the lawyer as advocate—directly says and affirms things. The lawyer makes the case for the client. He or she tries to explain, persuade and convince others that the client's cause should prevail. The lawyer lives with and within a dilemma that is not shared by other professionals. If the lawyer actually believes everything that he or she asserts on behalf of the client, then it appears to be proper to regard the lawyer as in fact embracing and endorsing the points of view that he or she articulates. If the lawyer does not in fact believe what is urged by way of argument, if the lawyer is only playing a role, then it appears to be proper to tax the lawyer with hypocrisy and insincerity. To be sure, actors in a play take on roles and say things that the characters, not the actors, believe. But we know it is a play and that they are actors. The law courts are not, however, theaters, and the lawyers both talk about justice and they genuinely seek to persuade. The fact that the lawyer's words, thoughts, and convictions are, apparently, for sale and at the service of the client helps us, I think, to understand the peculiar hostility which is more than occasionally uniquely directed by lay persons toward lawyers. The verbal, role-differentiated behavior of the lawyer *qua* advocate puts the lawyer's integrity into question in a way that distinguishes the lawyer from the other professionals.[8]

Fourth, and related closely to the three points just discussed,

[8] I owe this insight, which I think is an important and seldom appreciated one, to my colleague, Leon Letwin.

even if on balance the role-differentiated character of the lawyer's way of thinking and acting is ultimately deemed to be justifiable within the system on systemic instrumental grounds, it still remains the case that we do pay a social price for that way of thought and action. For to become and to be a professional, such as a lawyer, is to incorporate within oneself ways of behaving and ways of thinking that shape the whole person. It is especially hard, if not impossible, because of the nature of the professions, for one's professional way of thinking not to dominate one's entire adult life. Thus, even if the lawyers who were involved in Watergate were not, strictly speaking, then and there functioning as lawyers, their behavior was, I believe, the likely if not inevitable consequence of their legal acculturation. Having been taught to embrace and practice the lawyer's institutional role, it was natural, if not unavoidable, that they would continue to play that role even when they were somewhat removed from the specific institutional milieu in which that way of thinking and acting is arguably fitting and appropriate. The nature of the professions—the lengthy educational preparation, the prestige and economic rewards, and the concomitant enhanced sense of self—makes the role of professional a difficult one to shed even in those obvious situations in which that role is neither required nor appropriate. In important respects, one's professional role becomes and is one's dominant role, so that for many persons at least they become their professional being. This is at a minimum a heavy price to pay for the professions as we know them in our culture, and especially so for lawyers. Whether it is an inevitable price is, I think, an open question, largely because the problem has not begun to be fully perceived as such by the professionals in general, the legal profession in particular, or by the educational institutions that train professionals.

II.

The role-differentiated behavior of the professional also lies at the heart of the second of the two moral issues I want to discuss, namely, the character of the interpersonal relationship that exists between the lawyer and the client. As I indicated at the outset, the charge that I want to examine here is that the relationship between the lawyer and the client is typically, if not inevitably, a morally defective one in which the client is not treated with the respect and dignity that he or she deserves.

There is the suggestion of paradox here. The discussion so far has concentrated upon defects that flow from what might be regarded as the lawyer's excessive preoccupation with and concern for the client. How then can it also be the case that the lawyer *qua* professional can at the same time be taxed with promoting and maintaining a relationship of dominance and indifference vis-à-vis his or her client? The paradox is apparent, not real. Not only are the two accusations compatible; the problem of the interpersonal relationship between the lawyer and the client is itself another feature or manifestation of the underlying issue just examined—the role-differentiated life of the professional. For the lawyer can both be overly concerned with the interest of the client and at the same time fail to view the client as a whole person, entitled to be treated in certain ways.

One way to begin to explore the problem is to see that one pervasive, and I think necessary, feature of the relationship between any professional and the client or patient is that it is in some sense a relationship of inequality. This relationship of inequality is intrinsic to the existence of professionalism. For the professional is, in some respects at least, always in a position of dominance vis-à-vis the client, and the client in a position of dependence vis-à-vis the professional. To be sure, the client can often decide whether or not to enter into a relationship with a professional. And often, too, the client has the power to decide whether to terminate the relationship. But the significant thing I want to focus upon is that while the relationship exists, there are important respects in which the relationship cannot be a relationship between equals and must be one in which it is the professional who is in control. As I have said, I believe this is a necessary and not merely a familiar characteristic of the relationship between professionals and those they serve. Its existence is brought about by the following features.

To begin with, there is the fact that one characteristic of professions is that the professional is the possessor of expert knowledge of a sort not readily or easily attainable by members of the community at large. Hence, in the most straightforward of all senses the client, typically, is dependent upon the professional's skill or knowledge because the client does not possess the same knowledge.

Moreover, virtually every profession has its own technical language, a private terminology which can only be fully understood by the members of the profession. The presence of such a language plays the dual role of creating and affirming the membership of the professionals within the profession and of preventing the client from fully discussing or understanding his or her concerns in the language of the profession.

These circumstances, together with others, produce the added consequence that the client is in a poor position effectively to evaluate how well or badly the professional performs. In the professions, the professional does not look primarily to the client to evaluate the professional's work. The assessment of ongoing professional competence is something that is largely a matter of self-assessment conducted by the practising professional. Where external assessment does occur, it is carried out not by clients or patients but by other members of the profession, themselves. It is significant, and surely surprising to the outsider, to discover to what degree the professions are self-regulating. They control who shall be admitted to the professions and they determine (typically only if there has been a serious complaint) whether the members of the profession are performing in a minimally satisfactory way. This leads professionals to have a powerful motive to be far more concerned with the way they are viewed by their colleagues than with the way they are viewed by their clients. This means, too, that clients will necessarily lack the power to make effective evaluations and criticisms of the way the professional is responding to the client's needs.

In addition, because the matters for which professional assistance is sought usually involve things of great personal concern to the client, it is the received wisdom within the professions that the client lacks the perspective necessary to pursue in a satisfactory way his or her own best interests, and that the client requires a detached, disinterested representative to look after his or her interests. That is to say, even if the client had the same knowledge or competence that the professional had, the client would be thought to lack the objectivity required to utilize that competency effectively on his or her own behalf.

Finally, as I have indicated, to be a professional is to have been acculturated in a certain way. It is to have satisfactorily passed through a lengthy and allegedly difficult period of study and training. It is to have done something hard. Something that not everyone can do. Almost all professions encourage this way of viewing oneself; as having joined an elect group by virtue of hard work and mastery of the mysteries of the profession. In addition, the society at large treats members of a profession as members of an elite by paying them more than most people for the work they do with their heads rather than their hands, and by according them a substantial amount of social prestige and power by virtue of their membership in a profession. It is hard, I think, if not impossible, for a person to emerge from professional training and participate in a profession without the belief that he or she is a special kind of person, both different from and somewhat better than those nonprofessional members of the social order. It is equally hard for the other members of society not to hold an analogous view of the professionals. And these beliefs surely contribute, too, to the dominant role played by a professional in any professional-client relationship.

If the foregoing analysis is correct, then one question that is raised is whether it is a proper and serious criticism of the professions that the relationship between the professional and the client is an inherently unequal one in this sense.

One possible response would be to reject the view that all relationships of inequality (in this sense of inequality) are in fact undesirable. Such a response might claim, for example, that there is nothing at all wrong with inequality in relationships as long as the inequality is consensually imposed. Or, it may be argued, this kind of inequality is wholly unobjectionable because it is fitting, desired, or necessary in the circumstances. And, finally, it may be urged, whatever undesirability does attach to relationships by virtue of their lack of equality is outweighed by the benefits of role-differentiated relationships.

Another possible response would be to maintain that all human relationships of inequality (again in this sense of inequality) are for that reason alone objectionable on moral grounds—any time two or more persons are in a relationship in which power is not shared equally, the relationship is on that ground appropriately to be condemned. This criticism would solve the problem by abolishing the professions.

A third possible response, and the one that I want to consider in some detail, is a more sophisticated variant of the second response. It might begin by conceding, at least for purposes of argument, that some inequality may be inevitable in any professional-client relationship. It might concede, too, that a measure of this kind of inequality may even on occasion be desirable. But it sees the relationship between the professional and the client as typically flawed in a more fundamental way, as involving far more than the kind of relatively benign inequality delineated above. This criticism focuses upon the fact that the professional often, if not systematically, interacts with the client in both a manipulative and a paternalistic fashion. The point is not that the professional is merely dominant within the relationship. Rather, it is that from the professional's point of view the client is seen and responded to more like an object than a human being, and more like a child than an adult. The professional does not, in short, treat the client like a person; the professional does not accord the client the respect that he or she deserves. And these, it is claimed, are without question genuine moral defects in any meaningful human relationship. They are, moreover, defects that are capable of being eradicated once their cause is perceived and corrective action taken. The solution, so the argument goes, is to "deprofessionalize" the professions; not do away with the professions entirely, but weaken or eliminate those features of professionalism that produce these kinds of defective, interpersonal relationships.

To decide whether this would be a good idea we must understand better what the proposal is and how the revisions might proceed. Because thinking somewhat along these lines has occurred in professions other than the law, *e.g.*, psychiatry, a brief look at what has been proposed there may help us to understand better what might be claimed in respect to the law.

I have in mind, for example, the view in psychiatry that begins by challenging the dominant conception of the patient as someone who is sick and in particular need of the professional, the psychiatrist, who is well. Such a conception, it is claimed, is often inadequate and often mistaken. Indeed, many cases of mental illness are not that at all; they are merely cases of different, but rational behavior. The alleged mental illness of the patient is a kind of myth, encouraged, if not created, by the professionals to assure and enhance their ability to function as professionals. So, on this view, one thing that must occur is that the accepted professional concepts of mental illness and health must be revised.[4]

In addition, the language of psychiatry and mental illness is, it is claimed, needlessly technical and often vacuous. It serves no very useful communicative purpose, but its existence does of course help to maintain the distinctive status and power of the psychiatric profession. What is called for here is a simpler, far less technical language that permits more direct communication between the patient and the therapist.

Finally, and most significantly, the program calls for a concomitant replacement of the highly role-differentiated relationship between the therapist and the patient by a substantially less differentiated relationship of wholeness of interaction and equality. There should not, for instance, be mental hospitals in which the patients are clearly identified and distinguished from the staff and the professionals. Instead, therapeutic communities should be established in which all of the individuals in the community come to see themselves both as able to help the other members of the community and as able to be helped by them. In such a community, the distinctions between the professionals and the patients will be relatively minor and uninteresting. In such a community the relationship among the individuals, be they patients or professionals, will be capable of being more personal, intimate and complete—more undifferentiated by the accident of prior training or status.

Now, if this is a plausible proposal to make, it is possible that it is because of reasons connected with therapy rather than with the professions generally. But I do not think this is so. The general analysis and point of view is potentially generic; and certainly capable, I think, of being taken seriously in respect to the law as well as in respect to psychiatry, medicine, and education. If the critique is extravagant even when applied to psychiatry, as I think it is, I am more impressed by the truths to be extracted from it than I am by the exaggerations to be rejected. For I do think that professionals generally and lawyers in particular do, typically, enter into relationships with clients that are morally objectionable in

[4] On this, and the points that follow, I am thinking in particular of the writings of Thomas Szasz, *e.g.*, T. S. Szasz, The Myth of Mental Illness (1974), and of R. D. Laing, *e.g.*, R. D. Laing & A. Esterson, Sanity, Madness and the Family (1964).

virtue of the paternalistic and impersonal fashion in which the client is viewed and treated.

Thus it is, for example, fairly easy to see how a number of the features already delineated conspire to depersonalize the client in the eyes of the lawyer *qua* professional. To begin with, the lawyer's conception of self as a person with special competencies in a certain area naturally leads him or her to see the client in a partial way. The lawyer *qua* professional is, of necessity, only centrally interested in that part of the client that lies within his or her special competency. And this leads any professional including the lawyer to respond to the client as an object—as a thing to be altered, corrected, or otherwise assisted by the professional rather than as a person. At best the client is viewed from the perspective of the professional not as a whole person but as a segment or aspect of a person—an interesting kidney problem, a routine marijuana possession case, or another adolescent with an identity crisis.[5]

Then, too, the fact already noted that the professions tend to have and to develop their own special languages has a lot to do with the depersonalization of the client. And this certainly holds for the lawyers. For the lawyer can and does talk to other lawyers but not to the client in the language of the profession. What is more, the lawyer goes out of his or her way to do so. It is satisfying. It is the exercise of power. Because the ability to communicate is one of the things that distinguishes persons from objects, the inability of the client to communicate with the lawyer in the lawyer's own tongue surely helps to make the client less than a person in the lawyer's eyes—and perhaps even in the eyes of the client.

The forces that operate to make the relationship a paternalistic one seem to me to be at least as powerful. If one is a member of a collection of individuals who have in common the fact that their intellects are highly trained, it is very easy to believe that one knows more than most people. If one is a member of a collection of individuals who are accorded high prestige by the society at large, it is equally easy to believe that one is better and knows better than most people. If there is, in fact, an area in which one does know

[5] This and other features are delineated from a somewhat different perspective in an essay by Erving Goffman. *See The Medical Model and Mental Hospitalization: Some Notes on the Vicissitudes of the Tinkering Trades* in E. GOFFMAN, ASYLUMS (1961), especially Parts V and VI of the essay.

things that the client doesn't know, it is extremely easy to believe that one knows generally what is best for the client. All this, too, surely holds for lawyers.

In addition there is the fact, also already noted, that the client often establishes a relationship with the lawyer because the client has a serious problem or concern which has rendered the client weak and vulnerable. This, too, surely increases the disposition to respond toward the client in a patronizing, paternalistic fashion. The client of necessity confers substantial power over his or her wellbeing upon the lawyer. Invested with all of this power both by the individual and the society, the lawyer *qua* professional responds to the client as though the client were an individual who needed to be looked after and controlled, and to have decisions made for him or her by the lawyer, with as little interference from the client as possible.

Now one can, I think, respond to the foregoing in a variety of ways. One could, to begin with, insist that the paternalistic and impersonal ways of behaving are the aberrant rather than the usual characteristics of the lawyer-client relationship. One could, therefore, argue that a minor adjustment in better legal education aimed at sensitizing prospective lawyers to the possibility of these abuses is all that is required to prevent them. Or, one could, to take the same tack described earlier, regard these features of the lawyer-client relationship as endemic but not as especially serious. One might have a view that, at least in moderation, relationships having these features are a very reasonable price to pay (if it is a price at all) for the very appreciable benefits of professionalism. The impersonality of a surgeon, for example, may make it easier rather than harder for him or for her to do a good job of operating successfully on a patient. The impersonality of a lawyer may make it easier rather than harder for him or for her to do a good job of representing a client. The paternalism of lawyers may be justified by the fact that they do in fact know better—at least within many areas of common concern to the parties involved—what is best for the client. And, it might even be claimed, clients want to be treated in this way.

But if these answers do not satisfy, if one believes that these are typical, if not systemic, features of the professional character of the lawyer-client relationship, and if one believes, as well, that these are morally objectionable features of that or any other relationship among persons, it does look as though one way to proceed is to "deprofessionalize" the law—to weaken, if not excise, those features of legal professionalism that tend to produce these kinds of interpersonal relationships.

The issue seems to me difficult just because I do think that there are important and distinctive competencies that are at the heart of the legal profession. If there were not, the solution would be simple. If there were no such competencies—if, that is, lawyers didn't really help people any more than (so it is sometimes claimed) therapists do—then no significant social goods would be furthered by the maintenance of the legal profession. But, as I have said, my own view is that there are special competencies and that they are valuable. This makes it harder to determine what to preserve and what to shed. The question, as I see it, is how to weaken the bad consequences of the role-differentiated lawyer-client relationship without destroying the good that lawyers do.

Without developing the claim at all adequately in terms of scope or detail, I want finally to suggest the direction this might take. Desirable change could be brought about in part by a sustained effort to simplify legal language and to make the legal processes less mysterious and more directly available to lay persons. The way the law works now, it is very hard for lay persons either to understand it or to evaluate or solve legal problems more on their own. But it is not at all clear that substantial revisions could not occur along these lines. Divorce, probate, and personal injury are only three fairly obvious areas where the lawyers' economic self-interest says a good deal more about resistance to change and simplification than does a consideration on the merits.

The more fundamental changes, though, would, I think, have to await an explicit effort to alter the ways in which lawyers are educated and acculturated to view themselves, their clients, and the relationships that ought to exist between them. It is, I believe, indicative of the state of legal education and of the profession that there has been to date extremely little self-conscious concern even with the possibility that these dimensions of the attorney-client relationship are worth examining—to say nothing of being capable of alteration. That awareness is, surely, the prerequisite to any serious assessment of the moral character of the attorney-client relationship as a relationship among adult human beings.

I do not know whether the typical lawyer-client relationship is as I have described it; nor do I know to what degree role-differentiation is the cause; nor do I even know very precisely what "deprofessionalization" would be like or whether it would on the whole be good or bad. I am convinced, however, that this, too, is a topic worth taking seriously and worth attending to more systematically than has been the case to date.

[2]

MORAL RESPONSIBILITY IN PROFESSIONAL ETHICS[1]

GERALD J. POSTEMA*

Professor Postema argues for a new conception of professional ethics in which lawyers must acknowledge personal responsibility for the consequences of their professional conduct. He suggests that a new code of professional responsibility is required because the current Code allows lawyers to ignore the social and moral costs of their actions, and do as professionals what they would not do as individuals.

Lawyers, like other professionals, acknowledge gravely that they shoulder special responsibilities, and believe that they should conform to "higher" ethical standards than laypersons.[2] Yet, lawyers also claim special warrant for engaging in some activities which, were they performed by others, would be likely to draw moral censure.[3] Skeptical of this claim to special license, Macaulay asked "[w]hether it be right that a man should, with a wig on his head, and a band round his neck, do for a guinea what, without these appendages, he would think it wicked and infamous to do for an empire."[4] This conflict may trouble the layperson, but for the lawyer who must come to grips with his professional responsibilities it is especially problematic.

Montaigne offered one solution, the complete separation of personal and professional lives. "There's no reason why a lawyer . . . should not recognize the knavery that is part of his vocation," he insisted. "An honest man is not responsible for the vices or the stupidity of his calling."[5] The key to maintaining both professional

---

*Associate Professor of Philosophy, University of North Carolina at Chapel Hill. A.B., 1970, Calvin College; A.M., 1973, Ph.D., 1976, Cornell University.

[1] The concerns discussed in this essay were first suggested to me in discussions with several participants at the Institute on Law and Ethics sponsored by the Council for Philosophic Studies during the summer of 1977. Larry Alexander, Bernard Williams, and Gary Bellow were especially helpful. An earlier version of this essay was written as a background paper for the Philosophical Perspectives on Public Policy Project of the Center for Philosophy and Public Policy, the University of Maryland, College Park.

[2] "Lawyers, as guardians of the law, play a vital role in the preservation of society. The fulfillment of this role requires an understanding by lawyers of their relationship with and function in our legal system. A consequent obligation of lawyers is to maintain the highest standards of ethical conduct." ABA, Model Code of Professional Responsibility, Preamble, at 1 (1980) [hereinafter Code] (footnote omitted).

[3] For examples, see text accompanying notes 11-15 infra.

[4] T. Macaulay, Lord Bacon, in 2 Critical and Historical Essays 121, 152 (F. Montague ed. 1903).

[5] Quoted in Curtis, The Ethics of Advocacy, 4 Stan. L. Rev. 3, 20 (1951).

and personal integrity in the face of professionally required "knavery" was, Montaigne thought, scrupulously to keep the two personalities apart: "I have been able to concern myself with public affairs without moving the length of my nail from myself . . . . The mayor and Montaigne have always been two people, clearly separated."[6]

Montaigne's solution is tempting. Maintaining a hermetically sealed professional personality promises to minimize internal conflicts, to shift responsibility for professional "knavery" to broader institutional shoulders, and to enable a person to act consistently within each role he assumes. But for this strategy to succeed, the underlying values and concerns of important professional roles, and the characteristic activities they require, must themselves be easily segregated and compartmentalized. However, since there is good reason to doubt they can be easily segregated, Montaigne's strategy risks a dangerous simplification of moral reality. Furthermore, in compartmentalizing moral responses one blocks the cross-fertilization of moral experience necessary for personal and professional growth. This Article considers whether it is possible to follow Montaigne's suggestion and to separate one's private and professional personalities without jeopardizing one's ability to engage in professional activities in a morally and professionally responsible way. The central issue I address is not whether there is sufficient justification for a distinct professional code for lawyers, but whether, given the need for such a code, it is possible to preserve one's sense of responsibility. I argue that such preservation is not possible when a professional must adopt Montaigne's strategy in order to function well in his professional role. I contend that a sense of responsibility and sound practical judgment depend not only on the quality of one's professional training, but also on one's ability to draw on the resources of a broader moral experience. This, in turn, requires that one seek to achieve a fully integrated moral personality. Because this is not possible under the present conception of the lawyer's role, as exemplified by the Code of Professional Responsibility, that conception must be abandoned, to be replaced by a conception that better allows the lawyer to bring his full moral sensibilities to play in his professional role.

I

Moral Distance and the Perspective of the Responsible Person

It is not uncommon for lawyers to face dilemmas caused by the clash of important principles implicit within the professional code.

[6] Id.

A good example of this is the problem posed for a criminal defense lawyer by a client who announces a firm intention to perjure himself at trial.[7] Here, the deeply embedded principle of confidentiality[8] conflicts sharply with the equally important duty of candor before the court.[9]

But this is not the sort of clash Montaigne had in mind. Indeed, similar moral quandaries and conflicts are common outside of professional contexts. Rather, Montaigne draws attention to the conflict between principles of professional ethics and concerns of private morality. The requirements of professional ethics can sometimes move some distance from the concerns of private or ordinary morality, a phenomenon we might call *moral distance*. The range of practical considerations which alone are relevant to a proper ethical decision in a professional role is the *moral universe* of that role.[10] For many professional roles the moral universe of the role is considerably narrower than that of ordinary morality, and, when the two overlap, they often assign different weights to the same set of considerations. This often gives rise to conflicts, as the following cases illustrate.

The first example involves the duty of the criminal defense attorney to maintain client confidentiality. In the course of preparing a defense for a criminal trial in Lake Pleasant, New York, the client told his attorneys that he was responsible for three other murders unrelated to the pending case. The lawyers visited the location where one of the bodies had been hidden and confirmed the client's story. Nevertheless, they maintained silence for six months and refrained from disclosing the whereabouts of the body to the authorities or to the family of one of the victims, which had sought their help in locating the missing victim.[11] The duty of confidentiality, which here protects the client against self-incrimination, clearly forbade disclosure in this case,[12] even though the attorneys' personal inclinations were to disclose.

---

[7] See M. Freedman, Lawyers' Ethics in an Adversary System 27-42 (1975).

[8] See Code, supra note 2, Canon 4, especially EC 4-1, EC 4-5, DR 4-101(A), DR 4-101(B), DR 4-101(C)(3).

[9] See id. Canon 7, especially EC 7-27, DR 7-102(A)(4), (5), DR 7-102(B)(1). Also see ABA Project on Standards Relating to the Prosecution Function and the Defense Function § 7.7 (Approved Draft 1971).

[10] I borrow this term from Wasserstrom, Lawyers as Professionals: Some Moral Issues, 5 Human Rights 1, 2-8 (1975).

[11] People v. Belge, 83 Misc. 2d 186, 372 N.Y.S.2d 798 (Onondaga County Ct.), aff'd mem., 50 A.D.2d 1088, 376 N.Y.S.2d 771 (1975), aff'd per curiam, 41 N.Y.2d 60, 359 N.E.2d 377, 390 N.Y.S.2d 867 (1976).

[12] See Code, supra note 2, EC 4-1, EC 4-4. Also see Callan & David, Professional Responsibility and the Duty of Confidentiality: Disclosure of Client Misconduct in an Adversary System, 29 Rutgers L. Rev. 332 (1976). The prosecution argued that failure to report the deaths amounted to a criminal violation of the New York State Public Health Law, 83 Misc. 2d at 187,

The second example, illustrated by the case of *Zabella v. Pakel*,[13] concerns the lawyer's use of legally available defenses to circumvent enforcement of his client's moral obligations. At the time of suit, defendant Pakel was president and manager of the Chicago Savings and Loan Association. In earlier and less fortunate circumstances, he had borrowed heavily from his employee, Zabella. Pakel gave a note for the borrowed sums, but, before the debt was paid, he declared bankruptcy. Zabella sued Pakel in 1954, contending that the defendant had made a subsquent promise to pay the outstanding debt. Under Illinois law, a new promise is sufficient to block the defense of discharge in bankruptcy, but because Pakel's promise was not in writing the defendant was able successfully to assert the statute of limitations as a defense. Despite the moral obligation of the affluent Pakel to repay the old debt, the statute of limitations blocked legal enforcement.[14] Many lawyers would argue that for Pakel's lawyer to have failed to assert the statute of limitations defense would have been a gross violation of his professional responsibility.[15] Yet from the point of view of ordinary morality, the lawyer was implicated in the moral wrong done by his client. Professionally upright activities advancing the client's morally questionable, though legally sound, schemes are paradigmatic of the knavery to which Montaigne referred.

If we admit that some distance is likely to separate private and public morality, then several additional questions come to mind. How are these moralities related? How are conflicts between them to be resolved? Do they share a common foundation which could provide elements for resolution of the conflicts? One might seek a casuistry for a broad range of dilemmas that are likely to arise (which could then perhaps be taught to those preparing to enter the profession). Alternatively, one might seek some general account of the relationship between the principles governing each morality from which one could derive solutions to particular problems as they arise. The pres-

372 N.Y.S.2d at 799, which would render disclosure *permissible* under DR 4-101(C)(2). On more general moral grounds, however, it is hard to imagine that the ends served by the Health Code could outweigh the demands of confidentiality, if consideration of the much more significant injury to the families of the murdered women could not.

[13] 242 F.2d 452 (7th Cir. 1957), cited in Fried, The Lawyer as Friend: The Moral Foundations of the Lawyer-Client Relation, 85 Yale L.J. 1060, 1064 n.13 (1976).

[14] The *Zabella* court reasoned that "[o]f course, the jury was justified in thinking that defendant who then was in a position of some affluence and was the Chief Executive Officer of the Chicago Savings and Loan Association should feel obligated to pay an honest debt to his old friend, employee and countryman. Nevertheless, we are obliged to follow the law of Illinois." 242 F.2d at 455.

[15] See Code, supra note 2, EC 7-1, DR 7-101(A)(1).

ent approach to legal ethics, as embodied in the Code, largely utilizes the first strategy; philosophers tend to be partial to the second. Both can be useful, yet they both represent an approach to the problems posed by moral distance which is inadequate in important ways.

The first problem with these strategies is that they are only of limited usefulness in practice. Casuistry gives us solutions to isolated problems, but no strategy for resolving new problems. The systematic strategy is also not likely to help us in situations in which we experience the most puzzlement, since the moral dilemmas facing a lawyer generally cannot be reduced to a single perspective. Our personal and professional concerns do not have the collective uniformity necessary for the construction of a general scheme of principles and priority rules. On the contrary, our concerns are characterized by a complexity and a variety which resist reduction to a uniform scale.[16] As Thomas Nagel has argued, we are subject to moral and other motivational claims of very different kinds, because we are able to view the world from a variety of perspectives, each presenting a different set of claims. Nagel maintains that conflicts between perspectives

> [c]annot . . . be resolved by subsuming either of the points of view under the other, or both under a third. Nor can we simply abandon any of them. There is no reason why we should. The capacity to view the world simultaneously from the point of view of one's relations to others, from the point of view of one's life extended through time, from the point of view of everyone at once, and finally from the detached viewpoint often described as the view *sub specie aeternitatis* is one of the marks of humanity. This complex capacity is an obstacle to simplification.[17]

Are we left without any rational means for resolving this conflict? Nagel rightly resists this skeptical response.[18] The conflict Nagel describes shows only that it may be futile to search for a general reductive method or a clear set of priority rules to structure our basic concerns. There is always likely to be a significant gap between general practical theory and actual decision and practice.

---

[16] Perhaps one of the most serious general objections to Utilitarianism is that, although it professes to give full respect to all sources of value, it creates its simple normative structure by reducing all such values to a single dimension. The net effect is that either it distorts radically the world of human concerns, or it limits its scope to that range of values in which its simplifying assumptions are most natural. See generally S. Hampshire, Two Theories of Morality 25-26 (1977); R. Unger, Knowledge and Politics 86-88 (1975).

[17] Nagel, The Fragmentation of Value, in Mortal Questions 134 (1979). See also S. Hampshire, supra note 16.

[18] See Nagel, supra note 17, at 135.

In Aristotle's view, this gap is bridged by the faculty of *practical judgment*[19]—what he called practical wisdom.[20] Our ability to resolve conflicts on a rational basis often outstrips our ability to enunciate general principles. In doing so, we exercise judgment. Judgment is neither a matter of simply applying general rules to particular cases nor a matter of mere intuition. It is a complex faculty, difficult to characterize, in which general principles or values and the particularities of the case both play important roles. The principles or values provide a framework within which to work and a target at which to aim. But they do not determine decisions. Instead, we rely on our judgment to achieve a coherence among the conflicting values which is sensitive to the particular circumstances. Judgment thus involves the ability to take a comprehensive view of the values and concerns at stake, based on one's experience and knowledge of the world. And this involves awareness of the full range of shared experience, beliefs, relations, and expectations within which these values and concerns have significance.

In professional contexts there is much need for practical judgment in this Aristotelian sense. Judgment, however, is both a disposition—a trait of character—and a skill which must be learned and continually exercised. It is important, then, if we are seriously to consider matters of moral responsibility in professional contexts, that we pay attention to the conditions of development of this disposition and the exercise of this skill.

The second difficulty with the current approach to questions raised by the conflict between private and professional moralities is that it rests on a mistaken view of moral judgment and moral experience. Practical moral reasoning is wrongly viewed as strictly analogous to theoretical reasoning, the central objective of which is to arrive at correct answers to specific problems. This view of moral reasoning and experience is too narrow, for moral reasoning is not so singularly outcome-determinative. Our evaluations of ourselves and our actions depend not only on getting our moral sums right, but also on having the appropriate attitudes and reactions to the moral situation in which we act. Let me illustrate.[21]

Consider the truck driver who, through no fault of his own, hits and seriously injures a child. It may be correct to say that, since he

[19] See generally Aristotle, Nicomachean Ethics, bk. VI (H. Rackham trans. 1962).

[20] See S. Hampshire, supra note 16, at 28-39; Nagel, supra note 17, at 135. See also Hampshire, Public and Private Morality, in Public and Private Morality 29-33 (S. Hampshire ed. 1978).

[21] I borrow this example, for an entirely different purpose, from Williams, Moral Luck, 50 Proc. Aristotelian Soc'y 115, 124 (Supp. 1976).

drove with care and could not have avoided hitting the child, the driver is guilty of no wrong and thus is not blameworthy. However, consider the accident and the driver's involvement in it from his point of view. There is a very important difference between the driver's likely reaction and that of an uninvolved spectator. Both may feel and express regret, but the nature and behavioral expression of this regret will be quite different. The driver's direct, personal (albeit unintentional) involvement in the accident alters the structure of the moral situation and the driver's attitude toward it. The difference in the emotional responses of the driver and the spectator will be reflected in the way these feelings are expressed. The driver may attempt to make restitution in the hope that he can repair the injury he caused. The spectator may offer help, or contribute money for hospital bills, or even visit the child, but these actions would be understood (by him and by us) as expressions of pity, kindly concern, or perhaps generosity. From the driver, these same actions would be intended and understood as expressions of a special form of regret. Suppose, however, that the driver takes the attitude of the uninvolved spectator, perhaps expressing detached regret, but feeling no need to make restitution. He can rightly argue that he was not to be blamed for the accident, that he had done no wrong. In doing so, he could perhaps be rightly said to have gotten his moral sums right. But in asserting this defense quite sincerely and too quickly, he would reveal a defect of character—a defect much deeper and more serious than a lack of generosity. Morality seems to require not only that one be able to apply moral principles properly to one's own or another's conduct, but also that one be able to appreciate the moral costs of one's actions, perhaps even when those actions are unintentional. By "moral costs" I mean those features of one's action and its consequences touching on important concerns, interests, and needs of others that, in the absence of special justification, would provide substantial if not conclusive moral reasons against performing it.[22]

---

[22] One aspect of the failure of professionals in law to appreciate the moral costs of their actions is captured by G.K. Chesterton:

> [T]he horrible thing about all legal officials, even the best, about all judges, magistrates, barristers, detectives, and policemen, is not that they are wicked (some of them are good), not that they are stupid (several of them are quite intelligent), it is simply that they have got used to it.
>
> Strictly they do not see the prisoner in the dock; all they see is the usual man in the usual place. They do not see the awful court of judgment; they only see their own workshop.

Chesterton, The Twelve Men, in Tremendous Trifles 57-58 (1955).

Similarly, in cases in which obligations to other persons are correctly judged to be overridden by weightier moral duties, with the result that some injury is done, it is not enough for one to work out the correct course of action and pursue it. It is also important that one appreciate the moral costs of that course of action. This appreciation will be expressed in a genuine reluctance to bring about the injury, and a sense of the accompanying loss or sacrifice. It may even call for concrete acts of reparation: explaining and attempting to justify the action to the person injured, or making up the loss or injury to some extent. This is one way in which the moral status of the principle or right which was violated is acknowledged, and the moral relations between the parties affirmed and, when necessary, repaired.

Moral sentiments are an essential part of the moral life. The guilt or remorse one feels after mistreating a person is not merely a personal sanction one imposes on oneself after judging the action to have been wrong; it is the natural and most appropriate expression of this judgment. Similarly, the outrage we feel at injustice done to another and the resentment we feel at wrong done to ourselves are not just the emotional coloring of detached moral judgments, but the way in which we experience and express these judgments. Thus, morality is not merely a matter of getting things right—as in solving a puzzle or learning to speak grammatically—but a matter of relating to people in a special and specifically human way.

It must be admitted that these elements of practical wisdom and moral sentiment are not needed to understand the proper performance of duties in *some* professional or occupational roles. We need spend little time worrying about whether our understanding of the duties of bank clerks or auto mechanics properly allows for these elements. A person's moral faculties are not extensively engaged in the characteristic activities of these roles. In contrast, the characteristic activities of the lawyer's role demand a much greater involvement of the moral faculties.

For these reasons, we must approach the problems of professional ethics from a perspective that recognizes the importance of practical judgment and moral sentiment. The notion of professional responsibility should take on a different and broader meaning. The primary concern is not with the definition, structuring, and delimitation of a lawyer's professional *responsibilities* (his official concerns and duties), nor with those situations in which the lawyer is to be held professionally *responsible* (*i.e.*, liable to blame or sanction). Rather, the concern is with responsibility as a virtue or trait of character.[23]

[23] See Haydon, On Being Responsible, 28 Philosophical Q. 46, 46-57 (1978).

The focus, then, is on the notion of a *responsible* person—or perhaps better, on the notion of a person's *sense of responsibility*. My concern in the rest of this essay is to explore the ways in which institutional structures and public expectations, as well as the personal attitudes and self-conceptions of professionals, affect the development of this sense of responsibility.

II

MORAL DISTANCE AND THE CALL FOR "DEPROFESSIONALIZATION"

Before we proceed with the argument, however, we must consider briefly a more radical solution to the problems posed by the phenomenon of moral distance. It is sometimes argued that the dissonance between the dictates of professional and private morality is *itself* a symptom of a deep social and moral problem. The solution, it is claimed, lies in a "deprofessionalization" of professional roles[24] that would reduce all professional responsibilities to species of private morality. This view holds that it either is or should be the case that the duties and responsibilities of a professional are no different from those of any lay person facing a similar moral problem.

This approach to professional responsibility makes two serious mistakes. First, it rests on a mistaken objection to what we might call the "exclusionary character" of professional morality.[25] We have already seen that the moral universe of a professional role characteristically is narrower than that of ordinary morality. But since the moral universe defines the range of considerations that a role agent may take into account in choosing a course of action, it is possible that otherwise relevant considerations may be effectively excluded from the agent's deliberation. Thus, cases may arise in which an agent is required by his role to act without considering the full range of moral reasons before him; rather, he must consider only those moral reasons within his particular moral universe. Critics argue that this is both irrational and morally suspect since it denies the role agent his essential rational autonomy.

But it is not difficult to show that there is nothing inherently irrational or morally objectionable in this exclusionary character of professional morality. Some examples should make this clear.

---

[24] This appears to be the approach suggested by Wasserstrom. See Wasserstrom, supra note 10, at 12.

[25] A useful formal discussion of exclusionary reasons can be found in J. Raz, Practical Reasons and Norms 35-48 (1975).

Suppose I have a tendency to spend my paycheck frivolously, with the result that my monthly bills pile up unpaid. To avoid this dangerous situation I adopt the policy of paying bills first and spending on pleasure only what is left over. I know that in the absence of this personal policy, I am liable to be moved by immediate desires to postpone paying my regular bills. Suppose that after adopting this policy I come to believe, at the end of a very tiring month, that I deserve a weekend holiday, although I know I can afford it only if I postpone payment on several bills. I decide, however, by appealing to my policy, to pay the bills. In this case, the policy operates not as an additional factor to consider along with the good the holiday would do for me and the difficulty I will face if my bills are not paid, but as an exclusionary factor. Indeed, it may be true that this month no particular harm would come from my postponing payment of the bills. The policy, however, instructs me not to consider other factors; it excludes them from consideration and provides a reason for not acting on the balance of reasons in this case. Of course, the exclusionary policy must itself be supported by sufficient reasons, but they need not apply directly to the particular case. Similarly, the moral appropriateness of exclusionary reasons is evident in any standard case of promising. Suppose I promise to drive you across town to your doctor's appointment tomorrow. In this case, considerations of cost and inconvenience which otherwise might be sufficient to persuade me not to take the trip are excluded—the exclusion is not absolute. In neither of these cases, then, am I subject to a charge of irrationality or moral irresponsibility.

Second, the call for deprofessionalization fails to appreciate the important social value of professional roles having this exclusionary character. We design social institutions to perform important tasks and to meet social needs or serve important social values. To carry out these tasks we design specific roles within the institutional framework and entrust them with responsibility over a particular range of social concerns. The domain of practical concerns determined by the basic tasks of the role is the moral universe of that role. Thus, social and professional roles represent an important division of social and moral labor. And carefully defined boundaries of concern and responsibility are needed for the efficient and successful achievement of important social goals served by the division of labor.

Thus, there is nothing objectionable in general, nor anything unique, about the phenomenon of distance between private and public morality. Critical attention must be turned, rather, to the way in which the moral universe of a given role is defined and structured, and the effect this has on the professional's ability to act responsibly in the moral universe so defined.

III

Responsible Action Under the Standard Conception

The central problem I am concerned with is whether, given the fact of moral distance, it is possible to retain and act out of a mature sense of responsibility in a professional role. In this section, I argue that because of particular social and psychological features of professional roles, the pressures and tensions of acting and deliberating within such roles pose a serious threat to responsible professional behavior. In addition, I hope to show that the atrophy of the professional's sense of general moral responsibility is a serious and costly matter. If this argument is correct, we have discovered an important reason for radically rethinking the standard conception of the lawyer's role.[26] This standard conception[27] is marked by two central ideals:

(i) *Partisanship*: the lawyer's sole allegiance is to the client; the lawyer is the partisan of the client. *Within*, but all the way *up to*, the limits of the law, the lawyer is committed to the aggressive and single-minded pursuit of the client's objectives.

(ii) *Neutrality*: once he has accepted the client's case, the lawyer must represent the client, or pursue the client's objectives, regardless of the lawyer's opinion of the client's character and reputation, and the moral merits of the client's objectives. On this conception, the lawyer need not consider, nor may he be held responsible for, the consequences of his professional activities as long as he stays within the law and acts in pursuit of the client's legitimate aims.[28] Thus, the

---

[26] By "conceptions of the lawyer's role," I do not mean some abstract model of a lawyer's professional behavior. Rather I have in mind the more or less complex pattern of beliefs and attitudes which tend to structure a person's practical judgment and his view of his actions and relations to others, *i.e.*, his view of himself in the role. Although there is a personal or idiosyncratic element in any person's conception, nevertheless, because the role of lawyer is largely socially defined, significant public or shared elements are also involved. I shall concentrate on these latter elements, keeping in mind that they are shared elements in an individual's conception of himself in the role.

[27] Although my argument has general implications for the evaluation of conceptions of many professional roles, I shall restrict my attention here to what I shall call the standard conception of the lawyer's role.

[28] Samuel Johnson is often quoted with approval in support of this idea: " '[A] lawyer has no business with the justice or injustice of the cause which he undertakes, unless his client asks his opinion, and then he is bound to give it honestly. The justice or injustice of the cause is to be

proper range of the lawyer's concern—the boundaries of the lawyer's "moral universe"—is defined by two parameters: the law and the client's interests and objectives. These factors are the exclusive points of reference for professional deliberation and practical judgment. I contend that, far from encouraging the development and preservation of a mature sense of responsibility, the standard conception tends seriously to undermine it. To show why this is so I must sketch briefly what might be called "the problem of responsibility."

The problem is suggested in a rather grand way by Sartre in a familiar argument from his early existentialist period.[29] Sartre insisted that to take role moralities seriously is to fail to take responsibility for oneself and one's actions. The essential property of human consciousness, according to Sartre, is its absolute freedom—the capacity to define oneself in action independently of one's role or roles. Roles, however, come "ready-made," packaged by society. When acting in a role, one simply acts as others expect one to act. Simply to identify with one's role is to ignore the fact that one is free to choose not to act in this way. In Sartre's view, it is therefore essential that one be capable of walking away from one's role. Furthermore, although it is psychologically possible to identify deeply with one's role, doing so is, in Sartre's view, morally unthinkable and a form of bad faith. Identification is a strategy for evading one's freedom and, consequently, one's responsibility for who one is and what one does. By taking shelter in the role, the individual places the responsibility for all of his acts at the door of the institutional author of the role.[30]

Sartre's problem arises from the fact that in addition to moral distance, there is a second dimension—psychological distance—characteristic of the experience of persons who assume professional roles. Echoing Sartre, Goffman notes that

> in performing a role the individual must see to it that the impressions of him that are conveyed in the situation are compatible with role-appropriate personal qualities effectively imputed to him: a judge is supposed to be deliberate and sober; a pilot, in a cockpit, to be cool. . . . These personal qualities, effectively imputed and effectively claimed, combine with a position's title, where there is one, to provide a basis of *self-image* for the incumbent and a basis

decided by the Judge.'" Boswell's Journal of a Tour to the Hebrides, Aug. 15, 1773, at 14 (F. Pottee & C. Bennett eds. 1936) (quoted in M. Freedman, supra note 7, at 51).

[29] J.-P. Sartre, Existentialism and Humanism (P. Mairet trans. 1948).

[30] See generally id. at 48-58.

for the image [others will have of his role]. A self, then, virtually awaits the individual entering a position . . . .[31]

Psychological distance is especially characteristic of professional roles. As Goffman seeks to show in his essay, one can identify with, or distance oneself in varying degrees from, this available self-image. The more closely one identifies with one's role, the more one's sense of self is likely to be shaped by the defining features of the role.[32] At one extreme, maximal identification is characterized by an unquestioning acceptance of the duties and responsibilities of one's role. For the person who maximally identifies with his role, the response "because I am a lawyer," or more generally "because that's my job," suffices as a complete answer to the question "why do that?" One minimally identifies, on the other hand, when one conforms only to avoid the external consequences of failing to do so, in no way internalizing the role or its basic principles. Several possible intermediate states separate these extremes.[33]

Thus, in addition to the dimension of moral distance between private and professional morality there is the dimension of psychological distance between oneself, or one's moral personality, and one's role. Furthermore, these two dimensions are interrelated: the extent to which one identifies with one's role is a function not only of one's moral personality but also of the moral distance between role morality and one's private morality. The opposite influence is also possible. Acting and deliberating within the special moral universe of any role that involves a large investment of one's moral faculties will tend to shape one's moral personality and, thus, one's inclination to identify with the role. The problem of responsibility lies in the fact that as the moral distance between private and professional moralities increases, the temptation to adopt one or the other extreme strategy of identification also increases; one either increasingly identifies with the role or seeks resolutely to detach oneself from it. Under either extreme, however, one's practical judgment and sense of responsibility are cut off from their sources in ordinary moral experience. Yeats warned that "once one makes a thing subject to reason, as distinguished from impulse, one plays with it, even if it is a very serious thing."[34] We

---

[31] E. Goffman, Encounters 87-88 (1961).

[32] Consider, for example, the epitaph on a Scottish gravestone: " 'Here lies Tammas Jones, who was born a man and died a grocer.' " D. Emmet, Rules, Roles and Relations 154 (1966) (quoting W. Sperry, The Ethical Basis of Medical Practice 41 (1951)).

[33] I am indebted to Bernard Williams' lectures at the Insitute on Law and Ethics sponsored by the Council for Philosophical Studies in 1977 for the remarks at this point.

[34] Curtis, supra note 5, at 22 (1951) (quoting R. Ellman, Yeats 178 (1949)).

might say, paraphrasing Yeats, that the artificial reason of professional morality, which rests on claims of specialized knowledge and specialized analytical technique, and which is removed from the rich resources of moral sentiment and shared moral experience in the community, tempts the professional to distort even the most serious of moral questions.

The problem of responsibility is especially troubling for the legal profession. The risk of severing professional judgment from its moral and psychological sources is particularly strong in a profession that serves a system of institutionalized justice.[35] As a result, the problem of developing a sense of personal responsibility is critical for the legal profession. First, the factors inducing maximal psychological identification are strong.[36] Publicly dedicated to serving socially valued institutions, the lawyer occupies a key role in society, enjoying considerable social status. His claim to specialized knowledge and skill puts the lawyer in a position of power relative to his client. These facts, in addition to the important intrinsic satisfaction of exercising his special skills, encourage a high degree of role identification. As a result, principles of professional responsibility, originally justified on functional grounds, take on independent value and significance for lawyers. Professional integrity becomes a mark, often the most significant mark, of personal integrity.

Second, the characteristic activities of lawyering often require the lawyer to act in the place of the client, and thus require the direct involvement of the lawyer's moral faculties—*i.e.*, his capacities to deliberate, reason, argue, and act in the public arena. All professionals, and many persons in service-oriented occupations, do things for a client that the client is unable or unwilling to do for himself. But, unlike the lawyer, the physician or auto mechanic acts only to provide services for the client. The lawyer also acts as the client's

---

[35] See Bellow & Kettleson, The Mirror of Public Interest Ethics: Problems and Paradoxes, in Professional Responsibility: A Guide for Attorneys 219, 257-58 (1978):

> At the root of the dilemma is a professional ethic that requires a sharp separation between personal and professional morality. The lawyer is asked to do "as a professional" what he or she would not do "as a person"; to subordinate personal qualms about results in particular cases to the general rule of law and the bar's role within it. There is much to be said for such a combination of responsibility and neutrality, if the "law job" is to be performed. But it may be that over time, such a division between the personal and the professional will atrophy those qualities of moral sensitivity and awareness upon which all ethical behavior depends.

[36] See Elkins, The Legal Persona: An Essay on the Professional Mask, 64 Va. L. Rev. 735, 749 (1978), which argues that the pressure upon lawyers to identify with their role comes from a number of pervasive factors, including linguistic factors, specialized modes of reasoning, and even characteristic clothing styles.

agent. Although an individual may employ a physician or mechanic to operate on his body or his automobile, the work of these professionals is in no sense attributable to the patient or customer. When the lawyer acts to secure the client's interests, however, he often acts, speaks, and argues in the place of the client. He enters into relationships with others in the name of the client. When he argues in his client's behalf, he often presents his client's arguments; when he acts he is often said to be "exercising his client's rights." And what he does is typically attributable to the client.[37] Thus, at the invitation of the client, the lawyer becomes an extension of the legal, and to an extent the moral, personality of the client.

Since the lawyer often acts as an extension of the legal and moral personality of the client, the lawyer is under great temptation to refuse to accept responsibility for his professional actions and their consequences. Moreover, except when his beliefs coincide with those of his client, he lives with a recurring dilemma: he must engage in activities, make arguments, and present positions which he himself does not endorse or embrace. The lawyer's integrity is put into question by the mere exercise of the duties of his profession.[38]

To preserve his integrity, the lawyer must carefully distance himself from his activities. Publicly, he may sharply distinguish statements or arguments he makes for the client and statements on which he stakes his professional honor.[39] The danger in this strategy is that a curious two-stage distancing may result. First, the lawyer distances himself from the argument: it is not his argument, but that of his client. His job is to construct the arguments; the task of evaluating and believing them is left to others. Second, after detaching himself from the argument, he is increasingly tempted to identify with this stance of detachment. What first offers itself as a device for distancing oneself from personally unacceptable positions becomes a defining feature of one's professional self-concept. This, in turn, encourages an uncritical, uncommitted state of mind, or worse, a deep moral skepticism. When such detachment is defined as a professional

[37] As a result, serious questions arise when the lawyer acts negligently or irresponsibly. Is the client, thereby, committed to the consequences of such actions, of which he may not have been aware or did not approve? In general, the client is committed; failure of counsel to appear or respond may result in a default judgment as effectively as if the client never retained counsel in the first place. See Mazor, Power and Responsibility in the Attorney-Client Relation, 20 Stan. L. Rev. 1120, 1121-23, 1124 & n.24 (1968).

[38] Wasserstrom, supra note 10, at 14.

[39] See generally Simon, The Ideology of Advocacy: Procedural Justice and Professional Ethics, 1978 Wis. L. Rev. 30, 96; Code, supra note 2, DR 7-106(C)(4) (attorney prohibited from expressing personal opinions regarding, *inter alia*, the justness of a cause).

ideal, as it is by the standard conception, the lawyer is even more apt to adopt these attitudes.

The foregoing tensions and pressures have sources deep in the nature of the lawyer's characteristic activities. To eradicate them entirely would be to eliminate much of what is distinctive and socially valuable in these activities. Nevertheless, these tensions can be eased, and the most destructive tendencies avoided, if lawyers have a framework within which they can obtain an integrated view of their activities both within the role and outside it. The framework must provide the resources for responsible resolution of the conflicts that inevitably arise. The standard conception of the lawyer's role, however, fails notably on this score. Clearly, the standard conception calls for a sharp separation of private and professional morality in which, to quote Bellow and Kettleson, "the lawyer is asked to do 'as a professional' what he or she would not do 'as a person.'"[40] The conception requires a public endorsement, as well as private adoption, of the extreme strategy of detachment. The good lawyer is one who is capable of drawing a tight circle around himself and his client, allowing no other considerations to interfere with his zealous and scrupulously loyal pursuit of the client's objectives. The good lawyer leaves behind his own family, religious, political, and moral concerns, and devotes himself entirely to the client.[41] But since professional integrity is often taken to be the most important mark of personal integrity, a very likely result is often that a successful lawyer is one who can strictly identify with this professional strategy of detachment. That is, the standard conception both directly and indirectly *encourages* adoption of one or the other of the extreme strategies of identification. But, as we have seen, both strategies have in common the unwanted consequence that practical deliberation, judgment, and action *within* the role are effectively cut off from ordinary moral beliefs, attitudes, feelings, and relationships—resources on which responsible judgment and action depend. This consequence is very costly in both personal and social terms.

Consider first the personal costs the lawyer must pay to act in this detached manner. The maximal strategy yields a severe impoverishment of moral experience. The lawyer's moral experience is sharply constrained by the boundaries of the moral universe of the role. But the minimal strategy involves perhaps even higher personal costs. Since the characteristic activities of the lawyer require a large

---

40 See note 35 supra.

41 Cf. A. Neier, Defending My Enemy (1979) (belief in the higher value of the legal system *qua* system necessitates defending persons and causes antithetical to the lawyer's own beliefs).

investment of his moral faculties, the lawyer must reconcile himself to a kind of moral prostitution. In a large portion of his daily experience, in which he is acting regularly in the moral arena, he is alienated from his own moral feelings and attitudes and indeed from his moral personality as a whole. Moreover, in light of the strong pressures for role identification, it is not unlikely that the explicit and conscious adoption of the minimal identification strategy involves a substantial element of self-deception.

The social costs of cutting off professional deliberation and action from their sources in ordinary moral experience are even more troubling. First, cut off from sound moral judgment, the lawyer's ability to do his job well—to determine the applicable law and effectively advise his clients—is likely to be seriously affected.[42] Both positivist and natural law theorists agree that moral arguments have an important place in the determination of much of modern law.[43] But the lawyer who must detach professional judgment from his own moral judgment is deprived of the resources from which arguments regarding his client's legal rights and duties can be fashioned. In effect, the ideal of neutrality and detachment wars against its companion ideal of zealous pursuit of client interests.

Second, the lawyer's practical judgment, in the Aristotelian sense, is rendered ineffective and unreliable.[44] In section I, I argued that, because human values are diverse and complex, one is sometimes thrown back on the faculty of practical judgment to resolve moral dilemmas.[45] This is as true within the professional context as outside of it. To cut off professional decisionmaking from the values and concerns which structure the moral situation, thereby blocking appeal to a more comprehensive point of view from which to weigh the validity of role morality, is to risk undermining practical judgment entirely.[46]

Third, and most importantly, when professional action is estranged from ordinary moral experience, the lawyer's sensitivity to the moral costs in both ordinary and extraordinary situations tends to atrophy. The ideal of neutrality permits, indeed requires, that the

---

[42] This point was suggested to me by Philippe Nonet.

[43] See generally R. Dworkin, Taking Rights Seriously, ch. 4 (1977); H.L.A. Hart, The Concept of Law 199, 205-07 (1961); D. Richards, The Moral Criticism of Law 31-36 (1977).

[44] See text accompanying note 34 supra.

[45] See text accompanying notes 16-20 supra.

[46] This may explain, in part, the attitude of "ethical minimalism" among lawyers which many, both within and outside the profession, deplore. This minimalism is an understandable reaction, in light of the fact that there are few fixed and settled rules in the Code and the lawyer is effectively cut off from the resources needed to resolve the indeterminacies unavoidably left by the Code.

lawyer regard his professional activities and their consequences from the point of view of the uninvolved spectator. One may abstractly regret that the injury is done, but this regret is analogous to the regret one feels as a spectator to the traffic accident mentioned in an earlier example;[47] one is in no way personally implicated. The responses likely from a mature sense of responsibility appear morally fastidious and unprofessional from the perspective of the present Code. This has troubling consequences: without a proper appreciation of the moral costs of one's actions one cannot make effective use of the faculty of practical judgment. In fact, a proper perspective of the moral costs of one's action has both intrinsic and instrumental value. The instrumental value lies in the added safeguard that important moral dilemmas will receive appropriate reflection. As Bernard Williams argued, "only those who are [by practice] reluctant or disinclined to do the morally disagreeable when it is really necessary have much chance of not doing it when it is not necessary. . . . [A] habit of reluctance is an essential obstacle against the happy acceptance of the intolerance."[48]

But this appreciation is also important for its own sake. To experience sincere reluctance, to feel the need to make restitution, to seek the other's pardon—these simply are appropriate responses to the actual feature of the moral situation. In this way, the status and integrity of important moral principles are maintained in compromising circumstances, and the moral relations between persons are respected or restored.

Finally, the moral detachment of the lawyer adversely affects the quality of the lawyer-client relationship. Unable to draw from the responses and relations of ordinary experience, the lawyer is capable of relating to the client only as a client. He puts his moral faculties of reason, argument, and persuasion wholly at the service of the client, but simultaneously disengages his moral personality. He views himself not as a moral actor but as a legal technician. In addition, he is barred from recognizing the client's moral personality. The moral responsibilities of the client are simply of no interest to him. Thus, paradoxically, the combination of partisanship and neutrality jeopardizes client autonomy and mutual respect (two publicly stated objec-

[47] See pages 68-69 supra.

[48] Williams, Politics and Moral Chracter, in Private and Public Morality 64 (S. Hampshire ed. 1978). Milgram's well-known experiments underscore the commonplace that the more we are able to distance ourselves (often literally) from the consequences of our actions, the more we are able to inflict pain and suffering on others without moral qualms. See generally S. Milgram, Obedience to Authority: An Experimental View 32-43 (1974).

tives of the standard conception), and yields instead a curious kind of *impersonal* relationship.

It is especially striking, then, that Charles Fried, the most sophisticated defender of these central ideals of the standard conception, should describe the lawyer as a "special purpose" friend.[49] Indeed, it is the contrast between the standard conception of the lawyer-client relationship and the characteristics of a relationship between friends which, on reflection, is likely to make the deepest impression. The impersonalism and moral detachment characteristic of the lawyer's role under the standard conception are not found in relations between friends. Loyalty to one's friend does not call for disengagement of one's moral personality. When in nonprofessional contexts we enter special relationships and undertake special obligations which create duties of loyalty or special concern, these special considerations must nevertheless be integrated into a coherent picture of the moral life as a whole. Often we must view our moral world from more than one perspective simultaneously.[50] As Goffman points out, roles are often structured with the recognition that persons occupying the role fill other roles which are also important to them. Room is left for the agent to integrate his responsibilities from each role into a more or less coherent scheme encompassing his entire moral life.[51]

But it is precisely this integrated conception of the moral personality that is unavailable to the professional who adopts either the minimal or the maximal identification strategy. Either the moral personality is entirely fragmented or compartmentalized, or it is shrunk to fit the moral universe defined by the role. Neither result is desirable.

IV

Toward an Alternative Conception: The Recourse Role

The unavoidable social costs of the standard conception of professional legal behavior argue strongly for a radical rethinking of the lawyer's role. One alternative is a "deprofessionalization" of legal practice so as to eliminate the distance between private and professional morality. Deprofessionalization, however, would involve a radical

[49] Fried, supra note 13, at 1071-72.

[50] Tammas Jones, see note 32 supra, was not just a grocer; he was also, *inter alia*, a father, husband, friend, and neighbor. It was possible for him to relate to his family, customers, neighbors, and friends, not as a role-agent, but as a person, because it could have been recognized that his moral personality penetrated through his activities in his roles, and that these roles did not exhaust that personality.

[51] E. Goffman, supra note 31, at 142.

restructuring of the entire legal system, reducing the complexity of the law as it currently exists so that individuals could exercise their rights without the assistance of highly specialized legal technicians. But, setting aside obvious questions of feasibility, to discredit this proposal we need only recall that deprofessionalization ignores the significant social value in a division of moral and social labor produced by the variety of public and professional roles.

A second, more plausible alternative is to recognize the unavoidable discontinuities in the moral landscape and to bridge them with a unified conception of moral personality. Achieving any sort of bridge, however, requires that lawyers significantly alter the way they view their own activities. Each lawyer must have a conception of the role that allows him to serve the important functions of that role in the legal and political system while integrating his own sense of moral responsibility into the role itself. Such a conception must improve upon the current one by allowing a broader scope for engaged moral judgment in day-to-day professional activities while encouraging a keener sense of personal responsibility for the consequences of these activities.[52]

The task of forging a concrete alternative conception is a formidable one. To begin, however, it may be useful to contrast two conceptions of social roles: the fixed role and the recourse role.[53] In a fixed role, the professional perceives the defining characteristics of the role—its basic rules, duties, and responsibilities—as entirely predetermined. The characteristics may be altered gradually through social evolution or more quickly by profession-wide regulatory legislation, but as far as the individual practitioner is concerned, the moral

---

[52] David Hoffman, a nineteenth century legal educator in Maryland, offered a conception of lawyering in which the lawyer's sense of responsibility was central. 2 D. Hoffman, A Course of Legal Study (2d ed. 1836) (I an indebted to Michael Kelly for this reference.). Hoffman wrote: "My client's conscience, and my own, are distinct entities: and though my vocation may sometimes justify my maintaining as facts, or principles, in doubtful cases, what may be neither one nor the other, I shall ever claim the privilege of solely judging to what extent to go." Id. at 755. Furthermore, he insisted that:

> Should my client be disposed to insist on captious requisitions, or frivolous and vexatious defences, they shall be neither enforced nor countenanced by me . . . If, after duly examining a case, I am persuaded that my client's claim or defence . . . cannot, or rather ought not, to be sustained, I will promptly advise him to abandon it. To press it further in such a case, with the hope of gleaning some advantage by an extorted compromise, would be lending myself to a dishonourable use of legal means, in order to gain a *portion* of that, the *whole* of which I have reason to believe would be denied to him both by law and justice.

Id. at 754.

[53] S. Kadish & M. Kadish, Discretion to Disobey 31-36 (1973).

universe of his role is an objective fact, to be reckoned with, but not for him to alter.[54] Sartre, proponents of the standard conception, and advocates of deprofessionalization all rest their positions on the assumption that the defining features of each role remain fixed. But this assumption fits only some social roles. A bank clerk, for example, must follow set routines; little judgment is required, and he has no authority to set aside the rules under which he acts or alter these rules to fit new occasions.[55] This is not troubling because the sorts of situations one is likely to face in such a job lend themselves to routine treatment.

In contrast, in a recourse role, one's duties and responsibilities are not fixed, but may expand or contract depending on the institutional objectives the role is designed to serve.[56] The recourse role requires the agent not only to act according to what he perceives to be the explicit duties of the role in a narrow sense, but also to carry out those duties in keeping with the functional objectives of the role.[57] The agent can meet these requirements only if he possesses a comprehensive and integrated concept of his activities both within and outside the role. Role morality, then, within a recourse role is not properly served by maximal identification with one's role. Nor can the role agent minimally identify with his role so as to abandon or disengage his personal morality or basic sense of responsibility. Indeed, responsible professional judgment will rely heavily on a sense of responsibility.

If we perceive the role of the lawyer in our legal system as a recourse role, a viable solution to the problem of responsibility may be available. A recourse role conception forces the lawyer to recognize that the exercise of his role duties must fully engage his rational and critical powers, and his sense of moral responsibility as well. Although not intended to obliterate the moral distance between professional and private moralities, a recourse role conception bridges that gap by integrating to a significant degree the moral personality of the individual with the performance of role responsibilities. Most significantly, this conception prevents the lawyer from escaping responsibility by relying on his status as an agent of the client or an instrument of the system. He cannot consider himself simply a legal technician, since his role essentially involves the exercise of his *engaged* moral judgment.

---

54 See id. at 33-34.

55 Id.

56 Id. at 35.

57 Id. at 35-36.

V

OBJECTIONS AND REPLIES

Two initial objections to the recourse role conception should be addressed: (1) that it is paternalistic,[58] and (2) that it is unnecessary, since the standard conception adequately allows for the exercise of individual moral judgment by permitting the attorney to decide whether to accept or withdraw from representation.[59]

Both these objections are mistaken. Paternalism involves interfering with the actions of others or, in subtler cases, making judgments for others, for their own good. Engaging a lawyer's moral judgment in the day-to-day practice of law in no way entails paternalism—and will involve paternalism only if the lawyer himself holds strongly paternalistic moral views. There is an important distinction between evaluating alternatives in terms of the client's long range good and making decisions without the client's consent (or against his will), on the one hand, and exercising one's moral judgment regarding those alternatives, on the other. The recourse role conception is not paternalistic even in the very broad sense that the lawyer is encouraged to make the client's moral decisions for him. The moral judgments that the lawyer makes are made on his own behalf; he does not make the client's decisions. Indeed, it is an advantage of my proposal, in contrast to the standard conception, that it enables both lawyer and client to recognize and respect the moral status of the other. The lawyer-client relationship should not be any more paternalistic than a relationship between friends.

As to the second objection, it may be admitted that the Code of Professional Responsibility does provide some room for the individual lawyer to exercise moral judgment in the acceptance and withdrawal from representation. But the scope allowed for such judgment is limited, and the motivation skewed. The Code mandates refusal to accept employment only when the client clearly intends to bring an action "merely for the purpose of harassing or maliciously injuring any person,"[60] or seeks to bring an action for which no reasonable legal argument can be made.[61]

The lawyer may refuse to accept employment when his personal feelings are sufficiently intense as to diminish his ability effectively to

---

[58] See Fried, supra note 13, at 1066 n.17.

[59] See Freedman, Personal Responsibility in a Professional System, 27 Cath. U.L. Rev. 191, 193-95 (1978).

[60] Code, supra note 2, DR 2-109(A)(1).

[61] Id. DR 2-109(A)(2).

represent the client,[62] although the Code permits such refusal only in fairly compelling circumstances.[63] Once the lawyer has undertaken to represent the client, however, permissive withdrawal is allowed only in a few restricted circumstances,[64] none of which includes the conscience of the lawyer. Permissive withdrawal for what might be termed "moral reasons" is condoned only when the client insists upon presenting a claim or defense for which no reasonable legal justification can be advanced,[65] or when the client insists upon an illegal course of action.[66] Withdrawal for moral reasons is required only when the lawyer knows that the client is conducting the litigation solely to harass.[67]

Thus, in cases in which the Code permits the lawyer to refuse employment, the rationale seems to be that a lawyer who has scruples about the client's proposed legal action is not likely to be able adequately to serve his client.[68] And such scruples generally are not permitted at all once the attorney agrees to represent a client.[69] This point of view encourages the lawyer to steel himself against such scruples and to view them as strictly personal feelings which have no place in professional behavior—a kind of unbecoming moral squeamishness. It is hard to dismiss the thought that this reaction is at bottom morally cynical.

Charles Fried raises a more sophisticated objection to the conception of the lawyer's role developed above. On this point, he insists that the law must respect the autonomy and rights of individual citizens. According to Fried, one way we respect individual rights is through the creation of specific rules and institutions to protect them. But when the legal system is so complex that the ordinary person is unable to exercise his rights without an expert advisor, the interjection of a lawyer's moral judgment might prevent the individual from exercising fully these lawful rights. In this way, "the law . . . would

---

[62] Id. EC 2-30.

[63] Id. EC 2-26.

[64] See id. DR 2-110(C).

[65] Id. DR 2-110(C)(1)(a). Withdrawal is permitted for a number of other reasons, all unrelated to the present argument. These include, among others, failure by the client to pay fees, DR 2-110(C)(1)(f), and inability to work effectively with co-counsel, DR 2-110(C)(3).

[66] Id. DR 2-110(C)(1)(b), (c).

[67] Id. DR 2-110(B)(1). Withdrawal is mandated for a variety of morally neutral reasons, such as a conflict of interest with another client whom the lawyer is representing, DR 2-110(B)(2); see DR 5-105, or the lawyer's ill health, DR 2-110(B)(3).

[68] Id. EC 2-30.

[69] The Code *does* allow permissive withdrawal, however, if the client insists that the lawyer engage in conduct that is contrary to the lawyer's advice and judgment *and the matter is not before a tribunal*. Id. DR 2-110(C)(1)(e).

impose constraints on the lay citizen [implicitly] . . . which it is not entitled to impose explicitly."[70] Thus, Fried argues, although no rights are violated when a pornography venture fails because a person refuses on moral grounds to lend it funds, rights are violated when "through ignorance or misinformation about the law [because of an attorney's moral judgment] an individual refrains from pursuing a wholly lawful purpose."[71]

The problem with this argument is that while we might agree that individual autonomy and rights should be respected, we might still deny that it is the lawyer's moral as well as role duty to assist his client in any lawful exercise of his legal rights. Fried's mistake is to confuse *moral* rights with *legal* rights. He fails to distinguish the rights and sphere of autonomy defined by *morality* from the rights and area of free action defined by law. The area of legally permitted behavior need not coincide with that circumscribed as a matter of individual moral right. A lack of fit between legal and moral rights is most obvious when legal rights appear unjust or otherwise morally objectionable. But lack of fit may occur even when the legal system is morally ideal. For various reasons the law paints the canvas of legal relations, regulations, and rights with broad strokes. Many forms of social behavior otherwise harmful or morally objectionable are left unproscribed in light of the moral or social costs of enforcement.

Fried complains that if the services of the lawyer were restricted, the law would, in effect, implicitly impose constraints that it is not entitled to impose explicitly.[72] But this is not the case in the instances I am considering. For reasons of administrative efficiency, a particular restriction may not be imposed, but it does not follow that the lawmaker is not *entitled*—because it would violate someone's rights—to impose such a restriction.

Not all rights, powers, or permissions defined by the law protect moral rights. Fried's argument has force only for those legal rights that protect important individual moral rights and fundamental political liberties. It does not necessarily hold for other legal rights. My argument is not that the exercise of these legal rights is never justified. I merely contend that it is not always morally right for the individual to exercise these rights, and that it may, in particular instances, be wrong for a lawyer to help him. Thus, it is a matter of *moral argument* whether in particular cases it is appropriate for the

---

70 Fried, supra note 13, at 1073.
71 Id. at 1075.
72 Id. at 1073.

lawyer to assist in what may be considered a morally questionable exercise of clear legal rights.

However, Fried seems to qualify his commitment to the standard conception of the lawyer's role. He rejects the contention, advanced by proponents of the standard conception, that whatever is legally permissible for a lawyer is morally permissible as well.[73] He has no trouble with a lawyer who assists his client in exercising his legal rights when only the collective good or abstract interests are adversely affected.[74] But Fried is troubled by those activities of a lawyer that cause harm to specific persons known to the lawyer and client, such as the adverse witness who may be abused by the defense lawyer. To resolve this tension, he distinguishes between personal wrongs (wrongs *personally* committed by the lawyer in the course of his professional activities) and institutional wrongs (wrongs worked by the rules of the legal system).[75] However, in the absence of some independent principle by which to distinguish between personal and institutional wrongs, Fried seriously begs the very question at issue. The question can be rephrased: for what harms or wrongs done to specific individuals other than the client is the lawyer personally responsible, and what harms or wrongs must be laid at the door of the system itself?

Fried does suggest one answer, which turns on whether the description of the harmful action in question essentially refers to law or legal institutions. This principle can be illustrated by the difference between (a) abusing a witness in court and (b) exploiting unfairly the defense of the statute of limitations. In the second case, the harmful action is formally defined by the procedural rules of the legal system itself. Thus, legal institutions created the occasion for the action and are essential to the definition of the action itself. There is, for example, no action fitting the description "asserting the defense of the statute of limitations" outside a specific legal context, just as there is no action fitting the description "hitting a home run" outside the context of baseball. So, says Fried, the action is not personal, it is institutional—an action of the system, not of the individual lawyers.[76] In contrast, the act of abusing the witness is a personal act of the lawyer. Although it occurs in a legal context, it is an action that can be done both within and outside that context. There is nothing essentially institutional about it. Thus, Fried concludes, "[t]he lawyer is

---

[73] Id. at 1082-86.

[74] Id. at 1084-86.

[75] Id.

[76] Id. at 1085.

not morally entitled . . . to engage his own person in doing personal harm to another, though he may exploit the system for his client even if the system consequently works injustice."[77]

Fried's distinction between personal and institutional wrongs is open to criticism on two grounds. First, it relies too heavily on chosen characterizations. Consider, for example, a situation in which the lawyer is seeking to obtain custody of the children for the husband, his client, in a divorce proceeding. The lawyer knows that the wife has been conducting an adulterous affair for some time and that, under the law of the jurisdiction, this would disqualify her from obtaining custody. He also knows that the wife would be humiliated by having details of the affair brought out in open court. If he chooses to advance his client's interests and raise the issue of adultery, is he merely raising a point of law (an institutional action) or is he doing a personal wrong to the wife? The first characterization would pass Fried's test; the second might not. No important moral principle should rest on arbitrary distinctions between equally appropriate characterizations of the actions.

Second, there is the more fundamental problem of an individual's absolving himself of moral responsibility by shifting guilt to institutional shoulders. How can an action done within an institutional setting be morally appropriate, perhaps even morally required, when it is *wrong*? Fried suggests that responsibility shifts because the action is the action of the system—the institution—and not of the individual lawyer. Fried's reasoning seems to rest on the assumption that "if an action is essentially institutional then the good or bad consequences of the action are not attributable to the agent, but only to the institution." But, while it is important, for purposes of correction, to trace "institutional wrongs" back to the source, it does not follow that only the system may be blamed, or that the only possible action is to seek institutional reform. It is a mistake to insist that either the system is to blame or the individual agent is to blame. It is possible that moral criticism of both is appropriate. To rest blame with just one or the other suggests that when the system is to blame, there is nothing the individual can do about it but work to change the system, or the offending part of it. But that is not true: one can also avoid exploiting the defects of the law to the injury of others.

The lawyer must recognize that the institution acts only through the voluntary activities of the lawyer and client. The lawyer is not the instrument of the institution; rather the institution is the instrument

[77] Id. at 1086.

of the client and the client engages the lawyer to make use of the instrument.

It is far more desirable to recognize at the outset that the lawyer, as well as the client, bears at least some responsibility for harms done by both "institutional" and "personal" actions. The question, then, is whether in particular cases there is a moral justification for the harms done. Whether there is or is not will be determined by the substantive moral considerations relevant in the case. And it is these substantive moral considerations that the responsible lawyer must take into account in making his decision.

Part II

Neutral Partisanship: Justifications and Critiques

[3]

The Lawyer's Amoral Ethical Role: A Defense, A Problem, and Some Possibilities

Stephen L. Pepper

This essay presents a moral justification for the current generally accepted amoral ethical role of the lawyer. The justification is premised primarily upon the values of individual autonomy, equality, and diversity. Based upon these values, the author argues that the amoral role is the correct moral stance for the lawyer as a professional, is a "good" role. The essay then responds to two of the most frequent criticisms of that moral stance: the first based upon economic inequality and the fact that lawyers' services must be purchased; the second based upon the absence of the "adversary system" context for most lawyer work. The author then elaborates a serious problem created by the conjunction of the amoral role and the dominant legal philosophy of American lawyers, "legal realism." If the limit on a lawyer's conduct under the traditional amoral role is the law, then the realist emphasis on the indeterminacy and manipulability of "law" leave the lawyer in a difficult moral position. Finally, a series of possibilities are presented to deal with this problem, the most promising of which is the "moral dialogue" between lawyer and client as an adjunct to the amoral role.

Eleven years ago Richard Wasserstrom published a provocative paper focusing attention on the moral dimension of the lawyer-client relationship.[1] In the intervening decade the topic has received a great deal of attention both in the profession[2] and in the academy.[3] Much of Wasserstrom's

Stephen L. Pepper is professor of law at the College of Law, University of Denver, and during the 1987–88 academic year will be visiting professor of law at the Cornell Law School. A.B. 1969, Stanford University; J.D. 1973, Yale Law School.

This essay was the winning submission in the Association of American Law Schools 1985 "Call for Scholarly Papers" competition, and was presented at the 1986 AALS annual meeting, where it was commented upon by Professors Andrew Kaufman and David Luban. Those comments follow in this issue, along with a rejoinder by Professor Pepper.

1. Wasserstrom, Lawyers as Professionals: Some Moral Issues, 5 Hum. Rts. 1 (1975).

2. In 1977 the ABA formed the Commission on Evaluation of Professional Standards, charged with "a comprehensive rethinking of the ethical premises and problems of the profession of law" (Proposed Final Draft, Model Rules of Professional Conduct, Chairman's Introduction, 1981). The efforts of this group, known as the Kutak Commission, resulted in the ABA's adoption of a new code of ethics, the Model Rules of Professional Conduct, and in the Association of Trial Lawyers of America's proposal of an alternative code, the American Lawyer's Code of Conduct. This process involved numerous conferences and meetings, voluminous public comment and published commentary, and much revision. In relation to an underlying ethic, the general moral role of the lawyer, there is little difference between the prior ABA Code of Professional Responsibility and the new Model Rules. Hodes, The Code of Professional Responsibility, The Kutak Rules, and the Trial Lawyer's Code: Surprisingly, Three Peas in a Pod, 35 U. Miami L. Rev. 739, 746–750 (1981). References in this paper to the Code will not indicate the comparable portion of the Rules.

exposition concerned the role-differentiated morality of the lawyer-client relationship, what he referred to as the amoral professional role. Wasserstrom was critical, but "undecided," about the value of that role. This essay is a defense of the lawyer's amoral role.

The role of all professionals, observed Wasserstrom, "is to prefer . . . the interests of client or patient" over those of other individuals. "[W]here the attorney-client relationship exists, it is often appropriate and many times even obligatory for the attorney to do things that, all other things being equal, an ordinary person need not, and should not do."[4] This remains the generally accepted understanding within the profession of a lawyer's proper function. Once a lawyer has entered into the professional relationship with a client, the notion is that conduct by the lawyer in service to the client is judged by a different moral standard than the same conduct by a layperson. Through cross-examination, a lawyer may suggest to a jury that a witness is lying when the lawyer knows the witness is telling the truth. A lawyer may draft contracts or create a corporation for a client to enable the distribution and sale of cigarettes, Saturday Night Specials, or pornography. A lawyer may draft a will for a client disinheriting children should they marry outside the faith. The traditional view is that if such conduct by the lawyer is lawful, then it is morally justifiable, even if the same conduct by a layperson is morally unacceptable and even if the client's goals or means are morally unacceptable. As long as what lawyer and client do is lawful, it is the client who is morally accountable, not the lawyer.

Although this amoral role is the accepted standard within the profession, no generally accepted moral justification for it has been articulated.[5] This remains true despite heated academic discourse on the subject during the ten years following Wasserstrom's article, discourse symbolized by the question: Can a good person be a good lawyer?[6] The criticism of the amoral role has been extraordinarily diverse, ranging from economics through jurisprudence to religion.[7] The most common justification for the

3. E.g., G. Bellow & B. Moulton, The Lawyering Process—Ethics and Professional Responsibility (1981); M. Freedman, Lawyers' Ethics in an Adversary System (1975); G. Hazard, Ethics in the Practice of Law (1978); Schneyer, Moral Philosophy's Standard Misconception of Legal Ethics, 1984 Wis. L. Rev. 1529; Dauer & Leff, Correspondence, The Lawyer as Friend, 86 Yale L.J. 573 (1977); Fried, The Lawyer as Friend: The Moral Foundations of the Lawyer-Client Relation, 85 Yale L.J. 1060 (1976). See also sources cited *infra* note 7.

4. Wasserstrom, *supra* note 1, at 5.

5. Prominent descriptions and justifications are found in Curtis, The Ethics of Advocacy, 4 Stan. L. Rev. 3 (1951); Fried, *supra* note 3; and Freedman, Personal Responsibility in a Professional System, 27 Catholic U.L. Rev. 191 (1978). In some respects, the justification provided here is an elaboration and modification of those presented by Freedman and Fried.

6. The question, phrased slightly differently, is the first line of Charles Fried's article, *supra* note 3, at 1060.

7. See, e.g., Luban, The Adversary System Excuse, *in* D. Luban, ed., The Good Lawyer 83 (1984) (moral philosophy); M. Frankel, Partisan Justice (1980); T. Shaffer, On Being a Christian and a Lawyer (1981) (religion); Abel, Why Does the ABA Promulgate Ethical Rules? 59 Tex. L. Rev. 639 (1981) (socioeconomic analysis); D'Amato & Eberle, Three Models of Legal Ethics, 27 St. Louis U.L.J. 761 (1983) (moral philosophy); Rhode, Why the ABA Bothers: A Functional Perspective on Professional Codes, 59 Tex. L. Rev. 689 (1981) (socioeconomic analysis); Schwartz, The Zeal of the Civil Advocate,

role is framed in the language of the "adversary system," focusing on the justifiably different roles of the advocate and the judge.[8] Part I of this essay will suggest a far broader moral justification for the amoral professional role of the lawyer, the "first-class citizenship model." Part II will address two of the most common criticisms of the amoral role. Part III poses the serious difficulty for the model created when the amoral professional role is combined with the dominant legal realist view of the law. Part IV canvasses some possibilities for ameliorating the legal realism difficulty.

I. The First-Class Citizenship Model

As an introduction to the first-class citizenship model, I would like to begin with a brief explanation of the concept of professional obligation. The very idea of a profession connotes the function of service, the notion that to some degree the professional is to subordinate his interests to the interests of those in need of his services.[9] This orientation is suggested by the following seven characteristics that define the concept of a profession.[10]

1. A profession is a means of making a living.
2. A profession is based on specialized knowledge, training, and ability, often requiring intellectual labor and many years of higher education.
3. The services rendered by the professional, based upon this foundation of knowledge and ability, are necessary to individuals at various points in their lives and are frequently of the utmost personal concern (for example, services relating to physical health, liberty, religious salvation, or psychological well-being).
4. Because of the specialized knowledge involved, the quality of the services rendered by the professional is untestable from the perspective of the layman. The individual *needs* the service but is unable to evaluate it, and therefore the individual is *vulnerable* in relation to the professional.
5. The profession holds a monopoly on a service frequently needed by individuals, and as a result wields significant economic power.
6. The profession is largely self-regulated in determining and administering the qualifications for membership and in policing professional activities.
7. Part of the self-regulation usually includes ethical prescriptions that articulate a service orientation.

1983 A.B.F. Res. J. 543 (legal analysis); Simon, The Ideology of Advocacy: Procedural Justice and Professional Ethics, 1978 Wis. L. Rev. 30 (jurisprudence); Wasserstrom, *supra* note 1 (moral philosophy).

8. See, e.g., Freedman, *supra* note 3; Fuller & Randall, Professional Responsibility: Report of the Joint Conference, 44 A.B.A.J. 1159 (1958); Curtis, *supra* note 5.

9. B. Bledstein, The Culture of Professionalism 87 (1976); M. S. Larson, The Rise of Professionalism 56–63 (1977); W. E. Moore, The Professions: Roles and Rules 13–15 (1970).

10. These characteristics are derived from a similar definition provided by Wasserstrom, *supra* note 1, at 2 n.1. See also Bledstein, *supra* note 9, at 87; Larson, *supra* note 9, at x; Moore, *supra* note 9, at 4–22.

The sixth and seventh characteristics are the quid pro quo for the fact that the profession has a monopoly on and is making a living from a service the public needs but cannot evaluate.

The seven characteristics add up to an inherent advantage for the professional over those in need of his services and to a pervasive economic conflict of interest between the professional and those who need (and pay for) his services. As a remedy for this unbalanced conflict, there is a primary underlying professional obligation: When the client's interest and the professional's interest conflict, the professional is to forgo his interest in favor of the client's.[11]

The legal profession's ethical code reflects the factors and the conflict listed above. Much of the ABA's Model Code of Professional Responsibility (the governing document in over three quarters of the states) appears to be designed to enhance the economic well-being of the profession.[12] But much of it also appears designed to put the client's interest above that of the lawyer, to protect the client from the lawyer's self-interest. It is this second aspect of the legal profession's ethics with which this essay is concerned. Leaving aside the "guild" provisions, the role of the professional is to serve the client ahead of himself or herself. If anything justifies the asymmetrical power and opportunity sketched in the seven definitional elements listed above, it is this underlying ethic of professionalism. This ethic alone suggests that if a moral conflict between lawyer and client develops, the lawyer should honor the client's view. But this is not the argument to be presented here. This view of the theoretical service orientation of the professions only sets the stage.

The premise with which we begin is that law is a public good available to all. Society, through its "lawmakers"—legislatures, courts, administrative agencies, and so forth—has created various mechanisms to ease and enable the private attainment of individual or group goals. The corporate form of enterprise, the contract, the trust, the will, and access to civil court to gain the use of public force for the settlement of private grievance are all vehicles of empowerment for the individual or group; all are "law" created by the collectivity to be generally available for private use. In addition to these structuring mechanisms are vast amounts of law, knowledge of which is intended to be generally available and is empowering: landlord/tenant law, labor law, OSHA, Social Security—the list can be vastly extended. Access to both forms of law increases one's ability to successfully attain goals.[13]

The second premise is a societal commitment to the principle of individual autonomy. This premise is founded on the belief that liberty and autonomy are a moral good, that free choice is better than constraint, that each of

11. Morgan, The Evolving Concept of Professional Responsibility, 90 Harv. L. Rev. 702, 705 (1977).

12. *Id.*

13. L. Fuller, The Principles of Social Order 230–37 (1981); R. Summers, Lon L. Fuller 84–86 (1984).

us wishes, to the extent possible, to make our own choices rather than to have them made for us. This belief is incorporated into our legal system, which accommodates individual autonomy by leaving as much room as possible for liberty and diversity. Leaving regulatory law aside for the moment (and granting that it has grown immensely, contributing to the legalization to be mentioned below), our law is designed (1) to allow the private structuring of affairs (contracts, corporations, wills, trusts, etc.) and (2) to define conduct that is intolerable.[14] The latter sets a floor below which one cannot go, but leaves as much room as possible above that floor for individual decision making. It may be morally wrong to manufacture or distribute cigarettes or alcohol, or to disinherit one's children for marrying outside the faith, but the generality of such decisions are left in the private realm. Diversity and autonomy are preferred over "right" or "good" conduct. The theory of our law is to leave as much room as possible for private, individual decisions concerning what is right and wrong, as opposed to public, collective decisions.

Our first premise is that law is intended to be a public good which increases autonomy. The second premise is that increasing individual autonomy is morally good. The third step is that in a highly legalized society such as ours, autonomy is often dependent upon access to the law.[15] Put simply, first-class citizenship is dependent on access to the law. And while access to law—to the creation and use of a corporation, to knowledge of how much overtime one has to pay or is entitled to receive—is formally available to all, in reality it is available only through a lawyer.[16] Our law is usually not simple, usually not self-executing. For most people most of the time, meaningful access to the law requires the assistance of a lawyer. Thus the resulting conclusion: First-class citizenship is frequently dependent upon the assistance of a lawyer. If the conduct which the lawyer facilitates is above the floor of the intolerable—is not unlawful—then this line of thought suggests that what the lawyer does is a social good. The lawyer is the means to first-class citizenship, to meaningful autonomy, for the client.

For the lawyer to have moral responsibility for each act he or she facilitates, for the lawyer to have a moral obligation to refuse to facilitate that which the lawyer believes to be immoral, is to substitute lawyers' beliefs for individual autonomy and diversity. Such a screening submits each to the prior restraint of the judge/facilitator and to rule by an oligarchy of lawyers.[17] (If, in the alternative, the suggestion is that the lawyer's screening

14. H. L. A. Hart, The Concept of Law 27–28 (1961).

15. Law, The Messages of a Legal Education, *in* S. Gillers, ed., Looking at Law School 92, 104–5 (1984); Alschuler, The Search for Truth Continued, The Privilege Retained: A Response to Judge Frankel, 54 U. Colo. L. Rev. 67, 72–75 (1982); Freedman, *supra* note 5, at 204 (1978); Fried, *supra* note 3, at 1073; Wexler, Practicing Law for Poor People, 79 Yale L.J. 1049 (1970).

16. Access may be indirect. Thus a lawyer may serve as advisor to the union or the employers' trade organization, which in turn transmits wage and hour legal guidelines to member employees or employers.

17. Freedman, *supra* note 5, at 195; Wasserstrom, *supra* note 1, at 10–11.

should be based not on the lawyer's personal morality, but on the lawyer's assessment of society's moral views or on guidelines spelled out in a professional code of ethics, then one has substituted collective moral decision making for individual moral decision making, contrary to the principle of autonomy. Less room has been left for private decision making through a sub rosa form of lawmaking.) If the conduct is sufficiently "bad," it would seem that it ought to be made explicitly unlawful. If it is not that bad, why subject the citizenry to the happenstance of the moral judgment of the particular lawyer to whom each has access? If making the conduct unlawful is too onerous because the law would be too vague, or it is too difficult to identify the conduct in advance, or there is not sufficient social or political concern, do we intend to delegate to the individual lawyer the authority for case-by-case legislation and policing?

An example may help. Professor Wasserstrom implies that a lawyer ought to refuse to draft a will disinheriting a child because of the child's views concerning the war in Nicaragua.[18] "But," asks Professor Freedman, "is the lawyer's paternalism toward the client preferable—morally or otherwise—to the client's paternalism toward her children?" And, he asks further, is there any reason to substitute the diversity of lawyers' opinions on the issue of disinheritance based on political belief for the diversity of clients' opinions?[19] Ought we to have a law on the issue? If not, why screen use of the legal device of testacy either through the diverse consciences of lawyers or through the collective conscience of the profession? And if the law is clear but contrary to the lawyer's moral beliefs, such as a tax loophole for the rich or impeachment-oriented cross-examination of the truthful witness, why allow (let alone require) that the lawyer legislate for this particular person or situation?

It is apparent that a final significant value supporting the first-class citizenship model is that of equality. If law is a public good, access to which increases autonomy, then equality of access is important. For access to the law to be filtered unequally through the disparate moral views of each individual's lawyer does not appear to be justifiable. Even given the current and perhaps permanent fact of unequal access to the law, it does not make sense to compound that inequality with another. If access to a lawyer is achieved (through private allocation of one's means, public provision, or the lawyer's—or profession's—choice to provide it), should the extent of that access depend upon individual lawyer conscience? The values of autonomy and equality suggest that it should not; the client's conscience should be superior to the lawyer's.[20] One of the unpleasant concomitants of the view that a lawyer should be morally responsible for all that she does is the re-

18. Wasserstrom, *supra* note 1, at 7.

19. Freedman, *supra* note 5, at 194–95.

20. This is an echo of the underlying professional ethic presented at the beginning of part I. It also leaves one wondering whether there is any place for the *lawyer's* moral autonomy. The most commonly expressed focus for the lawyer's exercise of moral autonomy is in his or her choice of clients. This and

sulting inequality: unfiltered access to the law is then available only to those who are legally sophisticated or to those able to educate themselves sufficiently for access to the law, while those less sophisticated—usually those less educated—are left with no access or with access that subjects their use of the law to the moral judgment and veto of the lawyer.

II. The Critique and a Response

A. The Economic Inequality Criticism

The foregoing quickly leads to the observation that law is a public good in theory but not in fact, and that one of the key premises justifying the first-class citizenship model is therefore false. Like almost everything else in our society, access to law is rationed through the market—in this case, the market for lawyers' services. Thus, the rich have disproportionate access over the poor, and this is particularly unacceptable given the public nature of law and its implementing relationship to individual autonomy and first-class citizenship. This is the focus of the first criticism of the amoral role: it would be justified if everyone had access to "first-class citizenship" through a lawyer, but everyone does not. The drastic and fundamental inequality of means in America vitiates the moral justification for an amoral professional ethic for lawyers.[21]

Granting the truth of economic inequality does not, however, mean that the amoral role is a bad role, or that the lawyer currently fulfilling the role cannot be a good person. An analogous criticism might be made of the grocer and the housing contractor. Although food and shelter are (in our system) not public goods, they are more fundamentally enabling to autonomy than is law. Yet there is much less disquiet over the moral role of the grocer, housing contractor, or landlord than that of the lawyer.[22] We live in a primarily market system, not a primarily socialist system, and the contemporary problem in defining lawyers' ethics is likely to have to be answered in this market context. Lawyers cannot magically socialize the economy or legal services.

Another way of saying this, perhaps more to the point, is that there are two issues here: the distribution of legal services and the content of what is distributed.[23] The moral content of what is distributed—the ethical nature of the lawyer-client relationship once established—is the subject of this es-

more significant elements of the lawyer's moral autonomy are presented briefly below at secs. IV.D & E and part V.

21. J. Auerbach, Unequal Justice (1976); Abel, *supra* note 7, at 685–86 and sources cited at nn.250 & 255; A. Goldman, The Moral Foundations of Professional Ethics 124 (1980).

22. This may be explained by the relatively intimate interpersonal nature of the professional relationship and by the way a lawyer's integrity appears to be for sale. See the sixth element of Wasserstrom's definition of the professional and his discussion of the lawyer's hypocrisy, *supra* note 1, at n.1 & p.14.

23. For an interesting approach to the "economic inequality" issue and its nexus to law and legal services, and for an excellent overview which recognizes the distinction in the text, see Galanter, Why the "Haves" Come Out Ahead: Speculations on the Limits of Legal Change, 9 Law & Soc'y Rev. 95 (1974–75).

say. The distribution of access to the law (legal services) is a different subject. While the effort to make law a more truly public good is under way (or assuming it fails and we are left with the status quo), the other issue remains: what is to be the moral content of the legal services that are available? To suggest that transforming the amoral facilitator role of the lawyer into the judge/facilitator role follows from the insufficient availability of legal services is a non sequitur. Such a transformation would compound inequality upon inequality—first the inequality of access to a lawyer, then the inequality of what law that particular lawyer will allow the client access to.

One can argue that the judge/facilitator role will not compound inequality but, to the contrary, will balance power because the advantage accruing to those with access to the law over those without will be balanced by the restraint of the lawyer's moral screening of access to the law.[24] There are at least two reasons to react with skepticism to this argument. First, the inequality of distribution is neither complete nor uniform. At least some of the "outs" have had significant access to the law through lawyers.[25] Labor unions,[26] criminal defendants,[27] and civil rights organizations[28] are three prominent examples. Lawyers have played key roles in areas where many perceive gains to have been made in social justice.[29] Second, there is little likelihood of a large difference in moral perception between lawyers and their "in" clients.[30] Perhaps we need more (historical? empirical?) data: Looking back, would there have been more social justice, equality, or general welfare if lawyers had altered or withheld services on the basis of their own (largely middle- or upper-class) values? How would a moralistic as opposed to an amoral role for lawyers have affected 20th-century American social history? However one is inclined to answer such questions, to the extent that the first-class citizenship argument is otherwise valid, expansion and equalization of access to lawyers is a goal which is both consistent with and suggested by that argument.[31] Transforming lawyers into moral

24. This seems to be an implicit notion on the part of many. See, e.g., Auerbach, *supra* note 21; Luban, *supra* note 7; Wasserstrom, *supra* note 1.

25. Rabinowitz, The Radical Tradition in the Law, *in* D. Kairys, ed., The Politics of Law 310 (1982); A. Ginger, The Relevant Lawyers (1972); Sparer, Fundamental Human Rights, Legal Entitlements, and the Social Struggle: A Friendly Critique of the Critical Legal Studies Movement, 36 Stan. L. Rev. 509 (1984); Gabel & Harris, Building Power and Breaking Images: Critical Legal Theory and the Practice of Law, 3 N.Y.U. Rev. L. & Soc. Change 369 (1982–83).

26. See, e.g., Klare, Judicial Deradicalization of the Wagner Act and the Origins of Modern Legal Consciousness, 1937–1941, 62 Minn. L. Rev. 265 (1978); Sparer, *supra* note 25.

27. See, e.g., Bachmann, Lawyers, Law, and Social Change, 13 N.Y.U. Rev. L. & Soc. Change 1, 23–26 (1984–85). See generally Choper, Consequences of Supreme Court Decisions Upholding Individual Constitutional Rights, 83 Mich. L. Rev. 1 (1984).

28. Auerbach, *supra* note 21, at 263–68 (1976).

29. See note 25 *supra*.

30. Auerbach, *supra* note 21, at 14–39 (1976); Nelson, Ideology, Practice, and Professional Autonomy: Social Values and Client Relationships in the Large Law Firm, 37 Stan. L. Rev. 503 (1985).

31. Galanter, *supra* note 23, provides observations which appear equivocal on both the "amoral role" and the effect of expansion and equalization of access to lawyers. Compare *id.* at 114–19 with *id.* at 138–44.

screens for client access to the law, to the contrary, is a project quite problematic in its relation to equality of access to law.

Before moving on, one caveat related to the economic inequality criticism should be entered. The first-class citizenship model suggests that lawyers are a necessary item in a highly legalized society and that they should have an amoral role in relation to facilitating clients' wishes. It does not suggest how access to lawyers should be organized. The nature and extent of the legal profession's monopoly—for example, whether paraprofessionals should be allowed to practice independently, or whether unauthorized practice rules should be enforced against bankers, realtors, or accountants—is a separate question from that examined in this paper.[32] The term "deprofessionalization" can refer to either (1) the market-limiting nature of professional rules or (2) the amoral professional role.[33] The argument up to this point in this essay is that deprofessionalization in the second sense is a bad idea, but no position has been taken on deprofessionalization in the first sense.

B. The Adversary System Criticism

Much writing on the amoral role of the lawyer has dealt with the layperson's common conception of what lawyers do: criminal defense. The amoral role is justified by the need of the "man in trouble" for a champion familiar with the law to aid him in facing the vast resources of the state bearing down on him, attempting to seize his most basic liberties and put him in jail.[34] In this context, however, there is another champion, the prosecutor, with greater resources, opposing and balancing the lawyer's amorality. More important, there are a neutral judge and a jury whose roles are significantly less amoral than the advocate's. Critics of the lawyer's role have had a field day distinguishing this situation from civil litigation and from nonlitigation (what most lawyers are working on most of the time).[35] The critics suggest that a role justified by the rather unusual context of the criminal justice system simply is not justified in the far more common lawyer roles. Where there is no judge responsible for applying the law from a neutral stance, where there is no lawyer protecting those who may be victimized or exploited by another person's use of "the law"—in these situations the critics of the amoral role argue that the lawyer must take on the neutral judge's role and screen access to and use of the law. Their point is

32. The literature is vast. See, e.g., Rhode, Policing the Professional Monopoly: A Constitutional and Empirical Analysis of Unauthorized Practice Prohibitions, 34 Stan. L. Rev. 1 (1981); Morgan, *supra* note 11; Ehrlich & Schwartz, Reducing the Costs of Legal Services: Possible Approaches by the Federal Government, *reprinted in* A. Kaufman, Problems in Professional Responsibility at 582 (1st ed. 1976).

33. For a discussion of the latter sense of "deprofessionalization," see Simon, *supra* note 7.

34. E.g., M. Freedman, Lawyers' Ethics in an Adversary System (1975); D. Mellinkoff, The Conscience of a Lawyer (1973).

35. Luban's article, *supra* note 7, is entitled "The Adversary System Excuse." See also, e.g., Schwartz, *supra* note 7; Schwartz, The Professionalism and Accountability of Lawyers, 66 Calif. L. Rev. 669 (1978); Wasserstrom, *supra* note 1.

that a role modeled on Perry Mason does not fit the lawyer working for Sears drafting form consumer contracts.

It is therefore significant that the justification for the lawyer's amoral role sketched above has not once mentioned the adversary system, has not been based on any premise involving an opposing lawyer or a neutral judge or jury. In the usual justification of the lawyer's amoral role, the model is adjudication, and there is a difficult stretch adapting and applying this to the lawyer's office. In this essay, the model is the office lawyer advising about the law and implementing client goals through legally available devices, and one need not stretch to apply that model to litigation. Litigation is simply one of the available devices for implementing goals, like a trust or a corporation. When one focuses on a defendant, either civil or criminal, the moral validity of the autonomy and equality arguments is more apparent because the legal mechanism is being imposed on the individual rather than freely chosen, but the moral validity is not dependent on the defendant role. Thus, the arguments for the amoral role premised on the adversary system[36] supplement the first-class citizenship model in the litigation setting, and the critique based on the limited scope of the adversary system is largely beside the point under the first-class citizenship model.

Two further observations concerning the relationship between the first-class citizenship model and the adversary system model are apposite. First, as noted above, the criminal defendant is only a special instance of the first-class citizenship model. In the criminal context the moral value of full access to all that the law allows is simply clearer and more dramatic. However, because of what is at stake and the procedural safeguards of the adversary system (an opponent lawyer, neutral decision makers), the law may allow more in the criminal context. For example, the criminal defendant has the right to not incriminate himself and he suffers no legal liability for exercising that right. (The jury is told *not* to base convictions on the exercise of that right.) Outside the context of litigation, however, civil liability may be based on nondisclosure of incriminating facts in certain contexts, such as sales of securities under federal regulatory laws or the sale of a house under the common law tort doctrine of misrepresentation. Similarly, to take an example with which we began, the litigant through her lawyer may mislead the court with a cross-examination that intentionally and incorrectly implies the witness was not telling the truth on direct examination, and there will be no liability under the law for the client or the lawyer. In the nonlitigation context of selling a termite-ridden house, however, utilizing similar implications and half-truths to communicate the absence of termites may generate tort liability on the part of the client for misrepresen-

36. These arguments usually focus on the value of the adversary system in elucidating truth, Fuller & Randall, *supra* note 8, at 1160–61, and on the importance of protecting the dignity of the individual enmeshed in the judicial system, Freedman, *supra* note 3.

tation and an ethical violation on the part of the lawyer if she "assisted" the client in "fraudulent conduct."[37]

Second, the lines between criminal and civil litigation and between litigation and nonlitigation are not as clear as the critics suggest.[38] The criminal system pits "the state," with all its power, against an individual.[39] But the very point of civil litigation is to allow the private plaintiff to gain the power of "the state" to enforce her claim against the defendant, thus removing the need for, or utility of, acquiring private police or armies to enforce claims. Civil litigation is a contest over which side is to have the vast power of "the state" on its side in a dispute.

Certainly the distinction between litigation and nonlitigation is clearer, but even that line is not as bright as one might at first assume. When the consumer and Sears differ over the validity of a form contract or the misleading nature of advertising or displays, the disparity in power and means is huge. Moving across the line into litigation does equalize the power in both form and substance. But a good deal of that equalization is due to the presence of a lawyer. "Having a lawyer on your side" is a lot of what litigation implies. (To what extent would the filing of a complaint by a *pro se* consumer plaintiff against Sears change the balance of power?) Thus, the more significant transition—the brighter line—may be between having and not having a lawyer.[40] For the consumer to have access to the law through a lawyer *prior* to litigation would seem to be a more realistic possibility for equalizing power (or actualizing autonomy) than would an obligation on the part of Sears's in-house lawyer to function as a moral screen and filter for Sears's use of the law. This observation circles us back to both the first-class citizenship justification for the amoral role and to the economic inequality critique.

Before moving on from the adversary system criticism, it is appropriate to note that the adversary system image of the lawyer as the champion against a hostile world—the hired gun—is not the proper image for the general role of the lawyer presented here (although it may be the proper image for the criminal defense lawyer). Rather, the image more concordant with the first-class citizenship model is that of the individual facing and needing to use a very large and very complicated machine (with lots of whirring gears and spinning data tapes) that he can't get to work. This is "the law" that confronts the individual in our society. It is theoretically there for his use, but he can't use it for his purposes without the aid of

37. ABA Model Code of Professional Responsibility, DR 7-102(A)(7).

38. Weckstein, The Civil Advocate and the Multifaceted Functions of Dispute Settlement—Some Domestic and Cross-cultural Perspectives, 1983 A.B.F. Res. J. 577 (similarities between civil and criminal litigation and the consequent appropriate role of the lawyer).

39. E.g., Luban, *supra* note 5, at 92, 117; Wasserstrom, *supra* note 1, at 12.

40. Of course, part of the added power of having a lawyer on your side is the recognition that a lawyer brings with her the possibility—or the threat—of moving into litigation (and thereby gaining the power of the state). "Access to a lawyer" and the "potential for litigation" are, in this respect, two sides of one coin.

someone who has the correct wrenches, meters, and more esoteric tools, and knows how and where to use them. Or the image is that of someone who stands frustrated before a photocopier that won't copy (or someone whose car won't go) and needs a technician (or mechanic) to make it go. It is ordinarily not the technician's or mechanic's moral concern whether the content of what is about to be copied is morally good or bad, or for what purpose the customer intends to use the car.

III. The Problem of Legal Realism

This paper began with a moral justification for the lawyer's amoral ethical role. It then addressed, and for the most part rejected, two of the most common criticisms of that role. We turn now to a third, rarely articulated problem presented by the first-class citizenship justification for the amoral role. Up to this point in the discussion, access to the law as the primary justification for the amoral professional role has been presented with relatively little focus on what "the law" refers to. Three different facets of law have been recognized: (1) structuring mechanisms (trusts, corporations, civil litigation), (2) definitions of intolerable conduct (criminal law and litigation), and (3) regulatory law. The implication has been that the law is existent and determinable, that there is "something there" for the lawyer to find (or know) and communicate to the client. The "thereness" of the law is also the assumption underlying the commonly understood limit on the amoral role: the lawyer can only assist the client "within the bounds of the law."[41] This accords with the usual understanding of the law from the lay or client point of view, but not from the lawyer's point of view. The dominant view of law inculcated in the law schools, which will be identified here as "legal realism,"[42] approaches law without conceiving of it as objectively "out there" to be discovered and applied. A relatively little explored problem is the dynamic between the amoral professional role and a skeptical attitude toward law.

By "legal realism" I mean a view of law which stresses its open-textured, vague nature over its precision; its manipulability over its certainty; and its instrumental possibilities over its normative content.[43] From "positivism" modern legal education takes the notion of the separation of law and moral-

41. ABA Code of Professional Responsibility, Ethical Considerations 7-1 and 7-19. This approach pervades the Code. See, e.g., Disciplinary Rules 4-101(C)(2) and (3), 7-101(A)(1), 7-102.

42. Although perhaps misleading, the choice of the phrase "legal realism" derives from a perception that it will have the highest recognition level as descriptive of "the dominant view of law inculcated in the law schools." "We are all realists now" is a comment often heard from contemporary law professors. See, e.g., Kaufman, A Commentary on Pepper's "The Lawyer's Amoral Ethical Role," 1986 A.B.F. Res. J. at 654. Unfortunately, "legal realism" connotes rather different things to different persons. Robert Summers's usage, "pragmatic instrumentalism," is probably a better descriptive term. R. Summers, Instrumentalism and American Legal Theory (1982). My use of "legal realism" is intended to be more inclusive than Summers's use of "pragmatic instrumentalism," as the following paragraph elaborates.

43. See Cramton, The Ordinary Religion of the Law School Classroom, 29 J. Legal Educ. 247 (1978); Woodard, The Limits of Legal Realism: An Historical Perspective, 54 Va. L. Rev. 689 (1968).

ity: in advising the client, the lawyer is concerned with the law as an "is," a fact of power and limitation, more than as an "ought." From "legal realism" it takes the notion of law as a prediction of what human officials will do, more than as an existent, objective, determinable limit or boundary on client behavior. From "process jurisprudence" it takes an emphasis on client goals and private structuring, an instrumental use of law that deemphasizes the determination of law through adjudication or the prediction of the outcome of adjudication.[44] These three views of "the law" are mutually reinforcing rather than conflicting.[45] To the extent that legal education inculcates these views, "the law" becomes a rather amorphous thing, dependent upon the client's situation, goals, and risk preferences. What is the interaction between this view of the law and the view of the lawyer as an amoral servant of the client whose assistance is limited only by "the law"?[46]

The apt image is that of Holmes's "bad man." The modern lawyer is taught to look at the law as the "bad man" would, "who cares only for the material consequences."[47] The lawyer discovers and conveys "the law" to his client from this perspective and then is told to limit his own assistance to the client based upon this same view of "the law." The modern view of contract law, for example, deemphasizes the normative obligation of promises and views breach of contract as a "right" that is subject to the "cost" of damages.[48] Breach of contract is not criminal and, normally, fulfillment of a contractual obligation is not forced on a party (not "specifically enforced," in contract law terminology). The client who comes in with a more normative view of the obligation of contracts (whether wishing the lawyer to assist in structuring a transaction through a prospective contract or in coping with the unwelcome constraints of a past contract) will be educated by the competent lawyer as to the "breach as cost" view of "the law." Similarly, modern tort law has emphasized allocation of the "costs" of accidents, as opposed to the more normative view of 19th- and early 20th-century negligence law. Thus, negligence law can be characterized as establishing a right to a nonconsensual taking from the injured party on the part of the tort-feasor, subject once again to the "cost" of damages.[49] An industrial concern assessing and planning conduct which poses risks of personal injury or death to third parties will be guided by a lawyer following this view away from perceiving the imposition of unreasonable risk as a "wrong" and toward perceiving it as a potential cost.

44. See Simon, *supra* note 7, at 61–91; Ursin, Judicial Creativity and Tort Law, 49 Geo. Wash. L. Rev. 229, 234–37 (1981).

45. But cf. R. Summers, *supra* note 42 (differences between "process jurisprudence" and "legal realism"). The phenomenon I am describing is the (perhaps uneasy) synthesis of these three approaches that has come to characterize American legal education and, to at least a significant extent, the practice of American law.

46. The best discussion is to be found in Simon, *supra* note 7.

47. Holmes, The Path of the Law, 10 Harv. L. Rev. 457, 459 (1897).

48. Simon, *supra* note 7, at 48.

49. Calabresi, Torts—The Law of the Mixed Society, *in* B. Schwartz, ed., American Law: The Third Century 103 (1976).

There are, of course, variations in the extent to which legal realism will be encountered in a lawyer's office. One is more likely to find the cost-predictive view presented in relation to a contract problem than a tort problem,[50] and it is more likely to come from a lawyer advising a large corporate enterprise than one advising an individual.[51] But it is valid as a general suggestive model that most clients, most of the time, (1) will enter the lawyer's office thinking of law as more normative and more certain than does the lawyer, and (2) will go out having been influenced toward thinking of the law in terms of possible or probable costs more than they would have had they not consulted a lawyer.

From the perspective of fully informed access to the law, this modification of the client's view is good because it accords with the generally accepted understanding of the law among those who are closest to its use and administration—lawyers and judges. It is accurate; it is useful to the client. From the perspective of the ethical relationship between lawyer and client, it is far more problematic. First, the lawyer is to be an amoral technician who serves rather than judges the client. The lawyer is not the repository of moral limits on the client's behavior. Second, the law itself, as presented by the lawyer, also is not a source of moral limits. Rather, it is presented from the lawyer's technical, manipulative stance as a potential constraint, as a problem, or as data to be factored into decisions as to future conduct. Finally, in determining how far he or she can go in helping the client, the lawyer is instructed to look to that same uncertain, manipulable source: "the law." "Within the bounds of the law" sounds like an objective, knowable moral guide. Any second-year law student knows that as to any but the most obvious (and therefore uninteresting) questions, there will probably be no clear line, no boundary, but only a series of possibilities. Thus, if one combines the dominant "legal realism" understanding of law with the traditional amoral role of the lawyer, *there is no moral input or constraint in the present model of the lawyer-client relationship*.

Again, from the premises of the first-class citizenship model, this is as it should be. The client's autonomy should be limited by the law, not by the lawyer's morality. And if "the law" is manipulable and without clear limits on client conduct, that aspect of the law should be available to the client. If moral limits are not provided by the law and are not imposed by the lawyer, their source will be where it ought to be: the client. Morality is not to be

50. Viewing law in terms of "cost" entails perceiving enforcement as a part of the law. This is clear with Holmes's "bad man" view, and in his view that a contractual obligation entails only an obligation to pay damages for breach. It becomes more problematic when the lawyer is dealing with a potential criminal violation, rather than with contract or tort. See Luban, The Lysistratian Prerogative: A Response to Stephen Pepper, 1986 A.B.F. Res. J. 637, 647. Pepper, A Rejoinder to Professor Kaufman and Luban, 1986 A.B.F. Res J. 657, 669–73. Nonetheless, advice about enforcement has been considered part of the advice about "law" in general, and thus has been an accepted lawyer function. See, e.g., Panel Discussion, 35 U. Miami L. Rev. 639, 659 (1981) (comment of Prof. Geoffrey Hazard, Reporter, ABA Model Rules of Professional Conduct).

51. And it is quite unlikely to surface in reference to violent crime. See Simon, *supra* note 7, at 48.

inserted in the lawyer's office, its source either the lawyer or the law. Morality comes through the door as part of the client.

This shifts our focus from the lawyer and the law to the client. It should come as no surprise that many clients will come through the door without much internal moral guidance. Common sources of moral guidance are on the decline: religion, community, family. In a secularized society such as ours, religion no longer functions as the authoritative moral guide it once was. Geographic mobility and divorce have robbed many of the multigenerational moral guidance that families can provide. Small, supportive, usually continuous and homogenous moral communities are the experience of fewer and fewer people. The rural town, the ethnic neighborhood, the church attended for several generations, the local business or trade community (the chamber of commerce or the grocers' trade association)—all are the experience of a far smaller segment of the population than before.[52] Even the role of the public school in inculcating values may have declined.[53] For many, law has replaced alternative sources of moral guidance.[54]

Our problem now posits: (1) a client seeking access to the law who frequently has only weak internal or external sources of morality; (2) a lawyer whose professional role mandates that he or she not impose moral restraint on the client's access to the law; (3) a lawyer whose understanding of the law deemphasizes its moral content and certainty, and perceives it instead as instrumental and manipulable; and (4) law designed as (*a*) neutral structuring mechanisms to increase individual power (contracts, the corporate form, civil litigation), (*b*) a floor delineating minimum tolerable behavior rather than moral guidance, and (*c*) morally neutral regulation. From this perspective, access to the law through a lawyer appears to systematically screen out or deemphasize moral considerations and moral limits. The client who consults a lawyer will be guided to maximize his autonomy through the tools of the law—tools designed and used to maximize freedom, not to provide a guide to good behavior. If one cannot rely on the client or an alternative social institution to provide that guide, to suggest a moral restraint on that which is legally available, then what the lawyer does may be evil: lawyers in the aggregate may consistently guide clients away from moral conduct and restraint.

Assume client consults lawyer concerning discharge of polluted water from a rural plant. Client wants to know what the law requires, respects "the law," and intends to comply. Removing ammonia from the plant's effluent is very expensive. The EPA limit is .050 grams of ammonia per liter

52. Kaufman, Doubts About Justice, *in* H. E. Kiefer & M. R. Munitz, eds., Ethics and Social Justice (1970).

53. Moskowitz, The Making of the Moral Child: Legal Implications of Values Education, 6 Pepperdine L. Rev. 105, 107–14 (1978).

54. See Levinson, The Specious Morality of the Law, Harper's Mag., May 1977; Lessard, Notes and Comment, 53 New Yorker, May 23, 1977, at 27–28.

of effluent, and the EPA has widely publicized this standard to relevant industries. In addition to this information, however, lawyer informs client that inspection in rural areas of the state is rare and that enforcement officials always issue a warning (give a second chance) prior to applying sanctions unless the violation is extreme. Moreover, lawyer also informs client that it is known informally that violations of .075 grams per liter or less are ignored because of a limited enforcement budget. In such a situation, lay ignorance of legal technicalities and the realities of enforcement would seem to lead toward more obedience of "the law" (the .050-gram limit). Access to an amoral, "legal realist" lawyer leads toward violation of "the law." Given the model elaborated above, unless the client comes equipped with strong moral guidance, there will be no pressure to obey the law as written. (Worse, if the client is a corporate manager, she may be bound by her own amoral professional role which perceives shareholder profit as its primary guide.)

IV. Potential Answers to the Problem of Legal Realism

What follows is a brief canvassing of the major responses that might ameliorate the dilemma sketched above. The first two possibilities are societal responses that do not focus on the ethic of the lawyer-client relation, while the last three explore various approaches to lawyers' ethics.

A. Increased Societal Resources Applied to Law Enforcement

The first alternative is to accept the situation described above as either proper or unavoidable. To the extent that the pure "legal realist" view is the basis for conduct, law without enforcement is rendered meaningless. This in turn suggests the need for vast increases in resources devoted to law enforcement. Such a prospect is rather daunting in an era of insufficient government means. More important, the societal atmosphere likely to accompany such an emphasis on law enforcement is not pleasant to contemplate.

B. Rebuilding (or Creating Anew) Sources of Moral Authority and Guidance Other than Law

From right-wing fundamentalism through "values clarification" in the public schools to the renaissance in academic moral philosophy, the perceived need to revive or create sources of moral authority and guidance has become a pervasive societal concern. Commencing with the Enlightenment, secularization has progressively and thoroughly removed religion as the central source of moral authority in Western thought. Science and rationalism, whether taking the forms of logical positivism, anthropology, psychology, or scientism, are increasingly perceived as unable to answer moral and ethical questions. It is safe to say that the search for values and alternative methodologies to elucidate, compare, and validate values is and will remain one of the predominant intellectual (and perhaps political) themes of the last third of the 20th century. "Watergate" is often cited as the cause of the current academic interest in lawyers' professional ethics.[55] Both that scandal and our intellectual endeavors, however, are part of a larger and more important historical process. To the extent that values and sources of moral authority are rebuilt external to the law, the moral vacuum of the "amoral lawyer/legal realism" combination will be ameliorated.

As elaborated above, law itself as it is currently conceived is not a primary source of moral authority or guidance. It is possible that the dominant practical philosophy conveyed in the law schools will change, and lawyers' understanding of and approach to the law will change also. But this seems less likely than does a change in the understanding of the lawyer-client ethic. We therefore turn now to some of the possible changes in lawyers' professional ethics.

C. *The Lawyer as Policeman, Judge, and/or Deceiver*

The lawyer-client ethic analogous to the first possibility above, that of enhanced resources devoted to law enforcement, would alter the traditional balance of lawyer allegiance away from the client and toward society.[56] In the 1970s the SEC took such a position toward the securities bar. In essence it asserted that the lawyer in our hypothetical above would have had to report to the government consistent discharges above .050 grams per liter, regardless of the likelihood or nature of enforcement and regardless of whether his knowledge was based upon client confidences.[57] This is indeed to give policing responsibilities to the lawyer and, depending upon the client's understanding of the confidential nature of communications to a lawyer, perhaps makes the lawyer a deceiver.[58]

If the lawyer does not become a policeman, but instead injects morality by refusing to communicate the legal realism view of law to the client, there is still a significant problem. For the lawyer to communicate to the client a "thereness" and a normative obligation to a written law that is contrary to the lawyer's legal realist view of that particular law is to practice deception, deception in service to obedience of the law. Imagine, for example, a lawyer advising a couple for whom there are significant tax and economic advantages in living together unmarried, in a jurisdiction where fornication remains a crime on the books but is never prosecuted.[59] Is it not deception to fail to inform them of the benefits, or to inform them, but to add that the

55. See, e.g., T. Morgan & R. Rotunda, Professional Responsibility—Problems and Materials 1 (3d ed. 1984); Wasserstrom, *supra* note 1.

56. As Prof. Alschuler has aptly phrased this point, "Once lawyers became as loyal to opposing parties and to the public as they were to their clients, however, their clients would no longer have lawyers. The clients would only have judges—a whole series of them." Alschuler, *supra* note 15, at 72.

57. S. Gillers & N. Dorsen, Regulation of Lawyers: Problems of Law and Ethics 551–61 (1985), and sources cited therein.

58. Perhaps the best evocation of this is Freedman, *supra* note 3, ch. 3.

59. Morgan & Rotunda, *supra* note 55, at 179. The situation and the issue are not unreal. See, e.g., Doe v. Duling, 782 F.2d 1202 (4th Cir. 1986) (unenforced fornication and cohabitation statutes).

benefits are not available because the conduct would be criminal, but then to say nothing further?

To replace the amoral role with a moral responsibility role also transmutes the lawyer into an enforcement mechanism, although now it is not the written law but the lawyer's ethics which are being enforced on the client. The lawyer has become the judge of the client. This approach does ameliorate the dilemma by an injection of ethical constraint, but it does so at the expense of the moral values that inhere in the premises of the first-class citizenship justification elaborated above. That elaboration suggests that this would be a considerable price to pay because the values of individual autonomy, diversity, and equality are relatively fundamental to the traditional understanding of our society. Perhaps the expense is merited if one perceives the synergism of the lawyer's amoral role and the legal realist view of law as sufficiently destructive.

D. The Lawyer and Client in Moral Dialogue[60]

The fourth possibility emphasizes the utility of wide-ranging communication between lawyer and client. Instead of defining the client's goals in narrow material terms and approaching the law solely as means to or constraint on such goals, this view opens the relationship to moral input in two ways.

First, the lawyer's full understanding of the situation, including the lawyer's moral understanding, can be communicated to the client. The professional role remains amoral in that the lawyer is still required to provide full access to the law for the client, but the dilemma sketched above is ameliorated by moral input from the lawyer which supplements access to the law. The autonomy of the client remains in that she is given access to all that the law allows, but the client's decisions are informed by the lawyer's moral judgment.[61] Just as the lawyer/policeman role is the analogue in ethics to the alternative of enhanced resource investment in law enforcement, the dialogue role is one possible source for rebuilding moral authority aside from the law. While the lawyer still may not judge or police the client in the sense of screening access to the law, this view of the professional role does allow the lawyer the moral role of moral educator.

The second way the dialogue model infuses a moral element into the lawyer-client relationship is from the side of the client. The current situation minimizes the client's moral input as well as the lawyer's. The client comes in with a human problem (family, business, corporate, etc.); the lawyer defines it in legal terms, usually including a legal goal and legal means to that goal, all perceived from the amoral legal realist stance. Both goal and means may well be defined by the client's interests as presumed by the law-

60. For a general discussion of the ethical approach discussed in this section, see Shaffer, *supra* note 7. This approach is also reflected in the ABA Model Code of Professional Responsibility. See Ethical Considerations 7-1 through 7-8.

61. ABA Code of Professional Responsibility EC 7-7, 7-8.

yer: usually maximization of wealth or avoidance of incarceration.[62] More communication drawn from the client by an open lawyer may substantially qualify those presumed goals as well as limit means.[63] To the extent that the lawyer makes room in the professional relationship for a moral dialogue, the client's moral and ethical perceptions can affect decisions. Part of the dilemma sketched above was based on the limited extent of moral guidance with which many clients now come equipped; the dialogue model aims to draw out and actualize that which is there.

This paper began with the example of the lawyer cross-examining a witness known to be truthful in such a way as to suggest to the jury that the witness might be lying. Dialogue with the client may educate the lawyer to the fact that the client does not want to win that way, that the lawyer is wrong in assuming that winning by all lawfully available means is the task the client intended for the lawyer. To the contrary, the client may want to have "the facts" judged by "the law" and may have no desire to win if the truth does not lead to that conclusion. Or the client may believe that exposing the truthful witness to the implied accusation of dishonesty is a moral wrong of sufficient import to prevent its use even to gain that to which he believes justice entitles him. The client may simply not want to win by immoral means. Or, looking at the dialogue with the moral input coming from the lawyer, if the lawyer is the one morally troubled by such a cross-examination and the client is not, the lawyer's perception may engage or educate the client, or the client's overall regard for the lawyer may be sufficient for the client to agree that the tactic should not be used.

Two limits on the "moral dialogue" approach must be recognized. First, it is expensive. Such a dialogue requires time, and time is the lawyer's stock in trade. Either the client must be willing and able to pay for the expanded conversation at the lawyer's regular hourly rate, or the lawyer must be willing to accept a lower income. With traditional forms of legal services perceived as too expensive for the middle and lower classes, and a consequent shift occurring toward less expensive, more efficient structures for providing legal services, the dialogue model may be difficult (perhaps impossible) to incorporate as an integral part of the lawyers' professional ethic. It may be more likely to occur at the level of complex corporate practice because more time is devoted to analysis of legal alternatives. But even in this area

62. Simon, *supra* note 7, at 52–60; Freedman, *supra* note 5, at 200–201.

63. Gabel & Harris, *supra* note 25; Lehman, The Pursuit of a Client's Interest, 77 Mich. L. Rev. 1078 (1979); Fried, *supra* note 3, at 1088; Wexler, *supra* note 15, at 1062–66; but cf. Panel Discussion, 35 U. Miami L. Rev. 639, 643 (1981) (comment by panelist Chesterfield Smith, a former president of the American Bar Association, that clients pay him to tell them what to do, pay him to make choices, *not* to educate them so they can make the choices). See also Curtis, The Ethics of Advocacy, 4 Stan. L. Rev. 3, 6 (1951): "The upshot is that a man whose business it is to act for others finds himself, in his dealings on his client's behalf with outsiders, acting on a lower standard than he would if he were acting for himself, and lower, too, than any standard his client himself would be willing to act on, lower, in fact, than anyone on his own." Reprinted in C. Curtis, It's Your Law, ch. 1 (1954).

of practice, efforts to limit the costs of legal services have been rapidly expanding.

Second, client receptivity to the approach will vary with the context. The criminal defendant facing years in prison and represented by a public defender will be less open to the dialogue than will the corporate officer dealing with in-house counsel. Lawyers in some contexts may be simply unable to engage in dialogue with their clients; the larger the cultural and economic gap between lawyer and client, the less likely is meaningful moral dialogue.[64] Thus, both limits suggest there will be a spectrum of the kinds of legal practice for which the moral dialogue ethic is suitable or possible.

E. Conscientious Objection

Part I of this essay suggests a moral justification for the amoral role of the lawyer. That there is such a moral justification does not tell us how that justification will balance with competing moral values which may be present in any given situation. Assuming a lawyer feels bound (either morally or under legally enforced professional ethics) to the amoral ethic, he or she may perceive in a particular situation a higher value that supports conduct contrary to the lawyer role. Conscientious objection always remains an alternative in such a situation: one can recognize the moral and legal validity of the amoral role, but choose not to follow it. This possibility ameliorates the dilemma sketched above by injecting the moral perception of the lawyer into certain cases. In such cases, the lawyer's moral perception will screen the client's access to all that the law allows.

If such conscientious objection is not limited to extreme cases, however, it is little different from the lawyer as policeman, judge, and/or deceiver. To the extent the lawyer allows moral considerations to trump professional obligation, his role is no longer amoral. David Luban appears to have reached this point in his conclusion that the amoral role is supported only by very weak moral values.[65] He argues that in the absence of any countervailing moral value, the lawyer should follow the role. But if there is any valid moral objection to conduct mandated by the amoral role, he concludes that the role provides no justification. Part I above suggests, to the

64. Simon, *supra* note 7, at 55–60; Wexler, *supra* note 15, at 1052. Simon's article, quite possibly the best recently written on the professional ethics of lawyers, unfortunately tends to defeat itself with overstatement. For example, at n.69: "There are severe limitations on the extent to which a person, particularly a stranger, can understand with any depth the ends of another without actually sharing those ends." There is some truth to this point, but to use it as a basis for arguing for the deprofessionalization of lawyers is extreme. Common experience indicates that humans are better at communication than this suggests, and a properly trained lawyer is usually able to draw more from the client than Simon suggests is possible. Experience with a legal services office, a public defender, or a similar practice might move one toward Simon's position, but generalization from that experience to all of the practice of law is not warranted. One form of this tendency toward overstatement which weakens Simon's article is its perception of "contradiction" generally in lawyers' ethics where there may be only complexity, a flaw characteristic of much critical legal studies work. See R. Dworkin, Law's Empire 271–75, 441–43 (1986); Sparer, Fundamental Human Rights, Legal Entitlements, and the Social Struggle: A Friendly Critique of the Critical Legal Studies Movement, 36 Stan. L. Rev. 509, 516–19, 524 (1984).

65. Luban, *supra* note 7.

contrary, that the lawyer's amoral professional role has strong justification in several moral values. If this is true, conscientious objection should be rarely exercised by the lawyer.

The well-known "hidden bodies" case provides an example.[66] A criminal defendant revealed to his lawyers the location of the hidden bodies of two murder victims, and the lawyers visited the location to determine the accuracy of the information. The lawyers did not reveal this information for six months, even when it was personally sought from them by the parents of one of the victims. Normal morality would condemn such callous behavior. The amoral role demanded such behavior, for the lawyers were not legally obligated to disclose the information and they perceived it to be in the client's legal interest to delay divulging the information. Professor Luban's approach implies that normal morality should have been applied by the lawyers. The first-class citizenship model suggests the contrary, particularly in the context of criminal defense. Assume for a moment, however, that upon investigation by the lawyers, one of the victims was observed to be alive. Assume further that there was no legal or professional obligation to assist or reveal the existence and location of the live victim to others who would assist (which is quite possibly an accurate statement of the law). Here one has the kind of extreme case for which conscientious objection to the amoral role seems appropriate. Even if the client will be hurt by the lawyers' revealing the plight of the living victim, normal morality in this instance must outweigh the generally strong moral values underlying the amoral role.[67]

V. Conclusion: On the Moral Autonomy of the Lawyer

This paper began by presenting a moral justification for the lawyer's amoral professional role. It then turned briefly to two of the criticisms aimed at the amoral role: the economic one that focuses on the unequal distribution of legal service, and the "adversary system" one that focuses on the usual absence of a judge and the frequent absence of a second, counterbalancing advocate from the situations in which most lawyers function. The difficulty presented by the combination of the amoral professional role

66. People v. Belge, 372 N.Y.S.2d 798 (N.Y. Cty. Ct. 1975); Freedman, *supra* note 3, at 1; Morgan & Rotunda, *supra* note 40, at 192–93.

67. Alschuler, The Preservation of a Client's Confidences: One Value Among Many or a Categorial Imperative? 52 U. Colo. L. Rev. 349, 354–55 (1981). D'Amato & Eberle, *supra* note 7, at 784–85, draw the same line between not revealing the dead body and revealing the live victim, on the basis of a deontological model of legal ethics. They appear to assume that the conscientious objection alternative can be incorporated into lawyers' professional ethics, thereby avoiding the problem of violating the obligation to the client. It is difficult to understand how a legally binding ethics code (the current Code of Professional Responsibility carries legal sanctions) could impose an obligation to violate the law, a possibility implied by D'Amato and Eberle, *id.* at 795 (fugitive slave example). Perhaps they are thinking of a code of that which is not legally binding, *id.* at 793. Only the proposed American Lawyer's Code of Conduct, drafted by Professor Freedman, contains a provision allowing revelation of the live victim in the circumstances of the hypothetical in the text. That provision is included only as an alternative—it was not approved by the Commission. American Lawyer's Code of Conduct, Rule 1.6.

and the lawyer's "legal realism" was then elaborated. Last, some possible remedies for this problem were presented.

Where are we left? I would suggest that the moral values of autonomy and equality are imperative in relation to access to the law. Genuine autonomy is so dependent on access to the law, and inequality of access bears so directly on autonomy, that we are indeed dealing with a question of first- and second-class citizenship. This imperative is sufficient, in my view, to outweigh the problems presented by the amoral professional role.

Given this essay's stress on autonomy, it is fair to ask: Where in the amoral role is there a place for the lawyer's moral autonomy? Lawyers are far more intimately involved with and identified with their clients than grocers or landlords are with their customers and tenants. This causes much of the disquiet with the amoral role both within and without the profession. If the client chooses to be the "bad man," to do that which is lawful but morally wrong, does not the lawyer become a bad person, compelled by the amoral role to assist, yet intimately connected to and identified with the client's wrongdoing?

Part of the answer lies in the principle of professionalism sketched at the beginning of part I. Because of the large advantages over the client built into the lawyer's professional role, and because of the disadvantages and vulnerability built into the client's role, the professional must subordinate his interest to the client's when there is a conflict. That the conflict may be a moral one ought not change this precept. The lawyer is a good person in that he provides access to the law; in providing such access without moral screening, he serves the moral values of individual autonomy and equality. This ought to be enough, for the underlying professional ethic cautions that when there is a conflict between lawyer and client, the professional must remember that the raison d'être for his role is service to the client.

The rest of the answer can be found in those limited areas in which the moral autonomy of the lawyer can function compatibly with the amoral professional ethic. Initially, the lawyer has the choice of whether or not to be a lawyer. It should be clear that this choice involves important moral consequences.[68] Second, the lawyer has the choice of whether or not to accept a person as a client. This choice also involves the exercise of moral autonomy.[69] In light of the first-class citizenship model, exercise of the choice of client aspect of the moral autonomy of the lawyer is troubling if it leads to foreclosure of a person's access to the law. In that situation, the lawyer's autonomy results in second-class citizenship status for the denied individual.[70] Third, a large degree of moral autonomy can be exercised

68. Whether or not the choice is an educated one in most cases is unclear. While, as Wasserstrom observes, the amoral role may be "comfortable" for practicing lawyers, *supra* note 1, at 7, many law students I have encountered in Legal Profession courses are quite uncomfortable with the prospect of living such a role.

69. Law, *supra* note 15, at 103–4; Freedman, *supra* note 15, at 198–99, 204–5.

70. See Pepper, A Rejoinder to Professors Kaufman and Luban, 1986 A.B.F. Res. J. 657, 659–60.

through the lawyer-client moral dialogue. While there is a wide range of financial feasibility and client receptivity which will set limits on the extent of such dialogue, all lawyers have some opportunity in this area; and to a significant extent, each lawyer can take part in defining those limits. Fourth, conscientious objection is an ever present option within the realm of the lawyer's moral autonomy. These four areas combined create a meaningful field for the exercise of the lawyer's moral autonomy.

More important, if one adds together (1) the conscientious objection possibility, (2) the wide scope for moral dialogue, and (3) the inherent moral value of facilitating access to the law, the result, I believe is that the good lawyer can be a good person; not comfortable, but good.

[4]

PERSONAL RESPONSIBILITY IN A PROFESSIONAL SYSTEM*

*Monroe H. Freedman***

I.

In speaking to you today, I cannot be unmindful of the signal honor that you have shown me, as a member of a different religious faith, in inviting me to speak in honor of Pope John XXIII. Surely, though, that is not wholly inappropriate, for Pope John's concerns were truly catholic and his message of peace and of social justice was directed to the consciences and for the benefit of all humankind. Indeed, I could readily take as my text today a paragraph from *Pacem in Terris*:[1]

> The dignity of the human person . . . requires that every man[2] enjoy the right to act freely and responsibly. For this reason, therefore, in social relations man should exercise his rights, fulfill his obligations and, in the countless forms of collaboration with others, act chiefly on his own responsibility and initiative. This is to be done in such a way that each one acts on his own decision, of set purpose and from a consciousness of his obligation, without being moved by force or pressure brought to bear on him externally. For any human society that is established on relations of force must be regarded as inhuman, inasmuch as the personality of its members is repressed or restricted, when in fact they should be provided with appropriate incentives and means for developing and perfecting themselves.

---

* Delivered as the 13th annual Pope John XXIII Lecture at Catholic University Law School, Washington, D.C., October 28, 1977.

** former chairman, District of Columbia Bar Legal Ethics Committee; author, LAWYERS' ETHICS IN AN ADVERSARY SYSTEM (1975).

1. PACEM IN TERRIS, Encyclical Letter of Pope John XXIII, para. 34 (April 11, 1963).

2. Before the Women's Liberation Movement had become a significant force, Pope John stressed "equal rights and duties for man and woman," and recognized that women, consistent with human dignity, must have "rights befitting a human person both in domestic and in public life." *Id.* para. 15, 41.

II.

It is a singularly good thing, I think, that law students, and even some lawyers and law professors, are questioning with increasing frequency and intensity whether "professionalism" is incompatible with human decency—asking, that is, whether one can be a good lawyer and a good person at the same time. I have a special interest in that question because Professor John T. Noonan, Jr. (a personal friend, perceptive critic, and a previous speaker in this annual series) has drawn the inference from my book that I do not believe that a decent, honest person can practice criminal law or teach others to do so.[3] In fact, the title of today's paper derives directly from a challenge issued to me in the concluding paragraph of Professor Noonan's review of my book, urging that I write on "Personal Responsibility in a Professional System."[4]

At the same time I address the issue of professionalism and personal moral responsibility, I want also to discuss an integrally related question, one that is often expressed in terms of whether it is the lawyer or the client who should exercise "control" in the relationship between them. As it is frequently put: Is the lawyer just a "hired gun," or must the lawyer "obey his own conscience, not that of his client?"[5]

III.

Voicing a viewpoint prevalent in the profession, lawyers sometimes use the phrase "client control" (that is, control of the client by the

3. Noonan, Book Review, 29 STAN. L. REV. 363 (1977). Professor Noonan bases that inference, in substantial part, on my conclusion that a criminal defense lawyer will sometimes be compelled to knowingly present a client's perjury to the court and to argue it in summation to the jury. I base that conclusion on such considerations as the sixth amendment right to counsel, the fifth amendment privilege against self-incrimination, and the obligation of confidentiality, under which the attorney induces the client to reveal all relevant information with assurances that the attorney will not act upon that information in a way that will injure the client. Thus, I might ask rhetorically whether Professor Noonan believes that a good person can induce another to rely upon assurances of confidentiality, and then betray those confidences.

The difficulty, of course, is that the lawyer is frequently faced with conflicting moral obligations; here, either to participate knowingly in the presentation of perjury, or to violate the client's trust which the lawyer has induced (a problem that is discussed, more fully in M. FREEDMAN, LAWYERS' ETHICS IN AN ADVERSARY SYSTEM (1975)). In view of that kind of moral dilemma, a cynic might conclude that one cannot be a good lawyer and a good person at the same time. I do not believe, however, that one can properly be charged with immorality because one is presented with a moral dilemma. If so, the human condition is one of guilt without realistic free will. On the contrary, however, I believe that in such circumstances, the only immorality lies in failing to address and resolve the moral conflict in a conscientious and responsible manner.

4. Noonan, *supra* note 3, at 370.

5. Noonan, *The Purposes of Advocacy and the Limits of Confidentiality*, 64 MICH. L. REV. 1485, 1491 (1966) (quoting ABA CANONS OF PROFESSIONAL ETHICS No. 15 (1908)).

lawyer) in expressing their professional pride in maintaining the proper professional relationship. In a law school commencement address titled *Professionalism in Lawyering*, Clement F. Haynsworth, Jr., Chief Justice of the Court of Appeals for the Fourth Circuit stressed the importance of professional competence in handling a client's affairs; but Chief Justice Haynsworth went on to say that of even "greater moment" than competence on the part of a lawyer is the fact that:

> he serves his clients without being their servant. He serves to further the lawful and proper objective of the client, but the lawyer must never forget that he is the master. He is not there to do the client's bidding. It is for the lawyer to decide what is morally and legally right, and, as a professional, he cannot give in to a client's attempt to persuade him to take some other stand . . . [T]he lawyer must serve the client's legal needs as the lawyer sees them, not as the client sees them. During my years of practice, . . . I told [my clients] what would be done and firmly rejected suggestions that I do something else which I felt improper. . . .[6]

Surely those are striking phrases to choose to describe the relationship of lawyer and client—the lawyer is "the master" who is "to decide what is morally . . . right," and who serves the client's needs but only "as the lawyer sees them, not as the client sees them." Even more striking was the phrase once used by a sensitive and dedicated public interest lawyer, when he observed that as between the lawyer and client, it is the lawyer who holds "the whip hand."[7]

Thurmond Arnold, a prominent practitioner and a federal appellate court judge, held a philosophy similar to Chief Justice Haynsworth's. As described with approval by former Supreme Court Justice Abe Fortas, Arnold did not permit a client "to dictate or determine the strategy or substance of the representation, even if the client insisted that his prescription for the litigation was necessary to serve the larger cause to which he was committed."[8]

IV.

Critics of the legal profession argue not that such attitudes and practices are elitist and paternalistic, but rather, that not enough lawyers abide by them.[9] In an article on "Lawyers as Professionals: Some Moral

6. Haynsworth, *Professionalism in Lawyering*, 27 S.C.L.Q. 627, 628 (1976).
7. *See* Comment, *The New Public Interest Lawyers*, 79 YALE L.J. 1069, 1123 (1970).
8. Fortas, *Thurman Arnold and the Theatre of the Law*, 79 YALE L.J. 988, 996 (1970).
9. *See, e.g.*, J. AUERBACH, UNEQUAL JUSTICE (1976); M. GREEN, THE OTHER GOVERNMENT (1975).

Issues,"[10] Professor Richard Wasserstrom recalls John Dean's list of those involved in the Watergate coverup. Dean had placed an asterisk next to the names of each of the lawyers on the list, because he had been struck by the fact that so many of those implicated were lawyers. Professor Wasserstrom concludes that the involvement of lawyers in Watergate was "natural, if not unavoidable," the "likely if not inevitable consequence of their legal acculturation." Indeed, on the basis of Wasserstrom's analysis, the only matter of wonder is why so many of those on John Dean's list were *not* lawyers. What could possibly have corrupted the non-lawyers to such a degree as to have led them into the uniquely amoral and immoral world of the lawyers? "For at best," Wasserstrom asserts, "the lawyer's world is a simplified moral world; often it is an amoral one; and more than occasionally perhaps, an overtly immoral one."[11]

Professor Wasserstrom holds that the core of the problem is professionalism and its concomitant, *role-differentiated behavior*. Role-differentiation refers, in this context, to situations in which one's moral response will vary depending upon whether one is acting in a personal capacity or in a professional, representative one. As Wasserstrom says, the "nature of role-differentiated behavior . . . often makes it both appropriate and desirable for the person in a particular role to put to one side considerations of various sorts—and especially various moral considerations—that would otherwise be relevant if not decisive."[12]

An illustration of the "morally relevant considerations" that Wasserstrom has in mind is the case of a client who desires to make a will disinheriting her children because they opposed the war in Vietnam. Professor Wasserstrom suggests that the lawyer should refuse to draft the will because the client's reason is a "bad" one.[13] But is the lawyer's paternalism toward the client preferable—morally or otherwise—to the client's paternalism toward her children?

"[W]e might all be better served," says Wasserstrom, "if lawyers were to see themselves less as subject to role-differentiated behavior and more as subject to the demands of the *moral* point of view."[14] Is it really that simple? What, for example, of the lawyer whose moral judgment is that disobedient and unpatriotic children should be disinherited? Should that lawyer refuse to draft a will leaving bequests to children who

10. 5 HUMAN RIGHTS 1 (1975).
11. *Id.* at 2.
12. *Id.* at 3.
13. *Id.* at 7.
14. *Id.* at 12 (emphasis added).

opposed the war in Vietnam? If the response is that we would then have a desirable diversity, would it not be better to have that diversity as a reflection of the clients' viewpoints, rather than the lawyers'?

In another illustration, Wasserstrom suggests that a lawyer should refuse to advise a wealthy client of a tax loophole provided by the legislature for only a few wealthy taxpayers.[15] If that case is to be generalized, it seems to mean that the legal profession can properly regard itself as an oligarchy whose duty is to nullify decisions made by the people's duly elected representatives.[16] Therefore, if the lawyers believe that particular clients (wealthy or poor) should not have been given certain rights, the lawyers are morally bound to circumvent the legislative process and to forestall the judicial process by the simple device of keeping their clients in ignorance of tempting rights.

Nor is that a caricature of Wasserstrom's position. The role-differentiated amorality of the lawyer is valid, he says, "only if the enormous degree of trust and confidence in the institutions themselves (that is, the legislative and judical processes) is itself justified." "[W]e are today", he asserts, "certainly entitled to be quite skeptical both of the fairness and of the capacity for self-correction of our larger institutional mechanisms, including the legal system."[17] If that is so, is it not a nonsequitur to suggest that we are justified in placing that same trust and confidence in the morality of lawyers, individually or collectively?

There is "something quite seductive," adds Wasserstrom, about being able to turn aside so many ostensibly difficult moral dilemmas with the reply that my job is not to judge my client's cause, but to represent his or her interest.[18] Surely, however, it is at least as seductive to be able to say, "My moral judgment—or my professional responsibility—requires that I be your master. Therefore, you will conduct yourself as I direct you to."

A more positive view of role-differentiated behavior was provided in an article in the *New York Times* about the tennis star, Manuel Orantes:

> He has astounded fans by applauding his opponent's good shots and by purposely missing a point when he felt that a wrong call by a linesman has hurt his opponent.
>
> "I like to win," he said in an interview, "but I don't feel that I have won a match if the calls were wrong. I think if you're playing Davis Cup or for your country it might be different, but if I'm playing for myself I want to know I have really won."[19]

15. *Id*. at 7-8.
16. Wasserstrom acknowledges that concern but rejects it. *Id*. at 10-11.
17. *Id*. at 13.
18. *Id*. at 9.
19. N.Y. Times, Sept. 11, 1975, at 43, col. 8.

That is, one's moral responsibilities will properly vary depending, among other things, upon whether one has undertaken special obligations to one's teammates or to one's country.

Taking a different illustration, let us suppose that you are going about some pressing matter and your arm is suddenly seized by an old man with a long gray beard, a wild look in his eye, and what appears to be an enormous dead bird hanging around his neck, and he immediately launches into a bizarre tale of an improbable adventure at sea. If he is a stranger and you are alone on a poorly lighted street, you may well call the police. If he is a stranger but you decide that he is harmless, you may simply go on to your other responsibilities. If he is a friend or member of your family, you may feel obligated to spend some time listening to the ancient mariner, or even to confer with others as to how to care for him. If you are a psychiatric social worker, you may act in yet some other way, and that action may depend upon whether you are on duty at your place of employment, or hurrying so that you will not be late to a wedding—and in the latter case, your decision may vary depending upon whether the wedding is someone else's or your own. Surely there can be no moral objection to those radically different courses of conduct, or to the fact that they are governed substantially by personal, social, and professional context, that is, by role-differentiation. One simply cannot be expected, in any rational moral system, to react to every stranger in the same way in which one may be obligated to respond to a member of one's family or to a friend.

V.

Thus in an interesting and thought-provoking article, Professor Charles Fried has analogized the lawyer to a friend—a "special-purpose" or "limited-purpose" friend "in regard to the legal system."[20] The lawyer, thereby, is seen to be "someone who enters into a personal relation with you—not an abstract relation as under the concept of justice." That means, Fried says, that "like a friend [the lawyer] acts in your interests, not his own; or rather he adopts your interests as his own."[21]

The moral foundation upon which Fried justifies that special-purpose friendship is the sense of self, the moral concepts of "personality, identity, and liberty."[22] He notes that social institutions are so complex

20. Fried, *The Lawyer as Friend: The Moral Foundations of the Lawyer-Client Relation*, 85 YALE L. J. 1060, 1071 (1976).
21. *Id.*
22. *Id.* at 1068.

that without the assistance of an expert adviser, an ordinary lay person cannot exercise the personal autonomy to which he or she is morally and legally entitled within the system. "Without such an adviser, the law would impose constraints on the lay citizen (unequally at that) which it is not entitled to impose explicitly." The limited purpose of the lawyer's friendship, therefore, is "to preserve and foster the client's autonomy within the law."[23] Similarly, Professor Sylvia A. Law has written:

> A lawyer has a special skill and power to enable individuals to know the options available to them in dealing with a particular problem, and to assist individuals in wending their way through bureaucratic, legislative or judicial channels to seek vindication for individual claims and interests. Hence lawyers have a special ability to enhance human autonomy and self-control.[24]

She adds, however, that

> Far too often, professional attitude, rather than serving to enhance individual autonomy and self-control, serves to strip people of autonomy and power. Rather than encouraging clients and citizens to know and control their own options and lives, the legal profession discourages client participation and control of their own legal claims.[25]

The essence of Professor Fried's argument does not require the metaphor of friendship, other than as an analogy in justifying the lawyers role-differentiation. It was inevitable, however, that Fried's critics would give the metaphor of friendship the same emphasis that Fried himself does and, thereby, consciously or not, miss the essential point he makes, that human autonomy is a fundamental moral concept that must determine, in substantial part, the answers that we give to some of the most difficult issues regarding the lawyer's ethical role.

Thus, in a response to Fried,[26] Professors Edward A. Dauer and Arthur Allen Leff make some perceptive and devastating comments about the limited-purpose logic of Fried's metaphor of friendship. At the same time, however, Dauer and Leff express their own views of the

---

23. *Id.* at 1073. As Pope John expressed in the quotation I read earlier, "The dignity of the human person . . . requires that every man enjoy the right to act freely and responsibly." *See* note 1 *supra*. *See also* Bresnahan, *Ethical Theory and Professional Responsibility: Possible Contributions of Religious Ethics to Dialog about Professional Ethics of Attorneys*, 37 THE JUR. 56, 77 (1977), in which the author refers to the human being's fundamental freedom "decisively to dispose of self, and therefore also to affect one's world."

24. S. A. LAW, AFTERWORD: THE PURPOSE OF PROFESSIONAL EDUCATION, LOOKING AT LAW SCHOOL 205, 212-13 (S. Gillers ed. 1977).

25. *Id.*

26. Dauer and Leff, *The Lawyer as Friend*, 86 YALE L.J. 573 (1977).

lawyer's role and character, views which I find to be both cynical and superficial. They see an "invariant element" of the lawyer-client relationship as follows:

> The client comes to a lawyer to be aided when he feels he is being treated, or wishes to treat someone else, not as a whole other person, but (at least in part) as a threat or hindrance to the client's satisfaction in life. The client has fallen, or wishes to thrust someone else, into the impersonal hands of a just and angry bureaucracy. When one desires help in those processes whereby and wherein people are treated as means and not as ends, then one comes to lawyers, to us. Thus, if you feel the need for a trope to express what a lawyer largely is, perhaps this will do: A lawyer is a person who on behalf of some people treats other people the way bureaucracies treat all people—as nonpeople. Most lawyers are free-lance bureaucrats. . . .[27]

Despite that caricature, Dauer and Leff manage to conclude that "a good lawyer can be a good person." They do so, however, by defining "a good person" in the following limited terms: "In our view the lawyer achieves his "goodness" by being—professionally—no rottener than the generality of people acting, so to speak, as amateurs."[28] The best that can be said for that proposition, I believe, is that it is not likely to stop students with any moral sensitivity from continuing to ask whether it is indeed possible for a good lawyer to be a good person.

The most serious flaw in Professor Fried's friendship metaphor is that it is misleading when the moral focus is on the point at which the lawyer-client relationship begins. Friendship, like love, seems simply to happen, or to grow, often in stages of which we may not be immediately conscious. Both in fact and in law, however, the relationship of lawyer and client is a contract, which is a significantly different relationship, formed in a significantly different way.[29]

Unlike friendship, a contract involves a deliberate choice by both parties at a particular time. Thus, when Professor Fried says that friendship is "an aspect of the moral liberty of self to enter into personal relations freely,"[30] the issue of the morality of the decision to enter the

27. *Id*. at 581.

28. *Id*. at 582. Other observations by Professors Dauer and Leff are less witty but more substantive.

29. It is interesting to note that contract plays such a major role as a construct in political theory and in jurisprudence, but is overlooked in discussions of lawyer-client relations. Let me hasten to add, however, that I am not suggesting "The Lawyer as Contractor" as an all-purpose analogy. It is relevant to the question of the lawyer's personal moral responsibility in selecting (and rejecting) clients, but it may well be useless in other contexts.

30. Fried, *supra* note 20, at 1078.

relationship is blurred by the amorphous nature in which friendships are formed. Since entering a lawyer-client contract is a more deliberate. conscious decision, however, that decision can justifiably be subjected to a more searching moral scrutiny.

In short, a lawyer should indeed have the freedom to choose clients on any standard he or she deems appropriate. As Professor Fried points out, the choice of client is an aspect of the lawyer's free will, to be exercised within the realm of the lawyer's moral autonomy. That choice, therefore, cannot properly be coerced. Contrary to Fried's view, however, it can properly be subjected to the moral scrutiny and criticism of others, particularly those who feel morally compelled to persuade the lawyer to use his or her professional training and skills in ways that the critics consider to be more consistent with personal, social, or professional ethics.[31]

As I have stressed elsewhere, however, once the lawyer has assumed responsibility to represent a client, the zealousness of that representation cannot be tempered by the lawyer's moral judgments of the client or of the client's cause.[32] That point is of importance in itself, and is worth stressing also because it is one of the considerations that a lawyer should take into account in making the initial decision whether to enter into a particular lawyer-client relationship.[33]

VI.

In disagreeing with Professor Wasserstrom's criticism of role-differentiation, I did not mean to suggest that role-differentiation has not produced a degree of amorality, and even immorality, in the practice of many lawyers. The problem, as I see it, is expressed in the news item I quoted earlier regarding Manuel Orantes. Playing for himself, Mr. Orantes has earned an enviable reputation, not only for his athletic prowess, but also for his good sportsmanship—if you will, for his morality in his relations with his adversaries. Yet when he plays with teammates and for his country, he adopts different standards of conduct.

31. Such criticism might be answered on the grounds that everyone is entitled to representation, but that response is not conclusive as long as there is, in fact, another lawyer who is willing to take the case.

32. FREEDMAN, *supra* note 3, ch. 2.

33. *See* LAW, *supra* note 24, at 213-14. It is possible, of course, that a client will decide upon a course of conduct, not foreseeable as a possibility at the outset of the lawyer-client relationship, that is so morally repugnant to the lawyer as to make it impossible for the lawyer to continue without a serious personal conflict of interest. In that event, the lawyer is permitted to withdraw, but only upon taking reasonable steps to avoid foreseeable prejudice to the client's rights. *See* ABA CODE OF PROFESSIONAL RESPONSIBILITY, DR 5-101(A), EC 5-2, DR 2-110(C)(1)(e), DR 2-110(A)(2)(1974).

I think that Mr. Orantes is wrong, in a way that many lawyers frequently are wrong. I do not mean that in Davis Cup play he is not bound by special, voluntarily assumed obligations to others. On the contrary, he is bound by his role as teammate and countryman to accept the decision of his teammates, which may well be that each player should play to win, without relinquishing any advantage that the rules of the game and the calls of the judges allow. Where Orantes is wrong, however, is in preempting that decision, in assuming that their decision is that winning is all. Perhaps if he actually put the choice to them, Orantes' teammates would decide that they would prefer to achieve, for themselves and for their country, the kind of character and reputation for decency and fairness that Orantes has earned for himself. Perhaps they would not decide that way. The choice, however, is theirs, and it is a denial of their humanity to assume the less noble choice and to act on the assumption without consultation.

In day-to-day law practice, the most common instances of amoral or immoral conduct by lawyers are those occasions in which we preempt our clients' moral judgments. That occurs in two ways. Most commonly we assume that our function is to maximize the client's position—the client's material or tactical position, that is—in every way that is legally permissible. Since it is our function not to judge the client's cause, but to represent the client's interests, we tend to assume the worst regarding the client's desires. Much less frequently, I believe, a lawyer will decide that a particular course of conduct is morally preferable, even though not required legally, and will follow that course on the client's behalf. In either event, the lawyer fails in his or her responsibility to maximize the client's autonomy by providing the client with the fullest advice and counsel, legal and moral, so that the client can make the most informed choice possible.[34]

Let me give a commonplace illustration. Two experienced and conscientious lawyers, *A* and *B*, once asked me to help them to resolve an ethical problem. They represented a party for whom they were negotiating a complex contract involving voluminous legal documents. The attorneys on the other side were insistent upon eliminating a particular guarantee provision, and *A* and *B* had been authorized by their client to forego the guarantee if the other side was adamant. The other lawyers had overlooked, however, the fact that the same guarantee, more broadly and unambiguously stated, was provided elsewhere in the documents. Having agreed to eliminate the guarantee provision, with specific refer-

34. *Cf.* ABA Code of Professional Responsibility, EC 7-7 to 7-12, 7-26; DR 7-101(A)(1), DR 7-101(B)(1) (1974).

ence to a particular clause on a particular page, were *A* and *B* obligated to call the attention of opposing counsel to the similar clause on a different page? Or, on the contrary, were they obligated, as *A* put it, "to represent our client's interest, rather than to educate the lawyers on the other side?" Each of the lawyers was satisfied that, if he were negotiating for himself, he would unquestioningly point out the second guarantee clause to the other party. Moreover, each of them was more attentive to, and concerned about, questions of professional responsibility than most lawyers probably are—each of them, that is, was highly sensitive to the question of personal responsibility in a professional system. Nevertheless, it had occurred to neither of them that their professional responsibility was not to resolve the issue between themselves, but rather to present the issue to the client for resolution.[35]

Our discussion thus far has related to decisions that are clearly in the moral or ethical realm. What of tactical decisions? Are those significantly different and therefore within the lawyer's ultimate control?

At one time I had the notion, based on fantasy, that Alger Hiss had no involvement with Wittaker Chambers' nefarious activities, but that Hiss' wife did. Assuming such a case, imagine Mr. Hiss' lawyer advising him that the only way to defend himself would be to tell the truth about his wife's involvement, and Hiss replying that, in no way, directly or indirectly, was his wife to be brought into the case, even if it meant an erroneous conviction for himself. In those circumstances, I find it hard to believe that even Clement Haynsworth or Thurmond Arnold would insist upon conducting the case in such a way as to implicate the client's wife.[36]

---

35. Moreover, the attitude of *A* and *B* does not appear to be the result of what Professor Wasserstrom refers to as the "acculturation" of legal training and practice. I have used that illustration and others like it as classroom problems early in the first semester of the first-year contracts course and, consistently, students who have had minimal exposure to the corrupting influence of law school, and no experience at all as practioners, assume that the lawyer's proper function is to preempt the client's moral decision. As indicated by that response, and by other student responses to problems of lawyer's ethics, law teachers have a moral role to perform as an essential part of their professional responsibilities. *Cf.* Freedman, *Professional Responsibility of the Civil Practitioner: Teaching Legal Ethics in the Contracts Course*, 21 J. OF LEGAL EDUC. 569 (1969).

36. Compare, however, the report of a murder-kidnap trial of a group of Hanafi Muslims. According to the *Washington Post*, "the defendants are determined to share the guilt for crimes they may not have committed as a gesture of loyalty to their leader and belief in their faith." The *Post* quotes a defense attorney as saying, "They are willing to go down the tube for a principle."

Despite their clients' strong desires, which are based in part on religious conviction, the lawyers apparently intend to put on affirmative evidence and conduct adversary cross-examination of the group's leader (who is a co-defendant). The *Post* further reports that the lawyers believe themselves to be acting in accordance with their "duty to provide

Arguably, however, that case represents a moral decision rather than a tactical one. On the one hand, there is the client's love for and loyalty to his wife. On the other, there is the possibility of a wrongful conviction, and the likelihood that the client will give misleading, or even false, testimony in the effort to avoid implicating his wife.

A recent case in New Jersey, *State v. Pratts*,[37] would seem to come as close as possible to posing a tactical decision unencumbered by moral considerations. In that case, the lawyer representing a criminal defendant had interviewed a witness who had given the lawyer a statement helpful to the defense. The lawyer learned, however, that shortly thereafter the witness had given the prosecutor a different statement, damaging to the defendant. The lawyer's decision, therefore, was that the witness should not be called. For similar reasons, of course, the prosecutor also refrained from calling the witness.

The defendant disagreed with his lawyer. Fully aware of the risks of calling the witness, the defendant decided that the witness was part of the case he wanted presented on his behalf. Apprised of the situation, the trial judge accepted the decision of the defense attorney, and the witness was not called. The defendant was convicted.

On appeal, the Superior Court of New Jersey affirmed. The court stated the issue to be not "whether there was an abuse of discretion" by the trial judge, but "who was responsible for the conduct of the defense." The court held that "when a defendant accepts representation by counsel, that counsel has the authority to make the necessary decisions as to the management of the case."[38] Quoting a federal appeals decision, the court added that the defendant "has a right to be cautioned, advised, and served by [court-appointed] counsel so that he will not be a victim of his poverty. *But he has no right . . . to dictate the procedural course of his representation*."[39]

I think the court was wrong. At issue is not the lawyer's day in court, but the defendant's—the defendant's right to trial, right to due process of law, and right to counsel.[40] As the Supreme Court has noted, under the

what they think is the best defense possible," even though they are acting contrary to their clients' instructions. Further, the lawyers appear to have been encouraged in that view by the Bar Counsel of the District of Columbia Bar. Washington Post, July 10, 1977, § A at 1.

37. 145 N.J. Super. 79, 366 A.2d 1327 (1975), *aff'd per curiam*, 365 A.2d 928 (1976).

38. 145 N.J. Super. at 88, 366 A.2d at 1333.

39. Rogers v. United States, 325 F.2d 485,488 (10th Cir. 1963) (emphasis by the New Jersey court).

40. The decision recalls to mind the elderly attorney who said, "When I was younger and less experienced, I lost many cases that I should have won. Now that I am more experienced, I win cases that probably should be lost. So you see, in the long run, justice is done."

sixth amendment, "[t]he right to defend is given directly to the accused; for it is he who suffers the consequences if the defense fails."[41]

Indeed, I would put the *Pratts* case, too, in the realm of morality. In a society such as ours, an essential purpose of a criminal trial is to manifest respect for the dignity of the individual.[42] Further, as we have already noted, a central element of human dignity is personal autonomy, particularly in matters that affect our own lives as substantially as those in which lawyers are needed for assistance. Moreover, the "assistance" of counsel that is guaranteed by the sixth amendment is just that. In the words of the Supreme Court, "an assistant, however expert, is still an assistant. The language and spirit of the Sixth Amendment contemplate that counsel, like the other defense tools guaranteed by the Amendment, shall be an aid to a willing defendant. . . ."[43] Otherwise, "counsel is not an assistant, but a master," with the result that the right to make a defense is "stripped of the *personal character* upon which the Amendment insists."[44]

As against those weighty considerations of human dignity and autonomy, which find expression in the Constitution, what reasons are there for the attorney to control such a decision? In *Pratts*, there would have been some saving of time at the trial. On the other hand, in a case in which the defendant prefers not to call a particular witness whom the lawyer wants to call, the client's decision would conserve time. In either event, the time element would not appear to constitute a compelling reason to deprive the client of the opportunity to make the decision in a matter of such importance to him. I suspect, in fact, that the real reason lawyers prefer to make the final decision, and judges are inclined to give it to them, is professional pride, with the emphasis on the word pride.

---

41. Faretta v. California, 422 U.S. 806, 819-20 (1975).

42. *See* FREEDMAN, *supra* note 3, ch. 1.

43. Faretta v. California, 422 U.S. at 820.

44. *Id.* (emphasis added). The issue in *Faretta* was whether there is a constitutional right to waive counsel and proceed pro se. The Court held that there is such a right. In dictum, the Court said, "It is true that when a defendant chooses to have a lawyer manage and present his case, law and tradition may allocate to the counsel the power to make binding decisions of trial strategy in many areas. . . . This allocation can only be justified, however, by the defendant's consent, at the outset, to accept counsel as his representative." *Id.* at 820-21. Nevertheless, the cases cited by the Court (as well as the reasoning of *Faretta* itself) establish that basic rights cannot be waived by counsel without a voluntary and knowing consent by the defendant; moreover, those same cases strongly suggest that counsel can make no trial decision of consequence over the express objection of the defendant. *See* Brookhart v. Janis, 384 U.S. 1, 7-8 (1966); Henry v. Mississippi, 379 U.S. 443, 451 (1965); Fay v. Noia, 372 U.S. 391, 439 (1963). That understanding is reinforced by "right of privacy" cases which give constitutional status to "independence in making certain kinds of important decisions." *See* Whalen v. Roe, 429 U.S. 589 (1977).

That is, the lawyer does not want the judge or any colleagues present to think that he or she is so unskilled as to have called a witness who is so vulnerable to cross-examination. Insofar as the lawyer's response would be that the lawyer's real concern is with the client's welfare, I think it is another instance of misplaced paternalism.

VII.

One of the essential values of a just society is respect for the dignity of each member of that society. Essential to each individual's dignity is the maximization of his or her autonomy or, as Pope John expressed it, "the right to act freely and responsibly . . . act[ing] chiefly on his own responsibility and initiative [and] . . . on his own decision."[45] In order to exercise that responsibility and initiative, each person is entitled to know his or her rights against society and against other individuals, and to decide whether to seek fulfillment of those rights through the due process of law.

The lawyer, by virtue of his or her training and skills, has a legal and practical monopoly with respect to access to the legal system and knowledge about the law. Legal advice and assistance are often indispensible, therefore, to the effective exercise of individual autonomy.

Accordingly, the attorney acts both professionally and morally in assisting clients to maximize their autonomy, that is, by counselling clients candidly and fully regarding the clients' legal rights and moral responsibilities as the lawyer perceives them, and by assisting clients to carry out their lawful decisions. Further, the attorney acts unprofessionally and immorally by depriving clients of their autonomy, that is, by denying them information regarding their legal rights, by otherwise preempting their moral decisions, or by depriving them of the ability to carry out their lawful decisions.

Until the lawyer-client relationship is contracted, however—until, that is, the lawyer induces another to rely upon his or her professional knowledge and skills—the lawyer ordinarily acts entirely within the scope of his or her own autonomy. Barring extraordinary circumstances,[46] therefore, the attorney is free to exercise his or her personal judgment as to whether to represent a particular client. Since a moral choice is implicated in such a decision, however, others are entitled to

45. PACEM IN TERRIS, *supra* note 1.

46. The lawyer does undertake special responsibilities to society regarding the effective functioning of the legal system, and to that extent, the lawyer's autonomy may be circumscribed, e.g., by the obligation to represent someone who otherwise would be unrepresented. *See, e.g.*, ABA CODE OF PROFESSIONAL RESPONSIBILITY, EC 2-29 (1974).

judge and to criticize, on moral grounds, a lawyer's decision to represent a particular client.

Finally, those of us who teach law have a primary professional obligation to explicate the moral implications of the law in general and of lawyers' ethics in particular.

If we conscientiously carry out those personal and professional responsibilities, then I do believe that professionalism is consistent with decency, and I therefore conclude that one can indeed be a good lawyer and a moral person at the same time.

[5]

The Lawyer as Friend: The Moral Foundations of the Lawyer-Client Relation*

Charles Fried†

Advocatus sed non ladro,
Res miranda populo . . . .

Medieval anthem
honoring St. Ives

Can a good lawyer be a good person? The question troubles lawyers and law students alike. They are troubled by the demands of loyalty to one's client and by the fact that one can win approval as a good, maybe even great, lawyer even though that loyalty is engrossed by over-privileged or positively distasteful clients. How, they ask, is such loyalty compatible with that devotion to the common good characteristic of high moral principles? And whatever their views of the common good, they are troubled because the willingness of lawyers to help their clients use the law to the prejudice of the weak or the innocent seems morally corrupt. The lawyer is conventionally seen as a professional devoted to his client's interests and as authorized, if not in fact required, to do some things (though not anything) for that client which he would not do for himself.[1] In this essay I consider the com-

 This essay is part of a larger work on right and wrong, supported by the National Science Foundation under grant number SOC75-13506. Research assistance and suggestions were provided by Dan Polster and Jerrold Tannenbaum, students at the Harvard Law School. I am grateful for the comments of Gary Bellow, Sissela Bok, Alan Dershowitz, Philip Heymann, Andrew Kaufman, Robert Keeton, Thomas Nagel, Charles Nesson, Albert Sacks, and David Shapiro. I am especially grateful to the editors of the *Yale Law Journal* for their understanding, help, and encouragement. I wonder if any of them agree with what I say here. The National Science Foundation, of course, underwrites only the effort, not the conclusion.

† Professor of Law, Harvard University.

1. *See, e.g.*, J. AUERBACH, UNEQUAL JUSTICE (1976); M. GREEN, THE OTHER GOVERNMENT (1975).

Lord Brougham stated the traditional view of the lawyer's role during his defense of Queen Caroline:

> [A]n advocate, in the discharge of his duty, knows but one person in all the world, and that person is his client. To save that client by all means and expedients, and at all hazards and costs to other persons, and, among them, to himself, is his first and only duty; and in performing this duty he must not regard the alarm, the torments, the destruction which he may bring upon others. Separating the duty of a patriot from that of an advocate, he must go on reckless of consequences, though it should be his unhappy fate to involve his country in confusion.

2 TRIAL OF QUEEN CAROLINE 8 (J. Nightingale ed. 1821). A sharply contrasting view was held by law professors at the University of Havana who said that "the first job of a

patibility between this traditional conception of the lawyer's role and the ideal of moral purity—the ideal that one's life should be lived in fulfillment of the most demanding moral principles, and not just barely within the law. So I shall not be particularly concerned with the precise limits imposed on the lawyer's conduct by positive rules of law and by the American Bar Association's *Code of Professional Responsibility*[2] except as these provide a background. I assume that the lawyer observes these scrupulously. My inquiry is one of morals: Does the lawyer whose conduct and choices are governed only by the traditional conception of the lawyer's role, which these positive rules reflect, lead a professional life worthy of moral approbation, worthy of respect—ours and his own?

I. The Challenge to the Traditional Conception

A. *The Two Criticisms*

Two frequent criticisms of the traditional conception of the lawyer's role attack both its ends and its means. First, it is said that the ideal of professional loyalty to one's client permits, even demands, an allocation of the lawyer's time, passion, and resources in ways that are not always maximally conducive to the greatest good of the greatest number.[3] Interestingly, this criticism is leveled increasingly against doctors[4] as well as lawyers. Both professions affirm the principle that the professional's primary loyalty is to his client,[5] his patient. A "good" lawyer will lavish energy and resources on his existing client, even if it can be shown that others could derive greater benefit from them. The professional ideal authorizes a care for the client and the patient which

revolutionary lawyer is not to argue that his client is innocent, but rather to determine if his client is guilty and, if so, to seek the sanction which will best rehabilitate him." Berman, *The Cuban Popular Tribunals*, 69 COLUM. L. REV. 1317, 1341 (1969). And a Bulgarian attorney has been quoted as saying, "'In a Socialist state there is no division of duty between the judge, prosecutor and defense counsel . . . the defense must assist the prosecution to find the objective truth in a case.'" J. KAPLAN, CRIMINAL JUSTICE: INTRODUCTORY CASES AND MATERIALS 264-65 (1973).

2. The American Bar Association approved a revised *Code of Professional Responsibility* in 1969. In part that revision was a response to the criticism that the legal profession, by failing to make legal services more widely available, had not met its public responsibilities. J. AUERBACH, *supra* note 1, at 285-86. *See also Preface*, ABA CODE OF PROFESSIONAL RESPONSIBILITY.

3. *See* M. GREEN, *supra* note 1, at 268-69, 285-89.

4. *See* V. FUCHS, WHO SHALL LIVE? 60 (1974); Havighurst & Blumstein, *Coping With Quality/Cost Trade-Offs in Medical Care: The Role of PSROs*, 70 NW. U. L. REV. 6, 25-28 (1975). *But see* Fried, *Equality and Rights in Medical Care*, 6 HASTINGS CENTER REP. 29, 33-34 (1976).

5. *See* ABA CODE OF PROFESSIONAL RESPONSIBILITY CANON 7.

exceeds what the efficient distribution of a scarce social resource (the professional's time) would dictate.

That same professional ideal has little or nothing to say about the initial choice of clients or patients. Certainly it is laudable if the doctor and lawyer choose their clients among the poorest or sickest or most dramatically threatened, but the professional ideal does not require this kind of choice in any systematic way—the choice of client remains largely a matter of fortuity or arbitrary choice. But once the client has been chosen, the professional ideal requires primary loyalty to the client whatever his need or situation. Critics contend that it is wasteful and immoral that some of the finest talent in the legal profession is devoted to the intricacies of, say, corporate finance or elaborate estate plans, while important public and private needs for legal services go unmet. The immorality of this waste is seen to be compounded when the clients who are the beneficiaries of this lavish attention use it to avoid their obligations in justice (if not in law) to society and to perpetuate their (legal) domination of the very groups whose greater needs these lawyers should be meeting.[6]

The second criticism applies particularly to the lawyer. It addresses not the misallocation of scarce resources, which the lawyer's exclusive concern with his client's interests permits, but the means which this loyalty appears to authorize, tactics which procure advantages for the client at the direct expense of some identified opposing party. Examples are discrediting a nervous but probably truthful complaining witness[7] or taking advantage of the need or ignorance of an adversary in a negotiation. This second criticism is, of course, related to the first, but there is a difference. The first criticism focuses on a social harm: the waste of scarce resources implicit in a doctor caring for the hearts of the sedentary managerial classes or a lawyer tending to the estates and marital difficulties of the rich. The professional is accused of failing to confer benefits wisely and efficiently. By the second criticism the lawyer is accused not of failing to benefit the appropriate, though usually unidentified, persons, but of harming his identified adversary.[8]

6. For a description of the growth of such criticisms, see J. AUERBACH, *supra* note 1, at 275-88.

7. For a defense of an attorney's use of such tactics, see M. FREEDMAN, LAWYERS' ETHICS IN AN ADVERSARY SYSTEM 43-49 (1975). *See also* Curtis, *The Ethics of Advocacy*, 4 STAN. L. REV. 3 (1951).

8. The point really carries further than the distinction between benefit and harm. In the former case, though some particular person may have benefited had the distribution been efficient, it does not seem correct to say that for that reason this person had a right to the benefit which he was denied, or that this person was wronged by not receiving the benefit. Individuals do not acquire rights under policies which are dictated

The Lawyer as Friend

B. *Examples*

Consider a number of cases which illustrate the first criticism: A doctor is said to owe a duty of loyalty to his patient, but how is he to react if doing his very best for his patient would deplete the resources of the patient's family, as in the case of a severely deformed baby who can only be kept alive through extraordinarily expensive means? Should a doctor prescribe every test of distinct but marginal utility for every patient on public assistance, even if he knows that in the aggregate such a policy will put the medical care system under intolerable burdens?[9] Should he subject his patients to prudent testing of new remedies because he knows that only in this way can medicine make the strides that it has in the past?[10]

These problems are analogous to problems which are faced by the lawyer. The lawyer who advises a client how to avoid the effects of a tax or a form of regulation, though it is a fair tax or a regulation in the public interest, is facing the same dilemma and resolving it in favor of his client. So does the public defender who accedes to his client's demands and takes a "losing" case to trial, thereby wasting court time and depleting the limited resources of his organization. We

purely by considerations of efficiency. *See generally* Dworkin, *Hard Cases,* 88 HARV. L. REV. 1057, 1058-78 (1975).

Professor Anscombe makes the following suggestive argument: If saving the life of one patient requires a massive dose of a drug that could be divided up and used to save five other people, not one of those five can claim that he has been wronged, that the smaller dose of the drug was owed to him.

> Yet all can reproach me if I gave it to none. It was there, ready to supply human need, and human need was not supplied. So any one of them can say: you ought to have used it to help us who needed it; and so all are wronged. But if it was used for someone, as much as he needed it to keep him alive, no one has any ground for accusing me of having wronged *himself*.—Why, just because he was one of five who could have been saved, is he wronged in not being saved, if someone is supplied with it who needed it? What is *his* claim, except the claim that what was needed go to him rather than be wasted? But it was not wasted. So he was not wronged. So who was wronged? And if no one was wronged, what injury did I do?
>
> . . . .
>
> I do not mean that 'because they are more' isn't a good reason for helping these and not that one, or these rather than those. It is a perfectly intelligible reason. But it doesn't follow from that that a man acts badly if he doesn't make it his reason. He acts badly if human need for what is in his power to give doesn't work in him as a reason. He acts badly if he chooses to rescue rich people rather than poor ones, having ill regard for the poor ones because they are poor. But he doesn't act badly if he uses his resources to save X, or X, Y and Z, *for no bad reason*, and is not affected by the consideration that he could save a larger number of people. For, once more: who can say he is wronged? And if no one is wronged, how does the rescuer commit any wrong?

Anscombe, *Who is Wronged?*, 5 OXFORD REV. 16, 16-17 (1967) (emphasis in original).

9. *See generally* V. FUCHS, *supra* note 4, at 91-95; Fried, *Rights and Health Care—Beyond Equity and Efficiency*, 293 NEW ENGLAND J. MEDICINE 241, 244 (1975).

10. For discussions of this dilemma, see A. COCHRANE, EFFECTIVENESS AND EFFICIENCY (1972); C. FRIED, MEDICAL EXPERIMENTATION: PERSONAL INTEGRITY AND SOCIAL POLICY (1974).

The Yale Law Journal Vol. 85: 1060, 1976

tolerate and indeed may applaud the decision of a lawyer who vigorously defends a criminal whom he believes to be guilty and dangerous.[11] And I for one think that a lawyer who arranges the estate of a disagreeable dowager or represents one of the parties in a bitter matrimonial dispute must be as assiduous and single-minded in fulfilling his obligation to that client as the lawyer who is defending the civil liberties case of the century.

Illustrative of the second criticism (doing things which are offensive to a particular person) are familiar situations such as the following: In a negotiation it becomes clear to the lawyer for the seller that the buyer and his lawyer mistakenly believe that somebody else has already offered a handsome price for the property. The buyer asks the seller if this is true, and the seller's lawyer hears his client give an ambiguous but clearly encouraging response.[12] Another classic case is the interposition of a technical defense such as the running of the statute of limitations to defeat a debt that the client admits he owes.[13]

There is another class of cases which does not so unambiguously involve the lawyer's furthering his client's interests at the direct expense of some equally identified, concrete individual, but where furthering those interests does require the lawyer to do things which are personally offensive to him. The conventional paradigms in the casuistic literature deal with criminal defense lawyers who are asked improper questions by the trial judge ("Your client doesn't have a criminal record, does he?" or "Your client hasn't offered to plead guilty to a lesser offense, has he?"), a truthful answer to which would be damningly prejudicial to the client, but which the lawyer cannot even refuse to answer without running the risk of creating the same prejudice. There are those who say the lawyer must lie in defense of his client's interests even though lying is personally and professionally offensive to him.[14] The defense lawyer who cross-examines a complaining

11. *See* M. Freedman, *supra* note 7, at 43-49.

12. DR 7-102(A)(5) of the *Code of Professional Responsibility* states that a lawyer shall not knowingly make a false statement of law or fact in his representation of a client. The issue is how to apply this admonition in the context of negotiation, where deception is commonplace. *See* M. Meltsner & P. Schrag, Public Interest Advocacy: Materials for Clinical Legal Education 231-39 (1974).

13. For a striking example, see Zabella v. Pakel, 242 F.2d 452 (7th Cir. 1957), where the debtor asserting the technical defenses was a savings and loan association president, and the creditor was a man who had worked for him as a carpenter and had lent him money in earlier, less fortunate days.

14. Although Charles Curtis explicitly denounces lying to the court, his observation that the propriety of lying might depend on whether the question is asked "by someone who has a right to ask it" at least implies a possible qualification in the case of improper questioning by the court. Curtis, *supra* note 7, at 7-9. Monroe Freedman does not specifically address this problem, but his argument that an attorney's duty to safeguard

rape victim (whom he knows to be telling the truth) about her chastity or lack thereof in order to discredit her accusing testimony faces a similar moral difficulty. In some respects these cases might be taken to illustrate both principal criticisms of the traditional conception. On the one hand, there is harm to society in making the choice to favor the client's interests: a dangerous criminal may escape punishment or an appropriately heavy sentence. On the other hand, this social harm is accomplished by means of acting towards another human being—the judge, the complaining witness—in ways that seem demeaning and dishonorable.

II. The Lawyer as Friend

A. *The Thesis*

In this essay I will consider the moral status of the traditional conception of the professional. The two criticisms of this traditional conception, if left unanswered, will not put the lawyer in jail, but they will leave him without a moral basis for his acts. The real question is whether, in the face of these two criticisms, a decent and morally sensitive person can conduct himself according to the traditional conception of professional loyalty and still believe that what he is doing is morally worthwhile.

It might be said that anyone whose conscience is so tender that he cannot fulfill the prescribed obligations of a professional should not undertake those obligations. He should not allow his moral scruples to operate as a trap for those who are told by the law that they may expect something more. But of course this suggestion merely pushes the inquiry back a step. We must ask then not how a decent lawyer may behave, but whether a decent, ethical person can ever be a lawyer. Are the assurances implicit in assuming the role of lawyer such that an honorable person would not give them and thus would not enter the profession? And, indeed, this is a general point about an argument from obligation:[15] It may be that the internal logic of a particular obligation demands certain forms of conduct (*e.g.*, honor among

the attorney-client privilege requires the attorney to introduce his client's perjurious testimony would seem to extend to this situation. M. FREEDMAN, *supra* note 7, at 27-41. *Cf.* ABA COMM. ON PROFESSIONAL ETHICS, OPINIONS No. 287 (1967) (if attorney for defendant learns of previous criminal record through his communications with his client, he has no duty to correct misapprehension on part of court that client has no record).

15. That one assumes obligations to persons which cannot always be overridden by the benefits which would accrue from aiding some third person is a standard objection to utilitarianism. *See, e.g.*, W. ROSS, THE RIGHT AND THE GOOD 17-19 (1930).

thieves), but the question remains whether it is just and moral to contract such obligations.

I will argue in this essay that it is not only legally but also morally right that a lawyer adopt as his dominant purpose the furthering of his client's interests—that it is right that a professional put the interests of his client above some idea, however valid, of the collective interest. I maintain that the traditional conception of the professional role expresses a morally valid conception of human conduct and human relationships, that one who acts according to that conception is to that extent a good person. Indeed, it is my view that, far from being a mere creature of positive law, the traditional conception is so far mandated by moral right that any advanced legal system which did not sanction this conception would be unjust.

The general problem raised by the two criticisms is this: How can it be that it is not only permissible, but indeed morally right, to favor the interests of a particular person in a way which we can be fairly sure is either harmful to another particular individual or not maximally conducive to the welfare of society as a whole?[16]

The resolution of this problem is aided, I think, if set in a larger perspective. Charles Curtis made the perspicacious remark that a lawyer may be privileged to lie for his client in a way that one might lie to save one's friends or close relatives.[17] I do not want to underwrite the notion that it is justifiable to lie even in those situations, but there is a great deal to the point that in those relations—friendship, kinship—we recognize an authorization to take the interests of particular concrete persons more seriously and to give them priority over the interests of the wider collectivity. One who provides an expensive education for his own children surely cannot be blamed because he does not use these resources to alleviate famine or to save lives in some distant land. Nor does he blame himself. Indeed, our intuition that an individual is authorized to prefer identified persons standing close to him over the abstract interests of humanity finds its sharpest expression in our sense that an individual is entitled to act with something less than impartiality to that person who stands closest to him—the person that he is. There is such a thing as selfishness to be sure, yet no reasonable

16. I have discussed this problem elsewhere. C. FRIED, AN ANATOMY OF VALUES 207-36 (1970); C. FRIED, *supra* note 10, at 132-37. *Cf.* Schelling, *The Life You Save May Be Your Own*, in PROBLEMS IN PUBLIC EXPENDITURE ANALYSIS 127, 129-30 (S. Chase ed. 1968) (also discussing our greater concern for known, as opposed to unknown, individuals).

17. Curtis, *supra* note 7, at 8. Analogizing the lawyer to a friend raises a range of problems upon which I shall not touch. These have to do with the lawyer's benevolent and sometimes not so benevolent tyranny over and imposition on his client, seemingly authorized by the claim to be acting in the client's interests. Domineering paternalism is not a normal characteristic of friendship. This point is due to Jay Katz.

The Lawyer as Friend

morality asks us to look upon ourselves as merely plausible candidates for the distribution of the attention and resources which we command, plausible candidates whose entitlement to our own concern is no greater in principle than that of any other human being. Such a doctrine may seem edifying, but on reflection it strikes us as merely fanatical.

This suggests an interesting way to look at the situation of the lawyer. As a professional person one has a special care for the interests of those accepted as clients, just as his friends, his family, and he himself have a very general claim to his special concern. But I concede this does no more than widen the problem. It merely shows that in claiming this authorization to have a special care for my clients I am doing something which I do in other contexts as well.

B. *The Utilitarian Explanation*

I consider first an argument to account for fidelity to role, for obligation, made most elaborately by the classical utilitarians, Mill[18] and Sidgwick.[19] They argued that our propensity to prefer the interests of those who are close to us is in fact perfectly reasonable because we are more likely to be able to benefit those people. Thus, if everyone is mainly concerned with those closest to him, the distribution of social energies will be most efficient and the greatest good of the greatest number will be achieved. The idea is that the efforts I expend for my friend or my relative are more likely to be effective because I am more likely to know what needs to be done. I am more likely to be sure that the good I intend is in fact accomplished. One might say that there is less overhead, fewer administrative costs, in benefiting those nearest to us. I would not want to ridicule this argument, but it does not seem to me to go far enough. Because if that were the sole basis for the preference, then it would be my duty to determine whether my efforts might not be more efficiently spent on the collectivity, on the distant, anonymous beneficiary. But it is just my point that *this* is an inquiry we are not required, indeed sometimes not even authorized, to make. When we decide to care for our children, to assure our own comforts, to fulfill our obligations to our clients or patients, we do not do so as a result of a cost-benefit inquiry which takes into account the ease of producing a good result for our friends and relations.

Might it not be said, however, that the best means of favoring the

18. Mill, *Utilitarianism*, in THE PHILOSOPHY OF JOHN STUART MILL 321, 342-44 (M. Cohen ed. 1961).
19. H. SIDGWICK, THE METHODS OF ETHICS 252 (7th ed. 1907).

The Yale Law Journal Vol. 85: 1060, 1976

abstract collectivity is in certain cases not to try to favor it directly but to concentrate on those to whom one has a special relation? This does not involve tricking oneself, but only recognizing the limitations of what an individual can do and know. But that, it seems to me, is just Mill's and Sidgwick's argument all over again. There is no trickery involved, but this is still a kind of deliberate limitation of our moral horizon which leaves us uncomfortable. Do I know in a particular case whether sticking to the narrow definition of my role will *in that case* further the good of all? If I know that it will not further the general good, then why am I acting as the role demands? Is it to avoid setting a bad example? But for whom? I need not tell others—whether I tell or not could enter into my calculation. For myself then? But that begs the question, since if short-circuiting the role-definition of my obligation and going straight for the general good is the best thing to do in that case, then the example I set myself is not a bad example, but a good example. In short, I do not see how one can at the same time admit that the general good is one's only moral standard, while steadfastly hewing to obligations to friends, family, and clients. What we must look for is an argument which shows that giving some degree of special consideration to myself, my friends, my clients is not merely instrumentally justified (as the utilitarians would argue) but to some degree intrinsically so.[20]

I think such an argument can be made. Instead of speaking the language of maximization of value over all of humanity, it will speak the language of rights. The stubborn ethical datum affirming such a preference grows out of the profoundest springs of morality: the concepts of personality, identity, and liberty.

C. *Self, Friendship, and Justice*

Consider for a moment the picture of the human person that would emerge if the utilitarian claim were in fact correct. It would mean that in all my choices I must consider the well-being of all humanity—actual and potential—as the range of my concern. Moreover, every actual or potential human being is absolutely equal in his claims upon me. Indeed, I myself am to myself only as one of this innumerable multitude. And that is the clue to what is wrong with the utilitarian vision. Before there is morality there must be the person. We must attain and maintain in our morality a concept of personality such that

20. *See generally* D. Lyons, Forms and Limits of Utilitarianism (1965); J. Smart & B. Williams, Utilitarianism: For and Against (1973); Harrod, *Utilitarianism Revised*, 45 Mind 137 (1936); Mabbott, *Punishment*, 48 Mind 152 (1939).

The Lawyer as Friend

it makes sense to posit choosing, valuing entities—free, moral beings. But the picture of the moral universe in which my own interests disappear and are merged into the interests of the totality of humanity is incompatible with that,[21] because one wishes to develop a conception of a responsible, valuable, and valuing agent, and such an agent must first of all be dear to himself. It is from the kernel of individuality that the other things we value radiate. The Gospel says we must love our neighbor as ourselves, and this implies that any concern for others which is a *human* concern must presuppose a concern for ourselves.[22] The human concern which we then show others is a concern which first of all recognizes the concrete individuality of that other person just as we recognize our own.

It might be objected that the picture I sketch does not show that each individual, in order to maintain the integral sense of himself as an individual, is justified in attributing a greater value to his most essential interests than he ascribes to the most essential interests of all other persons. Should not the individual generalize and attribute in equal degree to all persons the value which he naturally attributes to himself? I agree with those who hold that it is the essence of morality for reason to push us beyond inclination to the fair conclusion of our

21. *See generally* C. Fried, An Anatomy of Values, 203-06; Rawls, *The Independence of Moral Theory*, 48 Am. Phil. Ass'n 17-20 (1975) (Kantian theory, as compared to utilitarianism, takes seriously basic moral fact of primacy of notion of individual personality).

22. . . . It is written (Lev. xix. 18, Matth. xxii. 39); *Thou shalt love thy neighbor* (Lev. *loc. cit.,—friend*) *as thyself*. Whence it seems to follow that man's love for himself is the model of his love for another. But the model exceeds the copy. Therefore, out of charity, a man ought to love himself more than his neighbor.

. . . .

We must, therefore, say that, even as regards the affection we ought to love one neighbor more than another. The reason is that, since the principle of love is God, and the person who loves, it must needs be that the affection of love increases in proportion to the nearness to one or the other of those principles.

. . . .

. . . As stated above . . . we ought out of charity to love those who are more closely united to us more, both because our love for them is more intense, and because there are more reasons for loving them. . . .

Accordingly we must say that friendship among blood relations is based upon their connection by natural origin, the friendship of fellow-citizens on their civic fellowship, and the friendship of those who are fighting side by side on the comradeship of battle. Wherefore in matters pertaining to nature we should love our kindred most, in matters concerning relations between citizens, we should prefer our fellow-citizens, and on the battlefield our fellow-soldiers. . . .

. . . .

If however we compare union with union, it is evident that the union arising from natural origin is prior to, and more stable than, all others, because it is something affecting the very substance, whereas other unions supervene and may cease altogether.

II Thomas Aquinas, Summa Theologica 1297-1301 (Fathers of the English Dominican Province trans. 1947).

The Yale Law Journal Vol. 85: 1060, 1976

premises.[23] It *is* a fair conclusion that as my experience as a judging, valuing, choosing entity is crucial to me, I must also conclude that for other persons their own lives and desires are the center of their universes. If morality is transcendent, it must somehow transcend particularity to take account of this general fact. I do not wish to deny this. On the contrary, my claim is that the kind of preference which an individual gives himself and concrete others is a preference which he would in exactly this universalizing spirit allow others to exhibit as well. It is not that I callously overlook the claim of the abstract individual, but indeed I would understand and approve were I myself to be prejudiced because some person to whom I stood in a similar situation of abstraction preferred his own concrete dimensions.

Finally, the concreteness which is the starting point of my own moral sensibility, the sense of myself, is not just a historical, biographical fact. It continues to enter into and condition my moral judgments because the effects which I can produce upon people who are close to me are qualitatively different from those produced upon abstract, unknown persons. My own concreteness is important not only because it establishes a basis for understanding what I and what all other human beings might be, but because in engaging that aspect of myself with the concrete aspects of others, I realize special values for both of us. Quite simply, the individualized relations of love and friendship (and perhaps also their opposites, hatred and enmity) have a different, more intense aspect than do the cooler, more abstract relations of love and service to humanity in general. The impulse I describe, therefore, is not in any sense a selfish impulse. But it does begin with the sense of self as a concrete entity. Those who object to my thesis by saying that we must generalize it are not wholly wrong; they merely exaggerate. Truly I must be ready to generalize outward all the way. That is what justice consists of. But justice is not all of morality; there remains a circle of intensity which through its emphasis on the particular and the concrete continues to reflect what I have identified as the source of all sense of value—our sense of self.

Therefore, it is not only consonant with, but also required by, an ethics for human beings that one be entitled first of all to reserve an area of concern for oneself and then to move out freely from that area if one wishes to lavish that concern on others to whom one stands in concrete, personal relations. Similarly, a person is entitled to enjoy

23. *See* G. Warnock, The Object of Morality 79-80 (1971); Nagel, Book Review, 85 Yale L.J. 136, 140 (1975).

this extra measure of care from those who choose to bestow it upon him without having to justify this grace as either just or efficient. We may choose the individuals to whom we will stand in this special relation, or they may be thrust upon us, as in family ties. Perhaps we recognize family ties because, after all, there often has been an element of choice, but also because—by some kind of atavism or superstition—we identify with those who share a part of our biological natures.

In explicating the lawyer's relation to his client, my analogy shall be to friendship, where the freedom to choose and to be chosen expresses our freedom to hold something of ourselves in reserve, in reserve even from the universalizing claims of morality. These personal ties and the claims they engender may be all-consuming, as with a close friend or family member, or they may be limited, special-purpose claims, as in the case of the client or patient.[24] The special-purpose claim is one in which the beneficiary, the client, is entitled to all the special consideration *within* the limits of the relationship which we accord to a friend or a loved one. It is not that the claims of the client are less intense or demanding; they are only more limited in their scope. After all, the ordinary concept of friendship provides only an analogy, and it is to the development of that analogy that I turn.

D. *Special-Purpose Friends*

How does a professional fit into the concept of personal relations at all? He is, I have suggested, a limited-purpose friend. A lawyer is a friend in regard to the legal system. He is someone who enters into a personal relation with you—not an abstract relation as under the concept of justice. That means that like a friend he acts in your interests, not his own; or rather he adopts your interests as his own. I would call that the classic definition of friendship. To be sure, the lawyer's range of concern is sharply limited. But within that limited

24. This argument is, of course, just a fragment which must be fitted into a larger theory. This larger theory would have to explain, among other things, what the precise contents of the various personal roles might be and how conflicts between personal roles are to be resolved. My later discussion of permissible and impermissible tactics in legal representation deals with this conflict in one context. A complete theory would also have to spell out the relation between personal roles and duties to the larger collectivity. These latter duties to man in the abstract as opposed to concrete persons are the subject of principles of justice. I have no doubt that such abstract duties exist and that they can be very demanding. Roughly, I would adopt something like the principles put forward in J. Rawls, A Theory of Justice 54-117 (1971). I would require, however, that these principles of justice leave sufficient scope for the free definition and inviolability of personal relations—to a greater extent perhaps than Rawls allows. These systematic concerns are the subject of a larger work from which the present essay is drawn. The relation of principles of justice to other aspects of right and wrong is a principal concern of that larger work.

The Yale Law Journal Vol. 85: 1060, 1976

domain the intensity of identification with the client's interests is the same. It is not the specialized focus of the relationship which may make the metaphor inapposite, but the way in which the relation of legal friendship comes about and the one-sided nature of the ensuing "friendship." But I do insist upon the analogy, for in overcoming the arguments that the analogy is false, I think the true moral foundations of the lawyer's special role are illuminated and the utilitarian objections to the traditional conception of that role overthrown.

1. *The Professional Role as Socially Defined: The Content of the Relation*

The claims that are made on the doctor or lawyer are made within a social context and are defined, at least in part, by social expectations. Most strikingly, in talking about friendship the focus of the inquiry is quite naturally upon the free gift of the donor; yet in professional relationships it is the recipient's need for medical or legal aid which defines the relationship. So the source of the relationship seems to be located at the other end, that of the recipient. To put this disquiet another way, we might ask how recognizing the special claims of friendship in any way compels society to allow the doctor or the lawyer to define his role on the analogy of those claims. Why are these people not like other social actors designated to purvey certain, perhaps necessary, goods? Would we say that one's grocer, tailor, or landlord should be viewed as a limited-purpose friend? Special considerations must be brought forward for doctors and lawyers.[25]

A special argument is at hand in both cases. The doctor does not minister just to any need, but to health. He helps maintain the very physical integrity which is the concrete substrate of individuality. To be sure, so does a grocer or landlord. But illness wears a special guise: it appears as a critical assault on one's person. The needs to which the doctor ministers usually are implicated in crises going to one's concreteness and individuality, and therefore what one looks for is a kind of ministration which is particularly concrete, personal, individualized. Thus, it is not difficult to see why I claim that a doctor is a friend, though a special purpose friend, the purpose being defined by the special needs of illness and crisis to which he tends.

25. This question might be more troubling in a socialist system in which the profit motive is theoretically subordinated to the service of the general good. But my argument is that the needs for which lawyers and doctors provide are significantly different in kind from those met by other economic agents. Therefore, my argument about doctors and lawyers should be general enough to apply in either a free enterprise or a socialist system.

The Lawyer as Friend

But what, then, of the lawyer? Friendship and kinship are natural relations existing within, but not defined by, complex social institutions. Illness too is more a natural than social phenomenon. The response here requires an additional step. True, the special situations—legal relations or disputes—in which the lawyer acts as a limited-purpose friend are themselves a product of social institutions. But it does not follow that the role of the lawyer, which is created to help us deal with those social institutions, is defined by and is wholly at the mercy of the social good. We need only concede that at the very least the law must leave us a measure of autonomy, whether or not it is in the social interest to do so. Individuals have rights over and against the collectivity.[26] The moral capital arising out of individuals' concrete situations is one way of expressing that structure of rights, or at least part of it. It is because the law must respect the rights of individuals that the law must also create and support the specific role of legal friend. For the social nexus—the web of perhaps entirely just institutions—has become so complex that without the assistance of an expert adviser an ordinary layman cannot exercise that autonomy which the system must allow him. Without such an adviser, the law would impose constraints on the lay citizen (unequally at that) which it is not entitled to impose explicitly. Thus, the need which the lawyer serves in his special-purpose friendship may not be, as in the case of the doctor, natural, pre-social. Yet it is a need which has a moral grounding analogous to the need which the physician serves: the need to maintain one's integrity as a person. When I say the lawyer is his client's legal friend, I mean the lawyer makes his client's interests his own insofar as this is necessary to preserve and foster the client's autonomy within the law. This argument does not require us to assume that the law is hostile to the client's rights. All we need to assume is that even a system of law which is perfectly sensitive to personal rights would not work fairly unless the client could claim a professional's assistance in realizing that autonomy which the law recognizes.

2. *The Asymmetry of Motive and Duty: The Form of the Relation*

The institutional origin of the lawyer-client relationship is not its only characteristic which suggests that the analogy to natural friendship

26. For a recent forceful statement of this conception of rights, see Dworkin, *Taking Rights Seriously*, in IS LAW DEAD? 168 (E. Rostow ed. 1971). *See generally* Dworkin, *The Original Position*, 40 U. CHI. L. REV. 500, 522-28 (1973).

is vulnerable. In natural friendship the ideal relation is reciprocal; in legal friendship it is not. The lawyer is said to be the client's friend insofar as he is devoted to his client's interests, but it is no part of the ideal that the client should have any reciprocal devotion to the interests of his lawyer. Furthermore, I have argued that our right to be a friend to whomever we choose is a product of our individual autonomy. But in legal friendship the emphasis has been on the autonomy of the client, and it is the client who chooses the lawyer;[27] yet it is the lawyer who acts as a friend in the relation. And as a final contrast to natural friendship, the usual motive for agreeing or refusing to provide legal services is money. Indeed, when we speak of the lawyer's right to represent whomever he wishes, we are usually defending his moral title to represent whoever pays.

But recall that the concept of legal friendship was introduced to answer the argument that the lawyer is morally reprehensible to the extent that he lavishes undue concern on some particular person. The concept of friendship explains how it can be that a particular person may rightfully receive more than his share of care from another: he can receive that care if he receives it as an act of friendship. Although in natural friendship I emphasized the freedom to bestow, surely that freedom must imply a freedom to receive that extra measure of care. And it is the right of the client to receive such an extra measure of care (without regard, that is, to considerations of efficiency or fairness) as much as the lawyer's right to give it, that I have been trying to explicate. Thus, the fact that the care in legal friendship systematically runs all one way does not impair the argument.

Yet the unease persists. Is it that while I have shown that the lawyer has a right to help the "unworthy" client, I have not shown that whenever the lawyer exercises this right he does something which is morally worthy, entitling him to self-respect? I may have shown that the law is obliged to allow the "unworthy" client to seek legal help and the lawyer to give it. But have I also shown that every lawyer who avails himself of this legal right (his and the client's legal right) performs a *morally worthy* function? Can a good lawyer be a good person?

The lawyer acts morally because he helps to preserve and express the autonomy of his client vis-à-vis the legal system. It is not just that the lawyer helps his client accomplish a particular lawful purpose. Pornography may be legal, but it hardly follows that I perform a morally

27. The lawyer is generally free to decline to serve for any or no reason. But even that freedom is qualified; there will be times when there may be a duty to serve, as when a court appoints the lawyer to serve or when his declining may leave a person unrepresented. *See* pp. 1078-79, 1086-87 *infra*.

The Lawyer as Friend

worthy function if I lend money or artistic talent to help the pornographer flourish in the exercise of this right. What is special about legal counsel is that whatever else may stop the pornographer's enterprise, he should not be stopped because he mistakenly believes there is a legal impediment. There is no wrong if a venture fails for lack of talent or lack of money—no one's rights have been violated. But rights *are* violated if, through ignorance or misinformation about the law, an individual refrains from pursuing a wholly lawful purpose. Therefore, to assist others in understanding and realizing their legal rights is always morally worthy. Moreover, the legal system, by instituting the role of the legal friend, not only assures what it in justice must—the due liberty of each citizen before the law—but does it by creating an institution which exemplifies, at least in a unilateral sense, the ideal of personal relations of trust and personal care which (as in natural friendship) are good in themselves.

Perhaps the unease has another source. The lawyer does work for pay. Is there not something odd about analogizing the lawyer's role to friendship when in fact his so-called friendship must usually be bought? If the lawyer is a public purveyor of goods, is not the lawyer-client relationship like that underlying any commercial transaction? My answer is "No." The lawyer and doctor have obligations to the client or patient beyond those of other economic agents. A grocer may refuse to give food to a customer when it becomes apparent that the customer does not have the money to pay for it. But the lawyer and doctor may not refuse to give additional care to an individual who cannot pay for it if withdrawal of their services would prejudice that individual.[28] Their duty to the client or patient to whom they have made an initial commitment transcends the conventional quid pro quo of the marketplace. It is undeniable that money is usually what cements the lawyer-client relationship. But the content of the relation is determined by the client's needs, just as friendship is a response to another's needs. It is not determined, as are simple economic relationships, by the mere coincidence of a willingness to sell and a willingness to buy. So the fact that the lawyer works for pay does not seriously undermine the friendship analogy.

3. *Institutional Clients*

Another possible objection to my analysis concerns the lawyer in government or the lawyer for a corporation. My model posits a duty

28. *See* ABA Comm. on Professional Ethics, Opinions 56 (1967) (Informal Opinion No. 334); ABA Code of Professional Responsibility EC 2-31, 2-32. *Compare id.* DR 2-110 (C)(1)(f) *with id.* DR 2-110(A)(2).

of exclusive concern (within the law) for the interests of the client. This might be said to be inappropriate in the corporate area because larger economic power entails larger social obligations, and because the idea of friendship, even legal friendship, seems peculiarly far-fetched in such an impersonal context. After all, corporations and other institutions, unlike persons, are creatures of the state. Thus, the pursuit of their interests would seem to be especially subject to the claims of the public good. But corporations and other institutions are only formal arrangements of real persons pursuing their real interests. If the law allows real persons to pursue their interests in these complex forms, then why are they not entitled to loyal legal assistance, "legal friendship," in this exercise of their autonomy just as much as if they pursued their interests in simple arrangements and associations?

The real problem in these cases is that the definition of the client is complicated and elusive. The fundamental concepts remain the same, but we must answer a question which so far we could treat as straightforward: Who is the client? It is the corporation. But because the corporation is an institutional entity, institutional considerations enter into both the definition of the entity to whom the loyalty is owed and the substance of that loyalty. This is dramatically so in the case of a government lawyer, since his client might be thought to be the government of the United States, or the people of the United States, mediated by an intricate political and institutional framework. So it is said that a United States attorney is interested (unlike an ordinary lawyer) not only in winning his case but also in seeing that "justice is done," because his client's interests are served only if justice is done. Since more and more lawyers have only institutional clients, the introduction of institutional concerns into the definition of the representational obligation is virtually pervasive. From this some would conclude that my argument is inappropriate or at least anachronistic. I insist that my analogy is the correct one, that it is applicable to the institutional client, but that it must be combined in a complicated though wholly coherent way with other arguments about who one's client is and how that client's interests are to be identified.

III. The Two Criticisms and the Friendship Analogy

A. *The Choice of Clients: The Question of Distribution*

It is time to apply the concept of legal friendship to the first of the two criticisms with which this essay began: that the lawyer's ethic of loyalty to his client and his willingness to pick clients for any and every reason (usually, however, for money) result in a maldistribution

The Lawyer as Friend

of a scarce resource, the aid of counsel. It is this criticism which the lawyer shares with the doctor. The preceding sections demonstrated at least this much: that legal counsel—like medical care—must be considered a good, and that he who provides it does a useful thing. But this first criticism in no way questions that conclusion. On the contrary, precisely because medical care and legal counsel are benefits to those who receive them, the critic blames the individual doctor or lawyer for not bestowing his skills in the way which best meets the social need. The notion of legal friendship helps us respond to this criticism.

The lawyer-client relation is a personal relation, and legal counsel is a personal service. This explains directly why, *once the relation has been contracted,* considerations of efficiency or fair distribution cannot be allowed to weaken it. The relation itself is not a creature of social expediency (though social circumstances provide the occasion for it); it is the creature of moral right, and therefore expediency may not compromise the nature of the relation. This is true in medicine because the human need creates a relation of dependence which it would be a betrayal to compromise. In the lawyer-client relation, the argument is more complex but supports the same conclusion. The relation must exist in order to realize the client's rights against society, to preserve that measure of autonomy which social regulation must allow the individual. But to allow social considerations—even social regulations—to limit and compromise what by hypothesis is an entailment of the original grant of right to the individual is to take away with the left hand what was given with the right. Once the relation has been taken up, it is the client's needs which hold the reins—legally and morally.

If I have a client with legal needs, then neither another person with greater needs nor a court should be able to compel or morally oblige me to compromise my care for those needs. To hold differently would apply the concept of battlefield emergency care *(triage)* to the area of regular legal service. But doctors do not operate that way and neither should lawyers. For it is just the point about emergencies and wars that they create special, brutal, and depersonalized relations which civilization, by its very essence, must keep from becoming the general rule of social life.[29]

So much for the integrity of the relation once it has taken hold. But what of the initial choice of client? Must we not give some thought to efficiency and relative need at least at the outset, and does this not

29. Fried, *supra* note 9, at 245.

run counter to the picture of purely discretionary choice implicit in the notion of friendship? The question is difficult, but before considering its difficulties we should note that the preceding argumentation has surely limited its impact. We can now affirm that whatever the answer to this question, the individual lawyer does a morally worthy thing whomever he serves and, moreover, is bound to follow through once he has begun to serve. In this he is like the doctor. So if there is fault here it is a limited fault. What would be required for a lawyer to immunize himself more fully from criticism that he is unjust in his allocation of care? Each lawyer would have to consider at the outset of his career and during that career where the greatest need for his particular legal talents lies. He would then have to allocate himself to that area of greatest need. Surely there is nothing wrong in doing this (so long as loyalty to relations already undertaken is not compromised); but is a lawyer morally at fault if he does not lead his life in this way? It is at this point too that the metaphor of friendship and the concept of self as developed above suggest the response. But this time they will be viewed from another perspective—the lawyer's as opposed to the client's rights and liberties.

Must the lawyer expend his efforts where they will do the most good, rather than where they will draw the largest fee, provide the most excitement, prove most flattering to his vanity, whatever? Why must he? If the answer is that he must because it will produce the most good, then we are saying to the lawyer that he is merely a scarce resource. But a person is not a resource. He is not bound to lead his life as if he were managing a business on behalf of an impersonal body of stockholders called human society. It is this monstrous conception against which I argued earlier. Justice is not all; we are entitled to reserve a portion of our concern and bestow it where we will. We may bestow it entirely at our discretion as in the case of friendship, or we may bestow it at what I would call "constrained discretion" in the choice and exercise of a profession. That every exercise of the profession is morally worthwhile is already a great deal to the lawyer's credit. Just as the principle of liberty leaves one morally free to choose a profession according to inclination, so within the profession it leaves one free to organize his life according to inclination. The lawyer's liberty—moral liberty—to take up what kind of practice he chooses and to take up or decline what clients he will is an aspect of the moral liberty of self to enter into personal relations freely.

I would not carry this idea through to the bitter end. It has always been accepted, for instance, that a court may appoint an available lawyer to represent a criminal defendant who cannot otherwise find

The Lawyer as Friend

counsel. Indeed, I would be happy to acknowledge the existence of some moral duty to represent any client whose needs fit one's particular capacities and who cannot otherwise find counsel. This is not a large qualification to the general liberty I proclaim. The obligation is, and must remain, exceptional; it cannot become a kind of general conscription of the particular lawyer involved. And the obligation cannot compromise duties to existing clients. Furthermore, I would argue that this kind of representation should always be compensated—the duty to the client who cannot afford representation is initially a duty of society, not of the individual lawyer. I go this far for a number of reasons. If the representation is properly compensated, then the very need to appoint a lawyer will be exceptional, an anomaly arising in one of two ways: a fortuitous perturbation in the law of supply and demand or a general, if not concerted, professional boycott of this particular client. If the first is the reason, then the lifetime imposition on any one lawyer will be slight indeed. If it is the second, then the assertion of a duty, oddly enough, serves to express and strengthen the principle of the lawyer's independence. For the moral position of the lawyer rests on the claim that he takes up his client's interests irrespective of their merits.[30] By accepting from time to time the duty to represent the undesirable, he affirms this independence.

But surely I must admit that the need for legal representation far exceeds what such an unstructured, largely individualistic system could supply. Are there not vast numbers of needy people with a variety of legal problems who will never seek us out, but must be sought out? And what of the general responsibility that just laws be passed and justly administered? These are the obligations which the traditional conception of the lawyer, with his overriding loyalty to the paying client, is thought to leave unmet. At this point I yield no further. If the lawyer is really to be impressed to serve these admitted social needs, then his independence and discretion disappear, and he does indeed become a public resource cut up and disposed of by the public's needs. There would be no justice to such a conception. If there are really not enough lawyers to care for the needs of the poor, then it is grossly unfair to conscript the legal profession to fill those needs. If the

30. Carried further, this argument would hold that, as to clients who are within his area of competence, are able to pay his fee, and create no conflict with existing clients, a doctor or lawyer is perfectly justified in taking whoever happens to be next in the queue in his waiting room. Places in the queue may be determined by luck, the price system, or even some bureaucratic method of assignment. The doctor or lawyer does no wrong if he chooses not to concern himself with how the queue was formed. For a more detailed discussion of the moral significance of queuing, see C. FRIED, *supra* note 10, at 132-37.

obligation is one of justice, it is an obligation of society as a whole. It is cheap and hypocritical for society to be unwilling to pay the necessary lawyers from the tax revenues of all, and then to claim that individual lawyers are morally at fault for not choosing to work for free. In fact, as provision of legal services has come to be seen as necessary to ensure justice, society has indeed hired lawyers in an effort to meet that need.

Finally, I agree that the lawyer has a moral obligation to work for the establishment of just institutions generally, but entirely the wrong kind of conclusions have been drawn from this. Some of the more ecstatic critics have put forward the lawyer as some kind of anointed priest of justice—a high priest whose cleaving to the traditional conception of the lawyer's role opens him to the charge of apostasy.[31] But this is wrong. In a democratic society, justice has no anointed priests. Every citizen has the same duty to work for the establishment of just institutions,[32] and the lawyer has no special moral responsibilities in that regard. To be sure, the lawyer like any citizen must use all his knowledge and talent to fulfill that general duty of citizenship, and this may mean that there are special perspectives and opportunities for him.[33]

B. *The Choice of Means*

More difficult problems are posed by the conflict between the interests of the client and the interests of some other concrete and specified person to whom the client stands in opposition. How does my friendship analogy help to resolve the conflict which a lawyer must feel if his client asks him to lie, to oppress, or to conceal—to do something which is either illegal or felt by the lawyer to be immoral?

1. *Staying Within the Law*

I have defined the lawyer as a client's legal friend, as the person whose role it is to insure the client's autonomy within the law. Although I have indicated that the exercise of that autonomy is not always consonant with the public interest, it does not at all follow that the exercise of that autonomy, therefore, must also violate the law. If the legal system is itself sensitive to moral claims, sensitive to the rights of individuals, it must at times allow that autonomy to be exercised in ways that do not further the public interest. Thus, the

31. *See, e.g.*, M. GREEN, *supra* note 1, at 268-72.
32. *See* J. RAWLS, *supra* note 21, at 333-91.
33. *See* ABA CODE OF PROFESSIONAL RESPONSIBILITY Canon 8.

The Lawyer as Friend

principle that the lawyer must scrupulously contain his assistance and advocacy within the dictates of the law seems to me perfectly consistent with my view of the lawyer as the client's friend, who maintains the client's interests even against the interests of society.

To be sure, there may have been and may still be situations where the law grossly violates what morality defines as individual rights; and there have been lawyers who have stood ready to defy such laws in order to further their client's rights—the rights which the law should, but did not, recognize. Whatever might be said about those cases, the lawyer's conduct in them travels outside the bounds of legal friendship and becomes political friendship, political agitation, or friendship *tout court*. But that is not the case I am examining. The moral claims which a client has on his lawyer can be fully exhausted though that lawyer contains his advocacy strictly within the limits of the law.

A critic who fails to see the importance of the lawyer's moral status in assisting the autonomy of his client, may also be inclined to complain that the constraints of the law restrain his advocacy of truly just causes too much. Such a critic has things wrong at both ends. Just as it is false to argue that the lawyer is morally reprehensible if he furthers the interests of some clients and not others or some purposes and not others, so it is false to assume that the lawyer fails to have the proper zeal if he does for his client only what the law allows. The distinction between the role of the lawyer as a personal adviser and that of the lawyer as a citizen and member of the community should be quite clear. It is by controlling what the law is and by varying the interests that clients may lawfully pursue that social policy should be effectuated; it is not by deforming the role of the lawyer as the client's legal friend and asking him to curb his advocacy in that relationship.

This explains why in a reasonably just system which properly commands the lawyer's loyalty, he must confine his advocacy to what the rules of advocacy permit. He may not counsel his client to commit a crime, nor to destroy evidence, nor to perjure himself on the witness stand. Of course, here as elsewhere there will be borderline problems. It may not be a crime to lie to the judge who has asked the improper and prejudicial question of the defense attorney, but the implicit or quasi-official rules defining the limits of the lawyer's advocacy may nonetheless forbid this. Nothing in my model should discourage the lawyer from observing such limits scrupulously.

A very difficult question would arise if the law imposed upon the lawyer an obligation first to seek and then to betray his client's trust, an obligation to do that which seems outrageous and unjust. I do not mean to say that the resolution of this question would be easy, but my

The Yale Law Journal Vol. 85: 1060, 1976

analysis at least clearly locates the area in which a resolution should be sought. For such laws, if they are to be opposed, ought to be opposed as are other unjust laws, and not because the lawyer is in general entitled to travel outside the constraints of the law in protecting his client's interests. Maybe in such a dilemma a conscientious lawyer would keep his client's confidence as would a priest or a natural friend; but if conscientiousness requires this, it requires it as an act of disobedience and resistance to an unjust law, rather than as a necessary entailment of some extreme view of the lawyer's general role.

2. *Immoral Means*

I come to what seems to me one of the most difficult dilemmas of the lawyer's role. It is illustrated by the lawyer who is asked to press the unfair claim, to humiliate a witness, to participate in a distasteful or dishonorable scheme. I am assuming that in none of these situations does the lawyer do anything which is illegal or which violates the ethical canons of his profession; the dilemma arises if he acts in a way which seems to him personally dishonorable, but there are no sanctions—legal or professional—which he need fear.

This set of issues is difficult because it calls on the same principles which provide the justification for the lawyer's or the friend's exertions on behalf of the person with whom he maintains a personal relation. Only now the personal relation is one not of benefit but of harm. In meeting the first criticism, I was able to insist on the right of the lawyer as friend to give this extra weight to the interests of his client when the only competing claims were the general claims of the abstract collectivity. But here we have a specific victim as well as a specific beneficiary. The relation to the person whom we deceive or abuse is just as concrete and human, just as personal, as to the friend whom we help.

It is not open to us to justify this kind of harm by claiming that personal relations must be chosen, not thrust upon us. Personal relations are indeed typically chosen. If mere proximity could place on us the obligations of friendship, then there would soon be nothing left of our freedom to bestow an extra measure of care over and above what humanity can justly claim. But there is a personal relation when we inflict intentional harm; the fact that it is intentional reaches out and particularizes the victim. "Who is my neighbor?" is a legitimate question when affirmative aid is in question; it is quite out of order in respect to the injunction "Do not harm your neighbor." Lying, stealing, degrading, inflicting pain and injury are personal relations too. They are not like failing to benefit, and for that reason they are laid under a correspondingly stricter regime than abstract harms to the collectivity.[34] If I claim respect for my own concrete particularity, I must accord that respect to others. Therefore, what pinches here is the fact that the lawyer's personal engagement with the client is urging him to do that to his adversary which the very principles of personal engagement urge that he not do to anyone.

It is not wrong but somewhat lame to argue that the lawyer like the client has autonomy. From this argument it follows that the lawyer who is asked to do something personally distasteful or immoral (though perfectly legal) should be free either to decline to enter into the relationship of "legal friendship" or to terminate it.[35] And if the client can find a lawyer to do the morally nasty but legally permissible thing for him, then all is well—the complexities of the law have not succeeded in thwarting an exercise of autonomy which the law was not entitled to thwart. So long as the first lawyer is reasonably convinced that another lawyer can be found, I cannot see why he is less free to decline the morally repugnant case than he is the boring or poorly paid case. True, but lame, for one wants to know not whether one *may* refuse to do the dirty deed, but whether one is morally *bound* to refuse—bound to refuse even if he is the last lawyer in town and no one else will bail him out of his moral conundrum.

If personal integrity lies at the foundation of the lawyer's right to treat his client as a friend, then surely consideration for personal integrity—his own and others'—must limit what he can do in friendship. Consideration for personal integrity forbids me to lie, cheat, or humiliate, whether in my own interests or those of a friend, so surely they prohibit such conduct on behalf of a client, one's legal friend. This is the general truth, but it must be made more particular if it is to do service here. For there is an opposing consideration. Remember, the lawyer's special kind of friendship is occasioned by the right of

34. This point is discussed in detail in Fried, *Right and Wrong—Preliminary Considerations*, 5 J. LEGAL STUD. (June, 1976; forthcoming). The notion that abstention from harming particular persons is a special kind of duty is expressed in Ross's concept of nonmaleficence. *See* W. ROSS, *supra* note 15, at 21-22.

35. DR 2-110(B)(1) of the *Code of Professional Responsibility* makes withdrawal *mandatory* if the attorney "knows or it is obvious that his client is bringing the legal action, conducting the defense, or asserting a position in the litigation, or is otherwise having steps taken for him, merely for the purpose of harassing or maliciously injuring any person." DR 2-110(C)(1)(c) and (1)(d) *permit* a lawyer to seek withdrawal if the client either "[i]nsists that the lawyer pursue a course of conduct that is illegal or that is prohibited under the Disciplinary Rules" or "[b]y other conduct renders it unreasonably difficult for the lawyer to carry out his employment effectively." For an argument that an attorney should make his own moral judgments about whether and how to represent clients, see M. GREEN, *supra* note 1, at 268-89. *See also* J. AUERBACH, *supra* note 1, at 279-82.

The Yale Law Journal Vol. 85: 1060, 1976

the client to exercise his full measure of autonomy within the law. This suggests that one must not transfer uncritically the whole range of personal moral scruples into the arena of legal friendship. After all, not only would I not lie or steal for myself or my friends, I probably also would not pursue socially noxious schemes, foreclose on widows or orphans, or assist in the avoidance of just punishment. So we must be careful lest the whole argument unravel on us at this point.

Balance and structure are restored if we distinguish between kinds of moral scruples. Think of the soldier. If he is a citizen of a just state, where foreign policy decisions are made in a democratic way, he may well believe that it is not up to him to question whether the war he fights is a just war. But he is personally bound not to fire dum-dum bullets, not to inflict intentional injury on civilians, and not to abuse prisoners. These are personal wrongs, wrongs done by his person to the person of the victim.[36] So also, the lawyer must distinguish between wrongs that a reasonably just legal system permits to be worked by its rules and wrongs which the lawyer personally commits. Now I do not offer this as a rule which is tight enough to resolve all borderline questions of judgment. We must recognize that the border is precisely the place of friction between competing moral principles. Indeed, it is unreasonable to expect moral arguments to dispense wholly with the need for prudence and judgment.

Consider the difference between humiliating a witness or lying to the judge on one hand, and, on the other hand, asserting the statute of limitations or the lack of a written memorandum to defeat what you know to be a just claim against your client. In the latter case, if an injustice is worked, it is worked because the legal system not only permits it, but also defines the terms and modes of operation. Legal institutions have created the occasion for your act. What you do is not personal; it is a formal, legally-defined act. But the moral quality of lying or abuse obtains both without and within the context of the law. Therefore, my general notion is that a lawyer is morally entitled to act in this formal, representative way even if the result is an injustice, because the legal system which authorizes both the injustice (*e.g.*, the result following the plea of the statute of limitations) and the formal gesture for working it insulates him from personal moral responsibility. I would distinguish between the lawyer's own wrong and the wrong of the system used to advantage by the client.

The clearest case is a lawyer who calls to the attention of the court a controlling legal precedent or statute which establishes his client's

36. *See* Nagel, *War and Massacre*, 1 PHILOSOPHY & PUB. AFF. 123, 133-34, 136 (1972); Fried, *supra* note 34.

position even though that position is an unjust one. (I assume throughout, however, that this unjust law is part of a generally just and decent system. I am not considering at all the moral dilemmas of a lawyer in Nazi Germany or Soviet Russia.) Why are we inclined to absolve him of personal moral responsibility for the result he accomplishes? I assert it is because the wrong is wholly institutional; it is a wrong which does not exist and has no meaning outside the legal framework. The only thing preventing the client from doing this for himself is his lack of knowledge of the law or his lack of authority to operate the levers of the law in official proceedings. It is to supply that lack of knowledge or of formal capacity that the lawyer is in general authorized to act; and the levers he pulls are all legal levers.

Now contrast this to the lawyer who lies to an opposing party in a negotiation. I assume that (except in extreme cases akin to self-defense) an important lie with harmful consequences is an offense to the victim's integrity as a rational moral being, and thus the liar affirms a principle which denigrates his own moral status.[37] Every speech act invites belief, and so every lie is a betrayal. However, may a lawyer lie in his representative capacity? It is precisely my point that a man cannot lie just in his representative capacity; it is like stabbing someone in the back "just" in a representative capacity. The injury and betrayal are not worked by the legal process, but by an act which is generally harmful quite apart from the legal context in which it occurs.

There is an important class of cases which might be termed "lying in a representative capacity." An example is the lawyer presenting to the court a statement by another that he knows to be a lie, as when he puts a perjurious client-defendant on the stand. There is dispute as to whether and when the positive law of professional responsibility permits this,[38] but clearly in such instances it is not the lawyer who is lying. He is like a letter carrier who delivers the falsehood. Whether he is free to do that is more a matter of legal than personal ethics.

A test that might make the distinction I offer more palpable is this: How would it be if it were known in advance that lawyers would balk at the practice under consideration? Would it not be intolerable if it were known that lawyers would not plead the defense of the Statute of Frauds or of the statute of limitations? And would it not be quite

37. Here I follow Augustine, *Lying*, in TREATISES ON VARIOUS SUBJECTS (R. Deferrari ed. 1952), and I. KANT, THE METAPHYSICAL PRINCIPLES OF VIRTUE 90-93 (J. Ellington trans. 1964).

38. *Compare* M. FREEDMAN, *supra* note 7, at 27-41 *with* Noonan, *The Purposes of Advocacy and the Limits of Confidentiality*, 64 MICH. L. REV. 1485 (1966).

all right if it were known in advance that you cannot get a lawyer to lie for you, though he may perhaps put you on the stand to lie in your own defense?

A more difficult case to locate in the moral landscape is abusive and demeaning cross-examination of a complaining witness. Presumably, positive law and the canons of ethics restrict this type of conduct, but enforcement may be lax or interpretation by a trial judge permissive. So the question arises: What is the lawyer *morally* free to do? Here again I urge the distinction between exposing a witness to the skepticism and scrutiny envisaged by the law and engaging in a personal attack on the witness. The latter is a harm which the lawyer happens to inflict in court, but it is a harm quite apart from the institutional legal context. It is perhaps just a matter of style or tone, but the crucial point is that the probing must not imply that the lawyer believes the witness is unworthy of respect.

The lawyer is not morally entitled, therefore, to engage his own person in doing personal harm to another, though he may exploit the system for his client even if the system consequently works injustice. He may, but must he? This is the final issue to confront. Since he may, he also need not if there is anyone else who will do it. Only if there is no one else does the agony become acute. If there is an obligation in that case, it is an institutional obligation that has devolved upon him to take up a case, to make arguments when it is morally permissible but personally repugnant to him to do so. Once again, the inquiry is moral, for if the law enjoins an obligation against conscience, a lawyer, like any conscientious person, must refuse and pay the price.

The obligation of an available lawyer to accept appointment to defend an accused is clear. Any moral scruples about the proposition that no man should be accused and punished without counsel are not morally well-founded. The proposition is intended to enhance the autonomy of individuals within the law. But if you are the last lawyer in town, is there a moral obligation to help the finance company foreclose on the widow's refrigerator? If the client pursues the foreclosure in order to establish a legal right of some significance, I do not flinch from the conclusion that the lawyer is bound to urge this right. So also if the finance company cannot foreclose because of an ideological boycott by the local bar. But if all the other lawyers happen to be on vacation and the case means no more to the finance company than the resale value of one more used refrigerator, common sense says the lawyer can say no. One should be able to distinguish between establishing a legal right and being a cog in a routine, repetitive

The Lawyer as Friend

business operation, part of which just happens to play itself out in court.

Conclusion

I do not imagine that what I have said provides an algorithm for resolving some of these perennial difficulties. Rather, what I am proposing is a general way of looking at the problem, a way of understanding not so much the difficult borderline cases as the central and clear ones, in the hope that the principles we can there discern will illuminate our necessarily approximate and prudential quest for resolution on the borderline. The notion of the lawyer as the client's legal friend, whatever its limitations and difficulties, does account for a kind of callousness toward society and exclusivity in the service of the client which otherwise seem quite mysterious. It justifies a kind of scheming which we would deplore on the part of a lay person dealing with another lay person—even if he were acting on behalf of a friend.

But these special indulgences apply only as a lawyer assists his client in his legal business. I do not owe my client my political assistance. I do not have to espouse his cause when I act as a citizen. Indeed, it is one of the most repellent features of the American legal profession—one against which the barrister-solicitor split has to some extent guarded the English profession—that many lawyers really feel that they are totally bought by their clients, that they must identify with their clients' interests far beyond the special purpose of advising them and operating the legal system for them. The defendants' antitrust lawyer or defendants' food and drug lawyer who writes articles, gives speeches, and pontificates generally about the evils of regulation may believe these things; but too often he does so because it is good for business or because he thinks that such conduct is what good representation requires.[39] In general, I think it deplorable that lawyers have specialized

39. The implications of this idea are particularly important for the so-called Washington lawyer (wherever he might be) who is hired to represent his client before agencies and legislatures contemplating new law. This may put us on one of the borderlines I do not pretend to resolve definitively, yet I think we can get an idea of how to think about these cases too. To the extent that such representation involves participation in a formal proceeding in which laws or regulations are drafted and technical competence is required, the task is *closer* to the traditional task of the lawyer as I have sketched it, and the legal friend concept is more appropriate. To the extent that the representation involves (wholly lawful) deployment of political pressures, inducements, and considerations, it is closer to being political action, and thus to requiring the kind of overriding concern for the common good that should motivate all political actors. Certainly it is absurd that a man should seek to be insulated from moral judgment of his accomplishments as a political string-puller or publicist by the defense that he was only doing it for money.

not only in terms of subject matter—that may or may not be a good thing—but in terms of plaintiffs or defendants, in terms of the position that they represent.[40]

There is a related point which cuts very much in the opposite direction. It is no part of my thesis that the *client* is not morally bound to avoid lying to the court, to pay a just debt even though it is barred by the statute of limitations, to treat an opposite party in a negotiation with humanity and consideration for his needs and vulnerability, or to help the effectuation of policies aimed at the common good. Further, it is no part of my argument to hold that a lawyer must assume that the client is not a decent, moral person, has no desire to fulfill his moral obligations, and is asking only what is the minimum that he must do to stay within the law. On the contrary, to assume this about anyone is itself a form of immorality because it is a form of disrespect between persons. Thus in very many situations a lawyer will be advising a client who wants to effectuate his purposes within the law, to be sure, but who also wants to behave as a decent, moral person. It would be absurd to contend that the lawyer must abstain from giving advice that takes account of the client's moral duties and his presumed desire to fulfill them. Indeed, in these situations the lawyer experiences the very special satisfaction of assisting the client not only to realize his autonomy within the law, but also to realize his status as a moral being. I want to make very clear that my conception of the lawyer's role in no way disentitles the lawyer from experiencing this satisfaction. Rather, it has been my purpose to explicate the less obvious point that there is a vocation and a satisfaction even in helping Shylock obtain his pound of flesh or in bringing about the acquittal of a guilty man.[41]

Finally, I would like to return to the charge that the morality of role and personal relationship I offer here is almost certain to lead to the diversion of legal services from areas of greatest need. It is just my point, of course, that when we fulfill the office of friend—legal, medical, or friend *tout court*—we do right, and thus it would be a great wrong to place us under a general regime of always doing what will "do the most good." What I affirm, therefore, is the moral liberty of a lawyer to make his life out of what personal scraps and shards of

40. In England barristers are regularly hired by the government in all manner of litigation, thereby accomplishing the many-sidedness I call for here. *See* Q. JOHNSTONE & D. HOPSON, LAWYERS AND THEIR WORK 371-75 (1967). Why should this not be done in the United States? Perhaps there is fear that this might simply become the occasion for a suspect form of patronage.

41. This point is due to Albert Sacks and Richard Stewart.

The Lawyer as Friend

motivation his inclination and character suggest: idealism, greed, curiosity, love of luxury, love of travel, a need for adventure or repose; only so long as these lead him to give wise and faithful counsel. It is the task of the social system as a whole, and of all its citizens, to work for the conditions under which everyone will benefit in fair measure from the performance of doctors, lawyers, teachers, and musicians. But I would not see the integrity of these roles undermined in order that the millennium might come sooner. After all, it may never come, and then what would we be left with?

[6]

Correspondence

The Lawyer as Friend

To the Editors:

We are, most of us, lawyers, or perhaps even worse, makers thereof. We would, most of us, also be good people if we could. It would be sad, socially and personally, if the act of being a lawyer necessarily conflicted in some way with being ethically "good." It will not do, however, either socially or personally, if we choose to avoid whatever necessary conflict there might be, not by changing the reality of ourselves, our profession, or our society, but by changing only the way we talk about who we are, what we do, and how we and those things function in modern American life. Thus, while we do not reject Charles Fried's conclusion[1] that good lawyers can be good people,[2] we must reject his route.

That route is roughly as follows. First, state the problem: "Can a good lawyer be a good person?"[3] Second, scotch the obvious initial response (variously phrased versions of "Why the hell not?") by pointing out that lawyers as lawyers occasionally do some morally disquieting things. In particular, they often choose their clients in a way that does not necessarily optimize—indeed, often seems antithetical to—group welfare;[4] and, in the name of serving the chosen client, they sometimes intentionally do grievous harm to other concrete individuals.[5] Third, take such an objection with tentative seriousness. Then, finally, overcome it by arguing: (1) a friend can do these nasty things and still be a good person; (2) a lawyer is like a friend; and, therefore, (3) a lawyer can be a good person. The only sticky parts are establishing that both (1) and (2) are true.

I

Let's start with friends. That's who a lawyer under this scheme will have to be like in order to be good. So first, what *is* a friend? Well, a friend is apparently a person who "acts in [someone else's] interests, not his own; or

1. Fried, *The Lawyer as Friend: The Moral Foundations of the Lawyer-Client Relation*, 85 YALE L.J. 1060 (1976). Fried's present work seems to be more or less a logical outgrowth, or at least a capitalizing upon the philosophical suggestions, of two of his prior books. C. FRIED, AN ANATOMY OF VALUES (1970); C. FRIED, MEDICAL EXPERIMENTATIONS: PERSONAL INTEGRITY AND SOCIAL POLICY (1974).

2. Or at least not worse people than people-in-general. *See* p. 580 *infra*.

3. Fried, *supra* note 1, at 1060.

4. "Critics contend that it is wasteful and immoral that some of the finest talent in the legal profession is devoted to the intricacies of, say, corporate finance or elaborate estate plans, while important public and private needs for legal services go unmet." *Id.* at 1062.

5. "Examples are discrediting a nervous but probably truthful complaining witness or taking advantage of the need or ignorance of an adversary in a negotiation." *Id.* (footnote omitted).

rather he adopts [someone else's] interests as his own."[6] Professor Fried, at any rate, "would call that the classic definition of friendship."[7] Being a friend, therefore, seems to involve undertaking a relationship very much like the one Professor Fried ascribes to lawyers, one which "permits, even demands, an allocation of . . . time, passion, and resources in ways that are not always maximally conducive to the greatest good of the greatest number,"[8] and authorizes "tactics which procure advantages for [some distinct other] at the direct expense of some identified opposing party."[9] If so, then friends might find it impossible to be good persons too.

But what if it could be shown that acting in ways not maximally conducive to the good of the greatest number, and knowingly inflicting harm on particular others, were not bars to the personal goodness of friends? That is exactly what Professor Fried tries to show. His argument proceeds in two stages, both of which demand the closest attention.

First, says Fried, it is clear that we may, each of us, choose to prefer ourselves over the collectivity. To deny that is to obviate all moral discourse, since moral ascription implies free and choosing beings—a conception totally incompatible with a duty always to act in the interest of the greatest social good. If we want to talk of morality, we must postulate the freedom to choose to act in a "nonutilitarian" way, at least with respect to ourselves. Therefore some selfish actions must be good; if all were bad, morality itself would be vacuous.

Next comes the jump from self-preferring to concrete-other-preferring. The critical passage is a short one:

> [W]e recognize an authorization to take the interests of particular concrete persons more seriously and to give them priority over the interests of the wider collectivity. One who provides an expensive education for his own children surely cannot be blamed because he does not use these resources to alleviate famine or to save lives in some distant land. Nor does he blame himself. Indeed, our intuition that an individual is authorized to prefer identified persons standing close to him over the abstract interests of humanity finds its sharpest expression in our sense that an individual is entitled to act with something less than impartiality to that person who stands closest to him—the person that he is.[10]

The aggregate move, then, is to redefine goodness by asserting nonutilitarian criteria. It is not "bad" to favor oneself and one's friends and relations over "the wider collectivity" (even if the latter needs your favor more; even if, indeed, you make it worse off by your self-and-buddies regard), because—well, because people in fact *do* favor friends and kinfolk over abstract people-in-general, and don't seem to feel guilty about it. So doing it can't be bad.[11]

6. *Id.* at 1071.
7. *Id.*
8. *Id.* at 1061.
9. *Id.* at 1062.
10. *Id.* at 1066.
11. Fried actually begins the argument by rejecting the utilitarian justifications for the "goodness" of friendship, noting quite rightly that such an instrumental justification

Correspondence

There are a number of unkind things that can be said about this argument.[12] Assume for the moment that grounding an ethical system on what people in fact believe and do were not twaddle.[13] Even given that, Professor Fried's ideas about how people feel about each other is most likely not sufficiently true. Is it accurate to say that one "surely cannot be blamed" for preferring one's own children as the objects of attention, if other people's children are actually starving? *How* expensive an education can one provide at the expense of others' lives, health, or even comfort? Do all or most people really deeply object to redistributive taxation, which cuts into their ability fully to favor themselves and their kin over other needs of other people? When they do, do they really not court blame, even from themselves? After all, while the currently preferred translation of "*caritas*" may be "love," most modern religions don't exclude from the concept the idea of a reasonably abstract charity.

We do, of course, believe that Professor Fried's "intuition" is to some extent correct. That one can, in most cultures, favor oneself and one's friends and relations *more than* abstract others without being labelled or feeling basically corrupt is, we think, an obviously accurate anthropological observation. But the difficult issue in all of those cultures is not really *if*, but who, in what ways, and how much. If one is going to try to validate as "good" some level of selective selfishness by pointing out that some level exists in fact in the relevant society (that is, if one is going to counter a thoroughgoing utilitarian standard by showing that hardly anyone always believes or acts that way), one is obliged to do more than point it out. For almost no one[14] believes that totally individualistic selfishness is "good" either.[15]

Professor Fried's key move, then, is to point out that unstinting utili-

cannot be validated empirically, and that its strictures are seemingly contrary to the normal expectations of modern life. *Id.* at 1067-68. This rejection is a potential source of embarrassment, however, since he eventually returns to quasiutilitarian props for a tottering nonutilitarian argument:

> [I]n engaging that aspect of myself with the concrete aspects of others, I realize special values for both of us. Quite simply, the individualized relations of love and friendship . . . have a different, more intense aspect than do the cooler, more abstract relations of love and service to humanity in general.

Id. at 1070.

12. Some of which are simply picky. For example, that it's ultimately circular, or at least self-sealing when isolated and extended a bit. It goes something like this. Question: "Can it ever be morally 'good' to lavish one's care on one concrete individual to the detriment of the wider social good?" Answer: "Yes, when that lavishing is done within the dyad of friendship." Definition of a friend: "Someone on whom such care is lavished." Conclusion: "We cannot gainsay any such selfish (socially nonoptimal) acts, since the doing of them makes the relationship one of (albeit, 'limited purpose') friendship, and friendship validates the doing."

13. While one of us has argued elsewhere that such an effort is ultimately doomed, *see* Leff, *Law and Technology: On Shoring Up a Void*, 8 OTTAWA L. REV. 536, 542 (1976); Leff, Book Review, 29 STAN. L. REV. 43 (forthcoming; Apr. 1977), a very sophisticated version of the effort has at least initial plausibility. *See* R. UNGER, KNOWLEDGE AND POLITICS (1975).

14. The qualification is in deference to arguments like those in R. NOZICK, ANARCHY, STATE AND UTOPIA (1974), but even in that work it is not clear how total is the commitment to total self-regard.

15. Including Professor Fried. *See* Fried, *supra* note 1, at 1062 n.8.

The Yale Law Journal Vol. 86: 573, 1977

tarianism (which he characterizes as treating everyone, including oneself, as an equal candidate for one's help and regard[16]) is hardly typical of human society; we all favor some people over others, notably ourselves. The more subtle "utilitarian" might answer that Fried has missed the point. What counts is not what people believe and do, but what they *ought* to.[17] But even if the "utilitarian" accepts the questionable idea that virtue is what we in fact want to do, and not something a bit more aspirational than that, he may still ask what the operational content of Fried's alternative self-and-favored-few ethic might be. The key question is not whether utilitarianism can be allowed to swallow all of ethics, but where "individual autonomy," Professor Fried's intuitionistic alternative, itself starts to gag.[18]

That question is particularly important to a critical view of Professor Fried's analysis because he is, at bottom, arguing that since people can favor their friends, even at substantial cost to nonfriends, lawyers can favor their clients the same way. Although Fried's argument, even before the shift from friend-friend to lawyer-client, seems to take some account of the possibility that this selective favoring is not permissible without limit,[19] the question of *creating* the friendship nexus is left all but unaddressed.[20] Can one totally arbitrarily (as a matter of "individual autonomy") choose whom one wants as a friend and then favor him? ("I wouldn't do this for

16. *Id.* at 1068-69.

17. Fried's essay exhibits, from time to time, some ambiguity about whether the metaphor of friendship is empirical or normative, making the argument a bit elusive, if not thaumatropic. At the critical points, however, the propositions seem to be empirical. If, on the other hand, Fried intended his statements to be ideals rather than facts, the flaws would be even more serious. It is curious enough to derive an ethical postulate from an empirical datum, but odder still to derive it from nothing. And finally, although Fried begins by rejecting utilitarian notions, *see* note 11 *supra*, he eventually does return to flirt with them.

18. There is, moreover, another bit of ambiguity in the structure of the argument. At times the "goodness" of acts of friendship seems to spring out of and around the relationship itself; at other times the goodness of the lawyer's acting seems to be predicated on the lawyer's autonomy as a person.

After the tour through love and friendship has nearly ended, Fried asserts that he has "argued that our right to be a friend to whomever we choose is a product of our individual autonomy." Fried, *supra* note 1, at 1074. We can't locate that argument exactly (*but see* p. 577 & note 21 *infra*), but even if we could we would be unimpressed: the autonomy argument is seriously flawed even as a matter of law, assuming (as we do) that law, too, expresses our collective sense of the "good" and the "wrong." True enough that one's choice of vocation is and should be unfettered by law. But equally true, the available choices are those among various callings all of which have some positive intrusions from felt social necessity. No one is ever coerced into becoming the manager of a public utility, but once one is that sort of person the freedom to refuse to deal equally with the public in that capacity is not unrestrained. Indeed, one might suppose that even professionals may not engage in those concerted refusals to deal which their autonomous collective hearts might otherwise desire. Law *and* morality limit autonomy all the time; indeed, that's what they're for. Citing the lawyer's autonomy-as-a-person therefore begs the important issues of whether autonomously following the biggest fee is sufficiently causative of social "bad" to justify its being marginally corralled.

19. *See* Fried, *supra* note 1, at 1066 (lying to save friends and relations).

20. It may again be the case that Professor Fried experienced some ängst about this lacuna, for when he returned to the two problem cases with which the essay began, he gave up on using friendship as the source of moral validation. To combine two criticisms (one regarding the missing link of choosing, and the other concerning the slippage in

Correspondence

anyone else, Ms. Borgia, but for old time's sake I'll see if I can free up a couple of bottles for you.")

Let us, however, pass on from the problems of choosing friends. For we are talking about lawyers, and we know how lawyers, most of the time, choose their clients. Assume then that the demands of individual autonomy[21] require that people be allowed to choose friends any way they want and then to favor them over nonfriends thereafter. *Is* a lawyer like a friend? Does the simile hold?[22]

Well, according to Professor Fried's own "classic definition of friendship": ". . . a friend . . . acts in your interests, not his own; or rather he adopts your interests as his own."[23] There is, therefore, at least one overlap

the logic of the argument), we should iterate the point just made, that none of this "friendship-acts" business goes to validate an initial *choice* of flush over impecunious potential clients; yet that very choice is the "test" which Fried has adopted for himself. To put it another way, suppose we were to admit, arguendo, that counseling dyads once undertaken imply duties like those of friendship, and that such duties deflect the claims of moral entitlement made by others. We still would not have gotten very far toward resolving the question of whether it is good to choose a wealthy businessman to be dyadic with as opposed to three or four (or even one) of the impecunious tenants of a slum. So what, that is to say, that lawyers may ideally be "friends" to such recipients as they may select? Fried's second problem case equally exposes the irrelevance of friendship. Even if it is "good" to injure *A* for the sake of *B* when *B* is already related by friendship, is it good to choose to be *B*'s friend when before the friendship sets in it is reasonable to believe that becoming *B*'s friend will necessitate doing harm to *A*?

All right, then. Maybe it is "good" for us to prefer ourselves, because we're us. And maybe we can even, morally, prefer our kin because no one else will, or because we're genetically programmed to do so, or whatever. But then, when we face the prospect of choosing other "friends," how can we validate that? "Friendship as good" doesn't take us very far, as the shift in Professor Fried's own argument makes clear.

21. *See* Fried, *supra* note 1, at 1078.

22. It might appear to the unsophisticated that this intermediate step is not strictly necessary. Since it was so easy to define a friend as good, why not just do the same for the lawyer? That is, why not just declare that since lawyers favor clients over the collectivity, and at the expense of particular others too, and don't feel guilty about it, then they can't be bad either? There are several problems with proceeding that way. First, it makes the callow prestidigitation of the original friendship-justifying move too painfully obvious. Second, insofar as the friendship move was worked by declaring human opinion to be the measure of goodness, the pseudoempiricism doesn't work nearly as well. Lawyers frequently do feel guilty about what they do for a living, and the public pretty thoroughly agrees that they ought to. So the metaphorical move is an absolute necessity for Professor Fried, for he must say that while human opinion and intuition defines the good, in this case it happens to be wrong. He cannot, that is, accept guilt and blame as the sole source of morality; he must convince people to change their views. And for persuasion there's nothing like the metaphor.

23. Fried, *supra* note 1, at 1071. It is meet to point out here that the metaphor fails to deflect the contrary common-sense notion that lawyers should sometimes be *more* constrained in pursuing their friendship than others need to be. If, for example, one prefers his friend to the collectivity when he is acting only as friend, he has typically injured others only in the sense that he has withheld from others what they may never have had to begin with. But when one acts as lawyer, he is often in the position of doing more than just lavishing protection on his client. His client, to put it crassly, often asks him to take away from some other person something which that other person already "has," or to give as little as possible in return. *See* p. 579 *infra*. We do not propose here that this observation is a sufficient basis upon which to establish an egalitarian ethic for lawyers. We mean only to indicate that Fried's route has done nothing much to establish the contrary position.

between reasonable perceptions of the friend-friend and the lawyer-client relationships. But note that even that single similarity comes about for the most part because Professor Fried has chosen totally to *define* friendship by reference to one (of many) of its indicia. In effect, a lawyer is like a friend even to this limited extent because, for Professor Fried, a friend is like a lawyer.

But let us pass even that by conceding that one of the indicia of some friendships is this lawyer-like adoption of another's interests. Ah, but the differences, oh my, the differences, between the affective commitment to friends' causes and the espousal of those of clients.

It is, for example, extremely rare that the lawyer's interest diverges from his client's during the course of representation. Under how many circumstances, after all, does it cost the lawyer anything to further his client's cause, except, of course, the use of his labor and time—for which the lawyer in any event is getting paid? One can think of short-run attorney-client conflicts of interest. If a lawyer chooses to go into contempt (and perhaps into jail) to preserve his client's secrets, that might present such a case. But even there the cost would seem to be only short-run; it can't be bad for business for the lawyer to show that much loyalty, and the "sacrifice," appropriately priced and discounted, might not be one at all.[24]

Moreover, except in reasonably rare circumstances, if the attorney finds espousing his client's cause too morally "costly," both the formal and unwritten standards of the profession permit him to get rid of the client.[25] Not always, of course, but under most real-world circumstances he can just resign the whole bother. And when there is a flat conflict between the attorney and his client, the same rules allow the attorney to be loyal to himself, even if that involves using the client's confidences against him.[26]

Still further, insofar as an attorney can predict in advance some conflict between his own interests or values and those of some potential client, he is almost perfectly free to refuse to take on that client in the first place.[27] Indeed, some of the most moralistic of commentators suggest that an attorney has a duty not to represent clients whose aims in life bruise the attorney's personal views of the right, the good, or the public interest.[28]

Even more striking than that, the attorney is in almost all cases allowed under the rules to find in one particularly important characteristic of the client perfect justification for refusing to serve—the client's lack of money.[29] Insofar as the lawyer allocates his energies and skills, his friendship within

24. There are other hypotheses as well about the motivations for such sacrifice: Perhaps it is fealty not to the client, but to the profession-cum-client; or to the structure of the system which requires confidentiality; or even, more selfishly, to one's own moral sense, operable whether or not there is a living client thus to be protected.

25. *See* ABA Code of Professional Responsibility DR 7-101; *id.* EC 7-9, 7-10. *But see id.* DR 2-110.

26. *See, e.g., id.* DR 4-101(C)(4).

27. *Id.* EC 5-2. *But cf. id.* EC 5-1 (lawyer's duties once lawyer-client relationship has been established).

28. The question is addressed in, among others, M. Freedman, Lawyers' Ethics in an Adversary System 49 (1975); and Califano, *The Washington Lawyer: When to Say No,* in Verdicts on Lawyers 187 (R. Nader & M. Green eds. 1976).

29. ABA Code of Professional Responsibility EC 2-25.

Correspondence

the legal system[30] is bought and paid for, if not in advance, at least at prudently planned intervals.

In addition, whatever the actual contingency and chilliness of the lawyer's relationship to his client, it is firm, wholehearted, and ardent compared to the client's reciprocal feelings and actions. A client has no legal, and most often no felt, duty to his lawyer (except to pay his fee) not shared by any other member of the public (*viz.*, not to commit a tort against him).

Thus the normal mode of the attorney-client relationship may better be described as follows: A lawyer is a person who, without expecting any reciprocal activity or inclination thereto, will attempt to forward or protect the interests of a client, within the rules of a legal system, so long as he is paid a sufficient amount to do so, and so long as doing so does not inflict any material unforeseen personal costs. That's "friendship"?

Thus almost the only similarity between the friend-friend nexus and the attorney-client one is Professor Fried's adoption-of-interests congruence, and even that depends mostly on trivializing the definition of friendship. True, metaphors do not assert identities. But there *are* limits. If it is proper to say a lawyer is like a friend, it is equally graceful to describe the ruddy complexion of one's beloved by "My love is as a pizza pie."

But once the power (such as it is) of the friendship metaphor dissipates, then all that is left is that a lawyer's autonomy[31] allows him to choose his clients as he will (mostly in such a way as to maximize his own income); and, once having chosen them in this self-serving way, he may, perhaps must, get what they want in any way that is not illegal (or in Professor Fried's terminology "insofar as this is necessary to preserve and foster the client's autonomy within the law"[32]). Why is it possible to do that and be "good" too? The answer is an interesting one: If the system of law is fundamentally just,[33] and if it provides that persons in the clutches of that system be fully represented, then it is not unjust (or morally bad) to do the representing, even if some of the things one must do in the course of that representation look not only not socially optimal, but downright nasty (like cross-examining a rape complainant to a quivering jelly about her prior chastity). That answer is interesting because it is so obvious; it is the ordinary rule-utilitarian lawyer-defending argument after all.[34]

Therefore, even Professor Fried's argument against the "utilitarian" critique of lawyering was at least partly disingenuous. There may indeed be some naive utilitarians in the world who would criticize lawyers for not seeking social optimization with each and every one of their professional decisions, but there are not many. Against such critics it is indeed easy to say (and Professor Fried indeed finally says) that while some *acts* are by themselves morally questionable, the system those acts serve and are part of is, if not perfect, morally better than any feasible alternative. But that

30. Fried, *supra* note 1, at 1071-72.
31. *Id.* at 1078-79; *see* note 18 *supra*.
32. Fried, *supra* note 1, at 1072.
33. Professor Fried quite rightly finds this to be a more interesting case to discuss than, say, Nazi Germany's legal system. *Id.* at 1084-85.
34. And there comes to be, after all is said and done, not much to distinguish Professor Fried from Dean Freedman. *See* M. FREEDMAN, *supra* note 28, at 43-49.

The Yale Law Journal Vol. 86: 573, 1977

opens up the following problem: What if the rule-utilitarian answers that it is the system—the rule—that is more unjust than it needs to be? Is it still "good" to serve a bad system within its own rules? Apparently it is, at least for Professor Fried. For when he actually gets to addressing the two charges raised against the goodness of lawyers—that they choose whom to help without regard to social optima and that they hurt determinate others while serving their some—it goes like this: (1) if choosing those who can pay is naughty, it is society's fault for not assuring that everybody can pay;[35] and (2) if a lawyer wrecks some third party in serving his client, "a lawyer is morally entitled to act in this . . . way even if the result is an injustice, because the legal system which authorizes both the injustice . . . and the formal gesture for working it insulates him from personal moral responsibility."[36]

II

All right, why the big fuss? What difference does it make? This, after all, is not the first time in history that someone lit on the wrong metaphor and pushed it, though not far, easily too far. Well, it matters because we are lawyers and, more exposed than that, teachers of lawyers, and it can do nothing but harm, to us and our clients, to distort what we are really doing, we *and* our clients. For (subject to some important qualifications to be discussed in a moment) lawyers and clients are not being "friends" to each other, and together they are not being "friends" to anyone else. Indeed, the relationship between lawyers and clients and, together, as to others is frequently almost the antithesis of friendship. It is often a relationship not of concrete humanity or friendly individuation but of bureaucratic manipulation, both of each other and, joined for the nonce, of others still. That is one of the reasons why lawyers are hated so much and why they are so frequently moved to hate themselves.

Let us suggest a different approach from Professor Fried's, just as an experiment. Instead of encasing something called "the lawyer-client relation" in an opaque abstraction pudding, let us try to picture—with just a little specificity—what it really is that clients ask lawyers to do for them, and what lawyers thereupon do.

Well, lawyers do lots of things for clients. They fill out forms, for instance, and draft documents—letters, contracts, memoranda, what all. They take part in negotiations with both governmental agencies and private parties. They tell clients what their chances are of getting into legal trouble with other people, including governments, if they do or don't do something, and suggest how they can arrange to get more or less what they want without those risks. When their clients are challenged at law on the grounds that they have already done something of the sort, lawyers try to eliminate or reduce recompense or punishment. When their clients believe that something nasty has been done to them, lawyers help them get protection, recompense, or revenge. All of these things lawyers do across the whole range of law, with respect to crimes, and torts, and contracts, and property, and domestic relations, and so on. In each instance they try to

35. Fried, *supra* note 1, at 1079.
36. *Id.* at 1084.

Correspondence

help their clients keep or get what under the law may very well be theirs, be it goods, money, or freedom.[37]

In most of these activities there is one invariant element. The client comes to a lawyer to be aided when he feels he is being treated, or wishes to treat someone else, not as a whole other person, but (at least in part) as a threat or hindrance to the client's satisfaction in life. The client has fallen, or wishes to thrust someone else, into the impersonal hands of a just and angry bureaucracy. When one desires help in those processes whereby and wherein people are treated as means and not as ends, then one comes to lawyers, to us. Thus, if you feel the need for a trope to express what a lawyer largely is, perhaps this will do: A lawyer is a person who on behalf of some people treats other people the way bureaucracies treat all people—as nonpeople. Most lawyers are free-lance bureaucrats, not tied to any major established bureaucracy, who can be hired to use, typically in a bureaucratic setting, bureaucratic skills—delay, threat, wheedling, needling, aggression, manipulation, paper passing, complexity, negotiation, selective surrender, almost-genuine passion—on behalf of someone unable or unwilling to do all that for himself.

This lawyerlike behavior, of course, need not always appear quite as icily nasty as its general description suggests. Especially when the client is an isolated person being injured by some true bureaucracy behaving like either a steamroller or a brick wall, helping the client looks and feels noble, even lovable. And when one thinks of those vast areas of lawyering not part of the usual litigation-fixated public image—planning, structuring, counseling—one tends to find relationships of lawyer and client, and of lawyer and client and third party, very much less bureaucratic and impersonal in technique, in purpose, and in tone.

But even conceding all that, and conceding that these "warmer" relationships do make up much more of legal practice than is usually realized, still, what lawyers do much of the time, even while only counseling, is help people who cannot in the particular instance relate successfully to each other as whole human beings to relate to each other as counters in each other's self-protecting and self-maximizing life plans.

Does that make lawyers bad people? Well, it does at least make them

37. We are not unmindful of alternative, and seemingly discrete, descriptions, which center about the "counseling" role of attorneys: "Counseling is a process that fosters party well-being. It is initiated by and because of the uncertainty and/or disagreeability relating to a party's experience." Redmount, *Humanistic Law Through Legal Counseling*, 2 CONN. L. REV. 98, 99 (1969). Goodpaster, Redmount, Watson, and Shaffer are the central expositors of such a view, which focuses on, as Shaffer might put it, counseling in the Sartrean sense of the word. Several points, however, should be made. First, each of these scholars presents the empathic viewpoint as a possibility and an aspiration rather than (like Fried) as a ubiquitous thing-in-itself. Secondly, the lawyer-client relationship, when it truly bears these empathic attributes, most often exhibits them *not* in circumstances that lead to the problematic cases Fried is discussing. And thirdly, this "better way" is indeed ultimately instrumental rather than either morally-validating or entered into for the purpose of creating the "special values" of love and friendship so central to Fried's analysis. *See* A. WATSON, PSYCHIATRY FOR LAWYERS 22-26 (1968); Goodpaster, *The Human Arts of Lawyering: Interviewing and Counseling*, 27 J. LEGAL EDUC. 5, 8-9 (1975). Dean Shaffer's work is both exemplary and abundant. *See, e.g.*, T. SHAFFER, THE PLANNING AND DRAFTING OF WILLS AND TRUSTS 1-27 (1972); Shaffer, *Christian Theories of Professional Responsibility*, 48 S. CAL. L. REV. 721 (1975).

people. The tendency for humans to treat each other as things to be manipulated is hardly an invention of lawyers, or for that matter of bureaucracy. Naturally, that's not the only way we treat each other. Love, social solidarity, even friendship do exist. Even "markets" are ambiguous as to whether they're conflictive or integrative, and markets often become "firms," which are even more ambiguous that way. But, by and large, deep relationships between whole persons do not typify human relationships in our society, and except for the usual "I-know-a-tribe-which . . ." exceptions, they don't seem to characterize the dominant mode of any other culture either. So if a good lawyer cannot be a good person, it is only because "good" is defined in such a way that achieving it is necessarily rather a rarity.

But, in addition, it does not make the "goodness" of lawyers any easier to see that they do what they do not, like friends, for ineffable reasons but coolly for cold cash. Much as we loathe the technique of using human intuition as a means of deciding what normative distinctions are "right," it is worth pointing out that most people do find some critical moral distinctions lurking in the difference between the motives of the lover and those of the whore, and that they can even contrast the avenger's impulse with the hit man's.[38]

Oddly enough, however, Professor Fried and we have reached pretty much the same conclusion—that a good lawyer can be a good person. We have just gotten there by materially different routes. In our view the lawyer achieves his "goodness" by being—professionally—no rottener than the generality of people acting, so to speak, as amateurs. In Professor Fried's view, the lawyer achieves his honorific status by behaving analogously to one rather nicer subset of human actors, the "friends." Associated with this split is another, or rather the same otherwise expressed: We see the lawyer as skilled at the impersonal dimensions of personal and social relations; Professor Fried sees him as an emotive specialist in personal, concrete "human" behavior, concerned with the "autonomy" of his clients. Professor Fried's lawyer is a friend; ours is not. Neither he nor we are wholly accurate. But let us say on behalf of our view that it explains something that Professor Fried's view makes inexplicable: the considerable degree to which the public, including our clients, distrusts and despises us. If lawyers are like friends, one would expect the public to notice. But they seem not to. It is, we suppose, possible that the public is just mistaken in its perceptions and will begin to see lawyers as friends once Professor Fried's corrective views get sufficient exposure.[39] But we are strongly inclined to

38. Or, to look at it yet another way, you don't need to love your hammer, for lovability is not its essence; its *areté* is to hit, and hit well, and most important, to hit not oneself, but what you want it to hit. A hammer that is perfectly willing to hit you, and would, but for the fact that you have bought it and thine enemy has not, may be used, but that is no reason at all to lavish love on it.

39. Three of the most significant studies of client attitudes toward lawyers are B. Curran & F. Spaulding, The Legal Needs of the Public (1974); J. Donnell, The Corporate Counsel (1970); and A Motivational Study of Public Attitudes and Law Office Management 65-76 (Missouri Bar/Prentice-Hall survey 1963).

Attitudes towards lawyers may change over time as the public (and the profession) change. At present, however, observations such as the following, from F. Marks, R.

Correspondence

doubt it. For it seems more likely that the public sees lawyers mostly aright, as the technically powerful embodiments of the public's own worst but often necessary instincts.[40] Indeed, if we are to keep on playing with allegedly clarifying metaphors, the lawyer can be seen, and is, we think, seen, not as friend, or even alter ego, but as alter id. In brief, a lawyer is one who helps indeed, but frequently what he helps to do is further his client's interest in reducing everyone and everything else into something to be escaped or consumed.[41]

III

Love *is* important to ethics. So are its cognates, like friendship and personal loyalty. It *is* a mistake to believe that one can be "good" if and only if one's caring is diffuse and hypothetical.

But love is not all there is to goodness. One can be too much a friend, to oneself or to another. More than that, the extent to which love and friendship are relevant to the evaluation of particular role behavior is, naturally, a function of whether or not love or friendship actually exists in that role. To defend a course of action as love-like or friendship-like when

HALLAUER & R. CLIFTON, THE SHREVEPORT PLAN 37 (1974), are typical of methodologically sound attitude surveys:

> It is questionable whether any large groups within our society, other than wealthy individuals and large business enterprises, voluntarily consult lawyers on a regular basis. For most people, consulting a lawyer is neither routine nor familiar, nor is it viewed as pleasant. . . .
>
> When an individual consults a professional, he feels a loss of control over both process and outcome . . . .

The matter of client attitudes and their implications for a society governed by law rather than tradition is explored more fully in a forthcoming work by one of us. L. BROWN & E. DAUER, PLANNING BY LAWYERS: MATERIALS ON A NONADVERSARIAL LEGAL PROCESS.

> 40. What does distinguish lawyers . . . is that they are feared and disliked—but needed—because of their matter of factness, their sense of relevance, their refusal to be impressed by magical "solutions" to people's problems. Conceivably . . . the ceremonial and mystification of the legal profession are, to a considerable degree, veils or protections underneath which this rational, all too rational, work of the lawyer gets done.

Riesman, *Toward an Anthropological Science of Law and the Legal Profession*, 57 AM. J. SOC. 121, 128 (1951). That is to say, clients use lawyers as ancient Arabs used goats (for Azazel); and lawyers toss it back on clients. Client: "That's up to my lawyer (and anyway, I can't be responsible since I don't understand all that stuff)." Lawyer: "The choices aren't mine, and the system demands that I protect my client." *See generally* L. BROWN & E. DAUER, *supra* note 39.

41. We might suggest in passing that if it is true that one of the key social roles of lawyers is to have everyone's worst impulses put into their skillful hands for execution, transference might help to explain the peculiar state of legal ethics. If people in society are projecting things about themselves which they don't much like, then one would expect them to punish those impulses by punishing the transferees. Direct punishment is hard: lawyers are too valuable to shun overtly. Far more subtle an approach would have it so that the lawyers punish themselves. One way to effect that (a way which we think is widely in effect) is to put the parties to be simultaneously used and hurt (*i.e.*, valued and punished) into a classic "double bind," a situation in which either course they take is "wrong." And one way to do that is to give them an ethical system complete with flatly contradictory commands—*e.g.*, (1) "Your obligation is to your client"; (2) "Your obligation is to 'justice' "—in a world in which, except by *coup de main*, no one can convince himself that he can always serve both at the same time.

it is, much of the time, no such thing, is not to explain reality, but to trump it with the slyly appropriated affect of an altogether different realm of relationship. That will not do. And that, we think, is what Professor Fried did.[42]

Edward A. Dauer
Associate Professor of Law
Yale University
Arthur Allen Leff
Professor of Law
Yale University

42. We did not, in text, comment on the narrowness of the question Fried set out to answer, mostly because we believe that, among scholars, criticizing the pragmatic relevance of a chosen topic is normally inappropriate. We do so now only to put Fried's essay in its proper place. Whether a lawyer can be a good person is a question that is philosophically interesting, perhaps even significant if extrapolated systematically. But it is not among the issues with which the profession and the society must presently grapple. As law continues to increase its jurisdiction over hitherto "un-lawed" areas of social and economic life, there arise increasingly serious real difficulties which must be addressed. A market system for the distribution of legal services may be thought to employ wealth as a modulator of access not only to justice, but even to those distributive shares that have been politically guaranteed. Yet, on the other hand, a nonmarket system may put at risk the putative clients' personal autonomies vis-à-vis government which a completely independent legal profession is thought to preserve. The arguments are complex, of course, but the issues are rather pressing. "The morality of the lawyer-client relationship" normally conjures up not whether one individual can be "good" and be a lawyer, but rather whether there is a need for some very fundamental restructuring of the reality of lawyering. The far more important question may be, indeed, whether a *society* with lawyers-for-fees can be "good."

Fried's other dilemma—which one might concretize by thinking of the humiliating cross-examination of the truthful victim in a rape case—is similarly more than just a philosophical imbroglio which might make the "good person" pause before choosing to be a criminal defense attorney. Its analysis necessarily implicates difficult reassessments of the balance of values which our juridical processes must encounter. The point is that there are problems enough to be wrestled with and pressing decisions presently to be made. Professor Fried's analysis contributes virtually nothing to the existing dialogue; he adopts, instead, the goodness of our present legal and organizational estates as givens. Some people don't. Thus even if lawyers are "good people," the temptation to beam sanctimoniously while clutching Volume 85, Number 8 of the *Yale Law Journal* will have to be resisted.

Author's Reply:

The editors of the *Yale Law Journal* have kindly offered me an opportunity to reply to Professors Dauer and Leff. It is not easy to do so; their essay, though unaccountably querulous in tone,[1] is like a pudding once described by Winston Churchill: it lacks a theme. Since I have already developed my position in detail in my original article, I shall confine myself here to noting what I believe are inaccuracies and misconceptions.

1. A small example, chosen at random: In note 1 the authors say that my article "seems to be more or less a logical outgrowth, or at least a capitalizing upon" some aspects of my other writings. The word "capitalizing" hints at some dark flaw. What are the authors getting at? Who knows? They seem to be generally annoyed with me.

[7]

4

The Adversary System Excuse

DAVID LUBAN

> Again, if we suggest that the agent should adopt as rule and incarnation of his conscience some extraneous interest, system or authority, serving henceforth that objectified Principle with punctual fidelity and unflinching zeal, we are no longer holding on to a morality of Conscience. . . . A conscience thus put out to lease is not conscience but the evasion of it, except for that specious semblance of conscience which may be discerned in one's blind obedience to the authority that happens to be in command.
>
> Aurel Kolnai, "Erroneous Conscience," in *Ethics, Value and Reality*, edited by Bernard Williams and David Wiggins (Indianapolis: Hackett, 1978), p. 7.

It is not the lawyer's responsibility to believe or not to believe—the lawyer is a technician. . . . Law is an adversarial profession. The other side is out to get your client. Your job is to protect your client and the nonsense they hand out in these ethics courses today—if the young

---

This much-traveled and often-revised paper has received the criticism and comments of too many people to acknowledge all by name. Portions were presented to the staff of the Center for Philosophy and Public Policy; the Center for Philosophy and Public Policy Working Group on Legal Ethics; the Ethics and Public Policy Workshop; and the Society for the Study of Professional Ethics 1981 meeting at the Western Division of the American Philosophical Association. I wish to thank the participants in these meetings for their helpful advice. Major repairs in the argument resulted from comments by Robert Fullinwider, Virginia Held, Douglas MacLean, George Sher, Henry Shue, and William Simon. Needless to say, the reader is safe in assuming that the inadequacies in what he or she now has in hand are entirely the fault of its author.

This research was funded in part by the Maryland Bar Foundation and NEH Grant No. EH-20045-81-0658. Neither sponsor should be held responsible for the views expressed in the paper.

> people listen to this kind of nonsense, there isn't going to be such a thing as an intelligent defense in a civil or criminal case.
>
> Roy Cohn, interview, *National Law Journal*, December 1, 1980, p. 46.

I. Introduction

Holding forth at table in 1831, Samuel Taylor Coleridge turned to the behavior of lawyers. "There is undoubtedly a limit to the exertions of an advocate for his client," he said, for "the advocate has no right, nor is it his duty, to do that for his client which his client *in foro conscientiae* has no right to do for himself."[1] Thirteen years later, William Whewell elaborated the same point:

> [E]very man is, in an unofficial sense, by being a moral agent, a Judge of right and wrong, and an Advocate of what is right. . . . This general character of a moral agent, he cannot put off, by putting on any professional character. . . . If he mixes up his character as an Advocate, with his character as a Moral Agent . . . he acts immorally. He makes the Moral Rule subordinate to the Professional Rule. He sells to his Client, not only his skill and learning, but himself. He makes it the Supreme Object of his life to be, not a good man, but a successful Lawyer.[2]

Whewell's position is not commonly acknowledged to be valid. George Sharswood, whose 1854 *Legal Ethics* is the great-grandparent of the current ABA Code of Professional Responsibility, wrote: "The lawyer, who refuses his professional assistance because in his judgment the case is unjust and indefensible, usurps the functions of both judge and jury."[3] A lawyer is not to judge the morality of the client's cause; it is irrelevant to the morality of the representation. That, I think, is the official view of most lawyers: the lawyer's morality is distinct from, and not implicated in, the client's. Murray Schwartz calls this the "Principle of Nonaccountability":

> When acting as an advocate for a client . . . a lawyer is neither legally, professionally, nor morally accountable for the means used or the ends achieved.[4]

Add to this the "Principle of Professionalism":

> When acting as an advocate, a lawyer must, within the established constraints upon professional behavior, maximize the likelihood that the client will prevail.[5]

and you get what is usually taken to be the professional morality of lawyers. Gerald Postema calls it the "standard conception of the lawyer's role";[6] William Simon says that these principles (which he calls the "Principle of Neutrality" and the "Principle of Partisanship") define partisan advocacy.[7]

Shortly after introducing these principles, Schwartz raises two points about them:

> It might be argued, that the law cannot convert an immoral act into a moral one, nor a moral act into an immoral one, by simple fiat. Or, more fundamentally, the lawyer's nonaccountability might be illusory if it depends upon the morality of the adversary system and if that system is immoral. . . . If either [of these challenges] were to prove persuasive, the justification for the application of the Principle of Nonaccountability to moral accountability would disappear.[8]

Schwartz raises these issues but does not address them. My purpose in this paper is to meet them head-on. I shall argue (1) that a lawyer's nonaccountability does depend on the adversary system; (2) that the adversary system is not a sufficient basis for it; and (3) thus, that while the Principle of Professionalism may be true, the Principle of Nonaccountability is not.

This, I believe, will defend the morality of conscience—the position of Coleridge and Whewell—against the claim that professional obligation can override it.

II. Institutional Excuses

On February 7, 1973, Richard Helms, the former director of the Central Intelligence Agency, lied to a Senate committee about American involvement in the overthrow of the Allende government in Chile. Santiago proved to be Helms's Waterloo: he was caught out in his perjury and prosecuted.[9] Helms claimed that requirements of national security led him to lie to Congress. We can only speculate, however, on how the court would have viewed this excuse, for in fact the case never came to trial; Helms's lawyer, the redoubtable Edward Bennett Williams, found an ingenious way to back the government down. He argued that national security information was relevant to Helms's defense and must be turned over to Helms, thereby confronting the government with the unpleasant choice of dropping the action or making public classified and presumably vital information. The government chose the first option and allowed Helms to plead guilty to a misdemeanor charge.[10]

I don't know if anyone ever asked Williams to justify his actions; had anyone attempted to do so, they would presumably have been told that Williams was simply doing his job as a criminal defense attorney. The parallel with Helms's own excuse is clear—he was doing his job, Williams was doing his—but it is hard to miss the irony. Helms tried to conceal national security information; therefore he lied. Williams, acting on Helms's behalf, threatened to reveal national security information as part of a tactic that has come to be called "graymailing." One man's ends are another man's means. Neither lying nor graymailing (to say nothing of destabilizing elected regimes) are morally pretty, but a job is a job and that was the job that was. So, at any rate, runs the excuse.

We may want to reject these "good soldier" excuses or we may find them valid and persuasive. That is the issue I shall address here. A second graymailing example will warm us to our topic:

> In instances [of merger cases involving firms in competition with each other] in which the [Federal Trade] commission's legal case looked particularly good and none of the usual defenses appeared likely to work, the staff was confronted several times with the argument that if they did not refrain from prosecution and allow the merger, one of the proposed merger partners would close down its operations and dismiss its employees. . . . Of course, the mere announcement of the threat to close the plant generates enormous political pressure on the prosecutor not to go forward. Ought lawyers to be engaged in such strategies for the purpose of consummating an otherwise anticompetitive and illegal transaction involving the joinder of two substantial competitors?[11]

On the lawyers' advice, the firms played a nice game of chicken: closing down by stages, they laid off a few workers each day until the FTC cried uncle.

What could justify the conduct of these lawyers? A famous answer is the following statement of Lord Henry Brougham:

> An advocate, in the discharge of his duty, knows but one person in all the world, and that person is his client. To save that client by all means and expedients, and at all hazards and costs to other persons, and, amongst them, to himself, is his first and only duty; and in performing this duty he must not regard the alarm, the torments, the destruction which he may bring upon others. Separating the duty of a patriot from that of an advocate, he must go on reckless of consequences, though it should be his unhappy fate to involve his country in confusion.[12]

This speech, made in his 1820 defense of Queen Caroline against King George IV's charge of adultery, was itself an act of graymail. Reminiscing years later, Brougham said that the king would recognize in it a tacit threat to reveal his secret marriage to a Catholic, a marriage that, were it to become public knowledge, would cost him his crown.[13] Knowing this background of Brougham's oft-quoted statement might make us take a dim view of it; it has, nevertheless, frequently been admired as the most eloquent encapsulation of the advocate's job.

Brougham's statement invites philosophical reflection for at first blush it is equally baffling to utilitarianism, and moral rights theory, and Kantianism. The client's utility matters more than that of the rest of the world put together. No one else's moral rights matter. Other people are merely means to the client's ends.[14] Moral theory seems simply to reject Brougham's imperatives.

They are, however, universalizable over lawyers, or so it is claimed. The idea seems to be that the role of lawyer, hence the social institutions that set up this role, reparse the Moral Law, relaxing some moral obligations and imposing new ones. In the words of an Australian appellate court, "Our system of administering justice necessarily imposes upon those who practice advocacy duties which have no analogies, and the system cannot dispense with their strict observance."[15]

The system of which the court speaks is the so-called "adversary system of justice." My main question is this: does the adversary system really justify Brougham's position? I hope that the example of Helms and his lawyers has convinced you that a more general issue is lurking here, the issue of what I shall call *institutional excuses.* We can state the main question in full generality in this way: can a person appeal to a social institution in which he or she occupies a role in order to excuse conduct that would be morally culpable were anyone else to do it? Plausibly, examples exist in which the answer is yes: we do not call it murder when a soldier kills a sleeping enemy, although it is surely immoral for you or me to do it. There are also cases where the answer is no, as in the job "concentration camp commandant" or "professional strikebreaker." Here, we feel, the immorality of the job is so great that it accuses, not excuses, the person who holds it.

This suggests that an important feature of a successful institutional excuse is that the institution is itself justified. I think that is partly right, but I do not think it is the whole story: I shall argue that the *kind* of justification that can be offered of the institution is germane to the success of the excuses it provides.

III. The Adversary System and the Two Principles

Sometimes a lawyer pursuing a case finds him or herself compelled to do something outrageous. Graymailing is one example. A second is the Lake Pleasant bodies case, in which lawyers Frank Belge and Frank Armani, having been told by their client Robert Garrow of two murders he committed, found and photographed the bodies but kept the information to themselves for half a year—this despite the fact that the father of one of the victims, knowing that Armani was representing an accused murderer, personally pleaded with him to tell him if he knew anything about his daughter.[16]

Such spectacular examples could be multiplied, but I think the point is made. A more important point is that it is not just the spectacular examples that are the problem—they only dramatize it. I dare say that all litigators have had cases where, in their heart of hearts, they wanted their client to lose or wished that a distasteful action did not need to be performed. The problem is that (recollecting Brougham's words) "to save that client . . . [the lawyer] must not regard the alarm, the torments, the destruction which he may bring upon others."[17] On the face of it, this is as terse a characterization as one could hope to find of amorality; it is reminiscent of Nietzsche's description of the old Teutonic code:

"To practice loyalty and, for the sake of loyalty, to risk honor and blood even for evil and dangerous things."[18]

The way it is currently phrased, in the ABA's Code of Professional Responsibility, is this:

> The duty of a lawyer, both to his client and to the legal system, is to represent his client zealously within the bounds of the law. . . . In our government of laws and not of men, each member of our society is entitled . . . to seek any lawful objective through legally permissible means; and to present for adjudication any lawful claim, issue, or defense.[19]

It sounds nicer than Zarathustra or Brougham, but in fact there is no difference: the zealous advocate is supposed to press the client's interests to the limit of the legal, regardless of the "torments or destruction" this wreaks on others.

Nor does the phrase "within the bounds of the law" mitigate this. For the law is inherently double-edged: any rule imposed to limit zealous advocacy (or any other form of conduct, for that matter) may be used by an adversary as an offensive weapon. In the words of former Judge Marvin E. Frankel, "the object always is to beat every plowshare into a sword."[20] The rules of discovery, for example, initiated to enable one side to find out crucial facts from the other, are used nowadays to delay trial or impose added expense on the other side; conversely, one might respond to an interrogatory by delivering to the discoverer several tons of miscellaneous documents, to run up their legal bills or conceal a needle in a haystack.

To take another example: rules barring lawyers from representations involving conflicts of interest are now regularly used by adversaries to drive up the other side's legal costs by having their counsel disqualified.[21] The general problem of double-edgedness is described by the novelist Yasunari Kawabata:

> When a law is made, the cunning that finds loopholes goes to work. We cannot deny that there is a certain slyness . . . , a slyness which, when rules are written to prevent slyness, makes use of the rules themselves.[22]

It is not just the rules governing lawyer conduct that are double-edged—double-edgedness is an essential feature of any law because any restraint imposed on human behavior in the name of just social policy may be used to restrain behavior when circumstances make this an unjust outcome. This is the unbridgeable gap between formal and substantive justice. David Mellinkoff gives these examples:

> The law intended to stop sharpers from claiming money that is not owed (the Statute of Frauds) may sometimes defeat a just debt, because the claim was not in writing.
>
> The law intended to stop a man from holding off suit until defense becomes impossible—memories grown dim, witnesses dead or missing—(the Statute of Limitations) may sometimes defeat a just suit, because it was not filed fast enough.

The law intended to prevent designing grown-ups from imposing on children (the defense of infancy) may defeat a just claim, because the man who signed the contract was 20 instead of 21.

The law intended to give a man, for all his misfortunes, a new start in life (the bankruptcy laws) may defeat a widow's just claim for the money she needs to live on.[23]

The double-edgedness of law underlines the moral problem involved in representing a client "zealously within the bounds of the law." If on the one hand this means forwarding legal claims that are morally dubious, as in Mellinkoff's examples, on the other, it means pushing claims to the limit of the law and then a bit further, into the realm of what is "colorably" the limit of the law.[24] "Zeal" means zeal at the margin of the legal, and thus well past the margin of whatever moral and political insight constitutes the "spirit" of the law in question. The limits of the law inevitably lie beyond moral limits, and zealous advocacy always means zeal at the margin.

It is at this point that the adversary system looms large, for it provides the institutional excuse for the duty of zealous advocacy. Each side of an adversary proceeding is represented by a lawyer whose sole obligation is to present that side as forcefully as possible; anything less, it is claimed, would subvert the operation of the system. The ABA code states the matter quite clearly: "The duty of a lawyer to his client and his duty to the legal system are the same: to represent his client zealously within the bounds of the law."[25]

Everything rides on this argument. Lawyers have to assert legal interests unsupported by moral rights all the time; asserting legal interests is what they do, and everyone can't be in the right on all issues. Unless zealous advocacy could be justified by relating it to some larger social good, the lawyer's role would be morally impossible. That larger social good, we are told, is justice, and the adversary system is supposed to be the best way of attaining it.

Indeed, it is misleading to call this Justification by the Adversary System an *argument*. It is more like a presupposition accepted by all parties before the arguments begin. Even lawyers with nothing good to say about the legal system in general believe that their current actions are justified or excused by the nature of the adversary system.

The point deserves to be labored a bit, for the universal acceptance among lawyers of the Justification by the Adversary System is a startling thing, a marvelous thing, a thing to behold. It can go something like this: one talks with a pragmatic and hard-boiled attorney. At the mention of legal ethics, he smiles sardonically and informs one that it is a joke. One presses the subject and produces examples such as the buried bodies case. The smile fades, the forehead furrows, he retreats into a nearby phonebooth and returns moments later clothed in the Adversary System, trailing clouds of glory. Distant angels sing. The discussion usually gets no further.

This portrait is drawn from life, but I do not tell the story just to be snide. It is meant to suggest that discussions of the adversary system usually stop where they ought to start, with a chorus of deeply felt but basically unexamined rhetoric.

What, then, is the adversary system? We may distinguish narrow and wide senses. In the narrow sense, it is a method of adjudication characterized by three things: an impartial tribunal of defined jurisdiction, formal procedural rules, and most importantly for the present discussion, assignment to the parties of the responsibility to present their own cases and challenge their opponents'.[26] The attorneys are their clients' agents in the latter task. The duty of a lawyer in an adversary proceeding is therefore one-sided partisan zeal in advocating his or her client's position. This in turn carries with it familiar collateral duties, the most important of which are *disinterestedness*[27] and *confidentiality*.[28] Each of these is best viewed as a prophylactic designed to enhance the quality of partisan advocacy: forbidding lawyers who have conflicts of interest from advocating a client's cause is meant to forestall the possibility of diluted zeal, and forbidding lawyers from divulging clients' confidences and secrets is meant to encourage clients to give their lawyers information necessary for effective advocacy. These duties of zeal, disinterestedness, and confidentiality—which I have elsewhere called the Three Pillars of Advocacy[29]—form the core of an attorney's professional obligations.

The structure of the adversary system, then—its fission of adjudication into a clash of one-sided representations—explains why Schwartz's Principle of Professionalism holds. But it explains the Principle of Moral Nonaccountability as well. If advocates restrain their zeal because of moral compunctions, they are not fulfilling their assigned role in the adversary proceeding. But, if lawyers must hold themselves morally accountable for what they do in the course of the representation, they will be morally obliged to restrain their zeal whenever they find that "the means used or the ends achieved" in the advocacy are morally wrong. Therefore, or so the syllogism goes, the structure of adversary adjudication must relieve them of moral accountability, and that is how the adversary system entails Schwartz's Principle of Nonaccountability—how, that is, the adversary system is supposed to provide an institutional excuse for moral ruthlessness.

All this holds (if hold it does) only within the context of adjudication. Lawyers, however, commonly act as though Schwartz's two principles characterized their relationship with clients even when the representations do not involve the courtroom.[30] Thus, there is a *wide* sense of the adversary system in which it is defined by the structure of the lawyer-client relationship rather than the structure of adjudication. When lawyers assume Schwartz's two principles in negotiations and counseling as well as courtroom advocacy, and attribute this to the adversary system, they are speaking of it in the wide sense.[31]

Lawyers often equivocate between the narrow and wide conceptions, appealing to the virtues of adversary adjudication in order to justify ruthless behavior on behalf of clients in nonlitigation contexts. Getting paid by the client, of course, makes it easier to ignore the difference between courtroom and other activities: $200 an hour has been known to buy a lot of Professionalism and will even stand in quite nicely for Moral Nonaccountability, especially around the first of the month—and an hour is an hour, in or out of court.[32] Rather than pursue this equivocation, however, I shall ask if an institutional excuse can be based on the adversary system conceived in the narrow sense. If problems crop up even there, certainly they will be worse outside of a legitimately adversarial institution.

IV. Criminal versus Noncriminal Contexts

I have suggested that the adversary system excuse may be only as good as the adversary system. The question of how good that is, however, is often ignored by discussions that stop where they ought to start. Indeed, there is a tendency among many people to treat reservations about the adversary system as assaults on the American Way. Monroe Freedman, for example, has written what is arguably the best modern book on lawyers' ethics.[33] He shows how the duty to put a perjurious client on the stand, or brutally cross-examine a witness known by the lawyer to be telling the truth, follows from the adversary system. But he defends the adversary system primarily by contrasting the nonadversarial systems in "totalitarian states" such as Cuba and Bulgaria, with American concern for the "dignity of the individual."[34] Left in their bare state, phrases like these can be only slogans.

Freedman's rhetorical point still contains an important argument. That argument is that zealous adversary advocacy of those accused of crimes is the greatest safeguard of individual liberty against the encroachment of the state. The good criminal defense lawyer puts the state to its proof in the most stringent and uncompromising way possible. Better, we say, that a hundred criminals go free than that one person be wrongly convicted.[35]

I think this is right as far as it goes, but as general defense of the adversary system, it is beside the point for two related reasons. The first is that it pertains only to criminal defense and thus is irrelevant to the enormous number of civil cases tried each year. The latter are in a way much more morally troubling. It inflicts no tangible harm on anyone when a criminal evades punishment. This is not to deny that people may be legitimately outraged (consider the Nixon pardon, the trial of Dan White in San Francisco, the acquittals of policemen that led to the 1980 riots in Miami). But no one's life is made materially worse off. However, when A wins an unjust personal injury claim against B, every dollar in A's pocket comes out of B's. A's lawyer, in my book, has a lot of explaining to do.

This point is worth emphasizing. Most people I have spoken with about lawyers' ethics assume that the paradigm of the morally dubious representation is the defense of the guilty criminal, the defense that gets a murderer back out on the street. This, I suspect, is a reflection of a perception of the justice system as primarily concerned with protecting the lives and property of Decent People (meaning us) from You Know Who (meaning you know who). It is You Know Who that needs watching, not the real estate speculator, the slumlord, the redliner, the discriminatory employer, the finance company, the welfare officials who won't give recipients their due, or the police.

It is this public preoccupation with crime and criminals, I think, that leads writers like Freedman and David Mellinkoff to focus their justifications of Broughamesque advocacy on criminal defense.[36] They are reacting to an assault from the Right, an assault that sees the rights of the accused as a liberal invention leading to anarchy. Now, emphasizing the role of lawyers in safeguarding individual liberty may indeed be the best defense against the Law and Order attack on lawyers. Criminal defense is, so to speak, the "worst-case scenario," and it might be assumed that any defense of advocacy that works there works everywhere else as well.

In fact, and this is my second point, criminal defense is a very special case in which the zealous advocate serves atypical social goals. The point is one of political theory. The goal of zealous advocacy in criminal defense is to curtail the power of the state over its citizens. We want to handicap the state in its power even legitimately to punish us. And so the adversary system is justified, not because it is a good way of achieving justice, but because it is a good way of hobbling the government and we have political reasons for wanting this. The argument, in other words, does not claim that the adversary system is the best way of obtaining justice. It claims just the opposite, that it is the best way of impeding justice in the name of more fundamental political ends, namely, keeping the government's hands off people. Nothing, of course, is wrong with that; indeed, I believe that Brougham's imperative may well hold in criminal defense. My point is merely that criminal defense is an exceptional part of the legal system, one that aims at protection rather than justice.

One might adopt Aristotelian language and say that the "final cause" of the adversary system is different in criminal and noncriminal contexts. In the latter, the primary end of adversary adjudication is legal justice, the assignment of rewards and remedies on the basis of parties' behavior as prescribed by legal norms. The adversary method is supposed to yield accurate accounts of past behavior and legitimate interpretations of the law. In the criminal context, on the other hand, the primary end of the adversary system is not legal justice but the protection of accused individuals against the state or, more generally, the preservation of the proper relation between the state and its subjects. (This suggests one qualification to what I have just said: some noncriminal matters, such as administrative hearings, can raise the same issues of state versus subject and should be treated similarly. The reader should therefore read "criminal context" as an abbreviation for "criminal and quasi-criminal contexts.")

It seems, then, that focusing on the adversary system in the criminal context obscures the issue of how it works as a system of justice, and for this reason I shall talk only about arguments attempting to vindicate it as a system of justice. There are two sorts of arguments: those claiming that the adversary system is the best way of accomplishing various goals (consequentialist arguments), and those claiming that it is intrinsically good (nonconsequentialist arguments). To begin, we shall look at three versions of the former: (1) that the adversary system is the best way of ferreting out truth, (2) that it is the best way of defending people's legal rights, and (3) that by establishing checks and balances it is the best way of safeguarding against excesses.

V. Consequentialist Justifications of the Adversary System

A. TRUTH

The question whether the adversary system is, all in all, the best way of uncovering the facts of a case at bar sounds like an empirical question. I happen to think that it is—an empirical question, moreover, that has scarcely been investigated, and that is most likely impossible to answer. This last is because one does not, after a trial is over, find the parties coming forth to make a clean breast of it and enlighten the world as to what *really* happened. A trial is not a quiz show with the right answer waiting in a sealed envelope. We can't learn directly whether the facts are really as the trier determined them because we don't ever find out the facts.

The kind of empirical research that can be done, then, is laboratory simulations: social psychology experiments intended to model the adversary proceeding. Obviously, there are inherent limitations on how closely such experiments can correspond to actual trials, no matter how skillfully they are done. In fact, the only experiments of the sort I know of are those of Thibaut, Walker, and their associates,[37] and these are far from perfect modelings of the adversary and "inquisitorial"—meaning French- and German-style—systems that they are comparing.[38] Even so, the results are instructive: they show that in some situations the adversary system works better while in others the inquisitorial system does, and furthermore, that the participants cannot tell which situation they are in. This would hardly surprise us: it would be much more astounding to discover a greater difference in veracity between the Anglo-American and Continental systems, for surely such a difference would after so many centuries have become a commonplace in our folklore.

Given all this, it is unsurprising to discover that the arguments purporting to show the advantages of the adversary system as a fact-finder have mostly been nonempirical, a mix of a priori theories of inquiry and armchair psychology.

Here is one, based on the idea, very similar to Sir Karl Popper's theory of scientific rationality, that the way to get at the truth is a wholehearted dialectic of assertion and refutation.[39] If each side attempts to prove its case, with the other trying as energetically as possible to assault the steps of the proof, it is more likely that all of the aspects of the situation will be presented to the fact-finder than if it attempts to investigate for itself with the help of the lawyers.

This theory is open to a number of objections. First of all, the analogy to Popperian scientific methodology is not a good one. Perhaps science proceeds by advancing conjectures and then trying to refute them,[40] but it does not proceed by advancing conjectures that the scientist knows to be false and then using procedural rules to exclude probative evidence.[41]

The two adversary attorneys, moreover, are each under an obligation to present the facts in the manner most consistent with their client's position—to prevent the introduction of unfavorable evidence, to undermine the credibility of opposing witnesses, to set unfavorable facts in a context in which their importance is minimized, to attempt to provoke inferences in their client's favor. The assumption is that two such accounts will cancel out, leaving the truth of the matter. But there is no earthly reason to think this is so; they may simply pile up the confusion.

This is particularly likely in those frequent cases when the facts in question concern someone's character or state of mind. Out comes the parade of psychiatrists, what Hannah Arendt once called "the comedy of the soul-experts."[42] Needless to say, they have been prepared by the lawyers, sometimes without knowing it. A clinical law teacher explained to a class that when you first contact a psychiatrist and sketch the facts of the case, you mention only the favorable ones. That way, he or she has an initial bias in your favor and tends to discount the unfavorable facts when you finally get around to mentioning them.

The other side, of course, can cross-examine such a witness to get the truth out. Irving Younger, perhaps the most popular lecturer on trial tactics in the country, tells how. Among his famous "Ten Commandments of Cross-Examination" are these:

- Never ask anything but a leading question.
- Never ask a question to which you don't already know the answer.
- Never permit the witness to explain his or her answers.
- Don't bring out your conclusions in the cross-examination. Save them for closing arguments when the witness is in no position to refute them.[43]

Of course, the opposition may be prepared for this; they may have seen Younger's three-hour, $425 videotape on how to examine expert witnesses. They may know, therefore, that the cross-examiner is saving his or her conclusions for the closing argument. Not to worry! Younger knows how to stop an attorney from distorting the truth in closing arguments. "If the opposing lawyer is holding the jury spellbound . . . the spell must be broken at all cost [sic]. [Younger] suggests the attorney leap to his or her feet and make furious and spurious objections. They will be overruled, but they might at least break the opposing counsel's concentration."[44]

My guess is that this is not quite what Sir Karl Popper had in mind when he wrote, "The Western rationalist tradition . . . is the tradition of critical discussion—of examining and testing propositions or theories by attempting to refute them."[45]

A skeptic, in fact, might try this scientific analogy: a beam of invisible electrically charged particles—charge and origin unknown—travels through a distorting magnetic field of unknown strength, then through an opposite field of unknown, but probably different, strength. The beam strikes a detector of undeterminable reliability, from which we are supposed to infer the nature and location of the beam's source. That is the adversary system at its worst.

Let us try another argument, this one taken from the ABA's official justification of the adversary system, the *Joint Conference Report* of the ABA-AALS. The heart of the argument is this:

> Any arbiter who attempts to decide a dispute without the aid of partisan advocacy . . . must undertake not only the role of judge, but that of representative for both of the litigants. Each of these roles must be played to the full without being muted by qualifications derived from the others. When he is developing for each side the most effective statement of his case, the arbiter must put aside his neutrality and permit himself to be moved by a sympathetic identification sufficiently intense to draw from his mind all that it is capable of giving,—in analysis, patience and creative power. When he resumes his neutral position, he must be able to view with distrust the fruits of this identification and be ready to reject the products of his own best mental efforts. The difficulties of this undertaking are obvious. If it is true that a man in his time must play many parts, it is scarcely given to him to play them all at once.[46]

Psychologically, the argument says, a nonadversarial trial is like trying to play chess against yourself: neither white nor black pieces get played very well, and second-rate games result.

The argument, however, begs the question. True, *if* the facts are best discovered by a battle between two conflicting points of view, then one person won't do as well at it as two adversaries. But to suppose that that is how factual inquiry best proceeds is simply to take as a premise that the adversary system is best, when that was supposed to have been the conclusion.

It is not, moreover, as attractive a premise as it appears at first glance. It trades on an ambiguity in the idea that the judge in a nonadversary proceeding must be the "representative for both of the litigants." It is true that the judge must take the *interests* and *legal claims* of both litigants into account in order to grant them due process of law: in this sense he or she must "represent" both of them. But that is not to say that the judge will find the facts by somehow balancing the parties' factual claims against each other as if these were the parties' interests. Is the best way to find out about an event to ask only parties who have special interests at stake in it? The *Joint Conference Report*, assuming that truth is gotten at by making sure that both sides' versions of every aspect of the story are represented, comes close to the undergraduate fallacy of thinking that because everyone has a right to his or her opinion, everyone's opinion on any topic whatsoever is equally worthy of being taken into account. Although frequently there are versions of the truth, truth does not necessarily come in versions. Thus, there is no reason to suppose that a judge making factual inquiries must "represent" the points of view of both litigants to be fair.

No trial lawyer seriously believes that the best way to get at the truth is through the clash of opposing points of view. If a lawyer did believe this, the logical way to prepare a case for trial would be to hire two investigators, one taking one side of every issue and one taking the other. After all, the lawyer needs the facts, and if those are best discovered through an adversary process, the lawyer would be irresponsible not to set one up. That no lawyer would dream of such a crazy procedure should tip us off that the *Joint Conference Report* premise is flawed.[47]

The *Joint Conference Report* employs two subsidiary psychological arguments as well. The first is that the adversary system will "hold the case . . . in suspension between two opposing interpretations of it,"[48] so the finder of fact will not jump to hasty conclusions. The second is that if the judge and not the lawyer had to "absorb" the disappointments of his or her theory of the case being refuted, he or she would be "under a strong temptation to keep the hearing moving within the boundaries originally set for it"; then it would not be a fair trial so much as a "public confirmation for what the tribunal considers it has already established in private."[49]

Let me reiterate that these arguments, however plausible they sound on paper, are untested speculations from the armchair. But let us suppose for the sake of argument that they are right. They still do not show why we must have an adversary system. Consider three other possible systems: (1) a three-judge panel, two of whom investigate and present the case from the points of view of the respective litigants, making the strongest arguments they can but also pointing out weaknesses in their side's case and strengths in the other; (2) a system like our own, except that the advocates are under an affirmative duty to point out facts or arguments in the other side's favor if the adversary is unaware of them (or, perhaps, a system in which the court awards attorneys' fees on the basis of how helpful they are in the overall search for truth); (3) the

French system in which one judge investigates the case beforehand and presents a dossier to the trial judge.

Now, I don't recommend any of these as a practical alternative to the existing adversary system; they have their drawbacks. But notice that (1) and (2) do just as good a job as the adversary system at holding the case in suspension, while all three do just as good a job at shifting the onus of being wrong away from the tribunal. All three, moreover, sever the search for truth from the attorney's need to win, which under the adversary system ties the attorney to the client's victory by bonds of self-interest. All three, therefore, are likely to avoid the most extravagant tactics currently employed by lawyers. The *Joint Conference Report* does not even consider this as a possibility.

Indeed, it seems to take as a premise the idea that truth is served by self-interested rather than disinterested investigation. "The lawyer appearing as an advocate before a tribunal presents, as persuasively as he can, the facts and the law of the case *as seen from the standpoint of his client's interest*" [emphasis added].[50] The emphasized phrase is accurate, but it gives the game away. For there is all the difference in the world between "the facts seen from X's standpoint" and "the facts seen from the standpoint of X's interest." Of course it is important to hear the former—the more perspectives we have, the better informed our judgment. But to hear the latter is not helpful at all. It is in the murderer's *interest* not to have been at the scene of the crime; consequently, the "facts of the case as seen from the standpoint of [the] client's interest" are that the client was elsewhere that weekend. From the standpoint of my *interest*, the world is my cupcake with a cherry on top; from the standpoint of yours, its streets are paved with gold. Combining the two does not change folly to truth.

All this does not mean that the adversary system may not in fact get at the truth in many hard cases. (Trial lawyers' war stories are mixed.) I suppose that it is as good as its rivals. But, to repeat the point I began with, nobody knows how good that is.[51]

B. LEGAL RIGHTS

It is sometimes said, however, that the point of the adversary system is *not* that it is the best way of getting at the truth, but rather the best way of defending individuals' legal rights. It is, in the words of the current attorney general of Maryland, "a celebration of other values" than truth.[52] Freedman points out that if the sole purpose of a trial were to get at the truth we would not have our Fourth, Fifth, and Sixth Amendment rights; that improperly obtained evidence cannnot be used against us and that we cannot be required to testify against ourselves indicate that our society considers other values more central than truth.[53] And, according to the theory we shall now consider, these other values have to do with legal rights.[54]

The argument is that the best way to guarantee that an individual's legal rights are protected is to provide him or her with a zealous adversary advocate who will further the client's interest.

This argument, we should note, is slightly different from Freedman's, according to which counsel by a zealous advocate is not merely the best way of defending one's legal rights, but is itself one of those rights.[55] That, of course, would make the adversary system necessary for the defense of legal rights, but only in the trivial sense that taking away counsel infringes a person's right to counsel and you can't defend a right by infringing it. Freedman suggests that adversary advocacy is a constitutional value,[56] but this is not obvious. The Constitution makes no explicit mention of the adversary system. Now, it may be, as Theodore Koskoff says, a "fact, so basic that the Constitution does not even mention it, that our system of justice is an adversary system."[57] Certainly the Supreme Court has asserted that we have an adversary system.[58] What is unclear is whether this means only that under an adversary system, due process of law requires adversary advocacy. It is not clear that the Court would find common-law tinkering with the adversary format a denial of due process, and it is not clear that a constitutional amendment would be required to change to a nonadversarial system. It is true that the Sixth Amendment gives persons accused of crimes the right to counsel, but this says nothing about the adversary system as such. If we used a nonadversarial system, the Sixth Amendment right could be fulfilled by giving the accused a nonadversary advocate.

The argument we are considering is rather that, right to counsel aside, adversary advocacy is the best defense of our *other* legal rights. The no-holds-barred zealous advocate tries to get everything the law can give (if that is the client's wish) and thereby does a better job of defending the client's legal rights than a less committed lawyer would do.

Put this way, however, it is clear that the argument trades on a confusion. My legal rights are *everything I am in fact legally entitled to,* not *everything the law can be made to give.* For obviously a good lawyer may be able to get me things to which I am not entitled, but this, to call a spade a spade, is an example of infringing my opponent's legal rights, not defending mine. Every lawyer knows tricks of the trade that can be used to do opponents out of their legal deserts—using delaying tactics, for example, to make it too costly for an opponent without much money to prosecute a lengthy suit even though the law is on his or her side.

To this it might be replied that looking at it this way leaves the opponent's lawyer out of the picture. Of course, the reply continues, no one is claiming that a zealous adversary advocate is attempting to *defend* legal rights: he or she is attempting to *win.* The claim is only that the clash of two such adversaries will in fact defend legal rights most effectively.

But what reason do we have to believe this, other than a question-begging analogy to eighteenth-century economic theories of the Invisible Hand, theories that are themselves myth rather than fact? Every skill an advocate is taught is bent to winning cases no matter where the legal right lies. If the opponent manages to counter a lawyer's move with a better one, this has precisely nothing to do with legal rights. In the Middle Ages lawsuits were frequently tried by combat between hired champions. Each was charged with defending the legal right of his employer, but surely the fact that one swordsman successfully fileted the other did not mean that a right was established. Now, of course judicial combat did not involve argument *about* rights. But neither does graymailing, "dollaring to death," driving up an opponent's costs by getting his or her law firm disqualified, peremptorily challenging a juror because he or she seems too smart, or even masking an invalid argument with what Titus Castricius called "the orator's privilege to make statements that are untrue, daring, crafty, deceptive and sophistical, provided they have some semblance of truth and can by any artifice be made to insinuate themselves into the minds of the persons who are to be influenced."[59]

It is obvious that litigators pride themselves on their won-lost record. The *National Law Journal* describes "the world's most successful criminal lawyer—229 murder acquittals without a loss!" and describes the Inner Circle, a lawyer's club whose membership requirement is winning a seven-figure verdict.[60] You never know, of course—maybe each of these cases really had legal right on its side. And when a coin comes up heads 229 times in a row it may be fair, but there *is* another explanation. Lawyers themselves do not see the point of what they do as defending their clients' legal rights, but as using the law to get their clients what they want.

It is true, of course, that one way for society to guarantee that lawyers do their best to defend their clients' rights is to commit them to defending every claim a client has to a right, whether valid or not. That kind of overkill is reassuring to each client, of course. But suppose we look at it from the point of view of the whole process, rather than of the individual clients. It is hard to see then why an adversary system is the best defender of legal rights. Why not, for example, a system in which both attorneys are committed to defending the legal rights of both parties, if they seem to be getting trampled? I am not recommending such a system: my point is only that we have no reason at all to believe that when two overkillers slug it out the better case, rather than the better lawyer, wins.

Let me be clear about what the objection is. It is not that the flaw in the adversary system as a defender of legal rights is overkill on the part of morally imperfect, victory-hungry lawyers. The objection is that under the adversary system an *exemplary* lawyer is required to indulge in overkill to obtain as legal rights benefits that in fact may not be legal rights.

At this point an objection can be raised to my argument. The argument depends on a distinction I have drawn between *what a person is in fact legally entitled to* and *what the law can be made to give.* But this is a suspect distinction because it is based on the notion that there are legal entitlements other than what the law in fact gives. American Realism, the dominant jurisprudential theory of this century, was primarily responsible for throwing cold water on the notion of entitlements-in-themselves floating around in some sort of noumenal never-never land. The law is nothing other than what the courts say it is.

The objection fails, however, for it cuts the ground out from under itself. If legal rights are strictly identical with what the courts decide they are, then it is simply false that the adversary system is the best defender of legal rights. *Any* system whatsoever would defend legal rights equally well, as long as on the basis of that system courts decided cases.

There is, however, a legitimate insight concealed in the Realist objection. Whether or not legal rights are anything beyond what the courts say they are, it is the courts that are charged with adjudicating them. And—the point continues—if lawyers were given discretion to back off from zealous advocacy, they would have to prejudge the case themselves by deciding what the legal rights actually are in order to exercise this discretion. Lawyers would be usurping the judicial function.

Now, it must be said that this insight cannot be used to defend the innumerable tactics lawyers use to force favorable settlements of cases outside of court; if anything, the argument should condemn such practices inasmuch as they preempt the adjudicatory process. Nor does it militate against requiring lawyers to disclose adverse information and arguments, since doing so does not usurp the judicial function. But I do not wish to focus on these points for I think that the insight contains an important argument for the adversary system that we have not yet considered.

C. ETHICAL DIVISION OF LABOR

This argument is no longer that the excesses of zealous advocacy are excused by appealing to the promotion of truth or the defense of legal rights. Rather, it is that they are excused by what Thomas Nagel calls "ethical division of labor." He says, in a discussion of the peculiarly ruthless and result-oriented role morality of public officials,

> that the constraints of public morality are not imposed as a whole in the same way on all public actions or on all public offices. Because public agency is itself complex and divided, there is a corresponding ethical division of labor, or ethical specialization. Different aspects of public morality are in the hands of different officials. This can create the illusion that public morality is more consequentialist or less restrictive than it is, because the general conditions may be wrongly identified with the boundaries of a particular role. But in fact those boundaries usually presuppose a larger institutional structure without which they would be illegitimate.

(The most conspicuous example is the legitimacy conferred on legislative decisions by the limitation of constitutional protections enforced by the courts.)[61]

The idea is that behavior that looks wrong from the point of view of ordinary morality is justified by the fact that other social roles exist whose purpose is to counteract the excesses resulting from role-behavior. Zealous adversary advocacy is justified by the fact that the other side is also furnished with a zealous advocate; the impartial arbiter provides a further check.

This is in fact one of the most commonly heard defenses for pugnacious advocacy: "he had a lawyer, too"; "I'm not supposed to do his lawyer's job for him"; or quoting Sharswood once again, "The lawyer, who refuses his professional assistance because in his judgment the case is unjust and indefensible, usurps the functions of both judge and jury."[62]

The idea is really a checks-and-balances theory, in which social engineering or "wise legislation" is supposed to relieve some of the strain on individual conscience. A functionary in a well-designed checks-and-balances system can simply go ahead and perform his or her duties secure in the knowledge that injuries inflicted or wrongs committed in the course of those duties will be rectified by other parts of the system.

Will this do the trick? The answer, I am afraid, is no. Suppose that a lawyer is about to embark on a course of action that is unjustified from the point of view of ordinary morality, such as attempting to win an unfair, lopsided judgment for a client from a hapless and innocent party. Or think of our second graymailing example. A zealous adversary advocate will do whatever he or she can to avoid the opposing counsel's attempt to foil his or her designs. But such an advocate surely cannot claim that the existence of the opposing counsel morally justifies these actions. Certainly the fact that a man has a bodyguard in no way excuses you for trying to kill him, particularly if you bend all your ingenuity to avoiding the bodyguard.

The problem is this. The checks-and-balances notion is desirable because if other parts of the system exist to rectify one's excesses, one will be able to devote undivided attention to the job at hand and do it better. It is analogous to wearing protective clothing in a sport such as fencing: knowing that one's opponent is protected, one is justified in going all out in the match. But in the adversary system the situation is different, since the attorney is actively trying to get around the checks and balances: here the analogy is to a fencer who uses a special foil that can cut through the opponent's protective clothing. To put the point another way, the adversary advocate attempts to evade the system of checks and balances, not rely on it to save his or her opponents.

There is another problem with the notion of ethical division of labor. It attempts to justify a system of roles by the fact that the system is self-correcting, in other words that injuries perpetrated by one part of the system will be rectified by another. Rectification, however, carries with it high transaction costs in terms of money, time, worry, energy, and (generally) an arduous passage through the bureaucratic straits. These transaction costs are, so to speak, a general background "noise" in the system, a penalty imposed on one simply for becoming embroiled in it. This can be justified only if the system itself is justified, but then the checks-and-balances argument seems merely to gild the lily. Had we found a justification for the adversary system on other grounds, we would not have needed to turn to the ethical division-of-labor argument to begin with.

A somewhat different division-of-labor argument has been offered by Virginia Held.[63] She argues that different institutional systems utilize different forms of moral argument; specifically, "deontological justification is especially characteristic of and appropriate to legal systems, teleological justification especially characteristic of and appropriate to political systems."[64] By "legal justification," Held is referring primarily to the sort of justification we expect judges to offer for their decisions; they are supposed to appeal to legal rules, not moral consequences. Since lawyers are also officers of the legal system, the argument might be extended to include them. In that case, lawyers would be justified in following the institutionally prescribed rule and forgoing consideration of wider moral consequences.

That this is a division-of-labor argument may be seen from Held's reason for holding it:

> The justification for such a division of appropriate forms of justification . . . seems to rest on a judgment that such a division, over time, is morally salutary. It provides an institutional balance, or system of checks within the social system which each system [legal and political] exerts upon the other, allowing both . . . more nearly to approach moral justification than could either system alone using no distinct form of justification.[65]

Now, this is certainly a plausible theory; however, I do not think it extends to the moral behavior of lawyers. Whichever form of moral argument one uses, deontological or teleological, one is still constrained by what I take to be a requirement on moral arguments in general: that the argument take into consideration the interests of and obligations toward all the parties in the situation. It's just that the judge and the politician do this in different ways and perhaps arrive at different results.

The defender of the adversary advocate, however, is arguing something different, namely, that the division of moral labor assigns the lawyer to take only the client's interests into account. This is neither a deontological nor teleological moral argument: such one-sidedness is not moral thinking at all. It will not do to say that the lawyer has a deontological duty to bracket all but the client's interests, for that begs the very question at issue, the question of what the lawyer's duties are.

This is a very troubling and difficult topic. The structure of bureaucratic institutions such as the legal system lends itself to divided responsibility. Those who write the rules, those who give the orders, and those who carry them out each have some basis for claiming that they are not at fault for any wrong that results. But this is unacceptable. As Hannah Arendt observed,

> In a fully developed bureaucracy there is nobody left with whom one can argue. . . . Bureaucracy is the form of government in which everybody is deprived of . . . the power to act; for the rule of Nobody is not no-rule, and where all are equally powerless we have a tyranny without a tyrant.[66]

If moral agency divides along lines of institutional authority, it seems to me that every agent in the institution will wind up abdicating moral responsibility. It is for this reason that division-of-labor arguments must walk a thin line between the legitimate notion that different patterns of moral thought are appropriate in different institutional contexts—what I take to be Held's point—and the unacceptable notion that moral responsibility is itself diminished or "divided down" by institutional structure.

A final division-of-labor argument exists different from those we have just been considering. This is the general line of argument of the *Joint Conference Report*. It is based on a point emphasized by the Realists, namely, that lawyers spend very little of their time or attention on actual litigation. Mostly they are involved in other activities: document-drafting, deal-making, negotiation, giving advice, and so forth. The *Joint Conference Report* seizes on this fact to argue for a separation of lawyerly functions, with a corresponding separation of norms of professional behavior in accord with the nature of those functions. The report restricts no-holds-barred zeal to the role of advocate, a role that, to repeat, lawyers do not occupy very much of the time. The real key to the lawyer's function in society, according to the report, lies not in litigation but in wise counsel and airtight draftsmanship, which make litigation unnecessary. As to the morally troubling cases, the lawyer is permitted or even required to advise the client against "a course of conduct technically permissible under existing law, though inconsistent with its underlying spirit and purpose."[67] This the lawyer does by reminding the client of the "long-run costs" of such conduct.[68]

I do not think we need to take this argument very seriously, for it trades on a sleight-of-hand and a key omission. The sleight-of-hand lies in the tricky phrase "long-run costs." Costs to whom? Society at large? I suppose some clients engaged in morally shady projects may be dissuaded by being told how they are harming society, but surely these are just the people least likely to listen. Perhaps the long-run costs are to the client, costs in the form of loss of respect in the community, hard feelings, inability to do business with people in the future, etc. But why suppose that these inevitably accompany morally unworthy litigation? It is a commonplace that we live in a litigious society, and the fact that a person or corporation makes effective use of an arsenal of legal weapons is not often held against him. We have, for better or worse, learned to expect such behavior, and ruthless, hard-driving entrepreneurship that eagerly goes to the legal mat is more likely to win respect than enmity if it is successful. You'd be surprised what a lot of money will do to make people like an amoral wheeler-dealer. The *Joint Conference Report*'s ominous rumbling about long-run costs is mere Panglossian piety, which harmonizes society's loss with the client's, when in fact society's loss is often the client's gain.

The argument also omits the key point that, after lawyers have offered their "quiet counsel," they will still have to press forward with the representation if the client won't be dissuaded. Perhaps the lawyer can say that he or she gave morality the old college try, and his or her heart is pure. Our worry, however, was not about impure hearts, but about dirty hands. And those haven't become any cleaner.

The *Joint Conference Report*'s theory that most lawyerly functions are nonadversarial is, I might add, bad sociology. Lawyers, I have suggested, commonly act as though *all* their functions were governed by the Principles of Professionalism and Nonaccountability. It follows, then, that lawyers commonly act as though all their functions were adversarial. This is true even of the counseling and drafting functions, the report's prime examples of nonadversarial legal activities. As Judge Frankel puts it, "if not combat soldiers—if, indeed, their main mission is to avoid combat—most lawyers pattern their advice and their arrangements by imagining who might sue whom for what, and with what chances of success."[69] If lawyers' "advice and arrangements" forestall litigation, this is because they were shrewd enough that potential adversaries are sure to lose. The counseling and drafting functions, in other words, work in daily life the way nuclear deterrents work in international affairs: they keep the peace, but it would be odd to call them "non-adversarial." You needn't look hard to see the bottom line.

Thus, the division of functions within a lawyer's own professional life fares no better than the division of functions within the legal system as a whole: neither is sufficient to provide the moral timbering of adversary advocacy.

VI. Nonconsequentialist Justifications of the Adversary System

It may be thought, however, that assessing the adversary system in consequentialist terms of how it will get some job done misses the point. Some social institutions, such as participatory democracy, are justifiable despite the fact that—maybe even *because*—they are inefficient. The moral standing of such institutions has a noninstrumental basis.

I wish to consider two nonconsequentialist justifications of the adversary system. The first and perhaps boldest is an attempt to justify the adversary system in the wide sense: it is the argument that the traditional lawyer-client relation is an intrinsic moral good. The second is a cluster of related arguments: that adversary adjudication is a valued and valuable tradition, that it enjoys the consent of the governed, and that it is thus an integral part of our social fabric.

A. ADVERSARY ADVOCACY AS INTRINSICALLY GOOD

When we seek out the services of a professional, it seems to me that we generally see more to the relationship than a mere quid pro quo. Perhaps this is because the quo may be of vital importance to us; perhaps it is because a lot of quid may be required to hire those services. In any event, we have the sense of entrusting a large chunk of our life to this person, and the fact that he or she takes on so intimate a burden and handles it in a trustworthy and skillful manner when the stakes are high seems commendable in itself. Nor does the fact that the professional makes a living by providing this service seem to mitigate the praiseworthiness of it. The business aspect moves along a different moral dimension: it explains how the relationship came about, not what it involves.[70] Finally, our being able to bare our weaknesses and mistakes to the professional and receive assistance without condemnation enhances our sense that beneficence or moral graciousness is at work here. Our lawyer, *mirabile dictu,* forgives us our transgressions.

Feelings such as these are quite real; the question is whether they have merely subjective significance. If they do not, if they mean something more, that may show that Schwartz's two principles, and thus the adversary system and the behavior it countenances, are themselves positive moral goods. Such arguments are, in fact, frequently made: they are based on the idea that providing service is intrinsically good. No finer statement of this exists, in my opinion, than Mellinkoff's. He sees the paradigm client as the "man-in-trouble."

> Cruelty, oppression, deception, unhappiness, worry, strain, incomprehension, frustration, bewilderment—a sorcerer's bag of misery. These become the expected. Then the saddest of all human cries: "Who will help me?" Try God, and politics, and medicine, and a soft shoulder, sooner or later a lawyer. Too many do.
>
> The lawyer, as lawyer, is no sweet kind loving moralizer. He assumes he is needed, and that no one comes to see him to pass the time of day. He is a prober, an analyzer, a scrapper, a man with a strange devotion to his client. Beautifully strange, or so it seems to the man-in-trouble; ugly strange to the untroubled onlooker.[71]

Charles Fried thinks of the lawyer as a "special-purpose friend" whose activity—enhancing the client's autonomy and individuality—is an intrinsic moral good.[72] This is true even when the lawyer's "friendship" consists in assisting the profiteering slumlord to evict an indigent tenant or enabling the wealthy debtor to run the statute of limitations to avoid an honest debt to an old (and less well-off) friend.

I mention Mellinkoff's and Fried's arguments together because, it seems to me, they express similar ideas, while the unsavory conclusion of the latter exposes the limitations of the former. Both arguments are attempts to show that a lawyer serving a client is engaged in an intrinsic moral good. Mellinkoff's, however, really shows something much weaker, that a lawyer serving a man-in-trouble is (even more cautiously: can be) engaged in an intrinsic moral good. If the client is one of Daniel Schwartz's graymailing companies,[73] or Fried's friends-in-need, we are confronted with no man-in-trouble, and the intuitions to which Mellinkoff's argument appeals disappear. Indeed, if these were the typical clients, the real men-in-trouble—the victims of these predators—might be better off taking their chances in the war of all against all than seeking to have their "autonomy" vindicated legally. The trouble with Mellinkoff's argument is that he makes clients look more pitiable than they are.

Fried, on the other hand, is willing to bite the bullet and argue that it is morally good to represent the man-in-no-trouble-in-particular, the man-who-troubles-others. Your friendly neighborhood anticompetitive multiglomerate is nobly served by a special-purpose friend who helps extract that pound of flesh. Fried constructs a "concentric-circles morality" in which, beginning with an absolute right to self-love based on our own moral standing, we work outward toward those closest to us, then to those whose connections are more remote. Fried's idea is that the abstract connection between a remote person (even a person-in-trouble) and the agent exercises too slight a claim on the agent to override this inclination toward concrete others. This justifies lavishing special care on our friends, even at the expense of "abstract others," and since lavishing care is morally praiseworthy, once we swallow the notion that a lawyer is a special-purpose friend we are home free with the intrinsic moral worth of the lawyer-client relation:

Several of Fried's critics focus on the fact that the friendship analogy is question-begging: Fried builds enough lawyerly qualities into his concept of friendship that the rest of the argument virtually writes itself.[74] It does seem to me, however, that the analogy captures, albeit in a distorted form, some of the legitimate notion of professionals as devoted by the nature of their calling to the service of their clients. Fried's analogy contains a grain of truth.

This does not, however, vindicate the adversary system. For the friendship analogy undercuts rather than establishes the Principle of Nonaccountability. We are *not* —except for Nietzsche's Teutons and G. Gordon Liddy—willing to do grossly immoral things to help our friends, nor should we be. Lord Brougham's apology may be many things, but it is not a credo of human friendship in any of its forms. Fried realizes the danger, for he confesses that

> not only would I not lie or steal for . . . my friends, I probably also would not pursue socially noxious schemes, foreclose the mortgages of

widows or orphans, or assist in the avoidance of just punishment. So we must be careful lest the whole argument unravel on us at this point.[75]

The method for saving the argument, however, is disappointing. Fried distinguishes between *personal* wrongs committed by a lawyer, such as abusing a witness, and *institutional* wrongs occasioned by the lawyer, such as foreclosing on widows. The latter are precisely those done by the lawyer in his or her proper role of advancing the client's legal autonomy and—preestablished harmony?—they are precisely the ones that are morally O.K. That is because the lawyer isn't really doing them, the system is.

This last distinction has not been very popular since World War II, and Fried takes pains to restrict it to "generally just and decent" systems, not Nazi Germany. With this qualification, he can more comfortably assert: "We should absolve the lawyer of personal moral responsibility for the result he accomplishes because the wrong is wholly institutional."[76]

This last sentence, however, is nothing but the assertion that institutional excuses work for lawyers, and this should tip us off that Fried's argument will be useless for our purposes. For consider: our whole line of argument has been an attempt to justify the adversary system by showing that the traditional lawyer-client relation is an intrinsic moral good. Now it seems that this can be established by Fried's argument only if we are permitted to cancel the moral debit column by means of an institutional excuse; but that can work only if the institution is justified, and we are back where we started.

Part of the problem is that Fried considers the wrong institution: the context of the lawyer's behavior is not simply the system of laws in general, which he assumes to be just and decent, but the adversary system in particular with its peculiar requirement of one-sided zeal at the margin. It is the adversary system and not the system of laws that shapes the lawyer-client relationship.

The more fundamental problem, however, is that Fried takes the lawyer to be the mere occasion rather than the agent of morally-bad-but-legally-legitimate outcomes. The system did it; it "was just one of those things difficult to pre-visualize—like a cow, say, getting hit by lightning."[77]

This is false in three respects: first, because it discounts the extent to which the lawyer has had a creative hand in advocating the outcome, at times even reversing the law—a skilled lawyer, after all, argues, advocates, bargains, and persuades. Second, because the system is not an abstract structure of propositions but a social structure of interacting human beings, so that the actions of its agents *are* the system. Third, because the lawyer is indeed acting *in propria persona* by "pulling the levers of the legal machinery."[78] Fried's image seems to trade on a Rube Goldberg insight: if the apparatus is complex enough, then the lever-puller doesn't really look like the agent. But that cannot be right. *I* chop the broccoli, whether I do it with a knife or merely push the button on the blender. The legal levers are pulled by the lawyer: no one else can do it.

B. THE SOCIAL FABRIC ARGUMENT

The remaining arguments are distinct but closely related. They are two variants of the following idea, which may be called the "social fabric argument":

> Regardless of whether the adversary system is efficacious, it is an integral part of our culture, and that fact by itself justifies it.

The first variation is based on democratic theory: it claims that the adversary system is justified because it enjoys the consent of the governed. The second variation is based on conservative theory: it claims that the adversary system is justified because it is a deeply rooted part of our tradition.

According to the social fabric argument, the moral reason for staying with our institutions is precisely that they are *ours*. We live under them, adapt our lives and practices to them, assess our neighbors' behavior in their light, employ them as a standard against which to measure other ways of life. Traditional institutions bind us—morally and legitimately bind us—because we assimilate ourselves to our tradition (Variation 2). In the language of political theory, we *consent* to them (Variation 1). They express who we are and what we stand for.

This way of looking at the adversary system is quite different from the claim that it promotes the discovery of truth, or the protection of legal rights, or the rectification of wrongs. Those arguments are consequentialist in character: they are attempts to justify the adversary system on the basis of what *it* does. The social fabric argument justifies it on the basis of what *we* do, or who we are. Let us look at the variants.

The *consent argument* claims that the adversary system is part of the social contract. The adversary system is justified because it enjoys the consent of the governed, the highest moral compliment that can be paid to it in a democracy. An immediate problem with the argument, however, is that we obviously do not *explicitly* consent to the adversary system. Nobody asked us, and I don't suppose anyone intends to. If the argument is to work, the consent must be *tacit* consent, and then we are entitled to wonder how we can tell that it has been given. One test is simply that, over an extended period of time, we have incorporated the institution into our shared practices. Michael Walzer makes this suggestion: "Over a long period of time, shared experiences and cooperative activity of many different kinds shape a common life. 'Contract' is a metaphor for a process of association and mutuality."[79]

There is a problem with this account, however: just because people do not have the energy, inclination, or courage to replace their institutions we should not conclude that they want them or approve of them. But unless they want them or approve of them, people's endurance of institutions does not make the institutions morally good. The verb "consent" can mean either "put up with" or "actively approve." Only the latter has the moral force required to show that the institution is a positive moral good, but only the former is revealed by the mere existence of "our common life."

To see this, recall the original point of consent theory—classically, the theory that we incur political obligations and forfeit political rights only through our own consent. The intuition behind consent theory is that human beings are morally autonomous. For classic consent theorists such as Locke this autonomy was expressed in the concept of natural right, but other conceptual vocabularies may be used to capture the same idea. In each version, regardless of vocabulary, consent theory assumes that coercion is prima facie wrong and that this prima facie wrongness may normally be overridden only by the fact that we have consented to submit to coercive institutions. It is a theory of governmental legitimacy that assumes government is illegitimate until proven otherwise, and that specifies the standard form of such proof: demonstration of the consent of the governed.

Such a demonstration—and this is the important conclusion of the preceding paragraph—shows that a coercive institution is *not illegitimate*, that it is *acceptable*. It does not show that it is *good* and thus does not provide an argument in favor of it. Think of this analogy: you ask me for a two-week extension on repaying some money you owe me. I grant the extension—I consent to it. That shows that you *may* wait two more weeks before repaying me, but it does not show that you *should* wait two more weeks, or that it is good for you to wait two more weeks.

Thus, the most we get from tacit consent arguments, such as Walzer's appeal to our "common life," is a demonstration that we are not obliged to dismantle the adversary system. To get anything stronger we must appeal to a different concept in democratic theory from consent: we must show that people *want* the adversary system. In Rousseau's language, we must show that having an adversary system is our "general will."

Does the adversary system pass such a test? The answer, I think, is clearly no. Few of our institutions are trusted less than adversary adjudication, precisely because it seems to license lawyers to trample the truth, and legal rights, and common morality. David Mellinkoff begins *The Conscience of a Lawyer* with a history of lawyer-hating that is quite eloquent in this regard. At one point he notes:

> The full force of the complaint is not alone the denial of truth, even coupled with avarice, but that with a God given talent the lawyer stands in the way of every man's birthright, the right to justice. The lawyer, in John Stuart Mill's phrase, is ready to "frustrate justice with his tongue."[80]

Is this because of the adversary system? Indeed it is, for it is the adversary system that makes zealous advocacy of the client's interests the pillar of professional obligation. The *Joint Conference Report* puts it best:

> At the first meeting of the Conference the general problem discussed was that of bringing home to the law student, the lawyer and the public an understanding of the nature of the lawyer's professional responsibilities. All present considered that the chief obstacle to the success of this undertaking lay in "the adversary system." . . . Those who had attempted to teach ethical principles to law students found that the students were uneasy about the adversary system, some thinking of it as an unwholesome compromise with the combativeness of human nature, others vaguely approving of it but disturbed by their inability to articulate its proper limits. . . . Confronted by the layman's charge that he is nothing but a hired brain and voice, the lawyer often finds it difficult to convey an insight into the value of the adversary system.[81]

Even law students, then, are suspicious of the adversary system (though not for long). There is irony here: the need to justify the adversary system lies, according to the *Joint Conference Report,* in the fact that no one seems to trust it or the conduct it countenances; our current argument purports to justify it by claiming that we all tacitly approve of it. The argument fails.

Seeing that it fails and why can motivate the second variation, which we may call the *tradition argument.* Consent theorists assume that we have no political obligations except those we consent to, but as Hume noted, "would these reasoners look abroad into the world, they would meet with nothing that, in the least, corresponds to their ideas, or can warrant so refined and philosophical a system."[82] On the contrary, as Hume argued, people commonly consent to institutions because they take themselves to be obligated to them, rather than the other way around. We feel that traditional institutions lay claim to us, even when they themselves originated through violence or usurpation.

The power of the past to move us and bind us is enormous; compared with such deep feelings, the ideas of consent theory seem shallow and alien to human experience. This criticism is most familiar in Burke (though it is implicit in Hume as well):

> Society is indeed a contract . . . —but the state ought not to be considered as nothing better than a partnership agreement in a trade of pepper and coffee, callico or tobacco, or some such low concern, to be taken up for a little temporary interest, and to be dissolved by the fancy of the parties. . . . It is . . . a partnership not only between those who are living, but between those who are living, those who are dead, and those who are to be born. Each contract of each particular state is but a clause in the great primaeval contract of eternal society. . . . The municipal corporations of that universal kingdom are not morally at liberty at their pleasure, and on the speculations of a contingent improvement, wholly to separate and tear asunder the bonds of their subordinate community, and to dissolve it into an unsocial, uncivil, unconnected chaos of elementary principles.[83]

A Burkean argument for the adversary system would appeal to its place in our traditions and claim that we are under a moral obligation to spurn "speculations of a contingent improvement" that would tear this tradition apart. There is much to be said for Burkean argument, if for no other reason than its rejection of a shallow and philistine conception of progress.[84] But it does not apply to the adversary system.

In the first place, it ignores the fact that there *is* no constant tradition: common law constantly modifies the adversary system. Indeed, the adversary advocate is a recent invention within that changing tradition. In Great Britain, criminal defense lawyers were not permitted to address the courts until 1836;[85] in America, criminal defendants were not guaranteed counsel until 1963.[86] Civil litigants are still not guaranteed counsel, even in quasi-criminal matters such as a state's attempt to take a child from its parent.[87] It is hard to see the adversary system as "a clause in the great primaeval contract."

In the second place, the adversary system is an ancillary institution compared with those with which Burke was concerned. In William Simon's words,

> I think the argument will seem rather out of proportion to the subject. It's one thing to talk about the dangers of utopian change when you're talking about ripping the whole society apart to restructure it from top to bottom. But there are plenty of ways of abolishing adversary ethics which from a larger point of view are really just marginal social reforms which, whether good or bad, hardly suggest the likelihood of Burkean dangers. It's like making a Burkean argument against no-fault or social security.[88]

The Burkean argument is in effect a demurrer to the demand that we justify the adversary system: it suggests that the system is too central to the "great primaeval contract" to be put to the justificatory test. To this argument the reply is simply that the tradition does not clearly incorporate the adversary system, and that the system is too marginal for us to let Burkean considerations permit the demurrer.

VII. The Adversary System Excuse

A. PRAGMATIC JUSTIFICATION

So far the course of argument has been purely negative, a persecution and assassination of the adversary system. By this time you are entitled to ask what I propose putting in its place. The answer is: nothing, for I think the adversary system *is* justified.

I do not, let me quickly say, have an argumentative novelty to produce. It would be strange indeed for a social institution to be justified on the basis of virtues other than the tried and true ones, virtues that no one had noticed in it before. My justification is rather a version of the tradition argument, but purged of its ideological overtones: I shall call it the "pragmatic justification" or "pragmatic argument" to suggest its affinity with the relaxed, problem-oriented, and historicist notion of justification associated with American pragmatism. The justification is this:

First, the adversary system, despite its imperfections, irrationalities, loopholes, and perversities, seems to do as good a job as any at finding truth and protecting legal rights. None of its existing rivals, in particular the inquisitorial system and the socialist system, are demonstrably better, and some, such as trial by ordeal, are demonstrably worse. Indeed, even if one of the other systems were slightly better, the human costs—in terms of effort, confusion, anxiety, disorientation, inadvertent miscarriages of justice due to improper understanding, retraining, resentment, loss of tradition, you name it—would outweigh reasons for replacing the existing system.

Second, *some* adjudicatory system is necessary.

Third, it's the way we have always done things.

These propositions constitute a pragmatic argument: if a social institution does a reasonable enough job of its sort that the costs of replacing it outweigh the benefits, and if we need that sort of job done, we should stay with what we have.

A cynic might say that the insight underlying a pragmatic justification is twofold: first, what has been called the Law of Conservation of Trouble, and second, the principle that the devil you know is better than the devil you don't. The suspicion is that even if the adversary system murders truth (and legal rights and morality) in its characteristic way, whatever we replace it with will do so in new and unexpected ways. Why, then, go through the trauma of change?

That this is a very relaxed sort of justification may be seen from the fact that it works equally well for the inquisitorial system in France and the socialist system in Bulgaria. A pragmatic justification is weak as well because it crumbles in the face of a demonstration that, contrary to what we believe, the institution is awful enough to replace. The argument, in other words, does not really endorse an institution—it only endures it.

Accepting a pragmatic justification of the adversary system, it should be added, does not commit one to a blanket conservatism. One can believe that our society should be drastically changed or that our legal system *in praxi* is hopelessly unjust and still accept that a changed society or overhauled legal system should utilize adversary adjudication. Thus, while the argument leads to a conservative conclusion, it does so in a nonideological way, and the conclusion extends no further than the institution for which the argument is offered.

In my opinion, many of our social institutions are like the adversary system in that they admit only of pragmatic justification. Some are not intended to serve any positive moral good; some serve it badly. That these institutions are not worth replacing may be a measure of nothing more than social lethargy and our inability to come up with a better idea; my point is that this *is* a real reason. A pragmatic argument is logically weak—it justifies institutions without showing that they are better than their rivals, or even that they are particularly good—but in practice it is overwhelmingly powerful. Institutions, like bodies, obey Newton's First Law.

B. PRAGMATIC JUSTIFICATION AND INSTITUTIONAL EXCUSES

Because this is so typical of institutions it is worth asking about the effect of pragmatic argument on the moral obligations of institutional functionaries (such as lawyers). The position I want to press is roughly that a social institution that can receive only a pragmatic justification is not capable of providing institutional excuses for immoral acts. To do that, an institution must be justified in a much stronger way, by showing that it is a positive moral good. A pragmatic argument, by contrast, need show only that it is not much more mediocre than its rivals.

Let me spell this out by criticizing what I shall call the Transitivity Argument, which goes as follows:

1. The institution is justified.
2. The institution requires its functionary to do A.
3. Therefore, the functionary is justified in doing A.

This plausible-looking defense of institutional excuses can be criticized by denying the first premise; however, I am accepting the pragmatic justification of the adversary system and thus accepting the premise. Or it could be criticized by attacking the second premise: thus, William Simon and Richard Abel have argued that the role morality of lawyers is so riddled with contradictions that it is impossible to derive any coherent set of professional requirements from it.[89] My strategy, however, is to deny that the conclusion follows from the premises. The institutional obligation is only a prima facie obligation, and the weaker the justification of the institution, the weaker the force of this obligation in overriding other morally relevant factors.

To get the argument underway, let us look at the way an institutional excuse might work when the institution is strongly justified, when it is a positive moral good.

Consider, as an example, a charitable organization whose sole function is to distribute food to famine-stricken people in impoverished areas of the world. We will call this the *institution*. Division of labor within it creates different jobs or *institutional tasks*, each of which has specified duties or *role-obligations*. These may be quite general: the logistics officer, for example, might have as his role-obligation procuring means of transporting food. To carry out the role-obligation, he must perform various actions, call them the *role-acts*.

Let us suppose that to get food to a remote village the logistics officer must obtain several trucks from a local, very powerful gangster, P. As it happens, P is involved in a number of unsavory activities, including a plan to murder a local man, because P wants to sleep with the man's wife. Imagine further that the logistics officer overhears P dispatching a murderer to kill the man that very night, that P discovers that the logistics officer has overheard him, and that P tells the officer that if the man is warned and escapes, P will not provide the trucks.

The officer is in a moral dilemma. Other things being equal, he is under a moral obligation to warn the man. Let us, at any rate, suppose that this is so. But here, if anywhere, we may wish to permit an institutional excuse. Suppose the officer complies with P's demand. Asked to justify this, he says, "My job is more important." This is an institutional excuse, the structure of which may be spelled out as follows: he points out that the role-act of complying with P is required by his role-obligation, which in turn is necessary to perform the institutional task, which (finally) is justified by the positive moral good of the institution—the saving of many innocent lives.

The general problem, which creates the dilemma, is that the propositions

> The institution is a morally good one

and

> The institution imposes role-obligations on its officers some of which may mandate morally bad role-acts

can both be true.

In such a case, the institutional excuse, fully spelled out, will take the form I have indicated: the agent justifies the role-act by showing it is required by the role-obligation, justifies the obligation by showing it derives from the institutional task, justifies the institutional task by appealing to the structure of the institution, and justifies the institution by demonstrating its moral goodness.

Let us apply this form of argument to a legal example. Freedman uses it in his analysis of the Lake Pleasant bodies case.[90] The lawyers' role-act (preserving the defendant's confidence) was required by the general duty of confidentiality (the role-obligation). This is justified by arguing that the duty is required in order to guarantee adequate criminal defense (the institutional task). (That argument is somewhat detailed, and I will not go into it here. Let me note that this stage of the argument is where most policy disputes in legal ethics are located.) The next step is to show that such defense is required by the adversary system, and this in turn, or so it is claimed and so I have agreed, serves the positive moral good of preserving individual rights against the encroachment of the state.

I am *not* claiming that an institutional excuse is inevitably appropriate when the institution is strongly justified. You and I may differ in our assessment even of the examples. I am claiming only that in such cases a difficult moral dilemma exists, from which an institutional excuse is one possible way out.

If, on the other hand, an institution is justified only by pragmatic argument, the sides of the dilemma do not have equal weight and the institutional excuse collapses. For in that case it reads as follows:

> It is true that I am morally wronging you. But that is required by my role-obligations, which are essential to my institutional task, which is necessary to the structure of the institution, which is justified
>
> because it is there.
> because it's the way we do things around here.
> because it's not worth the trouble to replace it.

This, I think, will not do. The excuse rests on an elephant that stands on a tortoise that floats in the sky. But the sky is falling.

Compare this real-life example with the Lake Pleasant case: A youth, Spaulding, badly injured in an automobile wreck, sued for damages. The conscientious defense lawyer had his own doctor examine the youth; the doctor discovered a life-threatening aortic aneurism, apparently caused by the accident, that Spaulding's doctors had not found. Spaulding was willing to settle the case for $6500, but the defense lawyer realized that if the youth learned of the aneurism he would demand a much higher amount.[91]

The defense lawyer concealed the information and settled for $6500. How could this be justified? Presumably, the argument would have to track Freedman's defense in the Lake Pleasant case, but the final step would be missing. In this case the adversary system is not strongly justified by the liberal argument about keeping the state's hands off people accused of a crime. No one is accused of a crime in this case. Uncharitably put, the basis of confidentiality here is the need to save money for a client or (more likely) an insurance company. Charitably put, it is that the adversary system is weakly justified—justified because it is there. That may be a reason to risk one's own life on a mountain, but it is not a reason to risk Spaulding's life in a law office.

It might be objected to this line of criticism that the pragmatic argument for the adversary system *is* a strong justification for it, even in noncriminal cases. After all, what better justification of the system can there be than saying that it performs a necessary function as well as any of its competitors? What absolute yardstick is used to measure it and find it wanting?

The answer to these questions has already been given in our discussion of the difference between the criminal and noncriminal contexts.[92] In the noncriminal context, the primary end of adversary adjudication is the assignment of rewards and remedies on the basis of parties' behavior as prescribed by legal norms: legal justice, rather than protection from the state, is the goal. The adversary method is supposed to yield accurate accounts of facts and legitimate interpretations of the law. *That* is the absolute yardstick: if the adversary system yields legal justice, it is a positive moral good. But, as I have argued, we have no reason to believe that it does yield legal justice in the hard cases.

An analogy may clarify this point. Scientists at times accept and use a theory because it is the best account going, even though they do not have much confidence in its truth. Such a theory is pragmatically justified in much the same way as the adversary system: it is as good as its competitors, some theory is necessary, and it is there. It's just that most scientists in the field think the theory will turn out to be false—and for that reason it is weakly, not strongly, justified.[93]

The general point is that some practices carry absolute criteria of success. The criterion of success for a scientific theory is truth; the criterion of success for mountain climbing is getting to the top and back. Other practices carry criteria that are merely relative (the fastest runner in the world is *ipso facto* a successful runner). A pragmatic argument strongly justifies only the latter sort of practices, but, if I am right, the adversary system is of the former sort.

Let us return to the two confidentiality examples. Their general point is that one can be excused from a moral obligation only by another moral consideration that outweighs it: an institution provides a moral excuse only if it has moral cachet. If the institution is justified only because it is there, it possesses only the minutest quantum of force to excuse an immoral act. The Transitivity Argument fails.

Another way to see this, derived from a point made by Gerald Postema and Bernard Williams,[94] can also be offered. Suppose that the Transitivity Argument were valid. Then it would not be immoral for lawyers to engage in ruthless, rights-violating activity. They would therefore have no occasion for moral regret at their actions. But, and this is Postema's and Williams's point, we want agents in "dirty hands" situations to feel regret at what they must do since otherwise they will not develop the sort of moral character that enables them to judge when they should refrain from ruthless action. It follows that we should accept the Transitivity Argument only if we are willing to accept lawyers who are incapable of turning off their own adversariality. But that is absurd, because such a lawyer would be unable to draw adequate lines in *any* sort of situation that requires normative judgment, and that is inconsistent with what it takes to practice law at all.

The basic problem with the Transitivity Argument is that it exempts officers of an institution from ordinary moral requirements that conflict with role-obligations, even though the institution itself is in place only because we have always done it that way. The result is to place conformity to existing institutions beyond the very possibility of moral criticism. This, however, is no longer justified conservatism: rather, it is fetishism of tradition.

Pragmatic arguments do not really praise institutions; they merely give reason for not burying them. Since their force is more inertial than moral, they create insufficient counterweight to resolve dilemmas in favor of the role-obligation. An excuse based on institutions justified in this way is simply a "good soldier" argument with little more to be said.

VIII. Conclusion and Peroration

By this point, I think, the argument has just about exhausted itself. It is time to summarize.

Perhaps the best way to see the import of the arguments I have been offering is not as an attack on the adversary system (for, after all, I have not suggested that it should be replaced) so much as an attack on an ideology consisting of these ideas:

1. The adversary system is the best system of justice ever devised.
2. It is a delicately poised instrument in which the generation of just outcomes depends on the regular functioning of each of its parts.
3. *Hence* the pursuit of justice morally obligates an attorney to assume a one-sided Broughamesque role.
4. The adversary system, in consequence, institutionally excuses lawyers from ordinary moral obligations conflicting with their professional obligations.
5. Broughamesque advocacy is, moreover, a cornerstone of our system of political liberties, for it is the last defense of the hapless criminal-accused against the awesome power of the state. To restrict the advocate is to invite totalitarianism.

I have argued, I hope convincingly, against the first four of these propositions. About the fifth a more cautious conclusion is in order. The argument it offers that the criminal defense lawyer "must not regard the alarm, the torments, the destruction which he may bring upon others" (Brougham, again) is rather persuasive, but only because of two special features of the criminal context: that we have political reasons for handicapping the government in its role as enforcer, and that the criminal defendant comes closest to the paradigm of the man-in-trouble. The argument, then, countenances adversarial ruthlessness as a blanket policy only in criminal and quasi-criminal defense, and thus only in these situations is the adversary system available as an institutional excuse. Criminal defense is the exception that proves the ordinary moral rule.

What does all this mean in noncriminal contexts, where this institutional excuse based on political theory is unavailable? The answer, very simply, is this. The adversary system possesses only the slightest moral force, and thus appealing to it can excuse only the slightest moral wrongs. Anything else that is morally wrong for a nonlawyer to do on behalf of another person is morally wrong for a lawyer to do as well. The lawyer's role carries no moral privileges and immunities.

This does not mean that zealous advocacy is immoral, not even when it frustrates the search for truth or violates legal rights. Sometimes frustrating the search for truth may be a morally worthy thing to do, and sometimes moral rights are ill served by legal rights. All I am insisting on is that the standards by which such judgments are made are the same for lawyers and nonlawyers. If a lawyer is permitted to puff, bluff, or threaten on certain occasions, this is not because of the adversary system and the Principle of Nonaccountability, but because, in such circumstances, anyone would be permitted to do these things. Nothing justifies doing them on behalf of a predator.

But, it will be objected, my argument leads to a paradox, for I have claimed to offer a vindication, albeit a weak one, of the adversary system, and therefore of the duties of partisan advocacy that it entails. Am I not saying that a lawyer may be professionally obligated to do A and morally obligated not to do A?

That is indeed what I am saying, but there is no contradiction here. The adversary system and the system of professional obligation it mandates are justified only in that, lacking a clearly superior alternative, they should not be replaced. This implies, I have argued, that when professional and moral obligation conflict, moral obligation takes precedence. When they don't conflict, professional obligations rule the day. The Principle of Professionalism follows from the fact that we have an adversary system; the Principle of Nonaccountability does not. The point of elaborating the former is to tell the lawyer what, in this system, professionalism requires—to say that it requires zeal, for example, even when cutting corners might be more profitable or pleasant. Professionalism can tell a lawyer not to cut corners; my point is that it cannot mandate him or her to cut throats. When moral obligation conflicts with professional obligation, the lawyer must become a civil disobedient.

Not that this is likely to happen. Lawyers get paid for their services, not for their consciences. But so does everyone else. As we do not expect the world to strike a truce in the war of all against all, we should not expect lawyers to. Shen Te, the Good Woman of Setzuan, says:

> I'd like to be good, it's true, but there's the rent to pay. And that's not all: I sell myself for a living. Even so I can't make ends meet, there's too much competition.[95]

That, of course, is the way the world is, and criticizing an ideology won't change the world. The point of the exercise, I suppose, is merely to get our moral ideas straight: one less ideology is, after all, one less excuse.

Notes

1. Samuel Taylor Coleridge, "Duties and Needs of an Advocate," in *The Table Talk and Omiana of Samuel Taylor Coleridge*, edited by T. Ashe (London: George Bell and Sons, 1888), pp. 140–41.

2. William Whewell, *The Elements of Morality, Including Polity*, 2 vols. (London: John W. Parker, 1845), vol. 1, pp. 258–59.

3. George Sharswood, *A Compend of Lectures on the Aims and Duties of the Profession of the Law* (Philadelphia: T. & J. W. Johnson, 1854), p. 84.

4. Murray Schwartz, "The Professionalism and Accountability of Lawyers," *California Law Review* 66 (1978): 673.

5. Ibid.

6. Gerald J. Postema, "Moral Responsibility in Professional Ethics," *New York University Law Review* 55 (1980): 73.

7. William Simon, "The Ideology of Advocacy: Procedural Justice and Professional Ethics," *Wisconsin Law Review* 1978 (1978): 36–37.

8. Schwartz, "Professionalism and Accountability," p. 674.

9. Mitchell Rogovin, "'Graymail': Shaded Variant of a Darker Hue," *Legal Times of Washington*, March 26, 1979; see Lawrence Meyer, "Justice Dept. is Examining Helms' Testimony on CIA," *The Washington Post*, February 12, 1975, pp. A1, A12.

10. Joe Trento, "Inside the Helms File," *National Law Journal*, December 22, 1980, p. 1.

11. Daniel Schwartz, "The 'New' Legal Ethics and the Administrative Law Bar," Chapter 10, this volume, pp. 247–48.

12. J. Nightingale, ed., *Trial of Queen Caroline*, 3 vols. (London: J. Robins & Co., Albion Press, 1820–21), vol. 2, p. 8.

13. David Mellinkoff, *The Conscience of a Lawyer* (St. Paul, Minn.: West, 1973), p. 188.

14. See Edward Dauer and Arthur Leff, "Correspondence: The Lawyer as Friend," *Yale Law Journal* 86 (1977): 581.

15. *Tukiar and the King*, 52 Commw. L.R. 335, 347 (Austl., 1934), quoted in Mellinkoff, *The Conscience of a Lawyer*, p. 273.

16. A lengthy discussion of this well-known case, with documents and interviews, is found in Patrick A. Keenan, ed., *Teaching Professional Responsibility: Materials and Proceedings from the National Conference* (Detroit: University of Detroit Press, 1979), pp. 233–324.

17. The damages to all concerned in the Lake Pleasant bodies case were considerable: the parents of the victims were anguished, the public aghast, the tourism business in Lake Pleasant harmed because of the unsolved disappearances, Garrow convicted and sentenced to 35-years-to-life, Belge and Armani nearly ruined.

18. Friedrich Nietzsche, *Thus Spoke Zarathustra*, in *The Portable Nietzsche*, edited and translated by Walter Kaufmann (New York: Viking Press, 1954), p. 171.

19. *ABA Model Code of Professional Responsibility* (1974 revision), EC 7–1.

20. Marvin Frankel, *Partisan Justice* (New York: Hill and Wang, 1980), p. 18.

21. See Martha Mills, "Motions to Disqualify: Caveat Advocatus," *Litigation* 6 (1979): 47–50 and, for a pioneering but not altogether satisfactory analysis, Lawrence Crocker, "Comment: The Ethics of Moving to Disqualify Opposing Counsel for Conflict of Interest," *Duke Law Journal* 1979 (1979): 1310–34. For general background, see "Developments in the Law—Conflicts of Interest in the Legal Profession," *Harvard Law Review* 94 (1981): 1244–1503.

22. Yasunari Kawabata, *The Master of Go*, translated by Edward Seidensticker (New York: Alfred A. Knopf, 1972), p. 54.

23. Mellinkoff, *The Conscience of a Lawyer*, p. 152.

24. *ABA Code*, EC 7–1 to 7–5 are clear on this point.

25. Ibid., EC 7–19.

26. See Murray Schwartz, "Professionalism and Accountability," p. 672; Lon Fuller, "The Adversary System," in *Talks on American Law*, edited by Harold J. Berman (New York: Vintage Books, 1961), pp. 30–32; Martin Golding, "On the Adversary System and Justice," in *Philosophical Law*, edited by Richard Bronaugh (Westport, Conn.: Greenwood Press, 1978), p. 105.

27. *ABA Code*, Canon 5.

28. Ibid., Canon 6.

29. David Luban, "Professional Ethics: A New Code for Lawyers?" *The Hastings Center Report* 10 (June 1980): 12.

30. A sophisticated attempt to characterize the principles of lawyers' ethics through the nature of the lawyer-client relationship rather than the adversary system is Charles Fried, "The Lawyer as Friend: The Moral Foundations of the Lawyer-Client Relation," *Yale Law Journal* 85 (1976): 1060–89. See also Charles Fried, *Right and Wrong* (Cambridge, Mass.: Harvard University Press, 1978), pp. 167–94.

31. Indeed, one of Schwartz's reasons for writing the article (see note 4) was to propose a reform according to which the principles do not apply in the context of negotiation. Currently, negotiation is seen as a subject calling for as much "hardball" as courtroom advocacy.

32. An attempt to argue that the real purpose of lawyers' codes of conduct is market-control from the supply side is Richard L. Abel, "Why Does the ABA Promulgate Ethical Rules?" *Texas Law Review* 59 (1981): 639–88.

33. Monroe Freedman, *Lawyers' Ethics in an Adversary System* (Indianapolis: Bobbs-Merrill, 1975).

34. Ibid., pp. 2, 4.

35. John Griffiths suggests that this way of thinking reflects "little more than the concerns of the middle class in connection with the rare occasions on which it has to fear prosecution." ("Ideology in Criminal Procedure *or* A Third 'Model' of the Criminal Process," *Yale Law Journal* 79 [1970]: 415.) It is clear, of course, that despite the official rhetoric of the bar indigent criminal defendants do not often get the zealous advocacy the rhetoric promises; it is hard to see, though, why it would not benefit them if they did get it, and thus why it is a strictly "middle class" concern. Griffiths's point seems to be that treating the exceptional case of genuine zeal as a paradigm simply reinforces a false liberal political philosophy "assuming the inevitability of a state of irreconcilable hostility between the individual and the state" (p. 413)—a political philosophy that is "middle class." Now, I do not wish to defend liberalism as a general political philosophy, for I think that trafficking in abstractions such as "the individual" and "the state" is essentially misleading. (For the same reason, I think that Griffiths's own proposal of the "fundamental reconcilability" of individual and state is as misleading as the position he attacks.) Neither is it true that *every* criminal defendant is equally set-upon by the state—think, for example, of the Watergate defendants. Thus, there *are* significant class differences in the way criminal procedure actually proceeds. Nevertheless, the liberal abstraction is a rather good first approximation of the relationship between defendant and state. Maurice Nadjari, lecturing his fellow prosecutors, told them that their "true purpose is to convict the guilty man who sits at the defense table, and to go for the jugular as viciously and rapidly as possible. . . . You must never forget that your goal is total annihilation" (quoted in Frankel, *Partisan Justice*, p. 32). If that isn't "irreconcilable hostility," what is? The criminal defense situation may, in fact, be the *only* one of which liberal political theory is true. The *real* objection to "Better a hundred criminals go free" is not that it is a middle class bromide, but rather that the middle class is so willing to abandon it the moment that a suspected mugger or burglar enters the docket.

36. In *The Conscience of a Lawyer*.

37. John Thibaut and Laurens Walker, *Procedural Justice: A Psychological Analysis* (Hillsdale, N.J.: Lawrence Erlbaum Associates, 1975).

38. See Mirjan Damaska, "Presentation of Evidence and Fact-finding Precision," *University of Pennsylvania Law Review* 123 (1975): 1083–106.

39. Karl Popper, *Conjectures and Refutations: The Growth of Scientific Knowledge* (New York: Harper & Row, 1963), pp. iv, 33–65, 114–19, 352, 355–63. See Marvin Frankel,

"The Search for Truth: An Umpireal View," *University of Pennsylvania Law Review* 123 (1975): 1036; and Monroe Freedman, "Judge Frankel's Search for Truth," *University of Pennsylvania Law Review* 123 (1975): 1060–61.

40. And then again, perhaps not. See Imre Lakatos, "Falsification and the Methodology of Scientific Research Programmes," in *Criticism and the Growth of Knowledge*, edited by Imre Lakatos and Alan Musgrave (Cambridge: Cambridge University Press, 1970); Paul Feyerabend, *Against Method* (London: New Left Books, 1975); and *Science in a Free Society* (London: New Left Books, 1978).

41. Feyerabend to the contrary (*Against Method, Science in a Free Society*). But his view is widely rejected, and anyway he does not claim that *truth* is the outcome of the process.

42. Hannah Arendt, *Eichmann in Jerusalem: A Report on the Banality of Evil* (New York: Viking Press, 1964), 2nd ed., p. 26.

43. Frank Moya, "The Teacher Takes the Final Exam," *National Law Journal*, November 17, 1981, p. 22.

44. Ibid.

45. Popper, *Conjectures and Refutations*, p. 352.

46. Lon Fuller and John D. Randall, "Professional Responsibility: Report of the Joint Conference," *ABA Journal* 44 (1958): 1160. Cited hereafter as *Joint Conference Report*.

47. A similar argument is used by William Simon, "The Ideology of Advocacy," p. 76.

48. *Joint Conference Report*, p. 1160.

49. Ibid., p. 1161.

50. Ibid., p. 1160.

51. For related arguments expressing skepticism about the truth-finding function of the adversary system, see Golding, "On the Adversary System and Justice," note 26 above, pp. 106–12; and Alan H. Goldman, *The Moral Foundations of Professional Ethics* (Totowa, N.J.: Rowman and Littlefield, 1980), pp. 112–16. Geoffrey Hazard, the Reporter who drafted the current ABA Model Rules of Professional Conduct, acknowledges that "there is no proof that the adversary system of trial yields truth more often than other systems of trial; that . . . is an article of faith, because there is no way to conduct a reliable experiment." "Rules of Legal Ethics: The Drafting Task," *The Record of the Association of the Bar of the City of New York* 36 (March 1981): 93.

52. Steven Sachs, untitled and unpublished speech, 1980.

53. Freedman, *Lawyers' Ethics*, pp. 3–4.

54. It should be noted that other values than truth and legal rights are also implicated in trial procedure. For example, in a personal injury negligence case evidence that the defendant has repaired the site of an accident after it happened is not admissible, even though it would indirectly establish that the defendant really had been negligent. The reason for this policy is that to do otherwise would discourage the repair and so enhance a menace to the public. It is thus an oversimplification to suggest that the whole purpose of the trial process is to protect the interests of the court (by getting at the truth) or the parties. The public interest is also involved.

55. Freedman, *Lawyers' Ethics*, pp. 3–4.

56. Ibid., p. 8. See also James L. Oakes, "Lawyer and Judge: The Ethical Duty of Competency," in *Ethics and Advocacy* (Washington, D.C.: The Roscoe Pound-American Trial Lawyers Foundation, 1978), p. 60, who argues that the adversary system is required by Article III and Amendments V, VI, and VII of the Constitution.

57. Theodore Koskoff, "Introduction" to *The American Lawyer's Code of Conduct Public Discussion Draft* (Washington, D.C.: The Roscoe Pound-American Trial Lawyers Foundation, 1980), p. ii.

58. See, for example *Hickman* v. *Taylor*, 329 U.S. 495, 514 (1946); or *Herring* v. *New York*, 422 U.S. 853, 857–58 (1974).

59. *The Attic Nights of Aulus Gellius*, translated by John C. Rolfe (Cambridge, Mass.: Harvard University Press, 1954), I. vi. 4–5 (quoted in Golding, "On the Adversary System and Justice").

60. Advertisement, *National Law Journal*, June 2, 1980, p. 30.

61. Thomas Nagel, "Ruthlessness in Public Life," in *Public and Private Morality*, edited by Stuart Hampshire (Cambridge: Cambridge University Press, 1978), p. 85.

62. Sharswood, *A Compend of Lectures*, note 3 above, p. 84.

63. Virginia Held, "Justification: Legal and Political," *Ethics* 86 (October 1975): 1–16.

64. Ibid., p. 11.

65. Ibid. It is this argument, justifying an institutional division of labor by its "morally salutary" results, that leads me to classify Held's theory as consequentialist, though it has nothing to do with simple utilitarian arguments. See also Chapter 3, this volume.

66. Hannah Arendt, *On Violence* (New York: Harcourt, Brace & World, 1970), p. 81.

67. *Joint Conference Report*, p. 1161.

68. Ibid.

69. Frankel, *Partisan Justice*, p. 4.

70. Fried, "The Lawyer as Friend," p. 1075.

71. Mellinkoff, *The Conscience of a Lawyer*, p. 270.

72. Fried, "The Lawyer as Friend," pp. 1068–73.

73. See text accompanying note 11 above.

74. See Dauer and Leff, "Correspondence: The Lawyer as Friend," note 14 above, pp. 577–78; Simon, "The Ideology of Advocacy," note 7 above, pp. 108–09.

75. Fried, *Right and Wrong*, p. 191.

76. Ibid., p. 192.

77. Galway Kinnell, *The Book of Nightmares* (Boston: Houghton Mifflin, 1971), p. 43.

78. Slightly paraphrased from Fried, *Right and Wrong*, p. 192 and "The Lawyer as Friend," p. 1085.

79. Michael Walzer, *Just and Unjust Wars: A Moral Argument with Historical Illustrations* (New York: Basic Books, 1977), p. 54.

80. Mellinkoff, *The Conscience of a Lawyer*, p. 12.

81. *Joint Conference Report*, p. 1159.

82. David Hume, "Of the Original Contract," in *Essays, Literary, Moral and Political* (London: George Routledge and Sons, n.d.), p. 272.

83. Edmund Burke, *Reflections on the Revolution in France* (Garden City, N.Y.: Anchor Books, 1973), p. 110.

84. My view here is heavily influenced by Walter Benjamin's brilliant but gnomic "Theses on the Philosophy of History," in *Illuminations*, edited by Hannah Arendt, translated by Harry Zohn (New York: Schocken Books, 1969). See particularly Thesis XV, p. 261.

85. Mellinkoff, *The Conscience of a Lawyer*, p. 47.

86. *Gideon* v. *Wainwright*, 372 U.S. 335 (1963).

87. See, most recently, *Lassiter* v. *Department of Social Services of Durham, N.C.*, 452 U.S. 18 (1981).

88. Letter to the author, January 31, 1981.

89. Abel, "Why Does the ABA Promulgate Ethical Rules?" note 32 above; Simon, "The Ideology of Advocacy," note 7 above.

90. Freedman, *Lawyers' Ethics*, chap. 1.

91. *Spaulding* v. *Zimmerman*, 116 N.W. 2d 704 (1962).

92. See pp. 91–93 above.

93. I am indebted to Victoria Choy for this point.

94. Gerald Postema, "Moral Responsibility in Professional Ethics," note 6 above, pp. 79–80. Bernard Williams, "Politics and Moral Character," in *Public and Private Morality*, edited by Stuart Hampshire (Cambridge: Cambridge University Press, 1978), pp. 61–65; Chapter 11, this volume.

95. Bertolt Brecht, *The Good Woman of Setzuan*, translated by Eric Bentley (New York: Grove Press, 1947), p. 24.

[8]

THE IDEOLOGY OF ADVOCACY: PROCEDURAL JUSTICE AND PROFESSIONAL ETHICS*

WILLIAM H. SIMON†

"If you want to take dough from a murderer for helping him beat the rap you must be admitted to the bar . . . ."

Rex Stout[1]

The system! I am told on all hands, it's the system. I mustn't look to individuals. It's the system. . . . I mustn't go to Mr. Tulkinghorn, the solicitor in Lincoln's Inn Fields, and say to him when he makes me furious by being so cool and satisfied—as they all do, for I know they gain by it while I lose, don't I?—I mustn't say to him, "I will have something out of someone for my ruin, by fair means or foul!" He *is not responsible. It's the system. But, if I do no violence to any of them. . . . I will accuse the individual workers of that system against me, face to face, before the great eternal bar!*

Charles Dickens[2]

Conventional morality frowns at the ethics of advocacy. Public opinion disapproves of what it considers the lawyer's most characteristic activities. Popular culture can reconcile itself to him only by pretending that all his clients are virtuous. The lawyer's response takes the form of a dialectic of cynicism and naiveté. On one hand, he sees his more degrading activities as licensed by a fundamental amorality lying beneath conventional morality. On the other hand, he sees his more heartening ones as serving an institutional justice higher than conventional morality. The two moods divide the profession as a whole, and the division can sometimes be seen in the professional lives of individual lawyers, as, for instance, when they turn from their paid efforts on behalf of what they admit to be private interests to their donated services on behalf of what they claim to be the public good.

The formal, articulate expression of the lawyer's response is the "Ideology of Advocacy." The purpose of the Ideology of Advocacy is to rationalize the most salient aspect of the lawyer's peculiar ethical orientation: his explicit refusal to be bound by personal and social norms which he considers binding on others. The most elaborate expressions of the

* I am grateful to many for advice and encouragement in connection with this essay. It would be impractical to name them all, but I must acknowledge special debts to Gary Bellow, Marc Galanter, Jeanne Kettleson, Leslie A.J. Simon, and Roberto Mangabeira Unger.

† A.B., 1969, Princeton University; J.D., 1974, Harvard Law School.

1. R. STOUT, IN THE BEST FAMILIES 199 (1950).
2. C. DICKENS, BLEAK HOUSE 228 (Signet ed. 1964) (emphasis in original).

Ideology of Advocacy occur in officially promulgated rules of ethics, in doctrinal writings on legal ethics, the attorney-client evidentiary privilege, and the constitutional right to counsel, and in writings on the legal profession.

Although this literature is voluminous, it is barren of any fundamental questioning of the ethical premises of legal professionalism. The profession has never been inclined to join issue on any but the most superficial level with the lay critique of these premises, and it presently seems less disposed toward reexamination of them than ever. The public disgust at the behavior of the lawyers in the Watergate affair has prompted an elaborate pretense of soul-searching on the part of the profession, but Watergate has in fact been an occasion for retrenchment and re-indoctrination, rather than reexamination. The profession has viewed Watergate as revealing problems regarding the enforcement of professional norms, but has refused to see it as raising questions about the validity of those norms. In the profession's current view, what is needed is not criticism of legal ethics, but rather more zealous propagation of those ethics through greater emphasis on the professional catechism in law school curricula and bar examinations.

Of course, there is a growing body of writing addressed to the profession which is critical of the conduct of lawyers and professional organizations. Yet, most of these discussions take place within the framework of the Ideology of Advocacy and do not involve criticism of its premises.[3] The more prominent of these discussions have been of two types. First, doctrinal writings on legal ethics and judicial procedure often take the form of a debate between the partisans of a "battle" model and the partisans of a "truth" model of adjudication. A famous example of this debate will be discussed in the next section.[4] These writings criticize certain kinds of conduct by lawyers as inconsistent with one or the other of these models. Yet, almost all of the distinctive ethical views of lawyers can be rationalized in terms of one or the other of the models, and the differences between them are greatly exaggerated in the debate. Both models accept the basic principles of the Ideology of Advocacy and are primarily concerned with defending those principles.

Second, there is a substantial body of sociology and social criticism which focuses on the legal profession. Some of this literature argues that lawyers compromise their clients' interests in order to advance their own

3. Important exceptions, which do involve criticism of the basic premises, are Bellow & Kettleson, *The Mirror of Public Interest Ethics: Problems and Paradoxes* (1977) (unpublished manuscript on file with author) [hereinafter cited as Bellow & Kettleson]; Griffiths, *Ideology in Criminal Procedure or A Third "Model" of the Criminal Process*, 79 YALE L.J. 359 (1970) [hereinafter cited as Griffiths]; Wasserstrom, *Lawyers as Professionals: Some Moral Issues*, 5 HUMAN RIGHTS 1 (1975).

4. *See* text accompanying notes 8-13 *infra*.

interests.[5] Other studies focus on an elite within the profession and argue that the elite has used professional ethics and organization to achieve prestige and economic privilege at the expense of the less powerful members of the profession and of the lower classes generally.[6] Studies which emphasize the exploitation of clients explicitly accept the Ideology of Advocacy and criticize lawyers for failing to live up to it. Although studies which emphasize elite domination purport to criticize legal ethics and professionalism, they do not deal with the basic principles expressed by the Ideology of Advocacy. Instead, they focus on principles such as restrictions on membership in the profession and prohibitions on advertising and solicitation. Such studies are concerned less with the nature of legal services than with their distribution.[7] In suggesting that the increased availability of legal services allegedly inhibited by professional ethics and organization would be desirable, these writings often rely on the Ideology of Advocacy. It is notable that writing from both perspectives often calls for reforms which would enlarge the size and power of the profession.

This essay attempts a critical examination of the Ideology of Advocacy. Section I outlines the basic principles of the Ideology. The following three sections are then devoted to a discussion and criticism of the jurisprudential doctrines with which these basic principles are defended. Each of these sections describes and criticizes one of the three most prominent versions of the Ideology. The descriptions of the three versions are not derived directly from officially promulgated doctrine or from the writings of any specific theorist. Rather, they are in the nature of ideal types, heuristic constructions which are intended to be representative of the prevailing thought within the profession about the ethics of law practice. The use of this procedure involves the risk that the ideal types will be taken for "straw men." Yet, the procedure is necessary in view of the absence of any coherent, systematic defenses of legal ethics. The

5. *See, e.g.*, D. ROSENTHAL, LAWYER AND CLIENT: WHO'S IN CHARGE? 106-16 (1974) [hereinafter cited as ROSENTHAL]; Blumberg, *The Practice of Law as a Confidence Game: Organizational Cooptation of a Profession*, 1 LAW & SOC. REV. 15 (1967) [hereinafter cited as Blumberg]; Skolnick, *Social Control in the Adversary System*, 11 J. CONFL. RES. 52 (1971) [hereinafter cited as Skolnick].

6. *See* J. AUERBACH, UNEQUAL JUSTICE: LAWYERS AND SOCIAL CHANGE IN MODERN AMERICA (1976) [hereinafter cited as AUERBACH]; J. CARLIN, LAWYERS' ETHICS (1966); Schuchman, *Ethics and Legal Ethics: The Propriety of the Canons as a Group Moral Code*, 37 GEO. WASH. L. REV. 244 (1968).

7. More radical criticisms of conventional law practice are sometimes made by partisans of public interest law. *See, e.g.*, Nader, *Law Schools and Law Firms*, 54 MINN. L. REV. 493 (1970); Comment, *The New Public Interest Lawyers*, 79 YALE L. J. 1069, 1119-37 (1970) [hereinafter cited as Comment, *The New Public Interest Lawyers*]. However, such criticism is often ambiguous. Like the works cited in the preceding note, it tends to focus disapproval on the professional elite and on its service to the dominant social groups. On the other hand, it sometimes urges lawyers not only to make conventional legal services available to the less powerful but also to devote their efforts to specific substantive ends and interests. Such criticism seems to hesitate between a critique based on the distribution of legal services, which would be compatible with the Ideology of Advocacy, and a critique based on the nature of legal services, which would involve a repudiation of the Ideology of Advocacy.

more general writing on jurisprudence has usually avoided the questions of legal ethics and professionalism. On the other hand, writing directly concerned with these subjects has tended to treat the issues in conclusory terms. So long as its doctrines are expressed only in an amorphous, fragmentary fashion, the Ideology eludes criticism. Even arguments which have been discredited after critical examination in other areas of law remain unchallenged as tacit assumptions in the Ideology of Advocacy. In order to criticize the Ideology, it is necessary to reconstruct the unstated or partially stated assumptions and arguments on which it depends.

The descriptions of the three versions of the Ideology of Advocacy are also intended to suggest the nature of the evolution of the ethical consciousness of lawyers over the course of the present century. Although the three versions of the Ideology of Advocacy all defend the same core of basic principles, each is based on different attitudes and commitments, and each describes and recommends a somewhat different style of law practice. Although all three versions exert influence today, each originated in a distinct historical situation and attained its greatest influence at a different time. The influence of the three versions has also varied significantly among different strata of the profession and in different areas of law practice. The three ideal types depart in some respects from some familiar categories of American legal history. For instance, writers identified with American Legal Realism will be cited in connection with all three versions. In part, such differences may be due to the overbreadth of the familiar categories, but they are also due more directly to the fact that the focus on this essay is more limited than that of writings on legal intellectual history in general. The present essay focuses on the way in which lawyers rationalize their departures from personal and social norms. Although, as will be shown, this issue depends on many other critical jurisprudential issues, it is partially independent of some issues.

The fifth section of the essay will attempt to formulate an overview of the subject matter from the critiques of the three versions of the Ideology of Advocacy and to describe the fundamental defects of all defenses of lawyers' ethics and legal professionalism. It will argue that the practices prescribed by the Ideology of Advocacy are inconsistent with the values invoked to justify those practices. At the base of each version of the Ideology of Advocacy is an appeal to an aspect of the fundamental value of individuality: autonomy, responsibility, dignity. Yet, in each instance, the practices and attitudes of professional advocacy subvert the norms of individuality in the interest of a repressive conception of social stability. The essay will argue that to take the value of individuality seriously would require the abandonment of the Ideology of Advocacy and of legal professionalism. Indeed, it will also suggest that respect for the value of law itself may require the repudiation of legal professionalism. The concluding section of the essay attempts to suggest an alternative approach to the problems of advocacy which might avoid the defects of the Ideology of Advocacy.

I. The Principles of the Ideology

> *There was tangled in these exchanges still another ever-recurring question. This was as to the range (if any) of values which would be said to be basic enough to be presented to students as demanding acceptance and respect in all circumstances. It was the view of Fuller, Mathews, Williams, Stone and others that there are, indeed, some values, certainly including the integrity of the judicial process from tampering, on which one single standard would be insisted upon. On this view, what must be taught on such matters is not merely the duty to participate, but the duty to participate by* supporting that particular form of social order.
>
> Julius Stone
> (reporting on the Conference for the
> Education of Lawyers for Their Public Responsibilities)[8]

Although certain issues of legal ethics are debated incessantly, the debates almost invariably take place within a framework of certain common, unquestioned principles. Consider the exchange between Monroe Freedman and John Noonan on what Freedman called "the three hardest questions" for the criminal defense lawyer. The questions concerned whether or not it is proper for a lawyer to attempt to discredit an adverse witness whom he knows to be telling the truth, to put a witness on the stand knowing he will commit perjury, or to advise a client in a manner likely to tempt him to commit perjury.

Freedman's answer to all three questions was affirmative.[9] The lawyer might argue with his client about the morality of such activities, but ultimately, he insisted, the lawyer must bow to his client's will. Freedman's argument focused on the notion of confidentiality. If the client thought that the lawyer would refuse to do anything which would mislead the trier, then the client would probably lie or withhold information in order to convince the lawyer that actions in his interest would not be misleading. But in order to present the best possible defense, the lawyer has to know all the facts. The client cannot know when it is in his interest to conceal or falsify information. Thus, the lawyer must have the confidence of the client. The only way to achieve this is to assure the client that he will not be prejudiced by telling his lawyer the facts. For the

8. J. Stone, Legal Education and Public Responsibility 34 (1959) (reporting on the Conference for the Education of Lawyers for Their Public Responsibilities, 1956) (emphasis in original).

9. Freedman, *Professional Responsibility of the Criminal Defense Lawyer: The Three Hardest Questions*, 64 Mich. L. Rev. 1469 (1966) [hereinafter cited as Freedman].

lawyer to refuse to follow the client's wishes after the facts had been revealed would betray the promise which had induced disclosure and would undermine the credibility of such promises in the future.

Freedman suggested that refusal to impeach accurate testimony would in some instances harm innocent defendants because evidence in itself accurate might still be misleading on the question of guilt. Yet, Freedman did not justify the conduct he advocated in terms of any contribution to the accurate determination of guilt or innocence. On the contrary, he relied on "policy considerations that at times justify frustrating the search for truth and the prosecution of a just claim" which are widely recognized in the legal system.[10] He pointed to the provisions in the Canons of Ethics that require adversary zeal and confidentiality. He noted that lawyers as eminent as Williston had recognized a professional duty to acquiesce in mendacity. And he emphasized the tacit sanction of mendacity in judicial procedures, such as the right of a defendant to plead not guilty regardless of his guilt.

Noonan congratulated Freedman on a candid and accurate portrayal of the working principles of a large segment of the profession, but he argued that these principles affront the dignity of the profession and the legal system by turning the lawyer into a "tool" of his client and the trial into an irrational battle.[11] Noonan criticized Freedman's reliance on the battle model of criminal procedure and advocated as more enlightened the truth model. In his view, the purpose of judicial proceedings is to produce wise and informed decisionmaking, and the lawyer's job is to assist the trier in this effort.[12] The lawyer's duty to advance his client's interests must be subordinated to the fundamental purpose of truth-seeking which brought the relationship into being. He must not therefore mislead the trier by introducing false testimony or discrediting accurate testimony. Moreover, this obligation applies even where the lawyer believes that by misleading the trier with respect to a particular piece of evidence he will promote a wiser and more informed decision on the ultimate issue. In addition to recognizing his duty to the goal of truth, the lawyer must recognize his auxiliary status in the quest for truth. The trial is structured as a whole to produce the most accurate results possible, and it functions best when each participant adheres to his own role. The lawyer is sometimes expected to exclude evidence, but his basic job is to introduce accurate evidence. The responsibility for assessing the weight of the evidence on the ultimate issue rests with the trier. For the lawyer to attempt to influence this assessment by deception on the basis of his own judgment of the evidence would be to transgress the limit of his own role and usurp the trier's function.

10. *Id.* at 1482.

11. Noonan, *The Purposes of Advocacy and the Limits of Confidentiality*, 64 MICH. L. REV. 1485, 1491 (1966) [hereinafter cited as Noonan].

12. *Id.* at 1487.

Freedman and Noonan differ less in their arguments than in the attitudes they bring to the subject. They illustrate the modes of cynicism and naiveté in which the Ideology of Advocacy is usually elaborated. In his article, Freedman casually assumes that the legal system routinely convicts innocent people. He shows no more indignation at this fact than he does discomfort at the fact that the measures he advocates will result in the acquittal of guilty defendants. He speaks of cases not in terms of justice or suffering, but in terms of probabilities of acquittal.

On the other hand, Noonan assumes that the legal system produces justice so dependably that the lawyer defending an innocent man need not even ask himself whether following the usual rules might lead to a disastrous ultimate result. He glosses over the aspects of the system which seem to institutionalize aggression and dishonesty. He seems to think that lawyers could transform the trial system from the battle model to the truth model simply by adopting a different attitude toward it.

Despite their differing attitudes, Freedman and Noonan both clearly assume four principles. These are the basic principles of the Ideology of Advocacy. Two are principles of conduct which prescribe attitudes and behavior. They appear on the surface of most discussions of advocacy. The other two are foundation principles which have to do with the way the principles of conduct are derived and applied. They rest below the surface of discourse on legal ethics, but they are nevertheless pervasive and important.

The first principle of conduct is the principle of neutrality. This principle prescribes that the lawyer remain detached from his client's ends. The lawyer is expected to represent people who seek his help regardless of his opinion of the justice of their ends.[13] In some cases, he may have a duty to do so; in others, he may have the personal privilege to refuse.[14] But whenever he takes a case, he is not considered responsible for his client's purposes. Even if the lawyer happens to share these purposes, he must maintain his distance. In a judicial proceeding, for instance, he may not express his personal belief in the justice of his client's cause.[15]

The second principle of conduct is partisanship. This principle prescribes that the lawyer work aggressively to advance his client's ends. The lawyer will employ means on behalf of his client which he would not consider proper in a non-professional context even to advance his own ends. These means may involve deception, obfuscation, or delay. Unlike the principle of neutrality, the principle of partisanship is qualified. A line

13. *See Professional Responsibility: Report of the Joint Conference*, 44 A.B.A.J. 1159, 1216-17 (1958) [hereinafter cited as *Professional Responsibility*].

14. W. FORSYTH, HORTENSIUS: AN HISTORICAL ESSAY ON THE OFFICE AND DUTIES OF THE ADVOCATE 387 (3rd ed. 1879); A.B.A. Op. No. 281; ABA CODE OF PROFESSIONAL RESPONSIBILITY, DR 7-101(B) (1976) [hereinafter cited as ABA CODE].

15. ABA CODE, *supra* note 14, at EC 7-24.

separates the methods which a lawyer should be willing to use on behalf of a client from those he should not use. Before the lawyer crosses the line, he calls himself a representative; after he crosses it, he calls himself an officer of the Court. Most debates within the Ideology of Advocacy concern the location of his line. Freedman and Noonan disagree on the location of the line, but they both take principle of partisanship for granted. Both men would probably agree that the lawyer should not reveal adverse evidence learned from the client even though it may be relevant and probative.[16] They would probably agree that he should exclude accurate, probative adverse evidence at trial whenever the rules of evidence permit.[17] They would agree that he should not hesitate to plead his client not guilty even when he knows the client has committed the crime with which he is charged, and they would probably agree that he should invoke the statutes of frauds and limitations to defeat otherwise valid civil claims.[18] Also, Freedman thinks, though Noonan disagrees, that the lawyer should present perjured testimony and discredit accurate testimony. Others have thought that partisanship warrants the use of dilatory procedural tactics, lying under almost any circumstances in which discovery is unlikely, and the citation of false precedents to the judge.[19]

The principles of neutrality and partisanship describe the basic conduct and attitudes of professional advocacy. The two principles are often combined in the terms "adversary advocacy" or "partisan advocacy", and this essay will adopt that usage. However, it should be noted that the two principles are distinct in important respects. Many occupational roles, for instance the bureaucrat and the doctor, are expected to serve the general public without regard to the ends of those who seek their help. Yet, they are not expected to engage in the partisan pursuit of individual ends. On the other hand, political representatives are expected to be partisan, but they are not expected to serve all comers without regard to their ends.[20] Only the lawyer seems to insist on making a virtue of both neutrality and partisanship.

16. *See id.* EC 5-1 to 5-24.

17. Freedman, *supra* note 9, at 1474-75; Noonan, *supra* note 11, at 1487-88; *see also* ABA CODE, *supra* note 14, at EC 7-20.

18. Freedman, *supra* note 9, at 1470; Noonan *supra* note 11, at 1489-90; *see also* H. DRINKER, LEGAL ETHICS 149 (1953) [hereinafter cited as DRINKER]; Thode, *The Ethical Standard for the Advocate*, 39 TEX. L. REV. 575, 589 (1961) [hereinafter cited as Thode].

19. DRINKER, *supra* note 18, at 83; LE DROIT DE LA NATURE ET DES NATIONS § XXI at 195-98 (French trans. 1747); Curtis, *The Ethics of Advocacy*, 4 STAN. L. REV. 3, 8 (1951); *but see* ABA CODE OF PROFESSIONAL RESPONSIBILITY, EC 7-23 and DR 7-102(A)(1), (A)(5).

20. Similarly, an adjudicatory procedure can adopt one principle without the other. The principle of neutrality was not involved in the highly partisan adjudicatory procedure of trial by battle which was used during the Middle Ages. *See generally* 2 F. POLLOCK & F. MAITLAND, THE HISTORY OF ENGLISH LAW 633 n.7 (1968 ed.). On the other hand, in the adjudicatory procedures of contemporary continental Europe, the principle of partisanship plays a muted role, while the principle of neutrality is enshrined. *See* D. RUESCHMEYER, LAWYERS AND THEIR SOCIETY: A COMPARATIVE STUDY OF THE LEGAL PROFESSION IN THE UNITED STATES AND GERMANY 85-87, 127-31, 143 (1973).

Two further principles, though less obvious, are also assumed by Freedman and Noonan. The first is the principle of procedural justice. In its most general usage, procedural justice holds that the legitimacy of a situation may reside in the way it was produced rather than its intrinsic properties.[21] Another aspect of the principle is that, given adequate procedures, one can act justly by conforming to them regardless of the consequences to which one's conduct contributes. In this essay, the term "procedural justice" is used more specifically to refer to the notion that there is an inherent value or legitimacy to the judicial proceeding (and to a more qualified extent, the entire legal system) which makes it possible for a lawyer to justify specific actions without reference to the consequences they are likely to promote. Freedman and Noonan tacitly embrace this principle. For both of them, the nature of the consequences to which the lawyer's actions may lead is irrelevant to the ethical decisions he must make. Freedman invokes procedural considerations which are explicitly indifferent to outcomes. Although Noonan refers to outcomes in his emphasis on truth-seeking, he clearly rejects the notion that any particular ethical decision can be made by determining which course of action is most likely to lead to the discovery of truth. Rather, Noonan insists that the lawyer must stay within the boundaries of his role regardless of whether doing so will promote the discovery of truth. For Noonan, the goal of truth legitimates the entire system of procedures and informs its design, but it does not determine specific ethical decisions. Such decisions are determined by procedural requirements.

The second foundation principle of the Ideology of Advocacy is professionalism. In its most general usage, the term professionalism refers to the notion that social responsibility for the development and application of certain apolitical and specialized disciplines should be delegated to the practitioners of these disciplines.[22] In this paper, the term is used more specifically to describe the notion that the law is an apolitical and specialized discipline and that its proper development and application require that legal ethics be elaborated collectively by lawyers in accordance with criteria derived from their discipline. Freedman and Noonan both assume this principle. They never doubt that the "three hardest questions" are in fact questions of *professional* ethics. They assume that the questions are to be resolved in terms of legal doctrine and that they should be resolved by lawyers collectively in their occupational capacities and not by lawyers individually in terms of personal or social norms or by broad-based political institutions.

Most of this essay, Sections II through IV, will be concerned with criticizing the kind of advocacy defined by the principles of neutrality and

21. B. Barry, Political Argument 97-98, 102-106 (1965) [hereinafter cited as Barry].

22. Carr-Saunders, *Professions*, in 12 Encyclopedia of the Social Sciences 476 (1934).

partisanship. Yet, the foundation principles of procedural justice and professionalism will remain in the background, and in Sections V and VI, the essay will return to them directly in order to discuss their relationship to each other and to adversary advocacy.

II. THE LAWYER AS CHAMPION (THE WAR OF ALL AGAINST ALL)

> BOSWELL: "*But what do you think of supporting a cause which you know to be bad?*"
> JOHNSON: "*Sir, you do not know it to be good or bad till the Judge determines it.*"
>
> James Boswell[23]

The fullest justification of the Ideology of Advocacy rests on Positivist legal theory. The term Positivist is used here to refer to the kind of theory which emphasizes the separation of law from personal and social norms, the connection of law with the authoritative application of force, and the systematic, objective character of law.[24] Positivism was the basis of the profession's conception of advocacy in the late 19th and early 20th centuries, and it is still an important component of the professional self-image of some lawyers, despite its repudiation in most areas by the intellectual leaders of the bar. Even lawyers who reject Positivism as a general jurisprudential theory are sometimes prone to fall back on it when justifying their professional roles.

A. *Positivist Advocacy*

The Positivist theory is constructed on the philosophical foundation laid by Thomas Hobbes.[25] In the Positivist view, society is an aggregate

23. J. BOSWELL, LIFE OF JOHNSON, *quoted in* 2 THE WORLD OF LAW 763 (E. London ed. 1960).

24. *See, e.g.*, J. AUSTIN, THE PROVINCE OF JURISPRUDENCE DETERMINED (Hart ed. 1954); H. HART, THE CONCEPT OF LAW (1961) [hereinafter cited as HART]; Holmes, *The Path of the Law*, 10 HARV. L. REV. 457 (1897) [hereinafter cited as Holmes]; Kelsen, *The Pure Theory of Law: Its Methods and Fundamental Concepts*, (pts. 1-2) 50 L.Q. REV. 474 (1934) and 51 L.Q. REV. 517 (1935).

There is no general jurisprudential work representative of the version of Positivism which has had the greatest impact on American legal history. As Karl Llewellyn wrote, "The older Jurisprudence . . . is one which the profession did not have occasion to particularly study; a lawyer just absorbed it, largely through the fingers and the pores, as he went along." Llewellyn, *On Reading and Using the Newer Jurisprudence*, 40 COLUM. L. REV. 581, 582-83 (1940). This jurisprudence, often called Legal Formalism, was the prevalent type of legal thought in the late 19th and early 20th centuries. In the field of applied doctrine, it is well exemplified by the majority opinion in Lochner v. New York, 198 U.S. 45 (1905), and by J. BEALE, A TREATISE ON THE CONFLICT OF LAWS (1916). Since Formalism included some natural law elements, it may not be strictly accurate to designate it as Positivist. Nevertheless, the elements of the Formalist system which bear on the issues of advocacy are consistent with the Positivist doctrine sketched here. For an early treatment of legal ethics from a Formalist perspective, see the letters of David Dudley Field *reprinted in* A. KAUFFMAN, PROBLEMS IN PROFESSIONAL RESPONSIBILITY 249-66, especially at 257-60 (1975) [hereinafter cited as KAUFFMAN].

25. T. HOBBES, LEVIATHAN (1651). *See*, L. FULLER, THE LAW IN QUEST OF ITSELF 19-26 (1940) [hereinafter cited as FULLER]; R. UNGER, KNOWLEDGE AND POLITICS 5, 37-38 (1975) [hereinafter cited as UNGER].

of egoistic individuals each pursuing his own ends. Government is an artificial creation, the basic function of which is to remedy the disorder which would result if the natural centrifugal tendencies of society went unchecked. Disorder is undesirable for two reasons. First, it makes for uncertainty, a constant fear about the future and an inability to plan one's activities so as to best attain one's ends. Second, it makes for oppression, the necessity of subordinating one's own ends to those of whomever is strongest at the moment. Since the need for order is the most basic of social needs and is shared by all men, a government which secures order has a claim to the loyalty of all its citizens.

Ends are natural, individual, subjective, and arbitrary. Social norms result from the random convergence of individual ends. By contrast, it is possible to construct a system of rules which is artificial, impersonal, objective, and rational. The best way to provide order is to create a sovereign (*e.g.*, monarch, legislature, party) which is neutral toward the various ends of the citizens and which acts through rules. Rules will give a regularity to social life and thus eliminate uncertainty. Oppression will be eliminated once power is concentrated in the hands of a neutral ruler. An obstacle remains. The legitimacy of the sovereign rests solely on the unique end of order which all share. Yet, from the point of view of each citizen, this end extends only to the orderly behavior of the others. People will constantly be tempted to violate the rules in order to pursue their own individual ends. No one will be willing to pay the price of resisting such temptation without some assurance that the others will also obey. The solution is to have the rules provide for the administration of rewards and punishments in a manner calculated to insure general obedience.

The rules will define for each citizen a private sphere of autonomy. Within this sphere, he need not account to anyone for his actions. So long as he remains within his sphere, he need not fear coercion by the sovereign. The sovereign's enforcement of the rules against the other citizens will insure that they do not trespass within his sphere. Where disputes arise, they must be resolved in accordance with the rules. Since the sovereign cannot itself apply the rules to every particular dispute, it must appoint judges to act on its behalf. It is important that the judges apply the rules with impersonal regularity. They must not refer to their own personal ends. Otherwise, they would create uncertainty, and their decisions would be oppressive. The rules cannot specify a specific result for each situation to which they apply, but the judge will be able to determine the proper result in any given situation because the rules have a systematic quality. The system may involve formal logic, linguistic analysis, empirical observation, or some combination of these methods. The system enables the judge to reason from the general prescriptions of the rules to particular results. The judge applies the rules to the factual premises of the given situation. The disposition of the case is dictated by the system. The judge has no discretion; he is bound by the system.

The need for lawyers in the Positivist theory arises from the strangeness of the law. Since the legal system is independent of personal ends and social norms, its prescriptions often appear alien. They may be very complicated, and the sovereign may find it convenient to express them in an esoteric language. Thus, the rules are not easily apprehensible. But the individual needs to know how he can further his ends without causing the sovereign to intervene with sanctions. Otherwise, he will be in the very state of uncertainty that government was supposed to remedy. Moreover, if other citizens can gain a superior understanding of the rules, they can use this knowledge to oppress him by maneuvering him into situations where sovereign power will operate to his disadvantage. The solution is to create a class of legal specialists and to require its members to serve every citizen regardless of his ends.

The function of the lawyer is to explain how, and under what circumstances, the sovereign will intervene in his client's life. The lawyer enables his client to pursue his ends effectively by predicting the likelihood of assistance or sanction which attaches to alternative courses of action. He does so by the same type of systematic reasoning which the judge uses to decide cases. From another perspective, this function can be described as informing the client of his rights. A right is an opportunity to invoke or resist the force of the sovereign in a certain way. Rights are defined by the rules of the legal system.

The lawyer's various other services as advocate are all ancillary to this basic task of prediction. In litigation, he simply sets in motion the system which vindicates (or refutes) his prior predictions. The lawyer presents the court with the factual premises to which the rules are to be applied. The outcome of the case is determined by the autonomous operation of the system of rules on these premises. At best, the lawyer anticipates the outcome; he does not determine it.

The lawyer's neutrality is essential to the proper performance of his basic task of prediction. Since the legal system is independent of personal ends and social norms, the lawyer's ends and his notions of social norms have no relevance to the prediction of the sovereign's actions. Because ends are individual, subjective, and arbitrary, if the lawyer attempted to take his ends into account in advising his client, he would reduce the accuracy of his predictions and the effectiveness of his services. If the attempt caused him to take an unrealistically liberal view of the scope of permissible conduct, the client would suffer unexpected state interference and would thus be deprived of a measure of the certainty which he was promised. If it caused him to take an unrealistically restricted view of the scope of permissible conduct, then the lawyer would be abusing his position to oppress his client.

The lawyer's partisanship arises from his duty to assist the client in the pursuit of his ends. The lawyer cannot legitimately recognize any limitation on this pursuit aside from the rules of the legal system.

The rule that the lawyer cannot reveal a confidence of the client without the client's consent is designed in part to enhance access to legal advice by insuring that the client will not be prejudiced by seeking such advice. It is also, more fundamentally, a reflection of the fact that the lawyer is, in effect, an extension of the client's will. Since he cannot consult his own ends or his own notions of social norms, the lawyer has no basis other than the interests of his client for deciding whether or not to reveal confidences. Noonan's criticism that the lawyer acts as a "tool" of his client is entirely correct but beside the point.[26] A tool is precisely what the client needs in order to invoke his rights and maximize his autonomy. The lawyer is not responsible for what he does because he is acting as the instrument of the client, and he should not be criticized for renouncing responsibility because, by doing so, he merely helps the client to invoke the rights which the system guarantees him.

B. *The Critique of Positivist Advocacy*

This summary does not begin to do justice to the rigor and elegance of the best expositions of Positivism. Yet, rigor and elegance are not sufficient to overcome the fundamental problems of Positivist theory, and these problems are as fatal in the most elaborate expositions as they are in the summary presented here. The Positivist version of the Ideology of Advocacy fails in two broad respects. First, Positivism's failure to take account of the problematical relation between substance and procedure undermines its promise to eliminate uncertainty and oppression. Second, Positivist notions about the relation between law and personal ends are inconsistent with the Positivist notion of the advocate's role. The Positivist version of the Ideology of Advocacy purports to show that the advocate enhances his client's autonomy. Yet, given Positivism's psychological assumptions, the advocacy it prescribes can only subvert this autonomy.[27]

26. Noonan, *supra* note 11, at 1491.

27. The disastrous consequences of Positivist advocacy to be described are in part hypothetical and in part actual. They are the consequences which *would* occur *if* the Positivist assumptions about the world and the legal system were correct and *if* lawyers behaved in the way Positivism suggests they should. In fact, the Positivist assumptions are wrong in important respects, and lawyers often do not behave in accordance with the Positivist prescriptions. *See* text following note 70 *infra*. However, no attempt will be made either here or in the critique of the other versions of the Ideology of Advocacy, to specify the discrepancy between assumption and actuality except generally and in passing. Most of the argument which follows is intended to show that the Ideology of Advocacy is untenable even on its own assumptions. On the other hand, much of the interest and plausibility of the argument lies in the fact that each version of the Ideology of Advocacy does to some extent accurately describe a familiar aspect of our social and legal experience, and the contradictions of the Ideology of Advocacy correspond to actual problems of the legal order and the society.

1. THE PROCEDURAL PROBLEMS

Procedure comes as something of an afterthought in Positivism, and the problems it creates are never fully acknowledged. Two procedural problems in particular—the problems of enforcement and access—represent serious dangers of uncertainty and oppression for which Positivism makes no adequate provision.

Positivist discussions of procedure begin with a belated recognition of a basic contradiction: in the Positivist system, the sovereign is both the only guarantee of order and the greatest threat to it. Since obedience to the rules does not come naturally, the sovereign must be charged with the power and duty to enforce them. But this task poses a terrifying prospect. The only effective means of enforcement involve torture, deprivation of liberty, invasion of privacy, or confiscation of property. These means are necessary both to get the information needed to determine that the rules have been violated and to deter future violations. Fact-finding holds the further danger that the sovereign will constantly be finding new evidence or revising his reasoning so as to upset previous determinations on which people have relied. Moreover, once the facts have been determined, there remains the further problem that the sovereign and its agents are likely to act inconsistently in applying the rules to different situations. No matter how elaborately the legal system is constructed, ambiguities will remain, and in choosing among alternative interpretations, the judges will act inconsistently, and will thus produce unpredictable results. Thus, within his own system, the Positivist finds the very danger of disorder which he had set out to remedy.

To meet this problem, Positivism proposes a second body of rules which limit the enforcement powers of the sovereign. As the purpose of the first set of rules is to impose regularity on conduct in the social world, the purpose of the second is to impose regularity on the actions of the sovereign. The first kind of rule is called substantive, and the second kind procedural. The procedural rules require that certain evidence be produced before the sovereign may act on the premise that a substantive rule has been violated. They limit the ways in which the sovereign can procure evidence and prescribe the manner in which it can be presented. They limit the authority of the sovereign to make and revise findings of fact and interpretations of rules. And they specify the sanctions which the sovereign may apply upon finding that the rules have been broken.[28]

The establishment of this second body of rules has a curious consequence. The substantive rules reflect the basic purpose of the system, the

28. *See* HART, *supra* note 24, at 89-96.

The question of how the enforcement of the procedural rules can be guaranteed is a further problem of Positivism and liberal political theory generally which is not considered here. *See, e.g.*, J. LOCKE, TWO TREATISES OF GOVERNMENT II § 242 (Laslett ed. 1960) (on the "Appeal to Heaven"); THE FEDERALIST PAPERS Nos. 47, 51 (J. Jay, A. Hamilton, J. Madison) (on the separation of powers).

securing of order in the social world. The procedural rules are designed to deal with a technical problem. Once the system is set into motion, however, the procedural rules play the more fundamental role. Order depends on the citizens' compliance with the substantive rules, and compliance depends on the application of sanctions by the sovereign. The application of sanctions is governed by the procedural rules. The key to the system is the operation of the sovereign, and the ultimate test of the legitimacy of any of the sovereign's acts is procedural. For the citizen, this means that compliance with the substantive law does not guarantee immunity from state sanctions. Nor does liability necessarily follow from violations of the substantive rules. The procedural rules legitimate results which may be substantively wrong. Having repudiated personal notions of justice at the outset of its system, Positivism ends by refusing to guarantee the citizen even the legal justice defined by the substantive law. All the citizen can count on is a day in court.[29]

The citizen's bewilderment may be a matter of indifference to the Positivist, but it is not so easy for him to shrug off another difficulty. The second body of rules has not solved the problem of disorder. The risk of disorder from the sovereign has been diminished only by impairing the efficiency of the sovereign's enforcement powers and hence by increasing the risk of disorder from the citizens. The procedural rules give the citizens a broad range of discretion. The existence of this discretion undermines the Positivist claim to secure order through the delegation of power to a neutral sovereign who exercises it through a system of rules. The citizens can use their procedural discretion to thwart the enforcement of the substantive rules and to affect the exercise of state power in accordance with their individual ends. Once the existence of this discretion is recognized, the actions of the sovereign appear to result, not from the neutral, systematic application of rules to given factual premises, but from the strategic exercise of procedural discretion by private parties.

29. Thus, when a man who has been duly convicted of a crime returns to the court with conclusive proof of his innocence, the Positivist judge replies:

> The Court is persuaded that . . . a grave miscarriage of justice has taken place. However, at the outset the Court is faced with the question of its power to grant relief. . . .
>
> The defendant's position is that in its totality the proceeding deprived him of his constitutional rights. However, he has not averted to . . . any impairment of any specific constitutional right or any unfairness upon the trial that would warrant a holding that due process has been denied.
>
> Essentially, the defendant is applying for relief upon the ground of newly discovered evidence. . . . However, this avenue is unfortunately closed since Rule 33 of the Federal Rules of Criminal Procedure . . . requires that a motion for a new trial based upon newly discovered evidence "may be made only before or within two years after final judgment."
>
> This time limitation, which has been rigidly enforced, works a great hardship in this case, for it is difficult to see how some of the vital evidence now presented could have been available to the defendant during the two year period . . . .
>
> It is with extreme reluctance that the Court is forced to the conclusion that it is without power to grant the application, but it may not exceed the limits of authority.

United States v. Kaplan, 101 F. Supp. 7, 11-14 (S.D.N.Y. 1951). This is the Positivist kiss-off: "I'd like to help, but my hands are tied."

For instance, the procedural rules which require that evidence be produced before sanctions can be applied and which limit the ways in which evidence can be obtained enable people to conceal violations of the substantive rules by not leaving evidence or by withholding or destroying it. The rules which govern evidence at trial enable people to thwart the enforcement of the substantive law by excluding or discrediting probative evidence or by introducing misleading evidence.[30] Procedural rules permit people whose claims have no substantive validity to put others to the risk of proof.[31] They enable people to frustrate enforcement by delaying and by imposing expenses on their adversaries.[32] They permit people to influence enforcement by strategic choices as to whether to initiate proceedings,[33] when to do so, and before which tribunal to do so.[34] They

30. *See, e.g.*, D. Oaks, *Studying the Exclusionary Rule in Search and Seizure*, 37 U. CHI. L. REV. 665, 736-39 (1970).

31. This is generally recognized as the usual and appropriate sitation in the criminal law. *See, e.g.*, Alschuler, *The Defense Attorney's Role in Plea Bargaining*, 84 YALE L.J. 1179 (1975) [hereinafter cited as Alschuler]; *see also* Simon, *Class Actions—Useful Tool or Engine of Destruction*, 55 F.R.D. 375, 389-90 (1972) [hereinafter cited as Simon].

32. Galanter, *Why the Haves Come Out Ahead: Speculations on the Limits of Legal Change*, 9 LAW & SOC. REV. 95, 119-22 (1974) [hereinafter cited as Galanter]; Schrag, *Bleak House 1968: A Report on Consumer Test Litigation*, 44 N.Y.U. L. REV. 115 (1969). *See, e.g.*, Halverson, *Problems in Settling the "Big Case" with the Government or the Private Plaintiff*, in REPRESENTING CORPORATE CLIENTS IN THE PROSECUTION OF GOVERNMENT AND PRIVATE ANTITRUST LAWSUITS (Massachusetts Continuing Legal Education—New England Law Institute 1976) at F.M. 42-44, 47-48 [hereinafter cited as Halverson]:

> PRACTICAL SUGGESTIONS ON SETTLEMENT STRATEGIES
> A. Private Plaintiffs
> 1. Monopolization Suits
> a. Take exhaustive discovery, particularly if your client has resources advantage, and concentrate on the plaintiff's market definition problems. . . .
> c. Show the plaintiff that it is not costless to sue. Counterclaim! . . .
> f. Remember private plaintiff looks at his pocketbook and not at so-called 'public interest', so make plaintiff worry about his pocketbook.
> g. If more than one private suit, get the weak one to trial fast and first and beat him.
> h. If exposure there, identify the needs of the plaintiff (often some kind offer to cease a particular practice, coupled with some cash), and then offer just enough to start the negotiation process . . . .
> Once the offer is there and the plaintiff's Board has seen months of attorneys' fees and corporate disruption, the plaintiff's Board will work in your favor, nudging the lawyers toward a compromise. . . .
> B. Government Suits
> 1. Monopolization
> a. Make certain that the government gets enough documents and data so that personnel on the team will turn over several times during the pendency of the action.
> b. Take advantage of the fact that your client is usually better organized and financed than the government.

33. In the criminal system, the sovereign retains prosecutorial discretion, but in the civil system, the procedural rules give such discretion to the citizens. Enforcement depends on the exercise of this discretion, and it has great potential to create disorder. People usually find it in their interest not to enforce their rights through the legal system. *See* Macaulay, *Non-Contractual Relations in Business: A Preliminary Study*, 28 AM. SOC. REV. 55 (1963). When they do not do so, others are likely to take actions and enter into relations in reliance on this pattern of non-enforcement. However, when someone's perception of his interests changes, he may decide to assert his rights in a manner which undermines the expectations of those who have relied on their previous failure to do so. For example, consider the

make it possible for some to influence rule interpretation by framing legal issues for decision in factual contexts favorable to the interpretation which suits their ends.[35]

J. Willard Hurst has described how the plutocracy in the late 19th and early 20th centuries used campaigns of multiple "diversionary lawsuits" to put pressure on adversaries and how it carefully framed test cases to present legal issues in a light favorable to the results it sought. Hurst emphasizes that the notion of litigation as a mechanism "to enforce rights and duties according to an existing body of 'law' " simply does not apply to these activities. This litigation was not a means of enforcing compliance with preexisting commands of the sovereign. It was "both an instrument of fixing policy and a tactical device in its execution."[36] The results were not determined by the operation of an autonomous system, but by the exercise of procedural discretion by private parties in the course of a free-wheeling struggle.

More recently, litigation has been used in this manner on behalf of lower- and middle-income individuals against dominant economic interests. The claim of spokesmen for large corporations that many recent class actions represent "legalized blackmail"[37] reflects an accurate perception that the procedure is not being used merely as a more efficient way of enforcing a substantive claim, but also as an instrument of private policy for the vindication of expectations which are not justified by the substantive law. The availability of the class action device may have a critical impact on the result independently of the substantive merit of the claim.[38] Analogously, the threat of mass assertions of due process rights by criminal defendants or welfare recipients is a potential instrument by which substantive concessions could be exacted from enforcement officials.[39]

---

situation of a landlord who enters into a lease in reliance on the tenant's pattern of non-enforcement of rights under a housing code. He may agree to a lower rent on the assumption that he will not have to meet code standards. Yet, the tenant retains the discretion to assert his rights under the code, and there may be no way for the landlord to be certain that he will not do so.

34. For an account of an elaborate strategy which may have been critically determinative of the outcome to choose a forum and a judge in a multi-million dollar personal injury action, see G. STERN, THE BUFFALO CREEK DISASTER 54-56, 84-86 (1976).

35. *See* J. HURST, THE GROWTH OF AMERICAN LAW: THE LAW MAKERS 34-51 (1950) [hereinafter cited as HURST]; Galanter, *supra* note 32, at 101.

36. HURST, *supra* note 35, at 349, 347-52.

37. Handler, *The Shift From Substantive to Procedural Innovations in Antitrust Suits*, 71 COLUM. L. REV. 1, 9 (1971).

38. Simon, *supra* note 31, at 389:

> The principal impetus for settlement comes from the atomic dynamics of large user class actions. When a firm with assets of, say, a billion dollars is sued in a class action with a class of several million and a potential liability of, say, $2 billion, it faces the possibility of destruction. A settlement offer may then be made of $20 million—or one percent of possible exposure. . . . What defense lawyer can tell his client that his probable success in any jury case is better than 100 to 1; no matter how little merit there is in plaintiff's claim?

39. *See* Alschuler, *supra* note 31; Rubenstein, *Procedural Due Process and the Limits of the Adversary System*, 11 HARV. C.R.-C.L. L. REV. 48 (1976); Subrin & Sutton, *Welfare*

Although the point is clearest in large-scale contests involving great interests, in fact almost all litigation has this instrumental, discretionary, *disorderly* character. In the vast majority of cases which are settled, there is not even a pretense that the result has been determined by the application of a system of substantive rules to given factual premises. The sovereign merely ratifies a result which the parties have negotiated by each giving up procedural discretion to injure the interests of the other.[40] Even when there is a contested judgment it will rarely appear as a mechanical vindication of substantive commands. More often, it will seem a consequence of a party's exercise of discretion, for instance, to plead not guilty, or to choose a favorable forum, or to appeal to the prejudices of the jury. On Positivist premises, given the existence of such discretion, every lawsuit is likely to be a form of "legalized blackmail."[41]

In creating a critical role for private discretion, procedure undermines the basic Positivist guarantee of order. Uncertainty becomes inevitable because the actions of the sovereign cannot be reliably predicted. The sovereign's actions are determined by procedural discretion. This discretion is not exercised by the citizens in any systematic fashion, but rather it is exercised instrumentally in the pursuit of their individual, subjective, and arbitrary ends. The problem is not just that procedure complicates the analysis. More importantly, the procedural rules create a situation in which outcomes depend on contingencies which are not susceptible to legal analysis. They depend on private decisions which are not controlled by the rules. Moreover, oppression still threatens. Positivism's claim to eliminate oppression is plausible only to the extent that people see state intervention as governed by a neutral system of rules. The system as a whole can be shown to be just vis-à-vis all the citizens, but no particular outcome can be shown to be just except by tracing it to the system. However, once the role of procedural discretion is recognized, the actions of the sovereign appear to be determined by private power.[42] As such, they constitute oppression.

Thus, to the extent that procedure checks public anarchy, it unleashes private anarchy. The debate within Positivism between authoritarians and libertarians is concerned with striking the balance between public and private disorder. Yet, by this point, Positivism has conceded its failure to secure the basic goal of order. Authoritarians and libertarians

Class Actions in Federal Court: A Procedural Analysis, 8 HARV. C.R.-C.L. L. REV. 21, 54-55 (1973); *see also* Arnold, *Trial by Combat and the New Deal*, 47 HARV. L. REV. 913 (1934).

40. *See* L. FRIEDMAN & S. MACAULAY, LAW AND THE BEHAVIORAL SCIENCES 162-70 (2d ed. 1977); Finkelstein, *A Statistical Analysis of Guilty Plea Practices in the Federal Courts*, 89 HARV. L. REV. 293 (1975).

41. *See* Leff, *Injury, Ignorance, and Spite—The Dynamics of Coercive Collection*, 80 YALE L. J. 1 (1970) [hereinafter cited as Leff].

42. *See generally* Galanter, *supra* note 32; Kennedy, *Legal Formality*, 2 J. LEGAL STUD. 351 (1973) [hereinafter cited as Kennedy].

merely claim to achieve an appropriate allocation of the incidence of disorder. The threat to the citizen from the sovereign has been alleviated only at the cost of aggravating the threat from his fellow citizens.

In the work of the Legal Realists, the tension between substance and procedure is recognized and discussed from within the framework of Positivism. The Realists saw clearly that rules are not self-interpreting and self-enforcing, and they acknowledged the impact of procedure in compromising the enforcement of substantive prescriptions.[43] Their writings suggest two strategies for dealing with the tension between substance and procedure without abandoning the basic Positivist premises. Neither is successful.

One strategy is to eliminate the distinction between substance and procedure by collapsing the two sets of rules into a single set. This can be done by reading the procedural rules as qualifications to the substantive rules. In this way, law can still be viewed as the prediction of the application of force from a unitary body of rules. The predictions simply become more complicated. This strategy seems to underlie some of the more familiar rhetoric of discussions of legal ethics. For instance, lawyers argue that a person has a "right" to plead the Statutes of Frauds or Limitations to defeat an otherwise valid claim or to object to probative hearsay because the rules authorize such actions.[44] And they insist that a person has a "right" to breach contracts because the law does not specifically enforce prohibitions of breach but merely imposes damages.[45] Significantly, however, such rhetoric rarely embraces the more extreme consequences of this line of thought. Lawyers never argue that a person has a right to commit murder so long as he does not leave behind proof beyond a reasonable doubt of his act. Nor do they assert that a person may lawfully swindle others if he flees to Brazil before the sovereign brings him to trial. Their reluctance to go this far has not been due to mere timidity. The distinction between substance and procedure reflects a real conflict within the Positivist system between the total dependence on the sovereign's power and the extreme danger from it. The procedural rules which are needed to limit the sovereign's power give discretion to citizens which undermines order. The experience of this discretion and of the disorder which it creates cannot be eliminated by a merely rhetorical or conceptual change.

Another strategy which Realism suggests is to make the sovereign's enforcement power more effective and to limit the discretion of citizens to

43. *See, e.g.*, J. FRANK, COURTS ON TRIAL: MYTH AND REALITY IN AMERICAN JURISPRUDENCE (1949) [hereinafter cited as FRANK]; Llewellyn, *Some Realism About Realism*, 44 HARV. L. REV. 1222 (1931).

44. *See, e.g.*, DRINKER, *supra* note 18, at 149; R. PATTERSON & E. CHEATHAM, THE PROFESSION OF LAW 86 (1971) [hereinafter cited as PATTERSON & CHEATHAM]; Thode, *supra* note 18, at 586-91.

45. *See, e.g.*, Holmes, *supra* note 24, at 461-62; *but see* HART, *supra* note 24, at 35-41.

manipulate the system.[46] But this approach merely turns the problem on its head. Limiting the discretion of the private parties only increases the discretion of the sovereign and thus enlarges the danger of disorder from that source. For example, if the rules were changed to abolish the discretion of criminal defendants to escape enforcement by excluding illegally seized evidence, the effective discretion of the sovereign to torture, wrongly imprison, and confiscate property in the quest for evidence would be enlarged greatly.

The second procedural dilemma of Positivism arises from the question of access to the legal system. Positivism recognizes that the strangeness and complexity of the law creates a new danger of oppression. The danger is that some will be able to anticipate state intervention better than others and that they will use their knowledge to the disadvantage of the less informed. Positivism's basic response to this danger is a promise to make counsel available to people regardless of their ends. Availability can mean either access for those who can pay, or some guaranteed level of access regardless of wealth. But neither approach is adequate.

Availability means merely formal access when Positivist legal theory is linked to the theory of the self-regulating market, as it commonly was in the late 19th and early 20th centuries.[47] According to this theory, each individual should be left to choose for himself which goods and services he will receive from the rest of society, but only within the limits of his wealth. The limits of his wealth should be determined by a series of bargains in which he sells his labor or whatever else he has for the best price he can get for it. In this view, legal services are merely another commodity which the individual can purchase or not according to his own schedule of satisfactions. Formal availability is the opportunity to use the proceeds of the sale of one's own labor to purchase legal services at the going rate. Under this standard, the lawyer's obligation is merely to make his services available to those who can pay for them.

This situation involves the citizen in a vicious circle. Because the process of economic bargaining is defined and regulated by the law, a person needs to know the law in order to understand his position and his options. In order to make the best bargains, he needs legal advice. Yet, in order to get legal advice, he needs to make good enough bargains to provide himself with the means to hire a lawyer. Contrary to the assumptions of those who advocate formal availability, legal services are not just another commodity, but rather a prerequisite to participation in the system. Where legal services are only formally available, the poor, who are unable to purchase legal services, may remain poor for precisely that reason. Their ignorance of the law puts them in an inferior bargaining

46. *See, e.g.*, FRANK, *supra* note 43.
47. *See* J. COMMONS, LEGAL FOUNDATIONS OF CAPITALISM (1924).

position which will prevent them from realizing the full value of their labor in the market.[48]

The profession's more recent response to the problem of access is to acknowledge some responsibility for making legal services available to those who cannot pay for them.[49] Yet, in terms of Positivist theory, this solution is little more plausible than the formal one. There is no practical way of equalizing access to legal services sufficiently to preclude oppression. The society is not prepared to make the enormous expenditures necessary to provide everyone with substantial access to legal assistance.[50] Although only a minority has substantial access at the present level of availability, the cost of maintaining even this level strikes many laymen as intolerably expensive. Moreover, cost seems to increase geometrically as the level of services grows, since formal disputes become not only more plentiful, but also more complicated.

Class representation is not a viable solution within the framework of Positivism to the prohibitive expense of individual representation. First, there is no reliable means of determining when the ends of individuals converge sufficiently to make them a class. Without a concrete factual basis for classification, the definition of classes inevitably involves resort to the personal ends of the people doing the defining, and thus creates uncertainty and oppression. The actual ends of many class members may differ sharply from the ends attributed to them by those who control the litigation.[51] Moreover, even where a genuine convergence of ends actually exists initially, class representation will itself disrupt this convergence by creating a conflict of interest between those who actually control the litigation and those who do not. The control of the litigation is an asset which those who possess can use to their own advantage at the expense of the other class members.[52] Finally, class representation tends, in practice, to favor those whose ends converge with others over those whose ends do not.

Thus, knowledge of the rules will necessarily be unequally distributed, and as a practical matter large numbers of people will be denied any substantial access to the legal system. Those who can afford a large amount of legal services will be able to use their superior knowledge to

48. *See* R. SMITH, JUSTICE AND THE POOR 241 (1919).

49. *See, e.g.*, ABA CODE OF PROFESSIONAL RESPONSIBILITY, EC 2-17 to 2-25.

50. One "conservative" estimate holds that "[i]t would require something on the order of a tenfold increase in the size of the *entire* bar to begin to provide the whole population with the legal services that the affluent presently enjoy." Bellow & Kettleson, *supra* note 3, at 57 (emphasis in original); *see generally id.* at 56-58.

51. *See, e.g.*, Bell, *Serving Two Masters: Integration Ideals and Client Interests in School Desegration Litigation*, 85 YALE L.J. 470 (1976) [hereinafter cited as Bell]; Stewart, *The Reformation of American Administrative Law*, 88 HARV. L. REV. 1667, 1762-70 (1975) [hereinafter cited as Stewart]; White, *The Abolition of Self-Help Repossession: The Poor Pay Even More*, 1973 WIS. L. REV. 503 [hereinafter cited as White].

52. *See, e.g.*, Simon, *supra* note 31, at 389-94 (1972); Comment, *The New Public Interest Lawyers*, 79 YALE L.J. 1069, 1124-25 (1970).

maneuver others into situations where the sovereign's interventions will benefit them at the expense of the others. It may turn out that the sovereign's interventions routinely serve the ends of those with superior knowledge of the rules.[53]

The problem of access is aggravated by the problem of enforcement. The citizen needs legal services not only to learn his rights, but also to enforce them against the trespasses of others. The advantaged can make far better use of their procedural discretion than the disadvantaged. They can engage in far more elaborate and sophisticated procedural strategies. They can use the procedural rules to increase the expenses of the disadvantaged in asserting their claims so that the latter must give up or compromise before their claims have been determined.[54]

At the same time, any attempt to alleviate the problem of access by increasing the availability of legal services will only aggravate the problem of enforcement. The expansion of legal services multiplies the number of people able to exploit their procedural rights so as to thwart the commands of the substantive law and escalates their ability to do so.

The problems of enforcement and access undermine the Positivist image of the lawyer. They make it implausible to portray the fundamental legal activity as the prediction of the actions of the sovereign. The lawyer does not merely anticipate outcomes, he makes them. This is so for two reasons. First, the notion of the lawyer as predicting events depends in large part on the notion of the law as a system with a momentum of its own, operating independently of the will and conduct of any particular actors. Yet, in fact, the outcomes of legal proceedings depend on strategic procedural choices in which the lawyer participates.[55] In becoming the tool of the client, the lawyer does not merely enable his client to vindicate expectations based on a determinate set of rights. Rather, he becomes an agency for the exercise of discretionary power. Second, the notion that the lawyer predicts events also depends on the assumption that there is no scarcity of legal services so that a lawyer's decision to represent a particular client has no significant impact on the distribution of legal knowledge. Yet, the problem of access refutes this assumption. The

53. *See* Galanter, *supra* note 32.

54. *See* Galanter, *supra* note 32; Halverson, *supra* note 32.

55. The Positivist view of the lawyer as merely anticipating the consequences produced by the autonomous operation of the legal system has receded in recent years, but it still persists in very prominent quarters. Defending the Ideology of Advocacy in the sphere of litigation, the Code states that, unlike the situation of counseling where a lawyer "assists his client in *determining* the course of future conduct and relationship," the courtroom advocate "must *take* the facts as he finds them". ABA CODE OF PROFESSIONAL RESPONSIBILITY, EC 7-3 (emphasis added). The implication is clear that, while in counseling the lawyer affects the outcome, in litigation the outcome arises directly from the operation of the system on the "facts" and does not depend on any action of the lawyer. *Compare* PATTERSON & CHEATHAM, *supra* note 44, at 135 *and* Thode, *supra* note 18, at 576-79 *with* HURST, *supra* note 35, at 349 ("[L]itigation as well as office work might be both an instrument of fixing policy and a tactical device in its execution.").

lawyer's acceptance of a particular client does not and cannot implement a condition of general availability. Availability will necessarily be limited, and the incidence of availability will be determined by the lawyer's decisions as to whom to represent. Lawyers' decisions as to whom to represent determine the distribution of legal knowledge, and hence, the distribution of power in the society. Whether or not a lawyer shares his client's interests, he influences the balance of power in favor of those interests by accepting him as a client.

2. THE TYRANNY OF ADVOCACY

The dilemmas of enforcement and access undermine the Positivist notion of the role of the lawyer in the legal system as a whole. They suggest that lawyers as a group cannot safeguard the general social interest in the elimination or containment of uncertainty and oppression. The Positivist notion of the lawyer's role also involves another perspective, that of the individual lawyer and his client. From this perspective, Positivism envisions the lawyer as enhancing the client's autonomy, as enabling the client to make the fullest use of his freedom to pursue his own ends. This latter perspective is to some extent independent of the larger one. For even after acknowledging the failure of the legal system to check uncertainty and oppression, the Positivist can still argue that the lawyer enables individual clients to pursue their ends more effectively within the limits imposed by both the legal system and social disorder. Yet this second perspective involves difficulties as serious as those of the first. Positivism fails to show that the lawyer can enhance his client's autonomy. Rather, it appears from Positivism's own premises that the lawyer who adheres to the Positivist version of the Ideology of Advocacy must end by subverting his client's autonomy. The problem is that the lawyer's task of explaining the impact of the legal system on the client's personal ends cannot be accomplished without some direct understanding of these ends. Yet, Positivism forbids the lawyer to seek or rely on such an understanding.

The lawyer purports to assist his client by using his objective knowledge of the precise, regular, mechanical operation of the legal system to predict the consequences of alternative courses of action. The lawyer assumes specific courses of action as factual hypotheses and reasons from them in accordance with the rules of the legal system in order to determine the consequences in terms of state action which follow from them. Yet by itself, this type of assistance is of little use to the client. The client is not interested in the consequences of *any* course of action. Of the infinity of possible courses of action, he is interested in only those which might advance his ends. Moreover, the client is not interested in *all* the consequences of a course of action. Of the infinity of probable consequences, he is interested in only those that will affect his attainment of his ends.

The Positivist version of the Ideology of Advocacy focuses on the person for whom the law is a mystery. Such a person, even if conscious of and articulate about his ends, would not know which aspects of them the lawyer would need to understand in order to gauge the impact of the legal system on his life. In order to isolate these aspects, he would need the legal knowledge for which he relies on his lawyer. The lawyer, on the other hand, has no reliable way of learning the client's ends on his own. Because these ends are subjective, individual, and arbitrary, the lawyer has no access to them.[56] Because the lawyer's only direct experience of ends is his experience of his own ends, he cannot speculate on what the client's ends might be without referring to his own ends and thus biasing the neutral predictive analysis he is supposed to perform. Any attempt to frame inquiries to the client concerning his ends or to interpret the client's ambiguous replies will necessarily involve the intrusion of the lawyer's own ends. Thus, consciously or not, the Positivist lawyer is faced with a dilemma: On the one hand, he cannot give intelligible advice to his client without referring to ends; on the other hand, he cannot refer to ends without endangering the client's autonomy, and thus, undermining the basic purpose of his role.

Today, in most areas of law practice, lawyers have repudiated Positivism. Even at the turn of the century, when the prevailing jurisprudence was Positivist, many lawyers who purported to subscribe to this jurisprudence ignored some of its assumptions and prescriptions in practice. Yet, there are some areas of practice where lawyers do operate on Positivist premises. In these areas, the Positivist dilemma is a real problem. Thus, Positivism has developed a strategy for dealing with the dilemma. Sometimes the strategy is acknowledged; more often, it is implicit. It can be found in a variety of discussions which view the legal system from a Postivist viewpoint.

The strategy is to impute certain basic ends to the client at the outset and to work to advance these imputed ends. This strategy drastically compromises the Postivist premise of the individuality of ends, but it seems to be the Positivist's only choice. The Positivists seem to assume that, if the ends imputed are sufficiently simple and sufficiently widespread, the risk of interference in the client's autonomy can be minimized. By imputing ends to the client at the outset, the lawyer obviates dangerous inquiries into the particular ends of the particular client. On the other hand, if most people actually do share the imputed ends to some degree, then the lawyer will usually advance the client's

56. *Cf.* S. WOLIN, POLITICS AND VISION: CONTINUITY AND INNOVATION IN WESTERN POLITICAL THOUGHT 341 (1960) ("The basic assumption [of liberal political thought], that each was the best judge of his own interests, rested squarely on the belief that no individual could truly understand another.").

actual ends when he works to advance the imputed ends. The ends which Positivism imputes are derived from the basic Positivist premise of egoism, but they go beyond this initial premise to emphasize characteristics of extreme selfishness. The specific ends most often imputed are the maximization of freedom of movement and the accumulation of wealth.

The notion that the advocate should serve, not the individual ends of the client, but rather certain standard ends imputed to him is implicit in cases dealing with the effectiveness of advocacy. The law of procedure repeatedly recognizes that critical decisions are made by the lawyer without any participation by the client.[57] Occasionally, such a decision results in disaster to the client, and the issue arises whether he has been represented effectively. This issue is often seen to depend on whether the lawyer's decision was strategically reasonable under the circumstances in which it was made.[58] A strategically reasonable decision is one well calculated to advance certain ends. Yet, these discussions often proceed in total ignorance of the actual ends of the particular client. Rather, the strategic reasonableness is assessed with respect to the imputed ends of Positivism. The lawyer is not criticized for failing to ascertain his client's ends, but only for failing to advance the ends which have been imputed to him.

In the area of the criminal law, lawyers and laymen have recognized increasingly the extent to which the lawyer dominates the client in conducting the defense. Yet, this recognition has led them, not to a re-examination of the premises of adversary advocacy, but to a re-invigorated defense of it in terms of the imputed ends. Thus, critics deplore criminal defense lawyers who fail to exercise their broad discretion more vigorously in order to make it more difficult for the state to coerce the client.[59] The interest in escaping conviction under any circumstances is not something which these critics have discovered after examining the lives of any particular clients. Rather, it is an end which has been imputed to the clients *a priori*.

This Positivist strategy is a complete failure. It can only precipitate, rather than mitigate, the lawyer's subversion of the client's autonomy. The Positivist's vague, crudely drawn psychological assumptions cannot begin to do justice to the specific complexity of his client's actual ends.

57. *See, e.g.*, RESTATEMENT OF JUDGMENTS §§ 126 (2)(e) & (f), 129 (a) (1942) (no relief from erroneous and inequitable judgment entered due to attorney negligence); *see also* Williams v. Beto, 354 F.2d 698, 706 (5th Cir. 1965) (The client "should know that in the course of a lawsuit there are many critical Rubicons at which the attorney must make finely balanced, often agonizing, decisions."). *See generally* Mazor, *Power and Responsibility in the Attorney-Client Relation*, 20 STAN. L. REV. 1120 (1968); Cover & Aleinikoff, *Dialectical Federalism: Habeas Corpus and the Court*, 86 YALE L. J. 1035, 1078-86 (1977).

58. *E.g.*, Estelle v. Williams, 425 U.S. 501, 514-15 (1976) (Powell, J. concurring); Henry v. Mississippi, 379 U.S. 443, 445-52 (1965); Finer, *Ineffective Assistance of Counsel*, 58 CORNELL L. REV. 1077, 1092-1116 (1973).

59. *See generally* Alschuler, *supra* note 31; Blumberg, *supra* note 5; Skolnick, *supra* note 5.

Unlike the hypothetical person assumed by the Postivist advocate, actual people have not just a few, discrete ends, but rather many ends which are interrelated in a complex fashion. Moreover, these ends are set in a social context in which the individual's fulfillment depends on his relations with others. Even assuming the basic Positivist psychology of egoism to be accurate, it would not follow that a person's ends could be reduced to a few crude presumptions. On the contrary, a person's fulfillment is likely to depend on a complex balance among many different satisfactions. Moreover, the attainment of individual satisfaction depends on the cooperation of others. Yet, Positivism is blind to all but the crudest ends, to the relations of ends among each other, and to the social relations on which personal fulfillment depends.

Thus, when the client comes to the Positivist seeking to protect the delicate rhythms of his private life from disruption by the mechanical operation of the state, the lawyer will implement the very result he was supposed to prevent. The lawyer explains to the client the probable impact of the state, not on the client's own life, but on the life of the hypothetical person assumed in the Positivist model whose simple, crude ends bear only the most problematical relation to those of the client. This advice is much worse than useless to the client. Though it will often be irrelevant to his ends, the client may not be in a position to reject it. The client of whom Positivism is most solicitous is the naive person, face to face with the alien force of the state, threatened with a massive disruption of his life. Confronted with the need to act in this strange situation, the client must make sense of it as best he can. The lawyer puts himself forth quite plausibly as the client's best hope of mastering his predicament. If he is to avoid being overwhelmed by chaos, he must acquiesce in his lawyer's definition of the situation. He must think in a manner which gives coherence to the advice he is given. He may begin to do this quite unconsciously. If he is at all aware of the change, he is likely to see it as a defensive posture forced on him by the hostile intentions of opposing parties, of whom his perception is mediated by the categories of his lawyer's framework of analysis.[60] His only strategy of survival requires that he see himself as the lawyers and the officials see him, as an abstraction, a hypothetical person with only a few crude, discrete ends.[61] He must assume that his subtler ends, his long-range plans, and his social relationships are irrelevant to the situation at hand. This is the profound and unintended meaning of Holmes's remark:

60. *See, e.g.*, L. AUCHINCLOSS, POWERS OF ATTORNEY 184-86 (1963).

61. On the process by which an individual comes to accept the others' definition of his situation, see J. SARTRE, BEING AND NOTHINGNESS 55-67, 252-302 (Barnes trans. 1952) [hereinafter cited as SARTRE]; Goffman, *The Moral Career of the Mental Patient*, in ASYLUMS: ESSAYS ON THE SOCIAL SITUATION OF MENTAL PATIENTS AND OTHER INMATES 127-169 (1961) [hereinafter cited as Goffman]; Lukacs, *Reification and the Consciousness of the Proletariat*, in HISTORY AND CLASS CONSCIOUSNESS 83-110 (Livingstone trans. 1971) [hereinafter cited as Lukacs].

> If you want to know the law and nothing else, you must look at it as a bad man, who cares only for the material consequences which such knowledge enables him to predict, not as a good one, who finds his reasons for conduct, whether inside the law or outside of it, in the vaguer sanctions of conscience.[62]

The role of the bad man, conceived as an analytical device for the lawyer, becomes, under pressure of circumstances, a psychological reality for the client.

The image of rational choice by the client in response to neutral analysis by the lawyer is the shabbiest fiction of the Ideology of Advocacy. The most vulnerable facet of Monroe Freedman's article, so often praised even by its critics as frank and realistic, is its thoroughly misleading presentation of the "three hardest questions" as subjects of meaningful choice by the client. Even where the issue is formally submitted to the client as a matter for his decision, the client's choice is determined, or at least strongly biased, by the way in which the lawyer defines the question.

Thus, a lawyer representing a murderer does not discuss society's feelings about the nature of the crime, the legitimacy of the state's attempt to punish him, the client's own views of his actions, or their effect on his life in society. In advising him about whether to cooperate with the authorities, he will not explain the complex functional and extrinsic policies behind the privilege against self-incrimination. As a scrupulous professional, all he can do is explain that, of two courses equally incomprehensible to the client, one will probably lead to prison and the other to release. Similarly, the good Positivist advocate does not explain that the obligation made unenforceable by the Statute of Frauds would be binding but for a formality. Neither will he inquire into the fairness of the bargain, the nature of the relationship between the two parties, or the effect of not paying on the client's future business dealings or his standing in the community. His analysis must leave the client to decide whether or not he wishes to be coerced by the state to pay a sum of money to the plaintiff.

Of course, in practice, lawyers often do not even go through the motion of presenting critical questions to the client as occasions for choice.[63] They decide the questions unilaterally in terms of the imputed ends of selfishness.[64] This practice seems entirely justifiable because

62. Holmes, *supra* note 24, at 459; *see* FULLER, *supra* note 25, at 93.

63. *See, e.g.*, ROSENTHAL, *supra* note 5, at 32 (survey of personal injury litigation in New York City indicating that critical decisions are routinely made by lawyers with little or no participation by clients).

64. *E.g.*, L. AUCHINCLOSS, THE PARTNERS (1974):

> She asked him to review one of her estate plans whereby the rich husband of an incompetent was enabled to set up a trust in such a way as to throw the bulk of his estate taxes on his wife's children by a prior marriage, leaving the trust principal intact for his own.
>
> "But the widow's property will all be gobbled up!"

when inquiries are made in the framework of the imputed ends, when only the considerations relevant to the "bad man" are mentioned, the answer is a foregone conclusion.

Despite its complete irrationality, this Positivist strategy for dealing with the problem of the inaccessibility of personal ends has become so widely accepted that many lawyers have come to equate the manipulation of the client in terms of imputed ends with neutral advice to the client on his rights. For instance, lawyers constantly express astonishment at the willingness of intelligent laymen, aware of their rights, to make inculpatory statements to the authorities. They can think of no other explanation for this phenomenon besides confusion or pressure from the interrogators, and they thus conclude that no one can be expected to make an "informed decision" on such matters without the assistance of counsel.[65] But the

---

> "I don't know what you mean by 'gobbled up,' Mr. Simmonds."
>
> "I mean that Mr. Pierson will have shoved the taxes that properly belong on his estate off on his wife's. His children will end up rich while hers are bust."
>
> "It's an odd situation, certainly. I think I have handled it to the advantage of my client."
>
> Ronny stared. "But does Mr. Pierson *know* about his wife's will and the effect of this?"
>
> Mrs. Stagg smiled thinly. "*One thing you'd better learn right away, Mr. Simmonds, is never to ask what clients know.* Mr. Pierson does not come to One New Orange Plaza for spiritual advice. He wants to look after his incapacitated wife with the minimum injury to *his* offspring. I think that is precisely what my plan will effect.

Id. at 32-33 (second emphasis added). Mrs. Stagg is engaging in the strategy of imputed ends. For her, the issue is whether or not the client wishes to save money for his family, and the answer is sufficiently self-evident to make formal inquiry of the client superfluous. For Mr. Simmonds, the issue is whether the client wishes to save money for his family at the expense of his wife's family. Mrs. Stagg thinks that putting the question this way makes impermissible assumptions about the client's ends. The desire to save money for one's own family is sufficiently simple and basic an end to be imputable to the client. On the other hand, the concern for more remote relatives would implicate far more particular and subjective considerations. Since this concern is clearly on the far side of the line which separates the realm of imputable ends from the realm of pure subjectivity, there is no more reason to present this consideration to the client than there is to ask him whether he wishes the trust assets to be invested in companies which do business with South Africa. In attempting to speculate on his client's actual ends, Mr. Simmonds has really been trying to foist his own personal ends on the client.

See also PATTERSON & CHEATHAM, *supra* note 44, at 86: "The layman might well view [pleading the Statute of Frauds] as being unfair, but the advocate does not. The duty of loyalty to his client requires the plea, regardless of the merits of the claim." Notwithstanding the fact that the client, presumably a layman, might regard the plea as "unfair," the authors do not speak of consulting him, and they assume that the Statute will be routinely pleaded when it is available. The "duty of loyalty" thus appears to be, not to the client's actual ends, but to the imputed ends.

65. *E.g.*, Griffiths & Ayres, *A Postscript to the Miranda Project: Interrogation of Draft Protestors*, 77 YALE L. J. 300 (1967). This article exemplifies the unconscious influence of ideological assumptions on empirical research. It is based on an actual, unstaged incident in which members of the Yale University community were interrogated individually on two occasions by agents of the FBI about their involvement in illegal draft protests. In the first series of interrogations, despite the fact that the agents gave *Miranda* warnings, all of those questioned discussed their involvement. After these sessions, those questioned attended a meeting at which they were then informed of their rights, this time in more detail and by a "friendly source," that is, three Yale law professors. At the subsequent interrogations, all refused to give any information to the agents. The authors attribute the change of mind to the "greater understanding" resulting from the meeting and suggest that the agents' *Miran-*

lawyer's assistance does not take the form of neutral information or the alleviation of pressure. Along with his knowledge of the law, the lawyer brings his own prejudices and his own psychological pressures. These derive from the conception of the roles of lawyer and client which is implicit in Positivism generally and in the strategy of imputed ends. As Justice Jackson put it, "[A]ny lawyer worth his salt will tell the suspect in no uncertain terms to make no statement to the police under any circumstances."[66] The Positivist lawyer is not an advisor, but a lobbyist for a peculiar theory of human nature.

Positivist lawyers fail to see that the kind of behavior they impose on their clients is meaningless when it originates in the lawyer's conception of his own role rather than in the will of the client. And yet, because the imputed ends cannot approximate the complexity of the client's actual ends, Positivist advocacy cannot join forces with the will of the client. This is so even in the area of criminal defense, where the Positivist case for an imputed end is strongest, but nevertheless insufficient. It may be true that the desire to escape criminal punishment is basic and widespread. But the standard adversary defense cannot be justified by routinely imputing such a general desire to every client. The actual and specific ends of even a purely selfish individual may not be served by an adversary defense. For instance, such a defense may merely prolong and intensify an ordeal regarded as more terrible than the threatened punishment.[67] Or it may make the punishment, if it should occur, more difficult

da warnings had been ineffective because they were mechanically and tersely given and because of psychological pressures inherent in the interrogation situation, stemming in part from middle-class habits of courtesy and cooperation and a natural fear of the alien, coercive force of the state. They conclude that mechanical recitals of the *Miranda* provisions by officials are not enough and that a person requires an "advocate" at interrogation proceedings.

The central thrust of the article is its portrayal of the psychological pressures involved in interrogation. It shows no awareness whatsoever of the possibility of pressure from a "friendly source" or an "advocate." Yet, from the authors' account of the incident, the following conclusions seem at least as plausible as theirs. First, the three friendly sources gave more than information: they also conveyed, tacitly or explicitly, the impression that cooperation with the FBI in an investigation into the political expression of students was contrary to the expected standards of behavior of members of a liberal university community. Second, the fact that the second interrogation was conducted under the indirect scrutiny of third parties, while the first was not, was a factor encouraging the students to refuse cooperation the second time when they had cooperated the first time. *Cf.* Darley & Latané, *When Will People Help in an Emergency*? 2 PSYCHOLOGY TODAY (Dec. 1968) (presence of third party observers inhibits willingness to take responsibility in an emergency). Third, put to the test, the students' middle-class instincts of cooperation proved stronger with respect to other students and faculty, members of the same upper-middle professional class to which the student subjects belonged, than with respect to the police, members of a lower social class and an occupational group held in low esteem by the upper-middle professional class.

66. Watts v. Indiana, 338 U.S. 49, 59 (1949); *cf.* Justice Jackson's remark on his experience of civil practice in Jamestown, N.Y., ". . . a lawyer there, if he was consulted on a matter, usually dominated the matter, no matter who the businessman was." E. GERHART, AMERICA'S ADVOCATE: ROBERT M. JACKSON 63 (1958).

67. *See, e.g.*, F. DOSTOEVSKY, THE BROTHERS KARAMAZOV, at 552-53 (Magarshack trans.

to endure by forcing the client to struggle against it and to deny its legitimacy.[68]

The Positivist psychology either makes advocacy impossible or forces the lawyer into the strategy of imputed ends. Because the imputed ends ignore the most important dimensions of the client's personality,[69] the strategy leads to the manipulation of the client by the lawyer in terms of the lawyer's own moral and psychological prejudices. In this manner, the lawyer becomes the agent of the result he was supposed to prevent. He subverts his client's autonomy.[70]

1958). During the investigation by the examining magistrate and the public prosecutor, Dmitry Karamazov's fear and discomfort increase as the officials emphasize his procedural rights:

> "You see, gentlemen," he said suddenly, restraining himself with difficulty, "you see—I listen to you and I seem to be haunted by a dream—you see, I sometimes have such a dream—a curious kind of dream—I often dream it—it keeps on recurring—that someone is chasing me—someone I'm terribly afraid of—chasing me in the dark at night—looking for me, and I hide somewhere from him behind a door or a cupboard—hide myself so humiliatingly—and the worst of it is that he knows perfectly well where I've hidden myself from him, but he seems to be pretending deliberately not to know where I am, so as to prolong my agony, to enjoy my terror to the full. . . . That's what you're doing now. It's just like that!"

68. *See, e.g.*, A. SPEER, SPANDAU: THE SECRET DIARIES 58 (R. Winston & C. Winston, trans. 1977): "Who could survive twenty years of imprisonment without accepting some form of guilt?"

69. If the imputed values of Positivism fail to approximate even purely selfish ends, *a fortiori*, they fail to take account of communitarian ends (e.g., the desire to be reconciled with one's fellows). It is possible, though not necessary, to interpret the Positivist emphasis on the egoism of the individual as a denial of the existence of communitarian ends. *See* S. LUKES, INDIVIDUALISM 99-106 (1973). Yet, such a denial would be unpersuasive. First, it would conflict with the fact that many people do experience such ends or at least profess to experience them and act as if they did. More fundamentally, it would conflict with the basic Positivist premise of the arbitrariness and individuality of ends. If ends are arbitrary, then there seems to be no logical reason for excluding any category of imaginable ends; and if ends are individual, then there seems to be no factual basis on which one individual could assert that another could not have a particular end. Yet, the imputed values of Positivist advocacy are completely inconsistent with communitarian ends, and Positivist advocacy is destructive of such ends. *Cf.* Griffiths, *supra* note 3, at 371-417 (contrasting adversary advocacy with the "family model" of criminal procedure).

70. A Positivist might attempt to avoid the criticism made here by qualifying or retracting the principle of the subjectivity of ends. He might assert that ends are sufficiently shared, or at least understood, so that even strangers can achieve some understanding of each other's ends. This being so, the lawyer could respect his client's autonomy by making strong efforts to come to an understanding of his ends. The Positivist might assert that, although many lawyers do engage in the strategy of imputed ends, there is nothing in Positivism, so revised, which requires that they do so.

I doubt that Positivist Advocacy can be made more acceptable by such a revision. In the first place, to the extent that the revision avoids the problem of the inaccessibility of ends, it becomes less plausible ethically than the version stated above. There are severe limitations on the extent to which a person, particularly a stranger, can understand with any depth the ends of another without actually sharing those ends. The language in which we describe ends is often vague and indeterminate. To understand its meaning in a specific context, one must often share the moral outlook of the person who uses it. *See* FULLER, *supra* note 25, at 92-95; UNGER, *supra* note 25, at 101. Thus, in order to suggest that the advocate can gain an understanding of his client's ends, the revision must assume a substantial degree of sharing of ends throughout the society. Yet, to the extent that such a sharing exists, the insistence that the advocate refrain from holding either himself or his client to personal or social norms becomes untenable. In the Positivist version, the ethical validity of adversary advocacy

C. *The Present State of Positivism*

Positivism has been repudiated as a general jurisprudential theory by most American lawyers, and the influence of the Positivist version of the Ideology of Advocacy on the practice and discourse of the legal profession has diminished substantially since the beginning of the century.

In the area of private law, the destructive tendencies of Positivist advocacy have been generally acknowledged. In this area, Positivism no longer provides the basic rationalization for the lawyer's partisanship and neutrality. Positivist notions have been banished almost entirely in theory and substantially in practice. They function largely as a fallback position for situations of unusual difficulty. As a general matter, Positivism has been superseded by a jurisprudence which emphasizes individual and social responsibility and shared values and which teaches sensitivity to the subtleties of personal factors and social relationships.[71] The new category of "counseling" in legal ethics and education reflects, not only the changed nature of legal practice, but the recognition of the need to curb the destructive tendencies of Positivist advocacy. The Ideology of Advocacy is now identified most readily with litigation, while new fields of expertise, such as negotiation, counseling, and arbitration, have among their primary purposes the avoidance of litigation.

On the other hand, Positivist notions of advocacy continue to play a significant, though somewhat ambiguous, role in criminal law, and to a lesser extent, in civil liberties and poverty law. The Positivist emphasis on normless strife seems to correspond to many lawyers' experience of practice in these areas. Moreover, in these areas, where lawyers frequently confront clients from very different social backgrounds, the Positivist

depends heavily on the premise that values are subjective, arbitrary, and individual. If there were a substantial sharing of values in society, then the reference to such values by judges and lawyers would not be likely to cause uncertainty. If lawyer and client did share values, then the lawyer's adherence to such values would not constitute oppression of the client.

In the second place, the notion that ends are inaccessible accurately describes the experience of lawyers in some areas of practice. This is particularly true in criminal law, where the client is likely to be from a different social background than the lawyer. Albert Alschuler has written, "Most criminal defendants do not understand our [sic] system of criminal justice and cannot be made to understand." Alschuler, *supra* note 31, at 1310. In this situation, Alschuler suggests, no meaningful choice by the client as to the exercise of certain procedural rights is possible. *Id.* If this is true, then it can only be because most defense lawyers do not understand their clients and cannot be made to understand. If the lawyer understood his client, he would be able to give him the information about the criminal justice system which the client would need in order to make an autonomous choice. The strategy of imputed ends is not merely a theoretical ploy. It is a response to the experience of the inaccessibility of client ends in actual practice. It seems unlikely that the problem can be solved merely by telling lawyers to try to learn their clients' ends.

71. *See* text accompanying notes 73-132 *infra*. *See, e.g.*, H. HART & A. SACKS, THE LEGAL PROCESS: BASIC PROBLEMS IN THE MAKING AND APPLICATION OF LAW ch. II (1958) (unbound edition prepared for classroom use) [hereinafter cited as HART & SACKS]; Cavers, *Legal Education and Lawyer-Made Law*, 54 W. VA. L. REV. 177 (1952); Stone, *Legal Education on the Couch*, 85 HARV. L. REV. 392 (1971) [hereinafter cited as Stone, *Legal Education*].

implication that the client's ends are inaccessible seems most solidly grounded. Some lawyers practicing in these areas have become sympathetic to the Positivist notion that social norms represent merely arbitrary convergences of individual ends and therefore cannot justify punishment or other forms of government coercion. They have thus been willing to pay homage to the Positivist notion that coercion can be justified only by a rigorously applied, impersonal system of rules. Yet, this homage is often ambiguous, and these Positivist notions sometimes seem to lead a precarious co-existence with other, inconsistent notions. For instance, many lawyers who discuss law in Positivist terms also seem to be aware that the state does not operate as a neutral mechanism to secure order, but that it is an instrument of uncertainty and oppression. They seem to feel that aggressive partisan advocacy is most justified when it is undertaken on behalf of the least powerful because it has the effect of partially redressing the imbalance of power and wealth in society.[72] To the extent that such lawyers come to justify their efforts in terms of service to particular individuals or groups and in terms of substantive, result-oriented criteria which are independent of the legal system, they have departed from Positivism and from the Ideology of Advocacy. Thus, in contemporary discussions, Positivist advocacy sometimes seems on the verge of changing into something radically different from the Ideology of Advocacy.

III. The Lawyer as Para-Bureaucrat (The Half-Hearted Appeal to Truth)

"It's not [the trial lawyer's] job to pursue the truth, but [to] pursue the process from which the truth emerges."

Charles Haar[73]

The justification of partisan advocacy as instrumental to the attainment of concrete social ends was a secondary theme in the Ideology of Advocacy at the beginning of this century. The conservative, formalist attitudes which prevailed among lawyers at that time were not hospitable to this type of argument. In the 19th century, utilitarian political philosophers had considered legal institutions in instrumental terms, but their considerations had led them to condemn adversary advocacy.[74] However, an instrumental version of the Ideology of Advocacy became increasingly prominent throughout the present century. Its victory over the Positivist view was formally acknowledged by the replacement of the Canons of

72. *See, e.g.*, Cahn & Cahn, *The War on Poverty: A Civilian Perspective*, 73 YALE L.J. 1317, 1335-36 (1964) (defending a basically Positivist style of advocacy—one which emphasizes that the lawyer has no access to his client's ends—on the basis of non-Positivist considerations of distributive justice).

73. Professor Charles Haar, Harvard Law School, *quoted in* The Boston Phoenix, Jan. 15, 1974 at 20 (commenting on James St. Clair's decision to represent President Nixon in the Watergate investigations).

74. *See, e.g.*, 7 THE WORKS OF JEREMY BENTHAM 473-80 (Bowring ed. 1962 reprint).

Ethics with the Code of Professional Responsibility.[75]

The instrumental approach was based on a jurisprudence which developed in opposition both to formalism and to the cynical, antijudicial attitude of the more extreme Realists. This jurisprudence, which had been elaborated in various ways in the writings of Pound, Brandeis, Fuller, Llewellyn, Freund, Hart and Sacks, and Hurst, among many others, was, at least until recently, the reigning philosophy in the law schools, and it continues to exert a powerful influence on the judiciary and the bar.[76] It is not as precise or as coherent a theory as Positivism, and it can be treated as a single doctrine only by ignoring substantial differences among the theories in question. Yet, there is an important core of agreement among these theorists. This core, which can be called Purposivism, has a more ambiguous relationship to the Ideology of Advocacy than Positivism, and some Purposivists, have at least partially repudiated adversary advocacy.[77] However, most Purposivists, when faced with the question, have committed their doctrine to the defense of adversary advocacy, and a Purposivist version of the Ideology of Advocacy has emerged from their work.

A. *Purposivism*

In the Purposivist view, society is populated not by atomistic egoists but by people held together by shared experiences and norms. The purpose of law is not just to maintain order, but also to coordinate the actions of citizens so as to further their common purposes as effectively as possible.

Unlike the subjective and individual values of Positivism, the social norms of Purposivism are intuitively perceived and accepted throughout the society. To a large extent norms are self-enforcing because people are spontaneously disposed to conform to them. Nevertheless, spontaneous conformity to social norms is insufficient to secure their fullest implementation. The most effective implementation of social norms requires the application of technique. Unlike norms, technique cannot be

75. The Code was promulgated in 1969, but it embodied ideas which had been considered and studied by the American Bar Association for decades. A particularly influential document from this long period of gestation is a report by a joint conference of the ABA and the Association of American Law Schools. *See Professional Responsibility*, *supra* note 13.

76. *See, e.g.*, L. BRANDEIS, *Business—A Profession, The Opportunity in the Law, The Living Law*, in BUSINESS: A PROFESSION 1-12, 313-27, 344-63 (1914) [hereinafter cited as BRANDEIS]; P. FREUND, THE SUPREME COURT OF THE UNITED STATES (1961) [hereinafter cited as FREUND, SUPREME COURT]; L. FULLER, THE ANATOMY OF THE LAW (1968); HART & SACKS, *supra* note 71; HURST, *supra* note 35; K. LLEWELLYN, THE COMMON LAW TRADITION: DECIDING APPEALS (1960); R. POUND, THE SPIRIT OF THE COMMON LAW, chs. 7-8 (1921); Freund, *The Legal Profession*, 92 DAEDALUS 689 (Dec. 1963); Pound, *The Lawyer as a Social Engineer*, 3 J. PUB. L. 292 (1954).

77. *See* Frankel, *The Search for Truth: An Umpireal View*, 123 U. PA. L. REV. 1031 (1975); Pound, *The Causes of Popular Dissatisfaction with the Administration of Justice*, 29 A.B.A. REP. 395, 404 (1906).

intuitively apprehended. Technique involves abstract cognition and requires aptitude, study, and training. The law is a technical apparatus for the advancement of social norms.

The application of technique involves the exercise of power. In contrast to Positivism, Purposivism does not require that power be monopolized by the state. Purposivism recognizes that lawyers and private citizens exercise power. The exercise of power by private citizens is justified by the same principle which legitimates its exercise by the state: its tendency to further the shared norms of the society.

Moreover, the exercise of power is not entirely constrained by rules. Rules are only one among a variety of legal tools for the advancement of social norms. Judges reach behind rules directly to the social purposes the rules are intended to serve, and when they find the rules wanting in the light of the relevant purposes, they abandon or modify the rules. The predictability of judicial decisions remains a goal of the legal system, but it has a different significance than in Positivism. First, the mechanical application of rules is not viewed as the best way to achieve predictability. Predictability can often be better achieved by appealing directly to the intuitively perceived shared norms of the society. Second, predictability is not the pre-eminent goal of the system. It must be weighed against competing purposes, and it may be occasionally sacrificed to them.

The lawyer's role is a social function designed to facilitate the advancement of norms through the application of legal technique. Legal technique involves the use of institutional forms to manipulate the social world productively. But the lawyer's role requires more than knowledge of legal technique. It also depends on his knowledge of the shared norms of the society. It is only through the intuitive normative understanding which the lawyer has by virtue of his membership and experience in the society that he can use legal technique productively.

In further contrast to Positivism, the role of the Purposivist lawyer is constructive, rather than predictive. He uses institutional forms to create generally rewarding patterns of interaction. He works in the interstices of the patterns created by legislators and judges. The individual's personal ends, though identical or compatible with those of others, are submerged in the minute practical considerations of his particular activity. The lawyer discerns these ends and houses them in an institutional form congruent with the larger patterns of the society. He thus links the concrete and particular with the abstract and general, but not through a system of rules held together by formal logic. He does so by bringing out the latent harmonies among different individual concerns and giving them a secure institutional foundation. His approach is technical and instrumental. He reasons not from rule to conclusion, but between ends (shared purposes) and means (institutional forms).

The implications of Purposivism for advocacy are not as immediately clear as are those of Positivism. Indeed, at first glance, Purposivism seems to present troubling difficulties for the Ideology of Advocacy. The most basic difficulty arises from the necessity of reconciling the Purposivist emphasis on shared values and social harmony with the large measure of social antagonism presupposed by the institutions of adversary advocacy. On the one hand, it is difficult to see how any substantial conflict could exist in a society founded on shared ends. On the other hand, given the existence of such conflict, it is difficult to see how it could be resolved in terms of shared ends, since conflict often arises from differing ends. It is particularly difficult to see how the institutions of adversary advocacy could resolve such conflict, since these institutions seem to preserve and engender social antagonism. In Positivism, where conflict is presumed to be natural and order depends on force, this fact is not an objection. But in Purposivism, where order depends on the tacit acceptance of social norms, the antagonistic nature of adversary advocacy seems a fatal defect.

Of the variety of more specific questions which Purposivism poses for the Ideology of Advocacy, two categories of questions are particularly significant. The first concerns what appear to be the different levels of responsibility imputed to the lawyer and to other citizens. The Purposivists attribute a large measure of responsibility to ordinary citizens for conforming spontaneously to intuitively apprehended social norms. This responsibility follows from the Purposivist emphasis on the value of the voluntary creative activity of the individual. The Purposivists believed that a great virtue of the social system they defended was that it enabled the society to secure the full benefits of this creativity by giving broad latitude to individual initiative, and they contrasted this sytem favorably to authoritarian or socialist systems in which individual initiative is stifled.[78] The Purposivists recognized that a concomitant to the principle of individual initiative is individual responsibility. If the Purposivists favored giving individuals broad discretion, they also expected them to be held responsible for their acts.[79]

The Purposivist emphasis on responsibility is strikingly evident in Purposivism's attitude toward retroactivity. In Positivism, a retroactive sanction, one which was not explicitly specified by a rule in effect at the time of the action in question, is completely arbitrary and unjustified. The Purposivists, on the other hand, recognized that rules are indeterminate, and they wanted the judge, not to shrink from the discretion this recognition implied, but to use it vigorously to further social ends. They were not disturbed by the fact that such a program would require the imposition of

78. *See, e.g.*, L. Fuller, The Morality of Law 162-77 (rev. ed. 1969); Hart & Sacks, *supra* note 71, at 111-12, 183-84; A. Mason, Brandeis: A Free Man's Life 141, 149-51, 160, 303-04, 359-60 (1946) [hereinafter cited as Mason].

79. *E.g.*, Hart & Sacks, *supra* note 71, at 263; Stone, *The Public Influence of the Bar*, 48 Harv. L. Rev. 1, 4 (1934) [hereinafter cited as Stone].

sanctions for violations of previously unformulated or ambiguously formulated commands.[80] They justified this retroactivity in terms of the individual's responsibility to respect the shared norms of the society. Unlike Positivism, Purposivism did not leave individuals free to flout the public interest in the interstices of formal rules.

Purposivism's emphasis on individual responsibility and its tolerance for retroactivity raise the question of how the lawyer can be blameless when he defends conduct for which the client can be punished. In Positivism, where the application of force is generally not retroactive, the only relevant consideration governing the lawyer's activities is that they be authorized by the applicable rules. It is of no importance that these activities may have led to a socially undesirable result because the system is not concerned with the social desirability of outcomes, and it would be subverted if lawyers tried to take account of such considerations. Things are different with Purposivism. Here decisions may be formally retroactive, but they are justified because they are based on social values known to the client and binding on him as a member of the society. Since the norms are also known to the lawyer and he is also a member of the society, his efforts to thwart their enforcement would seem to be as offensive as his client's violation of them. Unlike Boswell, the Purposivist lawyer does not need to wait for the judge to tell him so in order to know that certain kinds of conduct are wrong.[81]

There appears to be a similar discrepancy in Purposivism between the responsibilities of the lawyer and those of the judge. Purposivism repudiated the notion that judicial decisions were determined by the autonomous operation of legal rules. It insisted that decisions were in large part an exercise of power on the part of the judge and that this exercise could be justified only in terms of social norms. It refused to permit the judge to escape responsibility for his decisions by claiming that they had been compelled by the rules.[82] When a particular application of a rule leads to a result which frustrates its underlying social purposes, Purposivism expects the judge to reject it. On the other hand, in the adversary proceeding, the lawyer has no corresponding responsibility to ensure that rules are applied in a manner which furthers their underlying purposes. The adversary proceeding seems an inefficient method for the attainment of truth precisely because rules are so frequently applied in a manner which frustrates their basic purposes. For instance, if the purpose of the hearsay rule is to exclude inaccurate and misleading testimony, then why should the rule be enforced when the testimony in question,

80. *E.g.*, HART & SACKS, *supra* note 71, at 377-81, 574-76; Fuller, *The Forms and Limits of Adjudication*, in HART & SACKS, *supra* note 71, at 421-26 [hereinafter cited as Fuller, *The Forms and Limits of Adjudication*].

81. *See* text accompanying note 23 *supra*.

82. *See, e.g.*, HART & SACKS, *supra* note 71, at 515-46; Pound, *Mechanical Jurisprudence*, 8 COLUM. L. REV. 605 (1908).

though it falls within the language of the rule, is neither inaccurate nor misleading? In most situations, the judge has no way of deciding whether or not the testimony is misleading or inaccurate. But the lawyer often does. Why, then, should he not have the same responsibility Purposivists impute to the judge to see that the underlying social purposes are served by the enforcement of the rules he invokes?

A second important category of questions which Purposivism raises concerns the way values are perceived by the lawyer. This difficulty is illustrated by a passage in which Lon Fuller criticizes Holmes's quintessentially Positivist "bad man" theory. Fuller argues that Holmes's attempt to separate law and morals is untenable. First, to define legal analysis in terms of the calculations of the "bad man" is arbitrary. Most men do not think of the law in this fashion. They are concerned not only with state-imposed sanctions but with many other things, such as the good opinions of their friends and neighbors. Second, even an analysis which focuses only on predicting the application of state force cannot effectively separate law and morals. For the application of force will ultimately depend on the decision of a judge. Because legal rules are indeterminate, the judge will have to refer to the moral standards which underlie them in order to apply them to the case at hand. In order to anticipate the judge's decision, the lawyer himself will have to resort to these moral standards. Fuller concludes that if the lawyer is "[t]o be a good positivist, he will have to become a good natural-law lawyer."[83]

There is an ambiguity here. Does the natural-law lawyer merely do a better job than the Positivist, or does he have a different job? Is it just that by including values in his calculus he is able to derive a more accurate prediction of the probability of sanctions? Or are his efforts more evaluative than predictive because he reasons in terms of norms which he recognizes as binding on himself and his client as members of society? Like some contemporary analytical philosophers, Fuller contends that thought processes often discussed in terms of abstract cognition really make sense only in terms of the shared understandings and practices of the community to which the thinker addresses himself. But does the lawyer's membership in the community merely enable him to manipulate it more effectively; or does it constrain his activities?

The question is difficult. On the one hand, if the answer is that the Purposivist analysis merely provides more accurate predictions, then the argument against the Positivist separation of law and morals is trivial. Holmes was concerned with defending the objective character of the law and its basic emphasis on the prediction of the application of force. Moral values understood merely as data relevant to such predictions are different from moral values as they are usually understood, that is, as norms binding independently of the force behind them. The "bad man" obvi-

83. FULLER, *supra* note 25, at 95.

ously wants the most accurate prediction possible. On the other hand, if the answer is that the Purposivist analysis involves the recognition of norms binding on those who engage in the analysis, then it seems incompatible with adversary advocacy.

B. The Purposivist Accommodation to Advocacy

The Purposivists did not often recognize that their doctrine posed serious problems for the Ideology of Advocacy. This oversight was part of a general tendency on the part of Purposivism to ignore or minimize social conflict. For example, in the course of regretting the *Dred Scott* and *Pollock* decisions, Paul Freund once argued that the cases should have been decided on technical grounds without reaching the constitutional issues. He then concluded, "These were cases in which counsel were perhaps too eager for the settlement of burning issues."[84] Thus are events which historians have regarded as major battles in a class struggle reduced to a matter of technical confusion on the part of a neutral professional group.

When the Purposivists did not ignore conflict entirely, they tended to assume that the problems it presents had been superseded by the advent of a society in which any divergences between individual interests and social interests were almost automatically brought into line by the operation of public institutions. Hart and Sacks' *The Legal Process* illustrates this attitude. For instance, Hart and Sacks are sharply critical of the conduct of counsel for railroads, which in the 19th century sought to use their monopolistic power to contract out of negligence liability for freight damage and personal injury. This effort was thwarted eventually by judges, legislators, and government officials. Hart and Sacks argue that the railroad lawyers should have convinced their clients to work out voluntarily a fair arrangement with their customers. They conclude, "[h]ad members of the American bar in the last century taken this course, consider the aggregate of judicial, legislative, and administrative action that would have been unnecessary."[85] They never consider that the railroads' recalcitrance might have been profitable. Their reproach does not take the form of righteous indignation at the selfish, antisocial behavior of the railroad lawyers, but rather expresses surprise at their obtuseness in failing to perceive the inevitability of events which would bring self-interest and the public interest into line.

This Purposivist belief in the reconciliation of public and private interest was not a mere Panglossian intuition. It was closely related to the political developments culminating in the New Deal and to judicial reforms which the Purposivists had supported. The growth of government

84. FREUND, SUPREME COURT, *supra* note 76, at 149. For a contrasting view of *Pollack*, see A. PAUL, CONSERVATIVE CRISIS AND THE RULE OF LAW: ATTITUDES OF BAR AND BENCH, 1887-1895 (1960). *See also* FULLER, *supra* note 25, at 17.

85. HART & SACKS, *supra* note 71, at 263.

regulation and the decline of rule formalism in adjudication had made *ad hoc*, retroactive intervention to protect social interests a routine government activity. Formal rules no longer created pockets of discretion in which selfish individuals were free to flout the public interest. Thus, Adolf Berle suggested that Purposivism and the New Deal had mooted the issues of advocacy and that they would liberate "the bulk of the corporation bar from the profitable but mostly undistinguished bondage in which most of it lives" regardless of what position it took on these issues:

> At Columbia we teach . . . that there is an inchoate law affecting corporations holding market power, or on which the community has come to depend for some essential function, and that this inchoate law has recognizable criteria and principles. The moment these principles are seriously infringed, the state predictably intervenes. In that case an explicit rule of law presently results. Great and powerful interests cannot afford to risk being caught in a major infringement even though the rule has not become explicit.[86]

The Purposivist answer to the general question of the compatibility of conflict and shared values was to insist that conflict was a result of short-sightedness and confusion rather than of divergent norms, and to recommend that it be resolved simply by showing individuals that their true interests converged with the public interest. The principal theoretical underpinnings of this view of advocacy were the Purposivist notions of the separation of functions and the long run. The separation of functions purported to explain the apparent difference in the levels of responsibility attributed to the lawyer and to other citizens. The principle of the long run purported to explain how norms could be integrated into a technical, predictive analysis and yet still be understood as binding moral imperatives.

1. THE TECHNIQUE OF THE SEPARATION OF FUNCTIONS

The basic theory of the separation of functions is simple. Specialization into roles makes it possible to perform specific tasks more efficiently. This is so for two reasons: expertise and cognitive dissonance. First, there are limits to the amount of knowledge a person can absorb and the number of skills he can develop. Second, a person's understanding of a particular problem is limited by his tendency to develop preconceptions based on some aspects of the situation which distort his understanding of other aspects. The first factor limits the number of tasks a person can ever perform. The second factor limits the number of tasks a person can perform at the same time. Because of these factors, a person works most productively when he concentrates his efforts in a specific area. Yet, this specialization creates a new problem. Because a specialized role is

86. Berle, Book Review, 76 HARV. L. REV. 430, 431-32 (1962). *See also* HURST, *supra* note 35, at 355-56; PATTERSON & CHEATHAM, *supra* note 44, at 137-38.

designed to further only specific social values and needs, specialization creates the danger that the role occupants will pursue these values and needs at the expense of other values and needs outside the range of their role competences. This problem can be solved by coordinating the roles and functions so that each is confined to the sphere of operation where it is most effective and any deficiencies in the operation of one role can be remedied by the operation of the others. Thus, efficiency can be enhanced through specialization, while a proper balance among values and needs can be achieved by coordination.

The Purposivists saw the legal profession both as surrounded by coordinate, specialized roles and insitutions and as itself divided into specialized roles. While the value of specialization for other institutions, such as agencies and legislatures, rested in large part on expertise, the value of role specialization within the profession rested for the most part on cognitive dissonance. The two most important legal roles were the counseling and advocacy roles, and the distinction between them was a central pillar of the Purposivist version of the Ideology of Advocacy. This distinction was emphasized by the early Purposivists whose demands for the reform of the profession were prompted by the out-of-court activities of the corporate bar.[87] One of their principal criticisms of the *Canons of Ethics* was that the *Canons* were exclusively addressed to the lawyer's function as courtroom advocate and ignored his function as counselor and private law-maker. As Purposivism evolved, it developed a complex intra-professional separation of functions, which included not only the counseling and advocacy roles but also two other roles for which Purposivism won recognition: the government lawyer, and the lawyer pro bono publico.[88]

The Purposivist theory of the separation of functions was well explained by Fuller and his collaborators in the Joint Conference of the American Bar Association and the American Association of Law Schools which worked on the revision of the *Canons*. In their view, the purpose of advocacy is to promote "a wise and informed decision of the case." The utility of adversary advocacy in promoting such a decision lies in the application of the principles of specialization and coordination within the judicial proceedings:

> In a very real sense it may be said that the integrity of the adjudicative process itself depends on the participation of the advocate. This becomes apparent when we contemplate the nature of the task assumed by any arbiter who attempts to decide a dispute without the aid of partisan advocacy.
>
> Such an arbiter must undertake, not only the role of judge, but that of representative for both of the litigants. Each of these

87. *See, e.g.*, BRANDEIS, *The Opportunity in the Law*, in BUSINESS: A PROFESSION, *supra* note 76, at 339-41; Stone, *supra* note 79.

88. *See* ABA CODE OF PROFESSIONAL RESPONSIBILITY, EC 2-25, 7-13, 7-14, 8-1, 8-6, 8-9.

> roles must be played to the full without being muted by qualifications derived from the others. When he is developing for each side the most effective statement of its case, the arbiter must put aside his neutrality and permit himself to be moved by a sympathetic identification sufficiently intense to draw from his mind all that it is capable of giving—in analysis, patience and creative power. When he resumes his neutral position, he must be able to view with distrust the fruits of this identification and be ready to reject the products of his own best mental efforts. The difficulties of the undertaking are obvious.[89]

The practical consequence of such an undertaking is "that at some early point a familiar pattern will seem to emerge from the evidence; an accustomed label is waiting for the case and, without waiting for the proofs the label is promptly assigned." This results from the necessity of giving some pattern of coherence to the evidence, for "without some tentative theory of the case there is no standard of relevance by which testimony may be measured." Partisanship is seen as "the only effective means for combating the natural human tendency to judge too swiftly that which is not fully known." Thus, "[t]he arguments of counsel hold the case, as it were, in suspension between two opposing interpretations of it. While the proper classification of the case is thus kept unresolved, there is time to explore all of its peculiarities and nuances."[90]

Thus, the need for adversary advocacy arises not, as in Positivism, from divergent ends, but from the problem of cognitive dissonance. The separation of functions within the trial contributes to an informed decision by assuring that no aspect of either side's position will be overlooked. The advocate's partisanship is a psychological convention designed to enable him to achieve the benefits of specialization.

However, for the Purposivists, partisan advocacy was valuable only in certain situations, and the advocacy role was viable only as one of a number of specialized legal roles. A critical element of the Purposivist version of the Ideology of Advocacy was its emphasis on the residual nature of the function of advocacy. This emphasis follows from the Purposivist insistence that conflict is not the central element of social life. As Hart and Sacks put it, "The overwhelming proportion of the things which happen and do not happen in American society pass without any later question."[91] Adversary advocacy is needed only for that residuum of "trouble cases" as to which later question does arise. Adversary advocacy is not destructive in these situations because social relationships

89. *Professional Responsibility*, *supra* note 13, at 1160. (Fuller was co-chairman of the group which produced the report.) *See also* ABA CODE OF PROFESSIONAL RESPONSIBILITY, EC 7-19; Fuller, *The Adversary System*, in TALKS ON AMERICAN LAW 43-44 (Berman ed. 1971).

90. *Professional Responsibility*, *supra* note 13, at 1160.

91. HART & SACKS, *supra* note 71, at 312.

have already broken down, and private, voluntary efforts to restore them have failed.

In other situations, however, the Purposivists proposed to curb the principles of neutrality and partisanship and substitute new legal roles. The principle of specialization dictates a spectrum of ethical obligations to accord with different functions.

In the Purposivist view, the prototypical legal activity is counseling, rather than advocacy. The counselor most closely approaches the Purposivist ideal of the creator of mutually beneficial patterns of interaction. The counselor deals with individuals, but unlike the advocate's clients, they are not isolated individuals. Rather they are actual or potential participants in social relationships and institutions.

The fundamental ethical innovation which the Purposivists sought to establish was the counselor's affirmative duty to channel the client's egoistic impulses into socially desirable paths.[92] In this manner, they sought to find a middle way between the wholly public responsibilities of the civil servant and the aggressive partisanship of the adversary advocate. Unlike the civil servant, the counselor must be intimately concerned with, and sympathetic to, the special needs of particular people. Moreover, because the counselor does much of his work in the interstices of public policy, dealing with matters toward which public policy is indifferent, he has a greater range of discretion than the civil servant. Yet, unlike the advocate, the counselor does have an affirmative obligation to oppose his client's antisocial impulses. He can reconcile his obligations to his client and the public by focusing on the points of congruence between the particular interest of the client and the general welfare.

Yet the Purposivists realized that the added but limited responsibilities of the counseling role were not sufficient to enable the legal profession to play the most effective role it could in the social order. Rather than raise the counselor's public obligations still higher, however, and thus sacrifice the benefits of specialization, the Purposivists attempted to integrate more public responsibility into the profession through the government and the pro bono roles.

The government lawyer is at the opposite pole of the spectrum of legal roles from the advocate.[93] He is concerned entirely with the general welfare, and his responsibilities are entirely public. His role is closest to that of the civil servant in that the government lawyer should not direct his sympathies or energies toward any particular individual or group. His primary task, the enforcement of statutes, can be most effectively performed with a non-partisan attitude.

The pro bono lawyer also has primary obligations to the public at

92. *See, e.g.*, ABA CODE OF PROFESSIONAL RESPONSIBILITY, EC 7-3 to 7-5; PATTERSON & CHEATHAM, *supra* note 44, at 134-38; Thode, *supra* note 18, at 578-79.

93. *See* ABA CODE OF PROFESSIONAL RESPONSIBILITY, EC 7-13 to 7-14.

large, but these obligations are more limited than those of the government lawyer because the pro bono function is residual.[94] The job of the pro bono lawyer is to serve people and interests which have been slighted by the law enforcement efforts of the government and who have not gained effective private legal representation. In this task, he needs to be more sensitive to the needs and aspirations of particular groups than does the government lawyer, but in order to decide which of the potentially infinite number of unrepresented or underrepresented interests he should serve, he needs to take a public viewpoint. (Of course, once the pro bono lawyer has committed himself to a particular group or interest, he will assume the counseling or adversary role.)

Though none of these roles is sufficient to guarantee a satisfactory legal order, all of them can be coordinated so as to remedy the deficiencies of each. Lawyers will adopt the role most suitable to the situation at hand and, when the situation changes, will defer to a coordinate role. The Purposivists did not overlook that through incompetence or ill-will lawyers might deviate from the prescriptions of the separation of functions. But they were confident that deviations on the part of any one role could be rectified by the operation of the other roles. The task of checking excesses on the part of the others is built into the functional competence of each role.

While the Purposivists had criticized the application of neutrality and partisanship in the counseling sphere, they were not troubled by its application in the adversary sphere because they felt that in the judicial proceeding excesses of adversary zeal could be checked by the judge and the opposing lawyer.[95] They did not fear that the antagonistic tendencies of adversary advocacy would damage viable social relationships because they counted on the counseling role to keep such relationships out of the adversary sphere. The counselor is charged with a higher standard of public duty than the advocate to reflect the fact that he is subject to less direct scrutiny by opposing interests and public officials. Nevertheless, this ethical prescription is supplemented by pressures exerted from coordinate roles. If the counselor should attempt to further his client's interests at the expense of the interests of others, other lawyers in the advocacy, pro bono, or government roles would bring things back into line, either by causing him to reconsider or by precipitating the situation into the adversary sphere.

From this perspective, the difference in the ethical obligations imposed on the attorney, judge, and client appears as an application of the principle of specialization. The advocate's distinctive ethical orientation enables him to pursue his special tasks more effectively and thus to serve

94. *See* ABA Code of Professional Responsibility EC 2-25, 8-1 to 8-6, 8-9.

95. *See, e.g.*, Patterson & Cheatham, *supra* note 44, at 181; Brandeis, *The Opportunity in the Law*, in Business: A Profession, *supra* note 76, at 339-41; Thode, *supra* note 18, at 576-579.

better the social norms implicated in these tasks. His peculiar ethical orientation does not threaten other social norms because destructive tendencies on his part are checked by the operation of coordinate roles.

2. THE MORALITY OF THE LONG RUN

The principle of the separation of functions is complemented by the principle of the long run. The basic principle of the long run is that social norms should be pursued with a view toward achieving their greatest aggregate implementation over time, rather than toward an immediate, continuous implementation. The principle of the long run dictates that present sacrifices be suffered when they make possible greater future benefits. It prescribes that social norms be violated in particular instances as a means to the general welfare.

The principle of the long run is in marked contrast to the principles of Positivist legal theory. In Positivism, results must be immediately (even if only tautologically) just. Each legal decision must be rationalized on its own without reference to future consequences.

The Purposivist adoption of the morality of the long run was based on the realistic insight that in the modern world the achievement of most substantial social goals entails certain negative externalities. The operation of an airport requires that some suffer noise and smog.[96] The establishment of a criminal justice system requires that some innocent people be imprisoned.[97] Yet, such immediate negative results are eventually compensated for by greater positive ones. To refuse to tolerate such negative results would be to call a halt to progress. The short-run gains of such a refusal would be drastically outweighed by the ultimate decline in the level of satisfactions.

The notion of the long run underlies the Purposivist justification of the lawyer's role. Although Positivists often referred to the lawyer's role and particularly the rule of confidentiality as instrumental to the effective provision of legal services, the point was neither a difficult nor an important one because Positivism felt no need to rationalize the antisocial consequences produced by the lawyer's partisanship and neutrality. On the other hand, the Purposivist lawyer is not an extension of his client's will, but an agent of social welfare. The antisocial results of his activities cannot be rationalized as implementing the client's rights, for rights are themselves social functions.[98] These results must be seen as means to the greater long-run implementation of social norms. Thus, Purposivism emphasizes that, for every unjust result caused by the lawyer's refusal to

96. *See* Michelman, *Property, Utility and Fairness: Comments on the Ethical Foundation of "Just Compensation" Law*, 80 HARV. L. REV. 1165 (1967) [hereinafter cited as Michelman].

97. *See* Kaplan, *Decision Theory and the Factfinding Process*, 20 STAN. L. REV. 1065 (1968).

98. *See* Pound, *A Survey of Social Interests*, 57 HARV. L. REV. 1 (1943).

reveal his client's lies or crimes, a greater number of just claims are vindicated because of the greater access to legal services and the more effective presentation of claims which the rule of confidentiality makes possible.[99]

The principle of the long run provides an answer to the question of how the Purposivist lawyer can reject the viewpoint of Holmes' "bad man" and still acquiesce in his client's intentions to thwart the implementation of social norms. Like the other role occupants in the system, the lawyer perceives norms intuitively and regards them as binding on him, but only in the long run. Violations of social norms by lawyers in the performance of their professional role are merely means to advance social norms in the long run. Thus, the lawyer's neutrality operates only in the short run. It is a necessary concomitant to his commitment to social norms in the long run.

C. *The Critique of Purposivist Advocacy*

Once the Purposivist doctrine has made room for adversary advocacy, it looks more like Positivism than it did earlier. Law seems to have lost some of its organic ties with social norms and to have taken the form, if not of the conceptual system of the scientist, then of the mechanical system of the engineer. Once again, considerations of system appear to have compromised the lawyer's moral integrity.

However, even from this perspective, Purposivism promises much more than Positivism. First, the Purposivist system serves, and can be judged in terms of, a variety of concrete social ends, not just the unique, formal Positivist end of order. Second, in the counseling, pro bono, and government roles, the lawyer's service to shared norms is more direct and his experience of them more immediate than in the adversary role, which was the only one emphasized by Positivism. Third, the possibility of alternating among several roles gives the Purposivist lawyer an opportunity to bridge the gaps which separate the various functions and to enlarge the scope of his immediate experience of social ends.

Nevertheless, as in Positivism, a subtle shift of emphasis occurs when the Purposivist turns from general jurisprudential theory to legal ethics. In Positivism, the shift is from substantive rules to procedural rules. In Purposivism, the shift is from shared values to function.[100] The

99. *See* ABA CODE OF PROFESSIONAL RESPONSIBILITY, EC 4-1; Noonan, *supra* note 11.

100. Consider, the response of the Purposivist to the litigant whose claim is being denied despite its substantive justice:

> In any event, the policy of avoidance, if otherwise applicable, must prevail, despite hardship to the litigant and despite what is in other circumstances a strong policy in favor of authoritative and speedy pronouncement of governing rules. There are crucial differences . . . between the role of the Supreme Court in constitutional cases and the function of courts of general jurisdiction. The latter sit as primary agencies for the peaceful settlement of disputes and, in a more restricted sphere, as primary agencies for the vindication and evolution of the legal order. They must, indeed, resolve all controversies within their jurisdiction, because the alternative is

lawyer first sees his role in terms of social values. But then he learns the need to sacrifice these values to considerations of function. Properly understood, this phenomenon is no more than a foregoing of the short run in favor of the long run. Yet, it is inevitably experienced with a sense of tension and disappointment. Purposivism always begins exultantly with an attack on Positivism in the name of shared values, but it always ends soberly with an insistence on the need to defer to the constraints of function. Thus, Noonan opens his critique of Freedman with a celebration of the pursuit of truth as the lawyer's highest duty, but soon begins to caution the lawyer that this pursuit must stop when it reaches the line which separates the judge's role from his own.[101]

This sense of disappointment is not a mere side effect. It is a symbol of deep weaknesses in the Purposivist attempt to renovate the Ideology of Advocacy in terms of the principles of the separation of functions and the long run. First, the principle of the separation of functions cannot be effectively implemented. Second, the principle of the long run suffers from a serious ambiguity in its understanding of morality, or social values, and of the relationship of morality to technique. This ambiguity undermines Purposivism's claims both to legitimacy and to efficacy.

1. THE COLLAPSE OF FUNCTIONAL DISTINCTIONS

The basic defect of the principle of the separation of functions is the incompatibility of specialization and coordination. Purposivism insists on the efficiency of narrowing one's focus to a particular aspect of a situation. It also admits that the benefits of this specialization can be reaped only if the various limited perspectives can be coordinated from a broader point of view. Yet, the same reasons which make specialization efficient seem to make coordination impossible.

The rationalization of adversary advocacy in terms of the principle of specialization involves the Purposivists in the reverse of the difficulty which plagued the Positivist theory. Purposivism began with the important insight, ignored by Positivism, that in order to further his client's ends, the lawyer needs an intuitive grasp of them. But it begged an important question in reasoning from the premise that a single lawyer cannot fully discern the divergent views of two different people at the same time to the conclusion that partisan advocacy can effectively ascertain the truth. The argument fails to explain how the divergence of views is resolved. Purposivism never explains how the lawyer translates the

> chaos. The Supreme Court in constitutional cases sits to render an additional, principled judgment on what has already been authoritatively ordered. . . . Fixation on an individual right to judgment by the Supreme Court is, therefore, largely question-begging.

A. BICKEL, THE LEAST DANGEROUS BRANCH 173 (1962) [hereinafter cited as BICKEL]. This is the Purposivist kiss-off: "I'd like to help, but it's not my job." Compare this approach with that of the Positivists, at note 29 *supra*.

101. Noonan, *supra* note 11, at 1487-88.

insights achieved from a sympathetic consideration of his client's position into a form assimilable by the judge in an impartial consideration.[102]

It is true that the presence of advocates on each side may counterbalance any predisposition toward one side or the other which the judge might bring to the trial. In this way, advocacy makes for greater impartiality.[103] But this is not enough. The Purposivist must also show that the kind of impartiality enhanced by adversary advocacy is likely to lead to more accurate, socially efficient decisions. It is no virtue that adversary advocacy "hold[s] the case . . . in suspension between two opposing interpretations" while all the "peculiarities and nuances" are explored, unless it also increases the likelihood that the balance will ultimately be struck in favor of the correct interpretation.[104]

The Purposivist argument suggests no reason to believe that it does. In suggesting that partisan sympathy is necessary to fully understand a person's views, the Purposivist psychology of cognitive dissonance implies that no single person can ever simultaneously grasp the divergent views of different people. It would thus seem unlikely that a judge could ever fully understand both sides of the same case. If this is true, then Purposivist advocacy merely replaces prejudice with arbitrariness. The "familiar pattern" with which the trier begins may be subverted by the vigorous presentation of alternatives, but the pattern which ultimately emerges seems as likely to be the product of the distortions or obfuscations of one or both of the litigants as of anything else. In Purposivist terms, this displacement of the trier's initial prejudices by arbitrariness seems almost certain to be a loss in terms of the quest for truth. Prejudices, after all, are often very accurate, and in a world of shared values and common experiences, one expects "familiar patterns" to have a certain reliability.

Not only does Purposivism beg the question of the way the judge performs his job, but it misrepresents the way the lawyer performs his. The actual psychology of working lawyers does not conform to the model of partisan sympathy assumed by the Purposivist theory of cognitive dissonance. Practical discussions of litigation technique are full of warnings not to behave in precisely the manner that the Purposivist argument suggests the lawyer should act. They insist that a lawyer who accepts his client's version of the facts without being constantly sensitive to the

102. It should be noted that the problem of advocacy in Purposivism is in some ways distinct from the problem of rule interpretation. Purposivists sometimes suggest that the latter problem can be solved by a compromise method in which both rules and norms are taken into account. *Compare* HART & SACKS, *supra* note 71, at 155-68, *with* Kennedy, *supra* note 42, at 395-98. While such a method might justify the judge's role in resolving disputes, it does not justify the ethical and methodological division of labor between lawyer and judge. In order to explain this, two separate methods must be elaborated, and their congruence must then be shown.

103. *See* Thibaut, Walker & Lind, *Adversary Presentation and Bias in Legal Decisionmaking*, 86 HARV. L. REV. 386 (1972).

104. *Professional Responsibility*, *supra* note 13, at 1161.

possibility that he may be mistaken or lying, or who focuses on the arguments favorable to his client without making an equally vigorous attempt to anticipate those of his opponent, is likely to do a poor job regardless of the merits of the case.[105] For all its faults, the Positivist theory was a far more accurate description of the realities of adversary advocacy. Adversary advocacy tends more to encourage indifference toward the ends of the client than to encourage sympathy for them. The lawyer's analytical abilities are more compromised than enhanced by such sympathy.[106] The actual psychology of practicing lawyers in analyzing and preparing their clients' cases does not seem radically different from that of a judge trying to understand both sides with a view toward arriving at a decision. This psychology seems to contradict the contention that cognitive dissonance would compromise truth-seeking without adversary advocacy.

Yet even if it is assumed that the Purposivist psychology is accurate, the theory of the separation of functions is untenable both within the adversary sphere and within the legal system as a whole. The various roles in the system cannot be specified so as to permit their effective coordination with each other.

Purposivism suggests that roles are defined by lines. Within the lines, the role occupants are guided directly by social values, but when they reach the limits of the lines, they defer to other jurisdictions. But how are such lines to be drawn and understood? Two types of thought appear in Purposivism. First, there is the intuitive understanding of shared norms which all members of the society share. Second, there are a variety of technical skills possessed by various trained minorities which concern the use of institutional forms to advance the shared values. Neither of these types of thought can solve the problem of delineating the limits of role competences. Intuition cannot do the job because, in order to define the roles, one would need an understanding of the skills on which they were based. The roles are artificial; they are themselves instruments to social ends. Thus, technical knowledge is necessary to shape them. But one of the essential characteristics of technical knowledge is that it is specialized. Each particular skill is of no use in defining its relation to any other skill. The whole point of drawing the lines is to keep people within them, but it seems that they cannot be drawn unless people go beyond them.

One tempting solution to the dilemma is to delegate the task of line-drawing to some very generalized institutional competence, such as a philosopher-king, a constitutional convention, or a legislature. But this proposal only drives the Purposivist back toward the problem of formalism which he originally set out to escape. The lines will have to be

105. *See, e.g.*, R. Keeton, Trial Tactics and Methods §§ 9-10 (1954).
106. C. Curtis, It's Your Law 26 (1954) [hereinafter cited as Curtis].

expressed in a manner which can be understood by people who, because of the problem of specialization, have no direct, intuitive perception of their basis. The lines would take the form of rules. But the Purposivists have shown conclusively that rules are ineffective without some direct access to the understanding which lies behind them. When the Purposivists ignore their own insights and attempt to prescribe such lines, they fall into formalism and circularity.[107]

In the light of this dilemma, the Purposivist claim to rectify the inadequacies of the separate legal roles by coordinating them with one another is untenable. If cognitive dissonance limits the perspectives of the roles, then it also precludes the role occupants from perceiving the limits of their role competences. There is no way of confining the roles to the situations to which they are appropriate.

The counseling role is supposed to construct and maintain viable social relationships. It is supposed to do so by discouraging the client's short-sighted pursuit of his interests and channeling his energies along paths where these interests coincide with those of others. Yet, there is no reason to believe that the counselor will be able to recognize those short-sighted courses of action which are likely to bring his client into conflict with the interests of others. The counselor must seek an intimate and sympathetic understanding of his client's ends. The principle of cognitive dissonance suggests that this understanding must, at least to some extent, compromise his understanding of the interests of others. In constructing institutions and relationships, the counselor will thus interpret the interests of others in terms of his client's interests. He will be slow to see the points at which his client's short-term interests diverge from the interests of others. Failing to perceive such divergences, he may devote his talents to maintaining relationships which have become exploitative or destructive. In doing so, he may retard or prevent the appropriate transition of the matter from the counseling to the government or adversary spheres, where corrective action could be taken. Thus, he may perpetuate a socially undesirable situation. On the other hand, if timely intervention by other roles does occur, the problem will be rectified only at the cost of the kind of friction the counselor was supposed to prevent.[108] The basic

107. This is most dramatically evident in Purposivist critiques of the Warren Court. For instance, Philip B. Kurland introduces one such critique as follows: "I suggest that we ask whether, as the Warren Court has moved toward the legislative mode and away from the judicial mode of carrying on its business, it has endangered the capacity to perform its peculiar function." Kurland, *Toward a Political Supreme Court*, 37 U. CHI. L. REV. 19, 20 (1969) [hereinafter cited as Kurland]. Of course, since any "peculiar function" of the Supreme Court must be defined in terms of the "judicial mode," the reader is not surprised that the answer is that the departure from the latter endangers the former.

108. Brandeis, the first theorist of the counseling role, is also the source of striking examples of the problems which the principle of specialization poses for the notion of the counselor. In 1906, Brandeis acted on behalf of the United Shoe Machinery Company in successfully opposing a bill before the Massachusetts legislature which would have outlawed the tying clause in United's leases to shoe manufacturers. Brandeis argued that the clauses were in the interests of the public and the shoe manufacturers. In fact, as Brandeis

distinguishing feature of the counseling role is the lawyer's duty to divert short-sighted projects before they lead to the kind of behavior which requires litigation or government intervention. Yet, the counselor is unlikely to be able to perceive that projects which benefit his client immediately are short-sighted until litigation or government intervention is underway.

The advocate will not be able to insure that the destructive tendencies of his activities are confined to the area in which they are appropriate, that is, to situations in which beneficial relations have broken down irreparably. As the counselor will be slow to perceive divergences of interests between his client and others, so the advocate will be slow to perceive opportunities for reconciliation between his client and others. Once he adopts the perspective of partisanship, cognitive dissonance will blind him to chances to alleviate the costs of an adversary battle and to rescue viable relationships.[109]

The pro bono lawyer, in deciding where to allocate his services, will not be able to gauge what their impact will be once he has taken on a client and the relationship has assumed the form of counseling or advocacy. After he has taken on his client, particularly if he does so as an advocate, in order to represent the client's interests effectively he may be led to pursue a course which will jeopardize the public interest or the interests of other people who are not adequately represented. In attempting to decide how to remedy certain problems, he cannot be sure that he will ultimately not create worse ones.

Moreover, the semi-public orientation of the pro bono lawyer requires that he look at the world in terms of abstract notions of procedural

later acknowledged, the tying clauses were an oppressive exercise of United's monopoly power. Brandeis's biographer suggests persuasively that in 1906 his perception of the public interest and the interests of the shoe manufacturers was distorted by his close relation to United. His successful representation had the effect of preserving an exploitative relation by retarding intervention by the government. MASON, *supra* note 78, at 214-29.

Another example is the Lennox case in which Brandeis agreed with the insolvent Lennox that a member of the Brandeis firm would become trustee of his property for the benefit of creditors. Disputes later developed between Lennox and the trustee over how much Lennox would be paid for managing the property and over his father's obligation to turn over hidden assets. Ultimately, the trustee put Lennox into bankruptcy. Lennox and others alleged that Brandeis had accepted him as a client and then acted contrary to his interests in the administration of the assignment. However, the record indicates that Brandeis did not undertake to act on behalf of Lennox but rather on behalf of the creditors. Nevertheless, it seems fair to criticize Brandeis for failing to perceive the significance of the conflict between Lennox's interests and those of the creditors and for failing to emphasize to Lennox that he was not his lawyer and that the trustee might have to act contrary to his interest. Brandeis's identification with the creditors colored his perception of the interests of others involved in the situation. *See* Frank, *The Legal Ethics of Louis D. Brandeis*, 17 STAN. L. REV. 683 (1965); *see also* KAUFFMAN, *supra* note 24, at 109 n.3.

If one were to accept the Purposivist psychology of specialization upon which the counseling role and the separation of functions are based, one would have to regard situations of this sort as inevitable and typical.

109. *Cf.* Leff, *supra* note 41, at 18-19, 38-46 (discussing the destructive role of "spite" in collection litigation).

fairness. Unlike the counselor, he cannot be expected to be sensitive to the more subtle ways in which social relationships serve the concrete needs of the participants. (If he undertakes representation as a counselor, he may ultimately achieve such sensitivity, but if, as more commonly happens, he undertakes representation as an advocate, his perspective will soon be biased by partisan sympathy.) Since the pro bono lawyer's primary job is to enhance access to the legal system, he will be prone to frame issues in terms susceptible to legal resolution and to seek whatever legal remedies are available. He will thus be likely to ignore dimensions of problems which are not susceptible to legal resolution and to present the problems to the courts outside of their relevant social context. He will encourage the courts to intervene with judicial remedies in situations with which the courts are not equipped to deal and where judicial remedies may aggravate aspects of the problems over which courts have no control. The specialized perspective of the pro bono lawyer is likely to lead him to damage viable social relationships.[110]

Similarly, the government lawyer, whose orientation is public, will be prone to view matters from a formal, legalistic, bureaucratic point of view. In exercising his prosecutorial or administrative discretion, he is likely to ignore the value and effectiveness of informal, spontaneous patterns of cooperation, and his efforts are likely to damage such patterns.[111]

To rely on other roles to discern where any particular role goes wrong merely reverses the problem. Each role will naturally tend to detect the considerations for which it is responsible and to ignore the considerations with which the other roles are charged. For instance, when examining the counselor's performance, the advocate will naturally tend to find conflict; the pro bono lawyer, procedural unfairness; and the government lawyer, inefficiency or illegality. Even to the extent that these perceptions are accurate, they are likely to ignore the possibility that intervention may damage spontaneous, informal patterns of cooperation worked out by the counselor and naturally overlooked by the other roles.

110. A familiar example, which for present purposes can be taken as hypothetical, is the argument that the pro bono lawyer who brings lawsuits on behalf of poor tenants against landlords to compel compliance with housing codes worsens the plight of low-income tenants by compelling the landlords to raise the rent, or if the rents are already as high as the market will bear, to abandon the buildings. The court can compel compliance with the code, but the housing situation of the poor depends on other factors which it cannot control, such as the income of the poor and the level of investment in low-income housing. *See, e.g.*, Blum & Dunham, *Slumlordism as a Tort—A Dissenting View*, 66 MICH. L. REV. 451, 460-61 (1968). *See also* Bell, *supra* note 51 (arguing that school desegregation litigators have emphasized abstract notions of equal protection at the expense of concrete educational needs of blacks); White, *supra* note 51, at 503 (arguing that efforts to establish procedural rights of debtors will raise cost of credit to the poor). *See generally* Galanter, *supra* note 32 (suggesting that pro bono lawyers tend to overestimate possibilities for use of legal system to effect social change).

111. *Cf.* Jaffe, *The Effective Limits of the Administrative Process: A Reevaluation*, 67 HARV. L. REV. 1105, 1113-19 (1954) (the administrator develops a presumption in favor of regulation).

The phenomenon of cognitive dissonance which the Purposivists emphasize reflects a real problem which recurs in every area of law practice. Yet, the Purposivist scheme of separated functions merely institutionalizes the problem; it does not solve it. Purposivism fails because it treats what is really a moral and political problem as a psychological and technical one. The real source of the lawyer's dissonance is not his inherent mental limitations, but the weakness of the infrastructure of shared values on which Purposivism rests. The difficulty in coordinating the various specialized roles reflects the inability of the legal order Purposivism describes to reconcile private and public ends. Private individual ends are far more antagonistic than Purposivism allows. The public ends which actually are shared tend to be shallow, vague, and remote from the experience of individuals. This is the reason why in each of the roles and in the system as a whole, responsibility for private ends turns out to be incompatible with responsibility for public ends, or vice versa.

By treating the phenomenon of dissonance as a technical problem, Purposivism ignored the ethical and political issues raised by its proposal to integrate public responsibility into the lawyer's role. To accomplish this goal, it would have been necessary to work to establish a set of public norms of sufficient concreteness to serve as binding guides for private conduct. It would have been necessary to work to persuade people of the validity of these norms and to use power to institutionalize these norms and to block their frustration by purely private interests. Yet, to follow this route would have required a radical transformation of the role of the lawyer. Brandeis' career provides thrilling suggestions of what the Purposivist model could have been.[112] Yet, the model which ultimately triumphed in Purposivism is best represented, not by Brandeis, but by those New Deal lawyers who left government practice to become servants of large corporations, helping the corporations to manipulate in their own interests the agencies the lawyers had helped to establish in the public interest.[113] They could rationalize abandonment of the public interest by associating it with a role they no longer occupied. The Purposivist scheme of the separation of functions proves to be merely a set of alibis. Each lawyer can rationalize his refusal to face the ethical and political contradictions of law practice by assigning a critical portion of responsibility to some other role. The contradictions persist, but it becomes easier to ignore them.

The tensions in the separation of functions approach are most severe in the counseling role. The counseling role was the focus of the Purposivist claim to integrate responsibility to social norms into legal ethics. The most direct attempt to reconcile public and private ends was to be made in

112. *See generally* MASON, *supra* note 78.

113. *See, e.g.*, J. GOULDEN, THE SUPERLAWYERS 110-73 (1972).

this sphere. Yet, by underestimating the tension between private and public ends, by treating dissonance as a psychological problem, Purposivism usually ignored the difficult questions the counseling role raised. Much of the Purposivist literature was ambiguous as to whether the counselor might ever have a professional duty to actively oppose his client's antisocial projects. In the *Code of Professional Responsibility*, this ambiguity was resolved in a manner which confirms the bankruptcy of the separation of functions approach. The need to develop concrete guidelines for the counseling role squarely presented the draftsmen with the problem that any meaningful commitment to public norms would occasionally bring the lawyer into active opposition to his clients. The response was to reduce the distinction between advocacy and counseling to mere rhetoric.

Unlike the responsibility of the government lawyer, which is directly to public values,[114] the responsibility of the private lawyer under the *Code* is defined by "the bounds of the law."[115] But the *Code* emphasizes the fundamental Purposivist insight that the bounds of the law are uncertain and can be determined only by reference to social norms. This leads to the distinction between advocacy and counseling: "Where the bounds of the law are uncertain, the action of a lawyer may depend on whether he is serving as advocate or adviser. A lawyer may serve simultaneously as both advocate and adviser, but the two roles are essentially different."[116] But this distinction turns out to be of no practical significance. The ethical obligations imposed by the *Code* are generally consistent with the more Positivist approach attributed to the *Canons*:

> While serving as advocate, a lawyer should resolve in favor of his client doubts as to the bounds of the law. In serving a client as adviser, a lawyer in appropriate circumstances should give his professional opinion as to what the ultimate decisions of the courts would likely be as to the applicable law.[117]

As advocate, he will urge any position favorable to his client that is not "frivolous."[118] As advisor, he will continue to represent his client even if the client decides to ignore his advice as to what "would likely be the ultimate decisions of the courts."[119]

The *Code* refers to an "obligation to treat with consideration all persons involved in the legal process and to avoid the infliction of needless harm."[120] But no serious attempt is made to integrate this obligation into any specific prescriptions. The *Code* is quite clear on the

114. ABA Code of Professional Responsibility, EC 7-13 to 7-14.
115. *Id.* at EC 7-1.
116. *Id.* at EC 7-3.
117. *Id.*
118. *Id.* at EC 7-4.
119. *Id.* at EC 7-5.
120. *Id.* at EC 7-10.

priority of this obligation: "In the final analysis, however, the lawyer should always remember that the decision whether to forego legally available objectives or methods because of non-legal factors is ultimately for the client and not for himself."[121] Thus, in the final analysis, for all its rhetoric to the contrary, the *Code* abandons the attempt to distinguish advocacy from counseling and with it, the attempt to remedy the problems of the Ideology of Advocacy by integrating a responsibility to social norms into legal ethics. Ultimately, the *Code* falls back on a vision of the lawyer as the servant of private, individual will. In situations of conflict, where the critical decisions arise, it turns back to a notion of the "legal" defined in terms of the prediction of the authoritative application of force.

The *Code* does take one innovating step past the *Canons* in this area which reflects an approach typical of late Purposivism. The *Code* emphasizes the lawyer's discretion to dissociate himself from his client. Thus, it provides that the lawyer *may* "[r]efuse to aid or participate in conduct that he believes to be unlawful, even though there is some support for an argument that the conduct is legal."[122] This discretion is narrow in the area of advocacy, but broad in the area of counseling. But this is far from a significant step toward concretizing the counseling role. It does not solve any problems in terms of professional ethics, but rather simply withdraws certain problems from the area of professional ethics. The concern here is not to reconcile the client's proclivities with social norms, but to reconcile the client's proclivities with the lawyer's proclivities. The lawyer's perception of public values, which was once seen as the foundation of a new professional identity, is here given a purely private significance. To refuse to aid a client's anti-social plans, previously seen as a professional obligation, is here a mere personal privilege.

The *Code's* definition of the professional responsibilities of advocates and counselors almost entirely in terms of service to private ends reflects the ineffectuality of the Purposivist attempt to reconcile private ends and social responsibility in the separation of functions.

2. THE CONFLICT OF MORALITY AND EFFICIENCY

The morality of the long run fails to resolve the basic moral ambiguity of Purposivism. It cannot contain the doctrine's mutually subversive tendencies to view norms as values on the one hand and as facts on the other. In the Purposivist view, social norms, viewed as values, are ends in themselves. They are an important source of human satisfactions and the only source of the legitimacy of public institutions. But social norms, viewed as facts, are means. They are useful because people spontaneously conform to them and intuitively recognize their demands. They thus make it possible to have a social order which avoids the drawbacks of

121. *Id*. at EC 7-8.
122. *Id*. at DR 7-101 (B) (2).

totalitarianism and a jurisprudence which avoids the embarrassments of Positivism. Yet, these two ways of looking at values undercut each other. To perceive norms intuitively as values leads to the inefficiencies of the short run. But to perceive norms instrumentally as facts destroys the sense of worth and obligation which made them important in the first place.[123]

This theoretical difficulty corresponds to a practical dilemma. The more directly and immediately the society concerns itself with shared values, the more it limits its technical options and causes its institutions to stagnate. On the other hand, the more it unleashes its technical dynamism, the more it attenuates the experience of the values which are the basis of its legitmacy. The majority of Purposivists have tended to pursue the instrumental logic of Purposivism at the expense of its moral infrastructure. For that reason, the history of Purposivism has been a history of technical triumph (and the triumph of technicians) and of normative disintegration. Under the Purposivist version of the Ideology of Advocacy, the advocate has risen to greatest power and prestige at a time when the values he is supposed to further have declined.

The critical aspect of the morality of the long run is its approval of deliberate injustice. In the Positivist system, all outcomes are just by definition. The Purposivists recognize that this kind of perfect justice is a lawyer's mirage. Yet, they do not merely recognize the inevitability of failure, they accommodate themselves to it. They support a legal system which in particular situations often prescribes that social norms intentionally be sacrificed.

These sacrifices are justified in terms of the more remote but greater implementation of social norms which they make possible. The validity of such justification depends on the scarcely examined premise that the Purposivist technique includes some method of weighing effectively the relative values of present sacrifice and future benefit. The existence of such a method remains problematical. Yet, even if one could be demonstrated, it could not remedy the fundamental problem of the principle of the long run. In focusing on the relative value of the concrete *results* which follow from alternative decisions, the Purposivists ignore the impact of the *way* in which decisions are made on the experience of those involved. This impact is to diminish the sense of worth and obligation which attaches to the norms that provide the criteria of measurement. This impact cannot be assessed along with the other results in the weighing calculation because it arises in part from the calculation itself. It is inherent in the perspective of the long run.

123. The following discussion concerning the conflict of morality and efficiency draws on E. DURKHEIM, MORAL EDUCATION (Wilson and Schnurer trans. 1961); Williams, *A Critique of Utilitarianism*, in J. SMART & B. WILLIAMS, UTILITARIANISM: FOR AND AGAINST 77-150 (1973) [hereinafter cited as Williams]; Tribe, *Technology Assessment and the Fourth Discontinuity: The Limits of Instrumental Rationality*, 46 SO. CAL. L. REV. 617, 630-33 (1973) [hereinafter cited as Tribe]. *See also* D. WIGDOR, ROSCOE POUND: PHILOSOPHER OF LAW 207-32 (1974) (discussing tension between "organicism" and "instrumentalism" in Pound's writings).

In the judicial proceeding described by Purposivism, the litigant is brought to view social norms less as ends which he shares with others than as means to the advancement of interests which conflict with those of others. In the beginning, as the Purposivists assume, the litigant may feel that his personal concern implicates a generally shared norm. Thus, he may invoke a norm as a basis for the social recognition of his personal concern. Yet, he is soon disappointed. From the perspective of the long run, the court does not view his claim as a particular embodiment of a shared value, but rather as an opportunity for the general furtherance of a variety of social norms. The court does not recognize the litigant's personal concern in terms of a shared value, but rather manipulates the litigant in the interests of the larger society. A victory for the litigant does not mean the social vindication of his personal concern, but merely that allowing his claim has been found an adequate means for the advancement of social purposes (consider the exclusionary rule). Conversely, if the litigant loses, it is not because his claim is inconsistent with social norms, but merely because its denial is required in the interest of the long run (consider default procedures).

When social norms do not prove a vehicle for the social recognition of his personal concern, the litigant learns that social norms are neither shared, nor values. The failure to achieve recognition on the basis of norms emphasizes to the litigant his separateness. It teaches him that norms do not link his immediate personal concerns to those of the larger society. Yet, he also learns that the invocation of social norms produces somewhat predictable responses from social institutions. He discovers that he can use these norms to advance the personal concerns which he now feels to be separate and individual. He no longer perceives norms as ends or imperatives, but rather as facts and tools for the manipulation of society to serve his individual purposes.

Although the judicial decision plays an important role in this process, the process begins much earlier when the citizen is initiated into the proceeding. Purposivism expects and encourages the litigant to act not as an individual seeking justice but as a conduit for issues and arguments of public interest. The distinction is made clear in, for example, the case of ***Federal Communications Commission v. Sanders Brothers Radio Station.***[124] Apparently motivated solely by the hope of preserving a private economic advantage, a radio station owner sought to challenge the granting of a license to a competitor. The Commission refused to hear the challenge because the station owner's concern implicated no relevant social norm. The applicable statutes were not intended to protect owners from competition. The Supreme Court did not dispute this premise, but it considered that the social norm of good broadcasting might be served by the denial of the license. Thus, it ordered that the challenger be given a

124. 309 U.S. 470 (1940).

hearing so that he might try to show the Commission that this public interest would be served by the advancement of his individual interest. Although the *Sanders* case has a special significance in the law of standing, it expresses with unusual directness the general Purposivist notion of the litigant. Litigants are expected to pursue immediate individual interests by invoking the public interest. Thus, the guilty criminal defendant is permitted to invoke the public interest in the protection of the innocent by excluding certain kinds of evidence of his crime. Thus, the welching debtor is permitted to invoke the public interest in the protection of those who pay their debts by pleading the Statute of Frauds. The problem is that in this process the public interest becomes something remote from, and contradicted by, the experience of individuals.

The conduct and attitudes of the lawyer, as prescribed by the Ideology of Advocacy, play a critical role in this experience. The principle of neutrality encourages the view of social norms as data. In the light of the lawyer's attitude of authoritative indifference, norms are stripped of their ethical significance. The principle of partisanship encourages the client to view norms as a means to individual concerns. From the perspective of partisanship, social norms merely define technical options to be weighed in accordance with individual concerns. The consequence of this psychological transformation is disastrous. At just the moments when the individual's sense of solidarity with the society is most at stake, the lawyer deprives him of confirmation of his social identity in terms of shared values and hence undermines his satisfaction from the implementation of social norms. At just the moments when the individual's disposition to conform to social norms is weakest, the lawyer releases him from the pressure of the expectations of his fellow citizens and hence aggravates his antisocial dispositions.

It is futile to hope that the litigant's tendency to view social norms as instruments to selfish ends can be redeemed by a simultaneous sense of the long-run coincidence of his private ends with social norms, or that his altered attitude toward social norms will be confined to the sphere of litigation and give way to a renewed sense of the binding quality of norms upon his return to private life. In the first place, the relation between the litigant's actions and the long-run social welfare is a technical matter which can be determined only with technical knowledge. It cannot be assumed that the litigant has the expertise necessary to understand how his course of conduct will, in the context of the specialized Purposivist institutional apparatus, affect social norms in the long run. Thus, he does not experience his pursuit of his individual ends as advancing social norms. In the second place, the experience of the judicial proceeding is not something which the litigant can step into and out of in the manner in which the lawyer dons and removes his professional role. The dispute which is the subject of the proceeding arises from the litigant's private life, and its resolution will affect his private life. It has developed naturally and unpredictably; it cannot be contained within the artificial confines of a formal role.

Moreover, the morally corrosive impact of the long run is not confined to those directly involved in the "trouble cases" which require resolution in the adversary sphere. Even assuming that the non-advocacy legal roles could be designed to preserve a more immediate experience of social norms, the corrosive experience of the adversary sphere extends beyond the direct participants. Purposivists themselves have emphasized the importance of indirect participation by the general public in the judicial proceeding. For instance, they have argued that adversary advocacy is "essential to a sound development of public opinion" because it facilitates the public resolution of controversies in a manner which provides full public exposure of the issues. Without adversary advocacy, it is argued, "a fear arises that perhaps more might have been said for the losing side and suspicion is cast on the decision reached."[125] Yet such arguments ignore the impact that the spectacle of a litigant reaping a private profit, or escaping his obligations, in the name of a remote public interest has on the citizens' experience of social norms. This impact is inevitably to weaken their sense of satisfaction in, and obligation to, the norms in question.

The principle of the long run undermines the moral infrastructure on which Purposivism depends. It makes the Purposivist calculation of present sacrifices and future benefits meaningless. Such calculation depends on the use of social norms both as data concerning the likelihood of future conduct for the prediction of results and as criteria by which the value of competing results can be measured. A change in norms resulting from the application of Purposivist technique between the time the calculation is made and the time the benefits are supposed to accrue vitiates the calculation in two respects. First, the predicted results may not occur because essential conduct predicted on the basis of the original norms may fail to occur. Second, even if the predicted results do occur, they may be no longer considered, when measured in terms of the altered social norms, worth the past sacrifices. On a more general level, the cumulative effect of the repeated application of Purposivist technique in various areas of public life is to attenuate the experience of social norms throughout the society and thus to destroy the principal basis Purposivism recognizes for social cooperation.

The basic problem of the morality of the long run has been most clearly perceived in relation to the Warren Court's reforms of criminal procedure. These reforms created myriad opportunities for defendants to manipulate judicial procedures so as to frustrate, in the immediate in-

125. *Professional Responsibility*, *supra* note 13, at 1216; *see* Kaplan, *The Limits of the Exclusionary Rule*, 26 STAN. L. REV. 1027, 1035-36 (1974) [hereinafter cited as Kaplan].

stance, the social norms protected by the substantive criminal law. These reforms were often defended as appropriate means to more effective long-run control of official discretion, and the commentary of both critics and defenders has often taken the form of attempts to weigh present sacrifices against long term benefits of this kind.[126] Yet, commentators also have discussed the impact of procedures designed with a view to the long run on people's experience of the substantive norms of the criminal law. For instance, Paul Bator has pointed out that the elaborate procedural apparatus created by the Warren Court tends to diminish the defendant's sense of the validity of substantive norms and to preclude a sense of the legitimacy of the final outcome of his case:

> A procedural system which permits an endless repetition of inquiry into facts and law in a vain search for ultimate certitude implies a lack of confidence about the possibilities of justice that cannot but war with the effectiveness of the underlying substantive commands. Furthermore, we should at least tentatively inquire whether an endless reopening of convictions, with its continuing underlying implication that perhaps the defendant can escape from corrective sanctions after all, can be consistent with the aim of rehabilitating offenders. The first step in achieving that aim may be a realization by the convict that he is justly subject to sanction, that he stands in need of rehabilitation; and a process of reeducation cannot, perhaps, even begin if we make sure that the cardinal moral predicate is missing, if society itself continuously tells the convict that he may not be justly subject to reeducation and treatment in the first place. The idea of just condemnation lies at the heart of the criminal law, and we should not lightly create processes which implicitly belie its possibility.[127]

Yet, having thus appeared to recognize the problem, Bator fails to perceive its implications. The solution he proposes resorts to the very institutional formalism which is the source of the problem. He argues for greater emphasis on the principle of finality and more specifically, for the limitation of post-conviction review. But the problem lies not in the quantity of procedures, but in their quality, specifically, in the fact that they fail to respect the defendant's immediate, subjective sense of the relation between his conduct and social norms. In arguing for a limitation of post-conviction review, Bator assumes that the sense of guilt which is the moral predicate of the criminal law arises not from the defendant's understanding of what he has done, but from his understanding of the operation of judicial procedure. If the defendant has violated the criminal law, there is no reason to believe that the effect of adversary advocacy in undermining his sense of responsibility for his criminal acts can be

126. *See, e.g.*, Oaks, *Studying the Exclusionary Rule in Search and Seizure*, 37 U. CHI. L. REV. 665 (1970).

127. Bator, *Finality in Criminal Law and Federal Habeus Corpus for State Prisoners*, 76 HARV. L. REV. 441, 452 (1963).

reversed merely by cutting off the formal procedures at some definite point. The damage will have begun once the client is introduced to the criminal process through his lawyer's attitude of authoritative indifference, once he comes to see himself as a private attorney general empowered to escape the consequences of his acts in the name of a remote public interest. On the other hand, if the defendant has not committed the crime for which he has been convicted, finality is equally irrelevant. The suggestion that the defendant who knows he has been erroneously convicted should cease regarding himself as a victim of injustice and submit to his condemnation merely because he has exhausted procedures for review is monstrous. It could be followed only by giving up any sense of the meaningfulness of substantive standards of guilt and innocence.

D. *The Present State of Purposivism*

This critique of the Purposivist version of the Ideology of Advocacy is not conclusive. Purposivism has never been elaborated with sufficient precision or coherence to permit a conclusive refutation. Thus, doctrinal criticism must remain on the same impressionistic level as the theory itself.

In response to the criticism of the separation of functions, the Purposivist might still insist on a third type of thought, apart from the intuitive apprehension of norms or technical rationality, which could resolve the problem of coordination. Moreover, the Purposivist might insist that there is some method by which the morally subversive effects of the long run could be taken into account in general calculations of long-run social welfare.

But such arguments would not get Purposivism very far. For if Purposivism has yet to be refuted in theory, it appears to have been superseded by events. The increasing visibility of political conflict in recent decades has undermined the vision of fundamental shared values on which Purposivism was founded. Events have discredited both the technique of the separation of powers and the morality of the long run.

The theory of the separation of functions has been discredited by recent challenges to the institutional allocation of authority established by the New Deal, most notably, by the civil rights and public interest law movements. These challenges undermined the notion that the New Deal allocation was a technical, rather than a political achievement. When new political forces challenged the New Deal notions of the role competences of courts, agencies, and legislatures, the indeterminancy of role boundaries became apparent, and the concepts crumbled. When the federal judiciary destroyed the New Deal allocation, it attempted to justify its decisions in the language of institutional competence, and its critics responded by asserting that role boundaries had been transgressed. Yet, the debate has proved sterile, and many have come to feel that the critical decisions cannot be defended or criticized satisfactorily within the framework of the separation of functions. Thus, legal discourse has moved gradually away from this perspective.[128]

The morality of the long run has also fared ill. Purposivism has been severely criticized for slighting distributional considerations in its calculus of short-run sacrifices and long-run benefits, and for ignoring the tendency of benefits on the one hand and burdens on the other to cumulate in different sectors of the society.[129] Moreover, the fundamentally self-destructive quality of the principle of the long run is becoming increasingly apparent. The decline at all levels of society in both voluntary compliance with social norms and the sense of legitimacy of public institutions is one of the most striking facts of recent history.[130] This phenomenon appears to be in part a consequence of the design and operation of public institutions on the principle of the long run. Short-run violations of public norms have diminished respect for public institutions in situations where people cannot see how such sacrifices will be justified in the long run. Norms are increasingly seen as remote and abstract. From this perspective, the long-term benefits of social cooperation often seem too risky or remote to justify the short-run curbing of egoistic impulses which cooperation requires. Many people who are not inclined to conform to social norms in their private lives most vociferously condemn official institutions for their short-term infringements of social norms. This apparent contradiction is a natural response to the society's adherence to the morality of the long run. The further institutions drive values from the immediate experience of individuals, the more they undermine the basis of their own legitimacy.

The most notable attempts to shore up Purposivism in the face of this recent history have involved modifications of the basic assumptions of the doctrine. Purposivism has drifted toward a conservative historicism[131] on the one hand, and a liberal idealism, on the other.[132] The most critical change reflected in both perspectives is the muting of the classical Purposivist distinction between the natural infrastructure of shared values and the artificial superstructure of institutional forms. Institutional forms are no longer seen as artificial. They are portrayed as intuitively perceptible embodiments of either ideals or social practices. In this manner, the problem of coordination is avoided because general intuitive faculties can perceive role boundaries, and the problem of the long run is avoided because the operation of the institutions now has an inherent value. On

128. *E.g.*, Linde *Judges, Critics and the Realist Tradition*, 82 YALE L. J. 227 (1972) [hereinafter cited as Linde]; Stewart, *supra* note 51.

129. *See generally* Comment, *The New Public Interest Lawyers*, *supra* note 7.

130. *See* D. BELL, THE CULTURAL CONTRADICTIONS OF CAPITALISM (1976); A. GOULDNER, THE COMING CRISIS OF WESTERN SOCIOLOGY 275-77 (1970).

131. *See generally* BICKEL, *supra* note 100; Kurland, *supra* note 107.

132. *See* Fletcher, *Fairness and Utility in Tort Theory*, 85 HARV. L. REV. 537 (1972); Michelman, *supra* note 96.

the other hand, the institutional forms are still seen as partially instrumental. From the conservative perspective, they are useful because they embody almost the only shared values left in the society and thus represent the only alternative to anarchy. From the liberal perspective, they are useful because they protect minorities and procedural norms from the externalities which result as the majorities pursue substantive purposes.

To the extent that such doctrines escape the difficulties of role formalism and the long run, they often slide back into the difficulties of Positivism. Yet, at their most original, they point beyond both Positivism and Purposivism to a third version of the Ideology of Advocacy which is the subject of the next section.

IV. The Lawyer as Acolyte (The Sanctification of Ceremony)

> *[Thurman Arnold] put his finger on a matter too often overlooked: an impressive ceremonial has a value in making people* feel *that something is being done; this holds, whether the result is right or wrong; and there is some value in an institution which makes men content with fate, whatever that fate may be.*
>
> Karl Llewellyn[133]

The third version of the Ideology of Advocacy, which can be called Ritualism, has not achieved the preeminence of its predecessors. It is only one of several doctrinal responses to the decline of Purposivism. Yet, it is the most sensitive and ingenious response within the framework of the Ideology of Advocacy to the difficulties of both Positivism and Purposivism, and it comes closer than competing doctrines to resolving these difficulties. On the other hand, in creating new problems of its own, it shows the futility of attempting to reformulate the Ideology of Advocacy.

Ritualism responds to the critique of Positivism and Purposivism by changing the terms of the debate. It acknowledges the irrationality and inefficiency of the legal system, and then embraces it anyway. In a sense, it represents a synthesis of the two other versions, though only one of several possible syntheses. Ritualism refuses to follow Positivism in insisting that the legal system be viewed as independent of social ends; and it refuses to follow Purposivism in seeing the legal system as simply a means to such ends. The Ritualists suggest that judicial procedure be viewed as both means and end. Procedure can be seen as serving ends, but serving them less by producing them than by embodying them. This logical compromise is accompanied by similar compromises in politics and psychology. The Ritualists think the Positivists right in insisting on the presence of conflict in the social world. And they agree with the Purposivists that law is impossible without shared values. Thus, instead of strife on the one hand and harmony on the other, they propose to substitute the illusion of harmony. The Ritualists see with the Purposiv-

133. Llewellyn, *On Reading and Using the Newer Jurisprudence*, 40 Colum. L. Rev. 581, 610 (1940) (emphasis in original).

ists that men have other ends in common beside order, but they concede to the Positivists that it would be impractical to attempt to realize these ends. Thus, instead of retreat into private realms on the one hand and struggle for concrete social achievement on the other, they propose to substitute the performance of public ceremony.

A. *Ritualist Advocacy*

Among the adherents of Ritualism there are both cynics and naifs. Yet, the differences between them are superficial, and both groups share a common view of law and life. This view has been characterized by Charles P. Curtis and Roberto Mangabeira Unger, from very different perspectives, as Stoic.[134] It involves a faith in the immanent rationality of the world as it is, a determination to be modest in one's expectations of it, and a belief in social role as the natural locus of moral obligation.

Cynical Ritualism emerged in the writings of a few of the legal Realists who were not inclined toward Purposivism, and who did not join in the call to reform judicial procedure along instrumental lines to make it a more effective mechanism for the attainment of truth.[135] Rather, they adopted an attitude of bemused resignation toward the irrationalities of the system. The classical Positivists had taught that, though the legal system as a whole could be shown to be rational in terms of the overriding goal of order, particular results could not be evaluated by social criteria because the system was necessarily independent of society. Some Realists—most notably, Thurman Arnold—later suggested that particular results could not be criticized for precisely the opposite reason. They suggested that the system was submerged in society, where it served subliminal cultural needs too subtle to be susceptible to critical analysis. They explained that judicial procedures, including the advocate's role, served a dramatic function by expressing values which were deeply rooted, though only partially articulated, in the culture. These values, such as liberty, equality, and above all, individual dignity, are metaphysical abstractions which only complicate the practical affairs of life, but whose magical power over the culture is such that men cannot bring themselves to let go of them. Judicial procedure is perfectly designed to assuage the fears and longings engendered by such irrational attachments. By allowing these values to be symbolically enacted in its public forums, the society reassures its members that the values have not been forgotten and are still part of their lives. But by confining them to the realm of drama, it guarantees that they do not get in the way of the efficient fulfillment of material needs.

134. CURTIS, *supra* note 106, at 33-34; UNGER, *supra* note 25, at 179.

135. *See* T. ARNOLD, THE SYMBOLS OF GOVERNMENT (1935); T. ARNOLD, THE FOLKLORE OF CAPITALISM (1937); CURTIS, *supra* note 106; Fortas, *Thurman Arnold and the Theater of the Law*, 79 YALE L.J. 988 (1970).

The naive form of Ritualism has emerged more recently, sometimes in connection with discussions of the Warren Court's reforms in criminal procedure. The Warren Court and its supporters occasionally acknowledged that some of its holdings in this area could not be justified either as deductions from the language of the Constitution on the one hand, or as instrumental to the control of official discretion or the assurance of the accuracy of determinations of guilt or innocence on the other hand.[136] It was occasionally suggested that the procedures required by such decisions were justified by their service as expressions of fundamental moral values, such as individual dignity, trust, equality, and fraternity.[137] In Charles Fried's explanation, the trial is an end in itself in the same way that religious rituals and artistic performances are not means to ulterior purposes but are intrinsically valuable. The procedures enable the society to communicate to outsiders and to reaffirm to its members the kind of society it is and hopes to be. The rituals and performances cannot be viewed as means to this expression because they constitute it. The manner of expression and the content expressed are unintelligible apart from each other. The role of counsel is thus viewed as an expressive element in the expressive system of the trial. It is structured by the values the system embodies, and it contributes to the over-all expression as one of the musicians in an orchestra contributes to the performance of a symphony.

Fried does not limit his interpretation to criminal procedure. He suggests that the entire legal process be viewed as a system of such expressive structures, and the lawyer's role as at once implementing the system and constituting an expressive component of it. Ritualism adopts the entire structure of role formalism elaborated by Purposivism, but without the difficulties which this unacknowledged formalism caused in Purposivism. Having severed the roles from their instrumental bases, the Ritualists make a virtue of their formal qualities.[138] Roles and institutions are not functional components of a division of labor, but expressive elements of a performance. Because they are defined by shared norms rather than technique, their boundaries can be intuitively perceived without specialized training.

The principles of the Ideology of Advocacy occupy a prominent

136. *See, e.g.*, Miranda v. Arizona, 384 U.S. 436, 497 (1966); *but see* 384 U.S. at 517 (Harlan, J. dissenting); Linde, *supra* note 128.

137. C. Fried, An Anatomy of Values: Problems of Personal and Social Choice 123-135 (1970) [hereinafter cited as Fried]; Summers, *Evaluating and Improving Legal Processes—A Plea for "Process Values,"* 60 Cornell L. Rev. 1 (1974); Tribe, *Trial by Mathematics: Precision and Ritual in the Legal Process*, 84 Harv. L. Rev. 1329, especially 1391-2 (1971); Tribe, *Structural Due Process*, 12 Harv. C.R.-C.L. Rev. 267 (1975); *see also* Ball, *The Play's the Thing: An Unscientific Reflection on Courts Under the Rubric of Theater*, 28 Stan. L. Rev. 81 (1975) [hereinafter cited as Ball].

138. *See* Fried, *Two Concepts of Interests: Some Reflections on the Supreme Court's Balancing Test*, 76 Harv. L. Rev. 755 (1963) [hereinafter cited as Fried, *Two Concepts*]; Tribe, *Foreward: Toward a Model of Roles in the Due Process of Life and Law*, 87 Harv. L. Rev. 1 (1973).

place in both versions of Ritualism. The lawyer's neutrality makes it possible for everyone to have a lawyer and to participate in the legal system regardless of his ends. Neutrality thus expresses and implements the value of equality. Partisanship also expresses the value of equality. The vigorous presentation of alternative views by each side gives the trial the form of a contest between equals. Both principles are also closely linked to the value of individual dignity. Neutrality embodies a recognition that all individuals have rights regardless of their ends. Partisanship expresses the value of individual dignity by allowing the litigant wide latitude in the presentation of his case. The discretion allowed the litigant emphasizes the respect with which society views his claims, and perhaps also (from the naive point of view) a sense of trust in him.[139]

There are two interesting differences between the newer version and the earlier, cynical Ritualism. First, in the more recent version, the values expressed by the legal system are not mere sociological data, but, in part, ideals. They are not discussed in terms of purely empirical assertions, but in terms of a kind of moral discourse implicit in social life. Thus, the interpretation cannot be refuted merely by surveying the attitudes of the population any more than an art critic's interpretation of a work of art is refuted merely because some individuals do not see it that way. Second, unlike the cynical Ritualists, the newer Ritualists appear to include themselves in the culture whose values are thought to be expressed in the legal system. They do not pretend to hold themselves apart from what they describe. The new version thus completes the process of the erosion of the autonomy of the legal system and the submersion of it in society. The prevalence of procedure over substance, originally rationalized in Positivism as a response to the danger of public anarchy, is now explained as a manifestation of social harmony.

B. *The Critique of Ritualist Advocacy*

Two kinds of objections can be raised to the Ritualist version of the Ideology of Advocacy. First, it can be questioned whether the judicial proceeding is regarded, or should be regarded, as an embodiment of shared social values. Second, the propriety of the analogy of the judicial proceeding to theatrical or ceremonial performances can be disputed.

1. IGNORING EXPERIENCE

The cynical version of Ritualism depends on the assumption that the judicial proceeding functions to gratify beliefs actually held by the general public. Yet, it appears that this assumption is erroneous. Although Legal Realism, from which cynical Ritualism grew, purported to place a high value on systematic empirical research, the cynical Ritualists were

139. T. ARNOLD, THE SYMBOLS OF GOVERNMENT 128-48 (1935); FRIED, *supra* note 137, at 130-32.

generally content to rely on their intuition in the matter of lay attitudes toward the legal profession and judicial procedure. Had they been inclined to look seriously into the matter, they would have been surprised to find that the moral notions so readily attributed to the multitudes are in fact a matter of indifference to vast numbers, probably the great majority, of the American people.

In fact, the multitudes do not thrill to the ritual incantation and celebration of such values as equality and individual dignity. Indeed, of all the various manifestations of such values, none seems to have a more slender following than those which are specifically associated with the judicial proceeding. Moreover, not only does the judicial proceeding tend to be held in low esteem by the population as a whole, but it is even less well regarded by those who have actually had the experience of participating in it directly as litigants. The facts turn out to be not only a refutation of Arnold's theory, but something of a joke on him. Arnold seemed to assume that, while liberal professionals might be skeptical of adversary advocacy because of its shortcomings as a method of attaining the truth, the general public uncritically appreciated the judicial proceeding because it served popular political superstition. In fact, it appears that the attitudes which Arnold attributes to the nation as a whole are actually most typical of that minority to which the professionals themselves belong, the group which Herbert McClosky refers to as "the articulate classes."[140]

140. McClosky, *Consensus and Ideology in American Politics*, 58 AM. POL. SCI. REV. 361, 362 (1964) [hereinafter cited as McClosky].

In the past two decades, a large empirical literature on legal and political values and attitudes toward official institutions has developed. For a review of this literature, see Sarat, *Studying American Legal Culture: An Assessment of Survey Evidence*, 11 LAW & SOC. REV. 427 (1977) [hereinafter cited as Sarat]. The empirical research suggests a "remarkably weak commitment to what seem to be fundamental democratic ground-rules among the American people." F. GREENSTEIN, THE AMERICAN PARTY SYSTEM AND THE AMERICAN PEOPLE 9 (2nd ed. 1970). The surveys show a low level of commitment to values such as equality, freedom, and procedural fairness, particularly when the values are viewed in the context of specific situations rather than as general and abstract phrases. *See* Sarat, *supra* this note, at 470-72. (Sarat's conclusion that there is widespread commitment to equality as a "democratic norm", *id.* at 457, is contradicted by the surveys on which he relies, and appears to result from his failure to distinguish between the norm of equality and a feeling of envy or resentment. *Cf.* J. RAWLS, A THEORY OF JUSTICE 530-41 (1971); M. SCHELER, RESSENTIMENT (1961)).

Commitment to the values specifically associated with the judicial proceeding seems considerably lower than commitment to other political values. Many, and perhaps most, Americans are hostile to the Warren Court notions of the procedural rights of criminal defendants, particularly when such rights are perceived as frustrating the enforcement of the substantive law. *See* Kaplan, *supra* note 125, at 1035-36; Sarat, *supra* this note, at 447-48; *see also* F. GRAHAM, THE SELF-INFLICTED WOUND (1970). In McClosky's survey, 75.7% of a national sampling agreed with the statement: "Any person who hides behind the laws when he is questioned about his activities doesn't deserve much consideration." McClosky, *supra* this note, at 367.

Whether or not they hold such values, most people do not regard the trial as a satisfying expression of democratic values. Dissatisfaction with the courts is widespread, and most significantly, it is considerably more widespread among those who have actually had first-hand experience with the courts than among those who have had no such experience. *See*

The naive version of Ritualism depends less on assumptions about the views actually held by the public. Naive Ritualism was first elaborated when the Warren Court's most notable procedural decisions were producing a storm of hostile criticism throughout the country. In this situation, those who sought to justify these decisions could not comfortably appeal to prevailing social beliefs. Thus, the naive Ritualists did not insist that people actually respected equality, trust, and individual dignity or that they actually viewed the judicial proceeding as an expression of these values. Rather, they suggested that these values *should* be respected and that the judicial proceeding *should* be viewed in this way, in the same manner that a beautiful work of art should be appreciated and understood.

But if the Ritualist emphasis on the importance of such values as trust, equality, and individual dignity can be accepted with some qualifications, the Ritualist interpretation of the judicial proceeding as a dramatic expression of these values cannot. The public disdain for adversary advocacy does not arise from philistinism or insensitivity. It is a natural and perceptive response to the operation and design of the institutions prescribed by the Ideology of Advocacy.

The source of the Ritualist error is evident. In a limited sense, the trial *is* a ritual in which ideals *are* affirmed and celebrated. But it is not the ordinary citizen who participates in the celebration or who experiences the affirmation of trust, equality, and individual dignity. The litigants are not the subject of the ceremony, but rather the pretext for it.

Most litigants find the trial a completely irrational and oppressive experience. Far from seeing his dignity affirmed, the litigant is more likely to feel it is being assaulted. Far from celebrating mutual trust, the average litigant feels that he is involved "either in achieving or in checkmating chicanery . . . ."[141] Far from feeling engaged in a contest of equals, he is constantly reminded of his inferiority.

In fact, the celebration of trust, equality, and individual dignity in the judicial proceeding is done exclusively by, and for, the lawyers. The only manifestation of trust which occurs in the judicial proceeding is the willingness of the lawyers (and the judge) to rely on each other's professional honor. This willingness stands in sharp contrast to their attitude

Sarat, *supra* this note, at 441, 466-7. Some of this dissatisfaction is due to the fact that people perceive that procedural values are slighted in practice by the courts, but much of it is due to the fact that people are not committed to such values.

McClosky's study also indicates that a far greater portion of "the articulate classes" subscribes to liberal democratic values, including the norms associated with the judicial proceeding, than of the general population. McClosky mentions as defining characteristics of the articulate classes "education, S.E.S., urban residence, intellectuality, political activity." McClosky, *supra* this note, at 362. Other studies also suggest a higher level of commitment to democratic values and to courts among such articulates. Sarat, *supra* this note, at 466-72.

141. T. Veblen, The Theory of the Leisure Class 231 (Modern Library ed. 1934). Veblen attributes this attitude to the lawyer, ignoring that the Ideology of Advocacy enables him to feel that he has escaped to a higher moral plane.

toward the litigants and the general public. The lawyer often unflinchingly mouths his client's lies, but he holds himself and his legal brethren to a higher moral standard than that which he expects and encourages in ordinary citizens. Thus, in litigation, a critical moral distinction is drawn between statements of the client or of witnesses repeated by the lawyer, which are regarded with extreme skepticism, and statements backed by the lawyer's professional honor, on which other lawyers willingly rely.[142]

The elaborate patterns of courtesy and respect of the trial are entirely for the lawyer's benefit. In the courtroom, a place of special prominence from which laymen are excluded is reserved for the lawyers. Though the lawyer openly heaps contempt on the opposing party, he calls the opposing counsel a brother, refers to him with elegant courtesy, and criticizes him only with gentle circumlocution. The judge refers to the lawyer by titles such as counselor or officer of the court. Even where the judge must reprimand the lawyer, he honors him by assuming him to be bound by a code which the client is assumed to be incapable of understanding.

It may seem peculiar that the lawyer should routinely yield to the judge obsequies which, in almost any other sphere of life, would seem intolerably degrading. Yet, this exaggerated deference is really part of the ceremonial patterns which confirm the lawyer's distinctive dignity. The formal courtesy which the judge returns to the lawyer is all the more satisfying as coming from so exalted a source. As the European aristocracies confirmed their moral distinctiveness from the common people with elaborate ceremonies of deference for, and professions of loyalty to, the king, so the lawyer confirms his moral distinctiveness in acknowledging the judge as ***primus inter pares***. Nevertheless, the preeminent position of the king and the judge can become a threat to the dignity of the peers. In such instances, the peers may choose to appeal to the people against the exalted one. When the judge's position ceases to enhance his dignity, the lawyer can appeal in defiance of the judge to the jury. Although the case for permitting counsel a broad scope of argument to the jury is usually put in terms of the interests of the client, it is occasionally acknowledged that what is at stake is less the rights of the litigants than "the independence of the bar,"[143] that is, the ritual affirmation that the lawyer's honor is not entirely subordinate to the judge's.

The ritual incarnation of social values is accomplished by the lawyers and by the judge without any help from the litigants. It is the lawyers who perform the ceremony. It is they who assert rights and see their assertions recognized by the judge. They set the rhythm of the proceeding. In alternating turns, each shapes the trial, partly in accordance with

142. *Cf*. ABA Code of Professional Responsibility, DR 7-106 (C) (4) (lawyer is not to assert "personal opinion" that client's claim is valid).

143. M. Freedman, Lawyer's Ethics in an Adversary System 16 (1975) (quoting Lord Erskine).

his own itinerary and partly in response to his adversary's.[144] Out of this interplay of performances, a sense of resolution or wholeness may emerge and be crystallized and confirmed by the judge. To be sure, he gives judgment only to one side, but he expresses his conclusions in the terms established by both.

Throughout all this, the litigant, if he is well advised, will sit mutely and foolishly. If he should attempt to assert his individual dignity by speaking out, the judge will admonish him to let his lawyer do the talking.[145] If he should persist, he may be bound and gagged, or excluded entirely from the ceremony which is purportedly honoring his individuality.[146] Usually, the client will hesitate to do anything without furtive, whispering conferences with his lawyer. He will have to rise and sit awkwardly in accordance with the unfamiliar etiquette of the court.[147] The physical design of the courtroom, and particularly the bench where the judge sits, will intimidate him. Unaccustomed to striking the proper balance between sycophancy and assertiveness, he will stammer when addressing the judge.

The client's only opportunity to tell his own story is to take the stand. Yet, if he does so, his testimony will be rigidly controlled by the lawyers and the judge in accordance with a complicated body of rules which make no sense to him. He will be repeatedly interrupted, and he will be prohibited from saying much of what he wishes to say. But even the opportunity to make this expurgated, truncated personal statement can be had only at great cost. The litigant must submit to a cross-examination in which he is forced to respond, in accordance with a highly restrictive and peculiar logic and an oppressive etiquette, to a series of questions

144. *See, e.g.*, F. BAILEY & H. ROTHBLATT, FUNDAMENTALS OF CRIMINAL ADVOCACY 44 (1974): "As to your position as his attorney, make it clear [to the defendant] that you alone will control the strategy of the defense, decide what legal points are to be raised, determine what witnesses to call, engage in whatever discussions you deem necessary with the prosecution."

145. A litigant represented by counsel has no right to participate in the conduct of his trial either by examining witnesses or addressing the trier. *See* Annot., 67 A.L.R.2d 1102 § 3 (1959) (civil authorities collected); Annot., 77 A.L.R.2d 1233 § 4 (1961) (criminal authorities collected).

146. Illinois v. Allen, 397 U.S. 337, 343-46 (1970); *see generally* N. DORSEN & L. FRIEDMAN, DISORDER IN THE COURT ch. 6 (1973) [hereinafter cited as DORSEN & FRIEDMAN].

147. DORSEN & FRIEDMAN, *supra* note 146, at 276-77, report a survey in which more than half of 842 judges answering a question as to what a judge should do when a defendant engages in "passive insubordination," such as refusing to stand at the start of the proceedings or to address the judge as "your Honor," stated that the judge should hold him in contempt, that he should threaten contempt or some other sanction, or that he should lecture him on his bad manners. The authors quote one of the presumably more liberal judges who favored taking no action in response to passive disrespect by explaining, "Some don't stand up out of ignorance. If you landed on them then you would merely embarrass them and probably force them into taking a defiant attitude. I think that these small problems should be handled much in the same way as you deal with children." *Id.* at 111.

On the intimidation of *pro se* litigants in small claims courts, see Moulton, *The Persecution and Intimidation of the Low-Income Litigant as Performed by the Small Claims Court in California*, 21 STAN. L. REV. 1657 (1969).

designed to distort his position and perhaps also to abuse him personally. Testifying in an adversary proceeding is a humiliating experience. Witnesses are expected to tolerate abuse, condescension, and authoritarian discipline of a sort they would never willingly submit to in private life.

Except for such brief and unsatisfying participation, the litigant will be an alien spectator at his own trial. The language of the trial will be largely foreign to him.[148] It is not himself whom he will see represented, but a puppet manipulated by his lawyer in the character of "plaintiff", or "defendant". His lawyer will have dressed and groomed him in a manner calculated to please the trier. He will have drilled him in detail on how to behave throughout the proceeding so as to present an image consistent with the legal position the lawyer has taken.[149]

It cannot be denied that the Ritualist interpretation of the judicial proceeding has some social foundation. Indeed, Ritualism is a symptom of an important phenomenon: for many people, the judicial proceeding is the only meaningful, fulfilling ceremony which remains in contemporary society. But Ritualism errs in attributing this attitude either to vast majorities of the population or to the litigants. In fact, it is the lawyers and those members of the "articulate classes" who share the lawyer's values and can identify with his role who regard and experience the trial as ritual. The litigant is not the beneficiary of the trial, but the victim of it. His dignity and autonomy are sacrificed in order that his lawyer's may be celebrated.[150]

2. COLLAPSING RESULT INTO PROCESS

The Ritualist analogy of the judicial proceeding to drama and ritual

148. Alschuler, a strong proponent of defendants' rights, states that, "[m]ost defendants do not understand our system of criminal justice and cannot be made to understand." Alschuler, *supra* note 31, at 1310.

149. *E.g.*, A. AMSTERDAM, B. SEGAL, & M. MILLER, TRIAL MANUAL FOR THE DEFENSE OF CRIMINAL CASES (3rd ed. 1974):

> Finally, counsel should help the defendant to see ways in which he can best present himself to the jury as a likeable person, someone they can identify with and want to acquit. . . .
>
> Counsel should ask his client to dress for one of the pretrial interviews as the client will dress at the trial, so that the counsel can look him over. A lawyer who simply tells his defendant to "dress well" for trial and does not check out his choice of clothing in advance will often be horrified on the trial date to discover what the client considers "dressing well."

Id. at §§ 280-81.

150. The most serious attention to the moral psychology of the trial has been given, not by lawyers or legal scholars, but by novelists, and their conclusions often strikingly contradict the assumptions of Ritualism. One of the many anti-legalist themes of 19th century fiction is the view of the trial as crushing the dignity of the litigant by forcing him to conform to an artificial, alien discipline, and to recast his actions and his personality to flatter the vanity and appeal to the prejudices of the trier. The theme plays an important part in, for example, STENDAHL'S THE RED AND THE BLACK, bk. II, chs. 70-71 (1831), and in DOSTOEVSKY'S THE BROTHERS KARAMAZOV, bk. XII (1880). In addition, Dostoevsky emphasizes that the lawyer, in implementing the sacrifice of his client's moral integrity, uses the ritualistic aspects of the trial to gratify his own vanity. *Id.*

is ingenious and in some respects enlightening, but it is also fundamentally misleading. These analogies eliminate the problems of instrumentalism and the long run, but they do so in a question-begging manner. Dramas and rituals do not involve issues of instrumentalism and the long run because dramas and rituals do not produce distinct consequences; their purpose is not to alter the landscape against which they are played. But a trial does have a consequence; it is a decisionmaking procedure. It is designed to alter the landscape in a very precise fashion.

The significance of the Ritualist analogies can be clarified by comparing them to another possible analogy for the trial: the game. The anthropologist Claude Levi-Strauss has contrasted the notions of ritual and game thus:

> Games . . . appear to have a disjunctive effect: they end in the establishment of a difference between individual players or teams where originally there was no indication of inequality. And at the end of the game they are distinguished into winners and losers. Ritual, on the other hand, is the exact inverse; it *conjoins*, for it brings about a union (one might say communion in this context) . . . .[151]

Of these two alternatives, it is clearly the game which is the proper analogy for the trial. For the trial works to distinguish winners and losers. The Ritualist approach simply ignores that at the end of the trial one of the parties may imprison or coerce the other or deprive him of property. To ignore such facts is to commit the reverse of the mistake which the Ritualists attribute to instrumentalism. In Laurence Tribe's own rhetoric, it is to collapse result into process.[152]

The problem is not that procedures cannot be seen as expressive phenomena, but that the results which are produced by the procedures must also be seen as a part of what is expressed. The Ritualists cannot acknowledge this because, more often than not, the results of the judicial proceeding contradict the values which the procedures are supposed to express. It becomes more difficult to see the trial as a manifestation of social harmony when it is recalled that, at the end, one of the parties may inflict some sort of pain on the other. It becomes more difficult to see the trial as a "contest between equals" when it is recalled that its outcome will be determined in substantial part by the state of the substantive law and the nature of the available evidence. Where these factors put one party at a disadvantage, are they to be considered illegitimate handicaps? Suppose the result of the trial is that an ignorant person loses his savings through the enforcement of an unfair contract which he entered in reliance on the advice of the other party. What will have been said about trust? Suppose the result of the trial is that a person will be sent to a cesspool of

151. C. Levi-Strauss, The Savage Mind 32 (Chicago ed. 1966) (emphasis in original).
152. Tribe, *supra* note 123, at 630-33.

a prison. What will have been said about the dignity of the individual?[153]

The Ritualists can justify the trial only by detaching it from its social context and by closing their eyes to the practical consequences which the judicial system implements. This perspective is a real psychological possibility for the lawyer. For him, the trial does end when the procedures are exhausted. The rhythms of his life continue as before; he merely turns to another proceeding. But it is absurd to impute this perspective to the litigant. The litigant cannot ignore the outcome; he will suffer or benefit from it. After the trial, he turns not to another proceeding, but to the task of adjusting his life to the change which the trial has wrought.

The error of the Ritualist argument is very similar to the one exposed by Rousseau in his attack on the ceremonial defense of the theater. Rousseau points out that a ceremonial ethic detached from the reality of social life can only obfuscate moral understanding:

> I hear it said that tragedy leads to pity through fear. So it does, but what is this pity? A fleeting and vain emotion which lasts no longer than the illusion which produced it; a vestige of natural sentiment soon stifled by the passions; a sterile pity which feeds on a few tears and which has never produced the slightest act of humanity. . . . Tacitus reports that Valerius Asiaticus, calumniously accused by the order of Messalina, who wanted him to perish, defended himself before the emperor in a way that touched this prince very deeply and drew tears from Messalina herself. She went into the next room in order to regain her composure after having, in the midst of her tears, whispered a warning to Vitellius not to let the accused escape. I never see one of these weeping ladies in the boxes at the theatre, so proud of their tears, without thinking of the tears of Messalina for poor Valerius Asiaticus.[154]

Should not the Ritualist exultation in the trial as an expression of the dignity of the litigants also be likened to the tears of Messalina for poor Valerius Asiaticus?

3. THE JURISPRUDENCE OF RESIGNATION

For all their differences of mood, both the cynical and the naive versions of Ritualism share the basic defect of removing procedure from its context in the legal system and in society. Arnold adopts the stance of the objective social scientist so that he does not have to justify the irrational system from which he benefits as a lawyer. Fried takes the position of the abstract moral philosopher so that his justification can

153. John Griffiths points out the contradiction, in many contemporary writings on the criminal law, between the scrupulous concern for procedural justice and the indifference to the fate of the defendant once he has exhausted the procedures to which he is entitled. Griffiths, *supra* note 3, at 378-80.

154. J. Rousseau, Politics and the Arts (Letter to M. D'Alembert on the Theater) 24-25 (Bloom trans. 1960).

safely ignore the facts of suffering and bewilderment which the legal system produces. Arnold's thesis is founded on a sociological datum; Fried's on an aesthetic intuition. Yet, both foundations are weak. Arnold believes, without evidence and in defiance of fact, that people actually hold the views he would like them to hold. This is the naiveté of his cynicism. Fried implies that man's experience of shared values cannot go beyond ceremonial form, that result must be severed from process in order to create public ritual. This is the cynicism of his naiveté.

For the Positivists, the law was a zero-sum game in which one could win only at someone else's expense. For the Purposivists, it was a "dynamic pie" from which everyone could have a slice.[155] For the Ritualists, the law neither inflicts losses nor produces rewards; it offers consolation in terms of a pleasing rhetoric and imagery detached from social reality.

Ritualism represents a policy of resignation. It is based on a strategy of avoiding disappointment by moderating expectations of success and putting the best possible face on failure. Ritualism acknowledges the irrationality of adversary advocacy just enough to establish credibility. It glamorizes adversary advocacy just enough to discourage criticism.[156] As Alvin Gouldner writes of Erving Goffman's "dramaturgical" sociology, "[i]t is an invitation to the *enjoyment* of appearances."[157]

C. *A Revision: The Game Analogy*

In some respects, Goffman's dramaturgical sociology is more cynical than the jurisprudence of even the most cynical Ritualists, for Goffman seems indifferent to whether or not *any* of the actors in the dramas he describes actually believes in the part he plays. Yet, Goffman is interesting because he suggests a modification of Ritualism which might avoid some of the difficulties just mentioned. Though he has influenced some Ritualists, they have declined to follow the more radical aspects of his thought. Still, his ideas seem to be characteristic of the unarticulated attitudes of some lawyers.

Goffman's approach partly avoids the difficulties of conventional Ritualism, first, because it acknowledges a certain dissonance between the ostensible or surface meanings of formal patterns of interaction and the actual experience of the participants; and second, because it acknowledges that the formal patterns have distinct and concrete consequences.[158]

155. HART & SACKS, *supra* note 71, at 111.

156. This is the Ritualist kiss-off: "Things are not as bad as you think."

157. A. GOULDNER, THE COMING CRISIS OF WESTERN SOCIOLOGY 384 (1970) (emphasis in original) [hereinafter cited as GOULDNER]; *see generally id.* at 378-90.

158. *See* Goffman, *supra* note 61; *see also* E. GOFFMAN, INTERACTION RITUAL: ESSAYS ON FACE-TO-FACE BEHAVIOR (1967), especially at 48-56 [hereinafter cited as GOFFMAN, INTERACTION RITUAL]; E. GOFFMAN, THE PRESENTATION OF SELF IN EVERYDAY LIFE (1959) [hereinafter cited as GOFFMAN, PRESENTATION OF SELF].

Goffman sees the world as drama or ritual, but the performance is to a large extent false. The individual does not take on a role in order to express his harmony with the others, but to escape his terror of them. The mask which the individual puts on is not a message to his fellows, but a shield against them.

In Goffman's world of radical alienation, individual identity is so fragile and dessicated that every gaze from another person is perceived as a threat. Every social encounter is a crisis in which individuals struggle desperately to maintain their autonomy by erecting barriers to penetration by the others. In such situations, ritual and role provide breathing space. They shelter the individual from the siege of foreign gazes and temporarily relieve him from the constant pressure of having to improvise defenses.

This perspective can be readily applied to the judicial proceeding. By giving the proceeding a formal structure based on a moral rhetoric with which the participants have some familiarity, and by giving them fixed roles to play, the system offers the individual a little comfort and privacy in a situation of great stress. The litigant may welcome the identity which his lawyer fashions for him, for it frees him from the strain of adjusting his outward appearance to a new and frightening situation, and gives him a mask with which to shield his inner feelings from the intimidating presence of hostile strangers. He knows that he can satisfy everyone's expectations by adhering to the script. Similarly, by creating the formalized alliance of lawyer and client, the system enables the two actors not only to protect their separate identities from each other, but also to cooperate in the protection of their joint identity from the pressure of others.[159]

The principle of neutrality relieves the client from the pressure of having to account for himself to the lawyer. The principle of partisanship encourages the lawyer to run interference for the client against the advances of others. The lawyer is similarly benefited. Because he portrays himself to his client as indifferent to all purposes, he does not have to defend his own. Because he is expected to be partisan toward the ends of his client, he need not fear public criticism for his activities.

This line of thought travels some distance from the purer forms of Ritualism. It is like Purposivism in that it sees the proceeding as in part instrumental to an ulterior purpose. (Of course, in both pure Ritualism and the revision, the ritual might be described as instrumental to a particular mental state, but in pure Ritualism the mental state is more directly bound up with the ritual itself.) But this ulterior purpose is not the kind of purpose on which Purposivism usually focused, that is, concrete social achievements. The new version is like Positivism, in that it works to delineate pockets of autonomy within which the individual can exist

159. *See* GOFFMAN, INTERACTION RITUAL, *supra* note 158, at Ch. 2.

without accounting to others. But the pockets are much smaller, and they depend on a delicate balance of social forces, not just on state power. And the new view also suggests a compromise between the Positivist and the Purposivist visions of the social world. On the one hand, individuals are seen as alien and hostile, desiring barriers behind which they can isolate themselves from the others. On the other hand, they do not need much coercion to cooperate with each other. There is a spontaneous reciprocity of assistance in the task of safe-guarding order, which is now known, in Goffman's phrase, as "impression management."[160]

A second strength of Goffman's approach is that, though it often speaks in terms of drama or ritual, it is actually based on an analogy to game, as Levi-Strauss explains the term. Goffman does not overlook the fact that the patterns of interaction which he studies function to divide the society into winners and losers. Far from viewing such patterns independently of the results they produce, he insists on what he calls "consequentiality."[161] He recognizes not only that patterns of interaction are refuges for the harried ego, but also that they produce concrete social changes.

The game analogy rationalizes the contradictions between substance and procedure. The game is a social phenomenon in which the satisfactory quality of the outcome depends almost entirely on the proper implementation of procedures. People usually feel that when the rules are followed the outcome of a game is just, precisely because the rules have been followed. They usually are not inclined to assess outcomes in terms of an independent set of criteria. This is particularly true of the game of chance, where the only substantive criterion is negative: that the results have no discernible significance. It should not therefore be surprising that some philosophers find the game the most satisfying example of procedural justice.[162]

For many, the game analogy will appear dubious because the game appears to depend to such a large degree on chance and arbitrariness, and it appears remote from meaningful political activity. Yet, the game might be a useful metaphor for authoritative patterns of interaction, such as the judicial proceeding, to someone who believed that such patterns were arbitrary or had no substantial meaning. To see the central institutions of the society as constructed along the principle of the game of chance is to cease to hold the society to any substantive standards of meaning or consistency. To one willing to accept this conclusion, the game, particularly the game of chance, might be a satisfactory model for social institutions. If the central institutions of the society are viewed in terms of the game of chance, then the arbitrariness of the results they produce is a

160. GOFFMAN, PRESENTATION OF SELF, *supra* note 158, at ch. 6.
161. *See* GOFFMAN, INTERACTION RITUAL, *supra* note 158, at 151-61.
162. *E.g.*, BARRY, *supra* note 21, at 102-103.

virtue which proves the integrity of the system. On this view, the threat of contradiction would arise only if the results should actually produce meaningful patterns.

Abraham Blumberg's article, *The Practice of Law as a Confidence Game*, suggests that many criminal defense lawyers view the legal process in Goffmanian terms.[163] Charles P. Curtis has defended the view of law practice in terms of the game analogy as a special ethical prerogative of the lawyer. The lawyer, he suggests, is under much greater strain than the client because of his conflicting obligations to the public and to his client. The game analogy helps him to view his activities in a way which reduces the strain of his dual commitment. Thus, he writes, "Never blame the lawyer for treating litigation as a game . . . ."[164] On the other hand, Douglas Rosenthal's study of personal injury litigation suggests that lawyers lead clients to view the litigation in terms of the game analogy. Rosenthal emphasizes the passive nature of the client's role and his manipulation by the lawyer. He notes of one litigant: "The lawyer talked her into exaggerating her pain under oath by acknowledging that there were special 'rules' in the 'game' of trial tactics."[165] He quotes another as saying, "the lawyer is a reassuring presence who takes away your guilt feelings. He says, 'Hey, this is the way the game is played.' . . ."[166]

The greatest strength of the game analogy is its realism. It is more consistent with the actual experience of large numbers of people than the ritual or theatrical analogies. Moreover, it is a view which can be shared by both winners and losers, both lawyers and litigants. The lawyer is far more likely to be successful in inducing the client to see the litigation as a game than as a ritual.

Yet, the realism of the game analogy is not really a virtue, for the experience to which it defers is itself false and unworthy of respect. To encourage the client to see the results produced by the legal system as arbitrary is to discourage him from considering that they might have a meaning other than the one the legal system attributes to them. A litigant disposed to reflect on the meaning of the consequences produced by the legal system might decide that, while the judicial proceeding does not express such values as harmony, equality, and dignity, neither is it arbitrary. For instance, he might decide that it expresses such phenomena as cruelty, injustice, and oppression. The game analogy abandons the claim that there is any principle by which the way the system works to distinguish winners from losers can be justified, but in doing so, it also rejects the claim that there is any principle by which it can be criticized.

163. Blumberg, *supra* note 5.

164. CURTIS, *supra* note 106, at 35; *see also* Curtis, *The Ethics of Advocacy*, 4 STAN. L. REV. 4 (1951).

165. ROSENTHAL, *supra* note 5, at 45.

166. *Id.* at 171.

The game analogy subverts criticism of the legal system at the same time that it debunks the system.

Moreover, although the game analogy appeals to losers as well as winners, its appeal seems to be limited to the two extremes. As Alvin Gouldner writes of Goffman's sociology:

> A dramaturgical model . . . is for those who have already made it in the big game, or for those who have given up playing it. It has appeal to those members of the middle class who generally mask their alienation out of concern to maintain a respectable appearance and to those "dropouts" in the Psychedelic Culture who feel no need to conceal their alienation; both groups are alike in that they are not moved to protest against and actively oppose the system that has alienated them.[167]

Even more serious is the failure of the game analogy to distinguish between winners and losers in the attitudes it encourages toward the legal system. It induces the same kind of complacent cynicism in both the powerful and the weak. The game analogy admits that the actions of the litigants influence concrete consequences, as the actions of players influence who wins a game. However, it ignores the wide variation among the players in the legal system in the capacity to influence consequences. The problem is not so much that differences in power give some an advantage over others, since such power differences can be seen as the result of previous games. Rather, the problem is that the analogy conceals the extent to which people with power could, if they wanted to, stop playing the game, or attempt without great risk to alter its rules in accordance with some substantive standard of meaning. The game analogy encourages the winners to think of themselves as lucky but helpless beneficiaries of a situation they have not made and can do nothing about.

D. *The Finale: The Friendship Analogy*

In a recent article, Charles Fried has defended legal ethics in terms of yet another analogy: friendship. Unlike drama, ritual, and game, friendship is an analogy, not for the legal system, but for the lawyer-client relation itself. It is interesting because it illustrates a tendency to think of the lawyer-client relation as having a value apart from and even antagonistic to the legal system as a whole.[168]

Perhaps surprisingly, in view of the unalloyed naiveté of his earlier rhetoric, the newer article is full of statements associated with the most primitive sort of Positivism. Fried emphasizes the preservation of the client's "autonomy" as a basic purpose of the lawyer's role. He speaks

167. GOULDNER, *supra* note 157, at 386.

168. *See* Redmount, *Humanistic Law Through Legal Counseling*, 2 CONN L. REV. 98 (1969); Shafer, *Christian Theories of Professional Responsibility*, 48 S. CAL. L. REV. 721 (1975) [hereinafter cited as Shafer].

of lawyers' antisocial conduct in terms of pulling "legal levers" and of implementing the client's "rights." He explicitly recognizes and approves some of the lawyer's most unsavory activities such as helping the wealthy to exploit the poor or to avoid taxes.[169]

Yet, these points are peripheral to the basic thrust of Fried's new argument which is entirely foreign to Positivism. Fried's principal purpose is to defend lawyer-client relations as "good in themselves." As before, Fried is concerned with the embodiment of ideals such as "the ideal of personal relations of trust and personal care."[170] But now the relevant ideals are embodied, not in the legal system as a whole, but in the attorney-client relation itself. This relation is seen less as a component of a larger structure and more as an independent entity.

The defense of partisanship and neutrality as protecting an intrinsically worthwhile relationship is not new. In fact, it appears that the attorney-client evidentiary privilege was first rationalized in the 17th century precisely as safeguarding a valuable personal relationship. It was then argued that the rule of confidentiality followed from the more general principle that gentlemen do not reveal each other's confidences. However, in the following century the defense of confidentiality and legal ethics generally shifted to the claim that such principles are necessary to the proper functioning of the legal system as a whole.[171] Since that time, at least until recently, the Ideology of Advocacy has focussed on the alleged requirements of the system. The notion that lawyer-client relationships were intrinsically valuable remained a background theme, but it played small part in the public defense of legal ethics.

By contrast, Fried now attempts to rationalize legal ethics by emphasizing the personal worth of the relations defined by the professional norms of partisanship and neutrality. Fried suggests that partisanship is like friendship in that it involves "an authorization to take the interests of particular concrete persons more seriously and to give them priority over the interests of the wider collectivity." At the same time the lawyer's neutrality bespeaks a deference to the "concrete individuality" of the client which is similar to the deference one friend would show to another. The fact that the lawyer's concern is not reciprocated in kind by the client does not differentiate the relation from friendship. On the contrary, it exemplifies the lawyer's freedom to bestow and the client's "freedom to receive an extra measure of care" which also exists in friendship.[172] Fried argues that, after one has recognized in the lawyer-client relation the

169. Fried, *The Lawyer as Friend: The Moral Foundations of the Lawyer-Client Relation*, 85 YALE L.J. 1060, 1074, 1077, 1085 (1976) [hereinafter cited as Fried, *The Lawyer as Friend*]. For an excellent critique of this article, see Dauer & Leff, *Correspondence: The Lawyer as Friend*, 86 YALE L. J. 573 (1977).

170. Fried, *The Lawyer as Friend*, *supra* note 169, at 1075.

171. J. WIGMORE, 8 EVIDENCE §§ 2286-90 (McNaughton ed. 1961).

172. Fried, *The Lawyer as Friend*, *supra* note 169, at 1066, 1069, 1074.

qualities generally valued in friendship, one should accept the lawyer-client relation as good in itself.

The friendship analogy represents a substantial development beyond Fried's earlier work, but it is a development which exacerbates rather than remedies the flaws of the earlier work. The first flaw, as discussed above, was that Fried's idealized model of the judicial process did not reflect the actual experience of litigants. Fried's recent article totally blurs the distinction between the ideal and the actual and tries to pre-empt the vocabulary needed to establish it.

Fried writes: "[L]ike a friend [the lawyer] acts in your interests, not his own; or rather he adopts your interests as his own. I would call that the classical definition of friendship."[173] Now this is clearly an error. The classical definition of friendship emphasizes, not the adoption by one person of another's ends, but rather the sharing by two people of common ends.[174] Moreover, the classical notion of friendship includes a number of other qualities foreign to the relation Fried describes. These missing qualities include affection, admiration, intimacy, and vulnerability.[175] On the other hand, if Fried's definition is amplified to reflect the qualification, which Fried repeatedly acknowledges, that the lawyer adopts the client's interests *for money*,[176] it becomes apparent that Fried has described the classical notion, not of friendship, but of prostitution.

The conflation of the ideas of friendship and prostitution is typical of the moral obfuscation which pervades the article. For Fried, the problem of a doctor who must decide what to do for "a severely deformed baby who can be kept alive only through extraordinarily expensive means" is "analogous" to the problem of a lawyer who must decide what to do for a client who wants "to avoid the effects of a tax or a form of regulation." The task of helping a "disagreeable dowager" tyrannize her relatives deserves the same intensity of commitment as the task of "defending the civil liberties case of the century."[177]

173. *Id.* at 1071.

174. *See* ARISTOTLE, NICOMACHEAN ETHICS, bk. 8, especially at 218-23, 231 (Ostwald ed. 1962).

175. *Id.*; *see also* F. NIETZSCHE, *Thus Spoke Zarathustra* in THE PORTABLE NIETZSCHE 167-69 (Kaufmann ed. 1954) [hereinafter cited as NIETZSCHE]; W. SHAKESPEARE, THE MERCHANT OF VENICE, especially I:iii, ll. 131-38; IV:i, ll. 265-88.

176. "It is undeniable that money usually cements the lawyer-client relationship." Fried, *The Lawyer as Friend*, *supra* note 169, at 1075.

Fried adds, "But the content of the relation is determined by the client's needs . . . . So the fact that the lawyer works for pay does not seriously undermine the friendship analogy." *Id.* at 1075. This is unconvincing. The content of any commercial relation is determined by the buyer's needs. Of course, the lawyer's customers get "personalized" service, but so do the customers of tailors and insurance salesmen, if they can pay for it. Fried's suggestion that the lawyer is different because he feels obliged to continue to represent a client even when he becomes unable to pay is wrong. The profession recognizes no such obligation. *See* ABA CODE OF PROFESSIONAL RESPONSIBILITY, DR 2-110 (C) (1) (f) (lawyer may withdraw if client deliberately fails to pay fees); *see also id.* at DR 4-101 (C) (4) (lawyer may reveal client's confidences when necessary to collect a fee).

177. Fried, *The Lawyer as Friend*, *supra* note 169, at 1063-64. The nadir in the use of

Fried's lawyer is a friend in the same sense that your Sunoco dealer is "very friendly" or that Canada Dry Ginger Ale "tastes like love." The friendship analogy is one of those "self-validating, analytical propositions" which Marcuse describes as typical of "the closing of the universe of discourse":

> The unification of opposites which characterizes the commercial and political style is one of the many ways in which discourse and communication make themselves immune against the expression of protest and refusal. How can such protest and refusal find the right word when the organs of the established order admit and advertise that peace is really the brink of war, that the ultimate weapons carry their profitable price tags, and that the bomb shelter may spell coziness? In exhibiting its contradictions as the token of its truth, this universe of discourse closes itself against any other discourse which is not on its own terms.[178]

Marcuse's thesis that this style characterizes and rationalizes the flattening out of personality in contemporary society is amply confirmed by Fried's article. If Fried's earlier defense was a naive counterpart of Arnold's analysis, his recent one is a naive counterpart of Goffman's. Like Goffman, Fried celebrates the farnkly exploitative alliances of convenience between desperate, selfish little men. Fried explicitly strives to infuse with pathos and dignity the financial problems of the tax chiseler and the "disagreeable dowager." By collapsing traditional moral categories, this rhetoric reflects the homegenization of previously distinct personal characteristics. Fried can assert that the lawyer affirms the client's individuality because, like Goffman's protagonists, Fried's clients have almost no individuality. Any pretense to the contrary is abandoned by the middle of the article when Fried insists that corporations as well as natural persons are entitled to "legal friendship." After all, Fried argues, corporations are "only formal arrangements of real persons pursing their real interests."[179] Fried began his defense of the analogy by emphasizing that both friendship and the lawyer-client relation involve direct contact with a concrete individual. It now appears that these concrete individuals have so little individuality that a lawyer's relation to a "formal arrangement" can manifest the same qualities. Fried's final example of legal friendship involves friendship with a "finance company."[180]

"Orwellian" discourse to defend legal ethics occurs, not in Fried's article, but in Shafer's. *See* Shafer, *supra* note 168, at 738, 753, where the Code is analogized to "St. Matthew's Gospel" and the lawyer's attitude of neutrality to the "human experience Jesus identified as the source of his salvation."

178. H. Marcuse, One-Dimensional Man: Studies In the Ideology of Advanced Industrial Society 88, 90 (1964).

179. Fried, *The Lawyer as Friend*, *supra* note 169, at 1076.

180. *Id*. at 1086

The second major flaw in Fried's earlier work was its tendency to focus on judicial procedure to the exclusion of the consequences produced by the operation of the judicial system, that is, to collapse substance into process. The friendship analogy represents an even further narrowing of this focus. It focusses on the attorney-client relation to the exclusion, not only of substantive consequences, but of the other elements of the judicial proceeding as well. The most striking feature of Fried's position is that the "moral foundations of the lawyer-client relation" have so little to do with law of any kind.

For Fried, the legal system is a condition of the value of the lawyer-client relation, but it is not the source of this value. Legal friendship arises from the fact that the client has a special need for help in order to exercise the autonomy which the legal system guarantees. The fact that this autonomy is a moral value legitimates certain of the lawyer's anti-social conduct, but it does not give it the special pathos and dignity celebrated by the friendship analogy. These qualities arise, not from the specifically legal character of the client's need, but from the fact that the need is integrally related to the integrity of the person, that it is "implicated in crises going to one's concreteness and individuality."[181] Although Fried argues, somewhat half-heartedly, that the need is a special one which is different from needs for non-professional services,[182] he expressly indicates that the need for legal help is similar to the need for other professionals services, particularly, medical help.

Of course, the legal system defines the patterns and boundaries of the relation, but these patterns and boundaries seem to limit, more than to promote, the qualities emphasized by the friendship analogy. Fried does not contemplate that the lawyer do many things which friends might be expected to do for each other, such as to destroy evidence, lie to the court, or do anything else which would violate the law or the *Code of Professional Responsibility*. After first extolling friendship in glowing and unqualified terms, Fried breaks the bad news that the lawyer is only a "special-purpose friend."[183] Although the lawyer-client relation has

181. *Id.* at 1072.

182. Fried needs to make this argument to distinguish the lawyer from the friendly Sunoco dealer or the friendly insurance salesman, but the distinction is untenable. In the first place, while some clients, particularly the criminal defendant, can plausibly be viewed as involved in a "critical assault on one's person" or at least in a situation implicating their "concreteness and individuality," others cannot be so viewed. If a finance company's attempt to foreclose on a poor widow or a wealthy person's attempt to evade taxes—both examples used by Fried—can be viewed as implicating concreteness and individuality, then it is difficult to think of any effort to satisfy any desire which could not be so viewed. Moreover, Fried ignores the fact that for people who do not have secure employment or independent wealth it is precisely in the material dealings with landlords, employers, and bureaucrats that their individuality is most at stake. For most people individuality is jeopardized not by an ignorance of the law, but by an economic dependence which is largely sanctioned and implemented by the law. For them, concreteness and individuality would be better served by a friendly landlord than by a friendly lawyer.

183. Fried, *The Lawyer as Friend*, *supra* note 169, at 1071-72, 1080-87.

value apart from considerations of fairness and efficiency, that value must yield in some situations to the need to maintain the integrity of the legal system.[184] The legal system thus appears as a threat to the lawyer-client friendship.

The game analogy expressed a sense of the meaninglessness of the operation of authoritative institutions. The friendship analogy acknowledges their legitimacy, but emphasizes their remoteness. In an earlier example of the friendship analogy Charles P. Curtis wrote, "Justice is a chilly virtue. It is of high importance that we be introduced into the inhospitable halls of justice by a friend."[185] Fried asserts the intrinsic value of legal friendship against the "cooler, more abstract" notions of justice and social welfare.[186] The judicial proceeding no longer appears, as it did in Ritualism, as a warm, comfortable setting in which the litigant's identity is affirmed. It is cold and inhospitable. Affirmation is possible within the lawyer-client relation, but this relation is no longer harmoniously integrated into the larger system. As with Goffman, the relation shelters the participants against the harsh operation of the system.

Social norms no longer provide any kind of satisfaction. Rather they pose an intolerable burden, and even their ceremonial enactment is threatening. Fried argues against the Purposivist notion of responsibility—which he portrays in a Utilitarian caricature—as a "monstrous conception."[187] Where the classical Purposivists saw social norms as energizing creative individual behavior, the friendship analogy sees them as frightening individuals into retreat. The autonomy Fried celebrates is much different from the aggressive egoism portrayed in the classic Positivist writings. It is defensive and passive.[188]

184. Fried's article seems particularly incoherent at this point. At the beginning, the basic characteristic of friendship was portrayed as "an authorization to take the interests of particular concrete persons more seriously and to give them priority over the interests of the wider collectivity." *Id.* at 1066. Yet, in recognizing an obligation not to violate the law or the *Code of Professional Responsibility* on behalf of the client, the lawyer refuses precisely to give priority to his client's interests over "the interests of the wider collectivity." This obligation to the system seems incompatible with friendship as Fried himself has described it.

It is no answer to this objection to say that the legal system gives meaning to the client's autonomy by defining the rights which protect it and that, therefore, the lawyer respects his client's autonomy by respecting the law. For the law gives meaning to autonomy only in a very abstract and general sense, and it is precisely such abstract and general notions which Fried rejects in favor of commitment to the concrete interests of the particular client.

185. Curtis, *supra* note 106, at 1.

186. Fried, *The Lawyer as Friend*, *supra* note 169, at 1070.

187. *Id.* at 1078.

188. Fried also relies on the familiar distinction between wrongs "of the system" and the lawyer's "personal wrongs." The reasons why this type of rationalization is untenable have been discussed in the criticism of Positivism. *See* notes 29-42 *supra* and accompanying text. But Fried's version deserves further comment. He attempts to distinguish between the lawyer's putting the client on the stand to lie ("exploiting the system") and the lawyer's telling the lie himself ("engaging his own person in doing personal harm to another"). Putting the client on to perjure himself is all right because in doing so the lawyer is "like the letter carrier who delivers the falsehood." On the other hand, a direct lie is unethical

If the Ideology of Advocacy is a rationalization of the ethical orientation of lawyers, then the friendship analogy seems both its culmination and its finish. The lawyer's distinctive identity has emerged from behind the facade of the legal system and is now openly celebrated as an end in itself. The irony of this development is that at the same time that it celebrates the legal profession more openly than previous defenses, the friendship analogy also comes closer than previous defenses to acknowledging the failure of the legal profession to accomplish the task for which the lawyer's role was created in the first place, the reconciliation of public and private ends. Previously, the lawyer justified his role in terms of the resolution of individual differences through order, justice, welfare, or ceremony. Yet, in fact, to the extent that he was sensitive to outcomes at all, he experienced them not as resolutions, but as arbitrary concessions to one of two opposing spheres. In emphasizing the remoteness and coolness of public ends, the friendship analogy admits that the magic with which the lawyer once claimed he could resolve the clash of individual wills is a fraud.

Yet, the admission is only implicit. The friendship analogy diverts attention from failure by conflating the lawyer with a less problematical social role. The same effect occurs in the familiar comparison of the legal role with that of doctors (also used by Fried) or clergymen.[189] Such comparisons emphasize the commitment of all three professionals to individual clients, patients, or penitents against the claims of the collectivity, as illustrated particularly by the norms of confidentiality to which all three adhere. Yet, they gloss over a critical difference. The insistence of the doctor and the clergyman on maintaining the confidence of those they serve represents a commitment to the values with which their professional activities are concerned above competing social values. On the other hand, the lawyer's insistence on confidentiality represents a

---

because "every speech act invites belief." Fried, *The Lawyer as Friend*, *supra* note 169; at 1084-86.

Here are Fried's characteristic mistakes in striking form. First, the treason to actual experience: the competent trial lawyer must invite the trier's belief with his appearance and gestures just as much as with his speech, with the questions he asks and the way he asks them just as much as with the statements he makes. As Freedman writes, "[e]ffective trial advocacy requires that the attorney's every word, action, and attitude be consistent with the conclusion that his client is innocent." Freedman, *supra* note 9, at 1471. The ABA-ALI's *Civil Trial Manual* suggests that the trial lawyer "practice before a mirror on his mannerisms" and it observes that the advocate acquires his skills by "hard work and self-reformation." R. FIGG, R. MACULLOUGH, & J. UNDERWOOD, CIVIL TRIAL MANUAL 358 (1974). The distinction between speech and conduct is meaningless; personality is engaged in both, and in both it intentionally misleads. (On a more practical level, Fried ignores that the lawyer will have to argue explicitly to the jury that the client's lie is credible in his summation.)

Second, the suppression of consequences: Fried ignores that the client's lie—directed and affirmed by the lawyer—will, if successful, probably lead to an unjust result. The letter carrier analogy would be more truthful if the letter contained a bomb likely to blow up in the face of the recipient.

189. Fried, *The Lawyer as Friend*, *supra* note 169, at 1072-73; *see also* S. WILLISTON, LIFE AND LAW 272 (1940).

compromise *among* the values with which he is professionally concerned, or perhaps even a sacrifice of these values to extrinsic values. The doctor and the clergyman insist that for them health and salvation must take precedence over justice. The lawyer asserts that his relationship with his client must take precedence over justice, but in doing so he forgets that his relationship was originally defined and rationalized in terms of justice.

In the friendship analogy, the plaintive tone of Ritualism reaches its highest pitch. The lawyer tacitly concedes his failure, but rather than apologize for it, urges the society to lower its expectations. Unable to justify his role in terms of public means and ends, he urges that it be accepted as an end in itself.[190]

V. Procedural Fetishism

> *[T]he ubiquitous question asked, "Do you think the Rosenbergs were guilty?" is a wrong question and can only result in a wrong answer. The question should be "Do you think there was sufficient evidence warranting the jury, which sized up the witnesses, to decide tnat the Rosenbergs were guilty?"*
>
> Louis Nizer[191]

This section considers, briefly and tentatively, some of the broader implications of the critique of adversary advocacy. First, it argues that the most basic defect of the three versions of the Ideology of Advocacy is that the practices they prescribe engender a discontinuity between experience in the social world and experience in the world of ostensibly autonomous legal institutions. This discontinuity involves the alienation of the individual from his ends and actions. It thus leads to the subversion of the very values which the Ideology of Advocacy purports to safeguard: values such as individual autonomy, responsibility, and dignity. Second, this section speculates that an important, subsurface reason for the success of adversary advocacy is that it serves the goal of social stability by sublimating conflict. The characteristic form which this process of sublimation takes is the translation of issues of substantive law and justice into procedural issues. Although the Idology of Advocacy claims to serve individuality, this process of conflict sublimation actually subverts the norms of individuality in the interests of social stability. The argument concludes by suggesting that a different and no less realistic attitude toward conflict than the one which underlies the Ideology of Advocacy would lead to the abandonment of the Ideology of Advocacy. Both of the points made in this section refer to a phenomenon which can be called procedural fetishism.

190. *Cf.* Sartre's critique of Nietzsche's ethic of recurrence as a strategy of self-consolation for the philosopher's failure to change an intolerable situation: "[T]his man who is drowning demands that the instant of his choking last forever." J. Sartre, Saint Genet 349 (Frechtman trans. 1963).

191. L. Nizer, The Implosion Conspiracy 9 (1973).

A. *Discontinuity*

The practices prescribed by all three versions of the Ideology of Advocacy alienate the individual from his own ends and actions at the moments when his individuality is most at stake. In this situation, autonomy, responsibility, and dignity— the very norms the Ideology of Advocacy invokes in its own defense—are frustrated. The fatal discontinuity is inherent in the notions of procedural justice and professionalism and is implemented in practice by the principles of neutrality and partisanship.

The problem is manifested in the most salient contradictions of the three versions. Positivism promises to safeguard the autonomy of the individual. Yet, when the individual's autonomy is threatened, it thrusts him into a situation where he cannot make rational choices and must submit to the will of his lawyer. Purposivism promises to enhance social welfare by encouraging individual responsibility. Yet, at points of stress, Purposivism exacerbates centrifugal tendencies by encouraging individuals to regard values in a manner which strips them of their meaning and force. Finally, Ritualism makes only the modest claim to ceremonially affirm individual dignity. Yet, the ceremonies it prescribes turn out to be a mockery of individual dignity.

The common defect of the three versions is that they require that disputes be resolved in a specialized setting discontinuous with the one in which they arose, and in specialized terms discontinuous with those in which they were originally framed. Disputes arise in the social world in terms of rules, values, and practices associated with the substantive law. Procedural considerations such as finality, self-incrimination, notice, hearing, confrontation, repose, and standing, play little part in this context. However, when disputes resist voluntary resolution, they must be precipitated into a distinct, specialized setting in which these procedural considerations become dominant and dispositive.

The first consequence of the shift from the social world to the procedural world is the alienation of the individual from his ends.[192] Each version of the Ideology of Advocacy describes a different form of this phenomenon. In Positivism, because his own ends are assumed to be unintelligible to others, the individual must adopt the more familiar and limited ends which the legal system imputes to him in order to be recognized by the others, and to make sense of the situation. In Purposivism, the individual may retain his own ends, but he is pressured to abstract them from his experience, to look at them from a perspective which weakens their ethical force. In Ritualism, the individual is forced to watch and participate in a formal affirmation of his abstract individuality at the same time that his particular ends are being frustrated.

A further consequence of this shift from the social world to the

192. *See generally* Williams, *supra* note 123, at 77-150.

procedural world is the alienation of the individual from his actions.[193] In the social world, where individuals conduct disputes on their own behalf, they are conscious of creating and affecting the dispute through their own choices. The dispute appears to each disputant to proceed in accordance with actions which he and his adversary have taken, and the outcome of the dispute also appears to result from his and his adversary's actions. However, once lawyers move the dispute into the world of judicial procedure, this perspective changes. It seems to the disputants that the dispute has been taken out of their hands. Formal procedures seem to carry the dispute along with a momentum of their own. The client comes to see his actions as dictated by the requirements of procedures. He sees the lawyer's actions as representing, not the client's own choices, but rather features of an autonomous proceeding. The outcome of the dispute seems to have been determined, not by the client's actions, but by the autonomous operation of a system of rules, a mechanism of functional roles, or a ritual of ceremonial roles.

The Ideology of Advocacy cannot accommodate the autonomous, responsible, dignified individual. Such a person must be able to experience a set of ends as *his own* in the sense that they guide or explain his actions and constitute or contribute to his identity. Moreover, this experience must have some continuity over time. An individual does not make choices solely with regard to preferences of the moment, but rather with regard to ends which he has had and expects to have. This does not mean that a person's ends cannot change, but rather that when such change occurs a person's present ends are related to his past ends by a process of growth or development. Such change is continuous because it can be perceived, at least by the individual himself and often by others as well, as occurring within the framework of a single personality. A person who was merely the setting of a series of discrete transient desires would not be recognizable as an individual.[194]

In addition, an individual must be capable of conscious, deliberate action in furtherance of his ends. His actions can only be meaningfully related to his ends, and to him as an individual, if he has consciously and deliberately chosen to take the actions in the light of his ends.[195] Here too there must be continuity. A person's past choices will limit and influence his present choices, as his present choices will limit and influence his future choices. He must be capable of a continuous series of choices if he is not to blindly undo at night what he has purposefully accomplished by day.

The regime of procedural justice requires that this continuity be

193. *See generally* Lukacs, *supra* note 61, at 83-110.

194. *See* T. NAGEL, THE POSSIBILITY OF ALTRUISM ch. VIII (1970); SARTRE, *supra* note 61, at 462-67; UNGER, *supra* note 25, at chs. 1 and 5; Williams, *supra* note 123, at 93-118.

195. *See* H. HART, PUNISHMENT AND RESPONSIBILITY: ESSAYS IN THE PHILOSOPHY OF LAW ch. 4 (1968).

interrupted in situations of dispute. It radically abstracts the individual from the social context in which he created the dispute, and requires that he pursue it from a specialized, artificial perspective. It encourages him to forget what he has been and would like to be in the future, and to shape his concerns to the exigencies of the moment. It makes it impossible for him to relate the choices to be made in the procedural setting to the choices previously made, and expected to be made, in the social world. Underlying the disorienting experience of adversary advocacy is the client's sense of the autonomous, inherently legitimating force of procedure.[196] Because the judicial proceeding is designed to focus attention on its inherent norms, it subverts the participants' sense of their own ends. Because the pattern of the judicial proceeding is so formal and so alien to everyday social intercourse, it precludes active, coherent participation by the litigants.

The lawyer implements the discontinuity of procedural justice through the practice of neutrality and partisanship. Given the client's dependence on him, the lawyer, wittingly or not, will redefine the initial terms of the dispute in terms of his own procedural orientation. The fact that the lawyer presents himself (under the principle of partisanship) as sympathetic and committed to the client and yet (under the principle of neutrality) detached from and indifferent to his client's ends leads the client to view his own ends with detachment and indifference. The fact that (under the principle of partisanship) the lawyer is willing to take aggressive action on behalf of the client and yet (under the principle of neutrality) disclaims responsibility for the consequences of such action leads the client to see these consequences, not as results of his or his lawyer's choices, but as the products of autonomous forces.

Professionalism plays a critical part in this re-definition of the situation. The lawyer's formal and practical monopoly over access to the institutions of authoritative dispute resolution gives him a large measure of power over the client.[197] But the transformation of perspective can be accomplished only because the lawyer presents himself to the client, not

196. This psychology has been acknolwedged insofar as it affects the lawyer, but its impact on the client has geen generally ignored. *See, e.g.*, Parsons, *A Sociologist Looks at the Legal Profession*, in ESSAYS IN SOCIOLOGICAL THEORY: PURE AND APPLIED 380 (rev. ed. 1957) [hereinafter cited as Parsons]:

> The fact that the case can be tried by a standard procedure relieves . . . [the lawyer] of some of the pressure of commitment to the case of his client. He can feel that, if he does his best, then having assured his client a fair trial, he is relieved of responsibility for an unfavorable verdict if it comes. He may even take a case with considerable reservations about its soundness, counting on procedural fairness to protect the interests of the opponent.

197. It should be recalled that I am speaking of the relatively powerless and unsophisticated client. Of course, powerful, sophisticated clients are less likely to be dominated by their lawyers. But the arguments of the Ideology of Advocacy become inapplicable, or at least more implausible, to the extent that the client is powerful and sophisticated. The Ideology of Advocacy focuses on the relatively naive and unsophisticated client, and the validity of its prescriptions must stand or fall on their impact on that kind of client.

as an individual with ends and responsibilities of his own, but as the embodiment of a neutral specialized discipline. If the lawyer were merely an individual with personal ends, his definition of the situation would have no special priority. But because it is presented as standing above individual views, his professional view of the situation disarms defenses which might be raised to merely individual views, and lays claim to acceptance regardless of the client's personal views. Similarly, if the lawyer were an ordinary individual, he would be responsible for his actions, and his association with the client would not affect the client's responsibility for the client's own actions. But as an embodiment of a neutral, specialized discipline, the lawyer is a kind of filter through which the client's will is cleansed of responsibility. The client comes to see the lawyer not as an individual, but as a component in the procedural system. Thus, the consequences of the lawyer's actions on behalf of the client come to be seen as products of the system.[198] By creating this discontinuity whereby the client loses track of his own ends and his capacity to implement them, the Ideology of Advocacy precludes the most basic psychological prerequisites of individual autonomy, responsibility, and dignity.

It should be emphasized that the suggestion that legal experience should be continuous with other forms of social experience does not amount to a plea for a return to a pre-industrial communalism in which law is completely undifferentiated from other norms.[199] The values of individuality imply that law should be continuous with other social and moral experience, but not necessarily indistinguishable from it. Indeed, as I will emphasize below, liberal legal theory is correct in claiming that individuality and justice are best served by a distinctive form of law and legal experience which is differentiated from other categories of social norms and experience. The notion of continuity suggests only that people should be able to relate legal norms to other forms of understanding and experience in a coherent fashion. The critical point is that the law should be accessible to those who are governed by it. Thus, the notion of continuity is opposed, not to differentiation, but rather to specialization, that is, to the notion that the legal doctrine should or must be accessible only to a trained occupational minority, and that legal institutions should

198. *See, e.g.*, ROSENTHAL, *supra* note 5:

> If I had not had a lawyer here I would probably have settled for about $2,000 to cover my out-of-pocket expenses. But the lawyer is a reassuring presence who takes away your guilt feelings. He says, "Hey, this is the way the game is played; you take as much as you can get; it's what they expect; it's the way it's done." He takes upon his own shoulders the burden of your guilt—he's the professional. I hadn't thought of this before but it occurs to me now as what's [sic] involved.

Id. at 171 (quoting a plaintiff interviewed during a survey of personal injury litigation in New York City).

199. *Contra*, Diamond, *The Rule of Law Versus The Order of Custom*, in THE RULE OF LAW (Wolff ed. 1971). Neither does it amount to a plea for revolutionary socialist communalism. *But see* Pashukanis, *The Soviet State and the Revolution in Law*, in SOVIET LEGAL PHILOSOPHY (Babb trans. 1951).

or must be dominated by such a minority.[200]

Far from being a repudiation of modernity, the appeal to continuity is a plea for the fulfillment of a principle which is acknowledged or assumed in most legal thought as fundamental to modern law: what Hegel calls the "right of giving recognition only to what my insight sees as rational."[201] Like contemporary legal theorists, Hegel considered that, to be seen as rational by the litigants, a judicial decision must be justified in a manner accessible to the litigants in terms of norms which they understand as binding on them. In addition, it must embody active, meaningful contributions by the litigants to the proceeding from which it emerges.[202] Yet, unlike most contemporary theorists, Hegel saw the danger posed by a specialized legal system to the principle of continuity.[203] When access to the courts is monopolized by an occupational group and legal discourse becomes isolated from social norms,

> the members of civil society, who depend for their livelihood on their industry, on their own knowledge and will, are kept strangers to the law, not only to those parts of it affecting their

200. Sociological writing on law often obscures the tension between the notion that modern law is specialized and the notion that it serves a legitimating function by controlling the exercise of state power in a manner which citizens can perceive as rational. Some writers emphasize that modern law is specialized and discontinuous with social experience without considering the claims of modern legal systems to legitimate the actions of the state. *See, e.g.*, L. RUDOLPH & S. RUDOLPH, THE MODERNITY OF TRADITION 254-59 (1967); Nader, *Styles of Court Procedure: To Make the Balance*, in LAW IN CULTURE AND SOCIETY (L. Nader ed. 1969). On the other hand, other writers emphasize that the legitimating function of law in modern society requires continuity between legal and other social experience, but ignore the extent to which modern legal systems engender discontinuity. *See, e.g.*, FULLER, *supra* note 25; Fuller, *Human Interaction and the Law*, in THE RULE OF LAW (Wolff ed. 1971) [hereinafter cited as Fuller, *Human Interaction and the Law*]. For a discussion of legitimation which addresses the problem of discontinuity, see Tushnet, *Perspectives on the History of American Law: A Critical Review of Friedman's "A History of American Law"*, 1977 WIS. L. REV. 81, 100-02 [hereinafter cited as Tushnet].

201. G. HEGEL, PHILOSOPHY OF RIGHT 87 (Knox trans. 1952) [hereinafter cited as HEGEL].

202. *Id.* at 140-45; Fuller, *The Forms and Limits of Adjudication*, *supra* note 80, at 421-26.

203. The contradiction between the notion that the law serves democracy by enabling citizens to perceive as rational the exercise of state power, and the notion of law as specialized, is evident in late Purposivism. The later Purposivists often emphasized that the legitimation of the exercise of judicial power requires that courts establish the rationality of their decisions. They based this requirement on the nature of democracy and the right of citizens not to be subject to arbitrary power. They distinguished "law" from "fiat" on the ground that the former is bound to "gain reasoned acceptance." Bickel & Wellington, *Legislative Purpose and the Judicial Process: The Lincoln Mills Case*, 71 HARV. L. REV. 1, 5 (1957); *see also* HART & SACKS, *supra* note 71, at 665-67. Yet, in applying their theories, these writers were never less satisfied than when judicial decisions were most accessible to ordinary citizens. The criteria by which they tested the rationality of judicial decisions were drawn not from ordinary moral and political discourse but from the technical discourse of lawyers. *See generally* Arnold, *Professor Hart's Theology*, 73 HARV. L. REV. 1298, 1306-09 (1960) [hereinafter cited as Arnold]. In practice, the only audience from whom they insisted that decisions gain reasoned acceptance was the legal profession. The need for reasoned acceptance was said to stem from the moral and social imperatives of democracy; yet the test of reasoned acceptance was the satisfaction of a small elite.

> most intimate affairs, but also to its substantive and rational basis, the right itself, and the result is that they become the wards, or even in a sense the bondsmen, of the legal profession. They may indeed have the right to appear in court in person and 'to stand' there (*in judicio stare*), but their bodily presence is a trifle if their minds are not to be there also, if they are not to follow the proceedings with their own knowledge, and if the justice they receive remains in their eyes a doom pronounced *ab extra*.[204]

Not law, but rather the kind of law practice defined by the principles of professionalism and procedural justice engenders the discontinuity which subverts individual autonomy, responsibility, and dignity.

B. *The Sublimation of Conflict*

Ideologies are usually conceived as providing a facade of universality for particular group privileges and interests. I think that the Ideology of Advocacy functions to mask privilege and to rationalize domination, but I am not prepared in this essay to analyze in any detail the way it does so. Instead, I will suggest a related subsurface reason for its appeal: The Ideology of Advocacy rationalizes widely felt tensions and anesthetizes painful social choices. Since, in doing so, it functions to preserve the status quo and blunt efforts at social change, it benefits the dominant groups in society. Yet, it cannot be seen simply as an instrument of these groups, for the tensions it dulls seem to arise within as well as between groups, and the choices it rationalizes seem to have been made at several levels of society.

The Ideology of Advocacy is a tacit response to the tension between the norms of individuality and the goal of social stability. It is also a response to the often unacknowledged tension between the ideal of law and the goal of social stability. The nature of this response is to translate substantive concerns, which threaten to produce conflict, into more innocuous and manageable procedural concerns. In doing so, adversary advocacy promises to reconcile individuality and law with stability, but in fact it merely rationalizes the sacrifice of the former to the latter.

It may seem perverse to accuse the Ideology of Advocacy of selling out individuality when it attempts to justify itself primarily in terms of values associated with individuality. Yet, the critique of the Ideology of Advocacy has shown that, whatever its pretensions, the Ideology of Advocacy actually subverts the values of individuality. In this light, it is not implausible to suggest that the Ideology of Advocacy is strongly but tacitly committed to a competing goal, the goal of stability.

The goal of stability asserts the fundamental social value of formal,

204. HEGEL, *supra* note 201, at 145. Hegel's theory of the civil service as a "universal class", *id.* at 188-93, has flaws analogous to those he criticized in the theory of legal professionalism. *See* K. MARX, EARLY WRITINGS 100-16 (Vintage ed. 1975).

established institutions and practices. It defines itself in opposition, not to disorder, but to conflict. Conflict entails the mutual recognition of antagonistic wills. It involves conscious, deliberate action taken to further an end against an opposing end. Disorder, on the other hand, is merely randomness. Disorder represents a social failure, but it is a limited social failure which can be contained.[205] It does not call the entire structure of society into question. Conflict involves the assertion of claims which may challenge the ideological foundations of the social structure. It thus threatens the very existence of the established institutions and practices. For those who see stability as the fundamental social norm, the elimination of open conflict is the paramount social task.[206] However, this view presents a difficult problem for legal theorists. For there is a very sharp tension between the goal of stability and the ideal of law.

As far as the goal of stability is concerned, it is more important that conflict be eliminated than that it be eliminated in any particular way. An authoritative decision has value regardless of its content if it causes the disputants to cease to press their claims.

By contrast, the ideal of law prescribes that disputes be determined in a specific way. As elaborated in classical liberal theory, the ideal of law refers to substantive law. It is the notion that conduct in society should be governed in accordance with transcendent, universal norms.[207] The transcendent character of the law means that it stands above, and independent of, individual wills, including the wills of the people who make and apply the laws. The universal character of the law means that it applies to all citizens on similar terms and conditions. Although liberal theory has claimed that law secures stability, in fact law often is more a threat to stability than a guarantee of it. Law takes the form of rules or values. Yet, because rules are indeterminate and values are not fully shared, an official decision reached through the attempt to implement the ideal of law may not be accepted by the disputants as legitimate. The losers can always continue to appeal to their interpretation of the relevant rule or to the values to which they are committed. Unlike ideals of traditional or personal authority, the ideal of law itself may encourage a person who feels that a decision misinterprets a rule or violates a norm to reject the decision and continue his struggle. The transcendent character of the law invites the citizen to appeal beyond the particular official application of the law to the law itself. Moreover, unlike a decision based on tacit, ad hoc considerations, an authoritative decision which seeks to

205. For an illustration of the distinction between conflict and disorder, see Walzer, *Two Kinds of Regicide*, in REGICIDE AND REVOLUTION ch. 1 (1976).

206. *See* GOULDNER, *supra* note 157.

207. *See* FULLER, THE MORALITY OF LAW (rev. ed. 1969); F. HAYEK, THE CONSTITUTION OF LIBERTY 148-61 (1960); KANT, THE METAPHYSICAL ELEMENTS OF JUSTICE (Ladd trans. 1965); UNGER, *supra* note 25, at 72-76. The ideal of law is often closely associated with the ideal of popular or participatory government. *See, e.g.*, J. ROUSSEAU, THE SOCIAL CONTRACT 32-35, 80-87 (Hafner ed. 1947).

implement universal imperatives is likely to carry the issues beyond the immediate parties and make them a matter of contention throughout the society. Thus, far from resolving disputes, the attempt to implement the ideal of law may aggravate existing ones or even stimulate new ones.[208]

Modern social theory has focused on the tension between individuality and stability, and sociological writing often seems more or less explicitly to reject individuality in favor of norms more compatible with stability.[209] Although law is closely associated with individuality in American legal thought, the tension between law and stability is rarely acknowledged. Lawyers tend to be deeply committed to the goal of stability;[210] yet, the doctrines and principles which rationalize their privileges are based, to a large extent, on the norms of individuality. In this situation, lawyers are reluctant to confront the tensions between stability and law and to acknowledge openly that stability might require the sacrifice of law and individuality. Modern legal thought tends to rationalize the sacrifice of law and individuality, but tacitly, rather than explicitly. The sacrifice takes place under the cover of vague notions of legality which are flexible enough to contain the tensions without making them explicit. Sociologically minded jurisprudence often simply conflates the notions of law and stability without acknowledging the difficulties law poses for stability.[211]

A notable illustration of this tacit commitment to stability at the expense of law is the well-known passage of Hart and Sacks concerning "The Great Pyramid of Legal Order." The Pyramid is concerned entirely with dispute resolution. It consists of an ascending series of successively narrower stages: no dispute, informal dispute, private settlement, lawsuit initiated, summary judgment, judgment after trial, and disposition on appeal. Once they occur, "trouble cases" are shunted up the Pyramid until they terminate in "success, or at least . . . no trouble."[212] The

208. *See generally* BICKEL, *supra* note 100, at ch. IV (on the "passive virtues"); A. BICKEL, THE SUPREME COURT AND THE IDEAL OF PROGRESS (1970). *See also* E. THOMPSON, THE MAKING OF THE ENGLISH WORKING CLASS ch. 4, especially at 83 (1963); E. THOMPSON, WHIGS AND HUNTERS: THE ORIGINS OF THE BLACK ACT 258-69 (1976) [hereinafter cited as THOMPSON, WHIGS]:

> What was at issue was not property supported by law against no property; it was alternative definitions of property rights; for the landowner, enclosure, for the cottager, common rights, for the forester, the right to take turfs. For as long as it remained possible, the ruled—if they could fund a purse and a lawyer—would actually fight for their rights by means of law. . . . When it ceased to be possible to continue the fight at law, men still felt a sense of legal wrong: the propertied had obtained their power by illegitimate means.

Id. at 261.

209. *See* GOULDNER, *supra* note 157, at 91-92, 422-32; S. WOLIN, POLITICS AND VISION ch. 10 (1960).

210. *See* A. DE TOCQUEVILLE, DEMOCRACY IN AMERICA 245-58 (Mayer & Lerner eds. 1966).

211. *E.g.*, K. LLEWELLYN & E. HOEBEL, THE CHEYENNE WAY: CONFLICT AND CASE LAW IN PRIMITIVE JURISPRUDENCE chs. 10-11 (1941); Fuller, *Human Interaction and the Law*, *supra* note 200.

212. HART & SACKS, *supra* note 71, at 312.

difficulty with this vision is that it is not clear, in terms of Hart and Sacks's general theory, why the Pyramid should represent *legal* order. Elsewhere, Hart and Sacks repeatedly identify law with principles of institutional competence and social norms. Yet, the Great Pyramid seems to stand entirely apart from these considerations. It makes no difference to the vision of the Pyramid that the trouble cases may be eliminated without regard to institutional competence or shared norms. Hart and Sacks fail to take account of the fact that most disputants drop out of the climb up the Pyramid, not because they are convinced justice has been done, but because they are too weak, ignorant, or poor to pursue it. At one point, Hart and Sacks seem to acknowledge, in passing, that this may be the case, but they then go on to identify "the essence of the healthy functioning of any legal order" with the stifling of most conflict at the lower stages of the Pyramid.[213]

Another, more concrete illustration of the tacit response to the tension of law and stability is the case of *Walker v. City of Birmingham*,[214] in which the United States Supreme Court held that Martin Luther King and others could be punished for engaging in a constitutionally protected civil rights demonstration. The demonstration was intended, in significant part, to publicize the demonstrators' claim that certain established social practices prevailing in Birmingham violated the equal protection clause of the United States Constitution. This appeal to the ideal of law was perceived by local officials as posing an immediate threat of violence, and a more long term threat of destroying established social practices. The officials therefore sought and obtained an injunction against demonstration. The demonstrators believed that the injunction violated their rights of free expression under the first amendment, and they therefore proceeded with the demonstration despite the injunction. After being sentenced for contempt for violating the injunction, they urged the United States Supreme Court to reverse because the injunction was unlawful, and their conduct had been protected under the first amendment. This appeal to the ideal of law was perceived by the Supreme Court as posing a threat to established institutional patterns. The demonstrators, the Court noted, had failed to challenge the injunction through established judicial procedures. The Court thus held that, even though the injunction was illegal and the demonstrators' conduct was protected by the substantive law, they could be punished for "ignor[ing] all the procedures of the law and carry[ing] their battle to the streets."[215]

Of course, the Court in *Walker* did not consider that it was compromising law, and perhaps it is more fair to characterize its decision as relying on a conception of legality other than the ideal of law. This second conception of legality might be called the "rule of law." While

213. *Id*.
214. 388 U.S. 307 (1967).
215. *Id*. at 321.

the ideal of law views law as a regime of transcendent social norms, the rule of law views law as a regime of immanent institutional norms. The rule of law portrays law less as prescribing a desirable ordering of affairs in the social world, than as prescribing patterns of institutional propriety.[216] From the perspective of the rule of law, norms are less standards by which actual practices can be criticized than they are standards which inhere in the way things are actually done. Of course, the distinction is a matter of degree. Most discussions of the ideal of law acknowledge that legal norms are rooted in social practices at least to some extent. And from the point of view of the rule of law, social norms are sufficiently independent of the way things are done to make it possible to say on occasion that a particular action has violated the applicable norm. Nevertheless, the distinction is significant. The rule of law tends to portray norms as more closely bound up with the practices they govern than does the ideal of law. Moreover, the rule of law lacks the emphasis of the ideal of law on universality. It views law less as a moral basis for the public life of the entire society, and more as the province of public institutions and officials. While the ideal of law suggests that the primary obligation of officials is to secure justice in society, the rule of law suggests that their primary obligation is to safeguard the integrity of institutions. While the ideal of law emphasizes the active role of the citizen in interpreting and applying the law, the rule of law emphasizes the passive role of the citizen in respecting and acquiescing in the commands of legally constituted authority. The rule of law is a conception of legality far more compatible with stability than the ideal of law.[217]

216. Examples of works dominated by the perspective of the rule of law are A. BICKEL, THE SUPREME COURT AND THE IDEA OF PROGRESS (1970); MONTESQUIEU, THE SPIRIT OF THE LAWS (1748); Bickel, *Watergate and the Legal Order*, 57 COMMENTARY 19 (January 1974); Parsons, *supra* note 196. The contrast between the two points of view is particularly clear in Bickel's work on the Supreme Court, wherein the main theme is that the Warren Court naively concerned itself with the implementation of universal norms in society and betrayed its responsibilities to the canons of institutional propriety. *See* A. BICKEL, THE SUPREME COURT AND THE IDEA OF PROGRESS (1970).

217. This opposition can be resolved on the level of formal theory, but only at the cost of making theory irrelevant to experience. The theoretical reconciliation rests on the argument that the ideal of law can only be implemented in society through a specific institutional structure. *See* A. DICEY, INTRODUCTION TO THE STUDY OF THE LAW OF THE CONSTITUTION (10th ed. 1959). For example, the notion of a right suggests both a substantive entitlement to engage in an activity or to receive a benefit in society, and an institution to enforce the entitlement. Thus, adherents to the rule of law usually argue that by supporting institutions they are supporting corresponding substantive entitlements. There is theoretical force to the argument. The problem occurs when the theorists argue that *existing* institutions accomplish such a reconciliation between substantive and institutional norms. In the first place, the argument ignores that many institutional principles (*e.g.*, finality, standing, default, and prosecutorial discretion) explicitly compromise substantive prescriptions. Second, it ignores the pervasive experience in societies committed to legal ideals of a tension between substantive legal norms and the commands of authoritative institutions. People constantly find that substantive ideals are violated by authoritative institutions and that the ideal of law requires that institutions be defied or transformed.

Opposing notions of legality, similar to what are here called the ideal of law and the rule of law, are sometimes discussed as distinguishing opposing schools of legal thought. Yet, each of the three versions of the Ideology of Advocacy is characterized by the presence of both notions and by a surface ambiguity which conceals the tension between them. The rhetoric of the Ideology generally refers to "law" and "legality" without distinguishing between the ideal of law and the rule of law. Yet, the substance of the discussion often seems to rely on distinct and incompatible frames of reference. Indeed, the basic structure of many discussions of legal ethics involves a tacit transition from the perspective of the ideal of law to that of the rule of law. This transition usually appears as a shift from substantive to procedural considerations.

Positivism focuses on the substantive law as a system of social order. Yet, when the issues of advocacy arise, procedure turns out to be the basic key to the system. Purposivism begins by portraying procedure as an instrument to the attainment of substantive ends, but when the issues of advocacy arise, it finds itself rationalizing the sacrifice of substantive concerns to maintain the integrity of procedural institutions. Ritualism puts procedure in the forefront at the outset, but only as a partner in a marriage of procedure and substance. Yet as the ritualist theory is elaborated, substance is rapidly collapsed into procedure.

In all three versions, procedure is generally associated with stability. Procedural principles such as finality and standing are explicit responses to the impotence of substantive law to check the persistence and proliferation of conflict. In fact, the entire system of judicial procedure, as described and rationalized in the Ideology of Advocacy, may be seen as a response to the need to accomodate law to stability.

The regime of adversary advocacy is designed to sublimate conflict so that the sacrifice of substantive ideals is not acutely felt. Conflict is diverted from its social setting, where resolution is problematical, into a stylized setting designed, like a classical dramatic work, to lead inevitably to some definitive termination. The termination may then seem appropriately final in terms of the formal structure of the artificial setting, rather than in terms of the original social setting of the dispute. Unlike substantive formalism, procedural formalism does not depend entirely on abstract reasoning, but rather it is implemented by a concrete artificial world of sets and role players. Professionals move the disputants into the stylized setting and encourage them to transfer their energies and frustrations from the social world to the world of procedure. As their participation is channeled in this fashion, the procedures absorb their energies and numb their frustration. Thus, at best, the disputants acquiesce in the translation of the dispute into procedural terms and see the decision as legitimate merely because of its formal properties. At worst, the exhaustion and numbing which result from this stylized participation diminish their inclination to press their claims. Procedure enables them to "work out" their claims.[218]

As Lawrence Stone has noted in a discussion of the litigiousness of the Elizabethean aristocracy, the procedures worst designed to produce substantively legal or just results may be best suited to the task of conflict sublimation:

> From the point of view of the state the manifold inadequacies of the legal system had their advantages. So long as there was a remote prospect of ultimate victory, men would turn hopefully to the law as a weapon against their natural enemies. Once launched, the suit would with its complexity and prolixity consume their time, their energies, and their substance for years and years on end. The very deficiencies in the machinery of the law, its great cost, its appalling slowness, its obsession with irrelevant technical details, made it an admirable instrument for the sublimation of the bellicose instincts of a leisured class.[219]

The discontinuity which makes adversary advocacy so inadequate from the point of view of individuality is its principal strength from the point of view of stability. The design of adversary advocacy in terms of stylized aggression well serves the task of conflict sublimation. The client's own ends are reduced to crude pretexts for the standard partisan approach the lawyer takes on behalf of all his clients. The lawyer maneuvers the client into a role defined in terms of a formal, undifferentiated hostility. The client perceives the other party, not in terms of the other's concrete ends, but in terms of the formal, undifferentiated hostility which results from the other lawyer's partisanship. The litigant is discouraged from either considering his own ends or confronting those of the other party. The pre-condition of conflict—the mutual recognition of antagonistic wills—is thus precluded. The artificially stimulated aggression of adversary advocacy is sufficiently tractable to be channeled within the confines of a procedural pattern.

Adversary advocacy does not accomplish miracles. The typical losing party does not leave the trial with the feeling that, although the ends which he brought to the trial have been thwarted, he can still take satisfaction in the fact that he was given a "fair (that is, procedurally correct or elaborate) trial." He is not likely to feel that his day in court was an adequate substitute for the substantive benefit he did not get. Although this consideration is an important objection to the Ritualist claim that procedure is inherently satisfying, it does not substantially undermine the thesis that the regime of procedural justice functions to sublimate conflict. To sublimate conflict, it is not necessary that the

218. *See* Ball, *supra* note 137, at 107; Parsons, *supra* note 196, at 383.

219. L. Stone, The Crisis of the Aristocracy: 1558-1641, at 117-18 (Galaxy ed. 1967); *see also* Parsons, *supra* note 196, at 383.

litigant be satisfied, but merely that his energies and expectations be redirected. The goal of stability may in fact be well served when the litigant is left bewildered and exhausted, even though unhappy. As the analysis of the game analogy suggests, the cynicism often bred by adversary advocacy is far less threatening to stability than the kind of appeal to law made by the petitioners in ***Walker v. Birmingham***.

The contribution of the Ideology of Advocacy to stability does not lie solely in its ability to induce losers to accept their losses, but also in its ability to convince the winners of the legitimacy of their victories. It numbs doubts and anxieties which might lead the winners to re-examine and perhaps even challenge the practices from which they benefit. This effect is particularly important with respect to lawyers, who are among the biggest winners in the legal system. Lawyers tend to be wedded to established institutions and practices by self-interest, but many of them have the security and sophistication which might incline them toward criticism and change. By translating subversive substantive considerations into procedural ones, adversary advocacy dulls such inclinations.[220]

Procedural fetishism has become increasingly explicit in the Ideology of Advocacy. Procedural considerations appear in Positivism as an afterthought. They figure much more prominently in Purposivism, and they are explicitly dominant in Ritualism. This development reflects the growth of procedural fetishism generally in legal thought. As substantive legal doctrine has become increasingly politicized, as barriers once seen as separating substantive doctrine from the other academic disciplines and from social norms have fallen, lawyers have tended increasingly to think of the distinctive content of their discipline in terms of procedure. The claim that law is a specialized discipline, upon which lawyers' professional identity and organization rest, is often expressed in purely procedural terms.[221]

Some of the most important doctrinal developments of recent years are examples of the tendency to obscure conflict-threatening issues by focusing on procedure. The Jesuitical attention to criminal procedure of the Warren Court has diverted consideration away from fundamental doubts about the substantive bases for punishment, and about the character of existing penal institutions.[222] Similarly, attention to procedure in the area of government benefits has taken the place of attempts to

220. *See* Parsons, *supra* note 196; Tushnet, *supra* note 200, at 101; *cf.* Cahn & Cahn, *The War on Poverty: A Civilian Perspective*, 73 YALE L.J. 1317, 1335-36 (1964) (adversary advocacy enables lawyer to represent poor without being "apologetic about his middle class background").

221. *See, e.g.*, Joint Anti-Fascist Refugee Committee v. McGrath, 341 U.S. 123, 179 (1951) (Douglas, J., concurring) ("It is procedure that spells much of the difference between rule by law and rule by whim or caprice."); Freund, *Henry M. Hart, Jr.: In Memoriam*, 82 HARV. L. REV. 1595, 1596 (1969) (Hart viewed basic procedural considerations as a "kind of transcendent natural law, a law above laws, standing as the scientific process does to the mutable body of science itself").

222. *See* Griffiths, *supra* note 3, at 415-16.

confront growing doubts about the justice of the distribution of wealth.[223] Marc Galanter has analyzed a related phenomenon at the level of practice.[224] Efforts to provide legal services to the poor have focused on adjudication at the expense of organization-building, even though the latter promises more substantial benefits to the poor and is less conducive to lawyer-domination.[225]

Although procedural fetishism succeeds to a significant extent in sublimating conflict, it fails to reconcile stability and individuality. The Ideology of Advocacy begins by defending the ideal of law in terms of such values as autonomy, responsibility, and dignity, but ends by rationalizing practices which subvert these values, and hence any ideal of law which might embody them. The sacrifice of these values is a consequence of the effort to serve the pre-eminent goal of stability.[226]

Some level of stability is necessary to the benefits of society, but the cost of serving a goal of stability so shallow and fragile that it is threatened by any overt manifestation of conflict is great. Though conflict can jeopardize autonomy, responsibility, and dignity, some measure of conflict is essential to the development of these qualities. Individuality is a social phenomenon which develops through interaction with others, not merely the spontaneously cooperative interaction on which conservative jurisprudence and social theory focus, but friction-producing interaction

223. *Compare* Michelman, *The Supreme Court, 1968 Term—Foreword: On Protecting the Poor Through the Fourteenth Amendment*, 83 HARV. L. REV. 7 (1969) *with* Goldberg v. Kelly, 397 U.S. 254 (1970); *see also* Arnett v. Kennedy, 416 U.S. 134, 151-53 (1974). *Cf.* Reich, *The New Property*, 73 YALE L.J. 733 (1964). Reich's new property is defined largely in terms of the procedures which protect it. For an example in another area of the attempt to avoid difficult political issues by re-orienting doctrine toward procedural terms, see Monaghan, *First Amendment "Due Process"*, 83 HARV. L. REV. 518 (1970).

224. Galanter, *supra* note 32; Galanter, *The Duty Not to Deliver Legal Services*, 30 MIAMI L. REV. 929 (1976).

225. There are, of course, important qualifications to the argument of this section. First, I do not deny that the rule of law and notions of procedural justice can make, and have made, contributions to individual autonomy, responsibility, and dignity, particularly by restraining the crueler and more arbitrary excesses of state power. *See* THOMPSON, WHIGS, *supra* note 208, at 264-69. Nor do I deny that the Warren Court's procedural reforms were progressive developments toward a more humane and just society. Procedural considerations are not irrelevant to individuality, and they are not simply an ideological facade. Nevertheless, when and to the extent that procedural doctrines obscure substantive consideratons, they obfuscate understanding and inhibit action in a manner which can subvert individuality and justice. Even when procedurally oriented reform is progressive, it can inhibit change which would be more progressive.

Second, the argument that the type of legal thought and experience represented by the ideal of law has an inherent potential for conflict is not intended to suggest that this kind of legality invariably tends to produce conflict, much less that it invariably leads to justice. Obviously, the ideal of law can, and does, serve stability. Its affinity for conflict is a potential one, and the extent to which this potential is activated depends both on the content of the substantive norms and on surrounding social circumstances. The purpose of the present argument is simply to suggest that lawyers, at some level of consciousness, increasingly have perceived this potential as threatening, and that the Ideology of Advocacy has been part of their response to it.

226. *See generally* GOULDNER, *supra* note 157, at 218-24; *but see* FULLER, *supra* note 25.

which can flare into conflict. A society which treats all conflict as a threat sacrifices individual development to conformism and impoverishes both self-expression and social relations.[227] In such a society, where officially sanctioned patterns of behavior are perceived as coercively imposed, they engender cynicism and frustration. Where they are spontaneously adopted, they narrow the individual's perception of the world and of his own possibilities.

Remarks about the dangers of conformism for individuality have been a commonplace in American thought for a long time, though they rarely acknowledged the extent to which individuality entails conflict. Legal thought has accorded a high position to the goal of individuality, but it has accorded an even higher one to the goal of suppressing conflict. Lawyers have created a role for themselves which requires that, when individuality is most at stake—that is, when it involves conflict—they implement its systematic suppression in the interests of stability. If legal thought were to take seriously such values as autonomy, responsibility, and dignity, it would be led to ask whether, contrary to the common assumption expressed by Hart and Sacks,[228] the health of a legal system might depend on its willingness to tolerate conflict, even the persistent, proliferating conflict which leaves open wounds on the body politic. To entertain such a notion would be to take a long step beyond the Ideology of Advocacy.

The very least that can be said in favor of such consideration is that it might lead to the elimination of a great amount of the disorder which is artificially generated by the Ideology of Advocacy. The present system encourages the prosecution of claims which would not be pursued by people who were forced to seriously confront their own and society's values. It also causes the prosecution of sincere claims by means, such as delay and procedural fencing, which would not be used if the litigants were forced to make their own choices as to whether particular procedural decisions were justified in the light of the substantive ends at stake.

However, the elimination of this type of disorder will not be enough to justify abandoning the Ideology of Advocacy. The most important claim to be made against the system of procedural justice is that it frustrates the resolution of conflict in terms that would preserve the ideals of substantive justice. It teaches litigants to regard substantive norms as strategic props in a contest defined by procedure. The litigant ceases to take seriously either his own claim or that of his opponent. There is thus no possibility that he will experience either a settlement or an authoritative decision as a reconciliation of his claim either with that of the other party or with a higher norm. A favorable termination is a lucky coinci-

227. *See generally* D. RIESMAN, THE LONELY CROWD (1950) [hereinafter cited as RIESMAN].
228. HART & SACKS, *supra* note 71.

dence; an unfavorable one is a "doom pronounced *ab extra*."[229]

Genuine reconciliation would be possible only through the growth or development of one or both of the parties. In a setting where a party was conscious of his responsibility to press his claims in terms of substantive justice, he would be open to growth and development. It would always be possible that he might be led, through interaction with the other, to take a different view of his original claim. Procedural justice closes the possibilities of growth and development by forcing litigants into roles of stylized aggression.

The case against adversary advocacy rests in substantial part on the conviction that the pursuit of conflict is often better than its sublimation, that conflict can unleash creative energies, that it can promote understanding and personal growth, and that it can even lead to the sharing of values needed for its just resolution.[230] It can be hoped that the struggle for substantive justice will produce cumulative benefits which will some day make the resolution of conflict in terms of shared norms of justice a matter of routine. However, at present, newly unleased conflict is bound to prove tenacious. Thus, the rejection of procedural justice would entail the belief that enhanced conflict itself would better vindicate the values of autonomy, responsibility, and dignity than the anesthetized acquiescence induced by the regime of the Ideology of Advocacy.

If the notion of stability as the pre-eminent social goal were abandoned, it would not seem necessary to sacrifice the ideal of law to the rule of law. As E.P. Thompson writes, "law has not only been imposed upon men from above: it has also been a medium within which other social conflicts have been fought out."[231] Law can be valued, not as a mechanism of dispute resolution, but as an "arena of conflict."[232] Freed from the monopoly of the legal profession, law might provide a mode of public discourse and a framework for political action. Law conceived as a set of transcendent and universal public norms expresses the values of individuality. This is not to say that a conception of law or even a set of legal institutions can guarantee autonomy, responsibility, and dignity. But law

229. HEGEL, *supra* note 201, at 145.

230. The notion that conflict is essential to the development of both individuality and genuinely shared social values is central to the thoughts of Hegel, Mill, and some versions of psychoanalysis. *See, e.g.*, E. ERIKSON, IDENTITY: YOUTH AND CRISIS (1968) (on personal growth and creativity in the identity crisis); G. HEGEL, THE PHENOMENOLOGY OF MIND 228-240 (Torchbook ed. 1967) (on the attainment of freedom through the master/slave relation); H. MARCUSE, EROS AND CIVILIZATION: A PHILOSOPHICAL INQUIRY INTO FREUD 87-88 (Vintage ed. 1961) (on the development of individuality through Oedipal conflict); J. MILL, UTILITARIANISM, LIBERTY, AND REPRESENTATIVE GOVERNMENT 102-152 (Everyman ed. 1950) (on the attainment of, *inter alia*, moral truth through differences of opinion). For a recent defense of conflict and a critique of its sublimation in various areas of social policy and practice, see R. SENNETT, THE USES OF DISORDER (1970). *See also* the critical account of the sublimation of politics in modern social theory in S. WOLIN, POLITICS AND VISION ch. 10 (1960).

231. THOMPSON, WHIGS, *supra* note 208, at 267.

232. *Id.* at 264.

can inspire and shape efforts which may advance these values.[233] The gaps and indeterminacy of the law are not obstacles to this effort. They make room for creative effort and struggle. Nevertheless, it would remain possible that if conflict should lead to resolution, to genuinely shared values, then the gaps could be filled and indeterminancy lessened.

Incarcerated in the Birmingham jail for violating the injunction ultimately upheld in *Walker*, Martin Luther King reflected on the choice of the liberal middle class between stability and conflict, the ideal of law and the rule of law, and wondered whether "the Negro's great stumbling block in the drive toward freedom is . . . the white moderate who is more devoted to 'order' than to justice, who prefers a negative peace which is the absence of tension to a positive peace which is the presence of justice."[234]

VI. Conclusion: Non-Professional Advocacy

> *Is the inside-dopester an enemy, with his sympathetic tolerance, but veiled lack of interest, and his inability to understand savage emotions? Are they enemies, those friends who stand by, not to block but to be amused, to understand and pardon everything? An autonomous person of today must work constantly to avoid shadowy entanglements with this top level of other-direction—so difficult to break with because its demands appear so reasonable, even trivial.*
>
> David Riesman[235]

Showing that the Ideology of Advocacy is incoherent in theory and destructive in practice is not the same thing as showing that it should be abandoned. It remains to be shown that there is a more satisfactory alternative. There is an alternative implicit in the critique of the Ideology of Advocacy. The alternative can be called "non-professional advocacy." Although this essay cannot show conclusively that non-professional advocacy would prove more satisfactory, it can suggest the issues involved in the decision whether or not to adopt it. The choice between the Ideology of Advocacy and non-professional advocacy rests on one's view of the relative priorities of individuality and stability, and of the prospects

233. *See* Trubek, *Complexity and Contradiction in the Legal Order: Balbus and the Challenge of Critical Social Thought About Law*, 11 Law & Soc. Rev. 529, 545-69 (1977) [hereinafter cited as Trubek]. On the value of differentiated modes of discourse and interaction to individuality and to effective political action, see R. Sennett, The Fall of Public Man (1977).

The argument here is in some respects analogous to Theodore Lowi's critique of "pluralism." T. Lowi, The End of Liberalism: Ideology, Policy, and the Crisis of Public Authority (1969). Lowi urges the abandonment of interest group pluralism, a legislative version of procedural justice in favor of the ideal of law, although because of his somewhat naive attitude toward formalism, he does not fully acknowledge the issue of conflict.

234. King, *A Letter From Birmingham City Jail* in Civil Disobedience: Theory and Practice 79 (Bedau ed. 1969).

235. Riesman, *supra* note 227, at 256-57.

of reconciling the tension between them.[236]

Non-professional advocacy is difficult to describe with precision, but it is not at all mysterious. On the contrary, it relies on a style of thought and conduct with which everyone has at least some familiarity. The foundation principle of non-professional advocacy is that the problems of advocacy be treated as a matter of *personal* ethics. As the notion is generally understood, personal ethics presupposes two ideas diametrically opposed to the foundation principles of the Ideology of Advocacy. First, personal ethics apply to people merely by virtue of the fact that they are human individuals. The obligations involved may depend on particular circumstances or personalities, but they do not follow from social role or station. Personal ethics are at once more particular and more general than professional ethics. On the one hand, they require that every moral decision be made by the individual himself; no institution can define his obligations in advance. On the other hand, the individual may be called upon to answer for his decisions by any other individual who is affected by them. No specialized group has a monopoly which disqualifies outsiders from criticizing the behavior of its members. Second, personal ethics require that individuals take responsibility for the consequences of their decisions. They cannot defer to institutions with autonomous ethical momentum.

236. The principal thrust of the present argument is that adversary advocacy is incompatible with the norms of individuality to which it appeals. An alternative critique of the Ideology of Advocacy could be constructed on the basis of norms of community. *See* Griffiths, *supra* note 3. Such a critique would not necessarily be inconsistent with the present argument.

Individuality and community are best viewed, not as opposing norms, but rather as interdependent aspects of what Unger calls the Paradox of Sociability. UNGER, *supra* note 25, at 215-17. The notion of individuality depends on the norms of community because individuality is a social phenomenon. Because an individual's sense of self depends on recognition by others, individuality can flourish only in a community committed to the autonomy, responsibility, and dignity of each of its members. At the same time, the notion of community depends on the norms of individuality because it implies voluntary commitment to the values which are the basis of the community, and voluntary acceptance of membership in the community. For the members to exercise the voluntary choice necessary to form a genuine community, their capacities as individuals must be developed.

Thus, the notion of individuality discussed here implies a complementary rather than an antagonistic notion of community. For instance, I will suggest below that a style of advocacy which seriously respected individuality would be more likely to promote mutuality and altrusim in the judicial process than partisan advocacy. This is because people actually do hold communitarian values which partisan advocacy represses. To the extent that individuals do hold communitarian values, a style of advocacy which respected the litigant's own values and permitted him to act on them would promote both individuality and community. Moreover, even where they do not hold such values, a style of advocacy which respected the individual's capacity for personal growth would make possible the development of such values.

It may be objected that the notion of individuality discussed here is not the same one assumed by the Ideology of Advocacy. The objection is possible because the writing on partisan advocacy contains no analysis of the norms of individuality which it constantly invokes. But to be persuasive, the objection would have to elaborate an alternative notion of individuality which would be a plausible basis for an ethical or legal theory, and which would be consistent with the prescriptions of the Ideology of Advocacy. It seems unlikely that this can be done. *See generally* UNGER, *supra* note 25, at 211.

Personal ethics involve both a concern for one's own integrity and respect for the concrete individuality of others.[237] The non-professional advocate presents himself to a prospective client as someone with special talents and knowledge, but also with personal ends to which he is strongly committed. The client should expect someone generally disposed to help him advance his ends, but also prepared to oppose him when the ends of advocate and client conflict. If the two sets of ends coincide, then a strong alliance on behalf of these ends is possible. If the two sets of ends are irreconcilably opposed, then no relationship will be possible. It is essential that neither advocate nor client feel strong pressure to accept the other. Between the extremes of an alliance on behalf of entirely shared ends and a situation in which no relationship is possible, there is a broad category where one party will be able to win over the other to his position of where the parties will work out a compromise.

Non-professional advocacy does not preclude conflict. Conflict is possible both inside and outside of the relationship. Where their ends are opposed, the advocate may engage in conflict with the client (although

237. The concern for both one's own integrity and the integrity of others makes personal ethics somewhat problematical. It raises difficult questions in situations where one's own ends and the ends of others conflict. As I will suggest below, one of the ways in which personal ethics deal with such situations is by referring to social norms and institutions such as those associated with law. Conceived in this way, personal ethics differ from two other alternatives to professional ethics: radical individualist ethics and radical politicization.

Radical individualist ethics hold that moral decisions should be a matter of entirely autonomous, independent, and self-conscious choice by the individual decision-maker. *See, e.g.*, SARTRE, *supra* note 61; J. SARTRE, SAINT GENET (Frenchtman trans. 1963). From this point of view, social norms and institutions, and even the concrete ends of other people, are at best irrelevant and at worst oppressive constraints on the moral freedom of the individual. The radical individualist approach is unsatisfactory because it fails to take adequate account of the social dimension of individuality. Because the individual's sense of self depends on recognition by others, individuality depends on social relations. To a significant extent, individuality can only be expressed in terms which are meaningful to others. A person whose ethical choices were entirely independent of social norms and the ends of others could not have a coherent moral personality. See R. JACOBY, SOCIAL AMNESIA: A CRITIQUE OF CONFORMIST PSYCHOLOGY FROM ADLER TO LAING chs. 3, 5, 7, (1965) [hereinafter cited as JACOBY]; UNGER, *supra* note 25, at 215-22.

The approach of radical politicization holds that moral decisions should be entirely instrumental to the establishment of a new social order. *See generally* Lukacs, *Legality and Illegality*, in HISTORY AND CLASS CONSCIOUSNESS (Livingstone trans. 1971). From this point of view, existing social norms and institutions and the concrete ends of individuals are merely reflections of the injustice and repressiveness of the existing order. Moral decision on the basis of personal ethics must await the establishment of the new order. This view suffers from the defects of moralities of the long run. *See* text accompanying notes 123-27 *supra*. It treats existing norms, institutions, and personal ends as means to future ones, and hence collapses process into result. The problems of justice and freedom must be confronted in the course of social change; they cannot be deferred to an idealized future order. Moreover, the radical politicization approach ignores the extent to which the ideals for which it strives are themselves rooted in existing social norms and institutions and the concrete present concerns of individuals. To a significant extent, the realization of these ideals may require the resolution of problems and contradictions within the existing order. In relying solely on a vague idealized negation of the existing order, radical politicization begs the questions presented by these problems and contradictions. *See* UNGER, *supra* note 25, at 181-89, 250-52; Trubek, *supra* note 233.

obviously any large measure of conflict will end the relationship). Where their ends are shared, advocate and client may join together to engage outsiders in conflict. On the other hand, non-professional advocacy does not presuppose conflict any more than it presupposes the stylized aggression of the Ideology of Advocacy. The advocate may lead the client to modify or abandon a collision course so as to make voluntary, informal resolution possible. Indeed, one of the most important effects of non-professional advoacy should be to increase the client's concern for the impact of his conduct on others, and to enlarge the minimal role which norms such as reciprocity and community now play in attorney-client decisions.

If the major foundation principle of non-professional advocacy is that advocacy be deemed a matter of personal ethics, the major principle of conduct is this: advocate and client must each justify himself to the other. This justification need not embrace the person's entire life, but merely those aspects of it which bear on the dispute. Each must justify the goals he would pursue and the way he would pursue them. In this manner, the advocate-client relation is reconstructed in each instance by the participants themselves. It is not set in advance by formal roles. Such relationships will sometimes arise spontaneously, but they will often arise only after patient, step-by-step efforts. Advocate and client may become friends, not in Fried's sense, but in the more familiar sense of an intimacy made possible by shared ends and experience. Yet, friendship is not necessary to the relationship. The basic requirement is that each have respect for the other as a concrete individual. In addition, some sharing of ends will be necessary, but this sharing need not approach a complete coincidence of ends.

Trust is an important value in non-professional advocacy.[238] But it is not a formal, definitional property of the advocate-client relation. It is a quality which the parties must create or fail to create in each instance. When confidentiality may be important to the client, advocate and client should arrive at some understanding at the outset concerning this issue. The scope of confidentiality need not be defined for the entire relation at the outset. It can be defined in stages as lawyer and client gain greater understanding of each other. The client's claim to assurances of confidentiality is a strong one, and once assurances have been made, his claim that

238. The goal of trust does not arise, as Freedman and Noonan suggest, from the requirements of the legal system. Nonprofessional advocacy cannot justify confidentiality as protecting the client's capacity to invoke formal procedural rights. Nor can it accept the premise that confidentiality will enhance the capacity of the legal system to produce substantively desirable results. However, as Fried comes close to suggesting, the value of trust is implicated in any situation in which a dependent person seeks the help of another. The priority of confidentiality does not arise from the specifically legal character of the client's need, but simply from the facts that he has a need, and that he seeks the advocate's help. Legal norms will probably weigh against confidentiality more often than they will support it.

they be honored is much stronger still. Yet, these claims must be viewed in the context of other, potentially conflicting values. They must be considered in the context of the specific ends which the client seeks to further. The claim of a client who seeks legal services to exploit or oppress another cannot have the same priority as the claim of one who seeks to escape exploitation and oppression. This approach to the problem of confidentiality means that the client must take a risk in seeking an advocate, and that the advocate-client relation will sometimes end in betrayal.[239] This element of risk is inherent in any effort by lawyer and client to come to terms with each other as concrete individuals. It is in part because of this risk that trust, when it is created, can be a vital and concrete psychological reality rather than an empty, formal claim.

The non-professional relation is quite different from the "helping" or "accepting" lawyer-client relation described by recent writing which draws on the concepts and jargon of existentialist psychotherapy.[240] This writing is valuable because it recognizes that the task of understanding the client's ends is a difficult one, and that the client's consciousness of his own ends is shaped in the lawyer-client relation. It also acknowledges, at least partially, that the lawyer's posture of detachment can threaten, rather than safeguard, the client's autonomy. Yet, the relation of relatively intimate, sympathetic, and personal involvement prescribed by the psychotherapists is unsatisfactory. Although these writers purport to be concerned with respecting the client's concrete individuality, the style of practice they propose will often be more of a threat to it than traditional advocacy. As they describe him, the lawyer claims to be dedicated to his client's concrete individuality, but he does not present *himself* to the client as a concrete individual. Individuals have ends about which they care deeply. Even the most tolerant individual cannot view everyone's ends with the same undifferentiated sympathy. Yet, the psychotherapists seem to contemplate that the same homogeneous acceptance be dispensed

239. Since this statement is likely to outrage the pious professional more than any other, two points should be made to put it in perspective. First, even hard-line professional defenses of confidentiality contemplate some situations in which the lawyer will betray his client. ABA CODE OF PROFESSIONAL RESPONSIBILITY, DR 4-101(C)(3) (when client intends to commit crime); *id*. at DR 4-101(C)(4) (when client fails to pay fee). Second, most professional defenses of confidentiality rest on a moral formalism and absolutism which most people, including even most lawyers, reject in other areas of moral decision. The contradiction is strikingly evident in Freedman's work. *See* M. FREEDMAN, LAWYERS' ETHICS IN AN ADVERSARY SYSTEM (1975). Freedman fully appreciates the defects of formalist, absolutist moralities when it suits his purposes. He rails at length against "legalist-anti-utilitarian" moral views, which he associates with Kant, in arguing against people like Chief Justice Burger who assert that lawyers should never participate in the deception of the trier. *Id*. at 46-47. Yet, Freedman's own defense of confidentiality is quintessentially legalistic, anti-utilitarian, and Kantian in precisely the sense he rejects in Burger's argument. *See id*. at 1-5.

240. Goodpaster, *The Human Arts of Lawyering: Interviewing and Counseling*, 27 J. LEGAL EDUC. 5 (1975); Redmount, *Humanistic Law Through Legal Counseling*, 2 CONN. L. REV. 98 (1969); *see also* Shaffer, *Christian Theories of Professional Responsibility*, 48 S. CAL. L. REV. 721 (1975). For a critique of the psychological literature on which these articles draw, see JACOBY, *supra* note 237, at chs. 2-3.

indiscriminately to the exploiters and the exploited, the creative and the destructive, the smug and the despairing. No individuality of any depth could be expressed through such an attitude.

A relation defined in advance in terms of acceptance is more likely to be a relation of bureaucratic impersonality than one of respect and understanding.[241] It is doubtful that either lawyer or client would achieve a heightened understanding of the client's ends in a relation of this kind. The fact that the lawyer withholds or denies his private ends, while he seeks to ascertain his client's, undermines the credibility of his claim of loyalty to the client. The lawyer's posture of selflessness often will seem either false and hypocritical, or a defensive retreat to the refuge of role. In either event, the client will be led, as Goffman suggests, to retreat himself rather than, as the psychotherapists predict, to open himself to understanding by the lawyer. Moreover, the psychotherapists ignore that tension and even conflict is often essential to the growth of both self-consciousness and mutual understanding. The flaccid, undifferentiated sympathy so extravagantly dispensed by the psychotherapists may discourage precisely the kind of doubt, questioning, and reflection which would best enhance the client's understanding of his own ends. Non-professional advocacy must recognize that a relation of respect and understanding between autonomous individuals can rarely be an entirely accepting relation.[242] Respect and understanding will often depend more on resistance than on acceptance.

One of the most important questions raised by non-professional advocacy concerns the bases for the establishment of a relationship in the absence of a coincidence of ends. The question is not as difficult as it initially appears. In the first place, in many situations in which ends are not shared, there will not be opposition, but merely indifference. In these situations, there will be a large range of courses of action on which the parties will be able to agree. In the second place, even in those situations in which ends are actually opposed, there are a variety of quite familiar bases for compromise. These are the formal values of liberal theory, such as reciprocity, promise keeping, the ideal of law, and the ideal of representative government. These values do not provide a precise, objective, neutral mechanism for the resolution of differing ends. Moreover, they can never be dispositive by themselves. However, as values, they will often provide a substantial basis for an alliance between people with

241. *Cf.* RIESMAN, *supra* note 227, at 307-325 (on "false personalization").

242. Although the advocate-client relation will rarely assume the intimacy of friendship, Nietzsche's remarks about friendship are pertinent to it:

> If one wants to have a friend one must also want to wage war for him: and to wage war, one must be *capable* of being an enemy.
>
> In a friend one should still honor the enemy. Can you go close to your friend without going over to him?
>
> In a friend one should have one's best enemy. You should be closest to him with your heart when you resist him.

NIETZSCHE, *supra* note 175, at 168.

differing concrete ends. Consider, for instance, the ideal of law. The ideal of law has taken a battering in recent years, but it is still alive. We do not always know what the law says, and we sometimes feel that what it says is unjust. But there are many situations in which we do know what the law says and have no reason to think it unjust. At least in these situations, many people still feel that the ideal of law does have independent moral authority, that it can still provide a reason for doing something even when it conflicts with many more concrete ends. Thus, where the lawyer is convinced that the claim against his client is unsupported by law, or that his client's claim against another is supported by law, the ideal of law will often provide a basis for association even in the absence of a sharing of more specific, concrete ends.

Although non-professional advocacy rejects the determinative role of procedural considerations in the Ideology of Advocacy, it does not ignore procedural values entirely. The non-professional advocate recognizes that the *way* in which a dispute is settled or a decision made can be a matter of importance. In particular, he recognizes the strong value of assuring the client an opportunity to attempt to explain or justify himself publicly. Moreover, the non-professional advocate may encounter situations in which he feels that he cannot effectively assess his client's position, and thinks that a judge or jury would be in a much better position to do so after an adversary hearing.

Such procedural considerations provide a further basis for accommodation between parties with opposing ends. The non-professional advocate should take them very seriously. He does not, however, regard them in the same manner as the Ideology of Advocacy does. First, he will never consider them independently of the substantive legal and moral values involved. Unlike Freedman and Noonan, the non-professional advocate cannot answer any of the "three hardest questions" without knowing the nature of the result to which his decision is likely to lead. Second, the non-professional advocate considers procedural considerations as they arise in each case. He refuses to assume that such considerations are necessarily present in every case, or that when present they will invariably be advanced by any particular mode of conducting the case. The value of enabling the client to explain and justify himself in public is implicated only when the client sincerely wants to explain or justify himself and proposes to do so. The utility of adversary advocacy in facilitating informed decisionmaking is relevant only when there is some reason to believe that the truth is not clear, and that the judge will be in a better position to decide after a trial than the advocate is now. Neither of these procedural considerations can ever justify attempts to exclude probative evidence, to discredit testimony which is not misleading, or to engage in any of the routine procedural tactics designed to obfuscate rather than clarify the issues. There may be other considerations which would justify such actions, but they must be identified and considered in each case along with the competing considerations which favor the exposure of truth.

So far in this essay, the terms procedural justice and procedural values have been used to refer to norms associated specifically with the judicial process. The terms can also be used to refer to a more general notion which is also relevant to non-professional advocacy. This is the notion of a legitimacy or fairness arising from equality of access and participation in the society as a whole. Where there is substantial inequality and the lawyer can assist the relatively powerless to a greater measure of access and participation, this general notion of procedural justice will often provide a basis for advocate-client relationships in the absence of shared substantive values. The general notion of procedural justice will have a particularly strong claim on the advocate where his prospective client has little or no prospect of finding another advocate. In such situations, given the drastic inequality of power between lawyer and client, it will be unusually difficult to work out a genuinely voluntary relationship, and there is a great danger that the lawyer's insistence on his substantive ends may force the client to compromise his own in order to secure some measure of access and participation. For this reason, many who reject the determinative role of the specific notion of procedural justice contend that the general notion should be the exclusive basis of the advocate-client relationship, at least where the client is among the relatively powerless. From this line of thought, a modified version of the Ideology of Advocacy has emerged in the field of public interest law.[243]

Yet, non-professional advocacy cannot regard general procedural considerations as exclusively determinative of the advocate's ethical obligations even within the area of representation of the powerless. The importance of substantive considerations is most apparent in situations where the oppressed client proposes a course of action which will injure others who are equally powerless. In such situations, the public interest lawyer's appeal to procedural justice as a basis for representation is self-contradictory. He first commits himself to his client on the basis of his belief that institutional processes do not operate fairly, and then rationalizes the harm he does to others by asserting that institutional processes should be relied upon to protect their interests. Moreover, even where the client's course of action does not implicate the interests of other oppressed people, the interests of the client's own autonomy, responsibility, and dignity will sometimes require that the advocate insist on his own substantive ends.[244]

243. *See* Comment, *The New Public Interest Lawyers*, *supra* note 7, at 1110-37.

244. Although public interest lawyers are generally more sophisticated than conventional lawyers about client autonomy, they tend to commit the error of the Ideology of Advocacy in assuming that the lawyer's detachment from the client is the best guarantee of this autonomy. Thus, public interest lawyers warn their colleagues not to become politically involved with their clients. *Id.* at 1124 (citing to the California Rural Legal Assistance guidelines). They exhort lawyers to leave their "middle-class values" at home and to submit

Thus, non-professional advocacy rejects the foundation principles of professionalism and procedural justice entirely. Its response to the principles of conduct of the Ideology of Advocacy is more complex. The most important objections to the Ideology of Advocacy are addressed not to either of the principles individually, but to the stylized aggression which results from their combination. Non-professional advocacy rejects the notion that the advocate-client relation must invariably be characterized by both partisanship and neutrality, but it does not rule out the possibility that either principle might sometimes be relevant. There may be situations in which the non-professional advocate will find it appropriate to present to a tribunal a claim to which he is not willing to commit himself personally. And there may be situations in which he will find it appropriate to present a claim aggressively even to the point of engaging in obfuscation or deception. Yet, from the point of view of non-professional advocacy the two principles appear, not complementary, but antagonistic. Where the advocate is not committed to the cause of the client, aggressive methods will almost always seem improper. The non-professional advocate is likely to regard a strong commitment to a claim as a necessary condition to the use of such methods.

To a significant extent, non-professional advocacy avoids the critical problems of the three versions of the Ideology of Advocacy. The critical problems of Positivism are, first, that the advocate's conduct generates disorder throughout the legal system and the society because of the

to their clients' decisions and values. *See* Cahn & Cahn, *supra* note 72. They insist that for the lawyer to introduce his own substantive ends with any force into the relationship would be elitist or paternalistic. These views are fundamentally mistaken.

In the first place, the attitudes expressed toward "middle-class values" are inconsistent. Although the public interest theorists rarely specify these values, they often appear to have in mind conventional views on topics such as sex, honesty, and private property. Yet, the value of procedural justice is as middle class as any other value. *See* C. MACPHERSON, THE POLITICAL THEORY OF POSSESSIVE INDIVIDUALISM 186 (1962). Moreover, the attitude of diffidence toward one's own values, and of reluctance toward personal commitment, is also distinctively middle class. *See generally* RIESMAN, *supra* note 227, at chs. 5, 9. The public interest proponents do not hesitate to insist that this middle-class value and this middle-class attitude be incorporated into the advocate's role. They do not hesitate because they do not see this value and this attitude as impositions on the client. But, as this essay has tried to show, the lawyer's procedural values and his attitude of detachment do affect the way the client sees his situation, and thus can limit his practical options and subvert his autonomy.

In the second place, the public interest proponents fail to see that, far from guarding against elitism, their insistence on the lawyer's independence reflects an elitism of its own. The public interest lawyer assumes that the client should remain mired in the limitations of self-interest or class-interest while he himself is struggling to reach a higher moral plane which transcends egoistic and class orientations. *Cf.* F. NIETZSCHE, *Twilight of the Idols*, in THE PORTABLE NIETZSCHE 523 (Kaufmann ed. 1954) (arguing that the detached person is more exploitative than the political manipulator: "Perhaps he even wants a worse advantage: to feel superior to other human beings, to be able to look down on them, and no longer to mistake himself for one of them.").

In the actual practice of public interest law, the principle of procedural justice may be less destructive than it could be because it is frequently ignored. One suspects that public interest lawyers allow substantive considerations to enter into their practical decisions much more than they acknowledge in their theoretical discussions.

problems of enforcement and access; and second, that the advocate usurps the client's autonomy by redefining his situation in terms of procedural justice and forcing him to adopt the mask of the "bad man." Non-professional advocacy promises to mitigate, and perhaps even to resolve, the difficulties of enforcement and access. It mitigates the problem of enforcement by discouraging litigants from pressing insincere claims, and from pursuing sincere claims through the exploitation of obfuscatory and dilatory procedural devices. It mitigates the problem of access by encouraging the lawyer to consider concrete substantive and distributional norms in deciding where to commit his services. The effectiveness of non-professional advocacy in these respects depends in large part on the emergence of genuinely shared norms of fairness. At the least, non-professional advocacy makes possible the development of such norms and their incorporation within the legal system.

Second, the non-professional advocate can give his client advice which will enhance, rather than subvert, the client's autonomy. The non-professional advocate does not deny himself access to his client's ends. When there is sympathy and a sharing of values between lawyer and client, the lawyer's ability to consult his own ends, far from creating a risk of oppression, makes possible greater understanding of the client's position. Even when there is no sympathy, the non-professional advocate has an advantage. For he can engage his client in conflict; and conflict, even when unresolved, can lead to a greater depth of understanding between the participants than the stylized tolerance of the professional advocacy relation. Moreover, the non-professional advocate is less likely to dominate his client because he presents himself as an ordinary individual rather than as a manifestation of disembodied expertise. Thus, the client is aware of the contingency of the lawyer's definition of the situation. He does not see the lawyer as a component in a system of autonomous procedural institutions. He need not forget either that there is a broad range of choices open to him or that the actions which the lawyer takes on his behalf represent choices he (the client) has made and for which he is responsible.

The critical problems of Purposivism are, first, that the lawyer is a prisoner of various specialized perspectives which prevent him from seeing where the interests with which he is immediately concerned connect or conflict with other interests; and second, that the lawyer undermines the moral authority of social norms by encouraging the client to regard them as facts and to treat them instrumentally. Non-professional advocacy could avoid both problems. First, the non-professional advocate does not take any artificially limited view of his client's situation. He brings the full range of his understanding to bear on the issues. Second, the non-professional advocate represents, and puts forth, social values to the client to the extent that he (the advocate) himself holds these values. He may not require that his client adhere to them, but he will at least make the client aware of these values *as* values, not facts. Where social values are genuinely shared, and the client has some intuition of them, the lawyer's role will strengthen rather than undermine the client's commitment.

The critical problems of Ritualism are, first, that it celebrates a ceremony of individual dignity which contradicts the litigant's own experience of the trial as oppressive and manipulative; and second, that it ignores the client's fundamental concerns about the practical consequences of formal proceedings on his life. Non-professional advocacy eschews role playing and procedural formalism. It discourages the client's passive reliance on the lawyer, and encourages the client to take an active role in the conduct of his case. The non-professional advocate does not regard any particular procedures as intrinsically valuable, and he does not tend to push his client into any particular *mise-en-scène*. Moreover, non-professional advocacy insists on the significance of outcomes. It refuses to assess procedural options independently of the outcomes they produce.

Thus, non-professional advocacy has the critical virtue of preserving continuity of moral experience in the judicial process. The process still involves certain patterns of change. The formality of interaction increases as the dispute progresses. Certain procedural values may play a more important role in the later stages of the dispute. Yet, the basic terms of the dispute remain the ends of the individuals involved. The disputants need not lose sight of these ends or of the significance of their actions in relation to them.

Although non-professional advocacy could greatly alleviate the problems of adversary advocacy, it could not solve them alone. The problem of discontinuity stems from the specialization of the legal system. The ethical orientation of the Ideology of Advocacy is one of the most important aspects of this specialization, but it is not the only aspect. The prevailing patterns of the regulation of law practice, the practices of the courts, and the style and substance of legal rules and doctrine all promote specialization. All contribute to the alienation of the citizen from the law and to the weakening of his capacity for autonomous participation in the legal system and in society. The resolution of the problems which underlie adversary advocacy would require, in addition to a change in the attitude and style of practice by lawyers, a change in the structure of the legal system. The principles which support non-professional advocacy also support institutional reforms which would break down the professional monopoly over advocacy and other legal tasks, restructure courts and political institutions to enhance the ability of laymen to participate actively, and make legal rules and doctrine more accessible to ordinary citizens.[245]

245. A variety of such de-professionalizing reforms have been considered. Some focus

Yet, it seems unlikely that reform will ever completely abolish the problem of discontinuity. Ideally, everyone should be his own advocate, but this ideal does not seem capable of realization. The very existence of the occupation of the advocate pre-supposes some measure of alienation from law. Unlike the professional, the non-professional advocate can reduce, rather than aggravate, this alienation. Yet, except where advocate and client can develop a relation of genuine understanding and fraternity, he will not eliminate it. Except where the relation is based on shared substantive ends and experience, the client's dependence on the advocate will compromise his autonomy. It is important to recognize that, like the

---

on breaking down the professional monopoly over advocacy by: (1) lowering or eliminating the licensing requirements for law practice generally or for specific legal tasks (*see* Ehrlich & Schwartz, *Reducing the Costs of Legal Services: Possible Approaches by the Federal Government*, in KAUFFMAN, *supra* note 24, at 583-87 [hereinafter cited as Ehrlich & Schwartz]); (2) training non-lawyers to serve as advocates (*see* Lufler, Trubek, & Greenberg, *Meeting Legal Needs Without Lawyers—An Experimental Program in Advocacy Training*, (Center for Public Representation, Madison, Wis. 1977) [hereinafter cited as *Meeting Legal Needs*]; Wexler, *Practicing Law for Poor People*, 79 YALE L.J. 1049, 1055-59 (1970) [hereinafter cited as Wexler]); (3) giving non-lawyers authority to regulate the legal profession, for example, non-lawyers on disciplinary boards, legislatively promulgated ethical codes (*see* KAUFFMAN, *supra* note 24, at 522-23); and (4) reforming legal education to eliminate the emphasis on indoctrination in professional ideologies (*cf*. Stone, *supra* note 71).

Other possible reforms focus on decreasing dependence on legal services by institutional changes such as: (1) increasing lay instruction about law on both academic and practical (i.e., "do-it-yourself") levels (*see The Unauthorized Practice of Law and Pro Se Divorce: An Empirical Analysis*, 86 YALE L.J. 104 (1976) (student project); *see also* Wexler, *supra* this note); (2) requiring judges and court personnel to be more accomodating to *pro se* representation (*see* Note, *The Persecution and Intimidation of the Low-Income Litigant as Performed by the Small Claims Court in California*, 21 STAN. L. REV. 1657, 1663-75 (1969) [hereinafter cited as Note, *Persecution and Intimidation*]; (3) allowing represented litigants to participate actively with their lawyers in conducting their cases, for example, by examining witnesses or addressing the trier (*but see* Annot., 67 A.L.R.2d 1102 § 3 (1959); Annot., 77 A.L.R.2d 1233 § 4 (1961)); (4) instituting new procedures to facilitate *pro se* representation or establishing informal forums designed specifically for *pro se* assertion of claims (*see* Danzig & Lowy, *Everyday Disputes and Mediation in the United States: A Reply to Professor Felstiner*, 9 LAW & SOC. REV. 675 (1975); Note, *Persecution and Intimidation*, *supra* this note); and (5) re-orienting efforts to provide legal services to the poor away from litigation and toward organizing people to pursue their claims in the political process (*see generally* Galanter, *supra* note 32).

Still other possible reforms focus on decreasing the dependence on legal services by changes in rules and doctrine: (1) clarifying and simplifying the organization and language of legal rules and doctrine (*see* Bloomfield, *William Sampson and the Codification Movement*, in AMERICAN LAWYERS IN A CHANGING SOCIETY: 1776-1876 ch. 3 (1976); Ehrlich & Schwartz, *supra* this note, at 587-89); and (2) re-orienting the content of rules and doctrine away from specialized technical considerations, for example, from institutional formalism, toward social norms (*cf*. Arnold, *supra* note 203; Wright, *Professor Bickel, the Scholarly Tradition, and the Supreme Court*, 84 HARV. L. REV. 769 (1971).

The specialization of the law is not an autonomous phenomenon. The legal system is in large part a function of the larger social structure, and it could be transformed effectively only in connection with the transformation of other social institutions. Thus, the success of the reforms listed above would require that they lead to, or be accompanied by, further reforms designed to reduce alienation and enhance participation in other social institutions. *See* UNGER, LAW IN MODERN SOCIETY: TOWARD A CRITICISM OF SOCIAL THEORY 143-47, 176-81, 238-42 (1976); Galanter, *supra* note 32; Trubek, *supra* note 233.

soldier's, the advocate's occupation arises from social imperfection. This imperfection may be inevitable, but it is important that the advocate not feel that he has a vested interest in it. If the non-professional advocate is to perform his job, he must be willing and even anxious to work to diminish the power and importance of his own role in order to enhance the client's autonomy. For this reason, it may be desirable for the non-professional to be a part-time advocate, one whose primary means of livelihood is in some activity other than advocacy.[246]

The rejection of the Ideology of Advocacy in favor of non-professional advocacy would not guarantee progress toward the realization of the values of individuality in the legal system. Non-professional advocacy is a necessary, but not a sufficient, condition for the realization of these values. Progress toward this goal would depend on the particular ends which people brought to the judicial process, and on the extent to which the conflict unleashed by non-professional advocacy led to the enhanced sharing of concrete ends necessary to a social order in which individuality can flourish.[247] The change would thus require a certain amount of optimism, but if lawyers were seriously committed to the values of individuality, they could do no better than to abandon their professionalism.

This brief suggestion of the nature of non-professional advocacy leaves many problems to be worked out in theory and in practice. For the present, it will be sufficient to anticipate two of the more prominent objections with which the basic proposal will be met.

First, it will be argued that non-professional advocacy will make it more difficult or impossible for many to secure an advocate. Lawyers will decline to represent at least some people whose values they do not share. Those with unpopular views may thus find themselves without representation. Moreover, people will be unwilling to consult lawyers or to confide in them for fear of oppression or betrayal. Contentions such as these are among the oldest and most common arguments on behalf of professional ethics. One answer to them is that they are beside the point. Since the principal thrust of the critique of the Ideology of Advocacy is to show the destructiveness of legal services as they are now rendered, the possibility that reform might diminish the availability of legal services is hardly a disadvantage. Even if it were a disadvantage, it would seem plausible that it would be outweighed by the qualitative improvement which non-professional advocacy would bring.

There is a further answer to these contentions. The parade of horribles which they put forth as the hypothetical outcome of hypothetical reform is in fact precisely the situation which obtains *now* and which has obtained for the past century under the hegemony of the Ideology of

246. *See Meeting Legal Needs*, *supra* note 245.
247. *See generally* UNGER, *supra* note 25, at 183-85, 242-53.

Advocacy. There is now a wealth of empirical studies which confirm what most laymen have always known: only a tiny minority, composed almost entirely of the wealthy and the powerful, is assured or ever has been assured substantial access to legal services. The majority of the public distrusts and dislikes lawyers and seeks their help, if at all, only in connection with a few types of routine transactions or in desperate situations as a last resort. This distrust is well grounded; lawyers commonly pursue self-interest at the expense of their clients' interests.[248] The history of the profession mocks the contention that there is any connection between the Ideology of Advocacy and the adequate provision of legal services. In this dismal situation, the risks of reform are slight. At best, the abandonment of professional ethics, by broadening the lawyer's ethical perspective, will lead to a more equitable distribution of services than now exists. At worst, it is difficult to see how it could produce a less satisfactory situation than now exists.

Second, it will be objected that non-professional advocacy puts an unrealistically large moral and psychological burden on the lawyer. The constant responsibility for the consequences of his efforts on behalf of so many others with varying ends will generate a "role strain" which will make non-professional advocacy intolerable for lawyers.[249] The often voiced premise of this criticism—that the lawyer's conditions of work involve greater responsibility or ethical pressure than others—seems wrong. Most occupations involve, directly or indirectly, constant, and often intimate and confidential, dealings with strangers which implicate moral responsibilities. The real difference between the position of the lawyer and that of, for instance, the corporate bureaucrat lies not in the greater pressure on the lawyer, but in his greater freedom. The autonomy of the lawyer should not be exaggerated. Most lawyers work under conditions of bureaucratic routine. Nevertheless, compared with most other occupations, lawyers have achieved a remarkable measure of autonomy in their conditions of work. Not every lawyer has the opportunity to act like Brandeis, but some do, and many have more latitude in defining the nature of their work than the most powerful corporate executives. The strain which the lawyer feels results less from the weight of his responsibilities than from the weight of his freedom. The corporate executive sacrifices his personal values more easily because he perceives his choices as more limited. The lawyer must undertake more strenuous efforts to rationalize his compromises because the pressures on him to compromise are weaker. Non-professional advocacy merely asks the lawyer to make the most of the freedom he has.

The proposal to abolish legal professionalism will strike most law-

248. *See* AUERBACH, *supra* note 6; ROSENTHAL, *supra* note 5; Carlin & Howard, *Legal Representation and Class Justice*, 12 U.C.L.A. L. REV. 381 (1965); Sarat, *supra* note 140, at 435-38, 464-65, and works cited therein.

249. *See* Parsons, *supra* note 196, at 380.

yers as radical and unrealistic. But at least in some respects this impression is wrong. After all, it has become commonplace to speculate on the "death of law." It should not be surprising that such discussions rarely embrace the death of the legal profession; or indeed, that they often take place within the bastions of professional privilege and power.[250] For, legal professionalism thrives on contempt for the ideal of law. Yet, the ideal of law and the values of individuality have been a potent historical alliance, and they may well prove more tenacious than the most entrenched contemporary institutions. In this light, the death of the legal profession may be a more conservative and more practical alternative to the death of law.

250. *See, e.g.*, Is Law Dead? (E. Rostow ed. 1971).

Part III

Moral Psychology

[9]

Essay

The Legal Ethics of Radical Individualism

Thomas L. Shaffer*

> There's a magnifying glass all cracked and broken, and when you look at broken things through the lens you'd swear they'd turned whole again.[1]
>
> —Anne Tyler

Most of what American lawyers and law teachers call legal ethics is not ethics. Most of what is called legal ethics is similar to rules made by administrative agencies. It is regulatory. Its appeal is not to conscience, but to sanction. It seeks mandate rather than insight.[2] I argue here that

* Professor of Law, Washington and Lee University School of Law. B.A. 1958, University of Albuquerque; J.D. 1961, Notre Dame Law School; LL.D. 1983, St. Mary's University of San Antonio School of Law. I am grateful for the assistance of John Acuff, Mark H. Aultman, Milner S. Ball, Roger C. Cramton, Jane N. Farrell, Monroe H. Freedman, Stanley Hauerwas, Steven J. Hobbs, Louis W. Hodges, Burt Louden, Richard G. Marks, Stephen L. Pepper, Robert S. Redmount, Nancy J. Shaffer, Mary M. Shaffer, and Margaret Williams.

1. A. TYLER, THE ACCIDENTAL TOURIST 278-79 (1985).

2. *See* G. HAZARD, ETHICS IN THE PRACTICE OF LAW 15 (1978) ("The typical professional code of ethics presupposes that the profession has exclusive or substantial control over the process by which professional competence is attained and verified. It presupposes . . . that professional reputation must be maintained by good practice as a matter of professional survival."). The intellectual roots of this type of "ethics" seem to be in the sociology of professions:

> [Legal ethics is a] limited, bastardized version of ethics, an ethics culled from the ethos of professionalism. It is not the ethics known by philosophers and theologians, but . . . an ethics formed from the normative conventions and practices of those who do professional work. It is an ethics of work rather than an ethics of craft.

Elkins, *Ethics: Professionalism, Craft, and Failure*, 73 KY. L.J. 937, 946 (1984-1985); *cf.* Gewirth, *Professional Ethics: The Separatist Thesis*, 96 ETHICS 282, 300 (1986) (presenting an analysis of "ethics" in a professional-client relationship that confuses ethics with professionalism).

For an example of writing on "professional ethics," see THE LEGAL PROFESSION: RESPONSIBILITY AND REGULATION (G. Hazard & D. Rhode eds. 1985), an impressive collection of essays compiled for law students. The book identifies its purpose as an inquiry into "the legal profession as a serious academic subject," as opposed to the "formalist analysis, moralist polemics, and tepid apologia" of the past. *Id.* at 1. Consistent with that purpose, the book includes examinations of "the bar's social organization, . . . the premises underlying its regulatory efforts . . . [and] the social, economic, and ideological underpinnings of professional governance" from the perspective of "a variety of intellectual disciplines." *Id.* In the book, faith, religion, and theology are relevant, if at all, only as included in the discipline of history. Most of the "ethical" content of the book is regulatory, as distinguished from the philosophical ethics that interested, for example, Moses, Plato, Aristotle, Maimonides, Aquinas, Calvin, and Buber. Interestingly, the content is academically interdisciplinary from every point of view but the religious. The editors write and select as if none of their universities harbored schools of divinity, programs in theology, or departments of religious studies.

what remains and appropriately is called ethics has been distorted by the weaker side of an old issue in academic moral philosophy. This "weaker side" rests on two doctrines: first, that fact and value are separate; and second, that the moral agent acts alone; as W.H. Auden put it,[3] each of us is alone on a moral planet tamed by terror.[4] The influence of this philosophical position deprives legal ethics of truthfulness and of depth. As a principal example of the distortion, I use the case of lawyers employed by and for families, and by and for associations that use the metaphor of family to describe themselves.

Part I of the this Essay attempts to describe a different ethical theory, opposed to the separations of fact from value and of individuals

3. W.H. AUDEN, THE AGE OF ANXIETY: A BAROQUE EPILOGUE 17 (1947).

4. *See* A. MACINTYRE, AFTER VIRTUE 55-87, 107-20 (2d ed. 1984); REVISIONS 1, 16 (S. Hauerwas & A. MacIntyre eds. 1983); Wachbroit, *A Genealogy of Virtues* (Book Review), 92 YALE L.J. 564 (1983); Wachbroit, *Relativism and Virtue* (Book Review), 94 YALE L.J. 1559 (1985). The intellectual complaint is that the Scots and German Enlightenment, which enters our political and ethical thought through political institutions that ignore or neglect the religious tradition, caused moral philosophy to ignore, obviously, Moses and Jesus, and also, but not so obviously, Socrates and Aristotle. Clearly, though, Socrates' and Aristotle's ethics of character are as incompatible with the ethics of radical individualism as religious ethics. *See* Lehman, *Finding Our Way Back*, 29 AM. J. JURIS. 229, 232-33 (1984).

Legal ethics as an academic discipline has begun recently to notice moral philosophy; unfortunately, legal ethics also has begun to adopt moral philosophy's current biases. THE GOOD LAWYER (D. Luban ed. 1984), is an example. Luban's book is a set of essays balanced between those who accept and those who resist the distinction between fact and value and the individualism of the ethics of autonomy. As the editor poses the issues, however, the book emphasizes the conflict between the Kantian problem of universalism—something that MacIntyre finds unimportant, *see generally* A. MACINTYRE, *supra* (proposing a modern Aristoltelian ethic)—and the sociological argument that a professional role entails special morality, THE GOOD LAWYER, *supra*, at 2-3; *see also* Elkins, *supra* note 2, at 937 ("In structuring and defining human experience, the professions play an integral role in the delineation of experience as good/bad, healthy/sick, or legal/illegal."); Gewirth, *supra* note 2, at 282-86 (describing the thesis that professional duties differ from moral duties). Luban's dominant concern as a moral philosopher who focuses on legal ethics is the difference between a *procedural* and an *agency* view of the lawyer's role. That distinction, however, does not take seriously the importance of organic communities, *see infra* note 8, particularly in that the Luban book discusses procedures as bearing only on individuals, and agents as agents only for individuals. Luban thus reveals himself as "an empiricist of a certain type, [for whom] the fundamental and basic condition is human isolation, and relationship is a *derivative* fact which comes about only through inference." Fackenheim, *Martin Buber: Universal and Jewish Aspects of the I-Thou Philosophy*, MIDSTREAM, May 1974, at 46, 50 (emphasis in original). Luban's bias is evident even in his discussion of Judge Cardozo's opinion in Meinhard v. Salmon, 249 N.Y. 458, 464, 164 N.E. 545, 546 (1928) (holding that certain fiduciary relationships demand a higher loyalty than "the morals of the market place"). THE GOOD LAWYER, *supra*, at 8-14. Cardozo argued that the association of two business partners is organic, so that that *the law* will not allow a partner to keep a business opportunity to himself. *Id.* at 9.

Another important example of this focus on academic moral philosophy in "interdisciplinary" legal ethics is Stephen Pepper's essay, *The Lawyer's Amoral Role: A Defense, A Problem, and Some Possibilities* (Oct. 14, 1985) (unpublished manuscript), which was selected by academic judges in the Association of American Law Schools as the best paper submitted in a competitive call for papers for the Association's 1986 annual meeting. *Cf.* M. FREEDMAN, LAWYERS' ETHICS IN AN ADVERSARY SYSTEM 31-57 (1975) (dealing with, among other subjects, the "epistemology of legal ethics"); A. GOLDMAN, THE MORAL FOUNDATIONS OF PROFESSIONAL ETHICS 1-2 (1980) (discussing the necessity of special ethical norms in professional conduct).

from the community. Part II considers a bar association ethical quandary arising from what the modern ethics codes define as multiple-client employment. Part III first considers the same quandary under Rule 2.2 of the new *Model Rules of Professional Conduct*,[5] describing the lawyer as intermediary, and then assesses the influences of moral philosophy on that new rule. Part IV considers the quandary as it might have been viewed in the practice of Louis D. Brandeis. Part V concludes the Essay with an assessment of the ethics of radical individualism in terms of the religious tradition's influence on legal ethics.

I. The Ethical Context

Ethics properly defined is thinking about morals. It is an intellectual activity and an appropriate academic discipline, but it is valid only to the extent that it truthfully describes what is going on.[6] Those in contemporary ethics who concentrate on the importance of the truthful account argue first that fact and value are not separate—that stating the facts is, as Iris Murdoch put it, a moral act, a moral skill, and a moral art;[7] and second, that organic communities[8] of persons are prior in life

5. MODEL RULES OF PROFESSIONAL CONDUCT Rule 2.2 (1983).

6. J. FLETCHER, SITUATION ETHICS 84 (1966) (observing that ethics should put "a high premium on our knowing what's what when we act").

7. *See* Murdoch, *On "God and Good"*, in THE ANATOMY OF KNOWLEDGE 233, 243-45 (1969). "Stating the facts," however, is not a *prelude* to ethics; it *is* ethics. It requires discipline to eradicate from a description "the tissue of self-aggrandizing and consoling wishes and dreams which prevents one from seeing what there is outside one." *Id.* at 244.

8. The difference between a community and an organic community is a common theme in ethical writing, but the difference is suggested more often than it is defined. Maybe the distinction is better suited to illustration than to definition. Writers who describe or employ the distinction seem to have in mind three kinds of relationships among people that create *organic* communities.

First.—An organic community is created by people through the mutual practice of the virtues, and through mutual support in the pursuit of the good. For Aristotle, such associations are both the goal and the source of the virtue of friendship. ARISTOTLE, NICOMACHEAN ETHICS 271-72 (M. Ostwald trans. 1962). (Aristotle also makes the more problematical claim that political order rests on friendship, *id.* at 235-37, but that claim is not a claim about organic community.) Reinhold Niebuhr often spoke of Britain (he probably meant England) as organic in this way. *See* R. FOX, REINHOLD NIEBUHR 150, 170-74 (1985). Niebuhr also once attempted to define an "organic radicalism" for the Christian left in the United States. *Id.* at 172-73. In both cases, he seemed to associate "organic" with a communal practice of the virtues. An organic association also is possible among those who practice a craft or a profession. A. MACINTYRE, *supra* note 4, at 175-83. "Organic" in this sense is a metaphor, because the relationships it describes are constructed, not ordained or established, as a part of the constitution or structure of the community.

Second.—An organic community is created, sustained, and redeemed by God. An example is Israel, taken out of Egypt in the Exodus. *See* M. GOLDBERG, JEWS AND CHRISTIANS: GETTING OUR STORIES STRAIGHT 103-04 (1985). The church in Christian ecclesiology is another example. *See id.*; C. GREENHOUSE, PRAYING FOR JUSTICE: FAITH, ORDER, AND COMMUNITY IN AN AMERICAN TOWN 37-42 (1986); S. HAUERWAS, A COMMUNITY OF CHARACTER 59 (1981); Hauerwas, *The Church in a Divided World: The Interpretive Power of the Christian Story*, 8 J. RELIGIOUS ETHICS 55 (1980). "Organic" in this second sense sometimes is a metaphor (*e.g.*, in New Testament

and in culture to individuals—in other words, that the moral agent is not alone.

Exemplifying this second view committed to truthfulness is Anne Tyler's kidnapped housewife, Charlotte, in the novel *Earthly Possessions*.[9] When Charlotte reflects on her absent family, she understands and expresses to herself the truth about her individuality; she mixes fact and value, or rather, sees them correctly as mixed. She understands, through the moral art of seeing, that she does not face terror alone, even though she is alone: "I saw that all of us lived in a sort of web, criss-crossed by strings of love and need and worry. . . . It appeared that we were all taking care of each other, in ways an outsider might not notice."[10] Charlotte understands that to describe a fact is to describe a value. She sees that, when the bell tolls, and she is one of those who can hear it, it tolls for her. Seeing and hearing are moral arts; when she is successful at these arts, she hears the bell that says she is not an island.

In the practice of estate planning, for example, the facts that are available for moral description are death and property: property seen in the context of mortality, death seen in the context of owning things.[11]

references to the church as a body) and sometimes not (*e.g.*, in references to the *people* Israel or to the church as the people of God).

Third.—An organic community is recognized by people who discover a psychological or biological commonality in one another. The term "organic" (or "organismic") has been used in this way by humanistic psychologists. *See, e.g.*, A. MASLOW, TOWARD A PSYCHOLOGY OF BEING 189-214, 222 (2d ed. 1968) (characterizing this "belongingness" as an aspect of self-actualization). Reinhold Niebuhr also recognized this kind of community, noting in 1935 that the only "saving grace" of European fascism was its feeling for "the organic character of society," a feeling produced by "outraged truth avenging itself" on the excesses of individualism. R. FOX, *supra*, at 170. Individualistic psychologists apply the word "organism" to groups, *e.g.*, C. ROGERS, CLIENT-CENTERED THERAPY 481-533 (1951), thus implying that groups may have an *organic* life. Lewis Thomas perceives this organic communal life as a matter even of biology. *See* L. THOMAS, THE LIVES OF A CELL 11-16, 81-87, 102-06 (1975). This sense of "organic" is metaphorical or not depending on the nature of the characteristic that produces the commonality.

Whether "organic" is a metaphor or not, the term highlights the distinction between a *collectivity* and a *community*. A collectivity is mechanical; a community is organic. The Roman state, for example, was in concept and operation "a mechanism wearing the mask of an organism, an organism wearing the mask of the spirit," M. BUBER, ON JUDAISM 124 (1967), and "a contraction of the strayed will to community," *id.* at 125. Judaism, by contrast, "rejects the 'We' of group egotism, of national conceit and party exclusiveness, but it postulates that 'We' which arises from the real relationships of its components and which maintains genuine relations with other groups, the 'We' that may say in truth: '*Our* Father.'" *Id.* at 211 (emphasis in original). The collectivity (*i.e.*, chosen affiliations in an I-It world) is justified only as necessary to sustain an organic community of I-You relationships. M. BUBER, I AND THOU 124-26 (1970); *see also infra* note 48 (describing the relationship of "organic" in a religious focus).

9. A. TYLER, EARTHLY POSSESSIONS (1978).

10. *Id.* at 182. The critical fact is that Charlotte thinks of herself as *known*, and therefore not alone. *Cf. Psalms* 139:3-12 (praising God as One who knows the poet intimately); A. HESCHEL, BETWEEN GOD AND MAN: AN INTERPRETATION OF JUDAISM 57 (1959).

11. Death is a social, not only an individual, fact. Otherwise, the practice of estate planning would lose significance. Property is also a social fact. As a consequence, property laws reflect moral conclusions about the relationships among persons, and the importance of things for communities of

Radical Individualism

The way death is seen in estate planning is ownership—that is why we laugh at the cartoon that shows a fur-clad matron in the bank vault, the family safety deposit box empty in front of her, saying, "He took it with him!" The way ownership is seen in estate planning is in death—that is the paradox (if not the humor) in those old trust-administration cases in which the judges talk about long-dead settlors as people who own (present tense) the property and *can do* with it what they *want*.[12]

What reconciles death with the ownership of property is the family. The family is the lens through which we understand death as the death of an owner, and property as something owned by dead people. The family is the cracked magnifying glass that shows how things broken by discord and death are whole. The family is normally why people bother with estate planning—"normally" in the sense that, but for the family, estate planning would not be a legal subject.[13] The family is the cultural focus for the realization that estate planning is a worthwhile thing for people to do, because it reflects the hope that none of us will die alone. The human fact that is prior to the moral agency of which moral philosophy usually speaks[14] is the family; the moral art of description in the legal ethics of estate planning is the skill to describe a family.

This art applies as well to associations that account for themselves as if they were families. The skill for describing families holds moral promise beyond families for the human harmonies that describe themselves with family metaphors. I was, for example, thanked recently for patronizing "the Piedmont family," an incorporated airline company. I was for years employed in "the Notre Dame family," a not-for-profit Indiana corporation. I worship in what our pastor calls a parish family. I am affected, as all of us are, by aggregations of businesses that refer to themselves as families of companies. A lawyer for such an association is invited to take seriously his client's use of the metaphor of family, and to share in the hope that the members of the "family" have for one another

persons, including families. For analyses of these underlying moral conclusions, see Shaffer, *The Lawyer as Will Maker*, in FAMILY SYSTEMS AND INHERITANCE PATTERNS 87 (1982); Shaffer, *Slippered Feet Aboard the African Queen*, 3 J.L. & RELIGION 193, 198-99 (1985) [hereinafter Shaffer, *Slippered Feet*]; Shaffer & Rodes, *Law for Those Who Are to Die*, in NEW MEANINGS OF DEATH 291 (H. Feifel ed. 1977).

12. *E.g.*, Colonial Trust Co. v. Brown, 105 Conn. 261, 270, 135 A. 555, 560 (1926); Broadway Nat'l Bank v. Adams, 133 Mass. 170, 173 (1882); *In re* Pulitzer's Estate, 139 Misc. 575, 580, 249 N.Y.S. 87, 93, *supplemented*, 140 Misc. 572, 251 N.Y.S. 549 (N.Y. Sur. Ct. 1931), *aff'd*, 237 A.D. 808, 260 N.Y.S. 975 (1932); Saunders v. Vautier, 49 Eng. Rep. 282, 282 (1841).

13. See, for example, the titles of casebooks, such as O. BROWDER & R. WELLMAN, FAMILY PROPERTY SETTLEMENTS (1965); J. DUKEMINIER & S. JOHANSON, FAMILY WEALTH TRANSACTIONS (2d ed. 1978).

14. *See, e.g.*, S. HAUERWAS, CHARACTER AND THE CHRISTIAN LIFE 18-34 (1975) (discussing moral agency as the capacity to make choices that determine one's character).

that none of us need die alone. In accepting or refusing this invitation, the lawyer likely will act as a member of a professional association that accounts for itself, as its clients try to do, with family metaphors.

II. The Case of the Unwanted Will

I use, in teaching legal ethics, a series of quandaries that were posed in the *American Bar Association Journal* in 1979.[15] One of these quandaries describes John and Mary, a middle-aged couple with adult children. John and Mary want their wills drafted before beginning a vacation trip abroad. Based on John's instructions, the lawyer prepares a set of parallel wills, each leaving all property to the surviving spouse, or, if both are dead, to their children in equal shares. On a second visit to the law office, the lawyer presents the prepared wills to the couple, and John executes his:

> [T]he lawyer [then] suggests to John that he would like to be alone with Mary before she signs. John withdraws to another office. The lawyer asks Mary if the will is as she would have made it had her husband not been present at the conference and if the will were to be secret from her husband. She says no, that the will as drawn contains several provisions that are contrary to her wishes, and that she would change if her husband were not to know the ultimate disposition of her estate. However, she says that she would not be willing to precipitate the domestic discord and confrontation that would occur if her husband were to learn that she had drawn a will contrary to his wishes and in accordance with her own desires.[16]

You could say that the problem[17] never would have arisen had the lawyer not talked to Mary alone.[18] That description, of course, trivializes the problem, but many law students, and some ponderers of legal ethics, pose the quandary and the solution in just those terms.[19] From that

15. *The Case of the Unwanted Will*, 65 A.B.A. J. 484 (1979). I included an abridged version of these quandaries in my textbook. *See* T. SHAFFER, AMERICAN LEGAL ETHICS 313 (1985).

16. *The Case of the Unwanted Will*, *supra* note 15, at 484.

17. To describe *The Case of the Unwanted Will* as posing a moral problem or quandary is to make a moral judgment. *See* S. HAUERWAS, VISION AND VIRTUE 11-24 (1974); J. MCCLENDON, BIOGRAPHY AS THEOLOGY 13-38 (1974); T. SHAFFER, FAITH AND THE PROFESSIONS ch. 1 (1987); Pincoffs, *Quandary Ethics*, 80 MIND 552-55 (1971).

18. You also could say that the problem would have arisen differently had the lawyer felt it necessary in addition to talk to John, alone.

19. The comments of George W. Overton in the *A.B.A. Journal*'s discussion illustrate this trivial analysis: "[T]he custom of separating spouses at execution of wills, although not uncommon, is an anachronism, based on the notion that one spouse, presumably the husband, could coerce the other into an unintended result . . . ." *The Case of the Unwanted Will*, *supra* note 15, at 486. John C. Williams offered similar advice:

> The root of the conflict is Mary's problem. She doesn't like the will that was discussed in her husband's presence, but she doesn't want to disclose to him her dissatisfaction with it.

viewpoint, the immediately noticeable premises for the two judgments that there is a problem present, and that the problem is moral, are four. First, a lawyer's proper employment is by or for an individual. Second, employment by or for more than one individual is exceptional. Third, as a consequence, multiple party employment is necessarily superficial. Finally, the means for protecting the superficiality (or, if you like, the means for protecting the principle that employment is ordinarily and properly by or for individuals) is ignorance of any facts known to one of the individuals but not to the other.[20]

It follows from this typical analysis that the lawyer's moral mistake was in talking to Mary alone.[21] Otherwise, Mary's secret intention never would have come to his attention; her thoughts would be hidden, and that is appropriate because John's thoughts are hidden. Now that the lawyer *has* talked to Mary alone, he is in an impossible situation: he cannot allow John to board the plane with the mistaken belief that Mary agreed with what "they" had decided.[22] Nor, for the same reason, can he help Mary to make a different will.[23] And, of course, he cannot allow Mary to execute a will that does not do what she wants it to do.[24]

This principled analysis of *The Case of the Unwanted Will* fails because of what is prior to analysis: the moral art of description. The failure is sad and, I think, corrupting. It is corrupting, first, because it rests on an untruthful account of what is going on. What is present in the law

> This dilemma is Mary's and she should decide what to do about it. The lawyer, by meeting privately with Mary, has permitted her to transfer the problem to him.

Id. at 488. Mr. Williams also noted that the lawyer's conduct violated professional standards. *Id.* (citing MODEL CODE OF PROFESSIONAL RESPONSIBILITY DR 4-101, 5-105, EC 5-1, 5-14 (1980)).

20. For example, Mr. Williams claimed,

> It was a mistake for the lawyer to ask to meet privately with Mary before she signed her will. By doing so, he invited Mary to speak "confidentially" with him and opened the door to the dilemma that confronted him when Mary told him that she was dissatisfied with her will.

Id. In Mr. Williams' judgment, this conduct violated MODEL CODE OF PROFESSIONAL RESPONSIBILITY EC 5-14 (1980). *Id.*

21. Both commentators agreed. *See id.* at 486, 488.

22. That was Mr. Williams' view. *Id.* at 488 (citing MODEL CODE OF PROFESSIONAL RESPONSIBILITY EC 5-1 (1980) which states, "The professional judgment of a lawyer should be exercised . . . solely for the benefit of his client and free of compromising interests and loyalties."). Mr. Overton disagreed in part: "[T]he lawyer, if questioned by John, cannot lie to him, although I do not believe the lawyer has a duty to volunteer any information." *Id.* at 484.

23. *See supra* note 20. One of the commentators disagreed. Mr. Overton thought that the lawyer could help Mary make a new will, provided that he told John that he had done so. *The Case of the Unwanted Will*, *supra* note 15, at 486. Mr. Overton would not require the lawyer to disclose to John the *contents* of Mary's new will. *Id.* at 484. For Mr. Williams, though, Mr. Overton's solution did not provide "the full disclosure [to John] that the canons require." *Id.* at 488.

24. Both commentators agreed, although Mr. Overton would allow the execution of Mary's unwanted will if the lawyer first explained to her that the will "is unquestionably her will . . . and . . . [that] even if all their conversation were reproduced in court, it would not affect the validity of the will." *Id.* at 484.

office is a family, and this one-lawyer-for-each-person way of first seeing a moral quandary in this situation and then resolving the quandary with the ethics of autonomy (the ethics of aloneness) leaves the family out of the account.[25] The analysis looks on Mary as a collection of interests and rights that begin and end in radical individuality. Her affiliation with her husband, and with the children they have made and reared, is seen as a product of individuality(!), of contract and consent, of promises and the keeping of promises—all the consensual connections that lonely individuals use when they want circumstantial harmony. The employment of the lawyer is a result, then, of the links, the promises, the contract, the consent, and the need for circumstantial harmony. The family in the office is there only as the product of promise and consent. It is relevant to the legal business at hand only because the (radical) individuals, each in momentary and circumstantial harmony with one another, want it to be. The promise and the consent create the family.[26]

This description is offered by the legal ethics of radical individualism. It is sad, corrupting, and untruthful. An alternative argument is that the *family* created the promises, the contract, the consent, and the circumstantial harmony—not the other way around. The family is not the harmony; it is where the harmony (and disharmony) comes from. A truthful description of *The Case of the Unwanted Will* is that the lawyer's employer is a family. I suspect that that proposition will sound unusual in legal ethics, but my argument would be ordinary in other contexts. It treats, sees, and describes the family the way families are treated, seen, and described in the stories we tell, in the television commercials we watch, in the comics, and in our religious tradition. In these ordinary ways of accounting to ourselves for ourselves, it is the family that causes

25. Mr. Overton's comment illustrates the untruthfulness of the account. It begins, "The first question to be asked in all problems involving professional responsibility or ethics is 'Who is the client?' . . . John probably presumes that the lawyer is *his* . . . . The lawyer probably accepted the notion without clarification. The problem is that . . . Mary is the client . . . ." *Id.* (emphasis in original). Mr. Overton's perception denies the presence of a family (they are both *the* client), and then creates a quandary (for the ethics of autonomy), out of his denial of the presence of a family.

26. Mr. Williams thus distinguishes between a "happily married husband and wife [who are interested] in the continuity and development of their marital relationship" (*i.e.*, a family), and "the outcome of a particularly legal negotiation." *The Case of the Unwanted Will*, *supra* note 15, at 486. The reconciliation of the two views of people in the law office—of continuity in the organic community on the one hand, and a "particularly legal negotiation" on the other—rests, in his view, on the outcome of the lawyer's probing for conflicts between the couple. The organic community (family) is the client only if there are no conflicts. Describing a family in that way is comical. Mr. Overton suggests that lawyers explicate the assumption "that each of you has given me your wishes" in the joint interview for wills of spouses, but he would permit separate interviews "at the first meeting or immediately thereafter." *Id.* That suggestion is not funny, but it also rests on the view that momentary harmony creates the family. Its anthropology, therefore, is one of radical individualism. It depends on the exercise of autonomous, individual decision-making power. *Cf. infra* note 35 (suggesting an alternative anthropology of the family).

individuals to make the promises that begin, develop, and continue families. The family causes people to seek human harmonies and, consequently, to create more families, as well as associations such as businesses, clubs, and professions, that account for themselves with family metaphors.

The view of the family as organic and as prior to individuality is ordinary in other parts of our culture. The Hebraic religious tradition,[27] for example, regards the family as the nursery of the people of God.[28] Anne Tyler's modern novels,[29] like Jane Austen's nineteenth-century ones,[30] tell deep and interesting stories about family and culture. The truth here, however, is told in other and more ordinary places, including stories of real and fictional lawyers[31] and recent and popular novels that describe espionage as a family trade,[32] burglary as a (three-generation) family business,[33] and organized crime as a family and a web of families.[34] And, because understanding others as members and constituents of families generates a sense of shared experience, the final account of racial justice in twentieth-century America might depend more than we

27. I use "Hebraic" where other writers use "Judeo-Christian." The single term implies that the dominant American religious tradition is a single tradition, rather than two traditions that are causally related to one another, or that happen to have something in common. *See* Shaffer, *Jurisprudence in the Light of the Hebraic Faith*, 1 NOTRE DAME J.L. ETHICS & PUB. POL'Y 77, 78 n.4 (1984).

28. The significance of the family is evident particularly in the Jewish "master story," *see* M. GOLDBERG, *supra* note 8, at 25-131 (the Jewish "master story" is in *Exodus*), in the social organization of Israel after the death of Moses, when Israel was led by Joshua into the Promised Land. *See Joshua* 41:7-17. God dealt with Israel family by family. At the end, when it came time to renew the covenant between God and Israel in the new land, Joshua, in Israel, declared his allegiance in this way: "I and my family, we will worship the Lord." *Joshua* 24:15 (New English Bible). Joshua "spoke not as leader to his people but, in the cultural context . . . to all present as families . . . . He articulated the truth that the covenant with God exists directly between God and the most rudimentary social unit." McAlister, *Exodus and Community*, SOJOURNERS, Mar. 1986, at 36, 37.

Family physicians describe their patients and their power in communities in this Hebraic way; they care for families "in the larger sense." *See* Nemethy, *Doctor: A Profile of Contemporary Rural Practice*, VERMONT LIFE, Winter 1984, at 50, 53. *See generally* McPhee, *A Reporter at Large: Heirs of General Practice*, NEW YORKER, July 23, 1984, at 40 (presenting anecdotal evidence that doctors in rural communities counsel their patients as families, and as *in* families).

29. *E.g.*, A. TYLER, DINNER AT THE HOMESICK RESTAURANT (1982); A. TYLER, MORGAN'S PASSING (1980); *see also supra* notes 1, 9 and accompanying text (describing other Tyler novels).

30. For a discussion of Austen's novels, see A. MACINTYRE, *supra* note 4, at 169-74; J. WHITE, WHEN WORDS LOSE THEIR MEANING 163-91 (1984).

31. *See, e.g.*, T. SHAFFER, *supra* note 15 (discussing Harper Lee's Atticus Finch; Louis Auchincloss's Henry Knox and Mario Fabbri; Arthur Train's Ephraim Tutt; George V. Higgins's Jerry Kennedy; and others, and including biographies of Louis D. Brandeis, Farrington Reed Carpenter, Fanny Holtzmann, Justine Wise Polier, and others).

32. *See, e.g.*, J. CARROLL, FAMILY TRADE (1982).

33. *See, e.g.*, V. PATRICK, FAMILY BUSINESS (1985).

34. *E.g.*, *Protecting the Family*, TIME, Feb. 10, 1986, at 52. According to that article, organized crime families excuse lawyers' bribery, destruction of physical evidence, and betrayal of clients, under an ethic of loyalty in which the metaphor of family is the organizing insight. Thus, "to do the right thing means to protect the family . . . . It's a way of life." *Id.*

Texas Law Review Vol. 65:963, 1987

suppose on the black-family situation comedy on network television.[35]

III. Lawyer as Intermediary

The recently adopted *Model Rules of Professional Conduct* describe situations in which the lawyer acts as an "intermediary."[36] This formulation is remarkably ambiguous for a case such as *The Case of the Unwanted Will.* The *Model Rules* can be read to support the perception I treat as inadequate, untruthful, and corrupting—that is, the perception based on radical individualism. They can also be read to support the argument for taking deeper account of the family as the creator, rather than the product, of the human harmonies that are presented to lawyers in estate planning, and in legal work for associations that account for themselves with family metaphors.

The new rule offers a set of procedures for accepting employment from two or more individuals. The rule rests on the assumption that employment by individuals is the norm; it has to provide a behavioral checklist to make exceptional, multiple-client employment possible:

> (a) A lawyer may act as intermediary between clients if
> (1) the lawyer consults with each client concerning the implications of the common representation, including the advantages and risks involved, and the effect on the attorney-client privileges, and obtains each client's consent to the common representation;[37]

35. My view of the family is therefore anthropological. It is not normative, in the sense in which modern moral philosophy usually separates the normative from the descriptive. The family is not, always and everywhere, good teleologically; nor is it always and everywhere good for its members. The family is part of the way people are. (When the family is seen as ordained by God, perhaps it is good in an *ontological* sense, in the way that government, according to St. Paul, is good. *See Romans* 13:1-7).

My view of the family follows the second of the three views about "organic community" enumerated *supra* note 8. To describe, for example, black Americans in families therefore expresses a common experience that helps white Americans to understand black people, and that perhaps helps black people to understand themselves, in the way Anne Tyler's white characters come to understand themselves in families. *See supra* note 29 and accompanying text. James Cone makes a similar argument, theologically, in reference to black churches in America. *See* J. CONE, MY SOUL LOOKS BACK 57 (1982).

36. MODEL RULES OF PROFESSIONAL CONDUCT Rule 2.2 (1983). I am consulting this rule in two versions. The first is the form in which it originally was presented to the profession for comment: MODEL RULES OF PROFESSIONAL CONDUCT Rule 2.2 (Proposed Final Draft 1981) [hereinafter MODEL RULES (PROPOSED)]. The second is the form in which it finally was adopted by the House of Delegates of the American Bar Association: MODEL RULES OF PROFESSIONAL CONDUCT Rule 2.2 (1983) [hereinafter MODEL RULES].

37. The 1981 draft read "discloses to each client the implications of . . . and the effect on attorney-client privileges." MODEL RULES (PROPOSED), *supra* note 36, Rule 2.2. The phrase "multiple clients" was favored in the MODEL CODE OF PROFESSIONAL RESPONSIBILITY Canon 5, EC 5-15 to -19 (1985). Rule 2.2, however, favors "common representation," a choice that might support the argument that an organic community, or a "situation," can be a client. "Multiple client employment" is not a common Code phrase, but it seems to express the notions that (1) prototypical lawyer employment is employment by an individual and (2) employment for more than one person on the same matter is, in some sense, employment by each of them. *See generally supra* note 25 (quoting

Radical Individualism

(2) the lawyer reasonably believes that the matter can be resolved on terms compatible with the clients' best interests, that each client will be able to make adequately informed decisions in the matter and that there is little risk of material prejudice to the interests of any of the clients if the contemplated resolution is unsuccessful; and

(3) the lawyer reasonably believes that the common representation can be undertaken impartially and without improper effect on other responsibilities the lawyer has to any of the clients.

(b) While acting as intermediary, the lawyer shall consult with each client concerning the decisions to be made and the considerations relevant to making them, so that each client can make adequately informed decisions.[38]

(c) The lawyer shall withdraw as intermediary if any of the clients so requests, or if any of the conditions stated in paragraph (a) is no longer satisfied. Upon withdrawal, the lawyer shall not continue to represent any of the clients in the matter that was the subject of the intermediation.[39]

The *Model Rules*, unlike predecessor codes, canons, essays, and resolutions, eschew descriptions of morals. The authors and advocates of the rules have rooted out both the language and the discipline of ethical reasoning; these rules are not ethics but instead a set of regulatory mandates and prohibitions. As a consequence, the proposed rule on the lawyer as intermediary need not reveal its lonely-individual premise, if it has one. I think that Rule 2.2 does have a lonely individual premise, the premise of modern moral philosophy. The Rule's authors did assume that the normal employment of a lawyer is employment by a single individual,[40] and that, therefore, the profession needs a rule for the exceptional case in which a lawyer is employed by or for a group of individuals.[41]

one lawyer's assertion that the first issue in legal representation is determining who is the individual client).

38. The 1981 draft read "shall explain fully to each client the decisions to be made," rather than "shall consult with each client concerning the decisions." MODEL RULES (PROPOSED), *supra* note 36, Rule 2.2.

39. MODEL RULES, *supra* note 36, Rule 2.2. The 1981 draft read, "if the conditions stated in paragraph (a) cannot be met or if in the light of subsequent events the lawyer reasonably should know that a mutually advantageous resolution cannot be achieved." MODEL RULES (PROPOSED), *supra* note 36, Rule 2.2. This circumstantial test for commonality is radically different in moral implication from the test that gives any member of the group the power to end the group's common character as client.

40. MODEL RULES, *supra* note 36, Rule 2.2. The 1981 draft also prohibited the lawyer from continuing to represent one of the clients "unless doing so is clearly compatible with the lawyer's responsibilities to the other client or clients." MODEL RULES (PROPOSED), *supra* note 36, Rule 2.2.

41. Geoffrey Hazard describes this image of the lawyer in a lonely, individualistic, tamed-by-terror world:

> The picture of the lawyer . . . is that of a lone practitioner who must judge for himself what is right while engaged in intense competition . . . . The controls on his conduct . . . are almost entirely those of self-governance . . . . At the same time his vocational situation

It seems unlikely, for example, that the people who drafted and adopted the *Model Rules* would encourage a lawyer to exert herself to keep a client group together. The safer recourse, should fissures appear in the human harmony that first allowed the lawyer to be lawyer for the group, is to stand back, let things fall apart, and then take professional refuge from the falling debris by withdrawing from the representation. If the Rule had been invoked in *The Case of the Unwanted Will*, the lawyer would at any rate have learned, as he protected himself from the debris, not to focus attention on a will-making wife in the absence of her husband.

The comment to Model Rule 2.2 is more encouraging to those who might want to invoke the Rule for the proposition that families are prior to individuals, and, invoking it, to suggest that a lawyer should exert herself to describe the family and maybe to keep it together. When a lawyer follows the rule, she seeks "to establish or adjust *a relationship* between clients on an amicable and mutually advantageous basis."[42] None of the relationships given as examples is explicitly a family, or even a couple, married or not. Nevertheless, mediation is one of the professional skills mentioned; the development of mutual interests is one of the goals mentioned; the avoidance of complication is one of the benefits claimed for the employment; and situations "where the *clients'* interests are substantially though not entirely compatible" are given as prototypes of justified multiple-client employment.[43]

The comment can be read to describe families as we know them from our stories. If the comment to the Rule were invoked in *The Case of the Unwanted Will*, I see the possibility of an argument that the lawyer is lawyer for the family, and that what the Rule does is provide for the representation not of lonely individuals in circumstantial harmony, but of the harmony itself, or even of the communal source of the harmony.[44]

The moral premise of the regulatory rule with its behavioral check-

> . . . is one of dependency and vulnerability. Control of client misconduct will result, it is assumed, because conscience will surmount circumstance.

Hazard, *Conscience and Circumstance in Legal Ethics*, 1 SOC. RESP.: JOURNALISM L. MED. 36, 44-45 (1975). He is quoted in the business press as equating law-firm corruption with the loss of skepticism toward clients. *See A Question of Integrity at Blue-Chip Law Firms*, BUSINESS WEEK, Apr. 7, 1986, at 76, 80.

42. MODEL RULES, *supra* note 36, Rule 2.2 comment (emphasis added).

43. *Id.* (emphasis added). This language is cautious and regulatory. Compare Martin Buber's description of a marriage: "The You that is I for neither of them." M. BUBER, *supra* note 8, at 95. The husband or wife thus *is* an other—not a mirror.

44. Undermining the usefulness of the comment to Model Rule 2.2 is the statement in the preamble to the *Model Rules* that the comments "do not add obligations to the Rules but provide guidance for practicing in compliance with the Rules." MODEL RULES, *supra* note 36, scope. The comments provide *regulatory*, not moral, guidance. Nevertheless, courts previously have given coercive effect to moral admonitions such as the Ethical Considerations of the *Model Code of Profes-*

list is, I think, that the truly important and deep things in human life are individual and singular; they are matters of *autonomy*.[45] To put it another way, the highest good I can seek for a person on whom I focus my beneficence is that he be free—and free here means self-ruling and radically *not* committed.[46] The things that people share under this logic are relatively superficial; they are the harmonies that radically autonomous individuals *choose* to have. Employment by a group of persons is possible only if the lawyer stays with chosen harmonies. The employment is imperiled if the lawyer intrudes on these individualistic choices. If the employment will necessarily intrude on these choices, then the radically individualistic nature of the persons who are client(s) requires separate lawyers for each individual.

The competing premise—perhaps supported by the comment to the Rule—is that human harmonies do *not* rest on the choices of autonomous individuals; they rest instead on communities. Human harmonies are not chosen but given. As Abraham Joshua Heschel put it,

> [T]he self is a monstrous deceit . . . something transcendent in disguise . . . . I am endowed with a will but the will is not mine; I am endowed with freedom, but it is a freedom imposed on the will. Life is something that visits my body . . . . The essence of what I am is not mine.[47]

Organic[48] communities such as families are prior to individuals.

sional Responsibility. *See* R. ARONSON & D. WECKSTEIN, PROFESSIONAL RESPONSIBILITY 27-29 (1980). Courts eventually may give the same weight to the comments to the *Model Rules*.

45. *See* M. FREEDMAN, *supra* note 4, ch. 1; A. GOLDMAN, *supra* note 4.

46. *See* Dworkin, *Moral Autonomy*, in MORALS, SCIENCE, AND SOCIALITY 156 (1978) (exploring six meanings for the proposition, "A person is morally autonomous if and only if his moral principles are his own"); *see also infra* note 62 (detailing Dworkin's criticism of that proposition on the grounds that it is either trivial or objectively false).

47. A. HESCHEL, *supra* note 10, at 67. The ethical consequence of Heschel's statement is a truer regard for personhood, as opposed, perhaps, to individuality. The influential and even trendy enterprise described as "alternative dispute resolution" is one institution that depends on the denial of aloneness—that is, on the *fact* that a dispute is a fractured commonality, that the commonality is stronger than, and prior to, the fracture. *See* McThenia & Shaffer, *For Reconciliation*, 94 YALE L.J. 1660, 1664 (1985). The denial (or, perhaps, the overcoming) of aloneness is a matter of imagination—the ability to see another life as analogous. *See* P. ROSE, PARALLEL LIVES: FIVE VICTORIAN MARRIAGES 237 (1983) (quoting from George Eliot's memorial stone in Poet's Corner in Westminster Abbey: "The first condition of human goodness is something to love; the second something to reverence.").

48. Without denying my anthropological argument, *see supra* note 35, it is fairly clear that focus on the organic often, if not necessarily, is a focus from the religious tradition, *see supra* note 8. Looking at professional ethics from the religious tradition does not necessarily imply, though, consideration of God or ethical propositions in a way that academic categories identify narrowly as theological. Philosophy, from Plato through Kant, also considers God. The difference that focus on the organic can make is not the difference between philosophy and theology but the difference between seeing God as subject rather than an object. The religious tradition "does not understand [knowledge of God] as a noetic relation of a thinking subject to a neutral object of thought, but rather as . . . the genuinely reciprocal meeting in the fullness of life between one active existence and another." M. BUBER, ECLIPSE OF GOD 32-33 (1952). In the Hebraic tradition, "genuinely recipro-

Texas Law Review Vol. 65:963, 1987

The lawyer in *The Case of the Unwanted Will*, for example, did not err in turning his attention to Mary, in John's absence. (Nor would it have been a mistake to turn his attention to John, in Mary's absence; if evenhandedness is important, it would have been more evenhanded to talk privately with each of them.) The deep things to be found out about John and Mary, in particular the deep things involved in their will making, are family things.[49] Inquiring into deep family things is not only tolerated, but it is required by common representation, because *the client is the family*. Any other description is incomplete and, thus, untruthful and corrupting.[50] If an adequate account of what is going on in the family (to the extent that it has to do with their will making) requires talking to either or both parents alone, then talking to them alone is appropriate. If the family is well represented, it (that is, each person in it) will learn how to take Mary's purposes into account, because Mary is in the family.

Giles Milhaven demonstrates my point in an analysis of Bernard Malamud's novel *Dubin's Lives*.[51] In part, *Dubin's Lives* is the story of a man who has to choose between his wife and his mistress, and chooses his wife. He chooses not because he loves his wife rather than his mistress; he loves both. Rather, as Milhaven says, he loves a *life*. In "the Jewish matchmaking tradition, a man and woman . . . will in marriage . . . come to know and love each other's *lives*. Leaving father and mother, they will become one flesh . . . in their spontaneous, enduring desire to keep sharing *lives*."[52] Dubin's story denies "the assumption

cal meeting" is prototypically the meeting of God and community. *See* E. BERKOVITS, MAJOR THEMES IN MODERN PHILOSOPHIES OF JUDAISM 111 (1974); M. GOLDBERG, *supra* note 8, at 103-04.

The other side of the difference I mean to identify in this Essay tends away from community. The (modern) philosophical viewpoint "is the product of a consciousness which conceives of itself as autonomous and strives to become so." M. BUBER, *supra*, at 32. The religious tradition not only teaches something else, it also announces a moral objection to the striving for autonomy, on both religious and philosophical grounds, as idolatrous, as "the *worship* of freedom for its own sake," *id.* at 119-20, and as "[p]ower without faithfulness"—that is, the immoral use of persons as means to an end. M. FRIEDMAN, MARTIN BUBER: THE LIFE OF DIALOGUE 119 (1955). Thus Buber said that the price the West paid for the political consequences of the Enlightenment was the decay of *organic* forms of life such as family, village, and union in work. *See id.* at 123. We are left with the alienated world described by Franz Kafka. *See* M. BUBER, ON JUDAISM, *supra* note 8, at 131-32.

49. If will making is an example of "family things," then that fact also binds lawyers. The object of professional life is the goodness, not the freedom, of clients. Freedom is a necessary condition for goodness, but it is not the object of the enterprise. *See* Shaffer, *The Legal Ethics of Servanthood*, 8 SOC. RESP.: JOURNALISM L. MED. 34, 44 (1982); White, *The Ethics of Argument: Plato's* Gorgias *and the Modern Lawyer*, 50 U. CHI. L. REV. 849, 873 (1983).

50. *See* M. GOLDBERG, *supra* note 8, at 103 ("[A]ny description of human existence that denies or underestimates the full repercussions of the community's life for the life of an individual offers an account which is in the last analysis no more than a fairy tale.").

51. B. MALAMUD, DUBIN'S LIVES (1979).

52. Milhaven, *An Experienced Value of Marital Faithfulness in* Dubin's Lives, 12 J. RELIGIOUS ETHICS 82, 94-96 (1984) (emphasis added); *see supra* note 43.

Radical Individualism

that morality is something we create through individual choice rather than the shaping of our lives through the disciplined discovery of the good."[53]

To illustrate this shaping of lives in a disciplined discovery of the good, suppose in *The Case of the Unwanted Will* some further facts about Mary's purposes.[54] One of the couple's sons, Henry, was married for ten years to, and is now divorced from, a woman named Susan. Henry and Susan had children who now live with Susan, and Henry lives alone. John and Mary, however, remain fond of Susan and, despite the divorce, continue to be friendly with her. The lawyer's questions to John and Mary have brought this affection to the surface, but John, as is typical,[55] thinks of property and family together, and Susan no longer is in the family. During the joint interview, Mary sits silent while John says that they want "Henry's share" to go to Henry and, if Henry is dead, to his children. In the cases of the other children of John and Mary, says John, the child's share is to go to the child's spouse. What Mary says to the lawyer when they are alone, however, is that she wants her will to provide for Susan. Mary wants some of her family's property to be available for Susan, after Mary dies, when what is left of Mary will be in her fam-

53. S. Hauerwas, How Christian Universities Contribute to the Corruption of Youth: Church and University in a Confused Age, (Feb. 1986) (unpublished manuscript). Buber echoes the point:

> [I]nstitutions of . . . personal life cannot be reformed by a free feeling (although this is also required). Marriage can never be renewed except by that which is always the source of all true marriage: that two human beings reveal the You to one another. It is of this that the You that is I for neither of them builds a marriage.

M. Buber, I and Thou, *supra* note 8, at 95.

54. It is important to hypothesize *something* about Mary's purposes. (The *A.B.A. Journal's* discussion did not.) Otherwise, she is a problem rather than a person. One could suppose, for example, a Gilbert-and-Sullivan plot, in which Mary has borne a child early in life, before she met John. The child has been adopted or is otherwise being cared for by others (and is therefore in another family). Mary nevertheless wants to provide for him in her will.

A friend of mine who is in full time law practice suggests another possibility:

> I had a case where each spouse had children by a prior marriage. All of the children were adults. I prepared a rough draft of their wills in which they were treating each other's children equally with their own. One of the wife's two children then died. This had very unsettling effects and must have caused both of them to reexamine a lot of things. I am not sure of the thought process that took place, but each person then individually came to see me about the finalization of each person's will. In his will he disinherited two of his three children, leaving his estate to one child and the remaining child of his wife. The wife was not present when the husband made these decisions. The wife came to see me at a later time. Her husband had shown her his copy of his will. In her will, she left property to her child, the surviving spouse of her dead child, and her grandchild. In addition she also left property to her husband's children equally (including the two children her husband had disinherited). She also included a trust so that upon her death, her husband would be provided for, but would not have control over the assets . . . . She was not going to show him a copy. Perhaps she was looking through the cracked magnifying glass, seeing his and her family as a whole.

55. *See* Shaffer, *Slippered Feet*, *supra* note 11, at 196.

Texas Law Review Vol. 65:963, 1987

ily. Mary will be there, not because of a fictional notion about ownership, but because Mary did not die alone.

It is interesting to note how the narrative force of that statement about Mary's property changes as the case is described differently. Does Mary dispose of *her* property, *her family's* property, *her husband's* property, or *her children's* property? The point is that seeing and saying are moral and legal acts, and moral and legal arts.[56] The law is a language;[57] legal authority will support any one of these ways of speaking of this property, and any of the statements is a moral judgment, as, indeed, the word "property" is a moral judgment.[58]

Mary's conception of the family includes Susan, both now and after Mary dies. Mary sees her death and her property together; the lawyer's questions have caused her to do that. The lawyer's skill includes the moral art of seeing, of "knowing what's what when we act,"[59] and of training his client in that moral art.[60] Mary looks at her property and her death through the broken magnifying glass of her family, and now she sees Susan *in* her family. The lawyer has caused her to remember to see in this way through the broken magnifying glass that is her family.[61] The inquiry by the lawyer turned up this more truthful description of the family. Consequently, the lawyer's inquiry was a moral act, and the exercise of a moral art. To the extent that the quandary calls for a judgment about what the lawyer has already done, my argument is that he has begun to do a good thing. It is a good thing because it is a more truthful description of the reality that is the goal of the lawyer's work.[62]

56. *See supra* notes 7 and 12.

57. *See* J. WHITE, *supra* note 30, at 231-74.

58. *See id.* at 263-71; White, *The Conversational Process of the Law*, LAW QUADRANGLE NOTES, Summer 1985, at 26, 30, 31.

59. *See supra* note 6 and accompanying text.

60. *See supra* note 4. White, in a similar argument, says Jane Austen trains her readers in kindness. *See* J. WHITE, *supra* note 30, at 190-91.

61. This is not "the outcome of a particularly legal negotiation," *see supra* note 26, but an exercise in description, or the product of a vision of reality, *see supra* note 17.

62. To see Mary as self-ruling (autonomous) and essentially alone is untruthful. Dworkin argues that the formulation of the principle of moral autonomy is either trivial or false. *See* Dworkin, *supra* note 46, at 57-58. The principle of autonomy also is paradoxical:

> Consider the statement that moral agents ought to be autonomous. Either that statement is an objectively true statement or it is not. If it is, then there is at least one moral assertion whose claim to validity does not rest on its being accepted by a moral agent. If it is not, then no criticism can be made of a moral agent who refuses to accept it.

Id. at 161-62. Further, it is ahistorical and a false anthropology:

> From the temporal perspective the commitments of my earlier self must bind (to some degree) my later self. It cannot always be open for the later self to renounce the commitments of the earlier self. This implies that even self-imposed obligations create a world of 'otherness'—a world which is independent of my (current) will and which is not subject to my choices and decisions. The distance between my earlier and later selves is only quantitatively different from that between myself and others.

Id. at 164-65. It is unfactual, leaving culture out of account: "That I have obligations of gratitude to

Radical Individualism

It is more interesting, though, if *The Case of the Unwanted Will* must be seen as a quandary, to make it a quandary about what the lawyer should do now that the exercise of this moral art of seeing has described reality in such a way that the employment itself is a problem. Either multiple-client employment is no longer possible, or we must change our rule about when multiple-client employment is possible. The estate planning issue, therefore, is whether this family is equal to the truth of what it is. The legal ethics issue is whether this lawyer, employed by this family (which is now seen in this broken-magnifying-glass way), is to continue to have anything to do with the truth of what this family is.

I understand the objection that my way of describing the family, as the client, is patriarchal and therefore untruthful or unfair to married women. It is undoubtedly the case that much of conventional legal ethics is sexist. It is important nevertheless to identify the roots of the sexism, and to describe an ethic that is adequate to deal with sexism without being untruthful. I argue that the roots of sexism in legal ethics do not have to do with the family, or with the view of organic community that I urge here, but instead with the tellers of our stories. Fairness requires not stories that describe women outside of families, because our stories already say that that sort of story would be false,[63] but *women's* stories about families. With all our patriarchal self-deception, we property lawyers do seem able to accept the truth when it is described well. To know the truth, we need the stories told by Jane Austen, George Eliot, Anne Tyler, and family biographers such as Phyllis Rose[64] and Lis Harris[65]—not as a substitute for family stories told by Trollope and Faulkner, but in addition to and in enlargement of their stories.

IV. The Communal Context

A. The Lawyer for the Situation

The proposed ABA rule on the lawyer as intermediary apparently

my aged parents, of aid to the stranger attacked by thieves, of obedience to the laws of a democratic and just state, of rectification to those treated unjustly by my ancestors or nation are matters that are independent of my voluntary commitments." *Id.* at 165. Dworkin concludes his criticism: "It is only through a more adequate understanding of notions of tradition, authority, commitment, and loyalty, and of the forms of human community in which these have their roots, that we shall be able to develop a conception of autonomy free from paradox and worthy of admiration." *Id.* at 170. Stephen Pepper is attempting this "more adequate understanding" in legal ethics. *See* Pepper, *supra* note 4.

63. *See* Hauerwas, *supra* note 8, at 63.

64. P. Rose, *supra* note 47.

65. L. Harris, Holy Days: The World of a Hasidic Family (1985); *see also* M. Goldberg, Theology and Narrative, 13-15 (discussing C. Christ, Diving Deep and Surfacing 137 (1980)); Gilbert, *From Our Mothers' Libraries—Women Who Created the Novel*, N.Y. Times, May 4, 1986, § 7 (Book Review), at 30.

Texas Law Review Vol. 65:963, 1987

derives from Geoffrey Hazard's description of stories from the private law practice of Louis D. Brandeis.[66] Brandeis, however, did not say lawyer "as intermediary"; he said lawyer "for the situation."[67] Brandeis first used the singular word "situation" to describe a bankruptcy case involving a family business. This pattern of thought (and of practice), no doubt, was evident also in Brandeis' estate planning and probate and trust work for the Warren family. If his work is divided according to the norm that a lawyer is employed by the individuals in a family rather than by a family as a whole, then at one time or another Brandeis was lawyer for the senior Mr. Warren (founder of the family business), for Mr. Warren's wife, for Mr. Warren's estate, for the testamentary trust established in Mr. Warren's will, for temporary entities created (through Brandeis' work) to manage the family business, and for individual members of the family in the second generation.[68] Brandeis first used the word "situation" in the Senate hearings on his nomination to the Supreme Court, when he was defending himself against the charge that his representation during the bankruptcy of a family business demonstrated that he did not know who his client was.[69] In other words, Brandeis had violated the norm that a lawyer represents only individuals, except on extraordinary and necessarily superficial facts. He was asked who (singular) his client was. And, in answer, he chose the word "*situation*."

Joseph Fletcher later used the word "situation" to advocate a modern version of contextual religious ethics,[70] an ethics that puts particular stress on being truthful about what is going on, and that bases moral judgment on the context described in this truthful way.[71] The key point of distinction for present purposes is that contextual ethics denies the distinction between fact and value. When Brandeis used the word that Fletcher would use later—*situation*—he accomplished several things. He

66. G. HAZARD, *supra* note 2, at 58-68.

67. *See* Frank, *The Legal Ethics of Louis D. Brandeis*, 17 STAN. L. REV. 683, 702 (1965).

68. *See id.* at 699-703, 708-09.

69. *Hearings Before the Subcomm. of the Senate Comm. on the Judiciary on the Nomination of Louis D. Brandeis to Be an Associate Justice of the Supreme Court of the United States*, 64th Cong., 1st Sess. 287 (1916).

70. *See* J. FLETCHER, *supra* note 6, at 26-37.

71. *See supra* note 4. Fletcher made his argument within a modern school of ethics that exerts almost as much influence over religious ethics as Immanuel Kant's ethics of autonomy exerts over academic philosophical ethics. I mean the "school" (now in at least its fifth intellectual generation) of H. Richard Niebuhr of the Yale Divinity School, which is often identified as one part of a modern "ethics of responsibility." *See* A. JONSEN, RESPONSIBILITY IN MODERN RELIGIOUS ETHICS 140-46 (1968). *See generally* H.R. NIEBUHR, THE RESPONSIBLE SELF (1963). Fletcher, Hauerwas, and McClendon, *see supra* note 17, belong to that school, as does Goldberg, *see supra* notes 8, 65. The Niebuhr school's influence is manifest more in religious ethics than in academic moral philosophy, although the moral philosophers Pincoffs, *see supra* note 17, Murdoch, *see supra* note 7, and MacIntyre, *see supra* note 4, sympathize with much of it.

made a moral judgment about what was going on in the Senate hearings concerning a moral judgment he had made years earlier when confronted with the fact that the human harmony he had perceived or created was falling apart. Brandeis had decided originally that the human harmony was sufficient to be his client, and might have been (as the Warren family was) something prior even to the people he met when he decided that, together and not alone, they could be his client.

Brandeis thus looked at what he had done through a broken magnifying glass such as the Warren family, and he approved of it. The hounding senators failed in the attempt to make him ashamed of himself.[72] He rejected their implicit argument that a lawyer should be employed only by individuals. No doubt he considered, in rejecting the implicit argument, that the harmonies people create often become inharmonious, but he nonetheless decided that his initial hope for their harmony was justified. This hope, I take it, inspired Hazard to suggest a legal ethic to accomodate the harmony.[73] The harmony assumed importance because it rested in part on a common reality prior to the individuals with whom Brandeis dealt—the same individuals who later quarreled and used the law against one another—and in part on a hope for this common reality.[74]

Hazard understood from the Brandeis stories a coherent ethical argument about lawyers who are employed by groups, prototypically families. I infer that, in Hazard's opinion, the argument from the Brandeis stories was coherent enough to justify a new regulatory rule and a reasoned justification for the rule; the bar association politicians took it

72. Hazard suggests that one reason for the collapse of this attack on Brandeis was "concessions from other reputable lawyers that they had often done exactly as Brandeis." G. HAZARD, *supra* note 2, at 61. If Brandeis was wrong about "lawyering for the situation," then he certainly violated the rules of professional conduct. "But if Brandeis was right, and the record of good practitioners testifies to that conclusion, then what is required is not interdiction of 'lawyering for the situation' but reexamination of what is meant by loyalty to the client." *Id.* at 64.

73. *See id.* at 65 ("When a relationship between the clients is amenable to 'situation' treatment, giving it that treatment is perhaps the best service a lawyer can render to anyone.").

74. Lawyering for the situation is thus different from lawyering for an individual client. It provides no "structure of goals and constraints imposed from outside. The lawyer and the clients must create that structure for themselves, with the lawyer being an active participant." *Id.* at 66. This assertion is overstated to the extent that it fails to recognize that culture and tradition provide a structure of goals and constraints. My argument here is not sentimental; it is anthropological. *See supra* note 35. One of Iris Murdoch's fictional characters (Bradley Pearson) notices the structure of culture and tradition in a doleful, almost Calvinist way.

> The wicked regard time as discontinuous, the wicked dull their sense of natural causality. The good feel being as a total dense mesh of tiny interconnections. My lightest whim can affect the whole future. Because I smoke a cigarette and smile over an unworthy thought another man may die in torment.

I. MURDOCH, THE BLACK PRINCE 98 (1973).

from there.[75] If the result is ambiguous, as I think it is, it is not because the stories from Brandeis' life are ambiguous. Brandeis did not regret being a family lawyer. Nor did he regret the hope he had for families. He was, after all, by the time of the Senate hearings actively aware of his Jewish heritage, and, in Israel, "[t]he family is the nursery of the race."[76] He also was involved then in the Zionist movement, and in the American labor movement.[77] Both are things of families and of family metaphors.

Estate planning cases such as *The Case of the Unwanted Will* benefit more from Brandeis' understanding that a lawyer can be, and often is, a lawyer for the situation, than from the ABA's new regulatory rule, a pale vestige of Brandeis' understanding. We can transfer our insights from Brandeis' practice, and from what he said about it in retrospect, to the story of John and Mary in the law office. If John's and Mary's circumstances constitute a problem or a quandary, then the solution suggested by the Brandeis story is that Mary's secret purpose belongs *in* the family. Being a family means taking purposes and secrets into account, because being in a family means primarily that a person is *known*, even before she knows. (Susan is known; that fact presents the issue in the case.) The job of the lawyer for the family properly includes the description, in the language that is the law, of what a family knows, of what a family is, of what *this* family is. The job involves skills the lawyer, when young, may not have thought about—skills, though, that older lawyers use and teach to the young.

In *The Case of the Unwanted Will*, the most *irresponsible* thing a lawyer could do is to send either of these people to another lawyer, or both of them to two other lawyers. If that is the command of our professional ethics, or even the easiest available "solution" to the case from our regulatory rules, then our ethics and our rules are corrupting. They corrupt the family in general, and *this* family in particular. A lawyer following the rules is irresponsible because in fact, the family is the lawyer's client. The lawyer who sends the family away is not able to respond to his client. He is disabled by a false ethic and, and in trying to protect himself, he harms his client. My argument rests on the conviction that a family is something worth representing; the conviction is shown in, and is the product of, the stories we tell about ourselves, including deep and complex stories such as Anne Tyler's, and shallow and simple stories such as those we see on television.

75. Hazard, the reporter to the A.B.A. Commission on Evaluation of Professional Standards, was, I think, the principal intellectual force behind the early drafts.

76. S. COHON, JUDAISM: A WAY OF LIFE 166 (1948).

77. *See* A. VORSPAN, GIANTS OF JUSTICE 26 (1960).

Radical Individualism

In estate planning, and in much of business planning and corporate representation (to mention only a few examples), lawyers are invited to consider the changes that arise because members of families own things, gather wealth from things, and then grow old and die. If the social order is threatened by a disappearing moral consensus, or because our philosophers have so ravaged our language that we no longer can describe our moral consensus,[78] and if our organic communities are made fragile by the illusory promises of democratic liberalism, the result is not a world of lonely individuals, but a world in which groups like families are on cultural desert islands. As Robert N. Bellah and his colleagues describe this perception, "the family is no longer an integral part of a larger moral ecology tying the individual to community, church, and nation. The family is the core of the private sphere, whose aim is not to link individuals to the public world but to avoid it as far as possible."[79]

Anne Tyler's most recent novel, *Accidental Tourist*,[80] demonstrates Bellah's point. Macon's wife Sarah says to him: "If you could live any way you wanted, I suppose you'd end up on a desert island with no other human beings." Macon says that is not so: "I'd have you, and Ethan [his son], and my sister and brothers." And Sarah says, "But no people. I mean people there just by chance."[81] Sarah was not looking through the broken magnifying glass; Macon was. He knew he was not alone.

Collective isolation probably is not good politically, nor is it an adequate premise for a professional ethic that ignores the realities of the communities that we, in our communal isolations, have. These communities are what we present to our lawyers. Lawyers who are invited into such (to use Brandeis' word) situations are invited into sacred places. They are all the more sacred to the extent that these human harmonies somehow survive in a commonwealth of strangers. The moral principle, if we still need a principle after we see the reality, is that lawyers should endeavor in such places not to make things worse.

I confess that this view of the world seems to disturb law students;[82] it is, however, a view of things that brings nods of approval from the older lawyers I meet in professional gatherings—lawyers who have more experience than I or my students in ordinary, county-seat, Wednesday-afternoon law practice. It is possible—although this is boasting—that

78. *See, e.g.*, A. MACINTYRE, *supra* note 4, at 1-5; J. WHITE, *supra* note 30, at 278-85; REVISIONS, *supra* note 4, at 2-15.

79. R. BELLAH, R. MADSEN, W. SULLIVAN, A. SWINDLER & S. TIPTON, HABITS OF THE HEART 112 (1985) [hereinafter R. BELLAH].

80. A. TYLER, *supra* note 1.

81. *Id.* at 48-49.

82. *See* T. SHAFFER, TEACHER'S GUIDE TO AMERICAN LEGAL ETHICS 81-84 (1985).

the reason this perspective disturbs students is that it has moral substance for professional ethics, a subject that often has no substance except as a branch of administrative or criminal law. It is also possible that what is uncomfortable, in the family perspective on cases like *The Case of the Unwanted Will*, is the realization that the issues we identify as we discuss the morals of lawyers are sticky and uncertain. It is much easier for a lawyer to behave as if he were a clerk in a driver's-license office than to behave as someone who invites trust from families and then charges by the hour for accepting it.

What perhaps makes a family perspective on the law office appealing is not its ideology, but its truthfulness.[83] In estate planning, the family-lawyer perspective on will making (and on corporate practice) is relatively truthful because it takes account of the shared reality of death seen with property, and property seen with death; that shared reality is thus not a private fate or even an experience we need to talk about in the singular. We cannot take it with us, but we need not die alone.

B. *Values Destroyed by Death*

I have used in my teaching of wills and trusts a remarkable article from research psychology called *Values Destroyed by Death*.[84] Diggory and Rothman, the authors, asked several thousand people to choose from among seven consequences of dying the one that seems most distasteful.

> The consequence of my own death that seems to me most distasteful is:
> A. I could no longer have any experience.
> B. I am uncertain as to what might happen to me if there is a life after death.
> C. I am afraid of what might happen to my body after death.
> D. I could no longer care for my dependents.
> E. My death would cause grief to my relatives and friends.
> F. All my plans and projects would come to an end.
> G. The process of dying might be painful.[85]

83. *Cf. supra* text following note 62 (discussing the consequences of a society's acceptance of the untruthful ethics of autonomy). Bellah and his colleagues do not argue that Americans try to regulate their lives according to the ethics of autonomy or even that they accept the suppositions that lie behind liberal democratic political theory. *See* R. BELLAH, *supra* note 79. Instead, the connection between our traditions and the way we live our lives has faded, taking with it our power to explain what we do. As a consequnce, we can use only sappy words such as "lifestyle," and fatuous words such as "autonomy," to try to account for ourselves. These attempts at self-description and self-justification fail because we do not know what we are doing.

84. Diggory & Rothman, *Values Destroyed by Death*, 63 J. ABNORMAL & SOC. PSYCHOLOGY 205 (1961).

85. *Id.* at 205. I invite the reader to participate in this exercise. First, answer the question as if you had been casually stopped on the street. Then answer the question again as if you were a client talking to a lawyer about estate planning.

Radical Individualism

Diggory and Rothman reported that, when stopped on the street, people most often chose one of two answers:

A. I could no longer have any experience; and
E. My death would cause grief to my relatives and friends.[86]

In talking with will clients and with the lawyers who work with them I have found that there is a difference in answers to the question when it is put to persons involved in estate planning. According to my unscientific replication of the study, when people were thinking about estate planning the top answers were:

D. I could no longer care for my dependents; and
F. All my plans and projects would come to an end.[87]

I conclude that this disparity is evidence of two shifts. First, the concern about experiences becomes a concern for projects; the perspective changes from such things as "the Aspen ski experience" to working. Second, the concern for causing grief becomes a concern for the protection of families through wills, trusts, and life insurance.

In both cases, working at estate planning is a way to look at death and at property. The death of a property owner is not a private matter or a matter of survival through things. It is, rather, a matter of survival through those who are supported by work—usually (normally *and* normatively) through a family. The "situation" that Brandeis discussed,[88] when seen in cases like *The Case of the Unwanted Will*, is a reality as much as the people themselves. In fact, the family is the deepest and most pervasive reality in social life.[89]

86. *Id.* at 206-09.

87. *See* T. SHAFFER, DEATH, PROPERTY, AND LAWYERS 71-106 (1970).

88. *See supra* subpart IV(A).

89. The importance of the family even in modern social life is apparent in S. STOUFFER, COMMUNISM, CONFORMITY, AND CIVIL LIBERTIES (1963). Stouffer attempted to determine whether there was in America a national anxiety over communism, using an elaborate polling procedure that involved thousands of respondents and hundreds of interviewers. *See id.* at 15-19. The study found little anxiety about communism, even in the days of Senator Joseph McCarthy's anticommunist enterprise and the activities of the House Un-American Activities Committee. *Id.* at 54-55. Less than 1% of a sampling of Americans in several categories mentioned communism. *Id.* at 59, 68-70. The greatest aggregation of worry was, as Anne Tyler would have predicted, about the family. *Id.* at 59. 43% of the subjects said they were worried about personal matters that had to do with the family, with family matters collectively described, or with family businesses. *Id.* at 60. The family predominated in the responses that Stouffer quoted verbatim, even in those examples that were identified as personal (*i.e.*, individual) by Stouffer. *See id.* at 60-65 (most of the responses he classified as personal were related to support of dependents). Only 8% of Stouffer's respondents mentioned world affairs, and of those, most of the answers reflected or included concern about what would happen to members of the family in war. *Id.* at 81-82.

Stouffer's interview questions initially were open-ended, and then narrowed into the categories that had provoked the study. Here are examples of Stouffer's questions:

3. What kinds of things do you worry most about?

V. The Influence of the Religious Tradition

A. Paternalism

There are trends in both popular and scholarly views of families. The popular trends are evident, for example, in the movement over the last generation to television situation comedies about black families and away from series about doctors and lawyers, which in turn had replaced series about towering pine trees and cowboys in saloons. Fashion and change in fashion are evident among ethics scholars too—prominently with regard to what has been said about paternalism.[90]

Paternalism, in most writing on the professions, is a bad word. But *pater* (father) is not a bad word. The Hebraic religious tradition chose and retains the word, if only as metaphor, to describe God, despite the difficulty of a theology of patriarchy.[91] The description approximates with a family metaphor the understanding of the Hebrew prophets that the God of Israel is a God with feelings—the "divine pathos," as Abraham Joshua Heschel called it.[92] God's pathos means that He feels as a

5. Are there other problems you worry or are concerned about, especially political or world problems?

. . . .

7. . . . .

B. Were there other things? For example, did you talk about any dangers facing people in the United States?

8. Here is a list of topics which have been discussed in the papers recently.

A. Which ones do you remember talking about with your friends in the last week or so?

1. Atom or hydrogen bombs
2. Communists in the United States
3. Crime and juvenile delinquency
4. Danger of World War III
5. Farm prices
6. High prices of things you buy
7. High taxes
8. Negro-white problems
9. Possibility of another depression

X. Threats to freedom in the United States

Y. None of these, don't know

B. Which one on that whole list seems most important to you?—whether you talked about it or not.

C. Which one seems next most important?

Id. at 250.

Stouffer's study uncovered truths we do not see when we adopt the language of radical individualism. *See* R. BELLAH, *supra* note 79, at 84 ("We find ourselves not independently of other people and institutions but through them. We never get to the bottom of our selves on our own. We discover who we are face to face and side by side with others in work, love, and learning.").

90. For sources evaluating paternalism in health care, see J. CHILDRESS, WHO SHOULD DECIDE? PATERNALISM IN HEALTH CARE (1982); W. MAY, THE PHYSICIAN'S COVENANT: IMAGES OF THE HEALER IN MEDICAL ETHICS (1981).

91. *See, e.g.*, E. SCHUSSLER FIORENZA, IN MEMORY OF HER: A FEMINIST THEOLOGICAL RECONSTRUCTION OF CHRISTIAN ORIGINS 53-56 (1985); Wire, *Economics and Early Christian Voices*, 19 PAC. THEOLOGICAL REV. 15, 41-42 (1985).

92. A. HESCHEL, *supra* note 10, at 51 ("The ultimate is not a law but a judge, not a power but a father.").

father feels; the prophetic response to God is thus *sympathy*.[93] Father, consequently, is not a bad word; it cannot be. Writers on professionalism erred in thinking otherwise.

It is not a moral condemnation of standards of professional conduct, then, to call them "fatherly" (paternalistic); nor would it be a moral condemnation to call them "motherly" (maternalistic) or even parent-like (parentalistic). If we take our theological metaphors seriously, to analogize behavior to the parental is to fit it to our traditions. The retreat from parental metaphors in modern writing on professionalism is subject to two criticisms. First, the analysis has not proceeded deeply enough; writing on professionalism has been duped into announcing a moral principle when it should have been concerned with description—truthfulness—in the comparison of a professional person and a parent, and of the virtues of good parents and the failures of bad parents. Writing on professionalism should describe the moral reasons that we use family metaphors, in theology and in professional life and it then should turn those reasons into doctrine. Second, the condemnation of paternalism (parentalism) in modern writing on ethics in the professions is the product of the lonely-individual doctrine in philosophical ethics, and of the philosophical distinction between fact and value, particularly in its disposition to turn the parental metaphor into a moral principle.[94]

Radical individualism is the philosophy of an adolescent who wishes he had no parents. The school of moral philosophy that posits a parentless moral agent duped us into accepting an untruthful description of the world. I notice that untruthful description in *The Case of the Unwanted Will*, when legal-ethics commentators describe the woman making the will as a radical individual rather than as a wife, a mother, and a member of a family. The alternative is to understand enough about oneself and one's client to know that family words describe more than a set of social roles that a woman puts on as she might put on a hat.

The argument I make here is an argument from the Hebraic religious tradition. In Judaism, the family is not merely fundamental; it is ordained. God dealt with the family; He made a covenant with it. Israel is a family of families.[95] This "master story"[96] has innumerable implications, some obvious and some subtle, for Hebraic norms on sex, raising children, business and property, and inheritance. These implications

93. *See id.* at 116-24.

94. Paternalism in a narrow sense is consistent with the ethics of autonomy. *See* J. CHILDRESS, *supra* note 90, at 8-10 (giving the example of a father who respects his children). The ethics of autonomy speaks of these relationships in terms of freedom of choice.

95. *See supra* note 28.

96. *See* M. GOLDBERG, *supra* note 8; *supra* note 28.

turn on the moral teaching that a person alone is not complete; as the Midrash says, "He who lives without a wife lives without blessing, without life, without joy, without help, without good, and without peace."[97]

In Christianity, marriage is, in the Hebraic ethics of Jesus, so fundamental that it is sinful to dissolve it.[98] St. Paul's metaphors equate family and church, and speak of the church as the body of Christ.[99] The early Christian church was a patriarchy that tried to be open to notions of equality and partnership *within* the metaphor of family.[100] That aspiration was fundamentally Judaic: "[U]nity is a task . . . to endure means to be *one*."[101]

There are two ways to take account of the religious tradition in American legal ethics. One way is to note that the cultural deposits of most American lawyers include the religious tradition. Failing to take account of the tradition therefore is failing to be truthful. As Peter Berger put it, "The very least that a knowledge of religious traditions has to offer is a catalogue of heresies for possible home use."[102] That is, the religious tradition, when we are conscious of it, helps to keep us from repeating obvious moral mistakes and, more profoundly, it influences our behavior when we are not conscious of it. Berger thought that these influences were appropriate: "[I]n everyday life it is just as important that some things can silently be taken for granted as that some things are reaffirmed in so many words."[103] In that sense, law-office behavior probably rests on religious tradition in an ordinary and everyday way. The risk in Berger's reassurance, as Robert Bellah and his colleagues recently demonstrated, is that we will lose or distort influences that we do not bring into the light and make sense of.[104] The work of bringing moral influences into the light and making sense of them is the purpose of the discipline of ethics.

Muddled thinking about conflicts of interest in estate planning and in legal work for associations that account for themselves with the metaphor of family illustrates Bellah's point. This muddled thinking is like Gerald Dworkin's analysis of Sartre's World War II French patriot.[105] The patriot had to choose (as Sartre saw it) whether to stay at home in a

97. OUR MASTERS TAUGHT: RABBINIC STORIES AND SAYINGS 87 (J. Petuchowski trans. & ed. 1982) (quoting *Midrash Tehillim* LIX).

98. *See* 1 *Corinthians* 7:10-11.

99. *See Ephesians* 5:21-33.

100. *See* Norquist, *Family Dynamics in the Bible*, SEASONS, Summer 1984, at 3, 3.

101. A. HESCHEL, *supra* note 10, at 102-03.

102. P. BERGER, A RUMOR OF ANGELS 78 (1969).

103. *Id.* at 36.

104. *See supra* note 83.

105. Dworkin, *supra* note 46, at 159-60.

country occupied by the German army to care for his aged mother, or to join the Free French abroad. Sartre saw the story as posing a prototypical dilemma in the ethics of autonomy; he argued that the patriot had to choose what to do, and that the morals governing choice were morals because the patriot chose them.[106] Dworkin said that the dilemma existed only because of deeper moral realities: the family, and a nation that demanded patriotism.[107] To dispose of either of those realities is to dispose of the dilemma.

In *The Case of the Unwanted Will*, to dispose of the family in the will client's life, so that her relationship with her former daughter-in-law is a human harmony that stands independent of a larger harmony, is to eliminate the dilemma. She then will make her will alone; indeed she will probably not visit the office with her husband in the first place. To dispose of her continuing attachment to this other woman who in the law *is* no longer her daughter, is to say that she will accept the will that has been drafted for her. In either of those situations it would not occur to anybody that the law-office routine had anything moral about it. But, of course, and in *any* case, it does have something moral about it. Bellah's point is that we will lose the force of that reality if we lose the words to make ourselves aware of it. And as we lose the force of the reality of our harmonies, we lose the skill for seeing them in extraordinary cases, in, as Brandeis and Fletcher said, situations.[108]

The second way to take account of the religious tradition in legal ethics is not as a contribution to liberal democracy or a corrective to radical individualism, but as a radical alternative. As Stanley Hauerwas put it in reference to Christians, Christians should

> be the sort of people and community that can become a real option and provide for real confrontation for others. Unless such a community exists, then no real option exists. The manner of providing such an option, moreover, entails that Christians go to every land and every people in the hope that they can elicit a real confrontation on matters that matter.[109]

An interesting and parallel statement about Judaism could be made here, one that would show how Jews also provide an alternative to the world,[110] and how the Christian witness and evangelism to which

106. J. SARTRE, *Existentialism*, in EXISTENTIALISM AND HUMAN EMOTIONS 24 (1957).

107. Dworkin, *supra* note 46, at 160.

108. *See supra* Part IV(A).

109. S. HAUERWAS, *supra* note 8, at 105.

110. *See* M. BUBER, ON JUDAISM, *supra* note 8, at 124-25, 211; *see also* L. HARRIS, *supra* note 65 (Harris' narrative account of the religious lifestyle of a Hasidic family from Brooklyn, New York, presenting one example of a Jewish alternative in the world).

Texas Law Review Vol. 65:963, 1987

Hauerwas alludes has its roots in Israel, and in Jesus of Nazareth's life and death in a Jewish family.

Either account of the religious tradition's influence in legal ethics affirms the reality of the family metaphor: God is not a premise; He is the Father.[111]

I do not argue that one of these ways is as useful for legal ethics as the other. If I were to compare them, I would argue that only the latter view, the religious tradition explicated not as a corrective but as a radical alternative in the world of lawyers, is adequate. But either view identifies the religious tradition in ordinary, Wednesday-afternoon law practice.[112] Both ways show the fundamental importance of family to an adequate legal ethic in the culture of modern American lawyers.

The example I have used is an estate planning example. Estate planning is seen as family based rather more easily than personal injury claims or securities registration; in fact the irony of most writing about ethics in estate planning is that it describes family situations (as *The Case of the Unwanted Will* does), or encounters an association that wants to think of itself as a family, and then resolves them without reference to the family they claim and come from and go back to. Putting the family back into ethical discussion—*finding* it where it is or where it claims it wants to be —among lawyers would be, even in the most modest catalogue-of-heresies use of the religious tradition, a matter of describing what goes on. A radical use of Hebraic religious tradition would cut more deeply, affect more globally, and disturb profoundly. For that reason, even we believers do not like to think about it.

B. A Biblical Estate Planning Story

Judah was under siege by the powerful armies of Babylon. God told the prophet Jeremiah, and Jeremiah told Judah, that Jerusalem would fall and be destroyed and its people taken away in captivity. Jeremiah's countrymen imprisoned him for telling them about the fate of Judah. God then ordered Jeremiah to buy a piece of land—or, rather, to exercise his legal right to redeem land that had belonged to his uncle. Jeremiah obeyed: He paid for the land, obtained the deed from his cousin, and had the deed witnessed by his fellow inmates. Jeremiah then ordered his secretary, Baruch, to

111. *See* H. THEILICKE, BETWEEN GOD AND SATAN 40 (1958); *see also* M. BUBER, I AND THOU, *supra* note 8, at 129 ("[W]hat confronts us immediately and first and always . . . can only be addressed, not asserted.").

112. *See, e.g.*, Jones, *Lawyers and Justice: The Uneasy Ethics of Partisanship*, 23 VILL. L. REV. 957, 975 (1978).

> take these copies of the deed of purchase, the sealed and the unsealed, and deposit them in an earthenware jar so that they may be preserved for a long time. For these are the words of the Lord of Hosts the God of Israel: The time will come when houses, fields, and vineyards will again be bought and sold in this land.[113]

In this story, the symbol of the covenant that God will renew with His people, when He will "plant them in this land," is a Wednesday-afternoon legal transaction within a family. The transaction will lay proved in an earthenware jar until the family—the *family*, not the parties, who will all be dead by then—will come back to Jerusalem.

113. *Jeremiah* 32:1-25 (New English Bible).

[10]

Living in the Law

Anthony T. Kronman†

Introduction

Legal ethics is largely concerned with questions of moral permissibility. Is a lawyer morally permitted, for example, to destroy the character of an innocent witness through ruthless cross-examination or to withhold information, unknown to the authorities, regarding his client's participation in past crimes? A lawyer has a duty to advance the interests of his clients with maximum effectiveness, within the limits of the law,[1] and to do this must often perform actions that from a moral point of view may seem dubious or even indefensible. Whether, despite the appearance of impropriety, these actions are in fact morally allowable is generally assumed to be the central question of legal ethics.[2] Most affirmative

---

† Edward J. Phelps Professor of Law, Yale Law School. I presented an earlier version of this article as a speech at the Yale Law School on November 11, 1986. I would like to thank Alan Hirsch, Yale Law School Class of 1985, for his help in preparing this article for publication.

The traditional use of the male pronoun "he" to refer to persons of both sexes is a practice that has in recent years become a subject of controversy. Writers have adopted different strategies to deal with the problems they believe this practice presents. Some, for example, never use "he" alone, but always substitute "he or she" instead, and others alternate the use of "he" and "she," either randomly or in some regular way. The first of these strategies I find cumbersome and the second has always seemed to me (as a reader) more distracting than enlightening or refreshing. I have therefore elected to follow a modified version of the traditional practice, using "he" alone most of the time and "he or she" occasionally. Whatever its vices, this approach at least possesses the virtues of clarity and economy. When I use the pronoun "he" and its variant forms in a general or impersonal sense, I mean, of course, to refer to men and women alike.

[1] See Comment accompanying Rule 1.2 of the American Bar Association, Model Rules of Professional Conduct (1983) ("Model Rules"), noting that "[t]he client has ultimate authority to determine the purposes to be served by legal representation, within the limits imposed by law and the lawyer's professional obligations." The lawyer's professional obligations are quite limited; a lawyer is not, for example, supposed to lie to a tribunal or fail to make disclosures necessary to avoid a fraud on the court. Id., Rule 3.3.

[2] For works on legal ethics dealing primarily with issues of moral permissibility, see, e.g., L. Ray Patterson, Legal Ethics: The Law of Professional Responsibility (1982); David Luban, ed., The Good Lawyer: Lawyers' Role and Lawyers' Ethics (1983); Geoffrey C. Hazard, Ethics in the Practice of Law (1978); Monroe H. Freedman, Lawyers' Ethics in an Adversary System (1975); Gerald J. Postema, Moral Responsibility in Professional Ethics, 55 N.Y.U. L. Rev. 63 (1980); Murray L. Schwartz, The Professionalism and Accountability of Lawyers, 66 Cal. L. Rev. 669 (1978).

answers to this question appeal to the advantages of an adversarial system of adjudication and attempt to show that various actions that would indeed be objectionable if performed outside the context of such a system must be encouraged, or at a minimum allowed, if the advantages of the system as a whole are to be secured.[3] Arguments of this sort lead, in turn, to the further question of whether adversarial procedures are themselves morally acceptable, a question that grows directly from our doubts about the permissibility of the more specific things that lawyers do. These doubts culminate in uncertainties about the moral propriety of the adversarial system as a whole, and it is to this latter topic that Anglo-American writers on legal ethics have devoted the greatest attention—unsurprisingly, given their preoccupation with the issue of moral permissibility in general.

In this article, I raise, and attempt to answer, a question of a different sort. My question does not concern the moral justifiability of what lawyers do, but the reasons a person might have for choosing the life of a practicing lawyer in the first place.[4] What is it about the life of a lawyer that justifies the very large commitment which the decision to pursue it entails? Put differently, why should anyone care about being or becoming a lawyer, or leading the life to which the choice of law as a career confines one?

This question raises what is, in one sense, a subordinate problem, for it makes no sense to ask it unless we assume that the life of a practicing lawyer is indeed a morally acceptable one (which in turn presupposes that the actions a lawyer must routinely perform in the course of his or her professional duties are not themselves indefensible from a moral point of view). The life of a tyrant, as Socrates observed, may be immensely attractive, but since it necessarily involves wrongdoing, one can never have a reason to choose

[3] See, for example, Freedman, Lawyers' Ethics in an Adversary System (cited in note 2) (defending various seemingly unethical practices—withholding information about a client's previous crimes, presenting perjured testimony, "chasing ambulances"—on the grounds that they are needed to sustain the adversary system mandated by the Constitution and by humanitarian concerns). See also Stephan Landsman, The Adversary System: A Description and Defense (1984) (arguing that the adversary system is itself a good thing and that the lawyer's role in it therefore should be considered morally meritorious).

[4] For another, recent attempt to answer this question, see James Boyd White, The Study of Law as an Intellectual Activity: A Talk to Entering Students, in James Boyd White, Heracles Bow: Essays on the Rhetoric and Poetics of the Law 49-59 (1985) (suggesting that the life of a lawyer provides a particularly good opportunity to "learn both how to function in an inherited culture, as a member of it, and how to function at the same time as an individual," giving one "a double identity, as lawyer and as mind").

it in preference to a life of moral rectitude.[5] If the life of a lawyer were like a tyrant's—if it, too, inevitably entangled one in a web of wrongdoing—it would be difficult to see what could be said on its behalf. I shall assume, however, that this is not the case. It is true, of course, that lawyers sometimes act immorally, but in contrast to the tyrant they are not regularly required to do so by their work: moral evil is not an intrinsic feature of the goals they pursue or the actions they perform. I shall assume, in other words, that the life of a lawyer is one of those a person is morally permitted to choose. To say this, however, is only to say that such a life is among those one may choose without disgrace. It is not to offer any reasons for the choice itself or to suggest why one should care about becoming a lawyer rather than anything else. This latter topic is the one I propose to explore in this article. It is a topic that has been overshadowed, in the large literature on legal ethics, by the issue of moral permissibility. Yet I believe it is a subject of far greater personal importance to those in the profession, to those, that is to say, who have chosen to make their living in the law.

Why this topic has been ignored, to the degree it has, by those interested in legal ethics is itself an interesting question, but one I shall not pursue here. It is worth pointing out, however, that its neglect is by no means peculiar to the field of legal ethics but is broadly characteristic of modern moral philosophy as a whole (with a few notable recent exceptions). The philosopher Harry Frankfurt has observed that ethical theorists tend, in general, to be more concerned with questions of obligation and permissibility—what am I required to do and what choices do my moral duties allow?—than with the distinct problem of what it is that I have any reason to care about.[6] The general silence of moral philosophy on the subject of what we should care about suggests that this is a topic that falls outside the domain of ethics altogether, being largely a matter of personal taste, unassailable but also indefensible. To assume that this is so, however, is to trivialize many of the most agonizing questions of value that we face in our lives and to write out of ethics precisely those problems that stand most in need of our reflective scrutiny.

In the past few years, there has been a discernible reaction against this assumption on the part of many moral philosophers, particularly (and perhaps surprisingly) English-speaking philoso-

---

[5] See, for example, Plato, Gorgias *469-72 (W. C. Helmbold trans. 1952).

[6] See Harry Frankfurt, The Importance of What We Care About, 53 Synthese 257 (Nov. 1982).

phers trained in the analytic tradition. In addition to Frankfurt, I would mention Bernard Williams, Alasdair MacIntyre, Susan Wolf, Stuart Hampshire, Richard Wollheim, and Martha Nussbaum.[7] I write in the spirit of this reaction, and though my immediate concern is with lawyers and the lives they lead, it is my hope that what I say will contribute to the current revival of interest in the question of what it means, more generally, to live the life of a person,[8] to have the cares and commitments, the character traits and dispositional attitudes, that give the lives of persons their distinctive shape.

I. Instrumentalism

A. Money and Honor

What sorts of reasons might one give, then, for the decision to pursue a career in the law? It is best, perhaps, to begin with the answer that many will think the least respectable, even if they also consider it the most honest. A large number of lawyers undoubtedly believe that the life they have chosen is a desirable one because it offers great opportunities for wealth and prestige, for a disproportionate share of society's material resources and high professional status. Lawyers are generally well-compensated for their work and, though as a group they are often the object of popular vilification, tend, individually, to occupy positions of distinction in their communities. This, one might think, is reason enough to choose a career in the law, and other explanations can easily seem by comparison either unnecessary or disingenuous. Many, of course, will find this view repellent and judge the lawyer who candidly admits that his or her professional goal is money and honor and nothing else irresponsibly selfish. I, too, think this conception of the worth or value of law practice deficient, but would place the deficiency at a different point.

To enter the practice of law for money and honor alone is, at bottom, to view one's professional career as a vehicle for accumulating those things that are needed in other areas of life in order to acquire or accomplish what seems intrinsically important—important, that is, for its own sake and not as a means to

---

[7] See Bernard Williams, Moral Luck (1981); Alasdair MacIntyre, After Virtue: A Study in Moral Theory (1981); Susan Wolf, Moral Saints, 79 J. Phil. 419 (1982); Stuart Hampshire, Morality and Conflict (1983); Richard Wollheim, The Thread of Life (1984); Martha Nussbaum, The Fragility of Goodness (1986).

[8] I borrow the phrase "the life of a person" from Wollheim, The Thread of Life at 2 (cited in note 7).

some yet further end. The lawyer who takes this view of his practice treats it as a means to the things he truly cares about, the things that claim his attention, so to speak, at the end of the working day. In this general respect, however, he is no different from the rest of us, for we all do certain things not because we enjoy them or find them rewarding on their own terms but because they enable us to engage in other activities that do have these characteristics. Whether the lawyer who cares only about the pecuniary and honorific benefits of his professional work, who treats his profession as an instrumental good with no intrinsic value of its own, leads a life that in an overall sense is to be admired or regarded with pity and contempt, is a question that ultimately turns on the nature of the ends he uses the external rewards of his work to pursue. The corporate lawyer, for example, who works twelve hours a day at tasks he finds dull and unchallenging may nevertheless be leading a life that not only makes sense as a whole but even has appeal or a measure of nobility. Everything depends on what happens after hours and on whether this way of accumulating the instrumental goods needed to do the important things in life is preferable to the alternatives, both in terms of what it yields and what it takes. So a lawyer should not feel deeply ashamed to say that he is in it just for the money and prestige, though, to be sure, he must give us some account of what these things are for before we can decide whether his life is one we can admire. The question of whether he has reason to care about his professional career merges, at this point, into the larger and less focused question of whether he has reason to care about the things that give his life its meaning as a whole. He may or may not; what I want to stress is that this question is an open one even for the lawyer who values his profession not for what it is but for what it brings.

Still, as I have said, there is something deficient in this view. The deficiency lies, I think, in the breadth of the instrumental attitude that it endorses. No doubt, we must all take an instrumental attitude toward some of the things we do and even, in certain circumstances, toward other people (though our treatment of others as means—in the process of contractual exchange, for example—is usually circumscribed by obligations that reflect what might be called a noninstrumental conception of the other person).[9] What

[9] Consider, for example, a contract for the sale of goods. The purchaser, seeking to obtain a particular item as inexpensively as possible, looks to the seller solely for the fulfillment of his desire. The seller, wishing to maximize profit, views the buyer solely as a source of profit. The two regard each other as means, each being prepared to discard the other if a

makes the nakedly instrumental view of law practice that I have just described so unattractive is that it takes in too much of life, or more exactly, too much of what is important in life. This should first be understood in a purely quantitative sense. The lawyer who works the kind of hours at the kind of pace necessary to achieve great wealth or fame is likely to discover he has little time or energy left in which to pursue the things for whose sake he has made his professional career the instrument or vehicle. Faulkner, it is true, wrote *As I Lay Dying* in six weeks while working the night-shift in a boiler room, but his tasks were intermittent and mindlessly physical and, in any case, he was a genius. No matter how humdrum, the practice of law is always a mental exercise and often an emotional one, and the intellectual and spiritual resources that a lawyer has available for his extravocational pursuits, whatever they may be, are bound to be depleted in the course of his work itself—significantly so if the work is as long and as demanding of careful attention as it often is.

There is a second, nonquantitative sense in which the instrumental view is deficient and this, it seems to me, is more important still. The deficiency I have in mind can best be brought out if we begin by taking note of a basic fact about the nature of personal identity. Of the various things a person does, many have no bearing on who he is, on his character or personality; he would be the same person and have the same identity whether he happened to do them or not. I myself feel this way, for example, about washing the dishes and commuting to work. There are good reasons, of course, why I do these things but I am quite confident that I would be the same person if I had never done them or never did them again. To be sure, others may view these particular activities in a different light and think of them as being more directly connected with their own distinctive identities (though I must admit that I find this difficult to imagine). What seems to me indisputable, however, is the presence in every person's life of some rough division between those involvements and activities that constitute his character or personality, on the one hand, and those, on the other, that do not, between those that make someone the person he or she *is* and those one merely *has* or *does*.[10]

---

better offer comes along. Their exploitation of one another is nevertheless bounded in a number of ways, for example, by the doctrines of unconscionability and duress. These impose upon the parties a limited obligation to treat one another as ends in the context of what is otherwise a mutually instrumental transaction.

[10] I follow Michael Sandel's useful distinction between those traits, interests, abilities,

Now the whole of a person's professional life can, in theory at least, be placed on either side of this line. There is nothing, in the nature of things, that absolutely requires that the various activities of which one's professional existence is composed be character-forming in the sense I have suggested. I believe, however, that the practice of law exerts a very strong pull in this direction. To practice law well requires not only a formal knowledge of the law (a knowledge of what the legal realists termed the "paper" rules or rules "on the books"[11]) but certain qualities of mind and temperament as well. Most lawyers recognize this and recognize, too, that the qualities in question are also the ones that experience in law practice tends to encourage and confirm.

I shall have more to say, later in the article, about the nature of these qualities, about the way they are acquired, and the role they play in law practice. My central claim will be that they are traits of character, permanent dispositional attitudes rooted in the realm of feeling and desire. To accept this claim, however, is to acknowledge that these are qualities a person cannot lose or acquire without experiencing a change of identity. It is to accept the idea that to be a lawyer is to be a person of a particular sort, a person with a distinctive set of character traits as well as an expertise.[12] I believe that something like this is true, in a general way, of other professions as well and that the very notion of a profession—as distinguished from a mere technique—implies the possession of certain character-defining traits or qualities.[13] Whatever the case may be in other professional disciplines, however, it is the aim of this article to show that the dispositional habits which the practice of law both requires and encourages have a bearing not only on what a person can do (like the habit, say, of touch-typing) but on who he or she is as well (like the habits of generosity and temperance).

The instrumental view of law practice does not give adequate weight to this fact. If, in addition to requiring a large expenditure of time and energy, the practice of law also has an important influ-

---

and desires that are "mine" and those that are simply "me." See Michael J. Sandel, Liberalism and the Limits of Justice 55 (1982).

[11] The term "paper rules" was coined by Karl Llewellyn in A Realistic Jurisprudence—The Next Step, 30 Colum. L. Rev. 431, 451 n.18 (1930).

[12] For unflattering characterizations of those who possess expertise *without* character, see MacIntyre, After Virtue at 79-87 (cited in note 7); Max Weber, Politics as a Vocation, in H. H. Gerth and C. Wright Mills, eds., From Max Weber 72-128 (1946).

[13] For an excellent account of "professionalism," see Samuel P. Huntington, The Soldier and the State 8-10 (1957).

ence on the kind of person one becomes, then the professional lawyer has reason to worry about the intrinsic value of his career as well as its external or instrumental worth. It is perfectly legitimate to wonder whether the sort of person one is likely to become through long immersion in the law is the sort one may reasonably take pride in being or have reason to wish to become. The problem with the instrumental view is not that it answers this question one way rather than another, but that it fails to ask it altogether and thus obscures an important dimension of the commitment entailed by the choice of law as a career.

B. Public-Spiritedness

There is a second, equally familiar but more respectable way of justifying this choice. I have in mind the justification of law practice as a life of public service. In my view, this second justification often has the same central weakness as the first, though not as obviously nor to the same degree.

Some men and women choose the law because they are committed to the public good and believe that law, in America at least, is the most direct path to its attainment.[14] This attitude, of course, is compatible with a great diversity of opinion regarding the nature of the public good itself, and to subscribe to it one need not subscribe to any particular political orthodoxy (even an anarchist who believes in the abolition of law may consistently endorse it). I wish to make three points about this attitude, which might be called the "public-spirited" view of law practice. The first is that any lawyer who lacks it altogether is to that extent a professional failure. Lawyers or not, we all have certain basic obligations of citizenship that require us to attend, sporadically at least, to matters of public concern, to the overall well-being of the communities in which we live. Lawyers have these general obligations but they also have certain special responsibilities, deriving from their status or position, to preserve and perfect the legal institutions that in our society constitute a very large part of the public order itself.[15] I shall not attempt here to justify these special responsibilities or to describe their contours in more detail; the reasons for them are, I hope, self-

[14] Consider, for example, Anne Fagan Ginger, The Relevant Lawyers (1972); Roberto Mangabeira Unger, The Critical Legal Studies Movement, 96 Harv. L. Rev. 561 (1983).

[15] See Model Rules, preamble (cited in note 1) (noting that a lawyer is "a public citizen having special responsibility for the quality of justice. . . . As a public citizen, a lawyer should seek improvement of the law, the administration of justice and the quality of service rendered by the legal profession.").

evident, or nearly so.

My second point is that the public-spirited view, as I have called it, is not the only view capable of justifying the choice of law as a career. It is as much a mistake to think that the only ethically defensible conception of law practice is one that places the pursuit of the public good at the center of things as it is to think that lawyers have no special duties in this regard at all. Among those who practice law, some will find their moral fulfillment in the public interest, as some who belong to the wider community of citizens find theirs in a wholehearted commitment to politics. But just as it is wrong to think that a person can lead a morally respectable life only in case he chooses politics as his vocation, so it is wrong to assume that a lawyer who fails to carry his commitment to the public good beyond the point that his special, but limited, professional responsibilities require is somehow morally inferior to the lawyer who regards the attainment of these same values as the sole justification for all he does.

The third, and most important, point I want to make about the public-spirited conception of law practice is that it sometimes bears a resemblance to the instrumental view described above—or, more exactly, that it sometimes is a variant of that view and hence vulnerable to similar criticisms. At first glance, this may seem obviously false, for we tend to assume that the instrumental lawyer, the lawyer who works only in order to accumulate the resources he requires in his extraprofessional life, is a person motivated by selfish desires and characterized, above all, by a total lack of that feeling for the public good that distinguishes his public-spirited counterpart. But the difference between the two can be much narrower than our ordinary assumptions suggest. On the one side, for example, even the most thoroughgoing instrumentalist may use the material freedom he gains through work to pursue projects that, though lacking in public-spiritedness, cannot fairly be called selfish in the ordinary sense (like writing *The Life of Johnson*, for example, or working to achieve a Buddhistic selflessness through systematic meditation).

On the other side, an unbending devotion to the public good can sometimes be in theory, and often is in psychological fact, coupled with an instrumental view of the contribution one is expected to make toward it. The lawyer who chooses his career for public-spirited reasons alone may see himself merely as the instrument by which some communal good is to be achieved. He may even hate his work, find it dull and unrewarding in itself, but still consider it the most economical route to whatever political arrangements he values for their own sake.[16] Under other circumstances, he would perhaps have chosen another career and he may look forward to the abolition of the state, the law, and the class of professional lawyers.[17] For the time being, however, it is politically imperative that he continue to practice law, and the decision to do so will not seem to him irrational so long as the instrumental value of his work remains clear.

In this respect, the lawyer who views his career merely as a vehicle for justice or equality or some other public value bears a certain resemblance to the lawyer who regards his career as a means, say, to the production of musical comedies or the education of his own children. Both find the point of their professional work in something that lies outside it, and both may be inclined to view their choice of career as an accommodation to external necessity, which greater family wealth or a more just political system might have permitted them, quite happily, to avoid. To be sure, a public-spirited lawyer may find intrinsic satisfaction in his work if he believes that it not only leads to but actually constitutes an element of the public good. If a lawyer believes, for example, that the representation of indigent clients has moral value not only because it is likely to result in a fairer distribution of society's resources but because it is itself one part or aspect of what such a distribution includes, he will be more likely to think that his work has intrinsic as well as instrumental worth.[18] Whether he does in fact think this, however, depends on the particular conception of the public good to which he subscribes and not merely on the fact that he happens to take a public-spirited view of his own career. It is perfectly possible for someone to view all that he or she does for the sake of the public good as a necessary historical expedient that forms no lasting part of the public good itself, a ladder to be discarded once the goal has been attained, and there is evidence to suggest that some, at least, who count themselves among the public-spirited see the

[16] Consider, for example, Stephen Wexler, Practicing Law for Poor People, 79 Yale L. J. 1049, 1051-52, 1067 (1970) (noting that public interest law practice often "is not intellectually stimulating," acknowledging that "[m]uch of it is dull and routine," but nevertheless advocating it because "it is the only kind of practice which offers any hope of meeting the needs of poor people").

[17] See, e.g., Unger, 96 Harv. L. Rev. at 667-68 (cited in note 14); Harold Berman, Justice in the U.S.S.R. 28-29 (1963) (discussing Pashukanis's view that law will wither away after the socialist revolution).

[18] See, e.g., Wexler, 79 Yale L. J. at 1049 (cited in note 16) (people want to be poverty lawyers "because they have a moral concern which speaks . . . in favor of legal representation for everyone").

choice of law as a career in this perspective.[19]

To espouse such a view is to be public-spirited in a ruthlessly instrumental way, and any lawyer who does so in an effort to justify his professional existence runs the risks that I have associated with instrumentalism generally. Chief among these is the risk that he will fail to give due weight to the character-forming consequences of law practice, to the fact that by living in the law one not only accomplishes certain things but tends to become a certain sort of person as well. Most law students have a suspicion that this is so, but for the instrumentalist—whether of the public-spirited variety or not—the suspicion can easily become a nightmare if he or she has reason to believe that the traits of character formed in law practice are different from, or destructive of, the traits associated with whatever extraprofessional ends one happens to have embraced. The lawyer, for example, who lives for art may fear that his professional work will eventually dull his capacity for aesthetic understanding, and the lawyer who lives for justice may worry that too long an immersion in the balanced complexities of concrete cases will dissipate his passion for systemic reform. Both fears reflect a recognition of the fact that a lawyer's profession is part of his identity and can't be put on or off like a suit of clothes. For the instrumentalist, who finds no intrinsic satisfaction in his work, the realization that this is so poses a special challenge, and to meet it he may conclude that his views must be modified in certain fundamental ways.

Whether or not the public-spirited lawyer sees his career in an instrumentalist perspective, however, his conception of what gives it dignity and worth will not be shared by everyone in the profession. Though I do not find this disturbing in itself, it does raise an important question. For those who ask what reason they might have to choose the life of a practicing lawyer, or if they have already made that choice, who wonder what can be said on behalf of the lives they are now leading, but who find the instrumentalist view that I have sketched depressing and feel themselves, for whatever reason, unable to embrace the public-spirited conception of law practice—for those lawyers and would-be lawyers (a large fraction, I believe, of the profession as a whole), is there some other way of thinking about the life of a practicing lawyer that better explains its appeal? I think there is and will attempt, in the

[19] Roberto Unger characterizes modern leftist legal movements as aimed at "the merely instrumental use of law and legal thought for leftist ends." 96 Harv. L. Rev. at 666 (cited in note 14).

remainder of the article, to describe the alternative conception I have in mind. One of the main elements in the view I shall propose I have introduced already: this is the notion that law practice both requires and tends to encourage certain dispositional attitudes or traits of character, the notion, to put it differently, that a practicing lawyer not only possesses a set of distinctive skills but is likely to be a particular sort of person as well. It is the connection between this idea and the all-important, though obscure, concept of judgment that I want to examine in more detail. At the juncture of the notions of character and judgment there emerges a conception of law practice different from those I have so far considered, one that sees the value of what lawyers do, for the lawyers themselves, not so much in the fruits of their work as in the excellences of character their work requires them to develop and permits them to display.[20] Conceived in this way, the value of law practice is clearly something intrinsic to it, a fact that distinguishes the view I shall be developing from any form of instrumentalism, whether personal or political.

II. Judgment

My starting point is the phenomenon of judgment itself. By judgment I mean the process of deliberating about and deciding personal, moral, and political problems. We are all required to exercise judgment—almost continually about trivial matters and occasionally about very important ones. We all also recognize that some people have better judgment than others, and that the possession of good judgment is a virtue, a quality that reflects well on the person who possesses it in the way that other virtues, like courage or temperance, do. What is this virtue of good judgment that we are so accustomed to praising?

Given the pervasiveness of the phenomenon of judgment in our personal and political lives, one might assume that this would be a central question in moral and political philosophy but, interestingly enough, it is not. It is true that some philosophers (Aristotle in particular)[21] have addressed the subject, but none with

[20] The reverse argument—that law practice often *corrupts* character—is made in Andreas Eshete, Does a Lawyer's Character Matter?, in Luban, The Good Lawyer at 270-85 (cited in note 2).

[21] See Aristotle, Nicomachean Ethics *1139a-1140b. Useful discussions of Aristotle's theory of practical judgment may be found in John M. Cooper, Reason and Human Good in Aristotle 1-88 (1975); Norman O. Dahl, Practical Reason, Aristotle, and Weakness of the Will 61-73 (1984); Troels Engberg-Pederson, Aristotle's Theory of Moral Insight 188-222 (1983); David Wiggins and Amelie Rorty, Deliberation and Practical Reason, in Amelie

systematic thoroughness. Indeed, since Hobbes's rational reconstruction of political theory in the seventeenth century, the nature of judgment seems largely to have disappeared as a topic of interest among professional thinkers (with the one important exception of Kant[22]). The reasons for this are unclear, but it is a fact that anyone who takes up the subject today can expect only limited guidance from the past.

A. Deduction and Intuition

If we begin by reflecting on our own experience, it must be observed that one striking feature of the process of judgment is what might be called its "nondeductive" character. To make a judgment about how to behave in a given situation or in the context of a particular relationship is rarely, if ever, a matter simply of deriving the appropriate conclusion from a set of established maxims by means of a fixed method or procedure, of deducing the answer one seeks in the same way a geometrician deduces the truth or falsity of a proposed theorem by the rigorously exact technique we call "proof."[23] A judgment may be sound or unsound, but this cannot be established by deductive proof alone. There are, of course, situations in which a question is nominally raised as to what one should do where the answer follows immediately and unambiguously from some general rule of conduct to which one is already committed. Should I, for example, steal my friend's watch when I find it lying on a table? To grasp the right answer in situations of this sort, however, is not normally understood to require or reveal sound judgment, though some other virtue, like courage or steadfastness, may be involved.[24]

Good judgment, and its opposite, are in fact most clearly revealed in just those situations where the method of deduction is least applicable, where the ambiguities are greatest and the demand for proof most obviously misplaced. To show good judgment in such situations is to do something more than merely apply a general rule with special care and thoroughness, or follow out its

---

Rorty, ed., Essays on Aristotle's Ethics 221-40 (1980).

[22] For a discussion of Kant's theory of political judgment, based upon an inventive interpretation of his account of aesthetic judgment, see Hannah Arendt, Lectures on Kant's Political Philosophy (1982); Ronald Beiner, Political Judgment 31-71 (1983).

[23] See Thomas Grey, Langdell's Orthodoxy, 45 U. Pitt. L. Rev. 1, 16-20 (1983) (describing in detail the way Langdell and his followers attempted to apply the methods of geometry to legal doctrines and legal education).

[24] For a discussion of steadfastness and courage in the judicial arena, see Robert Cover, Violence and the Word, 95 Yale L. J. 1601, 1607 (1986).

consequences to a greater level of detail. Judgment often requires such analytic refinement but does not consist in it alone. That this is so is to be explained by the fact that we are most dependent on our judgment, most in need of *good* judgment, in just those situations that pose genuine dilemmas by forcing us to choose between, or otherwise accommodate, conflicting interests and obligations whose conflict is not itself amenable to resolution by the application of some higher-order rule. It is here that the quality of a person's judgment comes most clearly into view and here, too, that his or her deductive powers alone are least likely to prove adequate to the task.

If judgment is more than deduction, it is tempting to conclude that it must, to that extent, be a process of the very opposite sort, a process that usually goes under the name of "intuition." By intuition we normally mean a form of direct insight or apprehension distinct from any species of understanding at which one is able to arrive by reasoning alone. To be sure, intuitive insight may be preceded by a more or less elaborate process of abstract reflection. It is not itself, however, merely one more step in this same process, but represents instead a break with what has come before and the introduction of a radically different form of comprehension. We sometimes express this idea by saying that intuition is nonreflective, and in attempting to explain what we mean often find ourselves driven back to visual metaphors in an effort to express the peculiar immediacy of this mode of understanding. To have an intuition, we say, is simply to see that something is the case, to apprehend its obviousness in the same direct way that I apprehend, for example, the physical shape of the room in which I am at present sitting. Conceived in this way, intuition is analogous to vision—it is how we see things with the mind's eye—and while we all possess the power of intuitive insight to some degree, it also seems undeniable that the abilities of human beings fall, in this regard as in most others, along a scale, those with exceptional intuitive powers being able to see farther and more clearly than those of ordinary ability whose vision is by comparison clouded or confined.

If every problem requiring the exercise of judgment calls for an act of intuition at the critical moment of decision regardless of how long or how well one has deliberated about the problem in a reflective way, if, in other words, judgment always demands that at some crucial point one stop thinking and look instead, then the people who show good judgment will simply be those whose powers of intuitive vision are the most acute. There is obviously some truth in this, for we all know that clear thinking and good judgment are not the same thing. Yet the notion that judgment is a form of intuition, though not as obviously mistaken as the contrasting view that it is merely a species of deduction, is misleading too, and if anything, rather more discouraging.

It is more discouraging because it tends to bring inquiry to a halt. Since intuition itself is nonreflective in nature, it can easily seem intellectually inaccessible, one of those subjects that philosophers want badly to pursue but about which they have, and can have, nothing much to say. Intuition, it is sometimes said, is a mystery that can be experienced but never understood, at least in the way philosophers would like to understand it.[25] If one assumes this to be true and assumes, in addition, that judgment is at its heart an intuitive process, then it will seem less surprising that the subject of judgment should have been so rarely discussed in the long tradition of western political philosophy. The conclusion that judgment is not a fit topic for philosophical analysis is a troubling one, however, and seems inconsistent with the fact that many of the most basic problems in philosophy treat matters not fully transparent to reflective reason: the nature, for example, of aesthetic and religious experience, of death, love, imagination, and desire. Judgment is as suitable a subject for philosophy as any of these others, and given the large role it plays in our lives, as important. If the equation of judgment and intuition is understood to imply a contrary view, then that alone is reason to reject it.

The characterization of judgment as a form of intuition is also importantly misleading for the following reason. If judgment is conceived of as a process of reflection followed by a moment of intuitive insight, then our assessment of the soundness of a particular judgment can never depend on the reasons given to support it, since the goodness or badness of the judgment will be a function of its intuitive brilliance and originality and these are qualities that, by assumption, no reasoned argument can express. But as a matter of fact, in assessing the judgments that others make and even in evaluating the soundness of our own past decisions, we take into account the supporting reasons offered to explain and justify them. A person of good judgment is not someone who from time to time merely makes certain strikingly appropriate oracular pronouncements—that is what prophets and seers do—but who is able, as well, to provide a compelling framework of ideas for the decisions he or she arrives at. These decisions are not deducible by reason

[25] For a discussion of this claim, see Richard Rorty, Intuition, in 3-4 The Encyclopedia of Philosophy 210-92 (1967).

alone, but neither is their soundness entirely self-evident—something we either see or not depending on our own powers of intuitive comprehension. Good judgment, to put it differently, has an argumentative dimension which its equation with intuitive genius obscures.

There is a further reason why the equation of judgment and intuition is misleading. Intuition is today most often thought of as a gift: one either possesses it as part of one's original inventory of abilities or one does not and in either case there is little that can be done to alter the situation. This view, which in part reflects the characteristically modern association of intuition with art and artistic ability,[26] renders problematic the connection between intuition, on the one hand, and experience and character on the other. If intuition is a gift, we should expect to see evidence of it even in very young people; but the kind of intuitive insight that good judgment requires is universally associated with long experience and hence with age. There are prodigies in mathematics but none, as Aristotle notes,[27] in the field of practical affairs—which is a reason either to revise our notion of what intuition is or abandon the claim that judgment is intuitive in nature. Furthermore, if we view a person's intuitive abilities as a kind of gift, it is difficult to see what connection they can have with his character, which always takes time to develop and cannot be regarded as a gift at all. This would not raise a problem if good judgment were not thought to be as much a trait of character as an intellectual capacity. But for reasons I shall explain, we do quite properly view it in this way and hence must choose again between modifying our conception of intuition and qualifying the claim that judgment is best understood as a form of intuitive understanding.

B. Sympathy and Detachment

I have now considered two different ways of thinking about judgment—one that views it as a species of deduction and the other as a kind of intuition—and found both to be inadequate. The time has come for me to say something more positive about my subject. I propose to begin by examining more closely what a philosopher might call the "phenomenology" of judgment,[28] the felt

---

[26] See Jacques Maritain, Creative Intuition in Art and Poetry 223 (1953).

[27] Nicohmachean Ethics *1095a.

[28] I use the term in the loose sense that many philosophers do, and without any intention of endorsing the specific methods associated with the philosophical school that goes under the same name.

experience of judging itself. I mean to explore, more exactly, the experience of a certain sort of judging, the sort that we engage in when trying to make an important personal decision about our lives—the decision, for example, to get married, have a child, or pursue a particular career. First-personal decisions of this sort are not, of course, the only ones in which judgment plays a role; we must also exercise judgment in the advice we give to others and in the political choices that we make. It is difficult, in fact, to identify an area of our private or public lives that does not provide a theatre for the exercise of judgment or depend upon its proper use. The phenomenon of judgment has certain general features, however, which are most easily discernible in its first-personal form, and it is for this reason that I have chosen to begin my account of judgment at this point. When I return to the subject of political judgment later in the article, it will be my aim to show that what I have said about the structure of personal deliberation holds in the realm of politics as well.

We must all, from time to time, make hard personal choices—to get married or divorced, go to law school or drop out, support a parent or renounce a friend. If we find such choices difficult, it is usually because the alternatives seem in some fashion incommensurable. Each has its own balance of advantages and disadvantages and there is no common metric that permits us to assess their relative attractiveness in a decisive and unambiguous way. The choice that we must make cannot, therefore, simply be a matter of deduction or calculation, as utilitarians sometimes suggest. Nor is it a matter merely of waiting for the appropriate intuition, the one that will tell us what to do. We tend to deal with our personal dilemmas, even the intractable ones, in a more active and methodical way than that. Choices of the sort I have in mind call not for deduction or intuition but deliberation, which is another name for judgment. Indeed, it is precisely in situations of this kind, where the choice to be made is between alternatives not easily compared, that our reliance upon the faculty of judgment is most evident. In exercising this faculty, what exactly is it that we do?

The answer, I think, is something like the following. When faced with an important personal decision, I am frequently required to make what amounts to a choice among competing ways of life—different ways of life that might be mine though none of them, by assumption, yet is, at least in its fully developed form. To make such a choice, I must explore the alternatives in my imagination.[29] That is to say, I must make the effort to see and feel, from within, what each would be like were I to choose *it* rather than the others. The effort to do this is not unlike the everyday attempts we make to understand the experience of other people,[30] and it resembles, too, the attempt that historians and anthropologists make to understand those who are remote from them in time and cultural attitude.[31] In these latter cases, of course, it is other people and not ourselves that we are struggling to understand. But the self I will become if I embrace a certain way of life may very well seem, at the moment of decision, something of a stranger too, a person both familiar and remote in the way that other people often are. So to grasp the possibilities before me, even where they are only different ways of living my own life, I need the same sort of imaginative powers that are required to make sense of someone else's situation or experience. What is needed, above all else, is a certain measure of compassion, in the literal sense of "feeling with." I must make the effort, in choosing a life for myself, to feel along with each of the persons I might become the special cares and concerns, the risks and opportunities, that give the experience of that possible future self its own distinctive shape.

This is not always easy to do. Much in the experience of my imaginary future selves is bound to remain opaque to me, so opaque, in fact, that I fail even to notice how little I understand. And though I may have an abstract conviction that a particular way of life would be the best one for me, all things considered, my present affections may pull so strongly in another direction that I am unable to feel any genuine compassion for the person I believe I ought to be. Still, even with these qualifications, our powers of compassionate understanding seem sufficiently robust to carry us across the distances that separate us from others and from our own future selves and to permit us to take up—only partially, perhaps, but in a spirit of fellow-feeling—their preoccupations and concerns.

If a person who is faced, say, with a choice between alternative careers must make an effort to grasp in imagination each of the different ways of life these alternatives represent, if it is essential to his deliberations that he entertain their claims sympathetically

[29] See Anthony Kronman, Practical Wisdom and Professional Character, 4 Soc. Phil. & Pol. 203 (Aut. 1986).

[30] Max Scheler, The Nature of Sympathy 8-36 (1954).

[31] See Max Weber, Critical Studies in the Logic of the Cultural Sciences, in Edward Shils and Henry Finch, eds., The Methodology of the Social Sciences (1949).

and see each in the best possible light (the light in which one devoted to that way of life would see it), it is also necessary that he maintain a certain distance or detachment from the points of view he is attempting to understand. From each imaginative foray into a possible future career, he must be able to withdraw to the standpoint of decision, which is the standpoint he occupies at present. At least he must be able to do this if he is genuinely to make a decision among the alternatives rather than merely be swept along by the tide of feeling that any sympathetic association with a particular way of life—even if it is only an imagined way of life—can easily arouse. To ensure that this does not happen, to ensure that he remains sufficiently detached to survey all the alternatives from a vantage point different from any of their own internal points of view, it is necessary that he hold something in reserve even while making a maximum effort at imaginative understanding. The person faced with a hard choice must give each alternative its due; he must entertain all the possibilities by feeling for himself what is most attractive in each. But he must do this while withholding his commitment to any.

One way of expressing this idea is to say that the process of deliberation is peculiarly bifocal. Through one lens, the alternatives are seen not merely at close range but actually from within; through the other, all the alternatives are held at an identical distance.[32] As anyone who has ever put on a pair of bifocal glasses knows, it takes time to learn to shift smoothly between perspectives and the effort to do so can easily give one a headache. The same is true of deliberation: it is difficult to be sympathetic, and difficult to be detached, but what is most difficult of all is to be both at once. Yet it is in just this combination of opposite-seeming attributes that the process of deliberation consists. Deliberation is neither deduction nor intuition. It is the compassionate survey of alternatives viewed simultaneously from a distance, and those who show excellence in deliberation and whose judgment we value are the men and women best able to meet these conflicting requirements and to endure the often considerable tension between them.[33]

---

[32] The tension between these two points of view resembles the tension that Thomas Nagel describes in both thought and morality between the perspective of one's own self and that of the universe as a whole. See Thomas Nagel, The View from Nowhere 3 (1986).

[33] For a similar account, see Beiner, Political Judgment at 102-28 (cited in note 22).

C. Deliberation and Choice

To this last proposition, it may be objected that in ascribing sound judgment to a person we mean not only to imply that he or she is able to entertain an especially wide range of alternatives but able, as well, to make the proper choice among them. A person of sound judgment, it will be said, is one who regularly makes the right decision, a fact that my "procedural" account of judgment appears to ignore. I do of course agree that in attributing sound judgment to a person we are saying something about the sorts of decisions he makes as well as the deliberative procedures he employs in making them. I also believe, however, that these two aspects of judgment are connected and that the choices of a person who deliberates well—with sympathy and detachment—are themselves likely to be sound or practically wise in a sense that I shall now explain.

Someone faced with a difficult personal decision must make an effort, as I have said, to entertain the competing concerns that the possibilities before him represent; he must make an effort to enter, in imagination, each of the ways of life between which he will eventually have to choose. Now the critical term here is "entertain." What exactly do I mean by it? By entertain, I mean something different from and *less than* complete endorsement. To entertain a set of values is not to make them one's own without condition or reservation, but to take them up with a measure of detachment that sets these values apart from those to which one is at present actually committed. By the same token, however, I also mean something different from and *more than* a mere knowledge of the fact that the values in question happen to be the ones associated with a particular way of life. I may be said to have entertained a set of values, rather than simply taken account of their existence, only when I have succeeded in seeing them in a sympathetic light and have experienced for myself something of their power and appeal. Entertaining a value or concern, then, is an attitude midway between adopting it and merely acknowledging its existence. Though familiar to us all, this midway attitude is surprisingly difficult to describe. Perhaps the best we can do is say that it is the attitude of fellow-feeling, a term that suggests the combination of compassion and detachment I mean to emphasize.

It is helpful to think of the different ways of life that a person confronts when required to make an important decision about his future as representing different parts or aspects of himself, each part being developed in a way that requires the neglect or subordination of certain others.[34] Choices of this sort are inevitable in any moderately complicated human existence, and one of the great challenges of personal life is to discover the way of living that best accommodates all the different things one wishes to do and be. Since it is impossible to be them all, however, it is even more important to discover which way of life is most likely to preserve a relation of fellow-feeling or friendship, as Aristotle calls it,[35] among the different parts of one's own self, some of which must necessarily be subordinated for the sake of others. A person whose soul has, in Aristotle's phrase, "friendly feelings" toward itself,[36] a person whose parts are not openly at war or engaged in subtler contests of repression and revenge, possesses a quality of wholeness that is best described by the simple term "integrity." Most often, of course, we use this term to describe the steadiness of action and purpose, the reliability of character, the dignity of self-respect that a person shows in relations with others and in his or her conduct generally. It is difficult, however—if, indeed, it is possible at all—to sustain an outward constancy of this sort without the inward friendship of which Aristotle speaks. If a person's soul is divided against itself the pressures of the world are likely, in time, to explode whatever fragile truce has been established among its parts. The alternative is not the elimination of all conflict in the soul—after Freud we cannot hope or even wish for a psychic unanimity of this sort. Nor is it the kind of harmonic ordering of higher and lower parts that Plato proposes in the *Republic*,[37] an ordering that no longer has for us the naturalness it had for him. The alternative is sympathy toward oneself, and to a large degree it is on this attitude that the basic good of integrity depends.

Though the measure of integrity that a person achieves is in part, like most things, a matter of luck (including the luck of his original endowment of feeling and intelligence),[38] it is also a function of the various choices that he makes, for these are likely, over time, either to strengthen the friendly attitude that Aristotle describes or to encourage its opposite—self-hatred and a spirit of regret.[39] It is this difference, a difference in the consequences that

---

[34] This is of course an ancient metaphor. See Plato, Republic *435e-445e (Allan Bloom trans. 1968).

[35] Nicomachean Ethics *1168b.

[36] Id.

[37] Republic *444d.

[38] See Williams, Moral Luck at 20-39 (cited in note 7).

[39] Nicomachean Ethics *1150b. My account of the good of integrity draws heavily on Aristotle's analysis of the phenomenon of "moral weakness" or weakness of will. Id. *1145a.

important choices have for the achievement or preservation of integrity, that marks the line, in personal matters at least, between those decisions that show good judgment and those that do not. If we say, for example, that someone has shown good judgment in his choice of a career, it is not because the particular career he has chosen—the career, say, of a scholar, artist, athlete, or entrepreneur—is intrinsically superior to the others he might have pursued instead. We have no basis for making such comparisons, at least with regard to those ways of life that have a prima facie claim to worthiness (of which the number is large even if it is not infinite). There is, however, another way of understanding what is meant by the claim that a person has shown good judgment in making the decisions that have turned his life in one direction rather than another. To assert this is to claim that he has chosen a life which allows him the reasonable hope of a stable friendship among his different parts, among the interests he has had to abandon or subordinate and those at the center of his life (a condition of the soul which, though often associated with some rough matchup between a person's career and his abilities, may be present where the matchup is absent and missing where it exists). When we call a personal decision wise or say that it shows good judgment, what we mean is that it promotes integrity by increasing the chances that the person who has made it will be able to live with himself on amicable terms. In the domain of personal life, wise judgments lead to integrity and unwise ones to disintegration and regret. This is the only meaning these terms can have, in this domain at least, so long as we lack a scale along which to rank the worthiness of the different ways of life to which human beings may reasonably and responsibly devote themselves.

With one additional observation, I can complete my explanation of why those who deliberate well are also likely to make wise choices. I have said that excellence in deliberation requires a certain combination of sympathy and detachment; without these qualities, a person cannot entertain the different values associated with the ways of life between which difficult decisions compel him to choose. A person who deliberates with sympathetic detachment, however, will just for that reason be more likely to make those choices that increase his chances of living a life of integrity—wise choices, in the sense that term must be understood in first-per-

For an illuminating discussion of Aristotle's treatment of this subject, see David Wiggins, Weakness of Will, Commensurability, and the Objects of Deliberation and Desire, in Rorty, ed., Essays on Aristotle's Ethics at 241-66 (1980) (cited in note 21).

sonal matters. The reason is that all genuine deliberation, as distinguished from mere deduction and delphic intuition, demands the exercise of the very fellow-feeling in which integrity consists. To deliberate about a personal problem is to show this fellow-feeling toward oneself, and it is impossible to develop such an attitude and employ it regularly over any considerable period of time without becoming the kind of person for whom the attitude itself has value, the kind of person, that is to say, who thinks it important to try to understand concerns other than those that are at present most centrally his own and who takes pleasure in his ability to do so. A person like this is bound to value his integrity. Indeed, the pleasure he takes in his powers of fellow-feeling, in his ability to be at once sympathetic and detached toward his own conflicting concerns, is just another way of describing the experience of integrity itself. The person who deliberates well is likely, as a result, to have a taste for that special form of self-regarding friendship in which integrity consists and to choose for himself a life that assigns the good of integrity a central place. Or, to put the same point differently, someone who shows good judgment in the way he deliberates is likely to show the same good judgment in the decisions that he makes, which is what I have been trying to establish.

D. Judgment and Character

This last argument rests on a series of assumptions that I want to clarify before proceeding, even at the risk of repeating what I have already said. I have claimed that sympathy and detachment are crucially important features of first-personal deliberation and have suggested that together they make possible a form of understanding that is unattainable without them. It would be a mistake, however, to think that either this particular form of understanding or the qualities that make it possible can be adequately described in cognitive terms alone. The person who is able to entertain a certain way of life with sympathetic detachment does indeed know something that the person unable to adopt this attitude does not. What he or she knows, however, is what it is like to have that way of life as one's own, and this is a type of knowledge that can only be acquired by taking on, in a tentative way, the cares and concerns of the life itself.

We all recognize the difference between knowing, for example, that alcohol can change a person's behavior and knowing what it is like to be drunk. Even little children and lifelong teetotalers have the former sort of knowledge, but it takes some experience with alcohol to acquire an understanding of the latter kind. What distinguishes this second sort of knowledge is its affectual component. Such knowledge is more than merely cognitive, for it consists, in part at least, of a residue of feeling that can be described in propositions but acquired only through experience. The person who seeks, in a spirit of sympathetic detachment, to understand some way of life other than the one he happens to be leading aims at a similar kind of knowledge through the imaginative analogue of experience and to the extent he is successful, also takes away a residue of feeling. It is this that distinguishes his knowledge of the life in question from the knowledge he would possess if he merely understood, in the way an unsympathetic observer might, that those who lead it have certain attitudes and preferences. And just as the knowledge he acquires has an affectual component, so too the capacities he exercises in acquiring it have an affectual dimension as well; more exactly, they include certain capacities for feeling along with other, unambiguously cognitive powers. Sympathy is a capacity for the production of feeling, and detachment a capacity for the moderation or confinement of feeling. Both belong to the economy of our affective life and serve to regulate its forces. To deliberate well—which requires both sympathy and detachment—one must therefore be able not only to think clearly but to feel in certain ways as well. The person who shows good judgment in deliberation will thus be marked as much by his affective dispositions as by his intellectual powers, and he will know more than others do because he feels what they cannot.

Where these dispositions are habitual, they constitute traits of character, defining features of one's person. That this is so appears to be confirmed by our ordinary understanding of what is meant by the claim that someone possesses good judgment, for we generally interpret this as an observation about the person's character, about the kind of person he or she is, and not merely as a comment about his or her intellectual abilities. Character traits are generally associated with distinctive patterns of feeling, patterns of desire and aversion as well as modes of thought. On this familiar view, to have a particular trait is not only to hold certain beliefs or to think in a particular way, but to like some things and dislike others with steady regularity. What the person of good judgment habitually desires, and hence what defines this particular trait of character, we have seen already. In first-personal deliberation, at least, it is that wholeness of soul in which the good of integrity consists.

E. Politics

In my account of judgment I have, up to this point, been

speaking exclusively of the sort of judgment that individuals exercise in their own private lives with regard to their personal fates. Judgment also has a public face, however, and it is to this dimension of it that I now turn.

Many important human activities are pursued collectively and have goals that can be achieved only through the coordinated action of many individuals. Certain activities belonging to this broad class are further distinguished, however, by the fact that they have as their goal the well-being of some community or collectivity itself. To take a simple example, most of those who join a voluntary association (a political party or church society or museum foundation) are likely to do so because they believe in the association's goals and wish to see them realized. In almost every association of this sort, however, there will be some who are charged with responsibility for preserving the well-being of the association itself, for seeing that the rent is paid, circulars mailed, meetings held, and disputes among members (when they arise) resolved in the way that is best from the association's point of view. Those who bear these responsibilities have a set of special concerns that most members do not, concerns we may call "organizational" or "associational" to indicate that their focal point is the well-being of the whole community to which the individual members belong.

In many communities, of course, there is likely to be little disagreement among the members regarding the nature and purpose of their common enterprise (though the absence of such disagreement is always a contingent matter that is subject to change). Where there *is* disagreement about the character and aims of a community, however, the associational concerns of those who are responsible for maintaining its well-being assume a much greater scope and urgency. When this happens, we may say that the concerns in question become "political" in character. To be sure, this way of speaking is broader than ordinary usage might appear to warrant, and does not coincide with the familiar distinction between public and private activities. It does, however, mark out a class of endeavors that have something important in common and helps to explain what we mean when we describe the actions of people even in a private setting (a corporate boardroom, for example, or law school faculty meeting) as essentially political in nature.

Politics, broadly defined in the way I have proposed, includes a great deal. It certainly includes, for example, the administration of many private organizations—universities, foundations, and profitmaking corporations—as well as the management of cities, states, and nations. Each of these activities, of course, has special requirements of its own. To the extent they are political in the broad sense, however, all require judgment of a type that is analogous to the personal judgment each individual must exercise on his or her own behalf in the sphere of private life. What makes these two forms of judgment analogous is the fact that both have as their object the construction of a friendly or fraternal whole out of conflicting parts, in one case the parts of a single soul and in the other the parts of a community, the separate individuals who make it up.

In any given community, politics is the business of attending to the community's overall well-being, and the practitioners of politics will be most visible—and badly needed—when the aims or purposes of the community are in dispute. One who engages in politics must of course have some conception of what these aims or purposes are; without such a conception, political activity would literally be pointless.[40] In arriving at his own views, however, and in attempting to guide the community by them, it is essential that he exercise good judgment—which here, as in first-personal deliberation, requires both sympathy and detachment and the ability to combine the two. Before he decides in which direction his community should move and how current controversies about its future ought to be resolved, any would-be leader must survey the alternatives, place himself imaginatively in the position of each of the controversialists, and make an effort to see matters from their point of view. He must entertain their concerns in the sense suggested earlier. The different possible futures that an institution faces at every critical juncture in its history resemble the different ways of life between which an individual must choose at certain decisive moments in his own career. In the former case, as in the latter, what deliberation requires above all else is the effort to see each of these futures in its best possible light.[41]

Once this has been done, of course, a decision must still be made. But the standard by which we assess the wisdom of the choices in which deliberation terminates is the same here, in the political realm, as in first-personal matters. It is the mark of a wise or statesmanlike political decision that it enables the members of a community—its constituent parts—to live together in fellow-feeling despite the real differences of opinion that have divided them in the past and that will undoubtedly continue to divide them in

[40] See Weber, Politics as a Vocation in Gerth and Mills, eds., From Max Weber at 115-17 (cited in note 12).

[41] See Alasdair MacIntyre's account of the evolution and self-critical refinement of traditions in After Virtue at 222-23 (cited in note 7).

the future. Put differently, it is the sign of a wise political judgment that it promotes community, not through the construction of a false and unattainable unanimity, but in the only way that human beings with strongly divergent interests are ever likely to achieve it: by strengthening the capacity of each to entertain the views of those with whom he disagrees, a capacity that has traditionally gone under the name of political fraternity.[42] Fraternity is at once something less than unanimity and more than tolerance; like the midway attitude of sympathy, it belongs between these extremes of identity and indifference. Among the members of a community, we might say, fraternity is the analogue of integrity in the soul of a single person.[43] Those who know how to achieve these two related goods, and who have the desire to do so, may, with as much justification in the one case as in the other, and for essentially similar reasons, be said to exhibit the virtue of good judgment.

III. The Good Lawyer

At the end of Part I, after criticizing the instrumental and public-spirited conceptions of law practice, I suggested a third possible justification for the choice of a lawyer's life, one that locates the worth and appeal of such a life not in anything it leads to or produces but in the excellences of character that are demanded by and displayed in law practice itself. I suggested, in addition, that this third conception could best be approached through an analysis of the phenomenon of judgment, and in Part II examined this subject in some detail. My aim in Part III is to show that a proper understanding of the faculty of judgment gives lawyers grounds for believing in the intrinsic value of what they do and hence for choosing a life in the law, whatever other (instrumental and public-spirited) reasons they may have.

To achieve competence in the practice of law one must, of course, master a considerable body of doctrine and be familiar with the distinctive forms of argument the law employs. The truly distinguished lawyer, however, the one who is recognized by his or her peers in the profession as an exemplary practitioner and whose work is marked by subtlety and imagination, possesses more than mere doctrinal knowledge and argumentative skill. What sets such a lawyer apart and makes him a model for the profession as a

---

[42] See Aristotle, Politics *1280b-1281a, *1295b. For a discussion of these concepts, see Anthony T. Kronman, Aristotle's Idea of Political Fraternity, 24 Amer. J. Jurisprudence 114 (1979).

[43] See Plato, Republic *435e-449a.

whole is not how much law he knows or how cleverly he speaks, but how wisely he makes the judgments that his professional tasks require. When one lawyer wishes to praise the work of another, the compliment he is most likely to pay him is to say that he is a person of sound judgment. Nothing counts more among practicing lawyers than this. Indeed, if one looks mainly to the rhetoric of the profession[44] (which, at the very least, can tell us something about how lawyers see themselves), it would appear that chief among the virtues lawyers admire and believe essential to their work is the virtue of sound judgment or prudence, to use an older term whose meaning has undergone a radical alteration in modern times.[45]

Law is not, of course, the only activity in which sound judgment is highly valued. It is generally thought, for example, that an outstanding statesman or diplomat is distinguished by his possession of this same capacity. But whatever the case may be in other fields of endeavor, high achievement in the law is most often associated by practitioners themselves not only, or even primarily, with knowledge and intellect, but rather with the faculty of judgment, the power of deliberation and discernment that the most troubling cases invariably require and for which no doctrinal sophistication, or sheer intellectual brilliance, is ever a satisfactory substitute.

There is some danger of confusion here and I want, therefore, to make my position as clear as possible. My claim is that law practice is an activity (more exactly, an ensemble of related activities) that can be performed well or badly or merely adequately, and that to excel at these activities, one must possess the quality I

[44] See, for example, William Rehnquist, Sound Advice to Young Lawyers—and Older Ones Too, The Reporter 21-22 (Summer 1986) ("The senior partner in the law firm—the 'rainmaker'—does not know more about the law than the junior partners or the associates. But he has that indefinable something that makes clients turn to him, not just for an opinion on strictly legal matters, but for his judgment as to how they ought to conduct their affairs."); Judicial Conference—D.C. Circuit, 100 F.R.D. 111, 119 (1983) (remarks of Judge Cotter praising the sound judgment of Judge John Lewis Smith); Milton Freeman, Abe Fortas Was My Partner, The Reporter 17-18 (Dec. 1983) (praising Fortas's wisdom and sound judgment and noting that it was this quality of his that led the Supreme Court to appoint him defense counsel in the famous *Gideon* case: "They were seriously considering overruling a 21 year old precedent. They wanted counsel from a wise adviser as to the means of doing so without causing important conflict within the Court. He so understood his mission, and it was indeed accomplished with a unanimous judgment and three concurring opinions, all consistent with a calm and nondivisive resolution of the important problem.").

[45] Kant is largely responsible for this. In Kant's moral philosophy, the term "prudence," as a result of its equation with enlightened self-interest, loses its ancient meaning and takes on its characteristically modern one. See Immanuel Kant, Fundamental Principles of the Metaphysics of Morals 18-19, in Thomas K. Abbott, ed., Kant's Critique of Practical Reason and Other Works (1873).

call good judgment. I also mean to make a second and closely related claim: that the practice of law tends to promote the development of this same trait, for the general reason that long participation in any activity encourages those powers and abilities that excellence in the activity requires. From these two claims, it does *not* follow, and I do not mean to suggest, that anyone who practices law is bound to acquire good judgment, or that good judgment cannot be acquired outside the law in other professional disciplines or, indeed, through the experience of living generally. There are, as I have indicated, fields of endeavor other than the law in which good judgment is required and that tend, in turn, to foster it. There are also many people who learn good judgment outside the arena of work, in their private relations with family, friends and lovers. None of this, however, is inconsistent with the belief that some activities depend more than others on the exercise of good judgment (as distinguished from mere skill, which all complex activities require) and show a special tendency to call it forth in those who regularly perform them. Nor is it inconsistent with the claim that law practice is one of the activities belonging to this class. I maintain that it is, and maintain, as well, that good judgment, unlike mere skill, is a trait of character. The lawyer who accepts this last proposition can justify his choice of career in terms the instrumentalist cannot—as the choice of a way of life and type of character. That this same justification, or something close to it, is available to the practitioners of other professions (though not, I believe, to those engaged in every line of work) does not make it less available to lawyers or detract from the significance it has for them.

It remains to be shown that law practice does in fact require the exercise of good judgment, as lawyers generally assume. I have taken note of this assumption, and endorsed it, but so far have said nothing in its defense. Instead of defending the broad claim that a good lawyer must possess sound judgment, however, I shall defend three somewhat narrower propositions: that a good judge, a good counselor, and a good advocate must each possess this quality. These are, in Karl Llewellyn's phrase,[46] the three main "law-jobs" and it will be useful to decompose the global concept of law practice into them. Though lawyers do other things, these are their principal occupations and if it can be shown that good judgment is required in all three, we may reasonably conclude that it is needed

[46] Karl N. Llewellyn, The Normative, the Legal and the Law-Jobs: The Problem of Juristic Method, 49 Yale L. J. 1355 (1940).

in law practice generally.

I begin with adjudication. Judges are lawyers who have been selected from the ranks of their profession on the assumption that they possess in special measure the excellences of the profession as a whole. It is therefore natural to assume that these same excellences will be displayed with special clarity in the work they do. My claim is that a good judge is distinguished by his capacity for sympathetic detachment, by his possession of the two qualities that form the basis of good judgment generally. I shall argue that the same is true of counselors and advocates as well.

A. Judging

Before reaching his decision in a case, a judge must make an effort to see the claims of the parties before him in their best possible light, which means with as much sympathy as he is able short of actually endorsing any of the positions in question. It is not enough that a judge be an interpretive genius, a Hercules of the law who is able to construct out of the resources of his own intellect a deep and elegant theory to support his decision in the case at hand. It is also necessary that he appreciate what the decision means to the parties and to those who identify with or support them, for how he presents the decision, the words he chooses to explain and defend it and often the content of the decision itself, will depend on his estimate of its meaning to the parties and the groups they represent. This is something no mere comparison of the depth and elegance of different theories can reveal.[47] Only by sympathetically reviewing the case from the parties' own perspectives can a judge gain such understanding. In doing so, of course, he must also maintain his distance from the parties' concerns, and the great challenge in judging is to remain detached while simultaneously exercising a maximum of sympathy toward the parties and their conflicting claims. A judge who fails in the first respect shows bias or favoritism and one who fails in the second, hardheartedness—the twin vices between which every judge must thread his way.

A judge who succeeds in doing so is likely to see the function of his decisions in a certain light: to clarify the law and improve it, of course, but also to preserve the bonds of community that legal conflict often strains. He will do this by searching out solutions

[47] See generally Robert A. Burt, Constitutional Law and the Teaching of the Parables, 93 Yale L. J. 455 (1984).

that make it possible for the parties, and those who identify with them, to live on amicable terms even after a judgment has been rendered that places the prestige and power of the law on one side rather than another. Any judge habituated to the practice of sympathy will be inclined to view this last task as one of his chief responsibilities. The exercise of his own sympathetic powers is likely to awaken in such a judge an appetite for the fellow-feeling in which the community of law itself consists, and he will be anxious to do what he is able to establish and preserve it. A judge may be intellectually brilliant and socially farsighted, but what makes his judgments wise is another quality altogether—his own personal capacity to satisfy the conflicting claims of sympathy and detachment, and the tendency of his decisions to promote a similar attitude among the members of his community generally.[48]

B. Counseling

A lawyer representing a client is in a very different position from that of a judge. Judges are obliged to remain scrupulously neutral among the interests of those who appear before them, but lawyers are expected to show a zealous partiality toward the interests of their clients, to do what they are able, within the limits of the law, to advance these interests and to serve as their champion when they come into conflict with the interests of other parties. Yet like their counterparts on the bench, practicing lawyers are regularly required to exercise judgment in their professional work and the deliberative powers they employ in doing so are essentially the same. Soundness of judgment is needed as badly in the representation of clients as it is in the decision of cases and though the contexts differ, the nature of the faculty itself does not.

Consider, first, the work of a lawyer to whom a client has come seeking counsel regarding some contemplated course of action. Many people conceive, or perhaps I should say misconceive, the lawyer's role in situations of this sort to be purely instrumental: the client declares his objective and the lawyer (after researching the matter) tells him whether the goal in question is attainable by

[48] See the remarks of Dean Acheson in praise of Justice Cardozo, in Roger F. Jacobs, ed., 1 Memorials of the Justices of the Supreme Court 456-57 (1981) ("He was able to bring to the aid of judgment an appreciation of phases of life which he had not experienced and respect for the values and ideas of other men which he understood, even if he did not share. . . . This inner grace enabled [him] . . . to speak with understanding and tolerance of the conditions of men and ideas, and, at the same time, with a rugged practicality and common sense.").

legal means and, on the assumption that it is, outlines the most effective method of doing what the client wishes. A large part of law practice does consist, no doubt, in giving ministerial advice of this sort—but not the most interesting, or rewarding, or estimable part. For one thing, in addition to finding means for ends their clients have already set, lawyers regularly help to clarify these ends themselves and even on occasion act as midwives without whom the ends might never come to light.[49] By this I do not mean that lawyers function as their clients' conscience, passing moral sentence on their goals and plans (though every responsible lawyer recognizes that he or she must, from time to time, be prepared to do precisely this). What I mean is simply that clients often come to lawyers with confused or conflicting ends and that it is frequently part of a lawyer's job to help the client see what it is that he wishes to do and to decide whether, on reflection, he really wants to do it.

To design an efficient legal strategy for the attainment of some predetermined end requires a knowledge of the law and often considerable cleverness as well. Something more is needed, however, if a lawyer is to play a responsible role in helping his client identify and choose an appropriate set of ends in the first place. What is needed is judgment, the same combination of sympathy and detachment that a person must possess in order to deliberate wisely about his own ends. The wise counselor is one who is able to see his client's situation from within and yet, at the same time, from a distance, and thus to give advice that is at once compassionate and objective.[50] The merely clever[51] lawyer, the hired gun, is incapable of giving such advice, and though clients may rely upon his tactical assessments, they are unlikely to seek his counsel, or value his judgment, in matters where practical wisdom is required.

A second task that lawyers regularly perform, and one that also requires real judgment as distinct from mere cleverness or legal erudition is one that is analogous to the task of community-building that I have argued is an important part of the judicial enterprise. When a client wishes to embark with others on some common venture, it is the lawyer's job—or the job of several law-

[49] For an analysis of the role lawyers play in shaping preferences, as distinguished from merely executing them, see Cass R. Sunstein, Legal Interference With Private Preferences, 53 U. Chi. L. Rev. 1129 (1986).

[50] See Charles Fried, The Lawyer as Friend: The Moral Foundations of the Lawyer-Client Relation, 85 Yale L. J. 1060 (1976).

[51] See Aristotle, Nicomachean Ethics *1144a-1144b (distinguishing between cleverness and wisdom).

yers working together—to give the undertaking a legally effective form. In general, however, it is also the lawyer's job to find, or rather to invent, a framework of rights and obligations that will accommodate the different and frequently conflicting interests of those involved. The framework in question, whether it takes the shape of a partnership or contract or corporation, may quite properly be described as a community of sorts and the lawyers working to create it must know not only what the law allows and their own clients wish, but what the other members of the community want as well. This they can discern only through the exercise of a sympathetic imagination, and the lawyer who lacks such imagination will be handicapped in his efforts to fashion a community able to withstand even the mildest shocks that an unpredictable future holds in store. Every lawyer who has ever drafted a contract, or created a partnership, has participated in the foundation of a small commonwealth, and the excellences he requires in his work might be described as the excellences, in miniature, of a founding statesman. Chief among these is good judgment—the combination of sympathy and detachment that makes it possible to hold in view a range of different interests and to anticipate, in imagination, those arrangements most likely to preserve some measure of amicability among them.

C. Advocacy

Can it be said that advocates, like judges and counselors, require wisdom, rather than mere cleverness or cunning, in the work they do? This is an important question, for although the practice of law includes much more than advocacy in the narrow sense, it is advocacy that is most often taken, by lawyers and laypersons alike, to reveal the truth about the profession as a whole and the character of those engaged in it.[52] It is a question, moreover, which one might think must be answered in the negative, for it is unclear that practical wisdom, as I have characterized it, is in any sense required for the successful advocacy of a client's cause.

The job of an advocate, unlike that of a counselor, generally begins only when his client's interests have already been fixed with a high degree of certainty and his primary task cannot properly be described as that of building a community of any sort. Indeed, the

[52] See Schwartz, 66 Cal. L. Rev. at 672 (cited in note 2) (noting that non-advocate functions often are regarded "almost as exceptions to the primary role of lawyers as advocates").

aim of the advocate often seems to be precisely the opposite: to destroy communities (of contract, sentiment, and shared experience) for the sake of the particular interest he represents. It is thus hard to discern, in the work of an advocate, elements that correspond to those that in the fields both of adjudication and counseling call for the exercise of sound judgment and create room for its display. All an advocate needs, many have concluded, is the sheer manipulative power that Socrates had in mind when he described rhetoric, the art of the advocate who appears before juries and other assemblies, as a technique for making bad arguments appear good and vice versa.[53] An advocate must be cunning, he must know what will persuade and what will not, he must, perhaps, have a touch of ruthlessness and be prepared to say and do things that under other circumstances even he would regard as reprehensible. Where in the work of an advocate is there room for those qualities of sympathy and detachment, and for the spirit of community building, that I have identified with the faculty of judgment and claim is the mark of the practically wise?

It is tempting to respond that an advocate must often act as a counselor, for it is his job not only to champion his client's cause, but also to help him decide, at every stage along the way, whether to pursue some other, less combative course of action instead (by settling a claim, for example, or pleading guilty to a reduced criminal charge).[54] Here, as in the work of settlement itself, there is a need for something more than cleverness or cunning, and a place for practical wisdom. But this, it must be admitted, is an unsatisfying response, for it meets the charge that a successful advocate need not be practically wise merely by pointing out that lawyers rarely act in this capacity alone. This may be true—I happen to believe it is—but what of advocacy itself, considered independently of the other functions lawyers perform? Can it in any sense be said to require genuine wisdom as distinguished from slickness and a talent for manipulation?

It is possible, I think, to construct an affirmative answer to this question if one begins by taking seriously a puzzling remark that Aristotle makes in his treatise on rhetoric. According to Aristotle, the persuasiveness of a speech depends, among other things, on "the personal character of the speaker." "We believe good men more fully and readily than others," he observes, and notes that

---

[53] See Plato, Gorgias *455.

[54] See, for example, Andrew McThenia and Thomas Shaffer, For Reconciliation, 94 Yale L. J. 1660 (1985).

"this is true generally whatever the question is, and absolutely true where exact certainty is impossible and opinions are divided." Thus "[i]t is not true," Aristotle concludes, "that the personal goodness revealed by the speaker contributes nothing to his power of persuasion; on the contrary, his character may almost be called the most effective means of persuasion he possesses."[55]

This last observation, which seems flatly inconsistent with the Socratic portrait of the successful rhetorician as a person of unscrupulous cunning, states a truth of great importance. Among the people with whom we live and work, some we recognize as having greater probity, prudence, and compassion than others, and we tend instinctively to give their opinions greater weight than we give to the views of those who lack these qualities. If a person widely respected for sound judgment recommends that we pursue a particular course of action, or takes a position in an institutional debate, we treat his or her advice with special seriousness just because it comes from the person it does, regardless of its content. In this sense, our assessment of a person's opinions is always, in part at least, a function of our assessment of the person himself, though, of course, other considerations enter in as well. All moral and political argument is, to this extent, irreducibly *ad hominem*, from which it follows that anyone wishing to be effective in debate will have an interest in becoming the sort of person whose opinions are respected, that is to say, a person of good judgment.

To this it might be objected that all anyone really needs in order to be successful in debate is a reputation for practical wisdom and not the trait itself.[56] But a person's character is more difficult to conceal than this cynical advice implies. Our characters reveal themselves in all we do and are open to view, on the public surface of our lives, for everyone to see. Indeed, a person's character is often the first thing we feel with any confidence that we know about him. The reason is that our characters (unlike our beliefs and intentions, which are more easily concealed) have a dispositional dimension—more exactly, they consist in a set of dispositions or habitual desires. What we desire is generally harder to hide than what we think or intend, and the most difficult desires to conceal are those that have congealed into habits. The character a person possesses constitutes his habit of living, and though he may be intermittently successful in keeping it from view, it is likely to

[55] Aristotle, Rhetoric *1356a.

[56] This is the argument that Glaucon makes in order to force Socrates to give a more persuasive account of why justice is an intrinsic good. See Plato, Republic *360d-361d.

show through in most of what he does. Living out of character for any period of time is like living out of one's own skin, and about as difficult. One who seeks a reputation for practical wisdom without its substance is therefore likely to be seen for what he really is—a puppeteer dissembling to the world, the kind of person whose opinions we are unlikely to accept with trust or confidence.

But surely, it will be objected, none of this has any bearing on advocacy in law. The legal advocate typically argues his case before strangers who are unacquainted with his character and who have neither the time nor opportunity to learn much, if anything, about it. Moreover, though a person's character may reveal itself quickly in informal settings, the ceremonies of the law tend to conceal rather than accentuate the individual traits of those involved by requiring them to play already scripted parts.[87]

To this, I would reply as follows. One of the main responsibilities of a judge is to preserve the community of law, to discover and articulate the conditions under which political fraternity is possible. It is the judge's direct responsibility to do this; he must attend to the community of law, to its construction and preservation, and cannot simply assume that it will come into existence as the indirect consequence of what he does by means of an invisible mechanism of coordination. We are used to thinking of the advocate's role as a different one: the advocate's attention is directed to his client's welfare, and if his efforts promote the community of law they do so in a roundabout way by helping to ensure the effective operation of our adversarial system of adjudication. It is a commonplace, however, that to be successful in the representation of his client, a lawyer must imaginatively place himself in the position of the judge who will decide his case. (He must do this even in a jury trial, for it is a judge who will ultimately decide the controversy on appeal). If he cannot place himself in the judge's position and see the case from his perspective, an advocate will necessarily be limited in his ability to predict which of the arguments he might make on his client's behalf are most likely to meet with judicial favor, and thus be less effective in representing the client than he otherwise would be.

To be a good advocate, then, one must be in the habit of looking at one's own case from a judicial point of view, and since a judge's direct concern is with the community of law, an advocate who sees things from the judge's perspective and attends to his

[87] I borrow the idea of the law's ceremonial aspects from Thurman Arnold, The Folklore of Capitalism 211-17 (1937).

concerns will be careful to frame his own arguments so as to emphasize the congruence between his client's interests and the interests of the legal community as a whole. Every good judge knows the difference between a wise argument and a merely clever one. A clever argument shows inventiveness in the way it uses legal and other materials to promote a client's cause. A wise argument establishes a convergence between that cause and the community of law, the community the law both expresses and sustains and whose existence it is the special obligation of judges to protect. In the cases they decide, judges are likely to give arguments of the latter sort a special weight, for these are made from their own perspective and address the issue that is of paramount importance from a judicial point of view. Wise arguments, in short, win cases, and if you are an advocate, the only way to ensure that your arguments exhibit wisdom with any regularity is to acquire the habit of looking at your client's case from the point of view of a judge whose job it is to superintend the legal system as a whole.

If it is objected that an advocate can acquire a habit of this sort without, at the same time, acquiring the character trait I call good judgment—that he or she can become a connoisseur of judicial attitudes and perceptions without becoming judicious—my response is that this entirely ignores the dispositional aspect of adjudication and of judgment generally. In order to know what a judge is likely to say in any particular case, the advocate who imaginatively assumes his position must survey the conflicting interests that the case presents with the same sympathetic detachment the judge himself exercises. This is the only way an advocate can gain the insight on which the judge relies and hence the only way in which he can predict what the judge's decision in the case will be. But it is difficult to do this—indeed, I think it is impossible—without sharing in the affective dispositions that the judge's attitude of sympathetic detachment itself entails. And where such sharing becomes habitual, it, in turn, is likely over time to awaken in the advocate who imaginatively plays the role of judge a measure of the same desire for political fraternity that motivates the judge himself. Some of the judge's own good judgment will tend, in this way, to rub off on the advocate who is constantly straining to see his client's case from the judge's point of view. If he succeeds in doing so, it is likely that the advocate will eventually come to share the judge's dispositions, to care about what the judge cares about, and once these dispositions have become settled traits of character, to show the same good judgment that the successful judge displays.

In the beginning, of course, a lawyer may have only instrumental reasons for making the effort to see his clients' cases from a judicial point of view. Once he has acquired the capacity to do so, however, its exercise is likely to be, for him, a source of independent satisfaction. The same is true of many skills—of the skill, for example, of driving an automobile, or swimming, or even the mundane art of dressing properly. Initially, a person may wish to learn these things only for the sake of some external reward, like physical safety or parental approval, but in time he often grows to value them for their intrinsic interest and the pleasure they afford. Where the skill in question requires the controlled employment of certain affective attitudes—as the advocate's skill of predicting how a judge will view his case does—this general tendency for external goods to be supplemented by internal ones is likely to be particularly pronounced, for here the acquisition of the skill will typically be marked by a change of character, and this is something that can never be of merely instrumental importance to the person undergoing it.

It is only when an advocate has acquired the character trait of good judgment that he can be confident in his ability to see the world of legal disputes as a judge would see it and hence to distinguish wise arguments from merely clever ones. Advocates who do not possess this trait of character may be knowledgeable about the law and quick in argument, but their lack of judgment is a liability: it makes them less effective than they otherwise would be. In this sense we may with justification say that a successful advocate owes his triumphs, in part at least, to the character he possesses, to the fact that he is a person of a certain sort and not merely to his knowledge of the law or mastery of rhetorical techniques. To this extent, the truth of Aristotle's observation holds even here, in the realm of legal advocacy, where the occasions for displaying one's character are briefer and more ceremonial than in other areas of life.

I have now said enough about each of the three main branches of work in which lawyers are engaged—judging, counseling, and advocacy—to have made credible my claim that good judgment is indispensable in each. It is impossible, I believe, to be an outstanding lawyer in any of these fields if one lacks good judgment, and the sorts of tasks that lawyers perform tend in turn to cultivate this capacity by requiring its regular exercise. I do not mean to imply that all lawyers possess good judgment—many don't, of course—or even to suggest that a minimally acceptable competence is unattainable without it. It may be the case, for example, that a person's character is so decisively formed in a certain way by the time he comes to the law that no length of living in it can give him the traits of character I have just described. But none of this alters the basic fact that good judgment is for lawyers a professional ideal, a virtue that gives meaning and dignity to their craft precisely because the craft itself cannot be practiced well without it.[58]

Conclusion

To the question, then, of why one would ever choose to spend a lifetime in the law the following answer might be given. To live *in* the law, rather than *off* it,[59] is to submit to its discipline and to accept its ideals. Among these ideals is the attainment and exercise of good judgment or practical wisdom. To possess good judgment, however, is not merely to possess great learning or intelligence, but to be a person of a certain sort, to have a certain character, as well. It follows that to aim at practical wisdom can never simply be to aim at the appropriation of a skill whose mastery leaves its possessor fundamentally unchanged. To aim at practical wisdom is to aim at a particular conception of character and at the way of life associated with it. To the extent one's aim is true the result is

[58] Though I have said nothing in this section about the teaching branch of the profession, the message of my article is directed to teachers as well as practicioners of law. Indeed, in a sense, it is directed particularly to teachers, for one of the most striking characteristics of our leading law schools today is the attitude of contempt that prevails in them toward the old-fashioned virtue of practical wisdom. Why this should be so is a long and complicated story. One thing, however, is clear. The mistrust of practical wisdom and of arguments appealing to it, which is symptomatic of so much of contemporary legal scholarship, has led to a new and disturbing division within the profession as a whole, between the practicing bar and the professorate.

There will, of course, always be a separation of sorts between those who choose an academic career in law and those who practice their craft in some more worldly setting. In this country, such a separation has existed for at least a century, since legal education began to assume an academic character. In recent years, however, the separation has widened considerably. Most practicing lawyers still believe that excellence in the practice of law requires prudence or sound judgment, a view shared by those law teachers whose primary identification continues to be with the practicing bar. Many law teachers, however (including some of the most widely read and well-respected ones) take a different and more disparaging view of these qualities. In their view, an insistence on the importance of practical wisdom is to be regarded either as an ideological ploy or as a sign of scientific naivete. To be sure, practicing lawyers and law teachers inevitably will have different interests and aims. This difference in outlook becomes troubling, however, when it is accompanied by a loss of respect on the one side for the qualities of mind and temperament whose possession is regarded by those on the other as a badge of professional pride.

[59] See Weber, Politics as a Vocation in Gerth and Mills, eds., From Max Weber at 84 (cited in note 12) (distinguishing those who live "for" politics from those who live "off" it).

likely to be what Socrates in the *Republic* describes as a turning about of the soul, a transformation of one's own self, the development of a professional *persona*. Unlike some,[60] I do not regard this as a cause for regret or fear. Instead I see it as a source of pride, for the character that lawyers achieve if they live up to their professional ideals is itself an accomplishment of value marked by the attainment of a central human excellence.

There are, of course, other quite different modes of character and ways of life that are appealing too. I do not mean to suggest—what would in any case be absurdly presumptuous—that the life of a practicing lawyer is the best life anyone could lead. It is, however, one of the lives worth leading, and the virtue of practical wisdom that it holds up as an ideal is one of a small number of character traits to whose cultivation a person may reasonably devote the whole of his professional existence. A life lived in the law in this sense has intrinsic worth for the person living it. He need not look beyond his work to discover its point or find a reason for continuing, but finds reason enough in the work itself, and in the excellences he needs to do it well. Every defense of law practice that locates its good in something extrinsic to it follows a different strategy of argument and one, I think, that is bound to be less satisfying.

I have now answered the question with which I began. There is one last thought that I wish to add, however, a thought that haunts me as I think it must haunt anyone who is attracted to the view of law practice that I have defended here.

The world into which we have been born and in which it is our common fate to live is a world characterized, above all else, by what Max Weber called the process of rationalization.[61] In the countries of Western Europe and North America, every department of life—and this is as true of painting and poetry as it is of government and economic enterprise—has in the last century been rationalized or intellectualized to a degree unimaginable even to those Enlightenment thinkers who prepared the foundations for this development and acted as its early champions. Everywhere, even in areas of life where the intellect has always played at most a minor role, the claims of reason today enjoy a commanding priority over all others. By "claims of reason" I mean two things: first, a demand for intellectual transparency and second, for calculability.

---

[60] See, for example, Eshete, Does a Lawyer's Character Matter? (cited in note 20).

[61] Max Weber, Science as a Vocation, in Gerth and Mills, eds., From Max Weber at 155-56 (cited in note 12).

Only those activities and institutions that are based upon rules and processes that are fully accessible to the light of reason and that provide a framework for action calculable to the highest possible degree are rational in this twofold sense. All others are irrational, which today means either unworthy or in need of repair. Historically speaking, this is a novel idea though for us, as I have said, it is a fateful fact. The rationalization process that today carries our civilization forward has been gaining momentum for centuries, and like a powerful current it now sweeps us all along to a common destiny.

The law is as much caught in this current as everything else. Indeed, the law seems at times to be an accelerating force and has certainly supplied, out of its own particular resources, many of the main ideas that underlie the rationalization process as a whole.[62] There is much in our Anglo-American system of law, however, that is bound to seem anachronistic or even objectionable when viewed from the perspective of the claims of reason, and so to the extent these claims are taken seriously, there will be recurrent, and perhaps ultimately irresistible, demands that these irrational elements be purged. Among these elements, I am afraid, many will include the old-fashioned virtue of practical wisdom. Can practical wisdom remain a professional ideal in a legal world that has internalized the claims of reason?

There is, so far, only inconclusive evidence but it all points in the same direction—towards the transformation of legal education into a branch of social scientific training,[63] of the judiciary into a managerial bureaucracy,[64] and of the private law firm into a rationalized, profitmaking enterprise indistinguishable from any other economic organization.[65] These developments reflect, I believe, a common tendency toward increased rationalization in every branch of our profession, and the consequence has in each case been a weakening of the ideal of practical wisdom as a guiding professional norm. I do not know whether this tendency has a natural

[62] See Anthony T. Kronman, Max Weber 72-95 (1983).

[63] See John Monahan and Laurens Walker, Teaching Social Science in Law: An Alternative to "Law and Society," 35 J. Legal Educ. 478 (1985) (noting meteoric rise of social science teaching in the law schools from mid-1970s to today).

[64] See Richard A. Posner, The Federal Courts: Crisis and Reform 102-19 (1985); Owen Fiss, The Bureaucratization of the Judiciary, 92 Yale L. J. 1442 (1983); Wade H. McCree, Jr., Bureaucratic Justice: An Early Warning, 129 U. Pa. L. Rev. 777 (1981).

[65] See Ronald J. Gilson and Robert H. Mnookin, Sharing Among the Human Capitalists: An Economic Inquiry into the Corporate Law Firm and How Partners Split Profits, 37 Stan. L. Rev. 313 (1985) (analyzing law firm as profit-making organization).

limit, or whether it can be deliberately reversed if we make the effort, although I am inclined to think the answer to both questions is no. Beyond a certain point—and this is the thought that haunts me—the rationalization of the law is likely to turn us all, those who teach the law as well as those who make and practice it, into bureaucratic functionaries, characterless experts whose work requires knowledge, precision, and fairness, but never judgment in the sense that I have used that term here. When this happens, the only goods remaining to those who practice law will be external goods. Will it be possible, in the world of law that I fear is growing up around us, to answer someone who asks why he should choose a living in the law or think of it as anything more than a way of passing time and making money?

[11]

Portia in a Different Voice:

*Speculations on a Women's Lawyering Process**

Carrie Menkel-Meadow†

INTRODUCTION

As a scholar of the legal profession, I have asked whether the increased presence of women in the legal profession might lead to alternative ways of seeing what lawyers do and how they do it.[1] Will it be simply that more lawyers are women, or will the legal profession be transformed by the women who practice law? In recent years, two developments in feminist scholarship have offered insights which promise to shed some light on that question. This essay explores some of the potential applications to law of these two developments in feminist scholarship stated as speculative hypotheses for further study.[2]

The first of these developments in feminist scholarship is the self-conscious observation of how women's entry into formerly male-dominated fields has changed both the knowledge base of the field[3] and the

* This essay is a revised version of a paper presented to the annual meeting of the Law & Society Association in Boston (June 7, 1984) and of talks delivered at the 15th National Conference on Women & the Law in Los Angeles (March 29-31, 1984) and the Mitchell Lecture Series, Faculty of Law & Jurisprudence, State University of New York at Buffalo (November 20, 1984). I gratefully acknowledge the research assistance of Susan Nash and Laurie Taylor and the affiliational and intellectual support of Emily Abel, Grace Blumberg, Sheila Bob, Christine Littleton, Kitty MacKinnon and Fran Olsen. In addition, I especially thank editors Donna Peizer and Catherine Fisk for their extremely caring and responsible editing.

† Professor of Law, University of California, Los Angeles. A.B., 1971, Barnard College; J.D., 1974, University of Pennsylvania.

1 Menkel-Meadow, *Women as Law Teachers: Toward the Feminization of Legal Education*, in ESSAYS ON THE APPLICATION OF A HUMANISTIC PERSPECTIVE TO LAW TEACHING 16 (1981) [hereinafter cited as Menkel-Meadow, *Women as Law Teachers*]; Menkel-Meadow, *Women in Law?*, 1983 AM. B. FOUND. RESEARCH J. 189.

2 C. Menkel-Meadow & G. Blumberg, A Research Proposal on the Impact of Women on the Legal Profession and Law (1983) (a study-in-progress of how women behave as lawyers designed to test empirically some of the hypotheses contained herein). (The proposal is on file with the author).

3 A FEMINIST PERSPECTIVE IN THE ACADEMY: THE DIFFERENCE IT MAKES (E. Langland & W. Gove eds. 1981); A. RICH, *Toward a Woman-Centered University* in ON LIES, SECRETS AND SILENCE: SELECTED PROSE 1966-1978 125 (1979); Abel & Nelson, *Feminist Studies: The Scholarly Is Political*, 2 THE WOMEN'S REV. OF BOOKS 10 (vol. 4 Jan. 1985).

methodology by which knowledge is acquired.[4] Since our knowledge of how lawyers behave and of how the legal system functions is based almost exclusively on male subjects of study,[5] our understanding of what it means to be and act like a lawyer may be misleadingly based on a male norm. We need to broaden our inquiry to include the new participants in the profession so that we can discover whether our present understandings are accurate.[6] With more women lawyers available for study we may learn first, whether women perform lawyering tasks in ways different from men; second, whether our descriptions of what lawyers do may have to change to reflect different goals or task orientations; and third, whether the increased presence of women in the profession may have broad institutional effects. Current studies of gender differences in other fields offer a powerful heuristic for application to our understanding of the lawyering process.

The second development is a body of theoretical and empirical research in psychology and sociology. This research has postulated that women grow up in the world with a more relational and affiliational concept of self than do men. This concept of self has important implications for the values that women develop and for the actions that are derived from those values.[7] This research is controversial and is generating criticism from many different quarters.[8] I am not unsympathetic to some of

---

[4] C. GILLIGAN, IN A DIFFERENT VOICE: PSYCHOLOGICAL THEORY AND WOMEN'S DEVELOPMENT 6-23 (1982). Gilligan points out that much moral and psychological developmental theory (from Piaget, Kohlberg, and Erickson) is derived from studies using male subjects only.

[5] *See, e.g.*, J. HEINZ & E. LAUMANN, CHICAGO LAWYERS: THE SOCIAL STRUCTURE OF THE BAR (1982); J. CARLIN, LAWYERS ON THEIR OWN (1962). *Cf.* C. EPSTEIN, WOMEN IN LAW (1981).

[6] The present essay focuses on gender, but what I have to say about the exclusion of whole classes as subjects of study applies as well to minorities, ethnicities and other excluded, non-mainstream groups, such as the handicapped, lesbians and gay people.

[7] *See, e.g.*, C. GILLIGAN, *supra* note 4; N. CHODOROW, THE REPRODUCTION OF MOTHERING (1978); D. DINNERSTEIN, THE MERMAID AND THE MINOTAUR (1978); J. MILLER, TOWARD A NEW PSYCHOLOGY OF WOMEN (1976); N. NODDINGS, CARING: A FEMININE APPROACH TO ETHICS AND MORAL EDUCATION (1974); A. SCHAEF, WOMEN'S REALITY (1981). These are selected from a wider body of literature written mostly, but not exclusively, by women as a result of feminist interest in doing research in areas previously dominated by men. Most striking about these works from a variety of disciplines is the emphasis in each on women's affiliational or relational values. There is little agreement about the source of these values or attributes. Some authors find psychological, others sociological, causes; others do not posit a cause. But all of these authors have observed these attributes or values in women.

[8] One critique is focused on this research's failure to account for the political origin of these attributes. That is, some have argued that women exhibit caring and affiliational values because it is only natural for them to care about relationships in a world where women acquire status and power only in a derivative sense through their connection with men. This critique says we cannot know what women would value in a world where they are not oppressed. Comments by Catharine MacKinnon, Mitchell Lecture Series, State University of New York at Buffalo School of Law (Nov. 20, 1984), *reprinted in The 1984 James McCormick Mitchell Lecture: Feminist Discourse, Moral Values, and the Law—a Conversation*, 34 BUFFALO L. REV. 11, 20 (1985).

Another critique fears the political backlash from an effort to label qualities male and female in ways that may perpetuate old stereotypes and justify sex discriminatory laws. This is a variant of the current debate in feminist jurisprudence over formal versus substantive equality (or equal versus special treatment). *See, e.g.*, Note, *Toward a Redefinition of Sexual*

the criticism, which in part reflects a growing maturity and differentiation in feminist scholarship.[9]

I find persuasive, though not unproblematic, the notion that values, consciousness, attributes, and behavior are gendered,[10] *i.e.*, that some are identified as belonging to women and others to men. The attachment of gender labels is a product of both present empirical research[11] and social process. Thus, we may label the quality of caring a female quality, but note its presence in many men. Further, a man who exhibits many feminine qualities may be perceived as feminine, *e.g.* "He's too sensitive to be a good trial lawyer," or alternatively, an assertive woman may be met with remarks such as, "She's as sharp as any of the men on the team."[12] Attributing behavior characteristics to a particular gender is problematic, because even as we observe such generalizations to be valid in many cases, we risk perpetuating the conventional stereotypes that prevent us from seeing the qualities as qualities without their gendered context.[13]

The process is one that most feminists deplore because what is labeled female or feminine typically is treated as inferior, and is subordinated to what is labeled male or masculine. This is particularly true if the context in which they are found is one, such as the practice of law, which has itself traditionally been labeled male.[14] For the purpose of this essay I will assume that gender differences exist as they have been documented by such writers as Simone de Beauvoir, Carol Gilligan, Nancy Chodorow, Jean Baker Miller, Anne Schaef and others,[15] and will

---

Equality, 95 HARV. L. REV. 487 (1981) [hereinafter cited as Note, *Toward a Redefinition of Sexual Equality*]; Williams, *The Equality Crisis: Some Reflections on Culture, Courts and Feminism*, 7 WOMEN'S RIGHTS L. REP. 175 (1982); Olsen, *Statutory Rape: A Feminist Critique of Rights Analysis*, 63 TEX. L. REV. 387 (1985).

Yet another critique is that the qualities observed are the product of class, socio-economic relations or oppression and thus not necessarily gender-based. *See, e.g.*, Buck-Morss, *Socio-economic Bias in Piaget's Theory: Implications for Cross-Cultural Studies* in PSYCHOLOGY IN SOCIAL CONTEXT 349 (A. Buss ed. 1975).

Finally, Gilligan's work has been criticized on methodological and interpretivist grounds. *See* Broughton, *Women's Rationality and Men's Virtues: A Critique of Gender Dualism in Gilligan's Theory of Moral Development*, 50 SOC. RESEARCH 597 (1983); Flanagan & Adler, *Impartiality and Particularity*, 50 SOC. RESEARCH 576 (1983); Nails, *Social-Scientific Sexism: Gilligan's Mismeasure of Man*, 50 SOC. RESEARCH 643 (1983).

9 For an excellent typology of the different schools within feminism, see A. JAGGER, FEMINIST POLITICS AND HUMAN NATURE (1984).

10 S. DE BEAUVOIR, THE SECOND SEX (1953); C. GILLIGAN, *supra* note 4.

11 C. GILLIGAN, *supra* note 4; E. MACCOBY & C. JACKLIN, THE PSYCHOLOGY OF SEX DIFFERENCES (1974); Spence, *Changing Conceptions of Men and Women: A Psychologist's Perspective* in E. Langland & W. Gove, *supra* note 3.

12 Remarks overheard by the author by lawyers describing other lawyers.

13 One could argue that qualities or traits cannot exist without a gendered context or that all qualities and traits are gendered. In this view, the notion that there could be a neutral, objective, or genderless way to describe the qualities of lawyering is impossible.

14 "But the important question is what effect the presence of women as barristers in our courts would have upon the administration of justice, and the question can be satisfactorily answered only in the light of experience." *Re* Application of Bradwell, 55 Ill. 535, 542 (1869), *aff'd*, Bradwell v. Illinois, 83 U.S. 130 (1873). *See also* Schwartz, Brandt & Milrod, *The Battles of Clara Shortridge Foltz*, 1985 CAL. DEFENDER 7.

15 *See supra* note 7.

leave to others the important inquiry into the origins of these differences, be they biological,[16] sociological,[17] political,[18] or some combination of these. My perspective on this issue is that as long as such differences exist, studies of the world—here the legal profession—that fail to take into account women's experience of that world[19] are incomplete, and prevent us from having a greater repertoire of societal as well as individual choices.

An important part of this inquiry is whether it is yet possible to see if women conduct themselves as lawyers differently from men. I have commented elsewhere that just because there are increasing numbers of women in the practice and teaching of law,[20] we do not yet know whether women will transform the practice or themselves when they are found in sufficient numbers. Social research has indicated that those in token numbers may feel strong pressure to conform to the already existing norms of the workplace and to minimize, rather than emphasize, whatever differences exist.[21] Thus, when we look at women who are lawyers in 1985, we may be studying those women who have been successful in assimilating to male norms.[22] Although there is already some evidence of Portia-like[23] dissatisfaction with the present male voice,[24] more

16 R. BLEIER, SCIENCE AND GENDER (1984).

17 *See* Buck-Morss, *supra* note 8.

18 *See supra* note 8, especially MacKinnon article.

19 Catharine MacKinnon has pointed out that women do not yet "possess" a lawyering process that is their own—*i.e.*, not defined in relation to men's (in the possessive sense); thus for her it may be too early to talk about a "women's lawyering process." (Conversation with Catharine MacKinnon, March 25, 1985).

20 Menkel-Meadow, *Women as Law Teachers*, *supra* note 1. *See also* C. EPSTEIN, *supra* note 5.

21 R. KANTER, MEN AND WOMEN OF THE CORPORATION (1977); Kanter, *Reflections on Women and the Legal Profession: A Sociological Perspective*, 1 HARV. WOMEN'S L.J. 1 (1978); Spangler, Gordon & Pipkin, *Token Women: An Empirical Test of Kanter's Hypothesis*, 84 AM. J. SOC. 160 (1978).

22 *See* Note, *Toward a Redefinition of Sexual Equality*, *supra* note 8. On the question of the extent to which women speak in a different voice or use a different language (a disputed issue in feminist scholarship), see R. LAKOFF, LANGUAGE AND WOMEN'S PLACE (1975). Some would say that women have had to be bilingual in order to succeed in the male world, speaking both the prevailing male language as well as women's own language. In a recent speech, Carol Gilligan illustrated this point by reporting on a follow-up study of two of her subjects. At age 15 when Amy was asked again about the Heinz dilemma, *see infra* text accompanying notes 40-49, she answered in terms similar to Jake's (the "male" voice) and then asked, "Do you want to know what I really think?" and continued with a response similar to her earlier response at age 11. Comments by Carol Gilligan, Mitchell Lecture Series, State University of New York at Buffalo School of Law (Nov. 20, 1984), *reprinted in The 1984 James McCormick Mitchell Lecture: Feminist Discourse, Moral Values, and the Law—a Conversation*, 34 BUFFALO L. REV. 11, 36 (1984), this poignantly illustrates the ability of an adolescent girl being socialized to the male world by learning to speak in two voices. At this point, we can only wonder whether at some age Amy will stop asking if we want to hear what she really thinks.

23 Portia is one of the first women "lawyers" to be named in western culture. In *The Merchant of Venice*, Portia, disguised as a man (which is the only way she can argue the law), appears as a learned doctor of laws and eloquently pleads for mercy when others ask only for justice:

> But mercy is above is scept'red sway;
> It is enthroned in the hearts of kings,
> It is an attribute to God himself,
> And earthly powers doth then show likest God's
> When mercy seasons justice.

women lawyers may be necessary to form a critical mass that will give full expression to a women's voice in law (whether expressed exclusively by women or with men in another voice.)

Because our realization that women can transform a profession is quite new, I call what follows "speculations on a women's lawyering process." I hope to provoke further inquiry and dialogue on this subject as we begin to include women lawyers in our studies of the legal profession and the legal system. In addition, I hope to encourage those who wish to give expression to values and behaviors in the legal profession that are currently under-represented to do so, with the belief that this will produce a better legal system for lawyers, clients, and others who are affected by our legal institutions.

I. A Different Voice: Psychological Theories About Women

Several recent studies and books in psychological development have traced the implications of gender differences in psychological development for personality, moral development, child rearing, and ultimately, the very structure of major social institutions. The common theme that unites this body of work by psychologists such as Chodorow, Dinnerstein, Miller, Schaef, and most recently, Gilligan, is that women experience themselves through connections and relationships to others while men see themselves as separately identified individuals. In the view of Dinnerstein and Chodorow, these differences are the result of a childrearing system which is based on mothering, so that growing up is a process of identification and connection for a girl and separation and individuation for a boy.[25] Miller and Schaef, working as psychologists, heard women express values different from men's: vulnerability instead of strength, and responsiveness instead of independence.[26] Noddings and Gilligan, both professors of education, observed values of caring, responsiveness and relatedness in women, while they found values of principle, rights and universalism in men.[27] These observations and hypotheses led to the conclusion that women tend to see themselves as affiliated and related to others, while men are more likely to see themselves as separate,

W. SHAKESPEARE, *The Merchant of Venice*, Act IV, Scene 1, in THE COMPLETE SIGNET CLASSIC SHAKESPEARE 630 (S. Barnet ed. 1963). *See also* C. GILLIGAN, *supra* note 4, at 105.

24 *See, e.g.*, Fox, *Good-bye to Gameplaying*, JURIS DR. 37 (Jan. 1978) (a powerful critique of the games which the practice of law consists of, including the macho sporting ethic in litigation; the author speaks about why she gave up litigation practice); Rifkin, *Toward a Theory of Law and Patriarchy*, 3 HARV. WOMEN'S L.J. 83 (1980) (a more general and theoretical critique of the structure of law and legal systems as creations of men intending to protect and preserve patriarchical social relations).

25 *See, e.g.*, N. CHODOROW, *supra* note 7, and D. DINNERSTEIN, *supra* note 7.

26 *See* J. MILLER, *supra* note 7, and A. SCHAEF, *supra* note 7.

27 *See* C. GILLIGAN, *supra* note 7, and N. NODDINGS, *supra* note 7.

individualized, and different from (m)other. Although each of these writers came at their inquiry with different questions, their findings and theories are strikingly similar.[28]

Because Carol Gilligan's work is the most recent entry into this stream of research, and because it has already served as a powerful heuristic for legal studies,[29] I will explore, mostly by speculative analogy rather than by suggesting a possibly fallacious direct relationship, how, from a women's different voice in moral development, we might infer a women's different voice in legal processes.

In her book, *In a Different Voice: Psychological Theory and Women's Development*,[30] Gilligan observes that much of what has been written about human psychological development has been based on studies of male subjects exclusively. As a consequence, girls and women have either not been described,[31] or they are said to have "failed" to develop on measurement scales based on male norms.[32] Just as Gilligan has observed that studies of human psychological development have been centered on males, feminists have observed the law to be based on male values and behaviors. As Frances Olsen notes:

> Law is supposed to be rational, objective, abstract and principled, like men; it is not supposed to be irrational, subjective, contextualized or personalized like women. The social, political and intellectual practices that constitute "law" were for many years carried out almost exclusively by men. Given that women were long excluded from the practice of law, it should not be surprising that the traits associated with women are not greatly valued by law. Moreover, in a kind of vicious cycle, the "maleness" of law was used as a justification for excluding women from practicing law. While the number of women in law has been rapidly increasing, the field continues to be heavily male dominated.[33]

This phenomenon has also been noted by the sociologist Cynthia Fuchs Epstein, who observed that because white middle-aged men have been the demographic norm of "lawyer" for so long, we come to identify the characteristics of white middle-aged maleness as necessary for lawyering. We do not consider what the qualities of being a lawyer are independent of their identification with the male gender.[34] Thus, with

---

28 *See supra* note 7.

29 *See* Karst, *Women's Constitution*, 1984 DUKE L.J. 447 (1984); Schneider, *"In a Different Voice": Reflections on a Feminist View of Rights*, GEO. WASH. L. REV. (forthcoming); Spiegelman, *Court-Ordered Hiring Quotas After* Stotts: *A Narrative on the Role of the Moralities of the Web and the Ladder in Employment Discrimination Doctrine*, 20 HARV. C.R.-C.L. L. REV. (1985).

30 C. GILLIGAN, *supra* note 4.

31 *Id.* at 151-56.

32 *Id.* at 16.

33 F. Olsen, The Sex of Law (unpublished manuscript on file with the author).

34 C. EPSTEIN, WOMAN'S PLACE: OPTIONS AND LIMITS IN PROFESSIONAL CAREERS, 87-88 (1970).

males as the only source of our descriptions of lawyers,[35] what is normal, good or true is identified solely with how men behave in law,[36] a close parallel to Gilligan's conclusions in the area of moral development.

The male-derived model of moral reasoning and psychological development described by Gilligan values hierarchical thinking based on the logic of reasoning from abstract, universal principles. Gilligan measures her findings against the work of her colleague, Lawrence Kohlberg. His theory of moral development comprised of six "universal" stages[37] is based on a study of eighty-four *boys* from childhood through adulthood. Gilligan explains that when Kohlberg's model is applied to women, they tend to score at stage three, a stage characterized by seeing morality as a question of interpersonal relations and caring for and pleasing others.[38] In looking at moral judgments and hearing the "women's voice," Gilligan discovered that:

> [w]hen one begins with the study of women and derives developmental constructs from their lives, the outline of a moral conception different from that described by Freud, Piaget, or Kohlberg begins to emerge and informs a different description of development. In this conception, the moral problem arises from conflicting responsibilities rather than from competing rights and requires for its resolution a mode of thinking that is contextual and narrative rather than formal and abstract.[39]

An example drawn from Gilligan's work best illustrates the duality of girls' and boys' moral development. In one of the three studies on which her book is based,[40] a group of children are asked to solve Heinz's

---

[35] *See supra* note 5.

[36] *See* Note, *Toward a Redefinition of Sexual Equality*, *supra* note 8, at 499-508.

[37] L. KOHLBERG, THE PHILOSOPHY OF MORAL DEVELOPMENT (1981); L. Kohlberg, The Development of Modes of Thinking and Choices in Years 10 to 16 (Ph.D. Dissertation, Univ. of Chicago, 1958). Kohlberg's six stages of moral development begin with an egocentric focus on satisfying moral problems based on individual needs (stages one and two) and move to a more other/social identified focus on rules of obedience for public order and predictability and approval based on customs and understandings of social norms (stages three and four) and conclude with the use of principles, abstractions and universal, free-standing logic (stages five and six). *See* C. GILLIGAN, *supra* note 4, at 27. Specifically, Kohlberg's stages of moral reasoning are:

> Stage One: Punishment and Obedience Orientation (based on satisfying physical needs and avoiding punishment);
> Stage Two: Instrumental Relativist Orientation (based on satisfying instrumental needs);
> Stage Three: Interpersonal Concordance or "good boy-nice girl orientation" (based on efforts to please others);
> Stage Four: Law and Order Orientation (based on authority and rule orientation);
> Stage Five: Social Contract and Legalistic Orientation (based on general societal standards with utilitarian themes);
> Stage Six: Universal Ethical Principles (based on logical, universal and consistent principles of justice, reciprocity and equality).

Adapted from Kohlberg, *From Is to Ought: How to Commit the Naturalistic Fallacy and Get Away With It in the Study of Moral Development*, in COGNITIVE DEVELOPMENT AND EPISTEMOLOGY 151-231 (T. Mischel ed. 1971).

[38] C. GILLIGAN, *supra* note 4, at 18.

[39] *Id.* at 19.

[40] Gilligan's book is based on three separate studies. In the first study, Gilligan interviewed 25

dilemma, a hypothetical moral reasoning problem used by Kohlberg to rate moral development on his six-stage scale. The dilemma is that Heinz's wife is dying of cancer and requires a drug which the local pharmacist has priced beyond Heinz's means. The question is posed: should Heinz steal the drug?[41]

To illustrate and explain the differences between the ways boys and girls approached this problem, Gilligan quotes from two members of her sample, Jake and Amy. Jake, an eleven-year-old boy, sees the problem as one of "balancing rights," like a judge who must make a decision or a mathematician who must solve an algebraic equation. Life is worth more than property, therefore Heinz should steal the drug.[42] For Amy, an eleven-year-old girl, the problem is different. Like a "bad" law student she "fights the hypo"; she wants to know more facts:[43] Have Heinz and the druggist explored other possibilities, like a loan or credit transaction? Why couldn't Heinz and the druggist simply sit down and talk it out so that the druggist would come to see the importance of Heinz's wife's life? In Gilligan's terms, Jake explores the Heinz dilemma with "the logic of justice" while Amy uses the "ethic of care."[44] Amy scores lower on the Kohlberg scale because she sees the problem rooted in the persons involved rather than in the larger universal issues posed by the dilemma.[45]

In conventional terms Jake would make a good lawyer because he spots the legal issues of excuse and justification, balances the rights, and reaches a decision, while considering implicitly, if not explicitly, the precedential effect of his decision. But as Gilligan argues,[46] and as I develop more fully below,[47] Amy's approach is also plausible and legitimate, both as a style of moral reasoning and as a style of lawyering. Amy seeks to keep the people engaged; she holds the needs of the parties and their relationships constant and hopes to satisfy them all (as in a negotiation), rather than selecting a winner (as in a lawsuit). If one must be hurt, she attempts to find a resolution that will hurt least the one who can least bear the hurt. (Is she engaged in a "deep pocket" policy analysis?) She looks beyond the "immediate lawsuit" to see how the "judgment" will

---

students enrolled in a course on moral and political choice and interviewed them again five years later to explore issues of moral choice and the self in young adults. In the second study, 29 women were interviewed when they were making a choice about whether to have an abortion; twenty-one were interviewed again at the end of the year following the choice. In the third study, a sample of males and females matched for age, intelligence, education, occupation and social class at nine points across the life cycle, were questioned about their conceptions of self and morality, their experiences of moral conflict and choice, and their judgments about hypothetical moral dilemmas. *Id.* at 2-3.

41 *Id.* at 25-26.

42 *Id.* at 25-27.

43 *Id.* at 27-29.

44 *Id.* at 30.

45 *Id.* at 31.

46 *Id.* at 29-32.

47 *See infra* text accompanying notes 67-105.

affect the parties. If Heinz steals the drug and goes to jail, who will take care of his wife? Furthermore, Amy is concerned with *how* the dilemma is resolved: the process by which the parties communicate may be crucial to the outcome. (Amy cares as much about procedure as about substance.) And she is being a good lawyer when she inquires whether all of the facts have been discovered and considered.[48]

The point here is not that Amy's method of moral reasoning is better than Jake's, nor that she is a better lawyer than Jake. (Some have read Gilligan to argue that the women's voice is better. I don't read her that way.) The point is that Amy does some things differently from Jake when she resolves this dilemma, and these things have useful analogies to lawyering and may not have been sufficiently credited as useful lawyering skills. Jake and Amy have something to learn from one another.

Thus, although a "choice of rights" conception (life vs. property) of solving human problems may be important, it is not the only or the best way. Responsibilities to self and to others may be equally important in measuring moral, as well as legal decision making, but have thus far been largely ignored. For example, a lawyer who feels responsible for the decisions she makes with her client may be more inclined to think about how those decisions will hurt other people and how the lawyer and client feel about making such decisions. (Amy thinks about Heinz, the druggist, and Heinz's wife at all times in reaching her decision; Jake makes a choice in abstract terms without worrying as much about the people it affects.)[49]

In tracing through the sources of these different approaches to moral reasoning, Gilligan's analysis tracks that of Chodorow, Dinnerstein and Noddings.[50] Men, who have had to separate from their differently gendered mother in order to grow, tend to see moral dilemmas as problems of separateness and individual rights, problems in which choices must be made and priorities must be ordered. Women, who need not completely separate from their same gendered mother in order to grow, see the world in terms of connections and relationships. "While women thus try to change the rules in order to preserve relationships, men, in abiding by these rules, depict relationships as easily replaced."[51] Where men see danger in too much connection or intimacy, in being engulfed and losing their own identity, women see danger in the loss of connection, in not having an identity through caring for others and by being abandoned and isolated.[52]

---

[48] For a full discussion of Amy's and Jake's responses to the Heinz dilemma, see C. GILLIGAN, *supra* note 4, at 25-32.

[49] One critique of this exercise is that no one has asked for what Heinz's wife thinks about the situation. It is, after all, her life that is at stake. MacKinnon, *supra* note 8.

[50] *See supra* note 7.

[51] C. GILLIGAN, *supra* note 4, at 44.

[52] The same result may be observed even if one is not persuaded by the neo-Freudian model of

Both Gilligan and Noddings see differences in the ethics men and women derive from their different experiences of the world. Men focus on universal abstract principles like justice, equality and fairness so that their world is safe, predictable and constant. Women solve problems by seeking to understand the context and relationships involved and understand that universal rules may be impossible.[53]

The two different voices Gilligan describes articulate two different developmental processes. To the extent that we all have both of these voices within us and they are not exclusively gender based,[54] a mature person will develop the ability to consider the implications of both an abstract rights analysis and a contextualized responsibilities analysis.[55] For women, this kind of mature emotional and intellectual synthesis may require taking greater account of self and less account of the other; for men, the process may be the reverse. Such an integration[56] will not resolve all issues of personal development. Those who seek interdependence will not necessarily find it by the individualistic integration and reciprocity of reasoning styles proposed above. And if this integration fosters equality between the sexes, there still remains the problem of equity. As one of Gilligan's subjects observed: "People have real emotional needs to be attached to something and equality doesn't give you attachment. Equality fractures society and places on every person the burden of standing on his own two feet."[57] The different paths toward mature moral development for men and women[58] may give us more than

---

child development: boys may be encouraged by either parent to individuate and separate as a process of growing up, regardless of the relationship to the mother, simply because of stereotypic notions of appropriate childrearing. *See* J. KAGAN, THE NATURE OF THE CHILD (1984).

53 C. GILLIGAN, *supra* note 4, at 118.

54 *Id.* at 2-3. Some may see these voices simply as two different voices which are not necessarily gender-related. As Gilligan says:

> The different voice I describe is characterized not by gender but theme. Its association with women is an empirical observation, and it is primarily through women's voices that I trace its development. But this association is not absolute, and the contrasts between male and female voices are presented here to highlight a distinction between two modes of thought and to focus a problem of interpretation rather than to represent a generalization about either sex. In tracing development, I point to the interplay of these voices within each sex and suggest that their convergence marks times of crisis and change. No claims are made about the origins of the differences . . .

Id.

55 As a legal educator I have used this exercise heuristically to ask students how Amy would solve a particular legal problem and how Jake would solve the problem in order to suggest that these two perspectives lead to at least two possible solutions.

56 Integration should not mean submersion of one into the other so the second gets lost, as some fear androgyny might do by eliminating all gender. However, integration of sexual themes in our present world usually means the engulfing of the feminine by the masculine. As in marble cake, where there is never enough chocolate for the chocolate lover, integration of gender themes in our present world usually means the engulfing of the female by the male.

57 C. GILLIGAN, *supra* note 4, at 167. This is a quote from a male subject who, in expressing the pain of losing a relationship in which his experience of the relationship differed greatly from his girlfriend's, came to realize that relationships mean more than simple equality.

58 As men proceed from stages of ego to social to universal values on Kohlberg's scale, women progress through corresponding stages of self (survival) to other (responsibility) to care (of

one road to take to the same place, or we may find that there is more than one interesting place to go.

II. THE DIFFERENT VOICES OF LAWYERING

What does moral or psychological development have to do with the law? Gilligan's observations about male-female differences in moral reasoning may have a great deal to suggest about how the legal system is structured, how law is practiced and made, and how we reason and use law in making decisions.[59] I will speculate about each of these below but will focus primarily on the implications of these insights for the lawyering process.

Two sets of questions illustrate how we might think about the impact of two voices on our legal system as presently constituted and as it might be transformed. First, how has the exclusion, or at least the devaluation,[60] of women's voices affected the choices made in the values underlying our current legal structures? When we value "objectivity," or a "right" answer, or a single winner, are we valuing male goals of victory, exclusion, clarity, predictability?[61] What would our legal system look like if women had not been excluded from participating in its creation? What values would women express in creating the laws and institutions of a legal system? How would they differ from what we see now? How might the different male and female voices join together to create an integrated legal system?[62] Second, can we glimpse enclaves of another set of values within some existing legal structures? Is the judge "male," the jury "female?" Is the search for facts a feminine search for context and the search for legal principles a masculine search for certainty and abstract rules? It could be argued that no functional system could be either wholly masculine or wholly feminine, that there is a tendency for one set of characteristics in a system to mitigate the excesses of the other. Thus, the harshness of law produced the flexibility of equity, and conversely, the abuse of flexibility gave rise to rules of law to limit discretion. In this sense, the legal system could be seen to encompass both male and

both self and other). Men and women may need to go through different development processes to arrive at maturity, a suggestion which has been noted by scholarly psychologists as well as popular writers. *See, e.g.*, D. LEVINSON, THE SEASONS OF A MAN'S LIFE (1978); G. SHEEHY, PASSAGES (1976).

59 *See supra* note 29.

60 Some argue that women and all they value have been totally excluded from the legal system and from the world at large, *see* MacKinnon, *infra* note 86; others maintain that women and what they value are present, but devalued, *see* F. Olsen, *supra* note 33.

61 Predictability may be a male value since the male-dominated world of work may be more predictable than the largely female-dominated work of parenting.

62 As I have alluded to in *supra* notes 7 and 56, there is in this enterprise of labeling by gender a danger of creating further polarization rather than integration. Some polarization may be necessary before we can integrate, and indeed we are already situated in a world with more polarization than efforts to integrate.

female voices already. Yet, even though our present legal structures may reflect elements of both sets of values, there is a tendency for the male-dominated or male-created forms and values to control. Thus, equity begins to develop its own harsh rules of law and universalistic regulations applied to discretionary decisions, undermining the flexibility that discretion is supposed to protect.[63] Because men have, in fact, dominated by controlling the legal system, the women's voice in law may be present, but in a male form.

These two sets of questions explore a central issue, which is whether, to the extent that there are value choices to be made in the legal system, those choices will be differently made and with different results when the people who make decisions include a greater representation of women among their numbers. Some may prefer to see these different values as not necessarily taking gendered forms—I do. But even if the choices of values are not themselves gendered, it may be that women will favor one set of values over another in sufficient numbers, or with sufficient intensity, to change the balance at times.[64] Although existing structures give a glimpse of what the legal system could look like, we cannot yet know what the consequences of women's participation in the legal system will be—some fear the women's voice will simply be added on and be drowned out by the louder male voice; others fear an androgynous, univoiced world with no interesting differences.[65]

Perhaps by examining these issues in their concrete forms we can see how Portia's different voice might expand our understanding of the lawyering process. I will explore some of the tasks of the lawyer and skills that lawyers employ, and the larger adversarial system in which lawyering is embedded. The rules with which lawyers practice, which until recently have been articulated almost exclusively with male voices, will be examined so we can begin to speculate about how a woman's voice might affect the ethical rules which govern the profession and the substantive principles of the law. It is my hope that this preliminary review will spark more thorough and comprehensive research.

III. The Advocacy-Adversarial Model

The basic structure of our legal system is premised on the adversarial model, which involves two advocates who present their cases to a disinterested third party who listens to evidence and argument and declares one party a winner. In this simplified description of the Anglo-American model of litigation, we can identify some of the basic concepts

---

[63] *See, e.g.*, J. Handler, The Conditions of Discretion (forthcoming).

[64] This was the argument some suffragists made. It is heard currently in political analysis referred to as "gender gap." *See* B. Abzug, The Gender Gap (1984).

[65] *See, e.g.*, Olsen, *The Family and the Market: A Study of Ideology and Legal Reform*, 96 Harv. L. Rev. 1497, 1577 (1983).

and values which underlie this choice of arrangements: advocacy, persuasion, hierarchy, competition, and binary results (win/lose). The conduct of litigation is relatively similar (not coincidentally, I suspect) to a sporting event—there are rules, a referee, an object to the game, and a winner is declared after the play is over. As I have argued elsewhere,[66] this conception of the dispute resolution process is applied more broadly than just in the conventional courtroom. The adversarial model affects the way in which lawyers advise their clients ("get as much as you can"), negotiate disputes ("we can really get them on that") and plan transactions ("let's be sure to draft this to your advantage"). All of these activities in lawyering assume competition over the same limited and equally valued items (usually money) and assume that success is measured by maximizing individual gain. Would Gilligan's Amy create a different model?

By returning to Heinz's dilemma we see some hints about what Amy might do. Instead of concluding that a choice must be made between life and property, in resolving the conflict between parties as Jake does, Amy sees no need to hierarchically order the claims. Instead, she tries to account for all the parties' needs, and searches for a way to find a solution that satisfies the needs of both. In her view, Heinz should be able to obtain the drug for his wife and the pharmacist should still receive payment.[67] So Amy suggests a loan, a credit arrangement, or a discussion of other ways to structure the transaction. In short, she won't play by the adversarial rules. She searches outside the system for a way to solve the problem, trying to keep both parties in mind. Her methods substantiate Gilligan's observations that women will try to change the rules to preserve the relationships.[68]

Furthermore, in addition to looking for more substantive solutions to the problem (i.e., not accepting the binary win/lose conception of the problem), Amy also wants to change the process. Amy sees no reason why she must act as a neutral arbiter of a dispute and make a decision based only on the information she has. She "belie[ves] in communication as the mode of conflict resolution and [is convinced] that the solution to the dilemma will follow from its compelling representation. . . ."[69] If the parties talk directly to each other, they will be more likely to appreciate the importance of each other's needs. Thus, she believes direct communication, rather than third party mediated debate, might solve the prob-

[66] Menkel-Meadow, *Toward Another View of Legal Negotiation: The Structure of Problem Solving*, 31 UCLA L. Rev. 754 (1984).

[67] Gilligan notes that Amy recasts the problem because she hears a different question than Jake does when she is asked, "*Should* Heinz steal the drugs?" For Amy, the question is not whether he should obtain the drug, but how. C. Gilligan, *supra* note 4, at 31.

[68] *Id.* at 44.

[69] *Id.* at 30.

lem, recognizing that two apparently conflicting positions can both be simultaneously legitimate, and there need not be a single victor.

The notion that women might have more difficulty with full-commitment-to-one-side model of the adversary system is graphically illustrated by Hilary, one of the women lawyers in Gilligan's study. This lawyer finds herself in one of the classic moral dilemmas of the adversary system: she sees that her opponent has failed to make use of a document that is helpful to his case and harmful to hers. In deciding not to tell him about the document because of what she sees as her "professional vulnerability" in the male adversary system, she concludes that "the adversary system of justice impedes not only the supposed search for truth (the conventional criticism), but also *the expression of concern for the person on the other side*."[70] Gilligan describes Hilary's tension between her concept of rights (learned through legal training) and her female ethic of care[71] as a sign of her socialization in the male world of lawyering. Thus, the advocacy model, with its commitment to one-sided advocacy, seems somehow contrary to "apprehending the reality of the other"[72] which lawyers like Hilary experience. Even the continental inquisitorial model,[73] frequently offered as an alternative to the adversarial model, includes most of these elements of the male system—hierarchy, advocacy, competition and binary results.[74]

So what kind of legal system would Amy and Hilary create if left to their own devices? They might look for ways to alter the harshness of win/lose results; they might alter the rules of the game (or make it less like a game); and they might alter the very structures and forms themselves.[75] Thus, in a sense Amy and Hilary's approach can already be found in some of the current alternatives to the adversary model such as mediation.[76] Much of the current interest in alternative dispute resolu-

---

70 *Id.* at 135-36.

71 *Id.*

72 *See* N. NODDINGS, *supra* note 7, at 14.

73 The inquisitorial system contemplates a more active judge and is considered to be less adversarial and less controlled by combative attorneys than is the Anglo-American system. However, there is a great deal of scholarly debate about the accuracy of this picture. *See generally* M. SCHWARTZ, LAWYERS AND THE LEGAL PROFESSION, ch. 1 (1979).

74 The notion that the adversary system requires binary results may be somewhat exaggerated given the possibility of compromise in verdicts, *see* Coons, *Approaches to Court Imposed Compromises—The Uses of Doubt and Reason*, 58 NW. U.L. REV. 750 (1967), and the use of complex and creative remedies in some forms of major litigation, *see* Eisenberg & Yeazell, *The Ordinary and the Extraordinary in Institutional Litigation*, 93 HARV. L. REV. 465 (1980).

75 For example, Amy and Hilary may use mediation or pairs of judges in which one of the pair is a woman and the other a man. *See infra* note 101.

76 Mediation was first suggested by men. *See, e.g.*, O. COOGLER, STRUCTURED MEDIATION IN DIVORCE SETTLEMENTS (1978). However, to the extent that mediation is regarded as "soft," men who mediate are regarded as being somewhat like women (*e.g.*, nonanalytic and nonassertive) and are devalued accordingly, or treated as "social females," *see* Littleton, The Reconstruction of Sex Equality (1985) (unpublished manuscript on file with author). In my course on mediation and alternative dispute resolution, a disproportionate number of the students are women, indicating a high level of interest in mediation among women entering the legal profession.

tion is an attempt to modify the harshness of the adversarial process and expand the kinds of solutions available, in order to respond better to the varied needs of the parties. Amy's desire to engage the parties in direct communication with each other is reflected in mediation models where the parties talk directly to each other and forge their own solutions.[77] The work of Gilligan and Noddings, demonstrating an ethic of care and a heightened sense of empathy in women, suggests that women lawyers may be particularly interested in mediation as an alternative to litigation as a method of resolving disputes.[78]

Even within the present adversarial model, Amy and Hilary might, in their concern for others, want to provide for a broader conception of interested parties, permitting participation by those who might be affected by the dispute (an ethic of inclusion).[79] In addition, like judges who increasingly are managing more of the details of their cases,[80] Amy and Hilary might seek a more active role in settlement processes and rely less on court-ordered relief. Amy and Hilary might look for other ways to construct their lawsuits and remedies in much the same way as courts of equity mitigated the harshness of the law courts' very limited array of remedies by expanding the conception of what was possible.

The process and rules of the adversary system itself might look different if there were more female voices in the legal profession. If Amy is less likely than Jake to make assertive, rights-based statements, is she less likely to adapt to the male-created advocacy mode? In my experience as a trial lawyer, I observed that some women had difficulty with the "macho" ethic of the courtroom battle. Even those who did successfully adapt to the male model often confronted a dilemma because women were less likely to be perceived as behaving properly when engaged in

---

[77] There are many models of mediation being used in a variety of different contexts, but in its classic form the mediator's role is to facilitate communication between the parties so that they can reach their own solution to the problem. Mediation should not be confused, in this context, with arbitration, in which the third party acts more like an adjudicator and actually decides for the parties. *See, e.g.*, J. FOLBERG & A. TAYLOR, MEDIATION (1984); Riskin, *Mediation and Lawyers*, 43 OHIO ST. L.J. 29 (1982).

[78] Mediation has become a complex subject for feminists. Some feel that feminism and women have much to bring to the practice of mediation. *See, e.g.*, Rifkin, *Mediation from a Feminist Perspective: Promise and Problems*, 2 LAW & INEQUALITY 21 (1984). Other feminists see mediation as being harmful to the interests of women in contexts where they will be forced to compromise newly obtained legal rights or where there is an imbalance of power between the sexes, as in many domestic disputes. *See* Lerman, *Mediation of Wife Abuse Cases: The Adverse Impact of Informal Dispute Resolution on Women*, 7 HARV. WOMEN'S L.J. 57 (1984); Woods, *Mediation: A Backlash to Women's Progress on Family Law Issues*, 19 CLEARINGHOUSE REV. 431 (1985). My view is that mediation as a process is not necessarily good or bad for women's interests; it depends on who the mediator is and what model of mediation is being used. For instance, mothers frequently mediate between children they love equally. However, some disputes may need authoritative rulings to set precedents or to prevent the abuse of large disparities of power. *See* Menkel-Meadow, *For and Against Settlement*, 33 UCLA L. REV. 301 (1985).

[79] This principle of inclusion is given some recognition in the current rules on joinder of indispensible parties. FED. R. CIV. P. 19. Would women want more parties to be indispensible?

[80] *See* Resnik, *Managerial Judges*, 96 HARV. L. REV. 374 (1982).

strong adversarial conduct.[81] It is important to be "strong" in the courtroom, according to the stereotypic conception of appropriate trial behavior. The woman who conforms to the female stereotype by being "soft" or "weak" is a bad trial lawyer; but if a woman is "tough" or "strong" in the courtroom, she is seen as acting inappropriately for a woman. Note, however, that this stereotyping is contextual: the same woman acting as a "strong" or "tough" mother with difficult children would be praised for that conduct. Women's strength is approved of with the proviso that it be exerted in appropriately female spheres.

Amy and Hilary might create a different form of advocacy, one resembling a "conversation" with the fact finder, relying on the creation of a relationship with the jury for its effectiveness, rather than on persuasive intimidation. There is some anecdotal evidence that this is happening already. Recently, several women prosecutors described their styles of trial advocacy as the creation of a personal relationship with the jury in which they urge the jurors to examine their own perceptions and values and encourage them to think for themselves, rather than "buying" the arguments of one of the advocates.[82] This is a conception of the relationship between the lawyer and the fact-finder which is based on trust and mutual respect rather than on dramatics, intimidation and power, the male mode in which these women had been trained and which they found unsatisfactory.[83]

In sum, the growing strength of women's voice in the legal profession may change the adversarial system into a more cooperative, less

---

81 This "macho" trial ethic dominates the teaching of trial advocacy in programs such as the one offered by the National Institute for Trial Advocacy. Trial attorneys are taught to intimidate their witnesses, especially in cross-examination, to control the witness by never asking a question to which the attorney does not already know the answer, and to regard impeachment of a witness as a highly confrontational act. Ironically, some trial attorneys think that a non-confrontational impeachment process is frequently much more effective. *See, e.g.*, P. BERGMAN, TRIAL ADVOCACY IN A NUTSHELL (1979).

A trial judge once threatened to hold me in contempt of court for cross-examining a witness, even though opposing counsel had not made any objections, because he thought it "inappropriate for a young lady to be so argumentative." This is a good example of the stereotyping described by Epstein, *supra* note 34, at 87-88. Behavior that seems appropriate, indeed competent, for a male, is often seen as totally inappropriate for a female.

82 Women as Criminal Trial Attorneys, workshop presented at the Conference on Women in the Legal Workforce, University of Southern California, Los Angeles (March 19, 1983). Prosecutors who spoke of these competing images of trial lawyer styles work in an office that has just been ordered, as a result of a sex discrimination suit, to promote more women. Experienced women prosecutors in that office had seldom been promoted beyond a certain level though less experienced men had been. Could this have been because the women were not seen as fulfilling the male image of a good prosecutor? In the same city, a supervisor in the Public Defender's office has ordered the attorneys to try a certain quota of cases per year "to demonstrate to the DA how tough we are." *Id.*

83 The recent movie *All of Me* amusingly illustrates how women's consciousness might transform trial practice. While actors Lily Tomlin and Steve Martin inhabit the same male lawyer's body, they battle over whose trial ethics should prevail. Martin, as the stereotypic male trial attorney, is willing to use any argument or theory to win his case, while Tomlin is shocked and refuses to permit him to use an argument that is not factually correct, and that would hurt the other side.

war-like system of communication between disputants in which solutions are mutually agreed upon rather than dictated by an outsider, won by the victor, and imposed upon the loser. Some seeds of change may already be found in existing alternatives to the litigation model, such as mediation. It remains to be seen what further changes Portia's voice may make.

IV. Lawyers at Work: The Feminization of Law Practice

Does the female voice of relationship, care and connection lead to a different form of law practice? Although the present adversarial system may limit the ways in which concern for others may be expressed toward adversaries, the values of relationship and care may be expressed with one's work partners. In this area at least, we have some evidence that Portia's voice has had an influence. As Epstein has documented,[84] early attempts to form a separate feminist practice focused on establishing nonhierarchical organizations with participatory decision-making. This was a political expression of the psychological qualities observed by Gilligan in the relationships and connections that women lawyers sought to forge with each other while engaged in practices that pitted them against the traditional models. Some of these women lawyers were explicit in their rejection of male principles in the ordering of legal work.[85]

The historical source that helped create these feminist forms derives from perhaps the most original feminist methodology to date, the consciousness raising group. As Catharine MacKinnon has argued,[86] this partioular form of organization is more than a form; it is a methodology that creates knowledge from shared, collective experience. Communication occurs in a leaderless circle, and in some groups attention is paid to equality of presentation time and rotation of instrumental and affective tasks. There is a devaluation of expertise; everyone has life experiences from which something might be worth learning. Can this form of female organization of work affect the practice of law?

While hierarchy produces efficiency and individual achievement, as lawyers, Amy and Hilary might chose to emphasize other values such as collectivity and interpersonal connection. This attempt to work in a different way not only affects relationships within the working unit, but is also apparent in the work of feminists who seek to demystify law and the legal profession by working with clients on lay advocacy projects or self-representation.[87]

---

84 C. Epstein, *supra* note 5, ch. 9.

85 Fox, *supra* note 24.

86 MacKinnon, *Feminism, Marxism, Method and the State: Toward Feminist Jurisprudence*, 8 Signs 635 (1984); MacKinnon, *Feminism, Marxism and the State: An Agenda for Theory*, 7 Signs 515 (1982).

87 For an argument for the demystification of law, see Rifkin, *supra* note 24, at 84-88.

To illustrate the issues involved in a women's way of practicing law, consider the following example. My colleague Grace Blumberg, an expert in marital property law, was asked to write the first draft of an amicus brief in a case involving the legal treatment of a professional degree in a community property regime.[88] She describes the work on this effort with a group of California women lawyers as follows:

> The effort to transform a generally literate coherent brief into "proper form" took some 100 person hours, more than eight times the amount of time it took the author to write the brief. . . . The participants, leaving the author aside, seemed to get some substantial psychic rewards from this 100 hours spent mostly in conferences of two and three persons. They created an atmosphere of social intimacy between relative strangers. Although at least 90 percent of the time was spent hard at work, the atmosphere was of a social event. Food was always served even though it was not any discernible meal time. . . . Personal information and confidences were exchanged in the interstices of work. I was struck by the incongruity of my product (female)[89] and my process (male) and in contrast, their product (male) and process (female).[90] My product was revealing, tentative and dialectic. In contrast my process was individualistic and individual, highly concerned with the goal of efficiency and not at all interested in collaboration as an end in itself. In contrast, their product was extremely formal, authoritarian, concealing and impersonal. Their process was communitarian and communicative, full of feeling and interpersonal experience.[91]

The story of this brief-writing exercise also reveals another aspect of the women's lawyering process—concern for the interconnection of personal and professional life. In the "interstices of work," the lawyers engaged in this project shared information about their personal lives and brought sustenance to each other (intellectually, emotionally and nutri-

---

[88] The case was *In re* Marriage of Sullivan, 37 Cal. 3d 762, 691 P.2d 1020, 209 Cal. Rptr. 354 (1984), involving the question of whether a professional degree, in this case a medical degree, is community property for the purposes of allocating and dividing its proceeds at the time of marital dissolution. The author of the brief is an expert on the allocation of marital property and a feminist who saw one of the issues as protecting a woman's investment in her husband's degree by foregoing the opportunities to develop her own career and by working to support the acquistion of the husband's professional degree. The case raises interesting issues for professional women in deciding whether their affiliation is with the professional class, in which case they would probably see the degree as separate property, or with women as a class, who in the present world would stand to gain more from a holding that a professional degree is community property. The case was decided on hybrid grounds: the court recognized a right of reimbursement, but avoided deciding the community property issue. *Id.* at 768-69, 691 P.2d at 1025, 209 Cal. Rptr. at 358. The California legislature acted quickly to formalize the reimbursement treatment while the *Sullivan* case was pending before the Supreme Court.

[89] She considered her product to be female because it was scholarly, tentative, and not argumentative, but her process to be male because she worked alone as an expert and was concerned with efficiency in the process of completing the brief.

[90] The group's product was considered to be male because it was a traditional argumentative brief, stated in definite, authoritative terms, and their process to be female because of the collaborative and communitarian manner in which the work was done.

[91] Letter from Grace Blumberg to Carrie Menkel-Meadow (Jan. 10, 1982) (on file with the author).

tionally). Virtually every report of women lawyers discusses the impact of personal lives on professional lives and vice versa, where one finds almost no such reports in the descriptions and ethnographies of male lawyers.[92] The concern for the quality of life and the relation between one's work and one's personal life is consistent with the ethic of care and relationship exhibited by Gilligan's female subjects. To Jake, who can separate life and property, the division between work and the rest of one's life is easier. Indeed, the inability to individuate reported by Gilligan has been noted as sociologically dysfunctional for women lawyers who do not have enough "role virtuosity"[93] to separate different aspects of themselves so that they can convert from adversarial courtroom conduct in one moment to a collegial meal with opposing counsel in the next moment.

Perhaps the most salient feature of Portia's different voice is in the lawyer-client relationship, where the values of care and responsibility for others seem most directly applicable. Amy and Hilary, with their ability to "take the part of the other and submerge the self," may be able to enter the world of the client, thereby understanding more fully what the client desires and why, without the domination of what the lawyer perceives to be "in the client's best interest." More fully developed sensitivities to empathy and altruism, as reported by Gilligan and Noddings, may enable women lawyers to understand a fuller range of client needs and objectives. As we increasingly become aware that lawyers and clients may not have the same view of the world or what they want from that world,[94] the ability to examine *all* of the client's perspective becomes even more significant. Where the Jakes of this world may make assumptions about the primacy of economic and efficiency considerations of their cases, the Amys and Hilarys may see a greater number of issues in the social, psychological and moral aspects. Of course, in a fully mature and integrated vision of lawyering all of these aspects of the case would be considered important, as noted by one of Gilligan's subjects:

> It is taking the time and energy to consider everything. To decide carelessly or quickly or on the basis of one or two factors when you know that

---

[92] Menkel-Meadow, *Women in Law?*, *supra* note 1, at 195; *see also supra* note 5.

[93] Role virtuosity is the ability to perform a large number of potentially conflicting roles. C. EPSTEIN, *supra* note 5, at 288. Lawyers are expected to perform a large number of roles, some of which require one to play different roles with the same people, such as when an adversary on a case turns out to be a colleague on a bar association committee. Shakespeare aptly described the phenomenon of role virtuosity among lawyers:

> Please ye may contrive this afternoon
> And quaff carouses to our mistress' health
> And do as adversaries do in law,
> Strive mightily, but eat and drink as friends.

W. SHAKESPEARE, *The Taming of the Shrew*, Act I, Scene 2, in THE COMPLETE SIGNET CLASSIC SHAKESPEARE, *supra* note 23, at 340.

[94] *See* D. ROSENTHAL, LAWYER, CLIENT: WHO'S IN CHARGE? (1974); D. BINDER & S. PRICE, LEGAL INTERVIEWING AND COUNSELING (1977); Lehman, *The Pursuit of a Client's Interest*, 77 MICH. L. REV. 1078 (1979); Menkel-Meadow, *supra* note 66.

> there are other things that are important and that will be affected, that's immoral. The moral way to make decisions is by considering as much as you possibly can, as much as you know.[95]

Where a reluctance to make choices and universal judgments may prevent girls from reaching Kohlberg's fifth or sixth stages,[96] the tendency to personalize and contextualize problems may incline women lawyers to ask for more information on a broader range of subjects and thereby develop a fuller understanding of the context of the client's life. This, in turn, may make women better lawyers, especially in their relationships with clients and in their ability to see the human complexities of some legal problems.

V. Legal Reasoning and Rule-Making

In presenting their legal cases within a differently structured system, Amy and Hilary might reason about and plan their cases with a hope of expressing feminine values in their decision-making. Amy and Hilary might create different rules of the game. If Amy "fights the hypo" to learn more facts, might she not have a different conception of relevance and admissibility in deciding a dispute? If women are more concerned with the context in which the dispute is embedded, would they not search for more facts and be less concerned about creation of a precedent of universal applicability?[97] Gilligan suggests that women seek to reconstruct hypothetical dilemmas like Heinz's in order to get more information about the people and the places they live to avoid making abstract, formal judgments that might not work in particular cases.

Gilligan also points out that the insistence on more facts and on a more contextualized understanding of the dilemma helps the actor appreciate the social contingencies of the problem:

> Hypothetical dilemmas, in the abstraction of their presentation, divest moral actors from the history and psychology of their individual lives and separate the moral problem from the social contingencies of its possible occurrence. In doing so, these dilemmas are useful for the distillation and refinement of objective principles of justice and for measuring the formal logic of equality and reciprocity. However, the reconstruction of the dilemma in its contextual particularity allows the understanding of cause and consequence which engages the compassion and tolerance repeatedly noted to distinguish the moral judgments of women. Only when substance is given to the skeletal lives of hypothetical people is it possible to consider the social injustice that their moral problems may reflect and to imagine the individual suffering their occurrence may signify or their resolution

95 C. Gilligan, *supra* note 4, at 147.

96 *Id.* at 2-3.

97 Is the case-by-case development of the common law a more contextualized, female process, and the creation of statutory law a more universalistic, male process?

engender.[98]

These observations have implications for legal education as well as the practice of law. If the reconstruction of legal problems in their historical, psychological, and social contexts is useful for the "distillation and refinement of objective principles of justice and for measuring the formal logic of equality," then in preparing people to be lawyers, Amy and Hilary might include more interdisciplinary work as educationally relevant to law school.[99] Legal problems would be more likely to be seen as a "web," perhaps a seamless one, of multivariate causes and consequences, all requiring study.

According to Gilligan, Amy and Hilary have trouble judging disputes in a male-created context because of their difficulty in perceiving one right answer, and also perhaps because of the price they might pay in losing the approval of one of the parties.[100] Might more women judges affect the process of judging? Does the use of a jury provide a useful framework for a kind of judging where no single perception of the truth must prevail, but where a verdict is the product of a mediated consensus? If men and women approach the world with different substantive values, should each trial court have a team of judges, one male and one female?[101] If the male judge emphasizes justice, might the female judge pay attention to mercy, seeking that resolution "in which no one is hurt?"[102]

If Amy and Hilary use different considerations in their moral reasoning, would they create different ethical codes for the profession based on their different ways of engaging in moral reasoning? We have some evidence that Hilary would not place the same emphasis on the adversarial model of placing one's own client above the other if the result might be to hurt the other side (as well as to defeat a meritorious claim).[103] Would Amy and Hilary have adopted the original Kutak Commission's proposal[104] to increase the duty of a lawyer to reveal a client's wrongdoing if it caused harm to another? Would Amy and Hilary create rules about relationships between lawyers, based on mutual affiliation in the same profession, and requiring greater candor and fair-

---

98 C. GILLIGAN, *supra* note 4, at 100.

99 This argument parallels the critique of law and legal education made first by the legal realists and more recently by the Critical Legal Studies movement. *See, e.g.*, Frank, *Why Not a Clinical Lawyer-School?*, 81 U. PA. L. REV. 907 (1933); THE POLITICS OF LAW (D. Kairys ed. 1982) [hereinafter cited as Kairys].

100 *See* C. GILLIGAN, *supra* note 4, at 66.

101 I am indebted to Janet Lederman for exposure to the practice of this idea.

102 *See* C. GILLIGAN, *supra* note 4, at 105.

103 *See id.* at 135; *see supra* text accompanying notes 70-76.

104 *See* Commission on Evaluation of Professional Standards, Model Rules of Professional Conduct (Discussion Draft, Jan. 30, 1980). The rules as adopted by the American Bar Association in August 1983 were significantly different from this discussion draft in that requirements for mandatory *pro bono* work, mandatory disclosure of client wrong-doings, and a duty of fair dealing in negotiation were deleted in the final version.

ness in dealing with each other?[105] Would the conflict of interest rules or withdrawal from representation rules be different because of an ethic of care and affiliation that would lead to a different conception of client loyalty? Might a broader conception of the legal problem and its causes lead to less concern about the unauthorized practice of law and more toleration, if not encouragement, of work with other professionals and lay persons to solve those problems?

These are only a few of the available speculations about how our adversarial system might be affected by Portia's different voice. These and others not here mentioned await further expression and study as more women enter the legal profession and study its effects.

VI. The Substance of the Law: Lawmaking in a Different Voice

What if Amy and Hilary had been or could become lawmakers—whether legislators or judges—using a different voice in legal reasoning and lawmaking? Would the substance or principles of our laws be any different? This is a large question which occupies many of those at work on feminist jurisprudence.[106] I do not intend to take up this issue in any great detail here. I will simply explore some of the more obvious issues raised by the work reviewed in this essay and emphasize that most, if not all, of our laws are man-made. It might be useful to speculate on how different moral emphases might create new laws or express values other than those reflected in our current law.

My colleague Kenneth Karst has recently attempted to explore the implications of Gilligan's analysis for a "Woman's Constitution" by considering how women's values might infuse and perhaps change our conceptions of the meaning of the Constitution.[107] He suggests that women's concern for "webs of connection" might result in a more inclusive reading of the equal protection clause. Further, he suggests that the values in the Constitution may derive from a male conception of freedom that is expressed in terms of freedom *from* the interference of others. For example, the rights of liberty, property, due process and equality express a desire for separation from the government and from others. In essence, our basic liberties are expressed as individual liberties rather than as col-

---

105 *Compare* White, *Machiavelli and the Bar: Ethical Limitations on Lying in Negotiation*, 1980 AM. B. FOUND. RESEARCH J. 926 (1980) *with* Proposed Rule 4.2, Model Rules of Professional Conduct, *supra* note 104. The proposed rule, which would have required truthfulness in negotiation, was deleted from the final rules as approved by the American Bar Association.

106 *See* E. WOLGAST, EQUALITY AND THE RIGHTS OF WOMEN (1980); MacKinnon, *supra* note 86; Schneider, *supra* note 29; Rifkin, *supra* note 24; Scales, *Toward a Feminist Jurisprudence*, 56 IND. L.J. 375 (1981); Powers, *Sex Segregation and the Ambivalent Directions of Sex Discrimination Law*, 1979 WISC. L. REV. 55 (1979); Taub & Schneider, *Women's Subordination and the Role of Law* in Kairys, *supra* note 99, at 117.

107 Karst, *supra* note 29.

lective rights.[108]

Karst evocatively suggests that a women's voice of care and connection might lead to doctrinal changes in the areas of state action in discrimination law and in the state's affirmative duty to assist all its members to be able to fully participate in the community. Thus, our conception of state responsibility under the Constitution might be enlarged, and a conception of "responsibility" might supplement or replace altogether our notion of individualistic constitutional "rights."[109] Karst also suggests that the political context of lawmaking, particularly in the constitutional arena, would be more likely to be expressly involved in legal decision-making with a stronger women's voice by explicitly providing for more participation by women on the theory that they have something unique to contribute. Most interesting in Karst's analysis is the notion that the very terms of our constitutional and legal vocabulary might be redefined with a women's voice in greater evidence: words such as liberty, autonomy and equality might come to mean different things when expressed with a women's voice or looked at in a women's context. A few illustrations might illuminate these speculations.

Today, even the most important of "women's rights," the "right" to abortion, is framed exclusively in individualistic terms of privacy and professional decision-making. Would women constitutional lawmakers see these rights in other terms—in values of inclusion, connection, collectivity and social responsibility? Would a woman's concern over reproduction be seen as more her own and less the doctor's?[110] If the women's legal rights movement had not been forced to assimilate itself to a male-ordered constitution based on individual rights, it might have adopted different strategies for cases such as the pregnancy cases.[111] Women might have argued not for the right to be treated as having an individual disability, but for the requirement that society acknowledge and act on its collective responsibility for reproduction and its costs.[112]

Definitions of liberty would most likely be different if Amy and Hil-

---

108 Whether wittingly or not, in criticizing the individualistic and indeterminate nature of legal rights, Karst and Gilligan have aligned themselves with Critical Legal Studies scholars.

See, e.g., Schneider, *supra* note 29; Klare, *Judicial Deradicalization of the Wagner Act and the Origins of Modern Legal Consciousness*, 62 MINN. L. REV. 265 (1978); Freeman, *Anti-Discrimination Law: A Critical Review*, in Kairys, *supra* note 98, at 96; Kennedy, *The Structure of Blackstone's Commentaries*, 28 BUFFALO L. REV. 209, 211-14 (1979). *See also* Smith, *The Constitution and Autonomy*, 60 TEX. L. REV. 175 (1982).

109 Karst, *supra* note 29, at 493.

110 *See* Roe v. Wade, 410 U.S. 113 (1973).

111 *See* Geduldig v. Aiello, 417 U.S. 484 (1974); General Elec. Co. v. Gilbert, 429 U.S. 125 (1976). *See also* Freedman, *Sex Equality, Sex Differences, and the Supreme Court*, 92 YALE L.J. 913 (1983); Law, *Rethinking Sex and the Constitution*, 132 U. PA. L. REV. 955 (1984); Littleton, *supra* note 76.

112 I have alluded here to aspects of the debate about equal treatment versus special treatment (or formal versus substantive equality) that is being carried on in feminist theory circles. *See* Williams, *supra* note 8; Note, *Toward a Redefinition of Sexual Equality*, *supra* note 8. This is an important debate, but beyond the scope of this article.

ary sat on the Supreme Court.[113] The narrow definition of liberty as the possible loss of individual physical liberty would probably be enlarged to include the permanent disconnection from one's child as a sufficient denial of liberty to justify its legal protection through the appointment of counsel and other protections.[114]

As feminist jurisprudence has begun to explore such questions as the meaning of a "rights-based" strategy[115] for empowering women in society, we have learned that equality may not be sufficient in a world where one has the right to equal pay for equal work, but where equal work is not available. As equity and comparable worth have come to replace equality in some contexts, other staples of our jurisprudence may have to be reconsidered. Reciprocity connoting separable obligations may be replaced by interdependence connoting mutuality of need. Citizens could have a "right" to be connected, to belong, to be affilitated, to be cared for (an expanded social welfare program?), at the same time that they have the right to be free from coercion.

I do not mean to suggest that all women speak with a unified voice on these issues; already we have evidence that women lawmakers speak with many voices.[116] However, I do think that an increasing number of women's voices could or will alter our legal sensibilities and values. The issues are far too complex to be explored in detail here, but the discussion and debates about the laws that Portia's voice might create will affect the legal culture for some time to come.

VII. Directions for New Speculations

This brief and speculative discussion of how another voice might inform the law and the lawyering process may create more problems than it illuminates. Are these different voices gender-based or just two thematically different ways of looking at the world? If these are women's voices, why haven't they been heard yet, since there are an increasing number of women in all parts of the profession? Will the new voices become assimilated to the old before they are heard in the legal system? Have those women who have already become lawyers been socialized or self-selected to succeed with a man's voice? Have we sought to explain

113 I am aware that Sandra Day O'Connor sits on the Supreme Court, and that thus far she has not spoken in a different voice. What better proof could there be that the different voices are not exclusively gender-based and that success in the present world has required some assimilation to the male mode?

114 *See* Lassiter v. Department of Soc. Serv., 452 U.S. 18 (1981), in which the Supreme Court held that the termination of parental rights of an imprisoned mother did not constitute a sufficient liberty interest to require court-appointed counsel. This opinion demonstrates a particularly disconnected, individualistic conception of liberty. My speculation is that women judges might be more likely to see the connection to a child as a "liberty" interest.

115 *See* Schneider, *supra* note 29.

116 *See supra* notes 111-114.

too much by transposing psychological observations to the legal arena? And perhaps most importantly, how will the "women are different" argument play itself out in current legal disputes? Many of us feel the differences every day. What we deplore is when they are used to oppress or disempower us or when they are used as immutable stereotypes that prevent recognition of individual variations. We don't yet know how many of the differences will disappear in a world socially and legally constructed so that gender is not a basis for domination.[117] My point of view is that while we are observing the differences we might ask if we have something to learn from them. Whether or not the different voice is gendered, we might look at how our legal system might take account of a few more voices.[118]

The new voice may create its own problems and dilemmas—the values of care, responsibility and relationship present their own difficulties. Can we care for all? How many (our client, the other client, the other lawyer, the entire system) can we be responsible for at any one time? Are all relationships good, the unequal relationships to the same extent as the equal relationships? By caring too much for others, do we lose sight of ourselves? Will too much contextualism prevent the emergence of any general principles by which we can guide ourselves? These are among the difficulties we will have to confront when and if a women's voice in the lawyering process is heard.

It is increasingly important to examine whether and how Portia might speak in a different voice and how we might try to avoid descriptions of the legal world that commit a serious fallacy by using the part (the male world of lawyers) to describe the whole. We have a demanding research agenda ahead for the study of a women's lawyering process in legal education, in the practice of law, in the structure of the profession and the legal system, and in the doctrinal and substantive values of our laws.

---

117 *See* Wasserstrom, *Racism, Sexism and Preferential Treatment: An Approach to the Topics*, 24 UCLA L. REV. 581 (1977).

118 Other previously excluded voices, such as the voices of Black, Hispanic, Asian, gay or disabled lawyers, might also change the way we view the legal system some day when all have had a chance to express those voices and be heard.

Part IV

Ethical Ideals and Institutional Realities

[12]

Ethical Perspectives on Legal Practice

Deborah L. Rhode*

The moral content of legal practice has never lacked for critics. Plato's condemnation of the lawyer's "small and unrighteous" soul has echoed for millenia across a wide variety of cultures.[1] The invectives are familiar—attorneys are parasites on public disputes; their professional interest lies in amplifying rather than allaying controversy and in doing "for a guinea" what they would perceive "infamous to do for an empire."[2] Throughout this century, innumerable variations have issued on the theme of Louis Brandeis' 1905 Harvard address: The bar has allied itself with business in opposition to the public interest.[3]

From this historical perspective, the recent surge of animus towards lawyers seems unexceptional; the public assaults draw

---

* Professor of Law, Stanford Law School. B.A., 1974, J.D., 1977, Yale.

Financial support for this article was contributed by the Stanford Legal Research Fund, made possible by a bequest from the Estate of Ira S. Lillick, and by gifts from Roderick E. and Carla A. Hills and other friends of the Stanford Law School.

1. Plato, *Theaetetus*, in THE DIALOGUES OF PLATO 143, 175 (B. Jowett trans. 1937). A representative sample of six centuries of critiques appears in D. MELLINKOFF, THE CONSCIENCE OF A LAWYER 10–15 (1973). For discussion of American colonists' antipathy toward lawyers and attempts to restrict their practice, see, e.g., 1 A.H. CHROUST, THE RISE OF THE LEGAL PROFESSION IN AMERICA 71 (1965); 2 *id.* at 16–30, 49–50; C. WARREN, A HISTORY OF THE AMERICAN BAR 212–49 (1911). Efforts to purge lawyers in various societies are detailed in J. HAZARD, SETTLING DISPUTES IN SOVIET SOCIETY 1–3 (1960); V. LI, LAW WITHOUT LAWYERS 19–31 (1977) (China); D. RUESCHMEYER, LAWYERS AND THEIR SOCIETY 149–57 (1973) (Prussia).

2. Macaulay, *Lord Bacon*, in THE WORKS OF LORD MACAULAY 135, 163 (H. Trevelyan ed. 1866).

3. L. BRANDEIS, *The Opportunity in the Law*, in BUSINESS—A PROFESSION 313, 321 (1914) (address before the Harvard Ethical Society) ("[A]ble lawyers have, to large extent, allowed themselves to become adjuncts of great corporations and have neglected the obligation to use their powers for the protection of the people."); *see also* A.A. Berle, Jr., *Modern Legal Profession*, 9 ENCYCLOPEADIA OF THE SOC. SCI. 340, 342 (1933) (corporate firms "have contributed little to legal literature, social responsibility or public leadership; but they have been highly profitable and have safeguarded the position of the new business organizations"); T. VEBLEN, THE THEORY OF THE LEISURE CLASS 231 (1912) ("[t]he lawyer is exclusively occupied with the details of predatory fraud, either in achieving or checkmating chicane"). For more contemporary amplifications of the argument, see, e.g., J. AUERBACH, UNEQUAL JUSTICE (1976); VERDICTS ON LAWYERS (R. Nader & M. Green eds. 1976).

from a well-worn genre. What is unusual, however, is the extent of professional response. In the last decade, courts, commentators, and the organized bar have given unprecedented attention to legal ethics and etiquette.

Equally striking is the insular quality of that response. For the most part, the recent discourse on professional responsibility has evolved in a vacuum, inadequately illumined by moral theory and sociological research. Too often, the fundamental precepts of professionalism remain unexamined; arguments over candor, confidentiality, and client loyalty proceed without rigorous empirical or philosophical foundation. Most of the seminal work in legal ethics has focused on individual lawyer-client relationships that presuppose a considerable measure of personal autonomy, determinate objectives, and direct communication.[4] That paradigm bears little resemblance to the daily practice of a growing percentage of the profession. Approximately two-thirds of the bar, including 95% of recent entrants, now work within organizations of some sort, and perform the bulk of their services for entities rather than individuals.[5] In a substantial amount of legal practice, "the client" is not the "person with a problem" traditionally depicted in legal literature, but an organization with indeterminate or potentially conflicting interests. So too, the attorney often is not an independent moral agent but an employee with circumscribed responsibility, organizational loyalty, and attenuated client contact.

Under such circumstances, professional ideals that presup-

4. *See, e.g.*, Simon, *The Ideology of Advocacy*, 1978 WIS. L. REV. 30; Wasserstrom, *Lawyers as Professionals: Some Moral Issues*, 5 HUM. RTS. 1 (1975).

5. B. CURRAN, THE LEGAL PROFESSION OF THE 1980S: SELECTED STATISTICS FROM THE 1984 LAWYER STATISTICAL REPORT (1984); NATIONAL ASSOCIATION FOR LAW PLACEMENT, CLASS OF 1980, EMPLOYMENT REPORT AND SALARY SURVEY (1981), *discussed in* J. Taylor, Demographics of the American Legal Profession 17 (Feb. 1983) (unpublished manuscript presented at Harvard Law School Program on the Legal Profession). Between 1954 and 1975, the number of solo practitioners declined from roughly two-thirds to roughly one-third of the profession. Schwartz, *The Reorganization of the Legal Profession*, 58 TEX. L. REV. 1269, 1274 (1980); B. CURRAN, *supra*. Government and in-house counsel, who by definition serve organizational interests, now comprise 13% and 9% of the bar. *Id.* Among the third of the profession working in partnerships, most billable services are performed for businesses (51%) and governmental or other nonindividual clients (5%). Pashigian, *The Number and Earnings of Lawyers: Some Recent Findings*, 1978 AM. B. FOUND. RESEARCH J. 51, 79. *Cf.* Heinz & Laumann, *The Organization of Lawyers' Work: Size, Intensity, and Co-Practice of the Fields of Law*, 1979 AM. B. FOUND. RESEARCH J. 217, 225 (47% of total legal effort is performed for the corporate client sector).

pose personal autonomy and public responsibilities may prove difficult to reconcile with the internal dynamics of employing institutions. Moreover, much of the bar's partisan ideology derives its primary force from individualist values. It is by no means self-evident, as the profession's codes and commentary generally assume, that concerns of individual dignity and trust are equally implicated in all legal practice, irrespective of the client's size, structure, and objectives.

Any systematic attempt to explain or affect the ethical dimensions of contemporary legal practice will require a richer exploration of its ideological and organizational context. Thus, the following discussion examines recurring tensions in legal practice from both a normative and a sociological vantage. In particular, it explores the conflict among professional ideals, ideologies, and institutions. No such general survey can, of course, fully reflect the diversity of norms and tensions within a highly stratified profession. But neither is it possible to understand the ethical dimensions of any particular practice context without an understanding of the broader professional culture. By examining certain shared premises and structural pressures, the following analysis seeks to illumine some of the most persistent sources of normative conflict in legal practice.

The point is not, however, to imply that the bar is awash in ethical anguish on a daily basis. As the companion articles in this symposium suggest, much private practice involves technical and tactical assistance carrying little normative freight. The discussion here seeks not to magnify lawyers' moral conflict, but simply to force focus on its conceptual and sociological foundations. In so doing, the analysis is admittedly selective. Attention centers on the less laudable aspects of the professional climate. That focus should not be taken to denigrate attorneys' positive contributions in social ordering, nor to paint a monochromatic portrait of the legal landscape. But if, as the leadership of the bar repeatedly asserts, the profession is seriously committed to a "comprehensive rethinking of . . . ethical premises,"[6] it must give more searching scrutiny to its ethical dilemmas and to their institutional and ideological underpinnings.

To that end, the following discussion begins by exploring certain inherent tensions between professional ideals and ideolo-

6. Model Rules of Professional Conduct, Chairman's Introduction (Final Draft 1981), *reprinted in* A.B.A. J. 1299 (1981) [hereinafter cited as Model Rules (Final Draft)].

gies. Attention then turns to the institutional constraints that give rise to those conflicts. A final section explores alternative conceptions of legal practice and the context in which they might take root. Central to that reformulation is a theory of role that imposes greater personal responsibility for the consequences of professional actions. That enlarged sense of attorney accountability should, in turn, prompt a reexamination of adversarial processes, regulatory frameworks, and organizational structures.

I. Ideals and Ideologies

Particularly during the last century, the American bar has had considerable difficulty squaring the rhetoric and reality of legal practice. Professionalism, by conventional definition, presupposes a substantial degree of public commitment and private autonomy.[7] Most formal bar discourse has presupposed an Olympian detachment from parochial concerns and institutional constraints. Over the last century, attorneys have variously appeared as "sentinels," "ministers," and "high priests of justice," with eyes well-elevated "above the golden calf."[8] Though contemporary metaphors are more subdued, legal practice is still idealized as a self-directed calling, informed by "the spirit of a public service."[9]

Such rhetoric appears increasingly removed from the enterprise it purports to describe. As the profession's competitive ethos and partisan loyalties grow more pronounced, the pretense that the bar remains above trade becomes more difficult to accept. In responding to these trends, practitioners have displayed a mix of resignation, regret, and exhortation. Bar literature has long hosted laments for some happier era when law was a profes-

7. W. Moore, The Professions: Roles and Rules 5 (1970); *see also* Becker, *The Nature of a Profession*, in Education for the Professions 27, 38–39 (1962); Wilensky, *The Professionalization of Everyone?*, 70 Am. J. Soc. 137 (1964).

8. Story, Address Delivered Before the Members of the Suffolk Bar (1821), *excerpted in* P. Miller, The Legal Mind in America 63, 71 (1962) ("sentinels" and "ministers"); Jackson, *Law and Lawyers*, in P. Miller, *supra*, at 274, 283 ("sentinel," "guardian of morality," and "conservator of right"); People v. Beattie, 137 Ill. 553, 574, 27 N.E. 1096, 1103 (1891) ("minister"); Model Rules (Final Draft), *supra* note 6, Chairman's Introduction, at 4 ("minister"); T. Strong, Joseph H. Choate 130 (1917) ("high priest"); Brewer, *The Ideal Lawyer*, 98 Atl. Monthly 587, 591 (1906) ("[h]e looks above the golden calf"); *Report of the Committee on Code of Professional Ethics*, 29 A.B.A. Rep. 600, 602 (1906) ("ministers"); Address of Chancellor Kent before the Law Association of the City of New York (Oct. 21, 1836), *reprinted in* 16 Am. Jurist 471, 472 (1836) ("sentinels").

9. R. Pound, The Lawyer from Antiquity to Modern Times 14 (1953).

sion, not a business, and lawyers were stewards of societal values, not servants of private profit.[10]

To be sure, much contemporary commentary has a more prosaic tenor: Lawyers frequently cast themselves as simple technicians with a simple desire to conduct "the business as a business" according to the "morals of the market place."[11] Yet within the dominant ideology, professional ideals retain a toehold. Concerns for justice and aspirations to a public calling remain a prominent part of the bar's collective conscience. One of the profession's overriding objectives has always been, as a recent American Bar Association president affirmed, to prevent "the practice of law [from] becom[ing] just another business."[12]

Yet how that transformation can be averted is a subject on which most commentators are less forthcoming. Although the literature abounds with stinging accounts of seduced virtue, the prescriptions tend to be more tepid.[13] Rarely does an author venture beyond some brief evocation of traditional ideals and vague exhortations to selflessness. Nonetheless, the persistence of such rhetoric counsels against its dismissal as mere public posturing or rank hypocrisy. The intended audience is generally not laymen but lawyers, whose professional identities are shaped by idealized traditions as well as market realities. But if those traditions are to retain significant appeal, their adherents must con-

---

10. Margolick, *Lawyers from the Old School Losing Ground to New Breed*, N.Y. Times, July 17, 1982, at 21, col. 1, at 22, col. 6 (quoting Gerald Edelman) ("[A]dvocacy is going down the drain . . . . [T]he law has become a business, a trade. It's not a profession anymore."); *accord* Brown, *Misguided Lawyers*, N.Y. Times, Dec. 6, 1983, at A31, col. 1.

Such wistful retrospectives are by no means a recent phenomenon. *See* Stone, *The Public Influence of the Bar*, 48 HARV. L. REV. 1, 3 (1934) (evoking "pages of a glorious past" in which the bar's leadership was more committed to advancement of the public interest and less to profits from a successfully conducted business); *see also* E. SMIGEL, THE WALL STREET LAWYER 304 (1964) (discussing perceptions of Wall Street attorneys in the 1950s); Gordon, *"The Ideal and the Actual in the Law": Fantasies and Practices of New York City Lawyers, 1870–1910*, in THE NEW HIGH PRIESTS: LAWYERS IN POST-CIVIL WAR AMERICA 51 (G. Gawalt ed. 1984) (referring to legal practice around the turn of the century).

11. King, *The Law Gets Down to Business*, Boston Globe, May 17, 1983, at 37, col. 3, at 42, col. 5 (quoting Shepard Remis, Managing Partner, Herrick & Smith); Stewart, *Professional Ethics for the Business Lawyer: The Morals of the Marketplace*, 31 BUS. LAW. 463, 466–67 (1975).

12. Harrell, *Preserving Professionalism*, 69 A.B.A. J. 864, 864 (1983); *accord* Maxwell, *The Importance of Lawyers*, STUDENT LAW. J., Oct. 1956, at 5 (remarks at the time Maxwell was president of the ABA).

13. BRANDEIS, *supra* note 3, at 321 (quoting Bryce); *see also* Stone, *supra* note 10, at 1–14.

front the ideological and institutional constraints that war against professional values.

These institutional constraints are of varying dimensions. As Part II suggests, lawyers working within organizations or other professional subcultures are subject to shop norms and reward structures peculiar to each setting. Those internal norms and structures, in turn, respond to the external economic and social dynamics underlying lawyers' partisan status. For most attorneys, advancing client interests remains the primary means of securing financial success and professional status. A critical function of professional ideology is to make a virtue out of that necessity.

The following analysis explores the conventional justifications for lawyers' undivided partisanship—justifications that echo dominant communitarian and individualist strains in liberal political thought.[14] The communitarian approach builds on societal interests in informed dispute resolution. It posits adversarial processes as the best available means to secure results in accordance with applicable law. From this formalist perspective, zealous client representation appears essential to a well-ordered legal system. An alternative approach justifies such advocacy by reference to individualist values. In this framework, lawyers' unqualified partisanship serves to safeguard private spheres of dignity and autonomy. These adversarial ideologies work both to legitimate professionally expedient choices and to deny moral responsibility for their consequences. Yet each form of argument, and the ethical norms it has spawned, rests on premises requiring closer scrutiny.

In testing those premises, the following discussion draws from a variety of texts, including the ABA's *Model Rules of Professional Conduct* and some dozen volumes of accompanying bar and scholarly comment. The point is neither to debate particular formulations of the *Rules* nor to magnify their importance. Rather, such texts serve largely to illumine the incoherence of prevailing ideology. There are, to be sure, inherent limitations in any at-

---

14. The communitarian vision draws from classical sources, such as Aristotle and Plato's theories of the *polis* and Rousseau's notion of the general will. The individualist strand of liberal ideology is rooted in the work by Enlightenment philosophers and John Stuart Mill. For general accounts of the influence of these traditions on American political consciousness, see L. HARTZ, THE LIBERAL TRADITION IN AMERICA (1955); J.G. POCOCK, THE MACHIAVELLIAN MOMENT (1955); G. WOOD, THE CREATION OF THE AMERICAN REPUBLIC, 1776–1787 (1969).

tempt to generalize about professional mores from published sources. The diversity in perspective throughout the American bar will never be fully reflected in formal rules and rhetoric. Nonetheless, the dominance and continuity of certain forms of normative discourse suggest some common ground from which to begin analysis. Taken together, the bar's most recent debates on legal ethics illustrate the distance the professional ideology has moved from traditional ideals and their moral underpinnings.

A. *Formalism: The Adversary System's Invisible Hand*

Although most legal practice occurs outside any formal adversarial framework, justifications of partisanship often lean heavily on that paradigm. Underlying those justifications is a mixed formalist and free market conception of adjudicative processes. The bar seeks to resolve the contradiction between fidelity to a particular client and to the legal system as a whole by reference to a combative scheme of social ordering. The premise is that "truth" or the "right" result is attainable through competitive presentations of relevant factual and legal considerations.[15] Paralleling Karl Popper's concept of scientific rationality, the theory assumes that knowledge will emerge through a dialectic of conjecture and refutation.[16]

One of the strongest articulations of this claim appears in a report on professional responsibility by the Joint Conference of the American Bar Association and the Association of American Law Schools. The report's premise is that "[o]nly when [the trier of fact] has had the benefit of intelligent and vigorous advocacy on both sides can he feel fully confident of his decision."[17] Moreover, only when each side undertakes full responsibility for pre-

15. *See e.g.*, Frankel, *The Search for Truth: An Umpiral View*, 123 U. PA. L. REV. 1031 (1975) (discussing the need for modifications in the adversary system to place greater duties on lawyers to pursue the truth); MODEL RULES OF PROFESSIONAL CONDUCT Rule 3.4 comment [hereinafter cited as MODEL RULES] (effective adversary procedures contemplate competitive presentations by opposing parties); MODEL CODE OF PROFESSIONAL RESPONSIBILITY EC 7–19 (1980) (adversarial presentations enable tribunals to reach informed and impartial results).

16. K. POPPER, CONJECTURES AND REFUTATIONS: THE GROWTH OF SCIENTIFIC KNOWLEDGE (4th ed. 1972).

17. *Professional Responsibility: Report of the Joint Conference*, *reprinted in* 44 A.B.A. J. 1159, 1161 (1958) [hereinafter cited as *Report of the Joint Conference*]; *see also* Curtis, *The Ethics of Advocacy*, 4 STAN. L. REV. 3 (1951).

paring its case can the tribunal retain the neutrality essential for informed adjudication.

> Viewed in this light, the role of the lawyer as a partisan advocate appears not as a regrettable necessity, but as an indispensable part of a larger ordering of affairs. The institution of advocacy is not a concession to the frailties of human nature, but an expression of human insight in the design of a social framework within which man's capacity for impartial judgment can attain its fullest realization.[18]

A substantial part of the profession doubtless shares a more modest vision. An institutional framework that tolerates competing perspectives may simply appear as the logical means of coping with ambiguity and regularizing disputes in a pluralist social order. Nonetheless, even these more pragmatic constituencies often retain the conviction, articulated by the ABA's General Practice Section, that the "adversary system provides the best method we have been able to devise to determine truth" or its reasonable approximation.[19]

The most obvious difficulty with this premise is that it is neither self-evident nor supported by any empirical evidence. As Geoffrey Hazard, Reporter for the Model Rules Commission, candidly acknowledges, we have "no proof that the adversary system of trial yields truth more often than other systems of trial."[20] Neither is it intuitively obvious that truth is more often revealed by self-interested, rather than disinterested, exploration. The virtues of private initiative and judicial passivity come at a cost. Lawyers are concerned with the production of belief, not of knowledge.[21] Why assume, to paraphrase Macaulay, that the fairest results will emerge from two advocates arguing as unfairly as

18. *Report of the Joint Conference*, *supra* note 17, at 1161.

19. ABA General Practice Section, *Proposed Revisions of Model Rules of Professional Conduct*, 1 AMERICAN BAR ASSOCIATION MATERIALS ON MODEL RULES OF PROFESSIONAL CONDUCT, Item 519, at 5 (1982) [hereinafter cited as ABA MATERIALS]; *see also* M. FREEDMAN, LAWYERS' ETHICS IN AN ADVERSARY SYSTEM (1975); B. LEVY, CORPORATION LAWYER: SAINT OR SINNER? 159 (1961).

20. Hazard, *Rules of Ethics: The Drafting Task*, 36 REC. A.B. CITY N.Y. 77, 93 (1981); *see also* Luban, *The Adversary System Excuse*, in THE GOOD LAWYER 83 (D. Luban ed. 1983); Donagan, *Justifying Legal Practice in the Adversary System*, in *id.* at 123. For a critique of existing research on adversarial processes, see Damaska, *Presentation of Evidence and Factfinding Precision*, 123 U. PA. L. REV. 1083 (1975) (critiquing Thibaut, Walker, & Lind, *Adversary Presentation and Bias in Legal Decisionmaking*, 86 HARV. L. REV. 386 (1972)).

21. *See* PLATO, GORGIAS (T. Irwin trans. 1979), *discussed in* Kronman, *Forward: Legal Scholarship and Moral Education*, 80 YALE L.J. 955, 960 (1981).

possible on opposite sides?[22] That is not the way most countries adjudicate controversies, nor the way other professions conduct factual inquiry. Nor is it how the bar itself seeks truth in any setting outside the courtroom. In preparing for trial, for example, lawyers do not typically hire competitive investigators.

To retain plausibility, this defense of adversarial processes must proceed in a social and economic vacuum. The conventional paradigm presupposes combatants with roughly equal incentives, resources, and capabilities. How frequently those suppositions hold is open to question in a social order that tolerates vast disparities in wealth, renders most litigation enormously expensive, and allocates civil legal assistance almost entirely through market mechanisms. Under these circumstances, one would expect that the "haves" generally come out ahead.[23] Commonplace as this point must be to any practicing attorney, it is conspicuous only by absence in most official explications of adversarial premises. Only one submission to the Model Rules Commission questioned adversarial processes on grounds of unequal access to legal talent.[24]

The disparities in representation ignored by conventional paradigms are readily amplified under current practices. The adversary system's extensive procedural protections generate frequent opportunities for evasion, harassment, and delay. In large-scale litigation, principal pathologies include endless wrangling over peripheral issues, as well as over-and under-production of discoverable material. Pretrial proceedings too often give rise to casuistic constructions of discovery requests, disingenuous assertions of the attorney-client privilege, or "Hiroshima" responses to document demands (with any damaging items buried in a mass of trivia).[25] Although the bar's conventional response to such

22. J. FRANK, COURTS ON TRIAL 80 (1950) (quoting Macaulay). As David Luban has argued, adversary procedures, by permitting false conjectures and excluding truthful evidence, may often simply pile up confusion. Luban, *Calming the Hearse Horse: A Philosophical Research Program For Legal Ethics*, 40 MD. L. REV. 451, 469 (1981).

23. Galanter, *Why the Haves Come Out Ahead: Speculations on the Limits of Legal Change*, 9 LAW & SOC'Y REV. 95 (1974); *see* Wanner, *The Public Ordering of Private Relations, Part Two: Winning Civil Court Cases*, 9 LAW & SOC'Y REV. 293, 306 (1975) ("courts are vehicles by which organizational plaintiffs gain goods at the expense of individual defendants").

24. *See* Gillers (I–70), *General Comments*, 2 COMPILATION OF COMMENTS ON THE MODEL RULES OF PROFESSIONAL CONDUCT 12 (G. Hazard ed. 1980) [hereinafter cited as ABA COMMENTS].

25. Abuses include using formbook interrogatories of marginal relevance, encouraging deponents to revise their recollections, providing unresponsive answers, or disin-

problems has been that they "should be left to the procedural rules and sanctions of the court involved,"[26] these correctives have repeatedly proven inadequate. Sanctions are expensive to seek and administer, and judicial responses to adversarial imbalance or pretrial pugnacity are constrained by time, information, and perception of role.[27] Although recent amendments to the Federal Rules encourage greater use of discovery sanctions, such formal mandates are likely to have limited effect on the incentive and information structures that impede judicial oversight.[28]

These constraints on judicial governance are readily exploited by resourceful counsel. Many of the nation's most eminent law firms are noted for their skill in genteel procrastination. Among the most celebrated examples are Covington & Burling's 12-year delay of regulations governing peanut butter content, and Cravath, Swaine & Moore's 14-year defense of an antitrust case that, according to its chief litigator, involved thousands of exhibits, a 50,000-page record, and no real dispute about the facts.[29] Nor is delay the only pretrial pathology. The adversarial framework has often generated an ethos in which truth becomes more an obstacle than an objective. In a national survey of 1500 large-firm litigators, half of those responding believed that unfair and inadequate disclosure of material information prior to trial was a

genuously invoking the attorney-client privilege. For a recipe of further techniques, such as "concentration," in which one party reshuffles documents so that his or her adversary cannot locate relevant material, or "mixed cocktail," in which the attorney buries sought-after material in a warehouse full of other matter and invites the opponent to come and "visit for a spell," see Flegal, *Discovery Abuse: Causes, Effects and Reform*, 3 REV. LITIGATION 1, 23 (1982); *see also* M. FRANKEL, PARTISAN JUSTICE 18 (1980) ("the object always is to beat every plowshare into a sword"); note 155 *infra* and accompanying text (discussing the abuses which result from contingent and hourly rate fee structures).

26. Philadelphia Bar Association, *Evaluation and Report*, 2 ABA MATERIALS, *supra* note 19, Item 554, at 38 (discussing the problem of a lawyer destroying documents which he or she should know are relevant to a foreseeable proceeding).

27. *See* Sherman, *The Judge's Role in Discovery*, 3 REV. LITIGATION 89, 94–103 (1982); Brazil, *Civil Discovery: Lawyers' View of its Effectiveness, Its Principal Problems and Abuses*, 1980 AM. B. FOUND. RESEARCH J. 787.

28. For discussion of the modifications in the federal rules governing discovery abuse, see Miller, *The Adversary System: Dinosaur or Phoenix*, 69 MINN. L. REV. 1 (1984); *see also* Shapiro, *Some Problems of Discovery in an Adversary System*, 63 MINN. L. REV. 1055 (1979) (discussing the bar's responses to proposed rule changes).

29. The confession was Bruce Bromley's, before the Stanford Law School in 1958. *See* J. LIEBERMAN, CRISIS AT THE BAR 164–65 (1978). For discussion of Covington & Burling's creative lawyering, see M. GREEN, THE OTHER GOVERNMENT 136–50 (1975); *see also* M. WESSEL, SCIENCE AND CONSCIENCE 61 (1980) (quoting advice advocating exhaustive discovery given to antitrust attorneys).

"regular or frequent" problem.[30] Similarly, 69% of surveyed antitrust attorneys had encountered unethical practices in complex cases; the most frequently cited abuses were tampering with witnesses' responses and destroying evidence.[31]

As in Norman trial by combat, the prime objective in much contemporary litigation is to force the adversary to "cry craven" well before discovery of critical facts or adjudication by a neutral decisionmaker. The objective is frequently achieved. According to a survey of Chicago litigators, one in three cases was concluded without at least one party having discovered potentially significant information.[32] Since close to 90% of all civil cases are settled prior to trial,[33] and relatively little of lawyers' advocacy occurs in the presence of impartial adjudicators, the adversary paradigm offers an inadequate foundation for the partisanship role.

Even in full-dress hearings, it is questionable how often the invisible hand asserts itself. Bar ideology assumes that responsibility for ferreting out false testimony or for insuring "fair treatment" of unrepresented and inadequately represented opponents rests elsewhere.[34] If an unmeritorious claim prevails, the fault lies with the judge, the jury, or the litigant who failed to secure adequate counsel.[35] Yet such deflections of blame elide

30. S. Pepke, Standards of Legal Negotiations, Interim Report and Preliminary Findings (1983) (unpublished manuscript). Seventy-five percent of those surveyed indicated that incomplete information was a regular or frequent practice. *Id.* The median estimate of the number of attorneys who knowingly concealed information after having provided inaccurate or incomplete data was 20%. *Id.*

31. WESSEL, *infra* note 129, at 67 (quoting ABA Section of Antitrust Law, Tabulation of Responses to Complex Litigation Questionnaire 5 (Oct. 2, 1978)).

32. Brazil, *supra* note 27, at 816.

33. Approximately 94% of federal civil cases are settled prior to trial. BUREAU OF THE CENSUS, U.S. DEPARTMENT OF COMMERCE, STATISTICAL ABSTRACT OF THE UNITED STATES 189, table 316 (1984). The most comprehensive recent survey of state and federal cases with claims over $1,000 found that about 90% were settled or abandoned. Trubek, Sarat, Felstiner, Kritzer, & Grossman, *The Costs of Ordinary Litigation*, 31 U.C.L.A. L. REV. 72, 86 (1983).

34. Riverside County Bar, 5 ABA COMMENTS, *supra* note 24, Rule 3.6, at 2. In the view of one representative *Model Rules* commentator, to require counsel to decline to present testimony he reasonably believes false would obliterate the tribunal's role in finding facts. Whitaker (I–111), 4 ABA COMMENTS, *supra* note 24, Rule 3.1, at 2; *see also* Pepke, *supra* note 30 (finding that less than one-third of some 1,500 large-firm litigators believed that counsel had no duty to disclose that their clients had knowingly given false and material information at a deposition).

35. An apt illustration of the general approach appears in Douglas Rosenthal's study of the personal injury bar. After watching his adversary bungle a meritorious claim for injuries arising from a fractured skull, counsel for the defendant insurance

the inherent inadequacies of adversarial frameworks. Not all individuals have the information or resources to ensure an even contest, and neither the judge nor the jury may be well-situated to make appropriate adjustments. Carefully scripted court performances often bear limited resemblance to the actual facts triggering dispute. And conventional techniques of witness selection and preparation can easily yield guided tours down memory lane with predetermined destinations clearly in view.[36]

Despite a long succession of scholarship identifying such difficulties, the organized bar remains firmly wedded to the adversary ethos. With rare exceptions, commentators on the *Model Rules* found no evidence "that the champion system has ill served us,"[37] and resisted all proposed rules that might "undermine," "abrogate," or "fundamentally change" adversarial norms.[38] In response to this overwhelming professional consensus, the drafting commission eliminated an array of provisions designed to curb discovery excesses and to reduce the incidence of erroneous

company conceded that he would have preferred the plaintiff to win. He maintained, nevertheless: "I was just doing my job. . . . It's not my fault . . . . It's his lawyer's fault and [the plaintiff's] own fault for not getting a better lawyer like me . . . . If the client gets nothing it will be the jury's responsibility . . . ." D. ROSENTHAL, LAWYER AND CLIENT: WHO'S IN CHARGE? 82–83 (1974). Still, counsel was not entirely at ease with the analysis. All in all, it was a "dirty business." *Id.* at 82.

36. Prior to eliciting any facts, the lawyer often apprises the witness of relevent legal standards, other evidence, and tactical considerations that might affect his or her recollection. *See* FRANKEL, *supra* note 25, at 15 ("[E]very lawyer knows that the 'preparing' of witnesses may embrace a multitude of other measures, including some ethical lapses believed to be more common than we would wish . . . . [T]he process often extends beyond helping organize what the witness knows and moves in the direction of helping the witness know new things."); G. HAZARD, ETHICS IN THE PRACTICE OF LAW 132–34 (1978) (discussing the murky boundary between witness preparation and subornation of perjury, and the dubious assumption that cross examination will expose falsehood); FRANK, *supra* note 22, at 85 (suggesting that trials by a "preponderance of the perjury" are too frequent a phenomenon).

37. New Jersey Bar Association (0–19), *General Comments*, 1 ABA COMMENTS, *supra* note 24.

38. *See* Gonser (I–82), 4 ABA COMMENTS, *supra* note 24, Rule 1.13(b)(2), at 11 (rules requiring lawyers to disclose the unlawful activity of their clients would undermine a fundamental cornerstone of our legal system); ABA Commission on Evaluation of Professional Standards, Public Hearing of the Commission on Evaluation of Professional Standards 5 (1980) [hereinafter cited as Hearing] (statement by Sidney Rosdentcher, Chairman of the Committee on Professional and Judicial Ethics of the Association of the Bar of the City of New York) ("rules requiring the lawyer to give information or assistance to the other side would abrogate the adversary system"); Pike, *Don't Panic, Kutak Tells His Ethics Code Skeptics*, Nat'l L.J., Dec. 22, 1980, at 2, col. 3 (quoting Robert Kutak).

adjudication.[39] After these dilutions and deletions, the *Model Rules* do little more than incorporate general prohibitions on crime and fraud. Lawyers remain free to present evidence they believe is false or misleading, and to counsel clients' agents and employees to refrain from all voluntary disclosures.[40] Except in ex parte proceedings, counsel has no responsibility to apprise the tribunal of material facts.[41] The final version of the *Model Rules* even dropped provisions granting lawyers *discretion* to disclose evidence favorable to another party or to correct material misapprehensions. Only if failure to act would implicate attorneys in fraud may they make such disclosures.[42] Given these standards, the portrayal of lawyers as "ministers of justice" requires considerable poetic license.

Fundamental difficulties remain in adversarial premises as well as practices. Under conventional formalist accounts, just results emerge through the rational application of law to fact in the course of competitive presentations. Thus, the preamble to the *Model Rules* submits: "[W]hen an opposing party is well represented, a lawyer can be a zealous advocate on behalf of a client

39. *Compare* MODEL RULES OF PROFESSIONAL CONDUCT Rule 3.3 comment (Discussion Draft 1980) [hereinafter cited as MODEL RULES (Discussion Draft)] *with* MODEL RULES, *supra* note 15, Rules 3.1, 3.2 (1983). The discussion draft provided that lawyers should "not engage in any procedure or tactic having no substantial purpose" other than to delay other parties or to increase the burdens on them. In addition, under the draft, counsel should not initiate any action unless a "lawyer acting in good faith would conclude that there is a reasonable basis for doing so." *Id.*, Rule 3.3(b). The final version of Rule 3.2 states that a "lawyer shall make reasonable efforts to expedite litigation consistent with the interests of the client." The commission deleted language regarding increased burdens and relegated the prohibitions on tactics without "substantial purpose" to the comment. *Id.*, Rule 3.2 comment. Rule 3.1 permits a lawyer to bring a proceeding as long as it is "not frivolous." *Id.*, Rule 3.1. The rule contains no requirement that the claim have a "reasonable basis." *Id.*

Early drafts also granted attorneys discretion to turn over favorable evidence to an opposing party and to refrain from offering evidence if they doubted its veracity and authenticity. MODEL RULES (Discussion Draft) Rule 3.1(e). In addition, the Discussion Draft required that counsel in a civil case disclose adverse facts to a tribunal when, *inter alia*, disclosure "would probably have a substantial effect on the determination of a material issue." *Id.*, Rule 3.1(c). A lawyer was also to refrain from offering "without suitable explanation, evidence that the lawyer knows is substantially misleading." *Id.*, Rule 3.1(d)(3). During civil negotiations, attorneys would also be obligated to make disclosures "necessary to correct a manifest misapprehension of fact" resulting from their own or the client's previous representations. *Id.*, Rule 4.2(b)(2). Thus formulated, none of those rules were palatable to the organized bar, and were significantly altered or eliminated by the drafting commission. *See* text accompanying notes 40-42.

40. *See* MODEL RULES, *supra* note 15, Rules 3.3(c), 3.4.(f)(1).

41. *Id.*, Rule 3.3(d).

42. *Id.*, Rules 1.6(b)(2), 3.3(a)(2).

and at the same time assume that justice is being done."[43] In effect, this perspective conflates substantive and procedural justice. Thus conceived, the perspective is vulnerable to all the critiques of formalism that have become standard fare in modern jurisprudential analysis.[44]

Bar ideology makes no adjustment for the possibility that formalist application of legal rules may work injustice that other branches of government fail to redress. A recurring theme in bar rhetoric is that problems such as corporate immorality or adversarial imbalances are the responsibility of legislators, not lawyers.[45] Ad hoc attorney paternalism is considered an inappropriate response to systemic failures. Publicly accountable officials, not privately appointed Platonic guardians, should determine the appropriate corrective. If counsel's zealous representation impedes the control of hazardous products or toxic substances, the fault rests not with the attorney but with those who failed to pass the requisite standards or to appropriate sufficient funds for enforcement.[46]

Such genuflections to legislative process, however rhetorically reassuring, remain morally unpersuasive. Presumably, few lawyers are unaware of the inherent limitations in democratic procedures and regulatory solutions. Time lags in acquiring information and designing appropriate correctives are inevitable, and attorneys with access to confidential studies may often be more knowledgeable about injurious conduct far sooner than politicians or administrative officials. Even where problems are apparent, the costs of regulation may seem excessive, or interest group pressures and inadequate enforcement resources may prevent socially optimal resolutions. As long as disparities of wealth,

---

43. *Id.*, preamble at 2.

44. For two seminal critiques, see R. UNGER, LAW IN MODERN SOCIETY 204, 212, 238–42 (1976); Kennedy, *Form and Substance in Private Law Adjudication*, 89 HARV. L. REV. 1685 (1976).

45. *See* State Bar of Wisconsin, *Specific Comments and Recommendations on the ABA Final Draft of the Model Rules of Professional Conduct*, 2 ABA MATERIALS, *supra* note 19, Item 558, at 6 (remedies regarding corporate misfeasance should be left to the legislative process); *accord*, General Motors Corporation, 5 ABA COMMENTS, *supra* note 24, Rule 1.13, at 3; Section of Corporation, Banking, and Business Law, Letter to Robert J. Kutak (June 17, 1980), 3 ABA COMMENTS, *supra* note 24, at 8; *see also* Spilky, 2 ABA COMMENTS, *supra* note 24, Rule 8.1, at 9 (suggesting that representation of the indigent should be a societal, not professional, obligation); Villareal, 2 ABA COMMENTS, *supra* note 24, Rule 8.1, at 8.

46. J. GOULDEN, THE MILLION DOLLAR LAWYERS (1978). *But see* Hanover, *Corporate Lawyers Do Public-Interest Work*, Wall St. J., Feb. 23, 1984, at 28, col. 3.

knowledge, and power affect both the agenda and outcome of political debate, statutory solutions will imperfectly reflect societal values. Any legislative or administrative body may, as Duncan Kennedy notes, prove too "anaesthetized or simply overworked" to remedy obvious deficiencies in legal standards.[47] Nonetheless, the bar's adversarial premise equates justice with the mechanical application of these standards.

This constricted view of legal processes yields a correspondingly myopic perception of professional responsibilities. Within this framework, counsel need not contemplate any broader notion of justice than that defined by existing legal norms. Ironically enough, contemporary bar discourse depicts a far more circumscribed moral universe than that envisioned when formalist theories enjoyed higher regard. Nineteenth century commentary on legal ethics not only posited duties of law reform, but also expressly acknowledged that impartial application of civil law could occasionally result in "mistaken" or "perverted" judgments; for lawyers to lend assistance in these cases would be "revolting."[48]

By contrast, the bar's current code envisions a more stoic

47. Kennedy, *Legal Formality*, 2 J. Legal Stud. 351, 394 (1973); *see* F.H. Bradley, Ethical Studies 203 (2d ed. 1927); R. Unger, Knowledge and Politics 89–95 (1975); Postema, *Moral Responsibility in Professional Ethics*, 55 N.Y.U. L. Rev. 63, 86 (1980).

48. *See* Field, *The Study and Practice of the Law*, in The Golden Age of American Law 30, 33 (C. Haar ed. 1965). In 1844, when commenting on Lord Brougham's view that a lawyer's sole office was to serve his client, David Field observed:

> [A] more revolting doctrine scarcely ever fell from any man's lips. . . . It assumes that a man has a right to whatever the law will give him, that the law itself is so clear that it cannot be mistaken or perverted, and that he may rightfully avail himself of every defect in an adversary's proof . . . ; three propositions, every one of which is without foundation.

Id.; *see also* 2 D. Hoffman, A Course of Legal Study 755 (2d ed. 1836) (no lawyer is "privileged, much less obliged," to "arrest, or to impede the course of justice"); G. Sharswood, Professional Ethics (2d ed. 1860). Sharswood quotes with approval Chief Justice Gibson's conclusion that a lawyer is "bound by his official oath . . . [to act] with all fidelity to the court as well as the client; and he violates it when he consciously presses for an unjust judgment . . . ." *Id.* at 98. Sharswood further observes:

> There is no professional duty . . . which compels an advocate . . . to secure success in any cause, just or unjust; and when so instructed, if he believes it to be intended to gain an unrighteous object, he ought to throw up the cause, and retire from all connection with it, rather than thus be a participator in other men's sins.

Id. at 100–01.

Sharswood is not, however, entirely consistent on this point. Elsewhere in his essays he suggests that at least with respect to some claims and defenses, the lawyer should not arrogate the role of judge and jury. *See id.* at 82–83, 90–96, 105–07, 116–17.

stance. Reformist rhetoric is in decline. As long as attorneys continue representing a client, they are to "act with commitment and dedication to the interests of the client and with zeal in advocacy upon the client's behalf."[49] Although lawyers retain "professional discretion in determining the means by which a matter should be pursued,"[50] they should defer to the client regarding "the purposes to be served by legal representation."[51] If, during the course of representation, the client "insists upon pursuing an objective that the lawyer considers repugnant or imprudent," the lawyer has discretion but no duty to withdraw.[52]

What is disquieting about this formalist approach is not simply its implicit hierarchy of values, but also the absence of any significant controversy over its terms. That of itself suggests the extent to which professional ideology has become detached from society's more general ethical norms. Relieved of any responsibility for substantive justice, lawyers can come to view it as peripheral to their own sense of achievement. Litigation becomes a game or ritual, and as William Simon notes, such perspectives relieve the process of any necessity to generate fair or rational results.[53] Such a normative climate easily gives rise to the attitude expressed by one British barrister: "[I]t is sometimes more fun to have a bad case than a good one for it tests your powers of persuasion more severely. Certainly I have seldom felt better pleased than when I persuaded [the court] to come to a decision which I was convinced was wrong . . . ."[54]

This sporting theory of justice, however compatible with the profession's institutional incentives, fits poorly with its traditional ideals. Not only is such a perspective conducive to the procedural abuses described earlier, it seems fundamentally at odds with lawyers' aspirations to a public calling. To cope with that apparent contradiction, as well as with the vast range of representation in which adversarial safeguards are absent, bar ideology requires recourse to a second line of argument. This alternative approach legitimates partisanship norms not as in-

49. MODEL RULES, *supra* note 15, Rule 1.3 comment.

50. *Id.*

51. *Id.*, Rule 1.2 comment.

52. *Id.*, Rule 1.16(b)(3).

53. Simon, *supra* note 4, at 104–06, 124–30. For general discussion of the game analogy, see Leff, *Law And*, 87 YALE L.J. 989, 998–1005 (1978)

54. Lehman, *The Pursuit of a Client's Interest*, 77 MICH. L. REV. 1078, 1078 (1979) (quoting Hon. Lord Cross of Chelsea).

struments for achieving justice in particular cases, but as safeguards for values that are central to a just society.

B. *Individualism: Private Ends as a Public Calling*

The second premise of adversarial ideology is that lawyers' undivided client allegiance serves fundamental interests of individual dignity, privacy, and autonomy. From this essentially deontological perspective, justice depends not on the realization of substantively correct outcomes, but on the preservation of private rights. In Lord Brougham's classic formulation, the advocate "knows in the discharge of that office but one person in the world—[the] client and no other."[55] From this premise follow two corollaries. First, lawyers should remain neutral partisans who defend, not judge, their clients. In addition, norms that assist that partisanship function, such as those governing confidentiality, should assume precedence over other societal concerns.

The individualist premise, although frequently invoked, is almost never fully explicated in debates over professional responsibility. Most commentators on the *Model Rules* simply assume a societal preference for individual over collective interests. As in other rights-oriented discourse, the source of assertedly preeminent values remains unclear. Thus, the American Trial Lawyers Association reasons: "In a society such as ours, which places the highest value on the dignity and autonomy of the individual, lawyers serve the public interest by undivided fidelity to each client's interests as the client perceives them."[56] This non sequitur presupposes a societal consensus that may not exist for civil matters comprising the bulk of legal practice.

The force of the bar's deontological claims derives in large measure from the criminal defense paradigm, where the case for undiluted partisanship is most compelling. When individuals' lives, liberties, or reputations are so immediately at risk, our constitutional tradition has sought to guarantee that they have advocates without competing loyalties to the state. The justifications for that guarantee have generated an extensive scholarly dis-

55. CHEATHAM, CASES AND MATERIALS IN THE LEGAL PROFESSION 227 (1938) (quoting Brougham).

56. ROSCOE POUND AMERICAN TRIAL LAWYERS FOUNDATION [ATLA] CODE OF CONDUCT comment, at 202 (1981) [hereinafter cited as ATLA CODE OF CONDUCT]; *see also* MODEL CODE OF PROFESSIONAL RESPONSIBILITY EC 7-1 (1982) ("The duty of a lawyer, both to his client and to the legal system, is to represent his client zealously within the bounds of the law . . . .").

course that need not be rehearsed here.[57] Given the small number of attorneys actively engaged in criminal defense work, the critical question is whether professional norms appropriate in that context should serve as the paradigm for all legal practice. Yet the bar's exaltation of individualism remains heavily parasitic on the criminal defense role. In commenting on the *Model Rules*, the ABA General Practice and Corporate Law Sections cast the lawyer as a "champion against a hostile world" and a "fearless advocate" protecting individuals in their struggles with the state.[58]

Such rhetoric is not smoothly transposed to the social and economic landscape of most legal practice. To be sure, in some civil matters, the disparity of power between the parties, the potential for abusive state or private action, or the possible constraints on fundamental rights may raise concerns analogous to those at issue in criminal proceedings.[59] While the bar's contribution in those circumstances has been of enormous societal importance, such cases do not constitute the mainstay of legal work. Only a few lawyers are actively engaged in poverty, civil rights, civil liberties, or analogous litigation; a high percentage focus on problems of corporations and wealthy individuals.[60] In those more typical cases, even if the state is involved, the balance of

57. *See generally* Babcock, *Defending the Guilty*, 32 CLEV.-MAR. L. REV. 175 (1983); Freedman, *Professional Responsibility of the Criminal Defense Lawyer: The Three Hardest Questions*, 64 MICH. L. REV. 1469 (1966). For discussion of the distinctive features of the penal sanction and the importance of distinguishing the role of the lawyer in civil and criminal proceedings, see Schwartz, *The Zeal of the Civil Advocate*, in THE GOOD LAWYER (D. Luban ed. 1984) ("[T]he spectre of capital punishment . . . the often barbaric conditions of our penal institutions [and] . . . the unique stigma of conviction . . . have played profound roles in defining the responsibilities of defense lawyers in criminal cases."); Wasserstrom, *supra* note 4. *But cf.* Griffiths, *Ideology in Criminal Procedure or a Third "Model" of the Criminal Process*, 79 YALE L.J. 359 (1970) (critiquing adversarial premises in criminal contexts).

58. ABA General Practice Section, 1 ABA MATERIALS, *supra* note 19, Item 519, at 4; ABA Section of Corporation, Banking, and Business Law, 5 ABA COMMENTS, *supra* note 24, at 368–69 (detailing "battle" language used to describe legal contests between state and individual); 1 ABA MATERIALS, *supra* note 19, Item 519, at 8 (quoting Preamble, ATLA CODE OF CONDUCT, *supra* note 56, at 1).

59. As a practical matter, the financial and stigmatic consequences for the defendant in some civil actions may be more severe than for a twice convicted felon charged with some petty misdemeanor. Moreover, given the importance of deterring some forms of overreaching private and public conduct, a sharp disjuncture between civil and criminal advocacy norms should not be assumed. *See generally* Fried, *The Lawyer as Friend: The Moral Foundation of the Lawyer-Client Relation*, 85 YALE L.J. 1060 (1976). *But see* note 57 *supra*.

60. Laumann & Heinz, *The Organization of Lawyers' Work: Size, Intensity, and Co-Practice*

power is often rather different than the ABA's self-portrait assumes. When a Wall Street firm representing a Fortune 500 corporation squares off against a woefully understaffed state regulatory agency, it strains credulity to paint the corporate defender as a champion against offical tyranny.[61]

Moreover, as an explanation of the lawyer's role in private ordering, the appeal to tyranny seems rather forced. According to many commentators, any effort to place the "interests of society over the interests of the individual . . . [represents] a very significant move toward totalitarianism. It makes the lawyer an agent of the state."[62] Not only does this logic confuse social responsibility with social control, it condemns one form of domination only to license another. The specter of the "collectivist" state[63] serves to justify undivided partisanship in pursuit of private power, no matter how abusive. To assume that clients are entitled to assistance in any action not plainly prohibited collapses moral and legal rights. Only the most uninformed faith in legislative processes and unrefined concept of moral responsibility could sustain such a vision.

The individualist rationale retains force through a rarified conception of legal practice and a reified view of professional role. By assimilating all forms of legal assistance to a David and Goliath paradigm, the argument avoids testing its value assumptions against more realistic social and economic backdrops. From a rhetorical perspective, that assimilation makes eminent sense. It is far easier to defend a highly privatistic vision of the social good and the profession's responsibilities when the lawyer appears as protector of the persecuted rather than friend of the

of the Fields of Law, 1979 AM. B. FOUND. RESEARCH J. 217, 225; Heinz & Laumann, *infra* note 131.

61. *Compare* note 58 *supra with* Galanter, *Mega Law and Mega Lawyering in the Contemporary United States*, in THE SOCIOLOGY OF THE PROFESSIONS, LAWYERS, DOCTORS AND OTHERS 152 (R. Dingwell & P. Lewis eds. 1983).

62. Curley, *Lawyers Squabble About a New Code of Ethics; An Issue: How Confidential is Role with Clients?*, Wall St. J., Feb. 6, 1981, at 44, col. 1 (quoting Freedman, who explains objections to Kutak draft); *see also* Koskoff, *Proposed New Code of Professional Responsibility: 1984 is Now!*, 54 CONN. B.J. 260 (1980); Teschner, *infra* note 147, at 846.

63. ATLA CODE OF CONDUCT, *supra* note 56, at 1; *see also* Winokur, *Lawyers: Seekers of Truth or Advocates for Clients?*, San Francisco Examiner, Aug. 6, 1982, at A1, col. 2, A12, col. 1 (quoting Koskoff, Chairman, Commission on Professional Responsibility, American Trial Lawyers Association) (if you place "greater emphasis on truth," as does the Kutak draft, "you're doing what totalitarian and collectivist societies do").

finance company.[64] Yet highly abstracted encomiums to individualism fail to explain the wholesale appropriation of adversarial norms in the defense of organizational interests.

Among private practitioners, the traditional consensus has been that lawyers' societal responsibilities should be identical whether they represent institutions or individuals.[65] Yet no serious efforts have been made to justify that position or to confront its discontinuity with values underpinning the partisanship role. In much contemporary legal practice, it is by no means clear who constitutes the corporate "client." Nor is it self-evident that concerns of human dignity and autonomy are best served by lawyers' undivided commitment to organizational objectives, whatever the consequences to individual third parties, such as consumers, employees, or victims of environmental violations. The less adequately those individual interests are represented, the less convincing becomes the defense of undiluted client allegiance.

In any event, however persuasive one finds the abstract appeal to dignitary values, its status as justification for particular professional standards is far more questionable. When rules governing access to the legal system and fidelity to client interests are examined in social context, it is difficult to defend their formulation by reference to individualist concerns.

An obvious threshold difficulty with that defense involves the financial underpinnings of advocacy, a point on which most pro-

64. *Compare* Fried, *supra* note 59 *with* Simon, *supra* note 4, at 103–26 (critiquing the notion of lawyer-client relationship as moral equivalent of friendship).

65. *Model Rules* commentators frequently asserted the appropriateness of equal treatment of institutions and individuals. *See, e.g.*, ABA Section of Corporation, Banking, and Business Law, ABA COMMENTS, *supra* note 24, Rule 1.13, at 0.34; Wisconsin Bar Association, 2 ABA MATERIALS, *supra* note 19, Item 558, at 5; American College of Trial Lawyers, Committee on Legal Ethics, 3 ABA COMMENTS, *supra* note 24, Rule 1.13, at 0.43; Los Angeles County Bar Association, 3 ABA COMMENTS, *supra* note 24, Rule 1.13, at 0.47; Public Hearing on the Model Rules of Professional Conduct 7 (held in Honolulu, Hawaii, 1980) (testimony of Oscar Rubenhauser, President, Association of the Bar of the City of New York). Others saw no justification for imposing special responsibilities on lawyers representing corporate clients. *See, e.g.*, Poston (I–104), 4 ABA COMMENTS, *supra* note 24; Beverly Hills Bar Association, 1 ABA MATERIALS, *supra* note 19, Item 505, at 4 (Rule 1.13 resolution). Only the National Legal Aid and Defender Association took a different view. *See* National Legal Aid and Defender Association, 3 ABA COMMENTS, *supra* note 24, Rule 1.7(c)(2), at 0.52–12 (suggesting that the rule regarding confidentiality may be one "in which the obligations of counsel for a corporate entity differ from that of counsel for an individual—rich or poor"). For an analysis of possible distinctions in the professional duties owed to individuals and organizations, see Bellow & Kettleson, *From Ethics to Politics: Confronting Scarcity and Fairness in Public Interest Practice*, 58 B.U. L. REV. 337 (1978).

ponents of the adversary ethos are diplomatically silent. Almost without exception, *Model Rules* commentators who invoked fundamental values simply ignored the vast array of civil matters in which the stakes do not justify or the claimant cannot secure a "champion against a hostile world."[66] For example, in responding to a proposed Model Rule that would have mandated 40 hours per year of pro bono service, many critics simply denied that access problems existed:

> I know of no person or worthy cause that has been refused legal service in Malheur County, regardless of the ability to pay . . . . I have no reason to believe the same is not true of every other county in our state.[67]
>
> I know of very few lawyers who do not provide professional service at no fee or at substantial [sic] reduced fees . . . . The proposed rule also fails to take into consideration the very active legal services provided in most communities by the Legal Aid Societies which limits the pro bono work [that can be] done by the members of the large firms.[68]
>
> Manifestly, no necessity is demonstrated in the discussion draft. The [pro bono] rule is attempting to create a necessity where none has existed.[69]

In fact, numerous, frequently bar-sponsored, empirical studies reflect a rather less Panglossian portrait. Taken together, they depict a vast universe of unrepresented individual and public interests and woefully inadequate pro bono contributions by the private bar.[70] One ABA study estimated that individuals consulted lawyers on far less than one-third of "all the problems encountered that reasonably [could be] called legal problems." [71] Even before the Reagan administration cutbacks substantially reduced the Legal Services operating budget, its lawyers were handling at most 2 million of the 6 to 132 million legal problems annually encountered by persons below the poverty line.[72] Ac-

66. *See* text accompanying note 58 *supra*.
67. Stunz (I–120), 4 ABA COMMENTS, *supra* note 24, Rule 8, at 5.
68. Parsons (I–47), 2 ABA COMMENTS, *supra* note 24, Rule 8.1, at 8.
69. Lovell (I–93), 4 ABA COMMENTS, *supra* note 5, Rule 8.1, at 6–7.
70. *See* B. CURRAN, THE LEGAL NEEDS OF THE PUBLIC 261 (1977).
71. LEGAL SERVICES CORPORATION AND THE ACTIVITIES OF ITS GRANTEES: A FACT BOOK (1979). In 1980, the Council on Public Interest Law identified only 111 centers employing slightly over 711 attorneys that qualified as tax-exempt, nonprofit groups devoting at least 30% of their resources "to providing representation to otherwise unrepresented interests in court or administrative proceedings involving questions of important public policy." COUNCIL FOR PUBLIC INTEREST LAW, SURVEY OF PUBLIC INTEREST LAW NARRATIVE REPORTS 1, 5 (1980).
72. *Id.*

cording to the most comprehensive survey available, some three-fifths of sampled attorneys devoted less than five percent of their billable hours to pro bono pursuits, and almost one-third made no contribution at all.[73] The average investment of the bar as a whole was about six percent of billable hours, and much of that assistance was designed to accommodate existing or potential clients.[74] The vast majority of nonbillable services were rendered not to indigent individuals or public interest causes, but to friends, relatives, and organizations such as hospitals, Jaycees, and garden clubs.[75]

Efforts by the *Model Rules* Commission to inspire a somewhat heightened sense of *noblesse oblige* evoked outrage from the organized bar. Any mandatory public service proposal smacked of "involuntary servitude," "latent fascism," and an "improper intrusion into the lawyer's right of free determination."[76] To most commentators, the prospect of sacrificing any professional autonomy in the stand against "official tyranny" was plainly unacceptable. Accordingly, the drafters retreated to language simply exhorting lawyers to good works of undefined form or quantity.[77]

Other professional standards affecting unrepresented parties

---

73. Handler, Hollingsworth, Erlanger, & Ladinsky, *The Public Interest Activities of Private Practice Lawyers*, 61 A.B.A. J. 1388, 1389 (1975) [hereinafter cited as Handler].

74. *See id.*; P. Lochner, *The No Fee and Low Fee Legal Practice of Private Attorneys*, 9 LAW & SOC'Y REV. 431 (1975).

75. *Id.*; Handler, *supra* note 73.

76. *Model Rules, Initial Draft*, Legal Times, at 45, col. 4; *see* Lovell (I-93), 4 ABA COMMENTS, *supra* note 24, Rule 8.1, at 6–7. For a representative sample of the bar's objections to "involuntary servitude," see Pike, *Don't Panic Kutak Tells His Ethics Code Skeptics*, Nat'l L.J., Dec. 22, 1980, at 2, col. 2; *Kutak Panel Report: No Mandatory Pro Bono*, A.B.A. J. 33 (1981); *see also* McMaster (I-95), ABA COMMENTS, *supra* note 24, Rule 8, at 3 ("When I get through paying the onerous taxes that are imposed upon me I 'ain't got time' [sic] to play games with a do-good commission."); Spilky (I-57), 2 ABA COMMENTS, *supra* note 24, Rule 8.1, at 9 ("We are not willing to be drafted to work in matters for which we may not have previous experience or for [clients] for whom we may have no inclination or for causes with which we may have no empathy. We are opposed to the very idea that lawyers can be cammandeered [sic] as so much chattel to work as slave laborers."); Monahan (I-98), 4 ABA COMMENTS, *supra* note 24, Rule 8.1, at 8 ("I know of no other situation where mere employment is the basis for confiscation of one's property, be it money or time (excluding Cambodia under Pol Pot).").

77. Rule 6.1 of the MODEL RULES, *supra* note 15, provides:

> A lawyer should render public interest legal service. A lawyer may discharge this responsibility by providing professional services at no fee or a reduced fee to persons of limited means or to public service or charitable groups or organizations, by service in activities for improving the law, the legal system or the legal profession, and by financial support for organizations that provide legal services to persons of limited means.

reflect a comparable lapse in commitment to values of individual dignity and autonomy. For example, one regulation evoking almost no controversy among private practitioners prohibits the unauthorized practice of law.[78] Yet considerable empirical evidence indicates that the bar's sweeping prohibitions have significantly, and unnecessarily, impeded access to the legal system.[79] In this context, the profession's animating interest appears to be protecting its turf from lay encroachment, rather than maximizing opportunites for assertion of individual rights. Similarly, the interests of unrepresented litigants have little standing in official ideology. In response to vehement bar opposition, *Model Rules* draftsmen deleted provisions enjoining lawyers who appeared against pro se opponents from "unfairly exploiting . . . ignorance of the law or the practices of the tribunal," and "procur[ing] an unconscionable result."[80] Under the final draft, lawyers' sole responsibility when dealing with an unrepresented adversary is to avoid implying that they are disinterested and to make reasonable efforts to correct evident misunderstandings concerning their role.[81]

Why attorneys, particularly those representing organizational clients, should be so unconstrained in exploiting the ignorance of undefended opponents is not readily explicable from an individualist perspective. Neither the *Model Rules* Commission nor its critics confronted the implications of such unqualified partisanship in a society marked by grossly unequal access to legal services. Rather, commentators' overriding concern seemed to be that opposing parties "too cheap to hire a lawyer" should not be "coddled" by special treatment.[82] What these rules on unrepresented interests reflect is not simply an inconsistency in the bar's celebration of individualist values. Rather, such standards expose the fundamental inadequacy of any theory that defends par-

78. MODEL RULES, *supra* note 15, Rule 5.5.

79. *See* Rhode, *Policing the Professional Monopoly: A Constitutional and Empirical Analysis of Unauthorized Practice Prohibitions*, 34 STAN. L. REV. 1, 33 (1981) (noting that only two percent of over a thousand inquiries, investigations, and complaints processed by state bar unauthorized practice committees in 1979 arose from injured consumers, and reviewing the lack of empirical underpinnings for the bar's unqualified ban on lay practice); *see also* Christensen, *The Unauthorized Practice of Law: Do Good Fences Really Make Good Neighbors—or Even Good Sense?*, 1980 AM. B. FOUND. RESEARCH J. 159. *Compare* MODEL RULES (Discussion Draft), *supra* note 39, Rule 3.6; *id.* comment at 75.

80. MODEL RULES (Discussion Draft), *supra* note 39, Rule 3.6; *id.* comment at 75.

81. MODEL RULES, *supra* note 15, Rule 4.3.

82. Parsons (I–47), 2 ABA COMMENTS, *supra* note 24.

tisanship on individualist grounds, where partisans are allocated by market methods.

That inadequacy is perhaps most apparent in the bar's recent debates on confidentiality, which remained at the forefront of controversy throughout the *Model Rules* ratification process. Bar opposition ultimately forced the deletion of almost all mandatory disclosure requirements from the proposed *Model Rules,* including those requirements designed to prevent a client from committing an act that would result in death or substantial bodily harm to a third party.[83] In their final form, the *Rules* require disclosure by an attorney only where necessary to avoid assisting a client's criminal or fraudulent act in proceedings before a tribunal.[84] Lawyers may, but need not, reveal confidences in only two other circumstances: to prevent crimes likely to result in imminent death or substantial bodily harm, or to assert their own claims in a controversy with the client.[85] Thus official ideology not only permits but may require counsel to remain a silent witness to highly asocial conduct.

Absolving lawyers from disclosure obligations under such circumstances is not easily reconciled with individualist premises. Casting the lawyer's office as a secular "confessional for the troubled individual"[86] scarcely justifies its status as a haven for corporate prerogative. Particularly where the tradeoff is between shareholder profit and human safety, it is by no means obvious why organizational interests should occupy such a preferred position in defining counsel's ethical responsibilities.[87]

The profession's conventional defense of its limited disclo-

83. MODEL RULES (Discussion Draft), *supra* note 39, Rule 1.7(b).

84. MODEL RULES, *supra* note 15, Rule 1.6(b)(2), (3); Rule 3.3. In cases of false testimony, lawyers must first attempt to remonstrate with the client or to withdraw. Only if those efforts are unsuccessful may they make disclosures to the court. Attorneys are required to terminate any representation that will result in a violation of the law or of professional rules (including furtherance of criminal or fraudulent conduct), and may withdraw any previously rendered public opinions that they discover are incorrect. *Id.*, Rules 1.6, 3.3.

85. When representing organizational clients, lawyers have discretion to seek internal review of objectionable policies, but not to make external disclosures. *Id.*, Rule 1.13.

86. Koskoff, *supra* note 62, at 264.

87. As Christopher Stone has noted, stockholders disaffected with organizational policy can typically sell their interest with minimal effort. Individuals whose safety is at risk, such as those who are unwittingly exposed to hazardous wastes, working conditions, or product defects, "cannot remove themselves from the structure with a phone call." C. STONE, WHERE THE LAW ENDS 85 (1975).

sure obligations is too familiar to warrant extended exegis here. Nonetheless, the core arguments are readily summarized and reduce to two essential propositions: first, that any risk of disclosure would deter clients from freely confiding in counsel; and second, that the costs of such a chill on clients' access to legal assistance would outweigh any societal benefits. Such claims are not without some intuitive force. The public's distaste for tattling reflects deeply rooted convictions about the value of trust and candor in human relationships. The critical issue, however, is not whether those values are worth preserving, but to what extent they are reconcilable with fundamental interests in protecting innocent third parties. On this point, most professional discourse has been utterly unilluminating.

Defenders of broad confidentiality protections almost invariably assume what is to be proven, namely that *any* disclosure responsibilities would dismember lawyer-client relationships. Bar rejoinders to modest *Model Rules* proposals generally verged on the apocalyptic. The common assumption was that any qualification of confidentiality protections would "chill all client communications"; lawyers' access to "potentially sensitive information would be virtually eliminated," uprooting "a fundamental cornerstone of our legal system."[88] Only where lawyers enjoyed a relationship of "total trust [and] candor" could they effectively assist clients in conforming their conduct to legal mandates.[89]

Although rarely made explicit, the empirical basis for such assertions appears to be that attorneys' obligations are well known

88. Gonser (I–82), 4 ABA COMMENTS, *supra* note 24, Rule 1.13, at 11; *see also* Debate on Model Rule 1.6 Before the A.B.A. House of Delegates 23 (Feb. 7, 1983) (statement of John Elam, American College of Trial Lawyers); *see also* Virginia State Bar Association, *Report of the Special Committee on the Code of Professional Responsibility*, 2 ABA MATERIALS, *supra* note 19, at 547–51.

89. ABA Section of Corporation, Banking, and Business Law, 5 ABA COMMENTS, *supra* note 24, Rule 1.13(c), at 12 (corporate lawyers play a crucial "role in assisting and promoting management compliance with [the] vast array of statutes and regulations, federal and state, impinging on corporate activities. To discharge effectively this law compliance role, the corporate lawyer must have the total trust, which means total candor, of his management colleagues"); *see, e.g.*, New Jersey State Bar Association Special Committee, 1 ABA COMMENTS, *supra* note 24, at 0.19 ("[i]t is in the genuine public interest that clients be encouraged to consult frequently and freely with their lawyers, to inform themselves of their legal rights and obligations"); Association of the Bar of the City of New York, Committee on Professional and Judicial Ethics, 1 ABA COMMENTS, *supra* note 24, at 0.22 (existing confidentiality protection enhances lawyers' opportunities to make known the requirements of the law and to persuade clients to rectify past wrongs and behave legally and ethically).

and that any qualification would induce clients to suppress critical facts that they now divulge. Neither supposition is self-evident. Prior disclosure standards have been riddled with exceptions and indeterminacies, with which few laymen are familiar.[90] Moreover, many clients will withhold evidence of compromising conduct, regardless of the bar's formal rules or clients' perceptions of them.[91] What knowledge their counsel acquires will often be the product of paper trails and external corroboration rather than voluntary revelations. In any event, concerns about personal as well as organizational liability frequently leave clients with no practical alternative but to consult attorneys, and it is unclear how often some risk of disclosure would materially alter the terms of counsel's involvement.[92] From a historical and cross-cultural perspective, it appears that most professionals, including American lawyers, have managed to discharge confidential counseling functions without the absolute freedom from third-party obligations that the organized bar now claims.[93]

Thus, claims predicated on the lawyer's role as an institutional superego by no means justify the breadth of modern confidentiality protections. Given the scope of the attorney-client

90. *See generally* Rotunda, Book Review, 89 HARV. L. REV. 622 (1976); Rotunda, *The Notice of Withdrawal and The New Model Rules of Professional Conduct: Blowing the Whistle and Waving the Red Flag*, 63 ORE. L. REV. 455 (1984). To cite only the most obvious example, the ABA Code provision licensing disclosure of future but not past crimes has generated an expansive volume of incoherent and irreconcilable precedents in the area of ongoing illegality. As Charles Wolfram has suggested, predicting outcomes on the basis of reported decisions and ABA opinions had become something of a "law school parlour game." Wolfram, *Client Perjury*, 50 S. CAL. L. REV. 809, 837 (1977); *see also* text accompanying note 96 *supra*; Note, *Functional Overlap Between the Lawyer and Other Professionals: Its Implications for the Privileged Communications Doctrine*, 71 YALE L.J. 1226, 1232 (1962) (survey finding that most individuals either were unaware of the attorney-client privilege, or believed that it extended to other professional relationships).

91. *Hearings Before the Committee on Corporate Rights and Responsibilities*, 94th Cong., 2d Sess. (1976) (statement of C. Stone) (noting that in every case of corporate wrongdoing in a University of Southern California study, individual employers withheld compromising information).

92. G. HAZARD, ETHICS AND THE LAW 141 (1978) (noting that legal liabilities of organizations and management come close to making legal consultation a practical necessity).

93. *See, e.g.*, FREEDMAN, *supra* note 19, at 33 (Canadian legal profession); Tarasoff v. Regents of the University of California, 17 Cal. 3d 425, 551 P.2d 334, 131 Cal. Rptr. 14 (1976) (California Supreme Court) (psychotherapists); Regan, *Professional Secrecy*, in THE GOOD LAWYER, *supra* note 57, at 104–13 (clergy); M. Wald & R. Weisberg, Confidentiality Laws and State Efforts to Protect Abused or Neglected Children: The Need for Statutory Reform, (unpublished manuscript) (social workers). For most of its history, the Anglo-American bar functioned without a broad attorney-client privilege. *See* Hazard, *An Historical Perspective on the Attorney-Client Privilege*, 66 CALIF. L. REV. 1061 (1978).

privilege, little is known about the extent to which lawyers have managed to channel patrons along "proper paths."[94] Yet certainly the current incidence of illegal or hazardous corporate conduct suggests room for improvement.[95] It is at least conceivable that some qualified third-party responsibilities might incline attorneys toward greater activism in their prophylactic role.

Finally, it bears note that even the most fervent defenders of unqualified confidentiality have seldom pursued the logic of their position when attorneys' own interests are at issue. Few of the *Model Rules* evoked greater consensus than the provision allowing lawyers to reveal information necessary to collect fees or to establish their own position in a dispute with the client.[96] Yet nothing in the Commission's text or commentary explains why disclosures to protect lay victims will erode client trust, while revelations to secure attorneys' financial interests will not. In effect, the bar's selective endorsement of confidentiality exceptions concedes the empirical point at issue. Once one acknowledges that clients' general expectation of confidentiality can be maintained

94. Gerrie (I-21), 2 ABA COMMENTS, *supra* note 24, Rule 1.13, at 23–24 ("to place even discretionary [third-party] responsibilit[ies] on the general counsel creates an unhealthy relationship" and, to the extent such a relationship alienates the client, "the ability of counsel to assist organizational conduct along the proper path is weakened").

95. For example, in a 1980 *Fortune* survey of 1,037 companies that at some time between 1970 and 1980 had been listed among the 800 largest corporations in America, 11% had been convicted of at least one of the following five criminal offenses during that period: bribery, criminal fraud, illegal political contributions, tax evasion, or criminal antitrust violations. Ross, *How Lawless Are Big Companies?*, FORTUNE, Dec. 1, 1980, at 56, 58.

Noncompliance with environmental regulations, occupational safety standards, and labor relations requirements remains a perennial problem. The EPA has estimated that only ten percent of all hazardous waste disposal occurs in conformity with federal regulations. Beauchamp, *The Environment*, in CASE STUDIES IN BUSINESS, SOCIETY AND ETHICS 112 (T. Beauchamp ed. 1983). *Cf. GAO Reports Low RCRA Compliance, Little Enforcement Follow Up*, PESTICIDE AND TOXIC CHEMICAL NEWS, Oct. 12, 1983, at 13 (quoting General Accounting Office report on inspection and enforcement at hazardous waste facilities) (78% of the hazardous waste facilities for which data were available were not in compliance with applicable groundwater monitoring requirements). Of the companies engaged in repeated unfair labor practices, J.P. Stevens is perhaps the most notorious. *See* NLRB v. J.P. Stevens & Co., 563 F.2d 8 (2d Cir. 1977). For a more general discussion of labor violations, see Summers, *Past Premises, Present Failures, and Future Needs in Labor Legislation*, 31 BUFFALO L. REV. 9 (1982). For further discussions of corporate misfeasance, see C. STONE, *supra* note 87; Coffee, *Beyond the Shut-Eyed Sentry: Toward a Theoretical View of Corporate Misconduct and an Effective Legal Response*, 63 VA. L. REV. 1099 (1977); Vaughan, *Toward Understanding Unlawful Organizational Behavior*, 80 MICH. L. REV. 1377 (1982).

96. *See* Kutak, ABA Commission on Evaluation of Professional Standards, 1 ABA MATERIALS, *supra* note 19, Item 400, at 4–5 (noting that the confidentiality exception for lawyer-client disputes met with "almost universal consensus").

despite some limited risk of betrayal, it is unclear why the pecuniary concerns of lawyers should assume priority over the potentially more significant claims of third-party victims.

In short, the profession is scarcely well situated to make a disinterested assessment of the societal risks and benefits of less categorical confidentiality protections. The principal factors animating *Model Rules* commentators included the increased risk of financial liability[97] and the "dangerous diminution" of counsel's influence[98] that third-party obligations might entail. Had a less parochial constituency been passing on these issues, it might well have reached a different accommodation of the competing public concerns. When self-interest is not at issue, many professionals, including lawyers, have concluded that "the uncertain and conjectural character" of threats to client confidence should not take precedence over concrete risks to innocent third party victims.[99]

This is not, of course, to imply that tinkering with disclosure standards would in itself effect major changes in lawyers' perceived societal responsibilities. Whatever the bar's codified rules, avid policemen will not emerge among those whose salary and status flow directly from the targets of surveillance. In the face of strong economic, social, and cultural barriers to tattling, attorneys will inevitably resolve doubts in expedient directions.

---

97. Bar commentators consistently invoked the threat of civil liability as a necessary and sufficient basis for deleting third party protections. *See, e.g.*, STATE BAR OF CALIFORNIA, STANDING COMMITTEE ON PROFESSIONAL RESPONSIBILITY AND CONDUCT, REPORT CONCERNING A.B.A. MODEL RULES OF PROFESSIONAL CONDUCT 6 (1980). Other commentators targeted particular rules as objectionable. For a representative sample of these criticisms, see, e.g., Robinson, ABA Standing Committee on Lawyers' Professional Liability, 1 ABA MATERIALS, *supra* note 19, Item 528, at 7, 11 (citing, *inter alia*, rules governing meritorious claims and disclosures in negotiation as likely to cause unjustifiable increase in malpractice liability); New York State Bar Association, 2 ABA MATERIALS, *supra* note 19, Item 547, at 6, 7, 16, 20 (citing rules governing unconscionable contracts and disclosures of illegal corporate conduct as objectionable provisions that could create liability to third parties); Warner, Maricopa County Bar Association, 5 ABA COMMENTS, *supra* note 24, Rule 4.1, at 1 (making lawyers responsible for negotiation results would invite unjustified third party claims); Landau (I–33), 2 ABA COMMENTS *supra* note 24, Rule 4.3, at 2–3 (objecting to rules regarding negotiations as creating unique and unwarranted risks of liability).

98. Rosdeitcher, Association of the Bar of the City of New York, Committee of Professional and Judicial Ethics, 1 ABA COMMENTS, *supra* note 24, Rule 1.13, at 8; Medaglia & Wadlow, Bar Association of the District of Columbia, Young Lawyers Section, 5 ABA COMMENTS, *supra* note 24, Rule 1.13, at 20 (any guardianship responsibilities for attorneys will "diminish [their] role in future corporate matters").

99. Tarasoff v. Regents of the University of California, 17 Cal. 3d 425, 439, 551 P.2d 334, 346, 131 Cal. Rptr. 14, 26 (1976).

But it by no means follows that professional ideology should help to suppress those doubts by elevating prudential interests to ethical mandates.

Like its formalist counterpart, the individualist premise of partisanship enshrines an impoverished view of professional obligations. The premium placed on client loyalty and confidentiality affords maximum insulation from third-party claims or oversight. Yet the parochialism of these concerns is easily masked with an appealing individualist rhetoric. By invoking deeply rooted liberal values, the adversarial ethos retains force as the dominant vision of professional responsibility. But that vision, in conflating clients' legal and moral rights, sanctifies a form of private partisanship not readily reconciled with societal concerns or professional aspirations.

In seeking some more satisfactory reconciliation, the bar's final recourse tends toward a chastened skepticism. The ultimate move in many professional responsibility debates is to abandon any affirmative defense of existing norms, while challenging the plausibility of preferable alternatives.

C. *Skepticism: The Refuge of Role*

Arguments from skepticism fall into a variety of camps but share a common premise and pedigree. In essence, the premise is that lawyers neither can nor ought to make the factual and normative judgments that more rigorous ethical obligations would entail. The shared pedigree is a socialization experience that erodes conviction at every turn.

Professional education offers an extended exposure to the vagaries of legal doctrine and the frailties of its expositors. Faced with a steady succession of hard cases and unstable distinctions, aspiring students quickly discover that there are no "right" answers—there is "always an argument the other way and the devil often has a very good case."[100] Conventional law school courses not only demythologize doctrine, they also reinforce a skepticism about its underlying moral foundations. What appears patently inequitable in one instance becomes more problematic when the apparent correctives are generalized across broad categories of

100. Macaulay, Law School and the World Outside 25 (1982) (unpublished working paper); *see also* Cramton, *The Ordinary Religion of the Law School Classroom*, 29 J. LEGAL EDUC. 247, 253–59 (1978); Kennedy, *Legal Education and the Reproduction of Hierarchy*, 32 J. LEGAL EDUC. 591 (1982).

cases. For lawyers in practice, the appeal of agnosticism often increases. Pure victims and villains are hard to come by; factual uncertainties, extenuating circumstances, and normative dissonance confound all but the rarest cases.

In the face of such complexity, the bar's conventional response has been to retreat into a highly role-differentiated morality. Paralleling Emile Durkheim's classic formulation, contemporary ideology portrays the legal profession as a distinctive moral community, whose norms depart from ordinary conceptions of civic virtue.[101] From this perspective, the lawyer's function is simply to defend, not judge, the client. Accordingly, counsel assumes no moral responsibility for the ends to which his or her services are put.

Such a role definition has obvious appeal. As Richard Wasserstrom has noted, "the ethical problems that can arise within this constricted point of view are, to say the least, typically neither momentous nor terribly vexing. Role-differentiated behavior is enticing . . . precisely because it does constrain and delimit an otherwise often intractable and confusing moral world."[102] Yet this insular perspective comes at considerable social and individual cost. The extent to which a professional role should preempt personal responsibility bears closer scrutiny.

1. *The epistemological demurrer.*

Among the arguments from skepticism, one of the most common variants is epistemological; it denies lawyers' capacity to make the factual and legal determinations that certain normative judgments would entail. Invoking this incapacity, lawyers have resisted both legal and moral accountability for their participation in conduct later found to be fraudulent, misleading, hazardous, or unconscionable.[103] Given the inevitable indeterminancy

101. E. DURKHEIM, PROFESSIONAL ETHICS & CIVIL MORALS (1957).

102. Wasserstrom, *supra* note 4, at 9.

103. For protests regarding a *Model Rules* provision that would have barred lawyers from facilitating unconscionable transactions, see, e.g., Darby, New York State Bar Association, Banking, Corporation, and Business Law Section, 3 ABA COMMENTS, *supra* note 24, Rule 4.3, at 0.53; Forrow (1-17), 2 ABA COMMENTS, *supra* note 24, Rule 2.3, at 3; Welch, Omaha Bar Association, 3 ABA COMMENTS, *supra* note 24, Rule 4.3, at 0.54. For objections to other proposed standards regarding disclosures to prevent misrepresentation in negotiations, see American College of Trial Lawyers, 1 ABA MATERIALS, *supra* note 19, Item 503, at 33 (misrepresentation in negotiation); *see also* Avery, American College of Probate Counsel, 3 ABA COMMENTS, *supra* note 24, Rule 2.3, at 0.42 (questioning application of standards to attorneys who "suspect" but lack absolute knowledge

of facts and law, and the bounded rationality of individual assessments, the profession's preference has been to suspend judgment on client conduct. Thus one of the bar's most cherished literary allusions remains Samuel Johnson's response to Boswell:

> Sir, you do not know [a cause] to be good or bad till the Judge determines it . . . . An argument which does not convince yourself, may convince the Judge to whom you urge it: [A]nd if it does convince him, why then, Sir, you are wrong, and he is right."[104]

From a less positivist standpoint, it is equally plausible that Johnson was wrong. Given all the deficiencies of adversarial processes noted above, attorneys with access to privileged documents and unrehearsed narratives might frequently be better positioned than the court to resolve disputed issues. And since the vast majority of cases never reach a neutral decisionmaker, the lawyer's assessments, however flawed, will often assume controlling significance.[105]

Moreover, even on its own terms, the epistemological premise appears inadequate. To retain plausibility, it depends on a definition of knowledge more appropriate to the rigors of scientific debate than to conventional legal discourse. No system of governance could function if certitude became a requisite for liability. Since the law generally does not insist on omniscience, why should professional ideology require more? Yet with a more relaxed definition of knowledge, the skeptic's claim to ignorance borders on casuistry. In many instances, lawyers know, or ought to know, the merits of their client's claims.[106] And in any case, to concede the uncertainty of legal and factual assessments by no means establishes that counsel should be relieved from all responsibility for making them. When acting in legislative or judicial capacities, lawyers frequently assume that the general public

---

of illegalities). The bar's response to SEC efforts to impose professional liability for client misrepresentation is reflected in *Statement of Policy Adopted by American Bar Association Regarding Responsibilities and Liabilities of Lawyers in Advising with Respect to the Compliance by Clients with Laws Administered by the Securities and Exchange Commission*, 31 Bus. Law. 543 (1975); *see also* Lipman, *The SEC's Reluctant Police Force: A New Role for Lawyers*, 49 N.Y.U. L. Rev. 437 (1974); Lorne, *The Corporate and Securities Adviser, the Public Interest, and Professional Ethics*, 76 Mich. L. Rev. 425 (1978).

104. 2 Boswell, The Life of Johnson 47–48 (Hill ed. 1887).

105. *See* text accompanying note 32 *supra*.

106. Hazard, *supra* note 92, at 130; Anscomb, *Two Kinds of Error in Action*, in J. Thompson & G. Dworkin, Ethics 287 (1968) (intentional ignorance "where it is necessary and possible to know" is no defense).

can conform its conduct to indeterminate directives involving issues such as conscionablity, due care, or fair dealing. Attorneys charge substantial fees for construing such standards, and clients adjust their affairs daily in reliance on such advice. To argue that lawyers should be absolved from responsibilities that others routinely bear requires some further justification.

2. *The appeal to agnosticism.*

Perhaps the most common justification of professional amorality builds on a form of radical skeptism. While the epistemological claim invokes factual indeterminacy, the agnostic's appeal stresses normative uncertainty. Standards such as "the public interest" are thought too "nebulous" to guide conduct in cases of any complexity.[107] Such cases generally involve competing values, and lawyers can profess no "special expertise" in discerning the socially desirable balance.[108] For example, many disputes over safety and environmental regulations require complex trade-offs among cost, efficacy, consumer autonomy, and quality of life. What constitutes an acceptable level of risk or an appropriate societal corrective may admit of varying interpretations. In multinational contexts, the ethical issue can be still more complicated. To some observers, exporting products found unsafe for American consumption is the moral equivalent of genocide. To others, an imposition of Western standards on international markets becomes an act of cultural imperialism. Generalizing from such disputes, the skeptic inclines toward a perpetual suspension of judgment.

Appeals to agnosticism claim a respectable academic pedigree. For centuries, theorists have disputed the determinacy of

107. Krash, *infra* note 135, at 33; *see also* J. GOULDEN, THE SUPERLAWYERS 61 (1972) (quoting John Sapienza, partner, Covington & Burling: "The public interest—what is it? Who can define it?"); Cutler, *The Role of the Private Law Firm*, 33 BUS. LAW. 1549, 1551 (1978) ("I take a dim view of the idea that any right-minded lawyer can immediately detect which side of a legislative, regulatory, or litigation issue is the public interest side").

108. *See, e.g.*, GOULDEN, *supra* note 107, at 52 (quoting John Laylin, partner, Covington & Burling: "I'm a lawyer, not a reformer . . . . We are not presumptuous enough to pass judgment . . . ."); NEW YORK STATE BAR ASSOCIATION, REPORT OF THE SPECIAL COMMITTEE TO REVIEW A.B.A. DRAFT MODEL RULES OF PROFESSIONAL CONDUCT 24 (1981) (objecting to rules that would require a lawyer to be "the ultimate arbiter of his client's rectitude") [hereinafter cited as N.Y. ST. B.A. REP.]; Gerrie (1-21), 2 ABA COMMENTS, *supra* note 24, Rule 1.13, at 24 ("Lawyers, by training, . . . are by no means unique guardians of the 'public good'. . . . For the lawyers to arrogate such a role for themselves seems the height of arrogance.").

moral values and the appropriate means for discerning them. In the absence of divinely revealed truth, ethical argument appears inevitably inconclusive. No criteria for judgment are unassailable, and consensus about norms seems possible only at a level of abstraction that rarely resolves particular cases. For example, as much contemporary philosophical discourse makes evident, traditional utilitarian and Kantian approaches to moral philosophy yield highly indeterminate results.[109] Given the inevitability of normative dispute, a studied neutrality seems the prudent course. By what right should lawyers "play God" or "impose their own views about the path of virtue upon their clients"?[110]

Thus phrased, the agnostic's appeal has a convincing ring. The air of humility signals an appealing departure from the normal run of professional rhetoric. But underlying such self-effacement lies a considerable degree of self-deception, if not disingenuousness. To accept moral responsibility is not necessarily to impose it; not every exercise of judgment results in coercion. Unless the lawyer is the last in town, his or her refusal to aid certain endeavors will not necessarily preempt client choice. It may simply impose the psychological and financial costs of finding alternative counsel.

To be sure, in some instances, such attorney action will have coercive consequences. But the possibility of foreclosing other individuals' options or of adding to their expenses has not always inclined the bar to suspend judgment. If, for example, the nor-

109. To cite only the most obvious difficulty, Kant's categorical imperative mandates universalization, but little else. The question of which rules, once universalized, are desirable remains unanswered. *See* I. KANT, FOUNDATIONS OF THE METAPHYSICS OF MORALS 39 (1959); note 172 *infra*. For discussion of the lacunae left by Kant's approaches, see A. MACINTYRE, A SHORT HISTORY OF ETHICS 197–98 (1973); J.L. MACKIE, ETHICS 219 (1977). As a practical matter, utilitarian approaches may yield equally conjectural results. How one identifies and weighs all potential consequences of a given action is always open to challenge. *See* 2 F. HAYEK, THE MIRAGE OF SOCIAL JUSTICE 17–20 (1976); J. SMART & B. WILLIAMS, UTILITARIANISM, FOR AND AGAINST 140–50 (1973); UNGER, *supra* note 47, at 141.

110. Altman (I–17), 1 ABA COMMENTS, *supra* note 24, at 3; Auerbach, *Some Comments on Mr. Nader's Views*, 54 MINN. L. REV. 503, 505–06 (1970) (quoting Macaulay, *Law Schools and the World Outside Their Doors*, 54 VA. L. REV. 617, 626 (1968)). For comparable sentiments, see also Stewart, *supra* note 11, at 467 (suggesting that the ethics of the business lawyer should be no more than the morals of the marketplace); Krash, *infra* note 135, at 38 (asserting that counsel does not have the right to impose his views of the public interest on his client); N.Y. ST. B.A. REP., *supra* note 108, at 24 (postulating that a code of professional conduct should not define personal morality or the lawyer's responsibilities as a citizen). *But see* Macaulay, *supra* note 2, at 125 (generally applauding lawyers' use of their limited leverage to "channel behavior for good or evil").

mative dispute involves the profession's own regulatory policies, its level of self-effacement dips markedly. The organized bar has had no difficulty in discerning where the "public interest" lies when it comes to banning lay competition, minimizing lawyers' third-party responsibilities, or insulating professional governance from all external oversight.[111] Indeed, attorneys have even proclaimed themselves able to assess what sorts of youthful moral lapses should preclude individuals from aspiring to professional status.[112] In a vast range of more mundane circumstances, attorneys appear able to engage in normative dialogue. They continually draw lines, however fuzzy. "Sleazy" clients and "sharp" practices frequently figure in professional discourse. As Roberto Unger has noted, lawyers who insist that values are subjective are generally more than prepared to argue about policy as if a rational choice among competing values were possible.[113] In short, the bar's agnosticism has been highly selective.

Such inconsistencies do not, of course, undercut the agnostic's basic position; its inadequacies lie deeper. Few individuals are prepared to pursue the radical skeptic's claim to its logical extreme and suspend normative judgment on all forms of conduct.[114] That one is not paid to make such judgments does not generally operate as a moral excuse. The same is true for virtually every vocation outside the clergy. Moreover, a relativist or subjectivist approach to moral argument does not logically imply

111. For assertions regarding the "public interest" in banning lay practice, see Rhode, *supra* note 79, at 3–5, 9, 41, 59, 74. For analogous claims concerning society's interest in professional autonomy, see MODEL RULES, *supra* note 6, preamble at 2; *Law Poll: Self-Regulation, Some Lay Participation Still is Favored,* 69 A.B.A. J. 154 (1983) (finding that approximately three-fourths of attorneys responding believed that self-regulation "has proved successful and should be continued"). For a review of the bar's position on third party responsibilities, see notes 88, 89, 94, 97, 98 *supra* and accompanying texts.

112. Among the offenses bar character committees have recently found disabling are homosexuality, cohabitation, and discharges in bankruptcy. *See* Fla. Bd. of Bar Examiners Re N.R.S., 403 So. 2d 1315, 1317–18 (Fla. 1981)(homosexuality); Cord v. Gibb, 219 Va. 1019, 1022, 254 S.E.2d 71, 73 (1979) (overturning bar committee's denial of cohabiting applicant); Application of Gahan, 279 N.W.2d 826, 831–32 (Minn. 1979) (bankruptcy). For a critical review of the bar's role in this area, see Rhode, *Moral Character as a Professional Credential,* 94 YALE L.J. 491 (1985).

113. UNGER, *supra* note 47, at 95.

114. For suggestions that the record of Nazi Germany made radical skepticism less tenable, see B. RUSSELL, HUMAN SOCIETY IN ETHICS AND POLITICS 20 (1955); 1 M. GINSBERG, On the Diversity of Morals, in ESSAYS ON SOCIOLOGY AND SOCIAL PHILOSOPHY 98 (1956). For J. Habermas' critique of radical skepticism, see J. HABERMAS, LEGITIMATION CRISIS 102–11 (T. McCarthy trans. 1973); *see also* J. HABERMAS, COMMUNICATION AND THE EVOLUTION OF SOCIETY 95–129 (T. McCarthy trans. 1979).

indifference as the appropriate response.[115] To concede the indeterminacy of ethical analysis is not to establish its futility. On factual questions, lawyers frequently express convictions despite the possibility of error or uncertainty. And in some contexts, presumably even the most hardened agnostic will have greater confidence in making a normative than an empirical assessment. Confronted with the record in a major antitrust dispute, most general practitioners would doubtless feel more comfortable asserting that restraints on competition disserve the "public interest" than deciding whether a restraint in fact occurred.

In any event, many issues on which clients seek assistance inescapably require normative assessment. Client objectives are often multiple or indeterminate, and are shaped in part through dialogue with counsel. Analyzing potential liability or the merits of particular strategies will often demand more than "technical" judgments, and lawyers' own moral intuitions cannot help but color their decisions. To pretend otherwise misconceives an integral part of attorneys' counseling function. Particularly where clients' true "interests" are not self-evident, one of lawyers' greatest potential contributions lies in persuading individuals to act in conformity with their most socially enlightened instincts.

Appeals to agnosticism are problematic in one final respect. Those who refuse to pass judgment on a client generally seem to assume that such neutrality is value-free. But individuals cannot market their loyalty, avert their eyes to the consequences, and pretend they have not made a normative decision. To decline to take a moral stance is in itself a moral stance and requires justification as such. Thus the critical question is not by what right do lawyers impose their views, but by what right do they evade the responsibility of all individuals to evaluate the normative implications of their acts? Alternatively, by what right do clients circumscribe counsels' ethical duty?

3. *The restraints of role.*

When pressed for moral justifications of its amoral stance, the bar often invokes client sovereignty as an ultimate recourse. Such an appeal mirrors the individualist claims discussed earlier, and gives rise to the same difficulties. But some of the arguments, particularly those concerning organizational clients, have

115. B. Williams, Morality: An Introduction to Ethics 29 (1972); Moore, *Moral Reality*, 1982 Wis. L. Rev. 1061, 1064.

an additional dimension. The bar's conventional view is that counsel ought not to second guess policy decisons of corporate officers and directors; absent evidence of financial self-dealing, a lawyer's arrogation of normative authority would displace the appropriate mechanisms of corporate governance.[116] Such arguments presuppose that organizational authorities are, by definition, more able than counsel to assess the full ethical dimensions of their policies. That supposition appears questionable on a number of grounds.

Corporate structures inevitably tend to fragment moral responsibility. The impersonal character of bureaucracies, their departmentalized concepts of accountability, their claims of personal loyalty, and their devaluation of concerns not readily translated into relatively short-term advantages all conspire to circumscribe ethical vision.[117] Since prestige in the business world turns heavily on abilities to maximize organizational sales and growth, less tangible values are often discounted.[118] Indeed,

116. Elliot, *The Proposed Model Rules of Professional Conduct: Invention Not Mothered by Necessity?*, 54 CONN. B.J. 265, 276 (1980); *see also* Krash, *infra* note 135, at 37 (the client must make the ultimate policy decisions); New York County Lawyer Association, 2 ABA COMMENTS, *supra* note 24, Item 546 ("[i]t is the responsibility of the officers and directors of a corporation to decide what constitutes [the organization's] best interests"); B.B. Corporate Counsel, 3 ABA COMMENTS, *supra* note 24, Rule 1.13, at 0.45 ("[T]he role of the lawyer . . . is that of an advisor and of an advocate . . . The lawyer does [n]ot make the business or the policy decisions . . . ."); New York State Bar Association, 2 ABA COMMENTS, *supra* note 24, Item 547, at 12 (proposed *Model Rules* provisions regarding counsels' third-party responsibilities "are grounded upon an essentially fallacious conception of the lawyer as part of the machinery of corporate governance"); *see also* notes 108, 109 *supra* and accompanying text.

117. MacIntyre, *Corporate Modernity and Moral Judgment: Are They Mutually Exclusive?*, in ETHICS AND PROBLEMS OF THE 21ST CENTURY 122, 125–35 (K. Goodpaster & K. Sayre eds. 1979); *see also* A. GOLDMAN, THE MORAL FOUNDATIONS OF PROFESSIONAL ETHICS 230–70 (1980) (discussing tendency of business managers to reason in terms of profits rather than morality); Coffee, *"No Soul to Damn: No Body to Kick": An Unscandalized Inquiry into the Problem of Corporate Punishment*, 79 MICH. L. REV. 386, 410 (1981) (postulating that the corporate executive's risk of punishment by the corporation for nonprofit-oriented behavior may be much greater than the risk of punishment by the legal system for illegal conduct); Donaldson, *Accountability and the Bureaucratization of Corporations*, in PROFITS AND PROFESSIONS 215, 223 (W. Robinson, M. Pritchard, & J. Ellin eds. 1983) (noting that bureaucratization of corporations tends to weaken accountability).

118. Stone, *supra* note 87, at 85, 230. For discussion of various other bureaucratic pathologies that may displace long-term corporate goals or undervalue certain common interests, see generally R. MERTON, *Bureaucratic Structure and Personality*, in SOCIAL THEORY AND SOCIAL STRUCTURE 197–200 (1957) (analyzing the dysfunctions of bureaucracy); R. CYERT & J. MARCH, A BEHAVIORAL THEORY OF THE FIRM 28, 35–36 (1963) (discussing the unresolved conflict within organizations over appropriate goals); Warner & Havens, *Goal Displacement and the Intangibility of Organizational Goals*, 12 AD. SCI. Q. 539, 545 (1968)

within some corporate communities, the perception is that "the social responsibility of business is to make profits."[119]

Yet given market externalities and barriers to information, competition, legal redress, or political oversight, some divergence between private and public interests is inescapable. If corporate executives are convinced that "[s]afety doesn't sell,"[120] or if third-world nations lack the capacity to regulate hazardous corporate conduct, the human costs of profit maximization can be substantial. To be sure, lawyers have no special expertise in assessing such costs. But their distance from organizational incentive structures may at least permit a more disinterested perspective than that of corporate officers. By exploring the moral consequences of a client's contemplated actions, counsel may broaden the agenda of decisionmaking. Conversely, by declining that role, lawyers may compound the deflection of responsibility that too often characterizes organizational behavior. Clients can justify asocial action on the ground that counsel have pronounced it not unlawful, while counsel can rationalize their participation by deferring to client autonomy.

Professional ideology has not proven totally impervious to these concerns. The bar's official codes contemplate that lawyers' advice may appropriately encompass ethical considerations.[121] But if individual or organizational clients ignore such advice, the bar acknowledges no responsibility to withhold further assistance. Indeed, it is frequently asserted that lawyers ought not to withdraw from representation under these circumstances, given the risk that they would be replaced by those with less refined sensibilities, thereby insulating the client from conscientious advice.[122]

That argument is highly seductive; it elevates expedience to ethics. But the potential for self-delusion remains considerable. If the issues are truly significant, an individual who is prepared to express, but not to act on, moral convictions has limited influence. Surely in some cases, where the sunk costs of representation are substantial, the prospect of counsel's withdrawal will

(hypothesizing that clear, tangible goals tend to displace intangible organizational goals).

119. L. Silk & D. Vogel, Ethics and Profits 139 (1976).

120. Dowie, *Pinto Madness*, Mother Jones, Sept.-Oct. 1977 (quoting Lee Iacocca, Former Chief Executive, Ford Motor Company).

121. Model Rules, *supra* note 15, Rule 1.2, DR 7–101, EC 7–8.

122. *See* Hazard, *supra* note 92, at 136–49.

prompt the client to a more reflective inquiry than would otherwise ensue.

So too, the mores of the hypothesized successor-lawyer will always be conjectural. The risk of his or her venality is no greater than the risk that, over time, incumbent counsel's sensitivity may fade. Indeed, all of the social and psychological pressures noted previously make the posture of domesticated dissidence a hard one to sustain. But even assuming, *arguendo*, that counsel's withdrawal might result in a less refined replacement, that possibility cannot end the analysis. Neither public nor private sector decisionmakers are generally absolved from moral responsibility on the ground that their most plausible successor could have been worse.

Thus, the refuge in role provides a deceptive haven, and one that extracts a considerable personal price. When professional action becomes detached from ordinary moral experience, lawyers' sensitivity can atrophy or narrow to fit the constricted universe dictated by role.[123] The agnosticism that advocacy purportedly entails can readily become a defining feature of one's total personality. Such a perspective offers the illusion of freedom from responsibility, while in fact delimiting individuals' moral autonomy. At best, the result is likely to be a resigned submission. At worst, it can foster an enervating cynicism. Success is gauged by victories, not values, and professional idealism is dismissed as pompous rhetoric.

Yet underlying this role-differentiated retreat is a form of what Jean-Paul Sartre termed "bad faith."[124] The individual represents as necessary conduct that in fact is volitional. Among lawyers, the tendency is to defend normative passivity as an essential concomitant of their professional functions. This process is reinforced by a set of institutional constraints that preempt alternative visions.

II. Ideals and Institutions

The bar's prevailing ideology both reflects and rationalizes

123. Postema, *Moral Responsibility in Professional Ethics*, 55 N.Y.U. L. Rev. 63, 73–81 (1980); Wasserstrom, *supra* note 4.

124. J.P. Sartre, Being and Nothingness 86–116 (1956). For an explication of Sartre's use of this term and its relevance in moral philosophy, see, e.g., T. Anderson, The Foundation and Structure of Sartrerian Ethics (1979); P. Caws, Sartre 74–93 (1979).

certain institutional constraints of contemporary practice. The patronage structure and organizational context of much legal representation reinforces an unqualified partisan ethic while subverting the values on which that ethic rests.

A. *Patronage and Professionalism*

Most lawyers have, by definition, a derivative status; their incomes and reputations depend in large measure on accommodating clients. The effects of such dependency will obviously vary according to a broad range of factors, including the size, nature and competitiveness of the market, the lawyer's position within it, the demands of particular clients, and professional norms and values. In general, however, as an attorney's status and income become more closely tied either to representation of a single patron, or to success in a particular proceeding, the pressures to suspend normative judgment may intensify. Even in a large diversified practice, the ability to replace a major client will often be constrained by locale, specialization, the scale of certain litigation, or empire building by particular attorneys. And over time, much legal practice fosters marriages of convenience or genuine intimacy between patron and counsel. For example, Robert Nelson's study of Chicago firms revealed that lawyers in general spent about a third of their time, and corporate lawyers about half their time, on the client for whom they worked the most.[125] Such working relationships may amplify pressures for lawyers to demonstrate that they "are on [management's] side and not part of the problem."[126] Particularly under competitive circumstances, the likelihood of ethical tunnel vision increases.

To be sure, some countervailing prudential as well as normative considerations exist. A reputation for integrity remains a profitable commodity in many circles, and notorious impropriety may seriously devalue a practitioner's standing. Yet in other circles, some slight devaluation may prove desirable.

While no crude materialist account can capture the full complexity of ethical decisionmaking, it would be naive to suppose

125. Nelson, *Ideology, Practice, and Professional Autonomy: Social Values and Client Relationships in the Large Law Firm*, 37 STAN. L. REV. 503 (1985). For a general discussion of captivity in lawyer-client relationships, see T. JOHNSON, PROFESSIONS AND POWER 45–78 (1972); Nonet & Carlin, *Law: The Legal Profession*, 9 INT'L ENCYCLOPEDIA OF THE SOC. SCI. 66, 69–70 (1968).

126. *A Businessman's View of Lawyers: A Program*, 33 BUS. LAW 817, 833 (1978) (quoting statement of Thad Snell, vice-president and general counsel of U.S. Gypsum).

that the process remains impervious to market forces. Most recorded history is to the contrary, and the legal profession does not appear to be an exception. The Wall Street bar's unblinking deference to industrial magnates during the early twentieth century is too familiar to require retelling.[127] Nor is there a dearth of contemporary analogues. Even among well-established attorneys, different markets in morality have developed; street fighting as a sub-specialty has enjoyed modest commercial success.[128] While the pressures for normative compromise vary across practice settings, the data reviewed in Part I suggest that litigation can generate unusual levels of moral smog. Reported cases and surveys reveal a striking incidence of overly zealous representation ranging from garden variety discovery abuse to suppression of evidence and complicity in fraud or perjury.[129] So too, in matters involving securities or health and safety regulations, where the price of propriety may be unravelling major transactions or impeding highly profitable product distributions, the bar's performance has provoked considerable criticism.[130]

---

127. In summarizing the corporate bar's conduct during this period, William O. Douglas found an "almost perverted singleness of purpose with which [attorneys] have championed the cause of their clients . . . . That singleness of purpose has been wholly incompatible with . . . the welfare of the investors of the good of the public." Douglas, *Directors Who Do Not Direct*, 47 HARV. L. REV. 1305, 1329 (1934); *see also* note 3 *supra*.

For more dispassionate accounts of the bar's involvement in illegal conduct of robber barons and corrupt politicians, see, e.g., Gordon, *supra* note 10.

128. *See, e.g.*, P. HOFFMAN, LIONS IN THE STREET 20–21, 34 (1973); Bruck, *Enemy of the Maimed: Is He Anti-Human?*, AM. LAW., Sept. 1979, at 1 (discussing the attitudes and practices of "tough" defense attorneys in tort suits); *see also* HAZARD, *supra* note 92, at 134; note 129 *infra*.

129. For survey evidence, see text accompanying notes 30, 31 *supra*. For graphic individual instances, see, e.g., Roadway Express Inc. v. Piper, 447 U.S. 752, 754–56 (1980) (discovery abuse); Felts v. National Account Sys. Ass'n, Inc., 469 F. Supp. 54, 67 (N.D. Miss. 1978) (fraud); L.R. PATTERSON, LEGAL ETHICS: THE LAW OF PROFESSIONAL RESPONSIBILITY 10–55 (1982) (discussing Roberts v. Sears, Roebuck & Co., 573 F.2d 976 (7th Cir. 1978) (fraud)); M. WESSEL, SCIENCE AND CONSCIENCE 49–53, 60–62 (1980) (and sources cited therein); Kiechel, *The Strange Case of Kodak's Lawyers*, FORTUNE, May 8, 1978, at 188 (perjury); Kwitny, *Piper Deliberately Destroyed Evidence of Aircraft Defect, Federal Judge Rules*, Wall St. J., Apr. 2, 1984; Carley, *How Litton's Lawyers Hid Evidence 2 Years in Suit Against AT&T*, Wall St. J., June 21, 1983, at 1, col. 6; Hiltzik, *Abuse of 'Discovery' Phase Snarls Cases*, L.A. Times, Feb. 14, 1984, at 1, col. 4; Baron, *GNC Fined over Record Destruction*, L.A. Times, Apr. 27, 1982, § 4, at 1, col. 4.

Given the enormous difficulty in proving or sanctioning such misconduct, it is likely that reported cases grossly underrepresent the amount of serious misconduct.

130. *See, e.g.*, *In re* Carter, SEC Act Release No. 17,597 (Feb. 28, 1981); Kramer, *Clients' Frauds and Their Lawyers' Obligations: A Study in Professional Responsibility*, 67 GEO. L.J. 991 (1979); note 134 *infra*. A case generating considerable recent comment involved the OPM computer leasing scandal, in which counsel reportedly played a crucial

Although such criticism often attributes blame to lawyers' feeble moral fiber or crass material preoccupations, these reductionist accounts mischaracterize the range of forces at work. Much of what is problematic in legal practice springs not from venality but from factual or normative uncertainty, together with a tendency to resolve all possible doubts in a single, client-oriented direction. That tendency arises from a complex set of social and ideological as well as economic concerns. The American bar's pronounced specialization and internal stratification impedes commitment to interests transcending the lawyer-client relationship.[131] Professional ideology, as well as more informal processes of self-selection, socialization, and dissonance reduction, work to reinforce client allegiance. Much social science research confirms that proximity in working relationships more often breeds consensus than contempt.[132] The end result, as Nelson's study of Chicago practitioners illustrates, may be a strong coincidence in attitudes among counsel and clients.[133]

Yet as economic, social, and ideological forces converge to cement a patronage alliance, they diminish counsel's capacity for unbiased normative decisions. Under such circumstances, professionals may undervalue moral claims by non-clients, whose interests are directly implicated but inadequately represented in a given transaction. In addition, a reluctance to offend existing or potential clientele can play a dominant role in shaping an attorney's entire practice. Although the idealized vision of legal practice has always comprehended a serious commitment to law reform, attorneys have had difficulty becoming drum majors for

---

and unjustified role in consummating fraudulent financial agreements. Legal fees for the period in question totaled almost 7.9 million dollars, accounting for 60–70% of the law firm's revenues. *Report of the Trustee Concerning Fraud and Other Misconduct in the Management of the Affairs of the Debtor* (U.S. Bankr. S.D.N.Y. 1982).

131. RUESCHEMEYER, *supra* note 1, at 24; Heinz & Laumann, *The Legal Profession: Allied Interests, Professional Roles and Social Hierarchies,* 76 MICH. L. REV. 1111 (1978); Rueschemeyer, *Doctors and Lawyers: A Comment on the Theory of the Professions,* 11 CAN. REV. SOC. & ANTHR. 17, 23–25 (1964).

132. *See, e.g.,* R. PAVALKO, SOCIOLOGY OF OCCUPATIONS AND PROFESSIONS 101 (1971). Much psychological data confirm that individuals confronting conflicts tend to discount or reconstrue the less pressing concern to reduce dissonance. *See* L. FESTINGER, A THEORY OF COGNITIVE DISSONANCE (1957). *Cf.* Aronson, *The Theory of Cognitive Dissonance: A Current Perspective,* in COGNITIVE THEORIES IN SOCIAL PSYCHOLOGY: PAPER FROM ADVANCES IN EXPERIMENTAL SOCIAL PSYCHOLOGY 181 (L. Berkowitz ed. 1978).

133. Nelson, *supra* note 125, at 537.

justice where current or future client interests are at issue.[134] Similarly, while the bar's ethical codes have traditionally proclaimed an obligation to defend the unpopular, establishment lawyers have invoked that mandate more often to justify representing the disreputable wealthy than the discreditable indigent.[135] Though there have been many notable exceptions, the mainstream bar has generally avoided social pariahs with shallow pockets. To cite only the most obvious examples, almost all prominent practitioners declined loyalty cases during the McCarthy era; the profession, in Felix Frankfurter's phrase, gave a "miserable account of itself."[136] The southern bar's record on race cases was of a similar quality throughout much of this century, and the list of less celebrated recent illustrations is easily extended.[137]

That history reflects a mix of formal policy and informal accommodation. Many attorneys explicitly attempt, particularly in their pro bono practice, to avoid all "positional conflicts," that is, all matters that might prove adverse to an existing client's interest.[138] Other attorneys decline or fail vigorously to pursue claims in part because such action could jeopardize their standing with

---

134. Green, *ABA as Trade Association*, in VERDICTS ON LAWYERS, *supra* note 3, at 19; *see also* note 173 *infra*.

135. Krash, *Professional Responsibility to Clients and the Public Interest: Is There a Conflict?*, 55 CHI. B. REC. 31 (1974). When justifying its zealous representation of corporate clients interested in blocking health and safety regulations, the Washington bar makes frequent analogy to the defense of violent felons. As one Covington & Burling litigator responded to a hostile law student, "Would you represent Sirhan Sirhan?" M. GREEN, THE OTHER GOVERNMENT 279 (1975) (quoting Thomas Austern).

136. AUERBACH, *supra* note 3, at 254 (quoting Felix Frankfurter); *see also* Pollitt, *Counsel for the Unpopular Cause: The 'Hazard of Being Undone,'* 43 N.C.L. REV. 9, 9–14, 17–22 (1964).

In summarizing the record of the Association of the Bar of the City of New York, its historian noted that lawyers "who had the courage" to take loyalty cases during the McCarthy era "had not the stature; and of the few who had the stature, apparently not one had the courage." G.W. MARTIN, CAUSES AND CONFLICTS 277 (1970).

137. *See, e.g.*, Pollitt, *supra* note 136.

138. *See* Krash, *supra* note 135, at 45 (Most firms' pro bono policies reflect desire "not to step on the toes of their clients' important interests. [Firms] want to avoid economic conflicts or conflicts which would put them in a situation where they could be said to be disloyal to their clients."); Smith, *Empires of Paper*, TEX. MONTHLY, Nov. 1973, at 53, 100–02 (quoting Leon Jaworski: "How would a client who pays us a retainer react if he found that one of our boys was sitting on the other side . . . ?"); *see also* notes 139, 160 *infra*; Hullman, *Conflicts Disqualifications Caused Persisting Headaches*, Legal Times of Wash., May 5, 1980, at 88, col. 3 (relevant facts regarding potential positional conflicts include importance of client to the firm).

the business community.[139]

In a variety of circumstances, the patronage structure of legal practice reinforces partisan norms while compromising their normative premises. Although lawyers have long occupied an elevated status in American society, their perch has always been precarious. To a considerable extent, attorneys' rise in stature has been "built upon the foundation of their increased dependency."[140]

B. *Professional Values and Organizational Constraints*

The institutional structures of contemporary practice impose further restraints on professional autonomy. Growing numbers of lawyers work within organizations that increasingly resemble their clientele.[141] To varying degrees, these organizations display attributes that Max Weber associated with bureaucracies: fixed jurisdictional areas, generally ordered by rules; allocation of duties to those with specialized training; firmly ordered systems of hierarchy; and an ethos mandating institutional loyalty.[142] Those structures mesh poorly with ethical traditions that assume individual moral autonomy and commitment to professional, rather than organizational, objectives. While employees vary considerably in their accommodations of competing personal, professional, and bureaucratic values, certain common tensions are apparent.[143]

139. Macauley, *Lawyers and Consumer Protection,* 14 LAW & SOC'Y REV. 115, 136–41 (1979); *see also* W. HURST, THE GROWTH OF AMERICAN LAW 372–73 (1950) (discussing influence of business on lawyers in the nineteenth century).

140. Konefsky, *Introduction* to *The Papers of Daniel Webster,* at xxxix (A. Konefsky & A. King eds. 1982). For an account of the origins of this status, see M. LARSON, THE RISE OF PROFESSIONALISM: A SOCIOLOGICAL ANAYLSIS (1977).

141. Over one-third of the profession, including a majority of recent entrants, now works for private firms, and the scale of those institutions is increasing substantially. In 1959, only 37 firms had over 50 lawyers; 20 years later there were 200 such firms employing 22,000 attorneys. Nat'l L.J., Oct. 1, 1979, at 28–35; *id.*, Oct. 8, 1979, at 30–35. Approximately 13% of the profession now works in firms of over 20 lawyers. CURRAN, *supra* note 5. For analysis of the growth in scale of law firms see Galanter, *Mega-Law and Megalawyering in the United States,* in THE SOCIOLOGY OF THE PROFESSIONS: LAWYERS, DOCTORS AND OTHERS 152 (R. Dingwell & P. Lewis eds. 1983).

142. FROM MAX WEBER: ESSAYS IN SOCIOLOGY 196–99, 240 (H. Gerth & C.W. Mills trans. & eds. 1962).

143. *See* PAVALKO, *supra* note 132, at 190–92; Hall, *Professionalization and Bureaucratization,* 33 AM. SOC. REV. 92 (1968); Scott, *Professional Bureaucracies—Areas of Conflict,* in PROFESSIONALIZATION 265, 268–276 (H. Vollmer & D. Mills eds. 1966); Dribble, *Occupations and Ideologies,* 68 AM. J. SOC. 299 (1972). *See generally* A. DOWNS, INSIDE BUREAUCRACY (1967).

An obvious source of conflict is the competitive and hierarchical structure of much legal practice. For example, to maximize profits, law firms have generally organized in pyramid form, and have often kept the number of partners as low as recruitment and retention needs permit.[144] Promotion ratios differ, but surveys of major metropolitan areas indicate that anywhere from one-half to four-fifths of associates will not become members of the firm they initially enter.[145] Although no systematic information has been compiled concerning the number of attorneys who are formally or informally rejected, there often remains considerable competition for the salary, security, and status that partnership entails. While other legal practice settings may lack such intense up-or-out pressure, most have some form of competitive status distinctions. Of course, not all considerations influencing personal reputation and advancement will be equally subject to competition.[146] Nonetheless, at least two important factors are somewhat amenable to individual control: productivity and collegiality. Competition in these areas may compromise a broad range of personal and professional values.

While pressures to produce spring from a variety of causes, economic concerns undoubtedly rank high among them. Although preoccupation with profit is scarcely a recent phenomenon, it has become more overt. During much of the profession's early history, lawyers were expected at least to appear aloof from wordly concerns. Medieval traditions cast lawyers as missionaries of justice rather than mercenaries for hire, although it was appropriate for grateful litigants, like rescued maidens, to bestow some favor on their benefactors. Still, an "undue eagerness" for fees was not only deemed indelicate, but even provided grounds for disbarment.[147] Current mores are otherwise. Lawyers' obsessive

144. Nelson, *Practice and Privilege: Social Change and the Structure of the Large Law Firms*, 1981 AM. B. FOUND. RESEARCH J. 95, 126.

145. *Legal Scene*, Legal Times, Aug. 8, 1983, at 37–39 (New York: 20%; Washington D.C.: 28%; Los Angeles: 53%). These figures include voluntary departures, some of which are doubtless influenced by assessments of the likelihood of becoming a partner.

146. Success may turn in part on associates' race, sex, or ethnic backgrounds; their past achievements, family connections, or affinity for particular work; the fortuity of their assignments; and the employing firms' growth patterns. SMIGEL, *supra* note 10, at 96–98, 107–08; J. STEWART, THE PARTNERS 260, 295–96 (1983); R. SWAINE, THE CRAVATH FIRM AND ITS PREDECESSORS, 1819–1948 (1948); R. Nadelson, *The Pursuit of Partnership*, JURIS DR., June 1975, at 21–38.

147. W. FORSYTH, THE HISTORY OF LAWYERS 365 (1975). During the age of chivalry, professional norms encouraged the illusion that the strong (lawyers) would assist the weak (clients) in pursuit of justice without the lure of earthly recompense. Teschner,

pursuit of billable hours is sufficiently notorious to require little elaboration here. Folklore abounds with examples, some perhaps apocryphal, such as the Wall Street associate who recently managed, by exploiting time changes on a transcontinental flight, to bill more than 24 hours in one day.[148]

The pressures of productivity can generate various normative conflicts, many of which typically escape classification as "ethical" problems. From a personal vantage, the profit imperatives of large firm practice can be difficult to reconcile with meaningful family or pro bono commitments. Ervin Smigel's study of firms in the fifties revealed numerous examples of partnerships "lost on the New Haven railroad"; associates struggling to juggle late assignments and suburban home lives often mismanaged both. Nor have the pressures abated significantly. The norm for associates is over 1700 billable hours per year, and in large metropolitan areas is significantly higher.[149] Certain specialties, particularly litigation, impose additional demands due to erratic hours and protracted travel.[150] In a subtle, incremental fashion, the daily pressures of practice may finesse competing normative concerns. The Puritan ethic run amuck accounts in part for the homogeneity of law firm leadership. Female attorneys continue to assume a disproportionate share of domestic and child-rearing responsibilities that mesh poorly with the profit objectives of most private sector employers.[151] Some clients and colleagues

---

Lawyer Morality, GEO. WASH. L. REV. 789, 800 (1970). For descriptions of British etiquette concerning fees, see J. READER, PROFESSIONAL MEN: THE RISE OF THE PROFESSIONAL CLASS IN 18TH CENTURY ENGLAND 37 (1966) (discussing the pretense that gentlemen did not ask other gentlemen to pay for professional services); *see also* R. MEGARRY, LAWYERS AND LITIGANTS IN ENGLAND 57–60 (1962).

148. STEWART, *supra* note 146, at 70; *see also* M. MAYER, THE LAWYERS 330 (1966) (quoting Cravath, Swaine & Moore senior partner who denied that associates were overworked since "there wasn't a light on when I left at two this morning"). For Swaine's views on long hours, see Swaine, *Impact of Big Business on the Profession, An Answer to Critics of the Modern Bar*, 25 A.B.A. J. 89, 168 (1949).

149. *1982 Survey of Law Firm Economics*, 23 LAW OFF. ECON. & MGMT. 354 (1982). At Cravath, Swaine & Moore, associates billed an average of 2100 hours in 1981. AM. LAW., Mar. 1983, at 49.

150. New York lawyers involved in the Chrysler refinancing spent seven-day work weeks in the office for a substantial period. STEWART, *supra* note 146, at 223. One lawyer working on the IBM litigation joked that his children had forgotten his name and others acknowledged comparable sacrifices. *See id.* at 87, 211, 223.

151. *See generally* C. EPSTEIN, WOMEN IN LAW 206–12 (1981); note 152 *infra*. For example, a survey of Stanford law students and employers interviewing at Stanford Law School revealed that only one-fifth of the firms had any policies or experience with paternity leaves, while two-thirds had maternity leave poliices or experiences. Project, *Law*

resist part-time lawyers;[152] this resistance, together with other attitudinal and demographic factors, helps account for women's continued absence from firm partnership. A recent national survey of some 150 large firms revealed that only 8.3% of their attorneys were women partners.[153] Similarly, those with strong commitments to pro bono service often find their employing institutions more willing to praise than subsidize such efforts.[154] By choice or necessity, many lawyers with noncompetitive orientations or strong commitments to family or nonprofit pursuits drift out of firm hierarchies, leaving management composed largely of those who accept revenue-maximizing priorities. That selection process perpetuates a culture well insulated from alternative values.

Moreover, profit orientations threaten professional as well as personal commitments. Too often, neither clients nor legal institutions are well-served by the priorities that this ethos generates. The hourly fee structure of most private practice encourages production of any services for which parties are willing and able to pay. Contingent fee alternatives can create incentives to settle or

---

Firms and Lawyers with Children: An Empirical Analysis of Family/Work Conflict, 34 STAN. L. REV. 1263, 1268, 1273 (1982). Among law students, only 10% of males, but 57% of females, considered an employer's policies relating to family/work conflict to be an important factor in job choice. *Id.* at 1297. For general accounts of working women's asymmetrical share of family responsibilities, see, e.g., J. BERNARD, WOMEN, WIVES AND MOTHERS: VALUES AND OPTIONS 219–20 (1975); R. RAPPAPORT & R. RAPPAPORT, DUAL CAREER FAMILIES REEXAMINED 354–58 (1976).

152. *See, e.g.*, STEWART, *supra* note 146, at 70 (quoting Carroll Bumpers, Chairman of the Board, Greyhound) ("It really bothers me that my lawyer is going home to be with his family while [a Cravath partner] is figuring out how to kick the shit out of me.").

It is common for prominent women attorneys to return to work a week after their children are born and to refrain from acknowledging family commitments in a work context for fear their reliability under pressure will be doubted. *See* Bruck, *The Impeccable Carla Hills*, AM. LAW., Apr. 1983, at 84–87; Brill, *The Women Problem*, AM. LAW., Feb. 1983, at 9–10; *see also* Sylvester, *How Firms Cope With Motherhood*, Nat'l L.J., Nov. 7, 1983, at 1 (citing, *inter alia*, a recent Los Angeles survey finding inadequate maternity and child-rearing policies among most firms). *See generally* EPSTEIN, *supra* note 151.

153. Nat'l L.J., Dec. 20, 1982. Of those firms' 10,674 lawyers, 1,658 (15.5%) are women. Although women comprise 21% of the associates at the nation's 50 largest law firms, they represent only 2.8% of the partners at those firms. Project, *supra* note 151, at n.5; *see also* Burke & Johnson, *Women on the Way Up*, Nat'l L.J., Apr. 20, 1981, at 1, col. 1. Overall, approximately 20% of women in law firms are partners as compared with 44% of men. *See* Winter, *Survey: Women Work Harder, Are Paid Less, but They're Happy*, 69 A.B.A. J. 1384, 1385 (1983). Although women's relatively recent entrance into the profession accounts for a large measure of the disparity between male and female partnership status, the ratios at large firms suggest that other factors are also at work. *See generally* sources cited in note 152 *supra*.

154. *See* notes 71, 72 *supra*.

litigate where the client's interests dictate otherwise.[155] Depending on the press of other business, attorneys who charge by the hour may face considerable temptation to prolong certain tasks or to retain matters that they cannot complete efficiently. And clients are not always well situated to monitor counsels' performance.

As innumerable commentators have noted, these profit dynamics are a major cause of procedural incivilities.[156] At worst, among lawyers short on clients, legal strategies may reflect intentional meter-running, an abuse that litigators frequently report observing (though never committing).[157] At best, much paper churning and procedural shadow-boxing suggests a more subtle mixture of adversarial psychology, financial incentives, and perfectionist anxieties. As the level of dispute escalates, attorneys' own desires for retribution, if not victory, may skew their decisionmaking. After an educational process emphasizing the importance of preparation and indeterminacy of outcomes, most lawyers will prefer to leave no stone unturned, provided, of course, they can charge by the stone. For an attorney anxious to avoid overlooking details and underbilling hours, more is always better. For the client and the courts, the calculus may be otherwise.

Collegial as well as profit dynamics play a forceful role in reshaping values. Any organizational setting encourages team

155. D. ROSENTHAL, LAWYERS AND CLIENT: WHO'S IN CHARGE 96–100 (1974); Schwartz & Mitchell, *An Economic Analysis of the Contingent Fee in Personal Injury Litigation*, 22 STAN. L. REV. 1125 (1970).

156. As one prominent practitioner has explained,

> Pretrial is, economically, a dream come true for lawyers. Any number of idle hands can be put to work; the work can be scheduled to suit the firm's convenience and no experience is necessary to shuffle the papers—a new associate can be put immediately on the job . . . . If the Code were turned on its head to ban compensation based on hourly charges in litigated cases between two private parties, it is likely that the pretrial phase of each case would be cleaned up as fast as counsel could respectably push it to its conclusion.

J. BARTLETT, THE LAW BUSINESS: A TIRED MONOPOLY 75–76 (1982). For comparable diagnoses, see Rosenberg & King, *Curbing Discovery Abuse in Civil Litigation: Enough is Enough*, 1981 B.Y.U. L. REV. 579, 582 (attributing discovery problems in part to practices of billing by the hour); Rosenberg, *Discovery Abuse*, 7 LITIGATION 8, 9 (Spring 1981).

Pretrial harrassment can also serve client interests by exhausting the patience and resources of the opposing party. *See 1980 Amendments to the Federal Rules of Civil Procedure*, 446 U.S. 995, 997–1000 (1980) (Powell J., dissenting); Brazil, *Civil Discovery: Lawyers' Views of Its Effectiveness, Its Principal Problems and Abuses*, 1980 AM. B. FOUND. RESEARCH J. 787, 797–99; Miller, *supra* note 28.

157. *See* Brazil, *supra* note 156.

players, and the incentives in certain practice contexts can be particularly acute. Where legal partnerships entail lifetime commitments, senior attorneys will understandably be wary of advancing anyone who might have difficulty "getting along" with colleagues or clients.[158] The result has often been a stifling level of homogeneity. In the 1950s, associates of major New York firms were under considerable pressure not only to appear with the correct wardrobe and newspaper, but also to suppress views on morally freighted issues and to accept any work assignment, no matter how personally distasteful.[159]

Although such pressures to conform have clearly lessened over time, certain fundamental sources of tension remain. Few lawyers can fully set their own agendas. To be sure, attorneys have a range of subtle avoidance techniques that afford some insulation from objectionable matters. But diplomatic escape may not always be possible, or junior lawyers may have little reason to decline an assignment until well into a case, when they acquire substantial information regarding client or collegial conduct. Yet this is precisely the point at which disengagement becomes most difficult. As the sunk costs and social ties involved in the professional relationship increase, the taste for moral reflection or confrontation may diminish.

Even at the outset of representation, the pressures to accept an assignment may be substantial. Passing public moral judgment on a senior attorney's choice of clients or tactics is not always a costless enterprise, and the uncertainty of consequences increases the risk. For example, in Nelson's survey of Chicago law firms, only 16% of attorneys recalled ever refusing a case.[160] Although three-quarters of these lawyers also reported never having encountered an assignment contrary to their values, that absence of dissonance may itself be partly attributable to colle-

158. SMIGEL, *supra* note 10, at 332. *See generally* Smith, *supra* note 138; Stewart, *supra* note 11.

159. SMIGEL, *supra* note 10, at 320–22, 327. Junior attorneys who wore the wrong color combinations, forgot their garters, or got into "messy" social situations (*i.e.*, divorce), were also subject to considerable opprobrium. *Id.* at 317–19. It was unusual for an associate to decline an assignment for any reason other than that he was too busy. *Id.* at 321.

160. Nelson, *supra* note 125, at n.32; *see also* Reed, *The Lawyer-Client: A Managed Relationship?*, in THE SOCIAL DIMENSIONS OF WORK 420, 423 (C. Bryant ed. 1972) (finding that a random sample of Florida practitioners refused few cases for moral reasons; the matters most often rejected as "unpopular" were malpractice suits against fellow attorneys and representation of civil rights demonstrators).

gial socialization and post hoc rationalization.[161]

As attorneys ascend an organization's pecking order, the constraints on autonomy change in form, but not necessarily in degree. While the ability to decline cases or challenge conduct is greater, the costs of exit from either the institution or from particular relationships are higher. Power, status, and profit shares may often depend on alliances that constrict moral choice. As they increase in seniority, attorneys often lose job mobility and develop greater social, psychological and economic investment in their organization. Such attachments can yield normative as well as physical inertia.

This acculturation process is compounded by other aspects of legal practice. Attorneys working on fragmented aspects of a substantial matter may feel little accountability for its ultimate consequences. In hierarchical organizations, the sources of rationalization multiply; lack of experience, certitude, or formal responsibility supply ready grounds for suspending judgment. And once habituated to collegial norms and practices, a lawyer may have increased difficulty viewing them through moral lenses. Wayne Brazil's study of discovery abuse among Chicago litigators illustrates one such form of acculturation. Many attorneys who reported no problems in discovery procedures also indicated that they were encountering significant delays and evasiveness in obtaining information.[162] After a point, individuals can easily lose capacity to evaluate professionally accepted practices by publicly acceptable standards. Even where other attorneys' misconduct is evident, the costs of informing have generally appeared excessive; few lawyers have been willing to incur the risks and stigma of tattling, particularly since meaningful sanctions rarely result, and any benefits will redound largely to others.[163]

161. Nelson, *supra* note 125, at n.32. While self-selection may account for much of the absence of angst, other more subtle processes may also be at work. Theories of counter-attitudinal advocacy posit that individuals whose position calls for expression of values at odds with their own will often modify their original convictions. Chemerinsky, *Protecting Lawyers from their Profession: Redefining the Lawyer's Role*, 5 J. LEGAL PROF. 32 (1980). For accounts of individuals' tendency to reduce dissonance by reconstruing the less salient sources of pressure, see note 132 *supra*. Among lawyers, this tendency may take the form of radical skepticism toward morally relevant facts, or of resort to an adversarial ideology that would legitimate almost any client's representation. *See* text accompanying notes 55–124 *infra*. For an example of the potency of professional acculturation, see note 162 *supra* and accompanying text.

162. Brazil, *supra* note 156.

163. *See* note 168 *infra* and accompanying text.

These socialization processes are by no means unique to legal practice. Rather, they reflect a more general cultural ethos that discourages collective responsibility. Whistle blowers are unwelcome in most work environments, even where the societal costs of silence are acute. For example, studies of the medical profession reveal that doctors avoid confronting a colleague or reporting his incompetence except in the most exceptional and repeated instances of deviance.[164] Many public and private sector employees have remained comparably tight-lipped.[165]

The issue, however, is not whether legal practice is uniquely inhospitable to moral oversight, but how it can be made more accommodating. And the difficulty is that prevailing incentive structures contribute little to that enterprise. Competitive and patronage pressures converge to provoke and suppress normative conflict. For those experiencing dissonance, the path of least resistance is migration to other environments. Through that process, a variant of Gresham's Law asserts itself, leaving those most in need of ethical confrontation least likely to receive it. These instititutional forces are legitimized by an ideological construct that casts prudential interests as societal imperatives. To effect significant changes in professional mores will require a reconceptualization of the structures of legal practice and the ideologies that sustain them.

III. ALTERNATIVES

This is not the occasion for a full-scale blueprint of alternative formulations of professional roles. That is a larger enterprise and one approached with some wariness. As with any such reconstructive effort, it is not entirely clear what level of analysis would be instructive. A utopian vision will seem irrelevant to those coping with the current system, while incremental ameliorative strategies could further legitimate without fundamentally

164. *See, e.g.*, C. BOSK, FORGIVE AND REMEMBER 158–92 (1979); E. FREIDSON, DOCTORING TOGETHER 125–37 (1975); E. FREIDSON, PROFESSIONAL DOMINANCE: THE SOCIAL STRUCTURE OF MEDICAL CARE (1970).

165. *See generally* J. EDSALL, SCIENTIFIC FREEDOM AND RESPONSIBILITY (1972); D. EWING, FREEDOM INSIDE THE ORGANIZATION (1977); C. PETERS & T. BRANCH, BLOWING THE WHISTLE (1972); ROHR, ETHICS FOR BUREAUCRATS (1978); Bok, *Blowing the Whistle*, in PUBLIC DUTIES: THE MORAL OBLIGATIONS OF GOVERNMENT OFFICIALS (Fleishman, Liebman, & Moore eds. 1981); WHISTLE BLOWING (R. Nader, P. Petkas, & K. Blackwell eds. 1972); WHISTLE BLOWING: LOYALTY AND DISSENT IN THE CORPORATION (A. Weston ed. 1981).

altering existing norms. Yet it is precisely this concern, together with scholars' commendable sense of humility or less commendable distaste for vulnerability, that blunts serious reconceptual efforts. Until professionals are willing to engage in constitutive projects, the existing order wins by default. "But what's the alternative?" will remain the stopping point in too many discussions of legal ethics.

Thus the following analysis seeks to raise possibilities that may broaden the agenda of future dialogue. None of these proposals aspires to effect mystical transformations in professional mores. Absent major social reconstruction, the likelihood and impact of adjustments in legal practice remain quite limited. Still, pending the millenium, the task is to attempt a realignment of structural and ideological forces that will give professional ideals greater content in daily practice.

Meaningful renovation will require a broad range of adjustments. The problems examined in the preceding discussion stem from different roots and call for quite different responses. Some arise from the institutional dynamics of private practice, its adversarial framework, or bar regulatory structures. Related difficulties stem from a professional role definition that unduly confines moral vision. None of these difficulties are readily resolved. By drawing, however, on those normative traditions that have inspired lawyers' greatest societal contributions, the bar can seek modes of legal practice that more clearly exemplify its aspirations to a public calling.

A. *Structures*

The structural barriers to radical renovation appear substantial. As long as lawyers' services are allocated through market methods, problems of patronage and adversarial imbalance are inevitable. Yet it is difficult to conceive of radically different allocative structures that would unquestionably prove preferable, let alone politically feasible. Any sweeping entitlement system would raise enormous administrative difficulties. Legal need is a highly elastic, socially contingent concept. And since taxpayers are unlikely to tolerate subsidies for every conceivable claim or instance of disparate legal resources, some limiting principles appear essential. But who should design those principles, and by what criteria, remain highly problematic. A state-controlled system of access would create obvious potential for abuse: What passes for justice under authoritarian regimes does not commend itself for export. Nor does a judicially determined system of entitlements leap out as the obvious resolution. Courts are not particularly well-situated to determine the appropriate level of societal investment in legal process, as compared with other competing collective needs. Judges' professional acculturation cannot help but skew such assessments.

Yet to note these limitations is not to acquiesce in the existing distribution of legal services. Under current allocative structures, the higher socio-economic sectors are awash with lawyers, while the lower sectors are barely serviced. Within that system, any attempt to make justice less dependent on ability to pay is likely to be a progressive step. To that end, commentators have offered an array of partial correctives. Proposals to increase the legal leverage of underrepresented interests have included the creation of alternative forms of dispute resolution, the relaxation of anticompetitive constraints, and the expansion of subsidies through attorneys' fee awards, public grants, and private pro bono contributions.[166] Some, though insufficient, attention has focused on reconstructing adversarial processes and reward structures to render them less contingent on the capacities of counsel and the depths of clients' pockets. For example, European civil law procedures, which employ neutral as well as partisan modes of investigation, and which reduce financial incentives for pretrial abuses, might be adapted for some purposes in American tribunals.[167] Alternative fee structures, financial penalties, and cost-shifting arrangements also merit more serious consideration. The objective should be to minimize not only adversarial imbalances but also the societal waste that accompanies protracted belligerence among equals. If we are committed to retaining market-based structures of dispute resolution, we

---

166. *See, e.g., Reducing the Cost of Legal Services: Possible Approaches by the Federal Government, Report to the Subcomm. on Representation of Citizen Interests (Now Merged with the Subcomm. on Const. Rts.) of the Senate Comm. on the Judiciary*, 94th Cong., 1st Sess. (1975); M. FRANKEL, JUSTICE: COMMODITY OR PUBLIC SERVICE (1978); Johnson, Bice, Bloch, Drew, Kantor, Schwartz, & Tucker, *Access to Justice in the United States: The Economic Barriers and Some Promising Solutions*, in 2 ACCESS TO JUSTICE 913 (M. Cappelletti & B. Garth eds. 1978); Rhode, *supra* note 79.

167. Luban, *supra* note 20, at 93; LUBAN, THE SOURCES OF LEGAL ETHICS: A GERMAN-AMERICAN COMPARISON OF LAWYERS' PROFESSIONAL DUTIES 30 (1983); Frankel, *From Private Fights Toward Public Justice*, 51 N.Y.U. L. REV. 516, 525 (1976); Zeidler, *Evaluation of the Adversary System: As Comparison, Some Remarks on the Investigatory System of Procedure*, 55 AUSTL. L.J. 390 (1981).

must become more seriously committed to redressing market failures.

Moreover, the bar's demonstrated parochialism in enacting and enforcing ethical standards argues strongly for vesting regulatory power in a more balanced forum. Disciplinary sanctions are highly infrequent, and practitioners in established firms seem particularly immune from oversight.[168] As the most recent revisions of the *Model Rules* suggest, bar-designed ethical codes tend to mandate only those minimal responsibilities that most lawyers would willingly see enforced through disciplinary or civil liability proceedings. Yet as attorneys readily concede in other contexts, disinterested evaluation is impossible where the decisionmaker's status, income, and self-image turn on the result. An independent regulatory body, with broad-based representation, would be less susceptible to the fraternal concerns and tunnel vision that have impeded professional governance. Such an institution, by implementing stiffer standards and sanctions, might provide a way out of the current prisoner's dilemma. Under prevailing practices, competitive disadvantages too often attend socially desirable conduct.

Perhaps the only generalization applicable to all such proposals is that their design and evaluation ought not to rest solely under bar control.[169] A common danger is that minor tinkering

---

168. *See* NATIONAL CENTER FOR PROFESSIONAL RESPONSIBILITY, STATISTICAL REPORT REGARDING PUBLIC DISCIPLINE OF LAWYERS BY DISCIPLINARY AGENCIES, 1975–1978 (1979) (of 30,836 complaints triggering investigation in 1978, only 2.3% resulted in public sanctions and 0.3% in disbarment; 97% of consumer complaints in surveyed states were dismissed without investigation); Martyn, *Lawyer Competence and Lawyer Discipline: Beyond the Bar?*, 69 GEO. L.J. 705, 723 (1981); Steele & Nimmer, *Lawyers, Clients and Professional Regulation*, 1976 AM. B. FOUND. RESEARCH J. 917, 982.

The low incidence of disciplinary sanctions against lawyers in established firms is frequently acknowledged. *See* P. STERN, LAWYERS ON TRIAL 88–89 (1980); Garbus & Seligman, *Sanctions and Disbarment: They Sit in Judgment*, in VERDICTS ON LAWYERS, *supra* note 3, at 47 (quoting Orville Shell, past president of the Association of the Bar of the City of New York). To generate some empirical data on point, I, with the assistance of Stanford Law student Melanie Bronfman, surveyed all disbarments, suspensions, and public censures between October 1981, and December 1982, in three major jurisdictions which publish such information—Illinois, California, and the District of Columbia. Of the 125 attorneys for whom Martindale Hubbel information was available (59% of the total sample), none came from firms of more than seven attorneys; 81% percent were solo practitioners. Of the cited offenses, one-third involved neglect. Most of the other offenses concerned commingling (17%), misrepresentation (17%), and criminal convictions (16%).

169. *See* Rhode, *Why the ABA Bothers: A Functional Perspective on Professional Codes*, 59 TEX. L. REV. 689 (1981).

will simply paper over major structural deficiencies. Certain delegalization strategies may create a caste system of justice, token lay representation on regulatory bodies could mask professionally expedient choices, and minor improvements in access to legal assistance could deflect attention from the substantial imbalances that remain.[170] Given the organized bar's demonstrated distaste for altering adversarial or allocative structures, responsibility for reform cannot rest solely under professional tutelage.

That should not, however, be taken to minimize lawyers' role in the reconstructive enterprise. They are most intimately acquainted with abuses of the legal system and with the probable impact of reform. And they are the most plausible constituencies to seek certain forms of change. More humane and morally reflective working environments than those currently available to most practitioners are clearly feasible. Greater sensitivity to the consequences of representation, less competitive up-or-out promotion policies, fewer rigid status hierarchies, and increased options for those with competing family or public commitments, are not irreconcilable with reasonably remunerative legal practice.[171]

The task remaining is not simply to decry existing institutional arrangements; that form of discourse, as Montesquieu noted, may convince everyone and affect no one. The task is also to focus on structural alternatives, and to enlist individuals from varied vocational and academic backgrounds in that enterprise. Moreover, to a considerable extent, the possibility and effect of any institutional reforms will depend on changes in professional ideology. Without some tempering of the bar's attachment to regulatory autonomy and partisan mores, the barriers to pro-

170. Richard Abel argues that delegalization and informal modes of dispute resolution are a means of legitimating the inaccessibility of formal judicial protections. Abel, *The Contradictions of Informal Justice*, in 1 THE POLITICS OF INFORMAL JUSTICE 267 (R. Abel ed. 1982); *see also* J. AUERBACH, JUSTICE WITHOUT LAW? 115–47 (1983); Abel, *Socializing the Legal Profession: Can Redistributing Lawyers' Services Achieve Social Justice?*, 1 LAW & POL'Y Q. 5 (1979). For discussions of the cosmetic potential of token lay representation, see S. TISHER, L. BERNABE, & M. GREEN, BRINGING THE BAR TO JUSTICE: A COMPARATIVE STUDY OF SIX BAR ASSOCIATIONS 158–59 (1977); Rhode, *supra* note 79, at 58; Trubeck, *Public Advocacy: Administrative Government and the Representation of Diffuse Interests*, in 3 ACCESS TO JUSTICE 445 (M. Cappelletti & B. Garth eds. 1979); Wolfram, *Barriers to Effective Public Participation in Regulation of the Legal Profession*, 62 MINN. L. REV. 619, 642–43 (1978).

171. Many smaller and some larger partnerships have successfully institutionalized such arrangements. For example, Latham & Watkins, which in 1981 had 213 attorneys, democratic governance structures, and a high partner/associate ratio, also had the highest income per lawyer of large firms according to a 1981 Price Waterhouse survey. Stevenson, *Latham & Watkin's Youth in Management*, AM. LAW., Sept. 1983, Supp. at 6–10.

gress could prove impenetrable. Given the inherent limitations of any structural approach to adversarial imbalances and institutional pressures, much will depend on how attorneys perceive their societal responsibilities.

B. *Ideology*

As the preceding analysis suggests, current ideology miscasts professional expedients as moral necessities. Only through more candid acknowledgement of their divergence is a socially defensible accommodation likely to emerge. Neither formalist nor individualist justifications can sustain partisanship norms in their current, largely unqualified, scope. And a retreat into role fails even to confront, let alone resolve, the moral difficulties it raises.

A more ethically reflective form of legal practice will require different ideological foundations. Lawyers must assume personal moral responsibility for the consequences of their professional actions. At its most fundamental level, such a redefinition abandons Durkheim's faith in the ability of insular occupational communities to generate adequate normative visions. Given the tendency of parochial interests to skew ethical judgment, the justification for conduct must be tested by conventional techniques of moral reasoning. The rationale for professional action cannot depend on a reflexive retreat to role, which denies the need for reflection at the very point when reflection becomes most essential. To be convincing, professional judgments must withstand scrutiny by individuals seeking consistent, disinterested, and generalizable foundations for conduct.[172] Counsel should no longer categorically deflect responsibility to some governmental or private agent acting in a presumptively ideal regulatory system. Rather, attorneys must confront the consequences of their decisions against a realistic social backdrop, in which wealth,

---

172. *See* K. Baier, Moral Point of View: A Rational Basis of Ethics 107 (1958); P. Singer, Practical Ethics 10–11 (1979). The demand for universal principles of conduct forms the core of a variety of normative approaches ranging from Kant's reliance on the categorical imperative, Rawl's invocation of a "veil of ignorance," and Habermas' "ideal speech" situation. For a discussion of the parallels between Rawls' and Kant's approach, see Rawls, *Kantean Constructivism in Moral Theory*, 1980 J. Phil. 515. Habermas' framework classifies legitimate principles as those on which free and equal agents would agree after unlimited discussion in uncoerced circumstances. J. Habermas, *supra* note 114; *see* R. Geuss, The Idea of a Critical Theory: Habermas and the Frankfurt School 64–66 (1981).

power, and information are unevenly distributed, and democratic, adversarial, and market processes function imperfectly.

This reformulation of role in no sense contemplates that lawyers will become personally accountable for every adverse consequence that flows from client representation or collegial relationships. Under conventional ethical theories, moral responsibility depends on a variety of factors, including the significance of harm and the agent's degree of involvement, knowledge, and capacity to affect action. Nor does it follow that counsel must endorse a client's every objective or course of conduct before providing representation. Whether particular forms of assistance are defensible depends not only on the specific acts involved but also on their social and economic contexts, and on the principles at issue.

What distinguishes this framework is the insistence on an ethical predicate—on an attempt to justify systematically the consequences of professional action. That clients may have a "legal right" to engage in certain conduct or to invoke a particular procedure is conclusive neither of their moral right, nor of the appropriateness of counsel's aid. Lawyers cannot simply retreat to role in the face of larger normative questions. To cite only the most obvious example, attorneys who delay safety standards they would privately endorse, or who knowingly assist the distribution of products with significant undisclosed risks, are implicated in the human suffering that may result.[173] So too, in more common circumstances, counsel cannot continually resolve doubts in

173. For examples of corporate conduct that might have raised such questions, see M. GREEN, THE OTHER GOVERNMENT: THE UNSEEN POWER OF WASHINGTON LAWYERS 147–62, 273 (1975) (tobacco companies' resistance to placing warnings on cigarette packages); Elliott & Beauchamp, *Marketing Infant Formula*, in CASE STUDIES IN BUSINESS, SOCIETY, AND ETHICS, *supra* note 95, at 221 (distribution of formula to third world mothers incapable of safe use); Riley, *The Challenge of the New Lawyers: Public Interest and Private Clients*, 38 GEO. WASH. L. REV. 547, 563–65, 567–68 (1970) (marketing of Panalba); Hinds, *Report Questions Lilly Role on Drug*, N.Y. Times, Dec. 4, 1982, at 8, col. 1 (marketing of Oraflex); R. Rosen, Lawyers in Corporate Decisionmaking 102–03 (1984) (unpublished dissertation) (sales of chemicals with inadequate safety testing); *see also Competitive Problems in the Drug Industry, Part 6: Hearings Before the Subcomm. on Monopoly of the Senate Select Comm. on Small Business*, 90th Cong., 1st and 2d Sess. 2167–68, 2170–71, 2178–79, 2222–25 (1968) (distribution of chloromycetin for ten years without explicit warnings of potentially fatal side effects); M. VELASQUEZ, BUSINESS ETHICS: CONCEPTS AND CASES 37–42 (1982) (discussing Johns-Manville's continued distribution of asbestos without warning labels despite evidence of hazards); *see also* Zimmerer & Preston, *Plasma International*, in CASE STUDIES IN BUSINESS, SOCIETY, AND ETHICS, *supra* note 95, at 157 (blood purchased from poor Africans at $0.15 a pint resold for $25.00 a pint to disaster victims in third world countries).

favor of those with a history of revising reality, misplacing discoverable documents, or operating on the fringes of fraud. In effect, the attorney can no longer avoid responsibility for allowing client interests to trump all competing concerns.

Nor is the maxim "judge not" an adequate response to collegial misconduct. Participation in a common enterprise entails some accountability for the practices it tolerates and the values it engenders. Attorneys who blink at over-billing, misrepresentation, or procedural belligerence thereby legitimate forms of professional acculturation that are debilitating for practitioners as well as litigants.

To argue for individual assumption of responsibility, however, only begins analysis. The more difficult issue, which remains a highly contextual determination, is what that responsibility entails. Relevant factors include not only the magnitude and likelihood of potential harm and the attorney's capacity to affect it, but also the personal and social costs that corrective action would impose. Among those costs, the possible loss of client or collegial trust is entitled to weight. In some instances, an individual's dependency, or a lawyer's limited leverage and access to information, may make suspension of judgment the only practicable course.

So too, some limits to self-sacrifice demand recognition. To suggest that individuals are morally obligated to respond to every harmful consequence that they could potentially influence would impose paralyzing burdens. Conventional ethical theories do not posit that all humanity should live as Trappist monks, devote every discretionary dollar to famine relief, or pontificate at every possible opportunity.[174] Without some concept of supererogation, some "cut off for heroism," no significant realm of individual autonomy would survive.[175] If it is to provide useful normative guidance, a reformulation of professional role must remain sensitive to normal human capacities for altruism, as well as the psychological and economic pressures of legal practice.

Yet while professional ideology need not mandate canoniza-

174. J. FISHKIN, THE LIMITS OF OBLIGATION 78 (1982); C. FRIED, RIGHT AND WRONG 31–32 (1978); *see also* Feinberg, *Supererogation and Rules*, in DOING AND DESERVING: ESSAYS IN THE THEORY OF RESPONSIBILITY 3–7, 16 (J. Feinberg ed. 1970); Urmson, *Saints and Heroes*, in MORAL CONCEPTS 60, 70–73 (J. Feinberg ed. 1969). *See generally* T. NAGEL, THE POSSIBILITY OF ALTRUISM (1970).

175. FISHKIN, *supra* note 174, at 7–9, 170; *see also* Fried, *supra* note 59, at 1068–71.

tion, neither should it legitimate abdication. For lawyers to do for profit what they would deplore as decisionmakers cannot be justified simply by recourse to role. Under some circumstances, an attorney may be more able or inclined to make principled judgments than other individuals involved in the process. Depending on the context, the only acceptable course may be a refusal to aid, or an affirmative attempt to prevent asocial conduct.

Such contexts cannot, of course, be identified in the abstract. Yet to concede that decisionmaking will necessarily prove situational is not to embrace a totally relativist perspective. Given the heterogeneity of the American legal profession, collective adherence to some codified standards remains essential. Deference to established precepts such as honesty, fair dealing, or procedural civility is a necessary means of minimizing temptation and keeping normative ambiguity within reasonable bounds. Exhaustive evaluation of every act would yield a numbing moral perplexity.[176] Given the inevitable human tendency to skew ethical assessments in expedient directions, an *a priori* commitment to certain principles remains appropriate. What is critical, however, is that those precepts be themselves morally defensible in a world of regulatory imperfections and gross socioeconomic disparities. By that standard, as earlier discussion suggests, one cannot convincingly generate a principle that all clients are entitled to either unqualified confidentiality or the maximum neutral partisanship they can afford.

That is by no means to imply that systematic reflection will yield determinate resolutions, or to overlook the limitations of moral methodology noted earlier. But this concession need not invite paralysis. There may be no uncontrovertible answers, but there are better and worse ways of thinking about the questions. Thus, the attempt must be to create more channels within which serious normative dialogue can occur. Individuals must have ongoing occasions to confront ethical issues, to test their perceptions openly, and to raise concerns about client or collegial practices without professional risk. For that purpose, far more is needed than bar association advisory opinions or law firm conflict-of-interest committees. Rather, the profession must fashion structures within and across employing institutions that can en-

176. L. FULLER, THE LAW IN QUEST OF ITSELF 37 (1940); T. GREY, THE LEGAL ENFORCEMENT OF MORALITY 27 (1983).

courage collective support and a sense of responsibility for normative concerns.

C. *Socialization*

To proselytize for heightened moral sensitivity is always easier than to instill it. Any effort to jar professional consciousness will require a far greater investment of energies than either the organized bar or law schools have been willing to marshall. Apart from an infrequent inspirational address, most practitioners' formal exposure to ethical arguments has centered on the ABA's code of conduct. This text has formed the centerpiece of professional responsibility case law, bar examinations, and law school instruction. Yet for purposes of socialization, such official standards are demonstrably inadequate. As the principal draftsman for the *Model Rules* readily concedes, the final product is a code of conduct, but hardly of ethics.[177]

The danger is that it will pass for ethics. In that respect, the bar's insistence on minimal, enforceable standards may have missed the mark. No such code, however well-drafted, can definitively respond to the complexities of professional practice. Where a threat of formal sanctions is remote, as is generally the case in professional contexts, the most significant function of official codes will be symbolic and pedagogic. To the limited extent that codified precepts can affect behavior, an exclusively minimalist approach could prove misguided. The consequence may be socialization to the lowest common denominator of conduct that a highly self-interested constituency will publicly brand as deviant.

That prospect has rarely been confronted. Rather, the bar's primary concern (apart from disquiet at the prospect of any civil liability) has been that rules that set their moral sights too high would be routinely violated, thereby compromising the entire regulatory structure.[178] Standards out of step with frequent practices would encourage indulgence of individual lapses, and undermine commitment to code enforcement. Yet that logic has

177. Hazard, *Legal Ethics: Legal Rules and Professional Aspirations*, 30 CLEV. ST. L. REV. 571, 572–73 (1981).

178. White, *Machiavelli and the Bar: Ethical Limitations on Lying in Negotiations*, 1980 AM. B. FOUND. RESEARCH J. 926, 937–38; Luban (I–38), 2 ABA COMMENTS, *supra* note 24; *see also* N.Y. ST. B.A. REP., *supra* note 108, at 25 (recommending that the Commission on Evaluation of Professional Standards separate rules that are aspirational from those that are essential, in order to promote less rigidity and overregulation).

not been persuasive in many legal contexts, and its validity for professional regulation is not intuitively obvious. A high percentage of Americans habitually violate a variety of laws, most notably traffic and income tax statutes. No evidence indicates that society regards such laws as illegitimate or that innumerable violations have weakened support for enforcement of other criminal prohibitions. It scarcely can be assumed that some practitioners' evasion of rules regarding candor and civility would lead inevitably to benign attitudes toward commingling. Nor is it apparent that the most effective way of promoting ethical conduct within the profession generally is to delete provisions that a substantial minority would find onerous in some instances.

To be sure, a codified catechism that aspires too far beyond the capacity of "ordinary men on ordinary occasions" may seem irrelevant to the resolution of practical problems.[179] The ABA is not a plausible source for a Sermon on the Mount. Undoubtedly, the infusions of cant in the prior code have undermined its credibility in professional socialization. But it by no means follows that a less platitudinous document, expressing certain core notions of honest and equitable conduct, would generate comparable cynicism simply because many practitioners would occasionally stray from the prescribed path.

At the least, a more ethically rigorous code might perform a salutary function by sensitizing professionals to the full normative dimensions of their choices. Whatever the likelihood of enforcement, a collective affirmation of professional values may have some effect simply by supplying, or removing, one source of rationalization for dubious conduct. It becomes marginally easier to justify the use of substantially misleading evidence when the profession's formal norms decline to direct otherwise.[180] Conversely, standards pitched at a more demanding level can reinforce the lawyer who would prefer the ethical course but is reluctant to appear sanctimonious. Some of the now deleted *Model Rules* provisions, such as those regarding disclosure or pro bono obligations, might have served that purpose. At a minimum, such mandates could have afforded protective coloration to attorneys willing to do good but hesitant to cast themselves as do-

179. Urmson, *supra* note 174, at 60, 70; *see also* Rawls, *supra* note 172, at 76–80, 145.

180. *See* note 40 *supra* and accompanying text.

gooders.[181]

The difficulty with the current code manque—and the cases, commentary, and course instruction that parse it—is that together they may fortify the illusion that the profession's moral responsibilities have been adequately identified. Countering that perception and the passivity that contemporary institutional structures and incentives foster will require a different acculturalization process. Not only must control of bar codification be moved to less partisan quarters, but professional responsibility instruction must be reconceived. Legal ethics should be taught as ethics, not as etiquette or statutory exegesis. Law school courses and bar examinations that demand rote memorization of official standards merely trivialize the subject matter. For some years, the prevailing wisdom has been that one can pass most states' multiple choice ethics tests by resolving all doubts in favor of the second most ethical course of conduct. Whether or not apocryphal, such folklore points up the essential sterility of the exercise. Yet most jurisdictions rely on these exams to certify the "integrity" not only of initial applicants, but often of wayward attorneys as well. The assumption remains that mechanical recitation of bar standards can affect conduct ranging from Watergate abuses to commingling funds.[182]

Many law schools' professional responsibility efforts have been similarly misdirected. The role of such instruction should not, of course, be overstated. Even the most narcissistic academic might have difficulty with Harlan Fisk Stone's assertion that the character of the law school determines the character of the legal profession. Situational pressures and childhood socializations play a far greater role in resolving personal ethical issues than any transitory experience in academic institutions.[183] Yet

181. Respondents in one survey of 1,200 business executives indicated that the primary function of industry ethical codes would be to fortify individuals who would like to "refuse an unethical request impersonally." Brenner & Molander, *Is the Ethics of Business Changing?*, HARV. BUS. REV., Jan.–Feb. 1977, at 57, 68.

182. A survey of recent California cases reveals that disciplined attorneys are routinely required to pass the Professional Responsibility Examination as a condition of return to practice. *See* note 168 *supra*; *see, e.g.*, Segretti v. State Bar, 15 Cal. 3d 878, 544 P.2d 929, 126 Cal. Rptr. 793 (1976) (attorney suspended for five years because of his involvement in President Nixon's reelection campaign was required, as a condition of resuming practice, to pass the Professional Responsibility Examination).

183. Stone, *The Public Influence of the Bar*, 48 HARV. L. REV. 1, 14 (1934). *Cf.* Burger, *The Role of the Law School in the Teaching of Legal Ethics and Professional Responsibility*, 29 CLEV. ST. L. REV. 377, 388 (1980) (discussing Stone's proposition). The vast majority of

law school instruction clearly has some effect in instilling professional norms and attitudes, and is credited by substantial numbers of practitioners with assisting later resolution of ethical issues.[184] That is sufficient reason to attempt less arid curricular offerings than those currently in place.

Despite a steady succession of conferences, commissions, and commentaries lamenting the state of professional responsibility instruction, there have been too few advances beyond the "general piffle" that historically has dominated the field.[185] The "pervasive method" of instruction, in which ethical dialogue infuses the entire curriculum, has almost never proved pervasive. Instead, professional responsibility has usually been confined to a single, generally mandatory, course, rarely exceeding two class hours per week.[186] Such offerings have often vacillated between casuistic expositions of the ABA's text and desultory discussions of the instructor's anecdotal experiences. On the whole, students have perceived such courses as insufficiently rigorous and inattentive both to techniques of ethical decision-making and to issues regarding lawyers' societal role.[187]

---

surveyed Chicago attorneys believed that childhood training and peer influence were the most important factors in resolving ethical issues. *See* F. ZEMANS & V. ROSENBLUM, THE MAKING OF A PUBLIC PROFESSION 171–72 (1981); *see also* J. CARLIN, LAWYER'S ETHICS: A SURVEY OF THE NEW YORK CITY BAR 7–8, 61, 66, 84, 116–17 (1966) (finding situational pressures had substantial effect on New York lawyers' resolution of ethical issues). *See generally* LAW, JUSTICE AND THE INDIVIDUAL IN SOCIETY: PSYCHOLOGICAL AND LEGAL ISSUES (J. Tapp & F. Levine eds. 1977).

184. ZEMANS & ROSENBLUM, *supra* note 183, at 176 (finding that 42% of surveyed Chicago attorneys gave law school training some credit in helping to resolve issues of professional responsibility); *see also* Thielenn, *The Influence of the Law School Experience on the Professional Ethics of Law Students*, 21 J. LEGAL EDUC. 587 (1969) (discussing effects of law school in practitioners' resolution of ethical issues).

185. Costigan, *The Teaching of Legal Ethics*, 4 AM. L. SCH. REV. 290, 295 (1917) (Costigan was the author of the first casebook on legal ethics); *see* Clark, *Teaching Professional Ethics*, 12 SAN DIEGO L. REV. 249, 260 (1975). For a catalogue of the various commissions and commentary, see sources cited in Burger, *supra* note 183, at 391 n.68; M. KELLY, LEGAL ETHICS AND LEGAL EDUCATION 65–69 (1980); *see also* AMERICAN BAR ASSOCIATION, LAW SCHOOLS AND PROFESSIONAL EDUCATION: REPORT AND RECOMMENDATIONS OF THE SPECIAL COMMITTEE FOR A STUDY OF LEGAL EDUCATION OF THE AMERICAN BAR ASSOCIATION 7–13 (1980).

186. Goldberg, *1977 National Survey on Current Methods of Teaching Professional Responsibility in American Law Schools*, in TEACHING PROFESSIONAL RESPONSIBILITY: MATERIALS AND PROCEEDINGS FROM THE NATIONAL CONFERENCE 21, 22–23, 36 (P. Keenan ed. 1979) (finding that in approximately one-third of accredited law schools, professional responsibility was a one credit-hour course; in only 10% was it three or four credit-hours).

187. ZEMANS & ROSENBLUM, *supra* note 184, at 180; Pipkin, *Law School Instruction in*

A less impoverished approach to professional responsibility education will require more searching philosophical and sociological analysis. Given many law students' minimal background in ethics, some systematic exposure to the forms of moral reasoning is essential. In conjunction with that instruction, examination of normative issues through clinical experience, case histories, or well-crafted hypothetical problems, may sensitize students to ethical concerns before they enter practice and encounter pressures for particular resolutions. For example, forcing individuals to articulate principled justifications—that is, disinterested, consistent, and generalizable rationales—for common discovery practices or professional self-governance might prove a useful counterweight to subsequent socialization. Of equal importance is more sustained academic attention to the bureaucratic dynamics of various practice contexts and to the bar's history, regulation, and societal role. To avoid reinforcing a kind of dispirited cynicism, inquiry must focus not only on critiques, but also on alternative concepts of professional practice.

If that educational process is to have significant impact, it must extend well beyond the confines of any single course. Professional responsibility should in actuality, rather than in aspiration, be a pervasive part of legal education.[188] Even more important, it should become a matter of ongoing professional concern. Practitioners must begin to perceive ethical dilemmas not as aberrant, episodic events, but rather as the inevitable consequences of bureaucratic pressures, adversarial frameworks, and social inequalities. While not all souls are available for salvation, one can help fortify those genuinely in doubt by realigning socialization structures. To that end, the profession must create more opportunities for normative interchange not only in law schools, but also in law firms and bar associations. Affiliative structures within and across various legal subcultures could provide forums for greater professional introspection.

A central objective of all these proposals should be to counter the habituation to existing practices that has preempted alternative visions. G. K. Chesterton once suggested that abuses in the legal system arose not because individuals were "wicked" or

Professional Responsibility: A Curricular Paradox, 1979 AM. B. FOUND. RESEARCH J. 247, 257–59, 272–75.

188. Wasserstrom, *Legal Education and the Good Lawyer*, J. LEGAL EDUC. 155, 159–60 (1984).

"stupid" but simply because they had "gotten used to it."[189] Countering that acculturation process will require more sustained attention to its institutional and ideological foundations.

189. Chesterton, *The Twelve Men*, in TREMENDOUS TRIFLES 57–58 (1955).

[13]

BOOK REVIEWS

LAWYERS AS MONOPOLISTS, ARISTOCRATS, AND ENTREPRENEURS

LAWYERS IN SOCIETY. Edited by Richard L. Abel[1] and Philip S.C. Lewis.[2] Berkeley: University of California Press. 3 volumes.
Volume 1: THE COMMON LAW WORLD. 1988. Pp. xii, 399. $42.50.
Volume 2: THE CIVIL LAW WORLD. 1988. Pp. xiv, 459. $45.00.
Volume 3: COMPARATIVE THEORIES. 1989. Pp. xiii, 555. $40.00.

Reviewed by Mark J. Osiel[3]

I. INTRODUCTION

Two very different conceptions of the lawyer compete for ascendancy within Western society. Each claims both to describe the essential social role of the attorney and to prescribe the ethical standards entailed by it. The first conception enshrines the moral ideal of public service and conceives of the bar association — the expression of collective power — primarily as a necessary check against capitulation by individual attorneys in the face of antisocial demands by clients. The second conception upholds the ideal of loyalty to clients as the touchstone of professional ethics and conceives of bar associations as vigorous advocates for the legitimate interests of lawyers in a pluralistic society of freely competing interest groups. In recent years the leading scholarship on the legal profession in America has been primarily concerned with the normative defense of the first conception, the lawyer as "independent professional."[4] The prolific writings of Professor Richard Abel, however, constitute a sustained defense of the empirical resilience of the second conception. Although simplistic

---

[1] Professor of Law, University of California, Los Angeles.

[2] Senior Research Fellow, All Souls College, Oxford University.

[3] Associate Professor of Law, Tulane University. This Review was written while the author was a fellow in the Program in Ethics and the Professions at Harvard University. The author expresses his thanks for their comments to his co-fellows in the Program, as well as to Professors Sissela Bok, Mary Ann Glendon, Terence Halliday, Kenneth Kress, Michael Powell, Paul Starr, John Stick, Dennis Thompson, and Eliza Willis.

[4] *See, e.g.*, D. LUBAN, LAWYERS AND JUSTICE: AN ETHICAL STUDY (1988); Gordon, *The Independence of Lawyers*, 68 B.U.L. REV. 1 (1988); Simon, *Ethical Discretion in Lawyering*, 101 HARV. L. REV. 1083 (1988).

summaries appear to set the two scholarly agendas at odds, each actually stands to learn much from the other, as this Review argues.

Over the past decade, Abel has authored and edited several books and more than a dozen scholarly articles pursuing a single theme. The legal profession throughout Western society, Abel contends, underwent a transformation beginning in the mid-nineteenth century by which it reestablished its power upon new and more modern foundations. The Western world, increasingly distrustful of irrational bases of social privilege, began to require that attorneys provide reasoned defense of their prominence before the more skeptical public of a democratic society. The growth of the free market, moreover, subjected attorneys to increasingly competitive markets for their services. The bar met these twin challenges with a single response, Abel argues: it sought to reform the training, admission, and regulation of its members in a way that would also limit the growth of their numbers and the extent of overt competition between them. Lawyers sought to modernize the bases of their social advantage through, in a word, monopolization.

The volumes under review here develop this argument through an examination of the history and social structure of the bar in eighteen countries.[5] After introductions by the editors, the first two volumes, which address the common law and civil law "worlds" respectively, attempt to defend Abel's explanation of why lawyers have come to enjoy the degree of wealth and status that they do.[6] These essays describe in detail the legal profession's organization and composition, its methods of training and admitting new members, and its control over its markets throughout the world.[7] The third volume contains ten essays of a more theoretical nature. Although they cover a wide variety of themes, none seeks directly to refute Abel's argument.

Social scientists who study the legal profession have engaged Abel's developing argument respectfully and often sympathetically. But

---

[5] The comparative nature and geographical reach of these volumes is intended as a corrective to the parochialism of most sociologies of the legal profession, which have constructed theoretical accounts of the profession in "modern society" exclusively from the historical experience of England and the United States. *See, e.g.*, M. LARSON, THE RISE OF PROFESSIONALISM: A SOCIOLOGICAL ANALYSIS at xvii–xviii (1977) (arguing that professionalism "should present its 'purer' features in the Anglo-Saxon countries").

[6] Co-editor Philip Lewis does not appear to share Abel's near-exclusive preoccupation with the bar's efforts at market control, to judge from the short pieces in these volumes authored solely by him (vol. 1, pp. 1–22; vol. 3, pp. 27–79). Because Lewis does not offer an alternative framework, however, this Review focuses on Abel's theoretical argument.

[7] The impulse to examine how other legal systems handle a particular problem has often arisen from a perception of our own failure adequately to address it. Although this perception does not guide the comparative inquiry of Abel and his collaborators, the present Review indicates how the evidence they gather suggests that European societies have had greater success in securing ethical accountability from the bar — an experience from which the United States may have something to learn.

within the legal academy, Abel's prolific writings on lawyers will not be well received. Some will dismiss his work as merely an academic restatement of public antipathy toward the clubbish appearance of the organized bar in the more respectable form of a sociological "theory." Others will be skeptical of Abel's insistence on attributing the bar's anticompetitive practices, and the social advantages that these seem to have yielded, to the very nature of modern capitalism (vol. 1, p. 23). That attribution would appear to preclude effective reform of the bar without radical transformation, if not outright elimination, of the market system as a whole — an objective apparently favored by Abel,[8] but hardly anyone else.

This latter aspect of Abel's work has made many unwilling to engage his argument on its own terms. But his argument should be rejected only if it is mistaken, not because it suggests a more pessimistic prognosis for reform than most would prefer. Since many of the most illuminating insights of modern social thought (from Marx to Freud and Weber) have not been morally "uplifting," it is surely wrong to fault a provocative sociological argument for its refusal to put on a happy face. Effective schemes for changing the world require adequate interpretations of how it works, and adequate explanations of the social world have been fewer and harder to come by than appealing schemes for its reform. Developing such explanations demands a willingness to hold normative concerns in abeyance long enough to seek understanding of the workings of some unsavory aspects of social life. This is recognized by the most perceptive recent critics of American legal ethics, who acknowledge that their proposals for reform must be informed by a sociological analysis of the obstacles reform is likely to encounter and of the means by which these obstacles might be circumvented — an analysis that such critics readily confess to lacking.[9]

This Review maintains that current proposals for the reform of legal ethics cry out for sociological inquiry into the institutional underpinnings of ethical conduct. The results of such an inquiry would be helpful in anticipating the consequences of alternative reforms and hence in choosing among them. Abel's work significantly contributes to this task. By viewing the history of the organized bar as driven by the cravings of its members for wealth and status, Abel focuses upon just such structural roadblocks to reform. Even Abel's least sympathetic readers, after all, generally accept the empirical core of his argument — the claims that any excessive wealth enjoyed by lawyers must be due largely to the uncompetitive character of the

---

[8] *See, e.g.*, Abel, *A Socialist Approach to Risk*, 41 MD. L. REV. 695 (1982).

[9] *See* D. LUBAN, *supra* note 4, at xix; Gordon, *supra* note 4, at 30–31; Simon, *supra* note 4, at 1144. Hence Gordon stresses the need for a "historical sociology" of the "conditions of professional independence." Gordon, *supra* note 4, at 30.

markets for legal services and that such uncompetitiveness must have its historical roots in the bar's collective ability to impede entry to that market and to restrict competition among practitioners. This Review argues, however, that the monopolistic impulses of lawyers have played a relatively minor role in determining their wealth, status, and power in modern Western societies.

At first glance Abel's analysis of the anti-competitive practices of the organized bar may appear indistinguishable from the position long defended by neoclassical economists,[10] but Abel's differs significantly in two respects. First, unlike neoclassical economists, he does not view deregulation as a satisfactory solution to the problems of professional monopoly. Second, neoclassical economists contend that the monopolistic tendencies of professions will be progressively suppressed as capitalist principles of economic organization are adopted. Abel believes, by contrast, that capitalism and professional monopoly necessarily grow apace: the more that capitalist principles are adopted, the more powerful the countervailing political impetus toward professional monopoly. According to Abel, the competitive rigors of commercial society during the nineteenth century undermined the wealth and status that European lawyers had traditionally derived from their associations with landed and noncommercial interests.[11] With industrialization, land ceased to provide the principal source of wealth and status within society, and lawyers were compelled to compete in the marketplace — amongst themselves and with related occupations — for the business generated by modern commerce. Like many others, lawyers thus sought refuge from the more severe forms of market discipline.

Professionalization, in Abel's view, was a means to this end. It offered lawyers a way to protect their privileged status, but on terms compatible with the greater rationalism and democratic sensibilities of a modern industrial society. Lawyers could retain their social prominence only by improving their competence through increased educational requirements that imparted mastery of a more systematized body of knowledge. Because this covert monopolization by way of overt modernization represented the bar's response to a more competitive economy and a more democratic polity, such monopolization would have occurred throughout the democratic, capitalist world.

In most Western societies, however, lawyers have either refrained from seeking much monopoly, failed to achieve it when it was sought, lost it soon after it was obtained, won it for reasons wholly unrelated to those suggested by Abel's theory, or used it for ends inconsistent with what Abel views as its primary objective: wealth maximization.

---

[10] *See, e.g.*, M. FRIEDMAN, CAPITALISM AND FREEDOM 137–60 (1962).

[11] *See* Abel, *The Rise of Professionalism*, 6 BRIT. J.L. & SOC. 82, 82–89 (1979).

Lawyers have obtained their greatest wealth and status when they have devised new services and sought out new markets, even if such entrepreneurship initially increased the competition confronted by the bar. The differing social prominence[12] of lawyers in various Western societies is therefore attributable not to the relative success of their respective "projects"[13] of monopolization, but to the differing opportunities presented to them by industrialization during the nineteenth and early twentieth centuries and the differing propensity of national bars to seize such opportunities. Furthermore, the greater social prominence of common lawyers as compared to their civil law counterparts, which Abel and his collaborators demonstrate, can be largely attributed to the contrasting conceptions of legal reasoning and professional authority held by lawyers within the two systems. By reinterpreting Abel's own evidence and modifying his somewhat reductionist theoretical framework, one can develop a more coherent and better-supported understanding of the role of lawyers in Western society.

II. The Ideal of Independent Lawyering

Abel's argument has important implications for a number of current proposals for reform of legal ethics in the United States, particularly those that seek to reinvigorate the "independence" from client objectives on which lawyers have traditionally prided themselves. His analysis permits the inference that the bar's control over the markets for its members' services[14] can facilitate their independence by increasing their bargaining power over clients and potential clients (vol. 1,

---

[12] This term is used here as a shorthand for the wealth, status, and power of a profession, whenever there is no reason to believe that the acquisition of any one of these significantly jeopardizes acquisition of the other two. The term also refers to the scope of the activities within a society to which the expertise of lawyers is considered indispensable and in which lawyers consequently play central roles.

[13] Abel adopts this concept from M. LARSON, cited above in note 5, at 49–52, 104–05, on whose general argument he heavily relies.

[14] *See* R. ABEL, AMERICAN LAWYERS 40–126 (1989). Abel would certainly insist that such market control is at most a necessary condition, not a sufficient one, for the exercise of moral independence. But if market power is even a necessary condition for independent lawyering, Abel's findings on the social determinants of such power may be of greater significance to debates of more general concern than his own theoretical framework, which largely dismisses the independence ideal, permits him to appreciate. *Cf.* R. Gilson, The Devolution of the Legal Profession: A Demand Side Perspective (Feb. 20, 1990) (unpublished manuscript) (on file at the Harvard Law School Library) (arguing that lawyers' market control may have socially beneficial consequences because it increases attorneys' independence from socially retrograde demands by clients). This view is consistent with a longstanding minority position within economics. *See* Schumpeter, *Capitalism and Process of Creative Destruction*, in MONOPOLY POWER AND ECONOMIC PERFORMANCE 19, 31–35 (E. Mansfield ed. 1974) (contending that market control facilitates socially beneficial innovation by freeing business decisionmaking from the excessively short-run focus characteristic of perfectly competitive markets).

pp. 24–28, 189–200; vol. 2, pp. 9–18). But if lawyers have begun to lose control over their markets, as Abel contends, their hopes of exercising this traditional independence from, and restraint upon, their increasingly powerful clients recedes into implausibility; lawyers can only resist the loss of business when there are plenty of potential clients. In an increasingly competitive market even elite attorneys cannot preserve their independence merely through a self-conception as public-spirited "aristocrats" charged with infusing "higher," non-commercial values into a commercial society.[15] Yet it is that aristocratic ideal, democratized to reach beyond its patrician progenitors to a new middle class,[16] upon which contemporary critics of legal ethics seek to build their desired reforms.

To be sure, the ideal of the "independent professional" as public servant haunts the minds of many American lawyers, not just their academic critics.[17] The independent professional displays expert judgment while remaining relatively unspecialized and is thus familiar with the wide range of legal issues into which his clients' diverse endeavors draw him. He cultivates collegiality with professional peers without being diverted from his own life plan. He maintains independence from clients' interests while retaining and enhancing their business. He devotes serious attention to pro bono and periodic public service without enduring economic sacrifice, doing both "good" and "well" while not striving directly to do either. In this conception of the lawyer, practitioners are understood as integral components of a society's legal system who happen to be compensated by private payment, not as part of the market for human services whose services happen to involve interactions with the legal system.[18]

---

[15] On the aristocratic nature and origins of this ideal and its reality in the lives of many American lawyers during the late eighteenth and early nineteenth centuries, see R. FERGUSON, LAW AND LETTERS IN AMERICAN CULTURE 16–20, 66–78 (1984); A. DE TOCQUEVILLE, DEMOCRACY IN AMERICA 263–70 (J. Mayer ed., G. Lawrence trans. 1969) (13th ed. 1850); and Gordon, cited above in note 4, at 14–16.

[16] *See* Gordon, *supra* note 4, at 16 (concluding that "[o]ver the nineteenth century, the ideal [of professional independence] shed its aristocratic origins and became the ideology of a middle class searching for a source of prestige other than landed wealth or success in business"). Although the ideal itself was extensively embraced, it is unclear how far its realization ever reached beyond an elite circle.

[17]

> There are sound reasons to continue pursuing the goal that is implicit in the traditional view of professional life. Both the special privileges incident to membership in the profession and the advantages those privileges give in the necessary task of earning a living are means to a goal that transcends the accumulation of wealth. That goal is public service . . . .

Shapero v. Kentucky Bar Ass'n, 486 U.S. 466, 489 (1988) (O'Connor, J., dissenting).

[18] The continuing need for such independence, so conceived, is advocated in the writings of legal scholars, *see, e.g.*, R. ALEXANDER, P. BROWN & A. COX, THE LAWYER'S PROFESSIONAL INDEPENDENCE: PRESENT THREATS/FUTURE CHALLENGES (1984), moral philosophers, *see, e.g.*, A. GOLDMAN, THE MORAL FOUNDATIONS OF PROFESSIONAL ETHICS 90–137 (1980), and even

By what institutional means is the aristocratic ideal to be reinstated as the governing principle of the profession, and by whom? It seems that it is the intrinsic appeal to lawyers of this revived ideal that is to provide the primary impetus toward the self-transformation of that large majority of the American bar that primarily serves the interests of private business.[19] The cogency and coherence of the reinvigorated ideal, buttressed by the simple satisfaction derived from "doing good," are presumably to power the engines of a veritable revolution in the way that legal services are distributed within American society and in the way that the very purpose of the lawyer is understood. An entire theory of social change lurks implicit within this account: "true" ideas come to prevail within society because their power is intrinsically greater than that of "false" ideas.

The unabashed vulgarity of sociological approaches such as Abel's provides a much-needed corrective to this theory. Abel's "morally impoverished" view of human motivation readily acknowledges the influential and ineradicable role of aspirations to wealth, status, and power in social life. A sociological perspective suggests that if lawyers are to exercise independence from their clientele with a view toward advancing the public good, they must acquire not only morally defensible conceptions of their mission, but also institutional capacities for realizing it — in ways that do not require entirely disinterested motives. These capacities must rest in part on the bargaining power of individual lawyers vis-à-vis clients and potential clients, a power arising (for all but the most elite practitioners) from the collective control of the bar over the market for legal services. It is quixotic to predicate hopes for significant reform upon the capacity of moral philosophy to instill in lawyers an intellectual commitment to an ideal of public accountability that stands in powerful tension with their self-interest.

In contrast with such exclusively normative approaches, sociologists of the legal profession have been concerned with how lawyers have sought to make the realization of this ideal a genuine possibility in their lives.[20] Abel and his colleagues are therefore concerned with whether the attainment of that ideal has become increasingly difficult due to changes in the economics and organization of legal practice.

---

economists, *see, e.g.*, Kaplow & Shavell, *Legal Advice About Information To Present in Litigation: Its Effects and Social Desirability*, 102 HARV. L. REV. 567 (1989); R. Gilson, *supra* note 14.

[19] Roughly half of the work of lawyers in metropolitan Chicago, for example, is devoted to the representation and counseling of corporate clients. Another quarter is devoted to small businesses and the management of personal wealth. Only 18% is concerned with "personal rights." *See* Laumann & Heinz, *The Organization of Lawyers' Work: Size, Intensity, and Co-Practice in the Fields of Law*, AM. B. FOUND. RES. J. 217, 225 (1979).

[20] *See, e.g.*, R. NELSON, PARTNERS WITH POWER: THE SOCIAL TRANSFORMATION OF THE LARGE LAW FIRM (1988); Kagan & Rosen, *On the Social Significance of Large Law Firm Practice*, 37 STAN. L. REV. 399 (1985).

To know whether the traditional ideal retains any plausibility, it is necessary to uncover the social foundations on which it has rested, to inquire whether these foundations have eroded and how they might be reconstructed. The volumes under review help to answer this question with the clues they provide about why the lawyers of some societies acquired much greater independence from the power of large business than did others — and at what cost.

If lawyers in many Western countries were able to achieve crucial elements of the "independent professional" ideal, Abel and his collaborators suggest that they did so by restricting entry to their ranks and creating demand for their services. But during the last generation, Abel maintains, the profession virtually everywhere lost control over the market for its services (vol. 1, pp. 29–36, 65–66, 210; vol. 2, pp. 31–43). The ideal of the independent professional has become increasingly unsustainable as ever-greater proportions of law graduates in most societies have come to work in large formal organizations, public or private, as employers or employees (vol. 1, pp. 50–56, 223–25; vol. 2, pp. 38–40). Material success has required, as never before, that firms be administered increasingly like large businesses, with profound consequences for the human experience of the workplace.[21]

Abel's approach is favorably distinguished by its capacity to address — if not fully to answer — some of the hardest questions that other perspectives persistently evade. For instance, Professors William Simon and Robert Gordon[22] have both proposed strategies by which American attorneys might increase their margin of freedom for exercising independence from the antisocial demands of their clients, thereby infusing the public service ideal into their practice. Simon contends that the independence of lawyers can best be furthered by revising the profession's disciplinary rules to permit individual practitioners to act upon their assessments of the legal merits of their clients' positions, much as if they were judges.[23] But few attorneys could be expected to adhere to the model proposed unless virtually all were compelled to do so — a far more decisive departure from the existing regime than the proposal itself defends. Without such a change, the isolated practitioner would have to engage in public deception, concealing her discretionary practices from her clients.[24] We

---

[21] *See* R. ABEL, *supra* note 14, at 7, 135–39, 214–17; *see also* Gilson & Mnookin, *Sharing Among the Human Capitalists: An Economic Inquiry into the Corporate Law Firm and How Partners Split Profits*, 37 STAN. L. REV. 313, 313 n.1 (1985) (analyzing how the increasingly business-like management of large law firms has contributed to an annual growth rate in the industry of 12%).

[22] *See* Gordon, *supra* note 4; Simon, *supra* note 4.

[23] *See* Simon, *supra* note 4, at 1092–111.

[24] Such concealment would be incompatible with the "publicity principle," which requires that the principles governing the life of public institutions be susceptible to public defense

are therefore required to ask: what institutional changes are necessary to enable the individual attorney to practice in accordance with Simon's model, so that she would neither risk losing all her clients nor be required to deceive them? Simon concedes that the application of his model "depends on changes in the organization and economics of practice."[25] One wonders whether these changes would so extensively alter practice as to diminish the need for individual discretion of the sort proposed.

When social theorists of the past sought reinforcement for professional independence from the antisocial demands of clients, they turned to the professional community of peers as a buttress for collective standards of competence and responsibility.[26] In Simon's account, by contrast, the community of professional peers can offer little assistance. The possibility that independent lawyering by individual practitioners may require certain supports from the professional community and from the obligations it imposes upon members does not receive serious recognition. The most likely reason for this is the argument, closely associated with Abel,[27] that bar associations are hopelessly corrupted by their preoccupation with other, more venal purposes.

Gordon advances upon Simon's work by explicitly locating support for the ideal of independent lawyering within the profession's existing culture and social structure, rather than resting that ideal chiefly upon the good will of individual practitioners.[28] Regarding the profession's culture, he traces the persistence of the public service ideal through a long history of affirmation by leaders of the American bar, from President Lincoln to Justice Brandeis.[29] He thereby establishes its roots within the profession's self-understanding before invoking it for critique and renewal. More important, he identifies several features of the institutional structure of legal practice that create a measure of opportunity for the lawyer to exercise genuine independence, including

---

without becoming self-defeating. *See* E. KANT, *Eternal Peace*, in THE PHILOSOPHY OF KANT 430 (C. Friedrich trans. 1949); J. RAWLS, A THEORY OF JUSTICE 133, 177–82 (1971).

[25] Simon, *supra* note 4, at 1144.

[26] For a recent reformulation of this view, see Haskell, *Professionalism vs. Capitalism: R.H. Tawney, Emile Durkheim, and C.S. Peirce on the Disinterestedness of Professional Communities*, in THE AUTHORITY OF EXPERTS 180 (T. Haskell ed. 1983); *see also* S. FISH, DOING WHAT COMES NATURALLY 230 (1989) (arguing that, contrary to a prevalent view within the Critical Legal Studies Movement, "the alternative to 'conventional beliefs' within a professional community is not 'liberation,' but other conventional beliefs, urged not in a recently cleared space by a recently cleared vision, but in the institutional space that defines both the present shape of things and the possible courses of action by which that shape might be altered").

[27] *See, e.g.*, R. ABEL, THE LEGAL PROFESSION IN ENGLAND AND WALES 305 (1988) ("Professional associations are founded or activated in order to seek or defend material benefits and social status.").

[28] *See* Gordon, *supra* note 4, at 9–30.

[29] *See id.* at 1–10.

"diverse client base," "authority deriving from special contacts," "financial base," and "time."[30] But most of the conditions necessary for independence that Gordon identifies are conspicuously absent from the workplace confronted by the vast majority of American lawyers. The ideal of independence remains within realistic reach only for a small elite — an updated version of the Whig-Federalist, patrician elite from whom that self-understanding arose and whose substantial demise Gordon has so ably documented.[31] Even as to the elite, one is prompted to ask why the existing opportunities for independence that Gordon believes to exist in such abundance are so rarely seized.[32] In contrast, Abel's insistence upon confronting the workaday experience of non-elite lawyers ensures that he does not risk succumbing to wishful thinking, thereby minimizing the perhaps limited possibilities of the "actual" by seeking simultaneously to defend the enduring availability of an ancient "ideal."

The reform of legal ethics favored by Simon and Gordon not only eliminates the bar's obligation to serve client interests in a largely uncompromised fashion, but also threatens the stable association between large private firms and large private corporations that has proven so rewarding for many American lawyers since the turn of the century. It has been the largely unqualified obligations of loyalty to client interests and confidentiality with client information that have enabled the legal profession in the United States to consolidate so close and nonconflictual a relationship with private industry.[33] While the traditional common law rule on attorney-client privilege, for instance, afforded only relatively uncertain protection to many client confidences,[34] lawyers and their business clients sought increasing breadth and stability for this privilege during the late nineteenth century, thereby facilitating consolidation of a closer relationship between the

---

[30] *Id.* at 31–64.

[31] *See* Gordon, *"The Ideal and the Actual in the Law": Fantasies and Practices of New York City Lawyers, 1870-1910*, in THE NEW HIGH PRIESTS: LAWYERS IN POST-CIVIL WAR AMERICA 51 (G. Gawalt ed. 1984) [hereinafter Gordon, *The Ideal*]; Gordon, *Legal Thought and Legal Practice in the Age of American Enterprise, 1870-1920*, in PROFESSIONS AND PROFESSIONAL IDEOLOGIES IN AMERICA 70 (G. Geison ed. 1983) [hereinafter Gordon, *Legal Thought*].

[32] *See* R. NELSON, *supra* note 20, at 258 (indicating that very few attorneys in large firms admit to having ever challenged the morality of client conduct that they did not also believe to be unlawful).

[33] *See* Schudson, *Public, Private, and Professional Lives: The Correspondence of David Dudley Field and Samuel Bowles*, 21 AM. J. LEGAL HIST. 191, 192, 208–09 (1977) (discussing how the emergence of this relationship in the late nineteenth century prompted a redefinition of ethical standards within the American bar in the direction of increased client loyalty and reduced obligations to third parties); *see also* Rheinstein, *Leader Groups in American Law*, 38 U. CHI. L. REV. 687, 690–91 (1971) (describing how the legal advisors of industry and finance developed the law in favor of capitalistic interests).

[34] *See* Hazard, *An Historical Perspective on the Attorney-Client Privilege*, 66 CALIF. L. REV. 1061, 1069–91 (1978).

two than occurred anywhere else in the modern West. Where the ethical rules of conduct set greater limits on the lawyer's duty to protect client loyalty and confidentiality in deference to larger societal and third-party interests,[35] lawyers have not assumed such central roles as representatives of powerful businesses and have garnered a significantly smaller share of national assets. This is because they cannot be as thoroughly trusted to serve client interests with uncompromised fidelity.[36]

The ethical guidelines and professional self-understandings of lawyers evolved in tandem with the composition of their clientele.[37] Else-

[35] *See* M. DAMASKA, THE FACES OF JUSTICE AND STATE AUTHORITY: A COMPARATIVE APPROACH TO THE LEGAL PROCESS 142–44, 174–77 (1986) (contrasting the adversarial ethics of legal systems focused chiefly on dispute resolution with the nonadversarial conception of professional ethics in systems aimed primarily at policy implementation). Greater limits on client loyalty exist, for example, in Germany. *See* D. LUBAN, *supra* note 4, at 97 (indicating that excessive zealousness by German lawyers is limited by official fee structures determining compensation by the amount in issue, not by hours expended or by the results of the dispute); D. RUESCHEMEYER, LAWYERS AND THEIR SOCIETY: A COMPARATIVE STUDY OF THE LEGAL PROFESSION IN GERMANY AND IN THE UNITED STATES 127–29 (1973) (noting the much weaker restrictions on German attorneys than on their American counterparts concerning withdrawal from representation of current clients and the consequently greater independence of German private practitioners from clients who demand socially irresponsible conduct from counsel); Luban, *The Sources of Legal Ethics: A German-American Comparison of Lawyers' Professional Duties*, 48 RABELS ZEITSCHRIFT FÜR AUSLÄNDISCHES UND INTERNATIONALES PRIVATRECHT 245, 266–68 (1984) (observing the opportunities for attorneys' independence from clients created by other nonadversarial features of German civil procedure). The situation is similar in France. *See* E. SULEIMAN, PRIVATE POWER AND CENTRALIZATION IN FRANCE: THE NOTAIRES AND THE STATE 176–79 (1987) (observing the high tolerance for apparent "conflicts" among the interests of parties to a contract, all of whom are often represented by the same *notaire*, and the origins of such tolerance in the *notaires'* status as representative of public interests); Tomlinson, *Nonadversarial Justice: The French Experience*, 42 MD. L. REV. 131 (1983); *see also* Pina, *Systems of Ethical Regulation: An International Comparison*, 1 GEO. J. LEGAL ETHICS 797 (1988) (comparing similarities between the French and Spanish systems in this regard). Limits on client loyalty also exist in England. *See* P. ATIYAH & R. SUMMERS, FORM AND SUBSTANCE IN ANGLO-AMERICAN LAW 367 (1987) (noting the customary refusal of barristers to "coach" supporting witnesses or to discredit opposing witnesses whom they have no reason to believe are lying). The same has been observed of Canadian barristers. *See* M. ORKIN, LEGAL ETHICS 57 (1957).

[36] Hence, the rejection by the ABA House of Delegates of the Kutak Commission's recommendations for increased protection of "whistleblowing" by corporate counsel was influenced, in significant part, by the prediction that such reform would diminish the trust and responsibility that corporate clients are presently prepared to bestow upon their legal representatives. *See A License to Squeal?*, Wall St. J., Feb. 11, 1980, at A18, col. 1 (editorial); *see also* Rhode, *Ethical Perspectives in Legal Practice*, 37 STAN. L. REV. 589, 616 & nn. 97–98 (1985) (citing bar leaders' criticisms of proposals to weaken client confidentiality protections). For a discussion of how attorneys' self-interest is furthered by stringent norms of client loyalty, see Kaplow & Shavell, cited above in note 18, at 599.

[37] The fact of having acquired a business clientele surely created an "elective affinity" for ethical guidelines discouraging lawyerly conduct prejudicial to business interests. Conversely, the gradual transformation of lawyers' ethical standards in the direction of uncompromised client service, and away from the Tocquevillian ideal of civic statesmanship, authorized lawyers to

where in the Western world, where the principal client was the state itself, the lawyer's commitment to the public interest was necessarily built into his commitment to the client's interest. Further, in countries where the principal client has remained the "one-shot" criminal defendant or tort plaintiff, the client has not possessed sufficient bargaining power to condition his attorney's employment on the latter's acceptance of stringent standards of loyalty and confidentiality.

It is no mere oversight that leads Gordon and Simon largely to ignore the questions whether the social and economic underpinnings of "independent" lawyering actually exist or how they might be reestablished. The disinclination to address this question derives from their view that "there is no system"[38] — no fixed set of social and economic arrangements within or against which the lawyer must work. In keeping with the shifting *zeitgeist* of the legal academy, both authors demur from the older sort of root-and-branch criticism in which Abel continues to engage[39] in favor of identifying modest niches within existing institutions that will permit those of good heart to weather tough times.[40] A pragmatic approach to reformation of the legal profession need not deny, however, that certain institutions are more readily susceptible to significant change than others through isolated individual efforts. Nor need a genuinely pragmatic approach to rethinking legal ethics dismiss institutional obstacles to the realization of its ideals as merely "contingent" constrictions on our "political vision" — constrictions that drop like scales from the eyes of those bestowed with enough "social imagination."

Instead, a pragmatic approach would reveal that the structure of the adversary system and the powerful interests it has served are responsible for the insufficient independence from client interests that Simon and Gordon seek to cure and that make the problem so difficult for individuals to solve as individuals. Such a reemphasis on social structure would better acknowledge that the reformed actions we

---

give greater weight to pecuniary considerations in their choice of clients. *See generally* K. SCHEPPELE, LEGAL SECRETS: EQUALITY AND EFFICIENCY IN THE COMMON LAW 5 (1988) (observing how the legal right to keep secrets shapes "large parts of the social world by creating alliances and divisions" and thus often becomes a "tool of power").

38 Gordon, *supra* note 4, at 82; Simon, *Visions of Practice in Legal Thought*, 36 STAN. L. REV. 469, 497 (1984); *cf.* D. BELL, THE CULTURAL CONTRADICTIONS OF CAPITALISM 8–10 (1978) (observing the tendency of classic sociological thought to exaggerate the "systemic" character of modern society).

39 *See, e.g.*, Abel, *Law Without Politics: Legal Aid Under Advanced Capitalism*, 32 UCLA L. REV. 474, 528–34 (1985) (emphasizing the limited ability of state-sponsored legal assistance to advance the interests of poor and minority communities).

40 This prudential motivation is displayed, for instance, in Simon's admission that his preferred model of lawyering, by permitting the moral tempering of clients' avarice to be couched within the terms of existing law, is designed to make the ethical lawyer less "vulnerable both intellectually and practically." Simon, *supra* note 4, at 1114.

advocate for individuals must display some intelligible relationship to reasoned criticism of the institutions of legal practice and the distribution of legal services that we currently have and to reasoned defense of alternative ones.

Against this background of more influential ideas, Abel's perspective reminds us that the reforms we advocate ought to take into account the reasons why current practices came into being and have endured. It also enables him to suggest that the "actual" world of the legal profession for most within it may have come to diverge so profoundly from the historic "ideal" of independent lawyering that efforts to preserve a general belief in the possibility of living in accordance with that ideal cause it to operate primarily as an "ideology."[41] In other words, the maintenance of the ideal now leads, as Abel believes, chiefly to redoubled efforts within individual careers to achieve the ideal within the context of institutions that almost inevitably frustrate it. Lawyers are thereby deflected from addressing the more fundamental problems of such institutions.[42]

Because reformers such as Gordon and Simon wish to preserve the historical ideal of the independent professional as a banner to be carried into current battles,[43] they are reluctant to allow it to become besmirched with the label of ideology.[44] Conversely, because Abel believes lawyers should abandon their illusory hopes of attaining the independence ideal through careers within existing institutional frameworks, he seeks relentlessly to prove its demise as a workplace reality for most lawyers everywhere in the Western world. Because he thinks the traditional ideal now serves chiefly to prevent us from devising better ones, he strives to eradicate the last glimmer of hope among those who still aspire to realize it.[45] Such theoretical rigidity, however, prevents one from considering a more subtle and complex possibility: that the public service ideal of the independent professional functions simultaneously as an ideology, masking unpleasant institutional realities, and as a noble aspiration, prompting successful attempts at piecemeal improvement.

---

[41] Abel views the public service ideal of the independent professional as "ideological" not only because of its putative effect in eliciting public acceptance of lawyers' privileges, but also because it inhibits lawyers whose working conditions do not allow its realization from widening their primary identifications beyond the profession toward other occupational groups whose members labor under similar restrictions. *See* Abel, *supra* note 11, at 95–96. In this regard, Abel draws heavily upon M. LARSON, cited above in note 5, at 236–40.

[42] *See* Abel, *supra* note 11, at 94–96.

[43] *See* Gordon, *supra* note 4, at 68–83; Simon, *supra* note 4, at 1144 (defining the purpose of his scholarship as "redeem[ing] the traditional ideal from a series of jurisprudential mistakes").

[44] To unmask the ideal as ideology is to cut the last link between the present bar and all that has been most commendable in its patrician past.

[45] Thus, Abel gives no more than grudging, perfunctory acknowledgement to the fact that the traditional ideal continues at least occasionally to elicit from lawyers public-spirited efforts to chasten their clients' cupidity.

There are good reasons to examine the realistic opportunities for independence within the working world of non-elite lawyers. Given the prevalence of exaggerated expectations among those who have recently decided to become lawyers,[46] we should promote a realistic assessment of the less elevated features of much legal work and of the limited opportunities for moral autonomy it often presents. Even if the bureaucratic fate that Abel presents as their future may not reduce lawyers to "proletarians,"[47] recognition and discussion of that potential fate should be sufficient to deter many from locking themselves into what they may later view as an "iron cage."[48]

Empirical inquiries such as Abel's can also identify the social conditions under which lawyers have been able to attain the degree of independence from business desired by current advocates of the public servant ideal, with the hope of directing future reforms of the profession toward the reconstruction of these conditions or of their contemporary equivalents. The comparative sociology of the legal profession offers a unique vantage point from which to identify such conditions and hence to contemplate the corresponding reforms. For instance, Simon and Gordon suggest that the viability of the independent lawyering ideal has depended heavily on the willingness of attorneys to forego increased income in favor of the social status accorded to those who have performed public service.[49] The public service ideal would appear to retain some contemporary viability if it could be shown that lawyers, when compelled to choose, have regularly preferred status to wealth. That frequent preference is demonstrated below.[50] Before undertaking that task, however, it is necessary to indicate how Abel's work speaks not simply to normative debates over how to make the profession more publicly accountable, but also to explanatory debates about how lawyers acquired the power, wealth, and status that permit their present unaccountability.

III. Lawyers as Monopolists

A. *Tradition and Modernity in the Legal Profession*

Abel asserts the view, common to most schools of sociological thought, that over the last 150 years the bar was transformed from a

[46] *See* Gillers, *Great Expectations: Conceptions of Lawyers at the Angle of Entry*, 33 J. LEGAL EDUC. 662 (1983).

[47] *See* R. ABEL, *supra* note 14, at 32–33; R. ABEL, *supra* note 27, at 25.

[48] M. WEBER, THE PROTESTANT ETHIC AND THE SPIRIT OF CAPITALISM 181 (T. Parsons trans. 1958) (observing the seemingly inescapable spread of narrow specialization at work within formal bureaucracies and motivated exclusively by extrinsic reward). On the bureaucratization of law firms, see R. NELSON, cited above in note 20, at 205–29; and E. SPANGLER, LAWYERS FOR HIRE: SALARIED PROFESSIONALS AT WORK 65–69 (1986).

[49] *See* Gordon, *supra* note 4, at 41; Simon, *supra* note 4, at 1130.

[50] *See infra* pp. 2027, 2030–31, 2039–45.

"traditional" profession into a "modern" one.[51] A traditional profession identified new recruits through personal networks of kinship and friendship, while a modern profession becomes "a career open to talent." A traditional profession trained new members through apprenticeship; a modern profession transmits the most essential skills through formal education in a university. The skills of a traditional professional reflected craft-like "rules of thumb." Application of such rules was understood to require "practical judgment": perceptiveness in identifying the weightiest features presented by a case, the capacity to devise imaginative responses to these features, and a sense of appropriateness and proportion in choosing among such responses. The rules of competent practice under the traditional model were thus not reducible to rote routine, nor capable of being deduced from abstract theories. By contrast, the skills of the modern professional, Abel contends, derive from a body of knowledge that is rationally defensible, grounded either in scientific research or in theories that are logically coherent and empirically confirmed.[52] While the knowledge of the traditional professional is shrouded in secrecy or celebrated for its impenetrability, that of his modern successor is hailed as "transparent" to public inspection in, for example, university libraries and scholarly journals.

The traditional professional was highly dependent upon and deferential to his clients because the market that he served was limited to the small class of landed nobility.[53] The modern professional enjoys much greater independence from his clients because the broader distribution of societal wealth has greatly increased the effective demand for his services. The modern professional poses risks to clients on account of the genuine power of his expertise and the consequent perils of its incompetent or malevolent exercise. The traditional professional, by contrast, posed risks to clients due to the relative weakness and imprecision of the available knowledge on which he was compelled to rely. The mastery and application of modern forms of knowledge require only the "ordinary" virtues of probity, consci-

---

[51] *See* Abel, *supra* note 11, at 88–89 (contending that "traditional sources of prestige . . . [were] progressively undermined by the rise of the market, compelling professions to find new sources" and that "[t]he project of the nineteenth century professional reformers was to modify each of these sources of prestige, replacing traditional criteria by modern ones, those independent of the market by those dependent on market control"); *see also* M. BLOOMFIELD, AMERICAN LAWYERS IN A CHANGING SOCIETY, 1776–1876, at 137 (1976) (observing that an increasingly technical definition of lawyers' professional role "enabled them to rationalize their elite status in American society on grounds that made some sense even to radical democrats").

[52] Hence modern professionals are said to engage in "[a]ssimilating professional knowledge and training to the characteristics of the scientific model . . . [so as to] defend that body of knowledge against competing paradigms and [to justify] the high status of those who have mastered it." Abel, *supra* note 11, at 87.

[53] *See* R. ABEL, *supra* note 27, at 18; Duman, *The Creation and Diffusion of a Professional Ideology in Nineteenth Century England*, 27 SOC. REV. 113, 115 (1979).

entiousness, and industriousness. But the exercise of traditional forms of practical judgment drew upon more diffuse and extraordinary virtues of "character" that were difficult to detach from the distinctive personality and imaginative range of the individual practitioner. Greater expertise endows the modern professional with more authority to define the nature of his clients' problems and the proper method of their resolution (vol. 3, pp. 492–93). The combination of expertise and independence from clients, however, poses dangers of unaccountability (vol. 3, p. 312), that must be addressed by heightened training and admission standards. Because only professional colleagues can adequately judge the performance of their peers, moreover, modern associations are necessary to promulgate codes of responsible conduct and to serve as the vehicle of their enforcement.

The prestige enjoyed by the traditional professional stemmed from his association with the European landed classes, who assiduously maintained their distance from "trade" and strenuous labor.[54] In contrast, the prestige of the modern professional follows from the respect accorded within contemporary society to reason and science and hence to those whose work draws heavily upon these forms of knowledge. In neither traditional nor modern society has wealth diverged significantly from status. In traditional society, land was the only source of either. In modern society, the successful practice of a learned profession is a major source of both.

Modern history has allegedly witnessed a transformation in the social basis of the bar's power, wealth, and prestige from the traditional to the modern.[55] The debate concerns why these changes came about and what "ulterior" purposes were thereby served. Abel sides with an influential position in this debate, one which understands monopoly rent-seeking to be the principal goal of professionals in all fields.

B. *The Theory of Market Control*

The social transformation of legal professionalism just described was not decreed by the ineluctable dictates of efficiency, science, or reason. It occurred, Abel suggests, as part of an effort by lawyers to organize themselves into powerful associations and to lobby for the right to impose restrictions on entry into their ranks. The other elements of the transformation were chiefly means toward this end.

---

[54] *See* A. MAYER, THE PERSISTENCE OF THE OLD REGIME: EUROPE TO THE GREAT WAR 9–12 (1981).

[55] *See* Abel, *supra* note 11, at 89. This view is shared by sociologists of radically different political persuasions. *See, e.g.*, A. CARR-SAUNDERS & P. WILSON, THE PROFESSIONS 289–97 (1933) (comparing the status of the legal profession before and after the industrial revolution); M. LARSON, *supra* note 5, at 166–77 (describing changes in the legal profession in the United States over the last 150 years).

The systematization of a specialized body of academic knowledge requiring lengthy university education, as well as the institution of bar examinations, contributed to monopoly power by restricting the number of entrants to the profession. Prohibitions against unauthorized practice prevented other occupational groups such as accountants and real estate brokers from encroaching on lawyers' markets. And by prohibiting advertising and the cruder forms of client solicitation, codes of ethics restrained price-cutting by competing firms.[56]

The historical and comparative perspective afforded by these volumes makes it clear that the work lawyers do within any given society is not preordained. Although lawyers may seek to claim certain tasks as uniquely their own, these claims are often disputed by competing occupational groups and rejected by society at large.[57] By obtaining a monopoly over some of the services they offer, however, and by invoking the power of the state against those who trespass upon that monopoly, lawyers can safely secure a sheltered market. The evidence in these volumes suggests that although lawyers in the United States and England exercised powerful control over a segment of the national market for legal services during certain periods, this was neither the principal determinant of lawyers' wealth and status in those societies, nor the primary purpose of modernizing the profession elsewhere.

C. *Lawyers as Monopolists: Two Examples*

How well does Abel's theory of modernization through market control explain the historical record? The only situations in which there seems to be a prima facie case for the theory of market control are the United States between the 1870's and the 1960's and England between the 1840's and the 1940's. The American story is well

---

[56] *See* R. ABEL, *supra* note 14, at 119–22, 142–57; R. ABEL, *supra* note 27, at 30. Abel believes that codes of ethics contribute to lawyers' wealth and status primarily by suggesting their "altruism." The more influential recent critiques of American legal ethics, by contrast, have concentrated on the indefensibility of the codes' decidedly non-altruistic provisions and the tension between code provisions on client loyalty and confidentiality, on the one hand, and attorneys' moral duties to third parties and to society at large, on the other. *See* A. GOLDMAN, *supra* note 18, at 99–101, 110–11, 135–37; D. LUBAN, *supra* note 4, at 185–89; Bok, *Can Lawyers Be Trusted?*, 138 U. PA. L. REV. 913, 913 (1990). It is difficult to see how guarantees of client loyalty and confidentiality against third parties and society at large could be construed as altruistic and hence as motivated by a desire to legitimate the wealth and power of the bar in the public mind.

One may be tempted to dismiss Abel's argument summarily for its refusal to consider the possibility of positive consequences for the quality of legal services resulting from the introduction of formal law school education, public examinations, unauthorized practice prohibitions, and codes of ethics. Although Abel makes no effort to weigh the negative impact of such "reforms" against their presumably positive effects, however limited, the strengths and weaknesses of his argument can best be assessed by asking whether his sociological analysis is accurate on its own terms.

[57] *See* A. ABBOTT, THE SYSTEM OF PROFESSIONS 247–79 (1988).

known[58] and can be understood in terms compatible with Abel's theory. Under the Jacksonian view, which prevailed until very late in the nineteenth century, "anyone with natural genius who hustled could succeed at the bar."[59] As late as the beginning of World War I, not a single American state required attendance at law school as a condition for legal practice. In the late nineteenth and early twentieth centuries, leading lawyers established bar associations that gradually persuaded state legislatures to condition practice on the acquisition of a license. These associations imposed ever more stringent requirements for entry into practice: state-sanctioned bar examinations with declining rates of passage, formal inquiries into the "moral character" of candidates, and graduation from a law school accredited by the bar itself. The method of training new lawyers thus shifted from informal apprenticeships in law offices to formal education in universities. Law schools sought to "modernize" their curricula through the widespread introduction of Christopher Langdell's conceptualist "science."[60]

Bar associations ultimately acquired responsibility for disciplining errant members and began to formulate codes of ethics designed to replace mere etiquette and social custom as the standards by which the conduct of peers would be judged. In the 1920's, bar associations began to bring many claims against members of other occupational groups for "unauthorized practice" (vol. 1, p. 206). The wealth, status, and power of the legal profession grew considerably during this period,[61] as lawyers became the "new high priests" of the gilded age.[62]

Despite the apparent congruence of this history with Abel's theory, however, the modernization of the American bar was driven less by lawyers' desire for monopolistic rents than by their efforts to combat the perceived "commercialization" of the profession. It was the excesses of the corporate bar[63] that partly prompted the formation of the first urban bar association, the Association of the Bar of the City of New York.[64] Early professionalizers did not wish to jettison the traditional view of the lawyer as public statesman, as Abel's theory suggests, but to bridge the widening gap between that conception and the emerging role of lawyers as agents of large-scale business. They

---

[58] *See, e.g.*, J. HURST, THE GROWTH OF AMERICAN LAW: THE LAW MAKERS 313–22 (1950).

[59] Gordon, *Legal Thought*, *supra* note 31, at 86.

[60] *See* Grey, *Langdell's Orthodoxy*, 45 U. PITT. L. REV. 1 (1983); Stevens, *Two Cheers for 1870: The American Law School*, in LAW IN AMERICAN HISTORY 405, 416–41 (D. Fleming & B. Bailyn eds. 1971).

[61] *See* R. ABEL, *supra* note 14, at 158–65.

[62] *See* Gawalt, *Introduction*, in THE NEW HIGH PRIESTS: LAWYERS IN POST-CIVIL WAR AMERICA, *supra* note 31, at i, vii–xiv.

[63] *See* J. AUERBACH, UNEQUAL JUSTICE 40–41 (1976).

[64] On the early history of professional organization within the New York bar, see M POWELL, FROM PATRICIAN TO PROFESSIONAL ELITE at xiv, 6–16 (1988).

sought to reform judicial appointments and particular fields of legal doctrine so as to eliminate the corrupting influences of their own corporate clients.[65] Their aim was to preserve a prominent place for lawyers within the new corporate order, but one that would protect them from corruption. If the American bar reformed its institutional foundations in response to threats from nineteenth century capitalism, as Abel contends, they did so to defend their traditional ideals, not solely their rents.

It is even possible, as some historians contend, that "bar leaders were motivated more by a desire to defend a fading public image of the profession and its public role than by a positive conception of needed changes."[66] The professionalizers' intentions in this regard were consistent with the fact that the self-aggrandizing efforts of the bar never went nearly as far as those of physicians or other groups.[67] Indeed, it may well have been the *absence* of strong professional organizations that permitted the new corporate counsel elite to seize the economic opportunities presented by the advent of large-scale corporate activity, free of the restrictions regularly imposed by similar associations in Europe.[68] Contrary to the assumptions of Abel's theory, both the American and European experiences suggest that the embrace of corporate capitalism did not find unqualified support in strong bar associations.[69]

The efforts of the American bar to upgrade the status of its profession do not comport with a market control theory. To be sure, the

---

[65] On the role of business lawyers in the reform of incorporation statutes and bankruptcy laws, see Gordon, *Legal Thought*, cited above in note 31, at 100–10. On the intention of business lawyers to ground law in a more rational framework, thereby finding a more secure and defensible place for themselves, see Gordon, *The Ideal*, cited above in note 31, at 52–57.

[66] W. HOBSON, THE AMERICAN LEGAL PROFESSION AND THE ORGANIZATIONAL SOCIETY 44 (1986).

[67] According to Hurst:

> [The ABA was not] a pressure group that could show energy, internal discipline, or staff work comparable to the activity of the contemporary spokesmen organizations for industry, commerce, labor or agriculture, ... With few exceptions [lawyers] busied themselves with matters which they took up in isolation from the social context, and matters which were generally of secondary social importance . . . .

J. HURST, *supra* note 58, at 361.

[68] *See* Burrage, *Revolution and the Collective Action of the French, American, and English Legal Professions*, 13 LAW & SOC. INQUIRY 225, 250–52 (1988) (contrasting European and American bar associations and noting the advantages that the absence of strong professional organizations provided for the first generation of American corporate attorneys).

[69] That strong bar associations could have impeded efforts to commercialize legal practice is apparent from the fact that such associations are almost invariably dominated by the "elder statesmen" of the profession, who are generally less inclined to favor this type of change. *See* M. BLOOMFIELD, *supra* note 51, at 150–51 (observing that in the early nineteenth century journeymen practitioners regularly invoked the free market ideal as a rhetorical device with which to attack the noncommercial pretensions of the elder bar); ABA Comm'n on Advertising, Report to the House of Delegates 7 (Feb. 1979) (on file at the Harvard Law School Library) (showing that younger attorneys are more disposed to advertise than older lawyers).

establishment of the first bar associations is sometimes portrayed primarily as an attempt by patrician elites to impose WASP morality on the immigrants who comprised the "ethnic bar,"[70] thereby preserving the social status of the profession in the face of new challenges from a more democratic society. But bar associations faced an irresolvable dilemma whenever they sought to "raise" the moral standards of the ethnic bar. They were compelled to choose between admitting only the elite of the profession,[71] thereby sacrificing any hope of effective influence over the majority of practitioners or, alternatively, admitting so many lawyers[72] that the "moralizing" effect intended by the founders was diluted beyond recognition. Either way, if upgrading the social status of the profession through bar associations was an integral element in the reformers' efforts at modern rationalization, it failed miserably.

The history of reform in American legal education also fails to support Abel's thesis of monopoly rent-seeking. The relocation of legal education from the office to the university and the adoption of Langdell's legal "science" were sponsored not by bar associations but by law professors with concerns very much their own.[73] Langdell's "revolutionary" case method could scarcely be described as singularly reflecting the rational spirit of the modern world, deriving as it does from the casuistical methods of religious law.[74] Moreover, Langdell's view of legal reasoning as the rational systematization of a body of interrelated rules displayed fundamental continuities with traditional methods of Roman law scholarship.[75] In short, contrary to Abel's argument, the American bar did not modernize on the basis of any new universalistic technical principles.[76]

English solicitors took many of the same steps as their American counterparts towards modern professionalization (vol. 1, pp. 23–48).[77]

---

[70] *See* J. AUERBACH, *supra* note 63, at 62–64, 94–101.

[71] This was the policy adopted by the Association of the Bar of the City of New York. *See* M. POWELL, *supra* note 64, at 226–35.

[72] This was the policy adopted by the Chicago Bar Association. *See* T. HALLIDAY, BEYOND MONOPOLY 119–41, 319 (1987).

[73] *See* J. AUERBACH, *supra* note 63, at 74–101; W. JOHNSON, SCHOOLED LAWYERS: A STUDY IN THE CLASH OF PROFESSIONAL CULTURES 120 (1978); Auerbach, *Enmity and Amity: Law Teachers and Practitioners, 1900-1922*, in LAW IN AMERICAN HISTORY, *supra* note 60, at 549.

[74] *See* A. JONSEN & S. TOULMIN, THE ABUSE OF CASUISTRY: A HISTORY OF MORAL REASONING 91–136 (1988); *see also* Chase, *The Birth of the Modern Law School*, 23 AM. J. LEGAL HIST. 329 (1985) (noting that Harvard President Eliot favored Langdell's method for its "clinical" focus on the irreducible complexities of particular cases, as contrasted with prior emphases on abstract, scientific theory, the greater "modernity" of the latter notwithstanding).

[75] *See* Rheinstein, *supra* note 33, at 691–92.

[76] W. HOBSON, *supra* note 66, at 143.

[77] *See* R. ABEL, *supra* note 27, at 139–68, 177–96 (observing that English solicitors organized themselves so as to limit their numbers and increase standards, status, and salary).

Like American lawyers in the mid-nineteenth century, solicitors did not initially constitute a modern "profession." The bench directly controlled entry into practice and disciplined errant members on its own inherent authority. Solicitors were recruited on the basis of kinship or friendship ties, not by demonstrated talent or knowledge. They were trained through apprenticeships rather than through a formal system of education.

Modern efforts at professionalization began as early as 1833 with the introduction of formal lectures for articled clerks. The first professional examination followed in 1836. A second obligatory exam was added in 1861, and a third in 1906. The proportion of those who passed all three exams declined progressively as ever stricter standards were imposed, until by the outset of World War II only half of those taking any of the three tests was likely to pass (vol. 1, p. 27). It also appears that the incomes of solicitors rose appreciably over these years.[78] While the courts continued to set maximum fees for their services, the local law societies successfully imposed minimum fee schedules that closely approximated the judicially-imposed maximum.

Although Abel argues that his rent-seeking theory is applicable to English solicitors, the paucity of secondary materials — historiographical and sociological — precludes a thorough evaluation of his interpretation. The evidence Abel presents, however, suggests that efforts to establish a measure of market control have generally enjoyed only limited success.[79] For example, throughout the eighteenth and nineteenth centuries Scottish solicitors, faced with increasing competition from "law agents," repeatedly sought to limit the growth of their own numbers through a variety of controls. These efforts were almost entirely unsuccessful (vol. 1, p. 82).[80]

More recently, leaders of the Scottish solicitors sought to persuade their followers to adopt a rule requiring three years of experience before one could set up a private practice. They defended the proposed rule as a means of "quality control," but it would also have had the effect of limiting competition within the ranks. When put to a vote of practitioners, the proposal "was rejected by the profession because of its supply control implications" (vol. 1, p. 91); the professional association may have been reluctant to engage in market control

---

[78] *See id.* at 235–41.

[79] Indeed, given the sympathy for Abel's perspective displayed by most of the contributing authors, it is surprising to discover how little evidence of effective, organized conduct by bar associations that could meaningfully be called monopolistic the authors have been able to uncover from their respective national histories.

[80] On similar resistance in the United States to lawyers' claims of unique and indispensable expertise, see Bloomfield, *Lawyers and Public Criticism: Challenge and Response in Nineteenth Century America*, 15 AM. J. LEGAL HIST. 269 (1971).

that would have encouraged the government to intrude into its affairs.[81] Such failures to attempt monopolization in the first place tend to undermine Abel's thesis.

Lawyers in several Western societies do enjoy a measure of state-sanctioned monopoly, but the scope of that monopoly is invariably far smaller than that enjoyed by their American counterparts. Whereas American bar associations have vigorously sought prosecution against "unauthorized practice," and so have been "unusually imperial" (vol. 1, p. 206) in pressing for exclusive jurisdiction over legal counseling and advice, "laymen" in virtually all other Western countries may perform many of the "legal" services that American lawyers regard as uniquely their own.[82] The scope of lawyers' monopoly in other countries is generally strictly limited to activities such as advocacy in the highest courts (English barristers), the transfer of real estate (English solicitors, until recently), or the formal authorization of contracts and deeds (French *notaires*). "Nonprofessionals" who have considerable legal education but who did not graduate from law school or obtain an official license largely comprise the legal staffs of large organizations. They counsel individuals and organizations as to corporate and municipal finance, trust and probate administration, bankruptcy, and tax planning. They also draft wills and transfer stock and real estate.

To be sure, the individuals in such countries whom we would consider to be "lawyers" seek, like their American colleagues, to derive much of their income from these same services. But because the scope of lawyers' monopoly is too narrow to provide a comfortable income, they must compete with members of other groups who provide such services, groups whose members are often subject to fewer restrictions, such as accountants and bankers.[83] These groups, for example, are lawfully permitted to advertise and solicit, while lawyers generally are not (vol. 1, pp. 100–01; vol. 2, p. 138). The existence of this competition confirms that lawyers in most Western societies have either refrained from strong assertions of monopoly, failed to achieve it, or obtained it only over a very narrow portion of the total market they seek to serve.

---

[81] The likelihood of such intrusion has increased, as several countries have begun to apply their antitrust laws to lawyers' conduct (vol. 1, pp. 129, 142, 164). *See* Goldfarb v. Virginia State Bar, 421 U.S. 773, 780–93 (1975) (finding minimum fee schedules set by bar associations to constitute price-fixing under the Sherman Act); LEGAL SERVICES: A FRAMEWORK FOR THE FUTURE 37 (1989) (presentations to Parliament by the Lord High Chancellor) (recommending extension of "restrictive trade practice" legislation to cover the organized bar).

[82] *See* vol. 1, pp. 40 (England), 99 (Scotland), 136–37 (Canada); vol. 2, pp. 73 (Norway), 164 (Japan), 241 (Belgium), 264 (France), 424 (Brazil).

[83] Competition is often particularly intense between opposing sides of a national bar that is only incompletely "divided," that is, whose market boundaries overlap (vol. 1, pp. 81–82, 99 (Scotland), 254–55 (Australia); vol. 2, pp. 226 (Belgium), 306 (Switzerland); vol. 3, pp. 335–37 (France and England)).

IV. Lawyers as Aristocrats and Entrepreneurs

Abel views lawyers' efforts to gain monopoly power as part of their pursuit not just of wealth, but of social status. According to him, many of the bar's efforts succeed in achieving both at once. Advertising restrictions, for instance, preserve lawyers' income by deterring price-cutting and also maintain lawyers' social status by cultivating an image of noncommercialism. Similarly, encouragement of public subsidies for legal aid both portrays the bar as public spirited and generates business for its members.

The claim that monopoly has been a major source of both wealth and status reveals little about how the conflict between the two will be resolved. Indeed, one of the central disputes in sociological theory has concerned the relative weight to be accorded pecuniary and non-pecuniary motives in explaining human conduct, with the latter understood as the desire for social honor or esteem. A comparative sociology aimed at identifying the conditions under which non-pecuniary motivations acquire social weight would therefore do well to remain attuned to the changing relations between lawyers and landed elites in various societies.

If lawyers regularly faced the necessity of choosing between pecuniary and nonpecuniary values, a sociology of lawyers would have to offer some account of which they choose, and why. Abel does not address the possibility that lawyers' desire for social status, traditionally associated with their public service ideal, may temper monopolistic impulses directed at maximizing wealth.[84] Vigorous self-promotional efforts needed to attain market control frequently require transparently self-interested activities that detract from a noncommercial image.[85] It may first appear no less unflattering to suggest that lawyers are as preoccupied with status as with wealth. The pursuit of social honor, however, has often led to conduct that is far superior to wealth-maximization in its social effect, even if no more disinterested in its motivation. In arguing for the continuing viability of the conception of the lawyer as public servant, Simon and Gordon appeal explicitly to American lawyers' concern with enhancing their social status.[86] If no such concern existed, one could dismiss their strategy

[84] Abel elsewhere acknowledges that such a conflict occasionally arises. *See* R. Abel, *supra* note 27, at 287.

[85] Therefore one need not assume any altruism on the bar's part to doubt that it routinely seeks to maximize its wealth through monopoly. The chapter on Canada suggests that self-interest in preserving a noncommercial image may be sufficient in some circumstances to deter such efforts. The Ontario commission of the bar recently recommended that no prosecution for unauthorized practice be commenced except with the written consent of the attorney general of the province, for fear of "the transparent element of professional self-interest" (vol. 1, p. 137).

[86] *See* Gordon, *supra* note 4, at 32–33; Simon, *supra* note 4, at 1130 ("When ethical norms are successful, they confer prestige on those identified with them, and degradation on those perceived to violate them.").

as utopian. Given the aristocratic residue within professional culture, however, it may not be entirely unrealistic to hope that the modern impulse to maximize wealth might be subordinated to the traditional impulse to preserve social status, so as to permit the reinvigoration of the independence ideal. At the very least, that possibility becomes worthy of the serious consideration it receives here.

Even if, as Abel believes, collective efforts to increase wealth and status are mutually reinforcing and "inextricably related" (vol. 1, p. 24), he should offer some explanation for the contrary empirical evidence within these volumes. For example, English barristers enjoy greater social status than solicitors, even though solicitors earn a higher median income (vol. 1, p. 55). Because wealth has become the principal source of status in the contemporary United States,[87] it may be difficult for Americans to appreciate that in much of the world, prestige and respectability have long rested on other grounds.[88] Where landed classes retained great social status and political power, as they did throughout much of Western Europe until the First World War, lawyers often sought status and power through continued service to such traditional elites rather than to emergent industrial interests.[89] The central features of the legal profession in most European societies became established during the nineteenth century and were profoundly shaped by the lingering aristocratic sensibilities that pervaded it.

If lawyers sought, like capitalist entrepreneurs, to maximize their wealth, we would expect them to seek expansion of the scope of their markets to increase the economic returns they could yield. We would also expect them to exploit fully their existing monopolies. If, on the other hand, lawyers sought chiefly to preserve a social status based on aristocratic distance from the business world, we would expect to find little effort on their part to expand the scope of their markets or to exploit their existing monopoly with great vigor. Monopoly, in the latter case, would be less a sword for self-aggrandizement than a shield against commercializing pressures.

Which view would Abel adopt, if compelled to choose? He argues that what drives the social transformation of professionalism in the law is capitalism (vol. 1, p. 23). On all accounts, capitalism promotes

---

[87] *See* D. TREIMAN, OCCUPATIONAL PRESTIGE IN COMPARATIVE PERSPECTIVE 223–24 (1977).

[88] M. WEBER, *Class, Status, Party*, in FROM MAX WEBER: ESSAYS IN SOCIOLOGY 180, 186–94 (H. Gerth & C. Mills eds. 1948).

[89] *Cf.* A. MAYER, *supra* note 54, at 176–77 (noting the continued influence of the nobility within the civil and military bureaucracies in the early twentieth century). Since the noncommercial world view of landed interests continued to exercise pervasive influence over that of the European (and especially German) middle class and commercial elites, the advent of a substantial market for legal and other professional services for these new groups did not require that lawyers adopt an entirely receptive attitude toward business and modern industry.

a world view that devalues traditional sources of honor and prestige.[90] To the extent that capitalism comes to prevail within a society, these older values, like all other forms of aristocratic "sentimentality," drown "in the icy water of egotistical calculation."[91] Abel leaves little doubt about his position when he writes that "my primary concern will be the economic aspects of legal practice because I believe that for most lawyers law is a means of earning a living before it is anything else."[92] In short, Abel would almost certainly concur with the Dickens character who claimed that "the one great principle of English law is to make business for itself,"[93] a conclusion that Abel seeks to apply far beyond the British Isles. As discussed below, however, the view of lawyers as capitalist entrepreneurs may only explain the experience of the United States; the evidence in these volumes suggests that elsewhere the ideal of the lawyer as aristocrat more readily explains the development of legal practice.

A. Lawyers as Aristocrats

In contrast to Abel's position, the material his collaborators present demonstrates that lawyers in most Western societies have largely remained content with a form of social honor that does not depend upon acquiring the wealth available only through wholehearted engagement in the legal affairs of private industry. Indeed, elite lawyers in most countries have satisfied themselves with the traditional form of respectability available through service to the state or landed interests. For this reason, the legal profession has not sought — except little and lately — to transform the bases of its professional authority to assume more decisive roles within the central institutions of its societies (other than the civil service).

European and American lawyers have retained different but equally powerful elements of the model of "traditional professionalism."[94] In both cases, the evidence suggests that the predicted social transformation of lawyers occurred to a much more limited extent than Abel's theory would suggest. For example, Abel argues that lawyers and their professional associations will want to abdicate responsibility for the training of new practitioners to the universities in order to establish the rational, "scientific" basis of legal expertise. But

---

[90] *See, e.g.*, M. SAHLINS, CULTURE AND PRACTICAL REASON 126–204 (1976); J. SCHUMPETER, CAPITALISM, SOCIALISM, AND DEMOCRACY 123–25 (3d ed. 1950); Berger, *On The Obsolescence of the Concept of Honor*, in THE HOMELESS MIND 83 (P. Berger & H. Kelner eds. 1973).

[91] K. MARX & F. ENGELS, *Manifesto of the Communist Party*, in THE MARX-ENGELS READER 473, 475 (R. Tucker 2d ed. 1978).

[92] R. ABEL, *supra* note 14, at 12.

[93] C. DICKENS, BLEAK HOUSE 603 (N. Page ed. 1971) (1st ed. 1853).

[94] *See supra* pp. 2022–24.

in many countries lawyers have been exceedingly reluctant to cede such power to the university law schools.[95] Even where formal university education has long been required for entering practice, there have frequently occurred serious conflicts between academicians and practitioners over the extent to which young lawyers actually require extended exposure to anything but the most rudimentary elements of legal practice (vol. 1, p. 149).[96] Abel also predicts that lawyers will form national bar associations in order to lobby for their collective interests in market control. Yet lawyers in many countries have been reluctant to shift their loyalties from local bar associations, which serve primarily to promote the traditional purpose of informal collegiality.[97] An examination of the historical experience of four countries — England, Germany, France, and the United States — sheds light on the factors that have led lawyers in most Western countries to resist the very pressures towards commercialization and modernity that Abel asserts drove their efforts to professionalize.

English barristers have made only half-hearted motions towards modernization. Until recently, the process of qualifying to become a barrister had little to do with acquiring formal knowledge or technical skills (vol. 1, p. 25).[98] Only since the late 1970's has admission to the Inns of Court required a university degree, and that degree need not be in law. The Inns long resisted granting universities any significant responsibility for legal education,[99] and the leading universities resisted taking responsibility for education in "merely practical" subjects such as law and business.[100] The majority of those seeking to enter the bar have always preferred private "crammers" for legal study (vol.

---

[95] In several countries, admission to the bar has continued to require, even for those who may have received university law degrees, formal apprenticeship with a practicing master, during which the pupil labors under the master's guidance for several years (vol. 1, pp. 84–90 (Scotland); vol. 2, pp. 237–38 (Belgium), 302 (Switzerland), 424 (Brazil)). The growth of "clinical education" in American law schools may be viewed as a revival of traditional apprenticeship within the modern context of formal education. *See* R. ABEL, *supra* note 14, at 221–23.

[96] *See* W. JOHNSON, *supra* note 73, at 120–21 (United States); Engel, *The English Universities and Professional Education*, in THE TRANSFORMATION OF HIGHER LEARNING: 1860–1930, at 293, 297–98 (K. Jarausch ed. 1983) [hereinafter TRANSFORMATION OF HIGHER LEARNING]; McClelland, *Professionalization and Higher Education in Germany*, in *id.* at 306, 317.

[97] These local bodies, of much older vintage, have tended to view their functions as the informal encouragement of collegiality among members of the bar and the facilitation of fruitful professional contacts. The persistent power of these local loyalties finds no recognition or explanation in Abel's theory. But in many societies they have apparently deterred the formation of strong bar associations at the national level (vol. 1, pp. 60 (England), 85 (Scotland); vol. 2, pp. 237 (Norway), 272 (France)).

[98] *See* W. READER, PROFESSIONAL MEN: THE RISE OF THE PROFESSIONAL CLASSES IN NINETEENTH-CENTURY ENGLAND 22 (1966) (noting the Inns of Courts' requirement that an aspirant eat a stipulated number of dinners before becoming a barrister).

[99] *See* B. ABEL-SMITH & R. STEVENS, LAWYERS AND THE COURTS: A SOCIOLOGICAL STUDY OF THE ENGLISH LEGAL SYSTEM, 1760–1965, at 467–68 (1967).

[100] *See* W. READER, *supra* note 98, at 21–22, 28.

1, p. 27). The Inns still look to the universities not to provide instruction in the law, but primarily to preselect those of greatest talent and general promise. Furthermore, barristers have long been reluctant to adopt formal examinations as a requirement for entry, fearing that this measure would facilitate, rather than limit, admission (vol. 1, p. 27). The primary barriers to entry remain informal and uncodified. Similarly, no formal code of ethics for barristers has been promulgated.[101] Modern legal scholarship, as developed in the universities, exercises negligible influence over judges.[102] As a leading study of the English bar concludes, the approach of barristers to education, admission, and ethical self-regulation remains wedded to "18th century practice and institutions, and in many respects with an 18th century outlook."[103]

The theory of lawyers as monopolists might be thought to find support in the fact that lawyers in continental Europe enjoy an official monopoly over certain highly-coveted positions within the national civil service (as in Germany) or as semi-public appendages of it (the *notaires* of France, Belgium, Switzerland, and Italy). But the origins of these monopolies are entirely different from those Abel's theory anticipates; they were created by the state sua sponte, rather than in response to lawyers' lobbying efforts. There is little evidence, moreover, of serious movement among lawyers in these societies toward any thoroughgoing "modernizing" of the foundations of their social prominence.

In Germany, for instance, university training in the law was originally instituted by absolutist monarchs seeking administrators and judges to serve as loyal instruments of the executive will.[104] To be sure, the "public service ideal" did become central to the self-under-

---

[101] This is not to suggest that barristers lack relatively clear ethical standards. *See* P. ATIYAH & R. SUMMERS, *supra* note 35, at 362–63, 367–69. The failure to formalize such standards into a code against which the conduct of individual practitioners may publicly be judged nevertheless indicates the relative weakness of the modernizing impulse that is central to Abel's theory.

[102] *See* M. SHAPIRO, COURTS: A COMPARATIVE AND POLITICAL ANALYSIS 129 (1981).

[103] B. ABEL-SMITH & R. STEVENS, *supra* note 99, at 460; *see also* D. DUMAN, THE JUDICIAL BENCH IN ENGLAND 1727–1875, at 5, 174 (1982) (noting that the Inns have "retained their ancient constitutions and identities virtually intact" and have succeeded in repeatedly "withstand[ing] demands for institutional rationalization" from Parliament during the nineteenth century). Beyond the contexts of education, admission, and ethical self-regulation, greater modernization has occurred. By the early eighteenth century the English bar "was no mere dependency of the landed ruling elite; . . . in terms of social origins, urban links, geographical and social mobility, sources of income, life-style, and attitudes to work, its members displayed some remarkable bourgeois traits." W. PREST, THE RISE OF THE BARRISTERS: A SOCIAL HISTORY OF THE ENGLISH BAR 325 (1986). But such changes occurred before the emergence of nineteenth-century capitalism, so they antedate the competitive forces and monopolistic responses to which Abel ascribes them.

[104] *See* Friedrich, *The Continental Tradition of Training Administrators in Law and Jurisprudence*, 11 J. MOD. HIST. 129, 131–33 (1939).

standing of German lawyer-bureaucrats, but the ideal originated in a conception of the *civil service* as the principal defender of the national interest and common good,[105] a notion alien to the modern "independent professional" of sociological theory. The German self-conception was grounded in the increasing prestige and independence from executive control that the state's high-ranking lawyer-bureaucrats had come to exercise since the early nineteenth century.[106] Moreover, the authority of German lawyers derived from their self-portrayal as the antithesis of uncommitted technicians, as the only force within society capable of seeing beyond the distorted visions of self-interested social groups and their political representatives. This self-conception coincided perfectly with a judicial system that had been conceived less as a vehicle for the disinterested resolution of private disputes than for the implementation of state policy.[107] In short, the claims to power and privilege of German lawyers simply have not rested upon the sort of expert knowledge and efforts at collective aggrandizement that Abel describes.

French lawyers have been only slightly more disposed to reconstruct their powers upon exclusively "modern" foundations.[108] Courtroom advocates, the *avocats*, have traditionally taken great pride in the continuity of their "order" with its prerevolutionary predecessors (vol. 3, p. 334). The system of admission and training established in 1810 persisted until 1971 (vol. 3, p. 335), having been suspended only during the Vichy period. The *notaires* have retained and even expanded their state-sanctioned monopoly despite repeated challenges to their professional standing and have been scarcely more enthusiastic than the *avocats* about modernizing the basis of their privileges. The procedure whereby the law school graduate is admitted to notarial practice originated in the *ancien régime*. Although the French state issues the license necessary to practice, the license becomes essentially the private property of its recipient. Because the state rarely issues new licenses, a law school graduate may enter practice only by purchasing the existing practice of a licensed *notaire*, a policy directly derived from the "venality of offices" before the French Revolution.[109] Moreover, the *notaires* demanded virtually no academic qualifications for entry into their ranks until 1972, when the requirement of a

---

[105] *See* D. RUESCHEMEYER, *supra* note 35, at 12–14, 90–91, 101–02, 152, 165.

[106] *See* H. ROSENBERG, BUREAUCRACY, ARISTOCRACY, AND AUTOCRACY: THE PRUSSIAN EXPERIENCE, 1660–1815, at 190–228 (1958).

[107] *See* M. DAMASKA, *supra* note 35, at 147–80.

[108] For an examination of the distinctive French pattern of "corporative" state governance over the professions in general and lawyers in particular, see PROFESSIONS AND THE FRENCH STATE (G. Geison ed. 1984); Herzog & Herzog, *The Reform of the Legal Profession and of Legal Aid in France*, 22 INT'L. & COMP. L.Q. 462 (1973); Karpik, *Lawyers and Politics in France, 1814–1850: The State, the Market, and the Public*, 13 LAW & SOC. INQUIRY 707 (1988).

[109] *See* E. SULEIMAN, *supra* note 35, at 38–59.

university degree was first instituted. Through the 1960's few *notaires* sought to remain well informed concerning new statutes and regulations affecting their work. Their prevailing accounting practices were antiquated, and their methods for handling client funds were very often in gross violation of basic ethical guidelines.[110] Despite recurring public outcry about the pervasiveness of such corruption among *notaires*, the profession displayed little inclination to raise the ethical level of its practitioners, actions that Abel views as indispensable to the modern "professionalization project" (vol. 1, pp. 217–22).

Although Germany and France are often casually described as reflecting a single "European" or "civil law" approach to the social organization of the legal profession (vol. 2, pp. 4–8), the relation between the state, lawyers, and their markets has in fact been rather different in these countries. Unlike their German counterparts, lawyers in the French civil service have never constituted the largest or most prestigious branch of the profession, and attorneys within the civil service do not occupy the most powerful positions, which are peopled instead by the engineering and management graduates of the *grandes écoles*.[111] German lawyers receive their licenses directly from the state, while French attorneys receive theirs from a corporative association to which the state has delegated this function.[112] The *avocats* and even the *notaires* have prized and preserved a significant measure of independence from the French state. Yet if serving the state has not been the principal source of social status among French lawyers, neither has their status derived exclusively from the wealth that can follow from service to a vigorous business community. The French lawyer has sought to combine the independence of solo practice with the collegiality of membership in a corporative body possessing powers of self-governance and a monopolized market that is secure but very narrow.

These patterns of cross national variation can be explained to some degree by considering whether the emergence of modern industry preceded or followed the advent of a strong state (vol. 3, pp. 300–05). Where a strong nation-state preceded the creation of large-scale private enterprise, as in Germany, lawyers have staked their fortunes with the state. Because the state itself spearheaded the subsequent industrialization of the country, the lawyer-bureaucrats who administered state enterprises exercised great power and privilege.[113] Strict

---

[110] *See id.* at 91–97. The resistance of *notaires* to the adoption of more modern procedures in this regard was probably attributable to the greater ease with which the older methods permitted the concealment of fraud and embezzlement of client resources.

[111] *See* E. SULEIMAN, POLITICS, POWER, AND BUREAUCRACY IN FRANCE 73–75, 94–98, 131–35 (1974).

[112] *See* A. ABBOTT, *supra* note 57, at 197.

[113] Private wealth, however, continued to derive principally from the ownership of land, so the practice of law could not lead to wealth. *See* A. MAYER, *supra* note 54, at 26–28.

limits on the activities of private industry restricted the private lawmaking that arises from the everyday work of lawyers in counseling, drafting, and arguing about the interpretation of private agreements.[114]

By contrast, the bar in the United States has largely staked its claims with the private sector. Where the most powerful and dynamic force within society emerged from that quarter, the profession turned to commerce for legal work and social prominence.[115] By the time a state bureaucracy emerged in the United States,[116] other professional groups, particularly economists, had developed expertise useful to policy-makers, thereby precluding lawyers from winning a German-style monopoly over prominent civil service posts. During the late nineteenth century, however, American lawyers succeeded in defining as their own tasks central to the creation, financing, and operation of large-scale corporate enterprises.[117] The activities of joint-stock companies could not have provided so substantial a source of new employment for American attorneys had state enterprises served as the principal vehicles of industrialization.[118]

Although the French state did not play so aggressive a role in industrialization as did the state in Germany,[119] it played a much greater role than in the United States.[120] It is therefore not surprising

---

[114] By the late nineteenth century, the private bar in Germany had, to a limited extent, begun to serve (and to seek alignment with) the emergent interests of industry and commerce, but this merely led to countervailing efforts to preserve close governmental control (vol. 3, pp. 306–09). To this day, attorneys occupy a significantly smaller percentage of top positions within private companies in Germany than in the United States. *See* Miller, *American Lawyers in Business and Politics*, 60 YALE L.J. 66, 75–76 (1951); Priest & Krol, *Lawyers in Corporate Chief Executive Positions*, 14 INT'L J. SOC. L. 33 (1986).

[115] Bloomfield partially attributes the unique history of the American bar to "the insistence of an ever expanding bourgeoisie upon increased legal services." M. BLOOMFIELD, *supra* note 51, at 138.

[116] *See* S. SKOWRONEK, BUILDING A NEW AMERICAN STATE: THE EXPANSION OF NATIONAL ADMINISTRATIVE CAPACITIES: 1877–1920 (1982).

[117] The entrepreneurship of lawyers in this context consisted not merely in their aggressive capture of professional jurisdiction over a lucrative new area of work, but more specifically in their "creative destruction" of doctrinal and institutional obstacles to industrial and organizational innovation. *See* J. SCHUMPETER, *supra* note 90, at 83–86, 132. For a discussion of lawyers' successful efforts to erode traditional corporate control devices, see J. HURST, THE LEGITIMACY OF THE BUSINESS CORPORATION IN THE LAW OF THE UNITED STATES 65–86 (1970).

[118] More attorneys were employed by New York's Erie Railroad Company in 1870 than practiced in the entire state of New York at the time of the framing of the Constitution. *See* Schudson, *supra* note 33, at 209. In Germany, by contrast, the state gave financial support only to railroads closely conforming to its strategic military plans, and, because doctrines of sovereign immunity generally protected the state from suit, lawyers lacked the dispute-related work elsewhere generated by private development. *See* D. SCHOWALTER, RAILROADS AND RIFLES: SOLDIERS, TECHNOLOGY, AND THE UNIFICATION OF GERMANY 17–75 (1975).

[119] *See* D. LANDES, THE UNBOUND PROMETHEUS: TECHNOLOGICAL CHANGE AND INDUSTRIAL DEVELOPMENT IN WESTERN EUROPE FROM 1750 TO THE PRESENT 399–400 (1972).

[120] French rulers in the late nineteenth and early twentieth centuries were less inclined than

to find that French lawyers have occupied an intermediate position on the spectrum of lawyers' affinities between business and the civil service: more dependent than their American peers upon the link to officialdom, but lacking the power that German lawyers possessed within the state apparatus and fearful of its potential grasp upon them.[121] The continued ambivalence toward state control among French lawyers has roots in this early relationship.[122]

In sum, a first step toward improving Abel's theoretical account would be to note that the natural temperament of lawyers might better be characterized not as that of monopolists but of heliotropes: gravitating to the sources of power and privilege within society and occasionally employing monopoly to further that end. The patterns we have observed in the comparative history of the profession emerge clearly from the chapters on particular countries and the other scholarly literature that Abel has canvassed. Abel fails to take account of these (or other possible) patterns when proposing a general account of the place of the legal profession and the source of its powers within modern Western society. It appears that for Abel the only game that lawyers play is monopoly. The players vary only in their "tactics" (vol. 1, p. 23) and "strategies."[123] When they give up that game, they do not engage in any other game significant to a sociological theory of the profession. The contrasting historical patterns noted above would lead one to expect, however, that lawyers have merely seized the best opportunities for wealth and power presented to them by their nation's particular route into the modern world. Although this would represent an improvement upon the view of lawyers merely as rent-seeking monopolists, it would nonetheless remain a considerable oversimplification of the historical record.

B. *Lawyers as Entrepreneurs*

Abel's rent-seeking theory must be further modified to explain the remarkable reluctance of lawyers in many countries to seize the new opportunities that private industry offered them. It may be that the

---

American leaders to view the activities of private companies as necessarily conducive to the national interest. Far fewer applications for the formation of joint-stock companies were approved in France than in the United States and those only after considerable official scrutiny by the *Conseil d'Etat*. *See* A. ABBOTT, *supra* note 57, at 94, 165–66.

[121] Such a fear would not have been unfounded, for French rulers frequently sought to tamper in major ways throughout the nineteenth and early twentieth centuries with the professional associations of both *avocats* and *notaires* whenever their prices, quality of service, or political activities were judged unsatisfactory (vol. 3, pp. 328–35).

[122] *See* E. SULEIMAN, *supra* note 35, at 239–41 (describing the *notaires'* recent difficulties in seeking to maintain close relations with, but also autonomy from, the state agency providing oversight of their activities).

[123] *See* R. ABEL, *supra* note 27, at 286.

social location of lawyers within a given country is often established with relative permanency during an early but decisive phase of its political and economic development. But why have major shifts in the subsequent course of a society's development — shifts that presented lawyers with very different incentives — failed to lead lawyers to alter their social allegiances?[124]

The uniqueness of American legal history helps to make sense of the uniqueness of contemporary American lawyers in this regard. A salient theme in American legal historiography has been the story of how the bench and bar in the nineteenth century actively redefined the common law of tort, contract, and property, with the effect of facilitating the economic development of the country by the private sector.[125] Furthermore, in the late nineteenth and early twentieth centuries the American bar invented an unprecedented range of imaginative legal devices to facilitate the financing of large-scale corporations and the limitation of their liabilities.[126]

In no other Western country, however, have lawyers shown the same interest in placing their talents so wholeheartedly in the service of commercial activity. In England, for instance, both nineteenth-century barristers and solicitors largely "turned their backs on the industrial revolution" (vol. 3, p. 362), even though industrialization was effected by private companies. The English judiciary did not produce any wholesale transformation of common law doctrine, with a view to fostering industrialization, as took place in American courts.[127] The heliotropic antennae of the English bar were more

---

[124] After all, large businesses, independent of state-supported cartels, eventually came to dominate the economic life of continental Europe, as they did in England and the United States.

[125] *See* M. HORWITZ, THE TRANSFORMATION OF AMERICAN LAW 1780–1860 (1977); J. HURST, LAW AND THE CONDITIONS OF FREEDOM IN THE NINETEENTH CENTURY UNITED STATES (1956).

[126] *See* J. HURST, *supra* note 58, at 336. Abel is correct in suggesting that American lawyers have displayed concern with developing new markets for themselves, but he focuses on public subsidies for legal aid, which were actively opposed by bar associations in many countries (vol. 1, pp. 101 (Scotland), 106–07 (United States); vol. 2, pp. 135–36, 144 (Germany), 241 (Belgium), 280 (France)) and which merely expanded existing legal services. Of greater economic and political significance for the bar's social alliances was the development of *new* services for large corporations. The rise of large-scale industry at the turn of the century presented far more attractive opportunities for lawyers to market their services than did the advent of public legal assistance.

[127] Technological innovations, for example, enjoyed relatively weak patent protection in England during the decisive period of the industrial revolution, and hence were widely pirated. This is not to suggest that rigorous patent protection necessarily contributes to industrialization. But English courts did not interpret patent law in light of a social policy favoring economic development until the mid-nineteenth century, after the major industrialization had occurred. *See* H. DUTTON, THE PATENT SYSTEM AND INVENTIVE ACTIVITY DURING THE INDUSTRIAL REVOLUTION, 1750–1852, at 69–81 (1984). The hesitant and incomplete commitment of the English bench and bar to revising legal doctrine in light of the needs of modern industry reflected the ambivalence toward industrial society displayed by most elite and upper-middle-

attuned to continuing sources of aristocratic status than to emerging sources of modern wealth, despite opportunities and incentives to behave otherwise.

As states began to assume the regulation of social and economic life, moreover, lawyers were presented with the opportunity to take an active part, forging new markets for themselves. The initial English response to the rise of administrative law, for example, was profoundly different from that of American lawyers. Unlike American attorneys, neither barristers nor solicitors seized control of that body of law. English courts did not seek to develop a body of law to supervise executive procedures in the implementation of regulatory activities, as did their French counterparts through the *droit administratif.*[128] "[M]ost new and vital issues were left either completely in the hands of the increasingly powerful civil service, or if some adversary procedure were deemed necessary, governments came to prefer flexible, policy-conscious administrative tribunals to the more cumbrous and formalistic courts of law."[129] English lawyers apparently believed their prestige would suffer by their direct association with mid-level bureaucrats, just as they had earlier feared close association with businessmen and "trade." To have responded to the economic incentives presented by the new administrative state would have been "to suggest that many of the decisions they took were very similar to those undertaken by relatively humble civil servants,"[130] an occupational group that barristers, in particular, viewed as socially inferior to themselves.

Such failures to respond to market incentives are also attributable, in several cases, to the very success of the monopolization that Abel views as a means of maximizing wealth.[131] The history of English solicitors, for instance, illustrates how possession of monopoly can induce institutional lethargy.[132] Solicitors' control over entry into the field was achieved in part by regulations severely restricting the number of "clerks" that could take an apprenticeship at a given time. This inflexibility prevented solicitors from seizing the new markets for legal services presented by the growth of large-scale business and the state's regulatory activity in the late nineteenth and early twentieth centuries. Private industry turned to in-house counsel, while the state expanded the civil service.

---

class groups throughout the nineteenth and early twentieth centuries. *See* M. WIENER, ENGLISH CULTURE AND THE DECLINE OF THE INDUSTRIAL SPIRIT, 1850–1980, at 81–94, 157–66 (1981).

[128] *See* B. ABEL-SMITH & R. STEVENS, *supra* note 99, at 2.

[129] *Id.*

[130] *Id.* at 464.

[131] This is consistent with the standard textbook view concerning the disincentive effects of monopoly on innovation. *See* Stigler, *The Case Against Big Business*, in MONOPOLY POWER AND ECONOMIC PERFORMANCE, *supra* note 14, at 3.

[132] *See* A. ABBOTT, *supra* note 57, at 253.

Similarly, French *avocats* throughout the nineteenth century preserved strict "ethical" guidelines "prohibiting their members from having any business contacts or relationships with manufacturers or traders, from employment within a private corporation" (vol. 3, p. 324), and from service on corporate boards of directors.[133] Indeed, until 1971 French lawyers allowed nonprofessional groups, the *agents d'affaires* and *conseils juridiques*, to provide the basic legal services required by the growth of private industry (vol. 3, p. 324). The *notaire* believed that his office was "not and should not be a commercial venture," and he was expected to exercise his functions "without making a business of it."[134] The profession became "a prisoner of its monopoly" over documentary authorizations and "lost the initiative to do anything else."[135] In fact, one-third of the profession reported that they regularly turned away commercial clients because they lacked basic knowledge of applicable business law.[136]

When lawyers have moved into new markets, with a view to increasing their income, their new activities have regularly appeared to conflict with colleagues' desires to preserve the status of the profession. These anti-commercial impulses among lawyers originated in the *weltanschauung* of the landed classes, who historically provided a major market for the conveyancing business of French *notaires* and English solicitors,[137] and with whom leading lawyers regularly socialized throughout Europe. But these values have endured among lawyers long beyond the political demise of the social classes from which they initially sprang.

As recently as 1985, for instance, a major conflict arose within the Genevan bar over whether the full-time employment of licensed attorneys by commercial and industrial enterprises constituted a violation of the profession's ethical standards (vol. 2, pp. 304–06, 319). The "old guard" of courtroom advocates feared that such direct employment would deprive young attorneys of independence from their "clients," and would thereby prevent them from performing their foremost public responsibility as "officers of the court." A restrictive proposal went so far as to pronounce that the profession of law was "incompatible with . . . all profitable activity that preponderates over the practice of law . . . [and] all activity contrary to the dignity of

---

[133] *See* Karpik, *supra* note 108, at 717–18. The distance that French *avocats* sought to preserve from businessmen reflected the relatively low prestige accorded the latter during this period. *See* Landes, *French Entrepreneurship and Industrial Growth in the Nineteenth Century*, 9 J. ECON. HIST. 45, 54–61 (1949).

[134] E. SULEIMAN, *supra* note 35, at 53.

[135] *Id.* at 101.

[136] *See id.* at 101–02 & n. 23.

[137] *See* Mathias, *The Lawyer as Businessman in Eighteenth-Century England*, in ENTERPRISE AND HISTORY 151, 152 (D. Coleman & P. Mathias eds. 1984) ("Undoubtedly the land has been the greatest source of business for lawyers, whether in litigation or not, since medieval times.")

the bar" (vol. 2, p. 320). The animating passion of the old guard appears to have been the residual, aristocratic ambivalence about commerce. Yet fused with this rhetorical strain was a more civic-spirited critique, directed against the perceived erosion of the traditional ethos of the courtroom advocate as a spokesman for public concerns. In fact, the current Genevan code of ethics continues to prohibit advocates from combining their "professional," litigation-related activities with other "nonprofessional" ones (vol. 2, p. 320).[138]

The status consciousness of European lawyers not only made them reluctant to enter new commercial markets, but also led them to abandon existing markets that have seemed to taint them with the odor of "trade." French *avocats*, for example, voluntarily "withdr[ew] from the more mundane and marketable aspects of legal practice" (vol. 3, p. 334). They established ethical rules that prohibited them from representing clients in commercial transactions or negotiations, handling clients' funds, or joining boards of directors of private companies. "These restrictions encouraged a narrow, almost monastic, self-definition of their role" (vol. 3, p. 333). English solicitors similarly "sought to improve their status by withdrawing from unsavory work" (vol. 3, p. 365) such as debt collection, even when such work continued to be remunerative. Their professional association encouraged the abandonment of such work as "unsuitable for members of a profession."[139] In Germany, well-established and unchallenged ethical rules prohibited advocates from providing business advice along with legal counsel.[140]

The residual effects of a social hierarchy based on land and state power led lawyers in many countries to be remarkably passive or ineffective in surviving within increasingly competitive markets. This would appear to contradict a theory of the profession that portrayed it as ever-watchful of shifts in its market situation and vigorously defensive against threats to its market power. Abel argues that because English solicitors, for instance, face increasing challenges from the newly established occupation of licensed conveyancers, their situation "will compel" them "to reach out toward new clients, subject matters, and functions" (vol. 1, p. 64). Nevertheless, other lawyers in similar circumstances have not done so. English solicitors withdrew during the early twentieth century from competition posed by a wide

---

138 The capacity of the Genevan professional association to implement such restrictions probably cannot be attributed primarily to the association's monopoly power, which has been particularly weak in Switzerland. *See* Siegrist, *Professionalization with the Brakes On: The Legal Profession in Switzerland, France, and Germany in the Nineteenth and Early Twentieth Centuries*, 9 COMP. SOC. RES. 267, 279–91 (1986).

139 Burrage, *supra* note 68, at 228.

140 Rueschemeyer attributes such conduct to the reserved attitude of many German lawyers toward business. *See* D. RUESCHEMEYER, *supra* note 35, at 113–14.

range of legal-business counseling and retreated to their present concentration on land conveyancing. Concerns about social status apparently affected the direction of their retreat. They "may have chosen conveyancing because of its associations with land, rather than [debt] collections with its associations with trade and commerce."[141] In the nineteenth and early twentieth centuries English barristers displayed relative unconcern with the increasing tendency of bankers and financiers to remove many business disputes from the slowly moving legal system in favor of arbitration.[142] Similarly, in France *notaires* lost that portion of their business not covered by their official monopoly over the authorization of contracts for land transfer, marriage, leases, and loans during the 1950's and 1960's.[143] Although faced with a veritable invasion from many quarters, the *notaires* neither moved into new markets nor fought to protect the old.[144] Currently, European lawyers across the continent face unprecedented competition in the market for advice concerning the law of corporate and public finance. The foreign offices of the "Big Eight" accounting firms and Wall Street law firms have seized virtually the entire market during the last five years, partly in successful anticipation of European integration in 1992. The organized response of the European bar to this encroachment upon its most lucrative markets to date has been essentially nil.[145]

Contingent fees are prohibited as incompatible with the ethical stature of a profession in virtually all of the countries here described (vol. 1, p. 294 (Australia); vol. 2, pp. 142 (Germany), 375 (Spain)). The lawyer's right to obtain contingent fees is defended in the United States as a method for increasing public access to the judicial system. But in the eyes of European lawyers, the primary effect of such fees in the United States has been to increase the involvement of the attorney in his client's business affairs, thereby threatening the lawyer's independence from the pecuniary motivations of his clients. In none of these societies has the legal profession pressured for the abandonment of such restrictions on their potential market. This suggests that lawyers generally view their social status as resting upon public acceptance of their capacity to stand apart from the pecuniary motivations of the business world that they serve. The self-interested motive of status-preservation has in most places apparently stopped the legal profession from adopting contingent fees, the contrary economic interests of lawyers notwithstanding.

---

[141] A. ABBOTT, *supra* note 57, at 276.

[142] *See* B. ABEL-SMITH & R. STEVENS, *supra* note 99, at 2–3.

[143] *See* E. SULEIMAN, *supra* note 35, at 101.

[144] *See id.* at 96–97.

[145] *See* Y. Dezalay, Putting Justice Into Play on the Global Market 34–37 (B. Cheve trans. June 11, 1989) (unpublished paper presented at the 1989 Law and Society Association Conference) (on file at the Harvard Law School Library).

Furthermore, until recently in many Western societies there have existed severe restrictions on the size of law firms (vol. 2, p. 19).[146] It was the advent of "large" law firms in the United States toward the end of the nineteenth century that enabled the American bar to meet the burgeoning new demand for its services by facilitating specialization among lawyers and massive team work on large projects.[147] But in several European countries the private bar has been composed almost entirely of solo practitioners. Although in recent years Europeans have acknowledged that such a rule is unsuited to modern economic conditions, the size of law firms in Europe remains extremely small by United States standards (vol. 2, pp. 19–20). The self-imposed restrictions of European lawyers on the size of their firms has seriously impeded their ability to attract legal business from large private companies, whose legal departments have grown to resemble American law firms in size. If European lawyers had been acting primarily in pursuit of their material interests, as Abel's theory leads us to expect, it is difficult to see how they could ever have devised such rules and retained them for so long.

The "exceptionalism" of the American bar[148] stands out vividly against this comparative backdrop. In Europe, the social class that has always viewed itself as the principal carrier and defender of nonpecuniary values has been the landed aristocracy.[149] In America no less an observer than Tocqueville characterized lawyers of the 1830's in these same terms: their role, he suggested, was not only to temper the excessive enthusiasms of a democratic populace, but also to chasten the excessive acquisitiveness of the newly emergent elites in commerce, finance, and manufacture.[150] Although lawyers in the United States may continue to think fondly of themselves as the pre-Jacksonian aristocracy that Tocqueville celebrated, they quickly came to conduct themselves far less aristocratically than their counterparts elsewhere in the Western world. Tocqueville saw American lawyers, with

---

[146] *See, e.g., id.* at 40 (describing continuing limits on the number of partners in West German law firms).

[147] On the origins of large firms in the U.S. see Hobson, *Symbol of the New Profession: Emergence of the Large Law Firm 1870–1915*, in THE NEW HIGH PRIESTS: LAWYERS IN POST-CIVIL WAR AMERICA, cited above in note 31, at 3.

[148] American "exceptionalism" generally refers to the fact that the United States is the only major industrial society never to have experienced a large socialist movement. The exceptional weakness of socialism within both American labor unions and the party system has contributed, in part, to the exceptional strength of the bar. In Western societies where socialist movements have been strong, significant numbers of union leaders have been elected to political office, which has in turn diminished the proportion of lawyers in parliamentary bodies. *See* D. RUESCHEMEYER, *supra* note 35, at 71–75.

[149] *See* M. WEBER, MAX WEBER ON LAW IN ECONOMY AND SOCIETY 194 (M. Rheinstein & E. Shils eds. 1954) [hereinafter WEBER ON LAW].

[150] *See* A. DE TOCQUEVILLE, *supra* note 15, at 263–70.

their "preference for order and [their] natural love of formalities,"[151] as stepping willingly and naturally into the shoes of an absent aristocracy. But lawyers in older Western societies — where authentically aristocratic elements remained influential — displayed, in their continuing ambivalence about market society, far greater interest in donning aristocratic garb. The uniqueness of American lawyers has consisted precisely in their relatively unqualified embrace of the modern world of commerce and corporations, notwithstanding their initial doubts[152] and recurrent bouts of uneasiness.

Although Tocqueville may have been wrong about the details of lawyers' roles, he was right about his more central argument that the historical tide sweeping American society toward "democracy," a tide within which expanding commerce was to constitute a central current, would prevail. He surely would not be terribly surprised to learn that lawyers, too, eventually succumbed to its pull. Thus, from the start, Tocqueville's agenda for the American lawyer was riddled with irresoluble tensions. To exercise the aristocratic moral tempering that was his mission, the American lawyer had to acquire a powerful position within the large private enterprises that would come to dominate the modern economy. But to acquire a position sufficiently prominent to influence the course of corporate policy, he had to accept the essential underlying principles of the competitive economy. Only a few transitional generations could sustain these conflicting commitments within a single professional role.[153] But American lawyers were increasingly denied the possibility of leadership *within* the corporate world without becoming *of* it. By choosing to accept their role as corporate agents, American attorneys failed to fulfill the task that Tocqueville had set for them, but they fulfilled a role that brought them far greater social prominence than they could have hoped to garner in defending the enduring merits of anti-commercial values within an increasingly commercial society.[154] American attorneys did well to ignore the advice of that aristocratic French tourist.

The European experience suggests that American society may have been no better off if attorneys had followed Tocqueville's advice. To

---

[151] *Id.* at 263.

[152] *See, e.g.*, Schudson, *supra* note 33, at 207 (describing David Dudley Field's efforts to distinguish his view of legal ethics from Lord Brougham's then-famous argument for unqualified fidelity to client interests).

[153] *See, e.g.*, Gordon, *Legal Thought*, *supra* note 31, at 99 (describing the ethical dilemmas perceived by the first lawyers for large private corporations in America).

[154] Gordon describes their role as predominantly "technical." *See id.* at 77–81. But this characterization probably underestimates the influence that lawyers exercised over American industrialization by redefining the terms of their clients' problems and designing revolutionary forms of corporate organization. This subtle form of influence goes unacknowledged in the empirical studies that view the power of elite practitioners as stemming not from their expertise, but from the elite character of their clients. *See, e.g.*, J. HEINZ & E. LAUMANN, CHICAGO LAWYERS: THE SOCIAL STRUCTURE OF THE BAR 353–73 (1982).

be sure, European lawyers in the same period could not even have hoped to play the Tocquevillian role. A *real* aristocracy denied lawyers a preeminent place in government leadership outside the civil service. Because landed interests also largely controlled the status order of late nineteenth-century Europe, legal service to commercial enterprises could not provide as unequivocal a source of social honor as it did in America. The central role of the state in industrialization on the European continent, moreover, made the pursuit of wealth through legal service to private industry even more inaccessible. Faced with these constraints, it is scarcely surprising that European lawyers held themselves apart from commercial society for a much longer time than did their American counterparts and preferred both semi-aristocratic status (based on aloofness from "trade") and political power (garnered from high-ranking service within the state bureaucracy). If American lawyers failed as aristocrats, European lawyers failed both as aristocrats and as capitalist entrepreneurs. But because European lawyers therefore acquired significantly less social prominence, European society was able to deal more effectively than our own with the problem of their public unaccountability.

If American lawyers obtained a near-monopoly over certain services, it was because their relative lack of interest in traditional sources of status led them to devote their attention to developing legal instruments that could advance the purposes of the new corporate economy. The center of attention for European lawyers remained the social status that had long been associated with exercising state power and serving "the common good." To be sure, official monopoly helped preserve this more sedate, genteel style of life by limiting the competition that could easily have eroded it. But the monopoly enjoyed by lawyers had been created and maintained to advance entirely different purposes and did not prevent competing occupational groups from seizing more lucrative new markets and encroaching upon lawyers' traditional market shelters. The policy implications of these conclusions are clear: the greater autonomy from commercial interests sought by current critics of the profession has historically been obtained by lawyers only through greater dependence upon the state and landed interests or through significant sacrifices in social prominence. The fact that the bar in the modern West has sought status more frequently than wealth ultimately offers little comfort to reformers who dwell within societies where wealth eventually became the principal source of status.

This conclusion may prove useful in identifying a well-concealed ambiguity in the arguments for a rejuvenation of the historic ideal of lawyerly independence. If the primary purpose of such a rejuvenation is to increase the public accountability of lawyers, that this has elsewhere been accomplished only by severely limiting the bar's prerogatives of self-regulation and its members' opportunities for entrepreneurship, and by subjecting lawyers to increased state control or market competition (or both), should not for a moment weaken the resolve of the reformer. By "deprofessionalizing" lawyers into bureaucrats or forcing them to compete directly in the same markets with other occupations delivering overlapping services, European society has dealt more effectively than our own with problems of public accountability. But if an important reason for reviving the ideal of professional independence from commercial concerns is to make the practice of law less alienating and unsatisfying for its practitioners,[155] "cures" of this sort are likely to appear worse than the disease against which they are directed. Critiques such as Simon's and Gordon's have implied that a reinvigoration of the aristocratic ideal will enable lawyers both to do more "good" and to feel better about themselves and their work while so doing. By implying that there is no serious tension between increasing the public accountability of lawyers and increasing their freedom and autonomy, however, the current critiques of legal ethics evade the most difficult issue that lawyers (and the public) will face in choosing among specific proposals for reform.

Let us assume that the primary purpose of reforming the ethical codes governing the bar is to increase the accountability of private practitioners to non-clients. The preceding analysis suggests that it is difficult to eliminate the ethical deficiencies of such codes, for the persistence of these deficiencies in the face of repeated efforts to redress them, most recently by the Kutak Commission,[156] has not been due primarily to cognitive weaknesses in prior arguments for reform. The unique deficiencies of American legal ethics are chiefly due to the unique social history of the American bar — the unusually intimate relationship between the bar and large business that emerged after 1870. The code obligations of client loyalty and confidentiality that we have today merely give a stamp of approval to this relationship. Although Abel does not directly address the current critics of legal ethics, he explains how the problem they identify transcends the intellectual incoherence they so easily detect in the bar's standard defenses of its ethical codes.

---

[155] This purpose is openly acknowledged by current critics. *See, e.g.*, D. LUBAN, *supra* note 4, at 159, 169–70; Bok, *supra* note 56, at 921; Gordon, *supra* note 4, at 62–63; Simon, *supra* note 4, at 1131, 1137–38, 1144; *see also* R. Jack & D. Jack, MORAL VISION AND PROFESSIONAL DECISIONS: THE CHANGING VALUES OF WOMEN AND MEN LAWYERS 150–55 (1990) (demonstrating the intense dissatisfaction of women attorneys with an ethic of unqualified client loyalty).

[156] The Commission's recommendations notwithstanding, the ABA House of Delegates ultimately adopted a standard, codified in Model Rule 1.13(c), that permits disclosure of client confidences in even fewer circumstances than were permitted under the 1970 Model Code or the 1908 Canons of Professional Ethics. *See* Gillers, *Model Rule 1.13(c) Gives the Wrong Answer to the Question of Corporate Counsel Disclosure*, 1 GEO. J. LEGAL ETHICS 289, 303 (1987) (criticizing the restrictive latitude for in-house whistleblowing ultimately adopted by the Model Rules).

If the primary problem, then, lies in the social underpinnings of legal ethics rather than in their logical incoherence, effective reform might best be directed at these underpinnings. Such reform must be guided by some sociological analysis of constraints and opportunities, however, and that analysis would surely begin by asking why civil law societies were able to limit the social prominence of lawyers much more than common law countries in general and the United States in particular. After all, where lawyers have not acquired as much wealth and power as in the United States, their ethical guidelines have not grown to be as dismissive of the rights of non-clients.[157] If power tends to corrupt, the moral corruption of American legal ethics might best be understood as a product of the power American lawyers acquired over the definition and resolution of societal problems. For if American attorneys surpass their European counterparts in wealth, power, and status, this is attributable not only to their closer relationship to the business world, but also to their greater cultural authority over the definition and resolution of a wider range of societal concerns.

Those who are critical of judicial "meddling" in policy issues would advocate a reduced role for lawyers in defining and addressing such concerns.[158] At first glance, this criticism of the bar would seem entirely unrelated, perhaps even antagonistic, to that offered by Simon and Gordon. But objections from the "left" to lawyers' ethics might be best addressed as a by-product of answering objections from the "right" to lawyers' power and to the inefficiencies and institutional rigidities it has allegedly produced. The drawbacks of this sort of reform for lawyers may be so great that one risks forfeiture of one's membership in the professional fraternity even by entertaining it. That is no reason, however, to refrain from examining its potential advantages for those the profession ostensibly exists to serve. The remainder of this Review reinterprets the empirical material presented by Abel and his collaborators to suggest a sociological account of the unparalleled prominence acquired by lawyers in America. In so doing,

---

[157] *See supra* pp. 2018–20.

[158] *See, e.g.*, P. HUBER, LIABILITY 3–18 (1988) (attacking the product liability "explosion" as a disincentive to product innovation and a threat to international industrial competitiveness); Bok, *A Flawed System of Law Practice and Training*, 33 J. LEGAL EDUC. 570, 576–77 (1983) (complaining that most lawyers do not contribute to the growth of social wealth but only fight over its proper division); Horowitz, *Decreeing Organizational Change: Judicial Supervision of Public Institutions*, 1983 DUKE L.J. 1265 (attacking judicial insensitivity to social complexity and suggesting the inherent limits of courts in dealing with that complexity); Peters, *Tilting at Windmills*, WASH. MONTHLY, March 1988, at 6, 6 ("The truly horrible thing lawyers have done to our national life is to create situations . . . where one lawyer says we can't do the right thing because another lawyer would sue us.") Only the possibility of reducing the social prominence of lawyers, not its desirability, is addressed here. It is unclear, however, whether the good that lawyers do in American society could continue unaffected by a significant reduction in the societal scope of the law's concern and in the attendant prominence of the law as a profession.

it indicates some of the historical idiosyncracies, unsusceptible to easy emulation, that enabled continental Europe to increase the public accountability of lawyers by reducing their social prominence.

V. Common Lawyers and Civil Lawyers

A. *Differing Social Prominence*

There have been many anecdotal observations concerning apparent differences between the place of lawyers in common and civil law countries,[159] but these new volumes provide the first substantial data bearing on the issue. They fully support Abel's conclusion that "[t]he civil law world is dramatically different from its common law counterpart in every respect" (vol. 2, p. 4).[160] The content of civil legal education, for example, is "intensely theoretical" (vol. 2, p. 13) by common law standards, having been controlled for centuries by academicians. Many civil law countries do not require bar examinations, since the state university is thought adequately to control the quality of entrants. In fact, it is not bar associations, but the university and the state that set standards for entry into the ranks of practitioners. Civil lawyers work fewer hours and earn significantly less income than their common law counterparts. Moreover, they are distributed across the subdivisions of practice in very different proportions. The ratio of lawyers in the civil service to those in private practice is very much higher in civil law than in common law countries.[161]

These lawyer-civil servants often enjoy greater income and prestige than the private bar or in-house counsel. In fact, the most promising law school graduates have always been drawn into public service. Private practitioners are engaged almost entirely in solo or small firm practice. Moreover, they serve only a small segment of the legal market serviced by their common law counterparts. Their work is largely confined to the representation of individuals and small companies in litigation. Legal counseling is offered by several occupational groups, including but not limited to law school graduates.

---

[159] *See, e.g.*, J. Merryman, The Civil Law Tradition, 109–20 (1969); 1 K. Zweigert & H. Kötz, An Introduction to Comparative Law 213–26 (T. Weir trans. 1977).

[160] In relying upon a simple and largely undefined dichotomy between "common" and "civil" law countries, Abel and Lewis neglect the difficulties associated with identifying the essential features of the "civil law world" and with locating the legal systems of particular societies within it. *See* H. Berman, Law and Revolution: The Formation of the Western Legal Tradition 9–10 (1983) (stressing the essential unity of a "Western legal tradition" encompassing common and civil law systems). The present analysis employs the concept of "the civil law" only as an "ideal-type" — a conceptual construct derived from the descriptive accounts of comparative law scholars. That concept is not asserted to mirror perfectly the legal system of any particular society.

[161] The factual assertions in this paragraph and the following derive from vol. 2, pp. 1–31.

Although lawyers everywhere occupy elected office in highly disproportionate numbers relative to other occupational groups, those in civil law societies do so in significantly fewer numbers than in common law countries. When the tasks of the various "legal professions" within each civil law country are considered as a whole, the scope and societal significance of these responsibilities nowhere equals that of lawyers in common law countries, particularly in the United States. The relative narrowness of legally cognizable issues within civil law societies may mean not only that lawyers there are less wealthy, powerful, and prestigious, but also that the human experience of their work is often inferior: it seems, in a word, less *interesting*.

Although Abel notes these empirical findings, he offers little explanation for them, preoccupied as he is with the task of putting the profession's venality on international parade. The structure of his theoretical argument — stressing the essentially identical predicament faced by the bar in all democratic, capitalist societies — compels him to couch these observations as minor qualifications. The data he has gathered, however, permit several possible explanations. The attraction of European lawyers to a respectability derived independently from the world of commerce surely made them more reluctant to seize opportunities requiring that they thrust themselves aggressively into new areas of business. Because the most esteemed variety of civil lawyer has generally been the civil servant, those drawn to a legal career may have been persons who value security in their careers over the potentially greater rewards that follow from greater risk.[162]

The effect of these career trends on the development of the law by the judiciary has also been significant. Because lawyers who attain high judicial office have spent their entire careers within the civil service, they have had direct involvement in a much narrower segment of business life and political activity than that regularly encountered by common lawyers.[163] This may in turn have induced greater caution about interceding in ways that would push the law into new areas of economic and political life. Because civil law judges, moreover, are neither appointed by elected representatives nor obliged to stand periodically for elections themselves, as in many common law countries, the democratic legitimacy of their powers has stood on more precarious footing.[164] This has contributed to greater caution in the

[162] For a discussion of the risk-aversion and relative lack of ambition of most who choose a judicial career in Germany, and the consequences for decisionmaking on the bench, see Luhmann, *The Legal Profession: Comments on the Situation in the Federal Republic of Germany*, 20 JURID. REV. 116, 120–21 (1975).

[163] *Cf.* Rheinstein, *supra* note 33, at 689 (observing that the decisionmaking of common law judges often displays a "fine finger-tip sense for the needs of a given situation which they had developed through experience in political life").

[164] *See* J. DAWSON, THE ORACLES OF THE LAW 379–80 (1968).

exercise of their powers. Those who occupy higher judicial office in the common law world, by contrast, attain it only after considerable success in the private sector or in political careers to which they can readily return. This "escape hatch" also gives them greater independence from the constraints that other branches inevitably attempt to impose upon their adjudicatory activities.

Civil law academicians lead an even more cloistered life than civil law judges. Yet it is the academicians who have, since the Renaissance, been regarded as far more authoritative in the interpretation and development of the civil law.[165] They have traditionally been concerned almost exclusively with the conceptual elaboration and formal rationalization of doctrine, processes requiring little sensitivity to the factual nuances of concrete cases or to the societal interests they implicate.[166] Nineteenth-century scholars of the civil law became largely unconcerned about its responsiveness to the changing needs of the modern industrial economy.[167] This tendency was particularly acute in Germany, where the cultural ideal of *Bildung* placed humanistic learning, rather than the needs of commerce, at the core of professional self-definition.[168] This ideal was reflected in the Pandectists' view of law as a purely analytical, intellectual construct, a sealed system of logically interconnected propositions impermeable to the economic pressures of the business world.[169] That conception of law not only precluded German judges from transforming doctrine in order to facilitate economic development, but also thereby impeded German lawyers from insinuating themselves into the most powerful positions within the private corporations that would eventually come to dominate even the German economy. As Abel and Lewis observe, we do not know whether the conceptualist utopia of the Pandectists bore any relation to the "law in action" as applied by German practitioners of

---

[165] *See* A. WATSON, THE MAKING OF THE CIVIL LAW 171–74 (1988); WEBER ON LAW, *supra* note 149, at 198–223.

[166] J. DAWSON, *supra* note 164, at 455–57; J. MERRYMAN, *supra* note 159, at 40–49. On recent departures from this view, see M. CAPPELLETTI, THE JUDICIAL PROCESS IN COMPARATIVE PERSPECTIVE 9–24 (1989). *But see* H. BERMAN, *supra* note 160, at 561 n.6 (arguing that the importance of precedent and analogical reasoning in early modern civil law is often underestimated).

[167] *See* M. GLENDON, M. GORDON & C. OSAKWE, COMPARATIVE LEGAL TRADITIONS 52 (1985). However, certain concepts within the classical Roman law that influenced Western jurists centuries after the collapse of the empire, *see* J. DAWSON, *supra* note 164, at 113, facilitated the economic growth of early modern Europe. *See id.* at 458.

[168] *See* McClelland, *Professionalization and Higher Education in Germany*, in TRANSFORMATION OF HIGHER LEARNING, *supra* note 96, at 306, 317–18.

[169] *See* J. MERRYMAN, *supra* note 159, at 62, 92–96. Because the Pandectists codified an "essentially nineteenth century attitude" toward "the role of individual autonomy," *id.* at 92, they hindered later judicial adjustment of legal doctrine to the collective social concerns of the regulatory state in twentieth-century Europe.

the day to their more mundane and concrete affairs (vol. 3, p. 507). But as long as academicians of this ilk remained the chief source of guidance to judges in legal interpretation, the law could not easily expand into new areas of social life. Whatever new opportunities for work and wealth the evolving social needs of the time presented to lawyers were thereby lost. Differences in prevailing modes of legal thought may therefore have been decisive in influencing the differing social prominence accorded to lawyers in common and civil law societies.

The contemporary sociology of law has preferred to explain legal thought and doctrine by reference to "underlying" social forces,[170] that is, whenever thought and doctrine have not been merely dismissed as "marginal"[171] to the "law in action." It must therefore come as a considerable surprise to many legal sociologists, Abel among them, to discover the persistence of profound differences between civil and common law countries in the social position of lawyers, despite great similarity in the social and economic systems upon which such legal institutions are thought to be "based."[172] The reigning prejudices of legal sociology have thus deprived Abel of any explanation for the most striking and unambiguous empirical finding of these comparative volumes.

If the sociology of law has led Abel astray in this regard, the sociology of the professions has served him little better. In viewing lawyers from the general perspective of "the professions" at large, Abel has underestimated how the varying powers given to the law and legal institutions in different societies affect the roles of Western lawyers in the resolution of important economic and political problems (vol. 3, pp. 438–88). General theories of the professions will be valuable only if they remain sensitive to the differing types of expertise employed by various professions and to the fact that the knowledge which lawyers use in their work is a knowledge of law. Greater sensitivity to these considerations can be achieved by focusing on what sociological theory has had to say about the knowledge that professionals possess and how it contributes to their social prominence.

---

[170] At the risk of some oversimplification, it may be said that the most ambitious and influential theoretical accounts of the relation between social structure and legal doctrine have generally privileged the influence of the former upon the latter. *See, e.g.*, E. DURKHEIM, THE DIVISION OF LABOR IN SOCIETY 138–46 (G. Simpson trans. 1964); MARX & ENGELS ON LAW 108–44 (M. Cain & A. Hunt eds. 1979); R. UNGER, LAW IN MODERN SOCIETY (1976).

[171] *See* Trubek, *Where the Action Is: Critical Legal Studies and Empiricism*, 36 STAN. L. REV. 575, 578, 585 (1984).

[172] Scholars of comparative law will be much less surprised. *See, e.g.*, A. WATSON, *supra* note 165, at 1 (observing the continuing similarities among the legal systems of civil law societies, and their continuing differences from common law systems, "despite . . . overwhelming joint social and economic circumstances, such as the Industrial Revolution").

B. Precision vs. Indeterminacy in Legal Knowledge: Differing Foundations of Professional Authority

Sociological theories of modern professionalism, Abel's included, harbor a persistent ambiguity. On one hand, they assert that the legitimate authority of a modern profession rests on a body of rationally defensible knowledge grounded in scientific research or disciplined academic reflection. Practitioners are to apply this knowledge to the resolution of their clients' problems. On the other hand, the sociologists also claim that a modern profession's knowledge is distinguishable from that of competing fields, including those requiring equally sophisticated technical expertise, in that these other occupations require only the observance of an established routine, however complicated. In a profession, by contrast, the deployment of technical expertise is never regarded as sufficient to constitute satisfactory performance. Acceptable performance requires the exercise of complex judgment, in both the choice among alternative means toward a given end and in the proper harmonization of a client's often conflicting ends. This capacity is developed only gradually in the course of practice by observing and emulating more skilled practitioners. Without the necessity for complex judgment, there could be no justification for conferring upon a profession the autonomy its members enjoy to regulate and supervise their affairs.[173]

Such judgment is considered impossible to codify or transmit directly — certainly not through formal education, at any rate. In the case of law, for instance, it would be possible to reduce to "standard forms" the profession's accumulated knowledge about the contractual terms most appropriate to each of a series of recurrent commercial transactions. If such boilerplate were sufficient to satisfy clients' objectives, there would be little need for the regular exercises of practical judgment by which the individual attorney tailors the terms of such agreements to the complex aims of his client.[174] The organization of work in the profession has been influenced by this aspect of its knowledge. Even the largest organizations in which attorneys labor have traditionally been arranged in a relatively non-bureaucratic fashion,[175] in order to ensure that the personal autonomy necessary for the exercise of such complex judgment is respected.[176]

---

[173] *See, e.g.*, M. CALVERT, THE MECHANICAL ENGINEER IN AMERICA 1830–1910, at 225–62 (1967) (describing the effect of modern science in transforming engineers from autonomous craftsmen into bureaucratic functionaries).

[174] *See* E. SPANGLER, *supra* note 48, at 48–50 (observing the tension between lawyers' self-image as professional craftsmen and the extensive use of boilerplate).

[175] *See, e.g.*, R. NELSON, *supra* note 20, at 205.

[176] *See* Freidson, *Are Professions Necessary?*, in THE AUTHORITY OF EXPERTS, *supra* note 26, at 3, 23–24.

Although practitioners greatly esteem those who display particular virtuosity in practical judgment,[177] there is nevertheless some discomfiture about the mysterious character of this knowledge. "In his day-to-day practice [every competent practitioner] makes innumerable judgments of quality for which he cannot state adequate criteria, and he displays skills for which he cannot state the rules and procedures."[178] When asked to describe their methods of inquiry, lawyers speak vaguely of experience, trial and error, intuition, insight, imagination, or simply muddling through.[179] If every case were in all respects unique, it would be pure luck that led to its satisfactory solution, and so fortunate a result would have nothing to do with the use of expert knowledge. Sensitive appreciation of the nuances of particular cases bears little relation to the view of practice communicated in either sociological theory or in most "modern" professional schools, where it is often portrayed as the application of procedures derived from theories developed within the university. Practitioners quickly realize the inaccuracy of this picture of their work, but they invariably fail to offer a coherent account of that work which is consistent with prevailing notions of the modern bases of professional authority. In failing to rise to the level of an applied science, their field appears to descend into a "craft," thus depriving it of the authority that follows from a claim to apply abstract theoretical knowledge about its corner of the social universe.

How can it be that the legitimacy of a modern profession depends on both its application of rationally defensible knowledge and the presence of inherent defects in that knowledge, defects that necessitate recourse to mysterious and ineffable powers unrelated and even hostile to it? What may first appear only as logical incoherence in the theory

---

[177] For recent defenses of the continuing primacy in professional life of practical judgment over technical expertise in the application of formal knowledge, see Fried, *The Artificial Reason of the Law or: What Lawyers Know*, 60 TEX. L. REV. 35, 53–58 (1981); and Kronman, *Living in the Law*, 54 U. CHI. L. REV. 835 (1987).

[178] D. SCHON, THE REFLECTIVE PRACTITIONER: HOW PROFESSIONALS THINK IN ACTION 49–50 (1983).

[179] The independence of professional expertise from theoretical or scientific reason is apparent in the traditional axiom precluding a judicial finding of *non liquet*, that is, prohibiting a judge from abstaining to decide a case on the ground that the authoritative materials require no particular result. *See* C. FRIED, CONTRACT AS PROMISE 67 (1981). In this regard, professional practitioners differ from scientists and philosophers. As one legal scholar observes, "[s]cientists have the luxury of suspending belief if the available evidence is inadequate to warrant true beliefs," but "[l]egal actors typically do not have this option. They must act on the best available alternative under the circumstances, which need not include a reasonable alternative of doing nothing." Burton, *Law as Practical Reason*, 62 S. CAL. L. REV. 747, 788–89 (1989). Because professional expertise primarily offers "reasons for actions" (by practitioner and client), rather than "reasons for [true] beliefs," it has sometimes been recognized as a form of "practical" rather than "theoretical" reason. *Cf.* J. RAZ, PRACTICAL REASON AND NORMS 1–2 (1975) (analyzing the structure and role of reasons).

in fact reflects a degree of complexity in the social reality the theory seeks to explain.[180] The legitimate authority of the professions in modern society continues to rest heavily upon "traditional" forms of knowledge that were said by sociological theory to have been discredited and extirpated by the modern forces of rationalization. If the drive toward modern professionalism in the law has been much weaker than generally thought, this is manifested not only in the enduring commitment of European lawyers to aristocratic forms of status, but also in the commitment of common lawyers to highly traditional forms of knowledge and attendant claims to cultural authority.

These volumes suggest that lawyers have fared best where they have readily confessed that the knowledge they claim has been too vague and imprecise to offer the predictability and conceptual lucidity of a rational decision procedure. Lawyers have fared much worse where their knowledge has appeared too schematic and formalistic to deal adequately with the tangled net of circumstantial considerations presented by concrete cases. But if the cultural authority of the modern professional rests on her possession of a body of knowledge that can answer to the claims of reason, how can it be that lawyers enjoy greater authority in common law societies, where legal reasoning has made far more modest claims to intellectual transparency and calculability than in the civil law world? The answer is that the cultural authority of common lawyers has actually depended to a far greater extent on their powers of practical judgment than on bolder epistemological claims to an expertise that delivers univocal answers, solutions easily predictable and logically defensible beyond possibility of reasoned disagreement.

Practical judgment has been generally understood in the common law world to entail the capacity to perceive the circumstances in which a particular legal duty has a decisive claim and the actions that will best satisfy this duty.[181] The capacity for practical judgment inheres not merely in individuals, but also within the institution of the common law. That institution has traditionally been viewed as developing a set of ever-subtler distinctions that crystallize the judgment of the profession at large (the "infinite number of Grave and Learned men"[182]) and that facilitate the exercise of such judgment by its individual members.[183] Because practical judgment in the law speaks

---

[180] Abel partly acknowledges this complexity in observing that the public legitimacy of professional authority has depended on "a good balance of technicality and indetermination" (vol. 1, p. 64).

[181] *See* Kronman, *Practical Wisdom and Professional Character*, in PHILOSOPHY AND LAW 203 (J. Coleman & E. Paul eds. 1987).

[182] T. HOBBES, A DIALOGUE BETWEEN A PHILOSOPHER AND A STUDENT OF THE COMMON LAWS OF ENGLAND 55 (J. Cropsey ed. 1971) (1st ed. 1681).

[183] This helps explain why the societal demand for practical judgment has led the United

to the peculiarities of a concrete case, rather than to an abstract idealized situation, it does not rely primarily on the ability to make deductions along a chain of formal propositions, but rather on discernment in according appropriate weight to each element in a complex network of circumstantial considerations.[184] Because practical judgment cannot be reduced to a codified decision procedure susceptible to identical application by all, it is acknowledged that some lawyers and judges will inevitably display it in much greater degree than others.[185] Thus, the reputation of an individual judge for frequent prior displays of such judgment has been regarded as a legitimate consideration in assessing the authority to be accorded his rulings. In civil law societies, however, judicial opinions are not even generally signed,[186] in part because the only authority to which the judge may legitimately appeal is the law, not his personal reputation for insight.

Sociologists may be correct that a profession cannot attain social prominence if the knowledge it claims becomes either too precise or too untidy and craft-like. But the greater social prominence of lawyers in common law as compared to civil law societies suggests that the "traditional" features of common law adjudication have not threatened the professional authority of common lawyers nearly as much as the "modern" features of civil law systems have imperiled the authority of European attorneys.[187] To be sure, law professors in common law countries continue to be greatly troubled by the apparent "indeterminacy" of adjudication.[188] But it is striking that this diagnosis, so seemingly corrosive of lawyers' claims to professional authority, does not appear to have seriously penetrated the concerns of even the most thoughtful judges, practitioners, and bar association leaders, for all

---

States to seek it in lawyers, rather than in other occupational groups also claiming to provide it — groups whose knowledge base is more formalistic and theory-driven.

[184] *See* C. LARMORE, PATTERNS OF MORAL COMPLEXITY 5–9 (1987).

[185] This acknowledgement is much more readily reconciled with the traditional conception of professionalism than with the modern conception. *See supra* pp. 2023–24.

[186] *See* A. WATSON, *supra* note 165, at 176–77. There is consequently nothing analogous in the civil law world to the public familiarity in common law countries with the long history of famous judges whose decisions are seen to have shaped the course of national history. *See* 1 K. ZWEIGERT & H. KÖTZ, *supra* note 159, at 121.

[187] This conclusion and the ensuing arguments developed from it support a view within sociological theory stressing the enduring strength of tradition within contemporary Western societies, as against the myriad schools of social thought affirming the progressive demise of nonrational modes of human thought and association. *See, e.g.*, H. GADAMER, TRUTH AND METHOD (W. Glen-Doepel trans. 1979); E. SHILS, TRADITION (1981).

[188] "Indeterminacy" refers to the frequent inability of rules, principles, or shared understandings to determine when a particular legal duty exists and how it is correctly to be carried out. *See, e.g.*, Fiss, *Conventionalism*, 58 S. CAL. L. REV. 177 (1985); Kress, *Legal Indeterminacy*, 77 CALIF. L. REV. 283 (1989); Solum, *On the Indeterminacy Crisis: Critiquing Critical Dogma*, 54 U. CHI. L. REV. 462 (1987).

of whom threats to the authority of the profession are presumably a preeminent concern. It is the skill in practical reason and complex judgment that the practicing bar and bench most esteem in their peers[189] and that they believe to provide sufficient foundation for their preeminent position within an otherwise modern society.[190]

The differing social prominence of the bar in the civil and common law worlds is due to contrasting views within these systems over the degree of precision and certainty necessary to the exercise of professional authority. Since the early nineteenth century, civil lawyers, especially in Germany, have viewed "gaps" and "open texture" in legal doctrine as profoundly threatening to their conception of "the rule of law" and hence to their claims of expertise in the application of legal rules. Common lawyers, by contrast, have often seen in such ambiguities welcome opportunities for extending the law, and the interpretive authority of lawyers, into new terrain through creative analogy from existing doctrine.[191] If lawyers in the common and civil law worlds thus differ in their attitudes toward doctrinal ambiguity, they likewise differ in their conceptions of legal reasoning and the sources of law. Civil lawyers have historically viewed such reasoning as consisting largely of a syllogistic process whereby cases presenting unprecedented factual configurations are subject to the strict application of existing rules.[192] Even in periods favoring a relatively "formal" style of jurisprudence, common lawyers have generally dismissed

---

[189] The loss of professional stature resulting from the routinization of professional knowledge into technical formulae for problem-solving also helps explain differences in the social prominence of lawyers *within* the common law world. For instance, English barristers have preserved their monopoly of audience in certain courts more effectively than English solicitors have preserved theirs over land conveyancing, even though solicitors established their monopoly on much more modern, rational foundations. The explanation lies in the fact that the conveyancing skills of solicitors are more easily standardized into a list of invariant procedures, whereas the argumentative skills of barristers are not so easily subject to standardization. See *supra* pp. 2028–29, 2034–35.

[190] *But see* Kronman, *supra* note 177, at 874–75 (stressing the tension between traditional methods of common law argument and modern "claims of reason" requiring "intellectual transparency and . . . calculability"). According to Kronman:

> [Common law reasoning] is bound to seem anachronistic or even objectionable when viewed from the perspective of the claims of reason, and so to the extent these claims are taken seriously, there will be recurrent, and perhaps ultimately irresistible, demands that these irrational elements be purged. Among these elements, I am afraid, many will include the old-fashioned virtue of practical wisdom.

Id. at 875.

[191] For instance, the periodic judicial creation of new torts — such as the invasion of privacy or infliction of emotional distress — is accomplished through the imaginative reconstruction and extension of existing precedent. This is not to deny the genuine differences of opinion among common lawyers over the proper extent of judicial lawmaking. *See, e.g.*, M. EISENBERG, THE NATURE OF THE COMMON LAW 4–7 (1988) (contrasting the view of judicial lawmaking in common law adjudication as interstitial and necessary only to decide hard cases with the view of the judiciary as proactive in routinely "enriching" the supply of legal rules helpful to society).

[192] *See* M. CAPPELLETTI, *supra* note 166, at 51.

this view as excessively conceptualistic and insensitive to the need for legal rules to evolve over time.

For example, civil lawyers have been more inclined to view the process of statutory interpretation as essentially mechanical and to understand their own expertise and professional authority accordingly. This has often made them reluctant to look very deeply into underlying policies and principles[193] from which ambiguity and resulting disagreement about how to apply a statute are almost certain to emerge. European lawyers have believed their authority as professionals to rest upon the uncontentious character of a claim to have interpreted a statute "correctly." This is evident from the fact that appellate courts in civil law societies have generally prohibited dissenting and even concurring opinions.[194] Common lawyers have not been as troubled by the weighing and balancing of competing policies and principles bearing on the factual peculiarities of a case. Individual practitioners even view their professional acumen as enhanced by the imaginativeness with which they can discover ambiguity in a statute, exploiting it to their clients' advantage.[195] That opposing counsel is likely to offer a divergent interpretation of the statute is not thought to call into question the very existence of "the law" or of professional expertise in its interpretation. Indeed, the likelihood of such contentiousness is merely thought to offer public display of the necessity for seeking legal guidance, since neither of the conflicting interpretations is likely to have been apparent to the lay parties from the face of the applicable statute.[196]

---

[193] *See* M. DAMASKA, *supra* note 35, at 68. The causal relation between judicial caution and interpretive style is reciprocal. The traditional reluctance of civil law courts to intercede in as wide a range of controversial policy issues as their common law counterparts has made the "formal rationality" of syllogistic reasoning, with its appearance of distant isolation from such issues, peculiarly congenial to them. Conversely, the professional socialization of civil law lawyers into a "formally rational" mode of decisionmaking historically has made them reluctant to intercede in controversial societal disputes, in which the deficiencies of their preferred method of legal reasoning, with its inability to apprehend the terms of policy debate, would be transparent to all concerned. Dawson even suggests that in Germany the judicial retreat from policy-balancing into a formally rational mode of decisionmaking helped lawyers find a stable, albeit narrowly delimited, professional niche in a highly unstable polity. *See* J. DAWSON, *supra* note 164, at 457–60.

[194] *See* J. DAWSON, *supra* note 164, at 406. To sociologists who believe, like Abel, that the legal profession underwent a modernizing transformation by which it sought to acquire a more rational and scientific form of expertise, it ought to be a puzzling paradox that courts enjoy significantly greater cultural authority, and their "officers" greater social prominence, in societies where higher courts rarely speak with one voice and where open disagreement on the bench concerning the meaning of "the law" might be expected to cast into public doubt the very existence of any rationally defensible, value-free expertise in its interpretation.

[195] By contrast, in the self-understanding of civil lawyers, "it is not considered desirable that private counsel's talent should play a crucial role . . . . [T]here is relatively little scope for deployment of counsel's skill and ingenuity." M. DAMASKA, *supra* note 35, at 177.

[196] This is not to deny that within the common law world differing jurisprudential positions

The greater tolerance of common lawyers for doctrinal ambiguity, particularly in the United States, does not rest on their resignation to the inherently greater imprecision of reasoning from cases. Rather, it is based on particular social alliances and corresponding ethical norms that have led American attorneys to seek social prominence by turning that imprecision to the advantage of their clients and themselves. The stringency of their ethical guidelines on matters of client loyalty impelled American lawyers toward the imaginative discovery of doctrinal ambiguity where such ambiguity would otherwise have remained merely latent. In particular, the view of legal expertise as the skillful exploitation of doctrinal uncertainty would not have become so central to the self-understanding of American attorneys had their ethical guidelines encouraged them to view themselves, like many lawyers elsewhere in the West, primarily as "officers" of society.

Scholars of comparative law have observed that while civil lawyers have been intolerant of ambiguity, practitioners of the common law have reveled in it,[197] seeing it merely as revealing the indispensability of imagination and ingenuity in practical judgment.[198] As Simon observes, "much of the attraction and dignity of the professional life [in the common law world] has been associated with the challenge of such complex judgments,"[199] the irreducibility of professional expertise to categorical rule-application. Leadership in the worldly affairs of modern business and politics is still generally thought to require practical judgment more than theoretical understanding or scientific learning.[200] For this reason, the differing attitudes of common and civil lawyers toward ambiguity in legal reasoning have led to corresponding

---

may vary in how much disagreement can be accommodated without undermining the appearance or reality of the "rule of law." *See* R. DWORKIN, LAW'S EMPIRE 88–89, 136–39 (1986).

[197] A traditional toast at Sargeants' Inn Hall, since the 1760's, has been to "'the glorious uncertainty of the law.'" J. KATZ, THE SILENT WORLD OF DOCTOR AND PATIENT 165 (1984) (quoting 100 GENTLEMAN'S MAGAZINE 98 (1830)).

[198] Hence Kronman's account of practical judgment in legal interpretation, for instance, gives particular importance to the role of the "imagination." *See* Kronman, *supra* note 181, at 216–21. This view would be especially antithetical to conceptions of adjudication long prevalent in the civil law world.

[199] Simon, *supra* note 4, at 1132. Practical judgment, as I have used the term, does *not* refer to the "realist" capacity to "predict what courts will do," since the civil law and its practitioners claim that capacity in even stronger terms, though practical judgment occupies no comparable place in the self-understanding of civil lawyers. In exercising such judgment on behalf of clients, common lawyers do engage in predictions of official behavior, but only on the basis of how they expect the genuinely practical judgment of official decisionmakers to be exercised, rather than on the basis of the result one would expect from a formally rational decision procedure.

[200] *See* M. OAKESHOTT, EXPERIENCE AND ITS MODES 247–321 (1933); M. OAKESHOTT, RATIONALISM IN POLITICS 105 (1962) (arguing that the knowledge involved in effective political leadership, and in any form of worldly expertise, cannot be fully codified as rules or principles that would be useful to others in resolving concrete practical problems).

differences in the degree of social prominence that they have acquired. The scope of societal problems that have fallen within the jurisdiction of common law courts is larger than in civil law counterparts because the modes of legal reasoning accepted by common lawyers are far more capacious and make available to the advocate and the sympathetic judge a smorgasbord of imaginative arguments.[201]

Tocqueville was the first to observe how the divergence between common law and civil law forms of reasoning had influenced the relative social prominence of lawyers in different societies. While French civil "laws are often hard to understand," he wrote, "everyone can read them, whereas nothing could be more obscure and out of reach of the common man than a law founded on precedent."[202] This difference in the form and sources of law explained why American and English lawyers became "increasingly separated from the people, forming a class apart," Tocqueville believed.[203] "A French lawyer is just a man of learning, but an English or American one is somewhat like the Egyptian priests, being, as they were, the only interpreter of an occult science."[204] Max Weber made an even stronger assertion in this regard, arguing that barristers in early modern England had resisted the diffusion of Roman law in order to preserve their considerable social prominence, which they understood to rest upon their mastery of a more arcane and inaccessible form of expertise than that permitted by the more simplified, modernized import.[205] One would think that a comparative sociology of lawyers placing great weight on the bar's capacity for market control would therefore be drawn to national differences in the sources of law and methods of legal interpretation, insofar as these appear to affect the facility with which legal knowledge may be monopolized by members of a single occupational group. But Abel succumbs to the "trained incapacity"[206] that leads sociologists of law to seek an explanation for national differences in lawyers' roles in virtually everything but the law itself.

---

[201] Despite Kronman's predictions of declining public respect for the practical wisdom reflected in common law judgment and despite the increasing legislative encroachment upon ancient common law fields, there is evidence that judicial lawmaking remains viable and frequent even in nominally statutory areas. *See, e.g.*, G. CALABRESI, A COMMON LAW FOR THE AGE OF STATUTES 90–119, 163–66 (1982).

[202] A. DE TOCQUEVILLE, *supra* note 15, at 267.

[203] *Id.*

[204] *Id.*

[205] *See* WEBER ON LAW, *supra* note 149, at 202–03; M. SHAPIRO, *supra* note 102, at 104 (discussing Bentham's conclusion that "the common law was a mass of contradictions and illogicalities whose complexities were designed only to enrich the lawyers"). *But cf.* P. ATIYAH, PRAGMATISM AND THEORY IN ENGLISH LAW 80–81 (1987) (contending that the common law displays "a predilection for common sense [that] owes its origins to . . . the fact that much of the common law had to be developed in a form in which it could be made intelligible to juries").

[206] The term is Thorstein Veblen's. *See* T. VEBLEN, THE THEORY OF THE LEISURE CLASS 363–400 (1934).

National differences of modern history help explain the belief among civil lawyers that their authority as professionals depends on possessing a type of expertise permitting them a degree of anonymity, unanimity, and infallibility that common lawyers readily abjure. The worldly wisdom for which great judges in the common law world continue to be respected was claimed by lawyers and judges of the civil law as well, throughout the seventeenth century.[207] The general recognition of precedent, and of the accumulated practical experience it seeks to embody, made possible lawmaking powers in civil law courts, powers of which such courts were later stripped. In late medieval and early modern Europe, including Tudor and Stuart England, the tasks of legislation and adjudication were not fully differentiated, with courts and various parliamentary bodies possessing overlapping powers.[208] The straightforward, undisguised exercise of judicial lawmaking must therefore be understood as essentially a premodern phenomenon. Indeed, its survival within a few Western societies, particularly the United States, has been recognized as a historical legacy of a form of political life in which state power was much less centralized and democratized than today.[209] Yet it has been such judicial lawmaking, manifested in both the development of common law and in judicial review, that enabled American lawyers to establish the place of courts as an independent source of power and moral authority, and hence the place of lawyers as a profession with an expertise pertinent to an enormous range of societal issues.

It was the suppression of judicial power by the executive rulers of absolutist states and the legislative leaders of democratic revolutions that deprived civil law courts of their overt lawmaking powers and authority.[210] In Europe since the French Revolution, judicial lawmaking has been regarded as "inconsistent with democracy"[211] and hence politically unacceptable. The close ties between the French bar and the monarchy during the *ancien régime*[212] prompted revolutionary leaders, and the substantial areas of Western Europe that fell under their sway, to repudiate the notion that judges should make law through particularized judgment in identifying dispositive factual idio-

---

[207] *See* Bouwsma, *Lawyers and Early Modern Culture*, 78 AM. HIST. REV. 303, 314–17 (1973).

[208] *See* A. HARDING, A SOCIAL HISTORY OF ENGLISH LAW 229–32 (1966); 4 W. HOLDSWORTH, A HISTORY OF ENGLISH LAW 168–69 (3d ed. 1945); C. MCILWAIN, THE HIGH COURT OF PARLIAMENT AND ITS SUPREMACY at xi, 93–96 (1910).

[209] *See* S. HUNTINGTON, POLITICAL ORDER IN CHANGING SOCIETIES 102–13 (1968).

[210] *See id.*; *see also* J. DAWSON, *supra* note 164, at 375–80, 402 (discussing the French system).

[211] J. DAWSON, *supra* note 164, at 429.

[212] *See, e.g.*, L. BERLANSTEIN, THE BARRISTERS OF TOULOUSE IN THE EIGHTEENTH CENTURY (1740–1793), at 123–47 (1975); M. FITZSIMMONS, THE PARISIAN ORDER OF BARRISTERS AND THE FRENCH REVOLUTION 1–32 (1987).

syncracies in the cases before them. Judicial lawmaking and practical judgment remained little-acknowledged or defended until recent years[213] — long after those societies had defined the bar's professional powers. The lesser social esteem traditionally accorded to continental courts, and hence to those who practice before them, is surely attributable, in significant part, to the fact that judges have lacked the independence necessary actively to shape legal doctrine in accordance with evolving societal needs or to pass upon the constitutionality of other branches' actions.[214]

Revolutionary reformers admittedly intended to replace traditional notions of practical judgment with what they saw as a more modern, technical, and scientific method of legal reasoning. European codification was *not* designed to facilitate professional monopolization, however, but to accomplish the very opposite: to tame the power of the prerevolutionary bench and bar by making judicial decisionmaking wholly nondiscretionary and readily intelligible to the critical scrutiny of the newly enfranchised citizens of continental Europe.[215] Although their conception of professional expertise became more modernized than that of their American counterparts, European attorneys were able to exercise cultural authority over a much narrower range of societal concerns, constricting the scope of their professional domain. If the American bench and bar successfully asserted relevant expertise over a wider societal compass, this has been due less to their own efforts to reform and rationalize their privileges, as Abel argues, than to a national history in which judicial power did not suffer the severe chastening it elsewhere received from absolutist monarchs or revolu-

---

[213] *See* M. CAPPELLETTI, *supra* note 166, at 9. Just as judicial lawmaking in continental Europe after the French Revolution declined on account of its association with a discredited political regime, so too the reemergence of judicial lawmaking there since the Second World War stems from the discredited association of deference to the "political branches" and mechanical positivism with the capitulation of bench and bar under Nazi rule. *See* M. CAPPELLETTI, JUDICIAL REVIEW IN THE CONTEMPORARY WORLD at viii (1971); M. SHAPIRO, *supra* note 102, at 155.

[214] *But see* Merryman, *The Italian Legal Style III: Interpretation* in THE ROLE OF JUDICIAL DECISION AND DOCTRINE IN CIVIL LAW AND MIXED JURISDICTIONS 163, 172–76 (J. Dainow ed. 1974) (observing that civil law courts regularly engage, albeit *sub rosa*, in judicial lawmaking, which they view as necessary to achieve adequate results, even if such conduct is also inconsistent with the publicly accepted boundaries of the professional authority of judges).

[215] *See* A. WATSON, *supra* note 165, at 101, 113. The fact that mechanical jurisprudence was essentially imposed upon the European bar as a condition of political survival explains a curious paradox: although judicial administration is avowedly aimed much more at "policy implementation" in civil law than in common law societies (where dispute resolution retains greater centrality), judicial method is nevertheless far less receptive to explicit policy-balancing. *See* M. DAMASKA, *supra* note 35, at 147–80. The historic effort to limit the power of bench and bar also explains the paradox that although the French Revolution was inspired by and lent great support to doctrines of natural law, the jurisprudential legacy of the Revolution for nineteenth-century Europe was a particularly mechanical form of positivism. *See* J. MERRYMAN, *supra* note 159, at 16, 21, 153.

tionary legislatures. It was the peculiar way in which American lawyers devoted a traditional form of knowledge to ethically uncompromised service of modern economic objectives that explains the incomparable prominence they attained.[216] Although the epistemological claims of civil lawyers at first appear bolder, these claims enabled civil lawyers to acquire only modest social prominence. After the French Revolution deauthorized the exercise of practical judgment by the bar, civil lawyers had much less to offer in grasping the factual complexities of the most important problems of the day.

VI. Conclusion: Sociological Theory and the Legal Profession

Professor Abel commendably acknowledges that many of the countries discussed in these volumes do not fit his theory about the centrality of monopolistic behavior by lawyers within modern Western society. But he apparently believes that this concession does not require him to modify the theory in a way that would permit him to account for why, in its initial formulation, it fit so narrow a swath of space and time. The chapters on lawyers in particular societies reveal so many exceptions as to swallow the rule Abel seeks to prove. It is

[216] Most explanations for the social prominence of lawyers in the United States, including those of Abel and Lewis (vol. 3, pp. 478–93), focus almost exclusively on the unusual American *demand* for law and hence, it is assumed, for those formally trained and officially licensed to interpret it. *See, e.g.*, L. Friedman, The Republic of Choice: Law, Authority, and Culture 7–18 (1990). But increased prominence for lawyers follows neither logically nor empirically from increased legal regulation of social life. As the European societies discussed here indicate, the enormous proliferation of legal rights associated with the rise of the administrative welfare state in Europe did not spur an equal proliferation of work for lawyers. This was partly because the formalism of legal reasoning among civil lawyers prompted European political leaders to assign exclusive jurisdiction over many regulatory matters to policy-sensitive administrative tribunals, before which lawyers are often expressly prohibited from appearing. *See* Glendon, *The Profession and Practice of Law*, in 22 Encyclopedia Britannica Macropedia 863 (1988). Such European experience indicates that it is wrong to view "mega-lawyering" in America as a direct, unmediated response to the "mega-law" of the regulatory state, Galanter's view notwithstanding. *See* Galanter, *Larger Than Life: Mega-Lawyers and Mega-Lawyering in the Contemporary United States*, in The Sociology of the Professions: Lawyers, Doctors, and Others 152 (R. Dingwall & P. Lewis eds. 1983). Hence European thinking on "law and society" does not share the American concern over the excessive number or power of lawyers, in the way that it does share our concern over the possibly excessive legal regulation of social life. *See* J. Habermas, The Theory of Communicative Action 356–73 (1987); Teubner, *Introduction*, in The Juridification of Social Spheres 1, 3–4 (G. Teubner ed. 1987). In contrast to the prevalent emphasis on demand, the present analysis has stressed how lawyers have influenced the societal demand for their services by altering what they *supply*, by modifying doctrine to facilitate commerce and avoiding mechanical jurisprudence. But unlike the version of "demand creation" proposed by Abel, that suggested here is not seen to result from "conspiratorial" collective action by the organized bar.

therefore unacceptable to treat these societies as statistical "outliers" for which one may offer purely ad hoc explanations.

Comparative sociology is a field that has advanced neither by imposing a priori theoretical schema upon a recalcitrant reality, nor by innocently trying to stare straight into "the facts," unencumbered by any legacy of prior thought. If Abel can be praised for resisting the latter (and more common) error, he must be faulted for succumbing to the former. He has not sought, as comparative sociologists generally do, to develop and advance existing theoretical accounts by bringing them into a genuinely reflective interaction with empirical material from diverse national histories.[217] In fastening so insistently upon a single hypothesis about how lawyers act, he has unwittingly reduced the abundant "local color" of his cross-national material to a monochromatic black and white.[218]

Abel's theoretical approach is nonetheless provocative in implying that professional independence may partly rely upon the market power that the bar's monopolistic practices have permitted its members. His approach therefore offers important insight into the reduced opportunities for independent lawyering that recent declines in market power must bring in their wake. These insights can be preserved in a reinterpretation of Abel's data, which nonetheless accords greater weight to national differences in the encounter with the French and Industrial Revolutions. In accounting for cross-national variation in the social role of lawyers, a sensitivity to considerations of market power need not blind us to the continuing primacy of traditional over modern forms of expertise and authority in the common law world or to the longstanding priority of status over wealth in the collective aspirations and activities of attorneys in civil law societies.

This Review contends that where the decisive events of national history did not deprive the lawyers of a given society of their traditional authority as bearers of practical judgment, they did not vigorously strive, as Abel contends, to reestablish their authority on the more modern basis of a scientific expertise that could be taught only in universities. They did not strenuously seek to reform the selection, training, admission, and regulation of their members along more rational lines. Where such reforms have been achieved, they have more

---

217 For a collection of essays examining methods of comparative historical sociology, see VISION AND METHOD IN HISTORICAL SOCIOLOGY (T. Skocpol ed. 1984).

218 It should be said, however, that Abel does at least consider a somewhat wider range of theoretical approaches in his monographs on American and English lawyers than in the volumes under review here. *See* R. ABEL, *supra* note 27, at 3–32; R. ABEL, *supra* note 14, at 14–39. But it is precisely the experience of other Western societies, as suggested here, that most demands a broader theoretical perspective, and it is the experience of American lawyers and English solicitors on which Abel has built a prima facie case, at least, for his theory of lawyers as modernizing monopolists.

often been brought about in spite of, not because of, the intentions of lawyers. In societies where the modernization of legal education and admission was forced upon the bar, even this did not decisively shift the bar's center of attention from the state or landed interests toward private industry. Noncommercial sources of social status continued to entrance many European lawyers while emerging markets for law-related work were seized by other occupational groups. If lawyers were heliotropes, they were more often drawn to traditional sources of status than to modern sources of wealth, even after significant opportunities for the latter had begun to emerge. Thus, the heliotropic hypothesis per se can tell us only a little.

The most important policy implication of these observations is that the aristocratic ideal of independence from commerce, its recent revivalists to the contrary, will be difficult to recreate in contemporary America on terms satisfactory to most lawyers, and hence by the bar's efforts at self-reform. The professional fraternity has long acknowledged the need for periodic, internal criticism of the client aims that lawyers sometimes serve, even if the bar has been more wary of criticism of the doctrines of professional ethics permitting lawyers to direct their powers toward those ends. But the professional fraternity has been still less receptive to criticism directed not at the ends its power serves, but at the will to power itself — the yearning for social prominence, which remains unquestioned in even the boldest of recent proposals for the ethical reform of lawyers' roles.

The great power of American lawyers, however, originates in the very nature of the expertise they claim and in the underlying conception of professional authority that this entails. These would be very difficult to dislodge. We would have to transform not only the relation between law and commerce, but also the deepest presuppositions held by American lawyers about the nature of law and legal reasoning. The expectation that the power of lawyers in America could be significantly chastened by a few discrete reforms displays little awareness of the deeper roots of that power in the logical structure of the common law and the social history of American lawyers.[219] Abel is right to suspect that in the modern West, it required a revolution to reduce significantly the political power and moral unaccountability of the bar.

[219] To be sure, concrete proposals exist for reducing the amount of litigation and hence the role of lawyers in America, such as adopting the "English rule" requiring the losing party to pay both sides' attorneys' fees. In lieu of striving to restore the social status of the aristocratic ideal, public policy could more effectively reduce the power of courts (and thereby — through the European strategy — increase the moral accountability of lawyers) by the economic approach of altering incentives to litigate, since the possibility of litigation casts such a long shadow over the rest of lawyers' work. But the primary bases of political support for such reforms may not realistically be expected to arise from within the ranks of lawyers themselves.

Name Index

Abel, R. xxvi, 169, 461–518 *passim*
Arendt, H. 150, 159
Aristotle xxii, 32, 43, 148, 338, 342, 347, 360–1
Armani, F. 143
Arnold, T. xxviii, 83, 91, 241, 244, 251, 258
Atkinson, R. xviii, xxix
Auden, W. H. 298
Austen, Jane 305, 313

Bacon, F. xi
Bator, P. 237
Beauvoir, S. de 371
Belge, F. 143
Bellah, R. N. 317, 322, 323
Bellow, G. 42
Bennet, E. B. 141
Berger, P. 322
Berle, A. 217
Blumberg, A. 254
Blumberg, G. 386
Boswell, James 188, 214, 427
Bradley, F. H. xiii
Brandeis, L. D. xxvi, 211, 230, 292, 299, 314–16 *passim*, 317, 319, 323, 397, 469
Brazil, W. 445
Brougham, Lord Henry 142, 143, 144, 148, 162, 173, 413
Burke, Edmund 167

Caplan, L. xxiii
Caroline, Queen 142
Chesterton, G. K. 459–60
Chodorow, N. 371, 373, 377
Churchill, Winston 138
Coleridge, Samuel Taylor 140, 141
Cover, R. xxx
Curtis, C. P. xxii, 103, 241, 254, 260

Dauer, E. A. xxi, 87–8, 127–38
Dean, John 5, 84
Dickens, Charles 179, 485
Diggory 318, 319
Dinnerstein, D. 373, 377
Durkheim, E. xxvi, xxviii, 426, 451
Dworkin, G. 322, 323

Eliot, George 313
Ellmann, S. xviii, xix,
Epstein, C. F. 374, 385

Faulkner, William 313, 332
Fletcher, G. xxi
Fletcher, J. 314, 323
Flom, J. xxiii
Foras, A. 83
Frankel, M. E. 144, 160
Frankfurt, H. 329, 330
Frankfurter, F. 438
Freedman, M. H. xiii, xv, xvi, xvii, xx, 62, 81–95, 147, 148, 153, 154, 171, 183–7 *passim*, 205, 224, 285
Freud, Sigmund 375, 463
Freund, P. 211, 216
Fried, C. xi, xii, xiii, xx, xxi, xxii, 45, 49–52 *passim*, 86–9 *passim*, 97–126, 127–34 *passim*, 136, 138, 161–3 *passim*, 242, 251, 255–60 *passim*, 261, 282
Fuller, L. xxviii, 211, 215, 218–19

Galanter, M. 276
George IV, King 142
Gilligan, C. xxiv, xxv, 371, 373–9 *passim*, 381–3 *passim*, 385, 387–9 *passim*, 390
Goffman, E. 38–9, 45, 251–2, 253, 254, 255, 258, 284
Goldberg, R. 163
Goldman, A. xiii, xviii, xix
Gordon, R. xiv, xxvi, xxvii, 468–70 *passim*, 472–4 *passim*, 483, 500, 501
Gouldner, A. V. 251, 255

Haar, C. 210
Hampshire, S. 330
Harris, Lis 313
Hart, H. L. A. 211, 216, 219, 270–1, 277
Hauerwas, S. 323, 324
Haynsworth, C. F. 83, 91
Hazard, G. xxxi, 314, 315, 404
Hegel, G. W. F. 267–8
Held, V. 158
Helms, Richard 141, 143
Heschel, A. J. 309, 320

Hobbes, Thomas 188, 339
Holmes, O. W. 69, 204–5, 215
Hume, D. 166
Hurst, J. W. 195, 211

Ive, Saint xi

Jackson, R. M. 207
John XXIII, Pope 81–2, 94
Johnson, Samuel 427

Kadish, S. xxii
Kant, I. xi, xxii, 142, 339, 429
Karst, K. 390, 391
Kawabata, Y. 144
Kennedy, D. 411
Kettleson, J. 42
King, M. Luther xii, xiii, xv, 279
Kohlberg, L. 375, 376, 388
Koniak, S. xxx
Koskoff, T. 154
Kronman, A. T. xxi, xxii, xxiii, xxv, 327–68

Langdell, C. 478, 480
Law, S. A. 87
Leff, A. A. xxi, 87–8, 127–38
Lévi-Strauss, C. 249, 253
Lewis, P. S. C. 461, 504
Liddy, G. G. 162
Lincoln, Abraham 469
Llewellyn, K. xxviii, 211, 240, 355
Louis XII xi
Luban, D. xiv, xv, xvi, xvii, xviii, xix, xx, xxvi, xxix, 76, 139–78

Macaulay, T. xi, xii, 27, 404
McClosky, H. 244
MacIntyre, A. 330
MacKinnon, C. 385
Malamud, B. 310
Marcuse, H. 258
Marx, Karl 463
Mellinkoff, D. 144–5, 148, 161, 162, 165
Menkel-Meadow, C. xiv, xxi, xxiv, 369–93
Milhaven, G. 310
Mill, J. S. 104, 105, 165
Miller, J. B. 371, 373
Montaigne, M. de xxii, 27–9 *passim*
Mortimer xxii
Murdoch, Iris 299

Nagel, T. 31, 156–7
Nelson, R. 435, 437, 444
Nietzsche, F. 143–4, 162
Nixon, Richard 13, 147
Nizer, L. 262
Noddings, N. 373, 377, 378, 383, 387
Noonan, J. T. jr 82, 183–7 *passim*, 191, 224, 285
Nussbaum, M. 330

Olsen, F. 374
Orantes, M. 85–6, 89–90
Osiel, M. J. xxvi, xxvii, 461–518

Parfit, D. xxi
Parsons xxvi, xxviii
Patterson, L. R. xxxi
Pepper, S. L. xix, xx, xxviii, xxix, 57–79
Piaget, J. 375
Popper, K. R. 150, 151, 403
Postema, G. J. xiv, xv, xvii, xviii, xxi, xxii, xxix, 27–53, 140, 172
Pound, R. 211

Rhode, D. L. xvii, xx, xxv, xxvi, xxvii, 397–460
Riesman, D. 279
Rose, Phyllis 313
Rosenthal, D. 254
Rothman 318, 319
Rousseau, J. J. 250

Sacks, A. 211, 216, 219, 270–1, 277
Sartre, J-P. 38. 47, 322, 323, 434
Schaef, A. 371, 373
Schwartz, D. 162
Schwartz, M. xiv, 140, 141, 146
Shaffer, T. L. xviii, xix, xxi, xxiii, xxiv, xxv, xxvi, xxix, xxx, 297
Sharswood, G. 140, 157
Sidgwick, H. 104, 105
Simon, W. H. xiv, xvii, xviii, xix, xxi, xxvi, xxviii, xxix, xxx, 140, 167, 169, 179–293, 412, 468–70 *passim*, 472–4 *passim*, 483, 500, 501
Socrates xi, 366
Stone, H. F. 457
Stone, J. 183
Stone, L. 274
Stout, R. 179

Thompson, E. P. 278
Tocqueville, A. de xxvi, 497–9 *passim*, 513
Tribe, L. 249
Trollope, Anthony 313
Tyler, Anne 297, 300, 305, 313, 317

'nger, R. M. 241, 430

'alzer, M. 164
'asserman, D. xviii
'asserstrom, R. xiii, xiv, xv, xvii, xviii, xix, xx, xxvi, xxix, 3–26, 57, 58, 62, 84–5, 89, 426
'eber, M. 366, 439, 463, 513
'hewell, W. 140

Wiggins, D. 139
Wilkins, D. xxix
Williams, B. 44, 139, 172, 330
Wittgenstein, L. xxii
Wolf, S. xxi, 330
Wollheim, R. 330

Yeats, W. B. 39, 40
Younger, I. 150, 151

www.ingramcontent.com/pod-product-compliance
Lightning Source LLC
LaVergne TN
LVHW101438200926
848483LV00004B/399